CRACKING

the

PM CAREER

THE SKILLS, FRAMEWORKS, AND PRACTICES
TO BECOME A GREAT PRODUCT MANAGER

CRACKING THE PM INTERVIEW
How to Land a Product Manager Job in Technology

CRACKING THE CODING INTERVIEW
189 Programming Questions and Solutions

CRACKING THE TECH CAREER
Insider Advice on Landing a Job at Google,
Microsoft, Apple, or Any Top Tech Company

CRACKING
the
PM CAREER

JACKIE BAVARO

GAYLE LAAKMANN MCDOWELL
Founder and CEO, CareerCup.com

CareerCup, LLC
Palo Alto, CA

CRACKING THE PM CAREER

Published by CareerCup, LLC, Palo Alto, CA. Compiled Jan 21, 2021.

For more information, or to enquire about bulk or university copies, contact support@careercup.com.

Please report bugs or issues at crackingthepmcareer.com.

978-0-9847828-9-5 (ISBN 13)

To James—I love you infinity
- Jackie

To Davis and Tobin and their zillions of questions
- Gayle

WHAT'S INSIDE

FOREWORD BY MARISSA MAYER

PART A

FOREWORD BY MARISSA MAYER

PRODUCT MANAGEMENT IS one of the most central and pivotal functions in modern technology companies. Ironically, the PM role is also one of the least well understood. What are the responsibilities of a PM? How do you measure their success? What skills are the most important in a product manager? What should you expect from an interview? What is the path for advancement? In *Cracking the PM Career*, Gayle McDowell and Jackie Bavaro do an excellent job detailing the PM role, the requirements, how to thrive and excel, and what to expect as you embark on a PM career.

I spent 13 years at Google, joining in 1999 as an early employee. The company grew and evolved considerably during my tenure there, and, in 2002, I was one of the founding members of the PM organization. In total, I spent just over a decade as a product manager and leader. From that first hand experience, I can say that product management is an interesting, varied, and challenging role. Every day is different, every product is unique, and every product manager's approach and what they bring to the role is distinct. Further, the role of product manager varies considerably from company to company.

One of the most crucial skills required of a PM is managing through influence. Product managers rarely have management responsibilities over the engineers building the product. As a product manager, your responsibilities naturally flow to the product and managing to meet the market need. However, to meet the market need, you will need to convince the engineering teams to build the product, requiring you to use influence rather than authority. Each product manager will draw on their own toolset—persuasiveness, supporting data, user studies, design principles, relationship building—to achieve this. Managing through influence is one of the most important skills a product manager must develop and is also the most nuanced.

As I established Google's Associate Product Manager program, our vision was to hire new college graduates and train them to be great product managers in the specific way Google needed. That meant we needed to figure out which aspects of the role mattered most and how to support someone learning them. As *Cracking the PM Career* illustrates, the list of skills is long: communication, listening, organization, prioritization, studying users and markets, empathy, and so on.

In the APM program, we found that one of the best ways to learn these skills was to take raw talent (smart, strong technologists) and give them real hands-on experience, coupled with a lot of feedback and coaching. While all of the chapters of *Cracking the PM Career* are valuable and give depth of perspective, I suspect that many readers will find the Product Leader Q&As among the most helpful. These are real stories from well-respected product leaders in the trenches.

Cracking the PM Career acts as a roadmap to understanding product management and how to establish a successful career as a PM. I applaud Jackie (a Google APM alum) and Gayle in creating an in-depth manual to help those entering and mastering the field of product management.

MARISSA MAYER is the co-founder and CEO of Sunshine, a consumer technology startup that makes daily mundane tasks effortless. Previously, she served as the CEO and President of Yahoo, which she led from 2012 to 2017. During her tenure at Yahoo, she transformed its culture, grew it to one billion users, hired more than 5,000 people, and oversaw nearly 50 acquisitions.

Prior to Yahoo, Marissa joined Google as an early employee and its first woman engineer. She helped to found the product management organization. As VP of Search Products and User Experience, she led the product management for Search, Maps, News and other consumer products. She also founded and led Google's Associate Product Manager program. Google's APM program, an elite rotational program which hires new college graduates and trains them as product managers, was the first of its kind in the industry.

THE PRODUCT MANAGER ROLE

PART B

CHAPTER 1

GETTING STARTED

UNICORNS. I NEVER thought that I'd be at this point in my career and trying to justify their existence, but PMing is funny that way. Sometimes your product needs a mythical beast. Or, at least I thought so.

Let me explain.

At Asana, we had a secret feature where users could turn on unicorn celebrations when they completed a task. Customers were delighted. Who wouldn't love a literal unicorn flying across their screen?

It turns out that the people who thought it was a virus weren't so crazy about the introduction of this possibly diseased beast. Also, it did seem a bit goofy for our business customers.

I was stuck. Logically, their points made sense. It could be jarring for our more serious users, and I could see where a less tech-savvy person might reasonably mistake our clip-art unicorn for a symptom of a computer issue.

At the same time, I believed in this feature. It offered a little treat for a "job well done." The reception was fairly positive, and I thought this feature would boost word of mouth.

My believing in it wasn't enough though; it's not like I could demand that everyone do what I wanted.

As I had instructed my mentees so many times, a PM can't just issue orders. They have to develop the frameworks, gather the data, consider the risks, and motivate people to align along some vision, goal or task.

This is the essence of what makes PMing so thorny. There are such a variety of multifaceted problems with so many stakeholders. Sure, we get more skilled as our career progresses—but then we face more complex problems and bigger goals. It's like we're perpetually fumbling in the dark for the light switch, but only finding a little flashlight.

A HOPE THAT THIS BOOK ILLUMINATES.

A good PM has goals, and this book—being a product itself—is no exception. These are our goals.

Our goal is for this book to be the guide we never had.

As a fresh PM, starting out at Microsoft, I had mentors and advice—but it wasn't comprehensive. No one could sit me down and teach me all of what it means to be a PM, and what it takes to become a fantastic one. It's not that they didn't try; there's just too much to say. I couldn't envision how the complexity of my problems would evolve with my career path.

While I was at Google—starting in the APM program—I continued to learn a great deal about building awesome products. But the complexity of the decisions grew. No longer did my work fit into a clear structure with defined projects and preset deadlines. I now needed to work with my team to decide what projects to tackle and when they should ship. I was expected to manage stakeholders and strategy—as well as my own career. I gobbled up all the information my mentors fed me, but I still felt like I was messing it up as often as I got it right.

Our goal is for this book to be the guide our mentees never had.

I joined Asana as their 13th employee and first PM. Now, it truly felt like it was all on me. No longer did I have premade launch checklists and spec templates. There was no super senior PM I could look to to see if I was on the right track. I was wearing those shoes now.

Over eight years, as Asana grew to more than 500 employees, I rose into the head of product management role, overseeing the product roadmap and a team of 20 PMs. I launched Asana's APM program and aspired to do everything right that my mentors had, nothing they did wrong, and then add on a few bits of awesomeness too.

That's a ridiculous, lofty goal—impossible to achieve—but that's okay. I'd like to think that I came pretty close.

Over the years, I've learned and grown so much. I've been mentored and supported by amazing people. I've made mistakes and learned from them. I've had major successes and learned from them. I've written job ladders and hired PMs. And I turned all of this into mentoring and supporting PMs—as APMs freshly out of college, as PMs growing into more senior roles, and now in the form of this book.

Our goal is for this book to help more people become great product managers.

This book shares the skills, frameworks, and practices that my peers and I have painstakingly learned and honed over the years, so that PMs can spend less time reinventing the wheel. It delves into the mystery and ambiguity surrounding career progression so that PMs can focus on the right areas and reach their potential. It connects the dots on how to develop each important PM skill so that mentors can point their mentees towards actionable feedback.

Of course, there is no such thing as a perfect PM, and there's no such thing as a perfect mentor. But we hope that this book will make things a little bit easier. Read it cover-to-cover, or sample the sections you like, or let it sit on your desk as a reference to flip to—or have your mentees flip to—as needed. The choice is yours.

ON MYTHICAL BEASTS

As for the unicorn celebrations, it launched in the end. We aligned the team together under a broad agreement about testing and measuring customer reactions. A designer worked to make the design match our brand and added an explanation on the first unicorn, so it didn't get mistaken for a virus. And we launched initially just for personal use cases, though we promoted it to organizations later. Internal stakeholders were happy and customers were delighted.

Now, years later, as I write this book, I'm on the other side—checking tasks off on Asana, and watching unicorns shoot across the screen. Perhaps I'm biased, but it does give me a little smile every time.

HOW TO USE THIS BOOK

This book is for anyone who wants to become a great product leader. You might choose to read it straight through, but you can also skip around—we give you some pointers on doing that (pg 11).

In the book *Peak: Secrets from the New Science of Expertise*, Anders Ericsson and Robert Pool study the question of how people develop their potential and achieve greatness. The key takeaway is that your expertise is driven by the quality of your mental representations. For example, when chess grandmasters look at a chess board, they don't see a scattering of pieces; they see an in-progress game where white played the queen's gambit and black declined.

> To get the most out of this book, focus on developing your mental representations around products, businesses, and people. Create and refine your own frameworks. Apply deliberate practice by comparing your intuitive behaviors to those of the best PMs. When you do this well, new situations you're faced with won't feel like total unknowns. Instead, they'll each feel like a variation of a pattern you recognize.

With practice, you too will hear an engineer complain about technical debt and say, "Ah, this is the classic roadmap conflict caused by prioritizing disparate goals in a single ranked list, and easily solved with a balanced portfolio roadmap."[1] It doesn't quite have the ring of "the queen's gambit declined," but it will do.

PM SKILLS

Every company uses different top-level categories to describe the skills and attributes of great PMs. Fortunately, the underlying elements are remarkably consistent. All companies want you to efficiently deliver high-quality products that create customer and business impact without causing problems.

In this book, we've grouped the skills it takes to be a great product leader into five categories:

- **Product skills** help you design a high-quality product that delights customers and solves their needs.

- **Execution skills** enable you to run and deliver your projects quickly, smoothly, and effectively.

- **Strategic skills** improve your ability to set direction and optimize for long-term impact.

- **Leadership skills** allow you to work well with others and improve your team.

- **People management skills** come into play when you have an official responsibility to hire and develop people.

If your company organizes the skills differently, this chart will help you find the relevant section.

---

1   See "Prioritize competing goals with a balanced portfolio" on pg 200 if you're eager to jump ahead to this solution.

Skill Area	Includes
Product Skills	• User insights • Data insights • Analytical problem solving • Technical skills • Product and design sense
Execution Skills	• Project management • Minimum viable products (MVPs) • Scoping and incremental development • Product launches • Time management • Getting things done
Strategic Skills	• Strategy • Vision • Roadmaps • Business models • Goal setting • Objectives and key results (OKRs)
Leadership Skills	• Communication • Collaboration • Personal mindsets • Mentoring

People Management Skills	· Do you really want to be a manager?
	· How to become a manager
	· Recruiting
	· Coaching
	· Performance reviews
	· Product processes
	· Team organization

For each skill we've highlighted:

- **Responsibilities:** things you're expected to do.

- **Growth Practices:** mindsets and exercises you'll work on over time to improve the skill.

- **Frameworks:** mental models, tools, and reference material. This section comes first when the frameworks are a prerequisite to understanding the responsibilities.

> Responsibilities and growth practices that only come into play at more senior levels are marked with ⚡.

You can read through the PM skills in order, or jump to the area that you want to focus on. They can also serve as a starting point for conversations with your manager such as, "When you said I needed to be more user-focused, did you have one of these in mind?"

CAREER SKILLS

Being an excellent PM and launching great products isn't always enough to have a successful career.

In Part H: Careers, we'll cover everything you need to know about managing your career so you can translate your efforts into the recognition you deserve.

Topics include:

- PM career ladder

- How promotions work

- Setting career goals

- Working with your manager

- Optimizing review cycles

- Networking

- Career options beyond PMing

- Q&A with successful product leaders

PM Career Ladder

Unlike most leveling frameworks and PM career ladders, this book does not create a rubric that describes what each skill looks like at every job level.

Why?

Those types of rubrics are either unhelpfully vague or misleadingly specific. They either use subjective qualifiers or list bullet points that aren't applied consistently. Often, they just self-referentially describe the scope you've been assigned.

The underlying truth is that PM skills don't translate directly into levels. Instead, your level is determined by your scope, autonomy, and impact. The way you earn a promotion to the next level is by demonstrating autonomy and impact at your current scope and building trust that you can perform at a larger scope.[2]

The PM skills are incredibly important for becoming a better PM and launching great products, but they don't create a guide for how to advance.

In Chapter 32: The Career Ladders (pg 343), we paint a picture of what each level looks like, and how to advance to each one. We cover levels from associate product manager (APM) to head of product and describe the typical scope, autonomy, and impact expected at each level.

IF YOU'RE SHORT ON TIME...

If you don't have time to read this book cover-to-cover, here's where to start:

I'M NEW TO PRODUCT MANAGEMENT

If you're new to product management, congratulations, and welcome!

- Start with Chapter 2: The Product Manager Role (pg 13) to learn the basics about the product life cycle and what a PM does during each phase.

- Read Chapter 3: The First 90 Days (pg 21), focusing on the introductory meetings. The PM role is slightly different on each team, so these conversations are critical for learning what your teammates expect of you.

- Scan the "Responsibilities" for each PM skill to get a deeper understanding of the role.

I'M HAVING TROUBLE GETTING PROMOTED

Don't worry, this happens to many PMs who go on to have highly successful careers.

- Start with Chapter 32: The Career Ladders (pg 343) to learn the differences between each level, and concrete tips on how to get promoted.

- Read Chapter 34: Working with your manager (pg 378) (and other parts of the same chapter).

- Ask your manager or a trusted mentor to direct you to the PM skills you should focus on.

---

2   For higher-level promotions (such as to VP), there also needs to be a business need for a person of that level.

I'M A SENIOR PRODUCT LEADER

You can skip the basics, we've still got plenty of information for you.

- Take a look at Chapter 32: The Career Ladders (pg 343) to get a sense of how the roles change in the upper levels of product leadership.

- Scan each PM Skill for the responsibilities and growth practices marked with ⚡. Strategic Skills (pg 166) are especially important as you advance.

- Read Part G: "People Management Skills" (pg 282) for help with the operational excellence side of product leadership.

I WANT TO DEVELOP MY SKILLS AS A PM

You can focus on the areas you want to develop.

- Read the "Growth Practices" for each PM skill.

- Scan the "Responsibilities" and "Frameworks" for anything unfamiliar.

- Take a look at "Learning from feedback" (pg 385) to make the most of personalized feedback.

I WANT TO LAND A PRODUCT MANAGER JOB

This wasn't our core use case, but that doesn't mean you're in the wrong place.

- Read the core skills in Product Skills (pg 32), Execution Skills (pg 110), Strategic Skills (pg 166), and Leadership Skills (pg 214)

- Check out Chapter 49: Landing a Product Manager Job (pg 481) to learn a bit about interview questions

- Check out our first book, Cracking the PM Interview, which focuses on interview prep

ENJOY!

We hope you enjoy this book. We know it's a big one, so skip the sections that aren't as relevant. You can always come back to them later.

Feel free to drop us a line at gayleandjackie@careercup.com or find us online:

- twitter.com/jackiebo
- facebook.com/jackie.bavaro
- https://medium.com/@jackiebo

- twitter.com/gayle
- facebook.com/gayle
- https://medium.com/@gayle

CHAPTER 2

THE PRODUCT MANAGER ROLE

IF YOU ASK five people what a product manager is, you might get six different answers.

Some people say a product manager is a mini-CEO. Others say they're the advocate for the customer. Some say they're the glue that holds the team together. Others say they're the conductor of an orchestra. Some people say they're responsible for strategy, while others focus on user research and execution.

Why so many answers? For one thing, the role is complex and multi-faceted. For another, the role really is different at different companies. Product management is a "whitespace" role—the PM is responsible for anything that isn't covered by other people. Some PMs work with dedicated researchers, data scientists, product marketers, and copy-writers, while others have none of those, or limited access to one.

Here's our answer to what a product manager is:

> A PM is the person on a product team who is responsible for choosing the right problems to go after, defining what success looks like, and guiding their team to achieve successful outcomes.

They are responsible for the overall success of their product. It's a hugely influential role because the PM is the main person who decides what the product teams actually work on.

This role is all about out*comes*, not out*put*. To be a great PM, you can't just follow the steps; you need to reliably build and ship successful products.

THE PRODUCT TRIAD

One of the best ways to understand the PM role is in relation to the other roles at a company. As a PM, you work with many teammates who each have parts they're responsible for. You are responsible for making sure everyone's vision is aligned, all the parts fit together, and that nothing slips through the cracks. If there is a problem, it's your responsibility to—diplomatically—ensure it gets fixed. You must lead without authority, influencing people by using your vision, research, and analysis.

The core product team at most modern tech companies is called the **triad**: Engineer (or Tech Lead), Designer, and Product Manager.

- **Engineers** are responsible for the technical solution. They'll plan the data structures and algorithms that will make things fast, scalable, and maintainable. They'll write the code and tests.

- **Designers** are responsible for the solution from the user experience perspective. What will it look like? What are the flows, screens, and buttons? They'll make mockups or prototypes of how the feature should work.

- **Product managers** are responsible for selecting and defining *which* problems the team is going to solve, then ensuring the team solves them. They'll define what success looks like, and plan how to get there.

There are many ways to divide work within the triad. The split can vary depending on each person's level of experience, time at the company, skills, interests, and how heavy their workload is. For example, a junior designer might expect the PM to entirely define the problem and constrain parts of the solution, while a senior designer might be very involved in shaping the problem. It's helpful to have a detailed discussion about this when you start working with new people to ensure there aren't any mismatched expectations.

On the best teams, the triad works together in a close partnership. All three are involved from the very beginning. They share context, give each other feedback, and problem-solve together. Many times, they all agree on a decision, but if not, they should trust each other enough to defer to the person who is most responsible for that problem. They help each other out.

THE PRODUCT LIFE CYCLE

The day-to-day work of a product manager varies over the course of the product life cycle. Modern product development doesn't follow a strict linear structure, but in order to understand the PM role, it's helpful to group activities by phase.

In reality, these phases will overlap, occur out of order, and happen in iterative cycles. Every company has its own version, but this is the general pattern:[1]

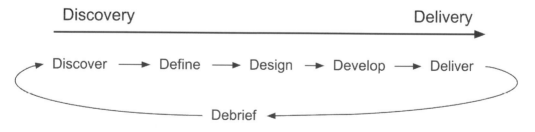

---

1   These phases expand upon the UK Design Council's "Double Diamond" model: https://www.designcouncil.org.uk/news-opinion/what-framework-innovation-design-councils-evolved-double-diamond

PMs often have two streams of work going at a time: one closer to discovery, and one closer to delivery.[2] This helps ensure that when the engineers finish their current work, there's no gap while the PM figures out the next thing to work on.

> Please note: determining key assumptions, creating hypotheses, and validating hypotheses occur during all stages.

Early on, the key hypotheses focus on the problem, customer needs, business needs, and market sizing. Later, the hypotheses center on the solution, usability, feasibility, and launch plans.

DISCOVER

Imagine your VP stops you in the hall one day and tells you that you need to add "export to PDF" functionality to your product this quarter. It's a straightforward idea, but it will take a few weeks to build in the existing codebase. You put your team on it and launch it without bugs, but no one uses it. Your annual review comes around, and you're blamed for the flop—not the VP who actually gave the order.

What went wrong?

You skipped product discovery and took your VP's solution too literally. The better path would have been to dig deeper and understand the underlying problem that they were trying to solve.

> This is a process called product discovery—when you figure out what problem you should go after.

All products start with an initial idea. It might be a problem you notice, a feature request, an underperforming metric, a new market to go after, or any number of other sources of inspiration. During discovery, you take that initial idea and expand your understanding of the customer's needs, problems, and goals.

> You're looking for a problem that's large enough to be worth solving, while feasible enough for your team to be successful.

Many launches fail because the team focused on the wrong problems. They misunderstood critical details of what the customer had told them, the pain of the problem wasn't big enough to overcome inertia, or they missed the bigger picture and only solved part of the problem.

A great example of this was the VHS versus Betamax video recording format war during the 1970s. Betamax clearly had better picture quality, but it turned out customers cared more about affordability and being able to record a full 2-hour movie. Betamax only had 1 hour of recording time. Better product discovery could have steered Betamax in the right direction.

Common tasks during the *product discovery* phase include:

- Reading through feature requests

---

2   Marty Cagan calls this "Continuous Discovery and Delivery" or "Dual Track Agile": https://svpg.com/continuous-discovery/

- Analyzing funnel metrics

- Interviewing customers

- Testing concept mocks

- Discussing long-term strategy

- Researching competitors

- Doing market analysis

- Holding brainstorming sessions

- Running design sprints[3]

Discovery is the magic tool for reliably creating successful products. Without product discovery, you're just hoping that the first idea you came up with, or that your executive told you to build, is a good solution for an important customer problem.

DEFINE

Imagine that you've invested a lot of time in product discovery, and brought your whole team along to many customer visits. Everyone is feeling great about the customer problems. When you start working with the designer on the solution, however, there are disagreements. Your designer came up with a beautiful solution that would take six months to build and is insisting that cutting anything means you don't care about customers.

What went wrong?

What went wrong here is that you weren't clear enough during the *define phase*. You didn't get alignment on the scope of the problem and what success actually looks like. You might have assumed that you'd start by tackling a small part of the problem in the first release, but your designer didn't know that.

> The define phase is when you narrow down the problem space to a specific, feasible slice, and frame it so it's ready for the team. You might have a hypothesis for a solution at this point, but it's just an illustration, not something you're committed to. During this phase, you'll be shaping the outcomes you're going after, and outlining the big picture so your team understands where this project fits in.

Common tasks during the *define* phase include:

- Prioritizing the problems identified in discovery

- Picking a target customer

- Mapping the customer journey

- Defining success metrics

- Creating a product vision

---

3   A design sprint is a great step-by-step process for pulling together all of the pieces of discovery: https://www.gv.com/sprint/

- Proposing a high-level roadmap

- Drafting an initial timeline

The culmination of the *define phase* is often some kind of review where the team gets the go-ahead for the work and people are assigned to the team.

DESIGN

Imagine your team is ready to start working on a well-defined problem of getting user photos during the sign-up flow, and your designer quickly sketches up a solution. It looks good, so, you give the go-ahead and the team builds it. Unfortunately, customers are

Betamax vs. VHS

confused by the flow and keep writing in to customer support. You realize a different approach is needed, and you rewrite the whole thing. What went wrong?

What went wrong in this scenario is that you didn't consider multiple solutions and test paper prototypes during the *design phase*.

> The design phase is not just about putting your ideas into pictures; it also includes expansive thinking and validating your ideas with real people. This includes both the user experience (e.g., mock-ups and visual prototypes) and the technical solution (design docs and technical prototypes).

Common tasks during the *design* phase include:

- Writing a spec

- Deciding what functionality is in or out

- Negotiating dependencies with other teams

- Whiteboarding with designers and engineers

- Giving feedback on design

- Running usability studies

Design activities usually start a bit before the *develop stage*, but for larger projects, they tend to overlap. For example, engineers might be implementing one part of the solution while the designer continues to work on another part. Or, the engineers will prototype a basic design and then work hand-in-hand with the designer to figure out how it should look and behave.

DEVELOP

Development is where you turn the ideas into working code. Depending on the team, the PM may have a lot of project management responsibilities during this phase, or the tech lead might take that on. In either case, surprises will inevitably come up and the PM will need to handle them to keep the team on track.

Common tasks during the *develop* phase include:

- Writing stories or tickets for engineering

- Determining which metrics to instrument and track

- Triaging bugs

- Checking in with teammates regularly to unblock them

- Trying out each feature as it's being built and giving feedback

- Keeping stakeholders and approvers up-to-date

The more responsive you can be to your team, the faster they'll be able to build the product.

DELIVERY

Delivery is where you roll out the solution to users. Some changes are quietly shipped without any fanfare, while others have a full go-to-market campaign.

A lot can go wrong during delivery, and it's up to the PM to make sure it doesn't. You don't want to find out that your product is buggy and takes down the servers on launch day. You don't want to surprise the sales and support teams with changes that they can't explain to customers. And you don't want to send out an email to thousands of people telling them to download an app that's not available in the app store yet (been there!).

Common tasks during the *deliver* phase include:

- Setting up validation phases such as internal dogfooding, beta testing, A/B tests, and stability tests

- Organizing the quality assurance (QA) process

- Working with launch partners to ensure everything is ready for launch (including gathering approvals)

- Partnering with marketing on the go-to-market plan

- Training salespeople and customer support

- Celebrating with the team.

Product delivery requires a lot of coordination and risk mitigation. Successful launches are a collaboration between product, infrastructure, marketing, operations, and many more departments.

DEBRIEF

While many people are eager to move on to the next new thing as soon as the product launches, it's not over yet. After the launch, it's important to measure how it went and learn from the project. Often, insights from the launch will drive the next round of product innovation.

Common tasks during the *debrief* phase include:

- Running a retrospective on what went well and what didn't

- Analyzing launch metrics

- Reading customer feedback on the launch

- Prioritizing "fast follow" work based on customer feedback

- Evaluating the launch success

- Sharing launch results with the company

- Planning for the next iteration

The time and energy you put into debriefing will help you grow as a PM and build your credibility.

OTHER ACTIVITIES

Beyond developing products, PMs are also expected to invest in their own personal growth and contribute to the rest of the PM team and company.

These tasks might include:

- Pitching and interviewing candidates
- Mentoring other PMs
- Writing high-quality peer feedback
- Participating in company processes like goal setting and status reports
- Reviewing specs from other PMs
- Answering incoming questions from other teams
- Presenting to important customers

- Meeting with customers regularly
- Sharing best practices and lessons learned
- Running company-wide processes
- Presenting at all-hands
- Participating in strategy discussions
- Attending industry conferences
- Staying up-to-date with PM best practices

HOW DO I BECOME A GREAT PRODUCT MANAGER?

Great product managers are those who reliably ship great products. Early in your career, you can get credit for developing your skills and showing potential, but eventually, your greatness will be measured by the impact of the products you ship.[4]

Luckily, to ship great products, you don't need to be a creative genius who's struck by inspiration in the shower.

> There are a lot of reliable frameworks and best practices that will improve your chances of shipping a successful product. The frameworks won't transform you into a great product manager overnight or guarantee that your products never fail, but they'll help you avoid the most common problems and give you some structure to start experimenting, reflecting, and improving. They are not a replacement for good judgment.

Becoming a great product manager can take years of practice and experience.

At first, you might feel like there are so many frameworks and best practices that it's impossible to know which one would be helpful at any given time. You might get caught up in the surface-level trappings of finding the right template or using the best agile methodology. It will take a lot of time to run your team

---

4   There's no scientific way to separate the impact of a PM from the strength of the rest of the team. In practice, managers give a lot of weight to peer reviews to understand how much the PM contributed to the results.

because you won't have the intuition on what steps can be skipped, or how to quickly get people on board with a plan. You'll catch some problems in later parts of development when they're more expensive to fix. Sometimes, product leadership will throw a wrench in things and require massive changes.

You might misunderstand part of the customer problem, or mess up part of the execution, causing the launch to miss its goals.

> Over time, you'll build up strong mental representations that help you quickly identify the right approach to any given problem.

You'll find that the PM work for each feature takes a lot less time as you hone in on the key pieces of work and need fewer iterations. You'll notice problems earlier, and learn to validate ideas to improve the quality and speed of your launches. You'll start to accurately predict what product leadership cares about, and learn to show your work early to avoid wasted work. You'll get better at digging deep into customer problems and executing smoothly, and you will hit your launch goals.

> Then, when you feel like you can launch features with your eyes closed, your role will change and you'll be a beginner again.

You'll be expected to take on more strategic responsibilities. It will feel like you need to prioritize apples against oranges while predicting the future of the fruit market. You'll be taking on multiple projects at once, many of which will require significant tradeoffs. There will be no way of pleasing all the stakeholders. People will ask for roadmaps and visions. With your team being asked to sign-up for absurdly ambitious goals, you'll wonder how you'll possibly find the time for everything.

You can make it through that adjustment period by getting comfortable with ambiguity, tough problems, and tradeoffs. You'll come to understand the company's business strategy and drive product strategy from it. Projects will take less of your time as you learn to empower the members of your team and earn the trust to take shortcuts. Stakeholders will feel like you understand them, so they'll be okay with the tradeoffs you have to make. You'll remove ego from the equation, and become okay with submitting work that's below your regular quality standards in order to make more time for strategy and vision. You'll figure out what it would take to make a significant impact, and drive conversations on the best path to follow.

> Around this time, you'll start to feel like a great product manager.

You can relax and enjoy your success, or take another leap into leadership roles. Good Luck!

CHAPTER 3

THE FIRST 90 DAYS

CLAIRE SHOWED UP at her new company ready to jump into action. Knowing how critical the first few months are, she wanted to show them that she could deliver an impact immediately. She wanted to get in some quick wins.

On her first week, Claire asked her engineering teams to bring all of their in-progress work to her for review. She knew the CEO was concerned about product quality, so she carefully tried out the products, filed dozens of bugs, and made a handful of usability suggestions. "Great!" she thought, "I'm already making a difference."

Then, Claire moved on to the upcoming work. She walked over to her designer's desk and tapped him on the shoulder. "Can you show me the mocks you're working on?" she asked. She reviewed them quickly and said, "Looks good! Can you please get me the final mocks by Friday." This team was really going to appreciate the way she ran a tight ship.

The next week, she was ready to present her spec for a new customer referral program, something she'd implemented twice before at previous companies. People came after her with question after question. How will this work for anonymous users? Is this legal in the UK? Won't this hurt our margins? Do our power users like this approach? What did customers say? Honestly, she didn't know.

After 30 days, when Claire got her first set of peer and manager feedback, she discovered that her "tight ship" was in shambles. Her teammates felt disrespected by the new processes, and frustrated that she hadn't protected them from the company's ever-changing requirements—which wasn't even on her radar. Her designer was frustrated by the constant interruptions and one-sided deadline setting. Her manager was disappointed that she hadn't spoken to any customers, and concerned that she hadn't submitted a roadmap yet—another task she was unaware of.

Ouch. Her eagerness gave way to impulsiveness, and she'd flubbed her first 30 days. Luckily, she still had 60 days to get things back on track.

She went back to each of her coworkers and apologized for rushing into things. "Can we start over again? Nice to meet you. Can you tell me about yourself?" She checked in with her teammates about what they were hoping she would work on. She met with her manager and wrote down a clear list of expectations, deliverables, and dates. Then she filled up her week with customer visits and spent her free time catching up on strategy documents and usage dashboards.

By switching out of "do, do, do!" mode and into learning mode, she was able to build up the context about how to help her team and what the company needed. Her team let go of the earlier objections—an apology always helps—and she regained the credibility she lost.

With her relationships restored, she worked with her team to develop a roadmap and started using it to push back against changing requirements. By the end of her first 90 days she'd launched several experiments to validate the team's direction, and was already delivering wins to customers.

> The first 90 days with a new team are crucial. Whether you're joining a large company or a small startup, this chapter will help you make the most of your first three months.

Overall, your goal for the first 90 days should be to set yourself up for long-term success on your new team. While it's beneficial to ramp up quickly and start delivering value early, you don't want to over-optimize on the short term. Some people mistakenly jump in and spend all their time finishing their first project quickly, instead of making space to learn the company and form strong relationships.

Take the time to lay the groundwork for the rest of your time on the team:

- Learn about the company, your team, and cultural norms.
- Learn about your product and customers.
- Align on the expectations for your role.
- Align on your onboarding plans and timeline with your manager and teammates.
- Form strong relationships with coworkers.
- Earn credibility.
- Get in some quick wins.

On the flip side, don't stir up trouble before you understand the team dynamics. You'll need strong relationships to get your job done, so you don't want to alienate anyone early on. It's fairly common for an eager new PM to end up inadvertently stepping on toes.

THE "I'M NEW HERE" ADVANTAGE

There are huge advantages to being new on a team.

When you're new, you can ask lots of questions. Make the most of, "Sorry, I'm new here so could you explain what that means?" or, "I might not have the full context, but can you tell me more about why we're doing it that way?" This applies to genuine questions, but it's also a powerful win-win technique for making suggestions in the early days.

Another advantage is starting relationships off on the right foot. There are a lot of "getting to know you" questions that are awkward to ask later on. If there's someone prickly who's had trouble with previous PMs, you can start out on the right foot with them.

Of course, being new also has disadvantages; you won't have earned credibility yet, and that makes your job a lot harder. Don't worry—you'll earn it again!

30/60/90 DAY ONBOARDING PLAN

In your first week or two, you'll want to put together an onboarding plan for your first 90 days and review it with your manager.

> The plan can be lightweight, but it helps to have something in writing when you're new. This is a key time when miscommunications or mismatched expectations tend to happen. Without a written plan, you might feel uncomfortable while ramping up, or your boss might think you're ramping up too slowly.

In creating your onboarding plan, ask for a list of people you should meet. Ask if there are specific topics you should discuss with them, and be sure to ask if there's any tension, conflict, or sore spots you should be aware of. The following list of people should get you started:

- Immediate team: designer, engineers, data scientists, and user researchers
- Other PMs on your team
- Your manager's peers
- Key stakeholders
- Cross-functional partners: sales, marketing, operations, infrastructure, quality assurance, business development, content writers, legal, etc.
- Anyone else who's generally good to know

Here's an example onboarding plan.

First 30 Days

HR & Company onboarding

- Employment forms, mandatory training, etc
- Read & watch materials about the company strategy and values

PM & Feature team

- Learn processes
- Get access to tools
- Learn about team's current plans & needs
- Shadow the current PM

Shadow onboarding buddy

- Sit next to them
- Watch their meetings
- Follow along on their communication

Meet coworkers

- Send out intro message

- Introductory 1:1s

- Daily check-ins with onboarding buddy

- Weekly 1:1s with manager

Become the expert on the customers and the product

- Join sales calls, onsite visits, and research sessions

- Read or answer customer support tickets

- Use the product, document first impressions, skim the help guide

Deliverables

- **Complete Starter Project:** Launch A/B test by week 3

First 60 Days

Feature team

- Take over as the primary PM, with reverse shadowing from the old PM

Meet coworkers

- Continue meeting with coworkers

Become the expert on the customers and the product

- Continue meeting with customers

Deliverables

- Run execution for September 10th launch

- Create quarterly roadmap for team by September 12th

First 90 Days

Feature team

- Lead team independently without reverse shadowing

Become the expert on the customers and the product

- Continue meeting with customers

Deliverables

- Hit team OKRs

INTRODUCTORY MEETINGS

Introductory meetings are a great way to start forming relationships and get off to a good start with your coworkers.

Relationships will be critical to your success as a PM. It's a lot easier to lead people through influence if you can show them that you understand their goals and care about them as people. This might be as simple as asking them about their personal interests and sharing some of yours - bonus if you have some in common! You might also want to share a bit about your past experience to quickly earn some credibility.

A second important goal of these meetings is to align on how you'll work together and how you'll split up the work. The PM role is a little different on each team, so you need to have a conversation about what is expected on this specific team.

Your manager

Your manager will be one of the most influential people in your career, so be sure to start off on the right foot. The more you understand them and what they care about, the better off you'll be.

Until you get to know your manager better, you can't go wrong by being friendly, curious, respectful, and enthusiastic to work with them.

You'll want to be completely aligned on expectations. Mismatched expectations are one of the top causes of failed onboarding. If you're having trouble bringing it up, try printing out the list of questions and asking to go over them at your next 1:1. If your manager doesn't set up regular 1:1 meetings, schedule them yourself.

About them:

- What is your working style?
- How would you like us to work together?
- How do you like to communicate; do you prefer written or in person?
- Do you have any pet peeves? Any things you love?
- What are your top goals for this year?
- How can I best help you with your goals?
- Is there anything else I should know about you?

About the role and expectations:

- How do you see my role?
- What makes a great PM?
- What does success look like to you?
- Do you have thoughts on what I should be doing in my first 90 days?
- Are there any important deliverables?
- Is there a project I should get started on first?
- How much are you expecting me to shake things up in the beginning vs. execute on the current plans?
- Are there any landmines or controversies to avoid?
- Do you have any ideas for quick wins where I could help the team?
- When is my first feedback or review cycle? Is there anything specific you'd like me to achieve by then?

- Is there a job ladder or leveling framework I could read?

- Are there any other expectations you have?

> You'll learn a lot about your manager by what they emphasize in their responses. Pay attention to any key phrases they use or ideas they repeat.

Some people will emphasize numeric results, while others emphasize teamwork or learning. Some like to see a lot of autonomy, while others want to be kept looped into the details until you've built up trust. Some care more about your relationship with the sales team, while others care more about your first-hand interactions with customers.

Be careful about how you talk about promotions and advancement. If you seem too focused on getting promoted, they might mistake you as being self-interested rather than user-focused or a team player.

Your onboarding buddy

Some companies will assign you an onboarding buddy. If not, you can ask your manager to recommend someone, or even approach someone directly. Ideally, your onboarding buddy is another PM on your team who has been at the company for a while. You want someone who knows how things work and won't judge you for asking questions. It's okay to have multiple onboarding buddies, for example, one person who's been at the company a long time, another who's on the PM team, and another who's eager to answer all your questions.

A great way to work with your onboarding buddy (especially a PM buddy) is to shadow them; sit next to them, ask them to invite you to their meetings, and have them loop you in on relevant communication. Ask them to talk out loud as they do their work—for example, explaining why they're answering a question in a certain way, sharing their tips for working with certain people, or explaining historical context about the product. By shadowing them in this way, you'll be able to pick up context, processes, and cultural norms.

In addition to any of the questions from the Manager section earlier, you might also ask:

- What should I know about my manager? Do they have any pet peeves? What's the fastest way to get on their good side?

- How do things actually get staffed and launched here? Who decides what's worked on? What kinds of approvals do people need?

- Do people really follow the official process? If they bend the rules, when and why?

- Are there any unspoken rules or cultural norms?

- Who are good role models?

- Are you in any fun groups or clubs at the company? Are there any you'd recommend for me?

Executives

It's great if you can meet with some executives while you're onboarding. At a large company, this might be your skip-level manager. At a smaller company, this might be the cofounders.

In general, since this might be one of the few times you meet one on one with them, the most important thing is to make a good impression. It's also a good idea to start forming a mental model of their perspective so you'll be able to predict what they care about later on.

An important part of making a good first impression is valuing their time. You don't want to ask informational questions that you could have looked up or should already know.

Here are some safe questions for an intro meeting:

- How are you feeling about the company goals?

- What keeps you up at night?

- What's your biggest challenge right now?

- Do you have any specific things you'd like to see me do in this role?

- What's your view of what makes a PM successful at this company?

Close teammates

For your closest teammates, such as your designer and engineering lead, you'll want to start by building a relationship, then making sure expectations are aligned, and finally, looking for opportunities to help the team.

Setting expectations is especially important with close teammates because the boundaries of the PM role vary greatly from team to team. You don't want to get a few months in and realize that your designer expected you to be providing long written documents, or that your engineering lead wanted to write the tickets herself.

Getting-to-know-you questions:

- Tell me about yourself. (Do you live near the office? Anything interesting going on outside of work? What do you do for fun? Do you like to travel? Etc.)

- What brought you to this company?

- What are you working on now? What are some of your favorite past projects? What are you looking forward to working on?

- What are your top goals for this year?

Aligning on expectations:

- How would you like to see us work together? What are your expectations for me?

- Are there things you've liked, or not liked, about working with people in my role before? Do you have any pet peeves?

- How often would you like to meet?

- How do you like to give and receive feedback?

- Is there anything you'd like to change about my 30/60/90 day plan?

Opportunities:

- How are you feeling about the team and how things have been going?

- Is there anything you're hoping to change about how the team works?

- Do you have any ideas for where I could find quick wins to help the team?

Everyone else

For everyone else, you'll want to focus on relationship-building and getting to know what's important to them.

General questions:

- Tell me about yourself.

- What are you working on? What are some of your favorite past projects? What are you looking forward to working on?

- What are your top goals for this year?

- How would you like to see us work together? Are there things you've liked, or not liked, about working with people in my role before?

- Is there anything I can do that would help you now?

DOS

Take advantage of your beginner's eyes

As Bryan Jowers, a VP of product, says:

> You only get to go through product purchase and onboarding once as a first time user. Be sure to document your emotions, what you understand, and don't understand.

Your notes could be useful in improving the product or even improving the onboarding process for the next hire.

Become the expert on your product and users

Get as much exposure to users and customers as possible. Meet with them in-person or on video calls. If your company has them, join sales calls and user research sessions. Answer support tickets. See what people are talking about on social media. Conduct your own interviews to understand why people are choosing your product and what challenges they're having with it. A huge part of your early credibility will come from your direct knowledge of the customer.

Another key area to become an expert in is your own product and technology. You'll want to make sure you understand not only your own feature area but also the broader product and how the various parts interact. If you don't deeply understand the product, you won't be able to spot opportunities, pitfalls, or important constraints.

Build credibility

It takes time for your teammates to begin to trust you and your judgment. One way to make it go faster is to share your thought processes and frameworks. Explain where your intuitions come from.

Get quick wins in early

Being helpful will help you to get off on the right foot. Often, you can take some grunt work off your teammates' hands, or you can help them complete something important that they've been putting off or struggling with.

As someone new to the team, you probably have extra time to spend on tedious tasks. You might find that a task they didn't want to do is a great learning experience for you. You can also ask your onboarding buddy for tasks you can pick up. This could be a bug they're handling, a small feature, or anything that will let you contribute to the team and get used to the processes in a scoped-down setting.

Look for ways to feel like you belong at the company

Join employee resource groups, social groups, sports teams, etc. Invite your coworkers out for coffee or lunch. The more you feel like you have friends at the company and feel like you belong, the happier you will be in the role in the long run.

Make it easy for people to give you feedback

New people aren't expected to get it perfect the first time. By explicitly checking in for feedback, you can make it easier for people to tell you what you're doing wrong and share their ideas of what "excellent" would look like, without it reflecting poorly on you.

You can ask, "Here's what I'm planning to change; does that sound good, or am I missing anything?" You can check in with your buddy or partners after a meeting and ask if they have any feedback, or what they feel amazing work would look like. You can hold a retrospective meeting after your first week to talk about what you want to change or continue as a team.

DON'TS

Don't start by telling people they're doing it all wrong

That's a quick way to alienate people. Instead, ask why they chose to do things that way, and be genuinely curious about their answer. Feel free to follow up with, "Did you consider doing it this other way?"

Don't shut people down—Say "yes, and…"

When you're new, you can get inundated with people asking for things or sharing their ideas for what you should do. A lot of those ideas won't be very good, or won't be high-priority. Instead of saying, "No, that's a bad solution," you can say, "Yes, I agree that's a problem worth solving." Even if your next sentence tells them it's not high on your list, they'll feel heard and be more willing to work with you in the future.

Don't try to make major changes right away

It's important to first listen and learn context before changing things. Then, when you're ready to make a change, be intentional about how you roll it out to bring the rest of your teammates along. Early on, try planting seeds of an idea rather than presenting a huge case.

Don't assume you need to maintain all previous decisions

New PMs often inherit a project in the middle of the product life cycle. Chances are, you'll disagree with some of the decisions the previous PM made, and you'll need to live with the product you ship. This situation calls for delicacy: talk to your manager and teammates to get a sense for how fixed the earlier decisions are. Sometimes you'll learn that the team is more than happy to change course, and other times you'll find out that they just want you to help them get the work out the door.

KEY TAKEAWAYS

- **Look before you leap:** The best use of your first 90 days is to learn as much as you can about the team, company, product, and customers. Take advantage of the extra time on your schedule to get a head start on the information that will help you succeed. Until you're ramped up on that, it will be hard for coworkers to trust your suggestions.

- **Get in a quick win:** While you still have a lot to learn, there are likely to be a few small, uncontroversial projects you can accomplish that make your coworkers feel glad that you're there.

- **Invest in relationships:** Good relationships will make your job easier and more fun. Take the time to get to know people at your company.

- **Be clear about expectations:** Each PM job is a little different, and misunderstandings are common in the first 90 days. Find out how people would like to work with you so you don't accidentally step on their toes or fail to pick up a responsibility they expected you to handle. Make sure you're clear with your manager about your top priorities and when deliverables are due. Put your plan in writing and share it so that everyone is on the same page.

PRODUCT SKILLS

USER INSIGHT

DATA INSIGHT

ANALYTICAL PROBLEM SOLVING

PRODUCT AND DESIGN SKILLS

TECHNICAL SKILLS

WRITING PRODUCT DOCUMENTATION

PART C

PRODUCT SKILLS

PRODUCT SKILLS

PRODUCT SKILLS ARE the foundation for designing high-quality products that delight users and solve people's needs. In this section, we'll develop the skills for making better product decisions.

- **User Insight** (pg 35) will teach us how to understand what people need and the problems they want a product to solve. We'll learn how to gather information from users and dig deeper to surface key insights. Finally, we'll explore the many types of user research.

- **Data Insight** (pg 50) will teach us how to review data, analyze it, and use it for better decision-making. We'll talk about how to look at company metrics, and explore A/B testing and statistics.

- **Analytical Problem Solving** (pg 63) will provide frameworks for making better decisions. We'll cover topics like systems thinking and learn techniques for tackling complex problems.

- **Product and Design Skills** (pg 76) will develop our product mindset and our ability to drive product decisions. We'll learn about prototyping and brainstorming, and how to prioritize product decisions.

- **Technical Skills** (pg 92) will teach you how to partner with engineers and how to better estimate development costs. It'll also offer a crash course in technology—APIs, deployment, SQL, algorithms, and more.

- **Writing Product Document** (pg 104) is exactly what it sounds like. This chapter will teach you best practices for writing specs and using them to improve your product.

You'll use product skills most heavily in the early phases of the product life cycle (pg 14), but they can come into play at any time.

CHAPTER 4

USER INSIGHT

ON MY FIRST product team, I read some support tickets and talked to a few customers on the phone. Mostly, however, I made decisions without ever talking to a real customer. Instead, I studied our product's personas, a small set of fictional people designed to represent the different types of customers. This was considered a best practice in 2004, but basically I was just guessing what customers would want.

Later, I saw how small errors in my assumptions became large problems for customers.

In one case, I'd saved engineering time by squeezing in a feature in a way that didn't pick up custom colors. I'd thought it might be a minor annoyance, but when I went on site with a customer I learned they would refuse to use the feature unless it matched their brand color. I had to patch their servers with their custom color to fix the problem.

In an even worse case, I learned that a piece of functionality I'd worked so hard to include (setting notifications for other users) was entirely undiscoverable. People complained that the feature was missing! We'd done the work but that didn't matter since people didn't know it was there.

These failures were a formative experience for me. I realized that my intuition could be wrong and started to believe that I needed to double check my assumptions. I'd thought I understood my users, but I didn't understand them enough.

This is user insight, and it's a core skill for you, as a product manager, to develop. You'll use that deep understanding and empathy to identify product opportunities and ensure solutions will meet your users' needs.[1]

RESPONSIBILITIES

SPEAK WITH USERS AND POTENTIAL USERS

Users are people. How do we get to know people? We talk to them!

---

[1] There's a bit of backlash against the term "user" because it can feel dehumanizing, but we use it in this book because the replacements like "customers," "readers," or "members" don't apply to all products.

Aim to speak with at least five to ten people when you start working with a new product, and add another five to ten people during each project. If your product has different types of users (such as authors + readers or riders + drivers), talk to five to ten of each type.

Live meetings, especially face-to-face, are better than asynchronous mediums like emails and surveys. Live meetings provide a depth of insight that written or pre-recorded sources lack. In a live meeting, you're learning brand new information. You absorb the emotional impact, and you can ask follow-up questions. Reading up on your company's existing user research is certainly important as well, but it's not a substitute for having conversations with people yourself.

Your goal is to become the expert on your users. Product management isn't like school, where you're solving problems with established answers. Rather, product management—or at least *effective* product management—requires you to learn new and unique insights about your area.

As you talk to people, focus on the insights—both expected and unexpected—so you can form a mental model of your users. Try to predict what people will say, and keep track of where your intuition is right and wrong. Over time, not only will your intuition improve, but you'll also develop a greater awareness of when your intuition is reliable, and when it might lead you astray.

Dig beyond surface needs

Imagine your company makes lasers, and your users—doctors—have a common complaint about these devices. The mechanical arms are too heavy! They are using these lasers to perform intricate surgery and the weight of the materials posed a significant challenge.

This was the situation Xanar and its competitors were in. The other companies heard the users' requests and responded to it with expensive investments in lighter metals and materials. Xanar, however, looked deeper. Doctors *asked* for a lighter arm, but the underlying *problem* was maneuverability.

With that in mind, Xanar merely counterbalanced the arm. The arm was no lighter (in fact, technically, it was *heavier*), but it was much more maneuverable.

People, as it turns out, do not always know what they want. They feel a "pain" and might translate that into a specific solution. Your job, in a sense, is to "un-translate" it. Listen to the feature request, and then figure out the underlying problem. This problem can then become part of the "job to be done" (pg 40).

As a PM, the deeper you go, the better you'll understand your customers and be able to steer the team towards solutions that work.

To probe deeper, try the following questions:

- Can you walk me through how you would use the feature you're requesting? What happens before you use it? What happens after?

- Is that task part of a larger goal?

- What are some of the challenges you run into with that task?

- Have you tried anything to help with this problem before? What stopped it from working? How are you solving the problem today?

- If we built this, would you switch to using it, or is there anything else you'd need?

- Here's how I understand the problem: [...]. Is there anything I missed?

Remember: we should listen to our customers, but that doesn't mean they're always right about the solutions they propose.

VALIDATE YOUR ASSUMPTIONS

Assumptions, left unvalidated, can be a dangerous thing. New PMs are often overconfident in their ideas or designs and fail to anticipate where things could go wrong.

Instead, treat your ideas and designs as hypotheses, and seek out lightweight ways to assess them. This could be via user studies, customer interviews, or sometimes just quick chats with friends or colleagues.

Louis Lecat, Head of Product at Algolia, shared a time when validating his assumptions with a prototype made a big difference:

> We were building a product to reorder search results and we assumed users would need to see attributes like price, margin, or discount.
>
> What we saw was unexpected; they reordered results based on how the items looked next to each other. They were optimizing for the global look and feel of the page, and not just for each item individually.

This led us to completely reorganize our roadmap. We were able to launch a successful product much faster than anticipated.

If you do things right, then early user testing will sometimes show that your idea was wrong. Treat this as a win! Not only did you prevent investing time and energy on the wrong path, but it also shows that your user testing is successful.

Here are some common areas for assumptions that are worth validating:

- Why users choose your product over an alternative

- Which features are must-haves vs. nice-to-haves

- How much time and attention users put into learning the product

- The impact of "minor" usability issues

- The discoverability of a feature

- The extent of the inertia to begin using the product

Read on for approaches to validate assumptions in "User Research" (pg 43).

PLAN STRATEGIC USER RESEARCH TO LOOK FOR NEW OPPORTUNITIES ⚡

As you advance in your career, you'll take on a more forward-looking, strategic role. No longer is PMing just about your assigned product area. Now, you'll need to look out at the horizon: What are adjacent customer problems for your product to tackle? How will this impact your product and its potential? How might external trends unlock new opportunities? What kind of research could validate or expand on these opportunities?

This strategic user research is often exploratory—you're not exactly sure what you're going to find. You're not asking about a specific feature; rather, you're trying to understand what people's lives and workflows are like. You'll ask open-ended questions like, "Tell me about the last time you…" or, "Walk me through how you made that decision."

There are a few different approaches you can take for strategic user research. You might go onsite with customers and watch them throughout their day. You can set up a diary study that runs over a few weeks, where paid participants take notes and record specific information whenever they do the activity being studied (for example, every time they plan a meal). Or, more simply, you can add some open-ended strategic questions to the usability sessions or customer visits you're already doing.

CREATE A USER-FOCUSED CULTURE ⚡⚡

At the higher levels of product leadership, you're responsible not only for your own user insight skills but also for those of your entire team.

Twilio found that having employees do stints in customer support greatly increased their empathy. As Jason Nassi wrote:[2]

> When they finish their support ticket training, new hires have a better handle on why some of our customers are so fanatic about Twilio, and how they can make a difference for other customers who might need some handholding to be equally successful.

Here are some ways to make your culture more user-focused:

- Require all PMs to answer support tickets occasionally.

- Put up a team leader board to track the number of customer visits.

- Bring customers into the office every week to speak with the team.

- Have a standing topic to share new customer insights during your team meeting.

- Put a customer insight section in the spec template.

- Ask about customer insights in product review.

- Be a role model; visit customers yourself and share the insights you've learned.

Note that this applies to your team as a whole. Yes, your PMs are the voice of the customer—but it's even better if your developers, testers, and other team members can be too.

GROWTH PRACTICES

CULTIVATE A BEGINNER'S MINDSET

The thing with getting good at a product is that, well, you're good at it. When using a product becomes familiar and easy (as it nearly always will be for its own PMs), it's easy to forget what it was like when the product was not familiar.

Practice putting yourself into the mindset of a beginner. Walk through the full product flow from beginning to end, imagining you're unfamiliar with the product. Where would you get confused? What phrases or icons wouldn't make sense? If you can do this effectively, you'll be able to quickly identify problems that new users would face.

---

2   Jason expands on this at https://www.zendesk.com/blog/new-employees-answer-support-tickets/.

To build this skill, pay close attention to what things you had to learn and what confused you when you were new. Watch user sessions with new users and learn the patterns where they struggled with features that power users understood.

CONNECT PRODUCT CHOICES TO CUSTOMER INSIGHTS

Understanding your customers would be a purely academic exercise if you didn't use your knowledge to make good product choices.

Be explicit about how customer insights drive product decisions. A key trait to possess is *intentionality*. Don't design wild ideas that came to you in a dream; rather, each part of the solution should be there for a reason.

New PMs often underinvest in making this connection explicit. It's easy to forget that engineers or executives aren't as immersed in customer insights as you are. They might have forgotten a key finding from research, or might not notice the same connections as you do.

In one case, we saw a PM make line-by-line annotations of the product design, connecting each decision back to an insight about customers so that everyone would understand the intentionality of the design. This arguably "obsessive" approach was a real hit; not only did people buy into her designs faster, but she also earned a reputation as a customer-centric PM. Her team felt confident that her future suggestions were well-reasoned, rather than just "feeling right" to her.

BUILD YOUR USER-FOCUSED INTUITION

Over time, you'll need to move from following a slow but thorough standardized process for gaining user insights, to a faster process, where you intuit which areas to focus on.

The way you build up this intuition is by observing a lot of user research and noticing patterns. Build up a list of mistakes that you or other PMs have experienced before. Reflect and debrief whenever things don't go well or you learn something surprising. Discussing insights with your team can also help to instill them in your memory and form patterns.

CATEGORIZE USER INSIGHTS BY PRIORITY ⚡

Do you fix all the usability issues you find? That's a tricky question. And the answer—like many things in life (and product management)—is: it depends.

When you have less experience, you should err toward fixing the usability issues you find. You typically have yet to establish credibility around your quality bar, and you're also generally more "in the weeds." It can be dangerous if your team perceives you as sloppy. So, yes, *do* focus on even the little usability issues.

However, as you move into higher-level roles, this same focus can backfire. You need to show that, yes, you value quality—but also that you have strong judgment about tradeoffs. Ask yourself about the impact and opportunity cost and be disciplined about which insights are worth investing in. To do this, you don't want to silently ignore low-priority insights. Instead, write down the work you're deciding to deprioritize.

To be clear, this does not mean that quality doesn't matter. It does, a lot! But the key is *balance*. A great PM knows when to delay launch by three weeks, because the newly discovered usability issue is *that* important.

EVANGELIZE YOUR CUSTOMER INSIGHTS ⚡

One habit that distinguishes senior PMs from more junior ones is the way they continually surface relevant customer information.

This could look like:

- Introducing a real-life example in a meeting.

- Pointing other PMs to relevant user research.

- Giving a company-wide talk on key insights.

- Presenting insights and their strategic implications to executives.

Share your knowledge to help your team and company make better decisions.

SURFACE THE KEY INSIGHT THAT UNLOCKS THE PROBLEM ⚡⚡

A JOKE ABOUT A GENERATOR

A company was having trouble with a large generator, and none of the engineers could diagnose the issue.

A contractor came in, listened to the machine for a bit, and then marked one part with chalk. "There's your problem," the contractor said. The engineers looked at the chalk mark and quickly realized the issue, which they then fixed. When the company received a $10,000 bill from the contractor, the manager balked and demanded an itemized bill. The contractor happily complied:

Chalk: $1

Knowing where to make the mark: $9,999

Excellent user insight looks a lot like that; it's seeing the connections between facts and realizing which pieces of information are relevant.

One way to get better at this is to proactively think about the implications of each new insight as you learn it. What past decisions would it change? What future decisions might it impact? By thinking about it ahead of time, you'll be more likely to remember it when it's relevant.

CONCEPTS AND FRAMEWORKS

JOBS TO BE DONE

You may know the age, location, and occupations of your users, but none of that tells you what *really* matters. What "job" are they trying to get done with your product?

This framework, popularized by Clay Christensen, is simultaneously simple and complex. Christensen explains:

> People don't simply buy products or services, they "hire" them to make progress in specific circumstances. They often buy things because they find themselves with a problem they would like to solve.

Consider, for example, customers of a music app. What job are they trying to get done?

The naive answer is that (duh!) they want to listen to music. But if that were the case, then you could just pull out any ol' music. Or let the user pick songs to add to a playlist.

The more complex answer—depending on the app and your users—might be, "I want to create a good vibe for my next party. Something that my friends will like and that will set an upbeat mood." With *that* answer, we lead to a new solution: "How do we surface enjoyable playlists for specific moods?"

The Jobs To Be Done (JTBD) framework is a way of looking at customer motivation and behavior.[3]

To write a user story or use case in the JTBD framework, you can use this template:

> When I <situation>, I want to <motivation>, so I can <expected outcome>.

For example, "when I am throwing a party, I want to play upbeat music, so that my friends and I will have a good time."

When you talk to potential customers, try to discover what "job" they are hiring your software to do. Dig deep. Ask *why*?

CUSTOMER JOURNEY

The Customer Journey framework describes the stages people go through during the life cycle of using a product. Intuitively, we know that these stages exist, yet many PMs only focus on later stages.

Consider a simplistic example of how it might look for an app like Netflix.

- **Awareness:** I discover (probably years ago) that Netflix exists.

- **Consideration:** I find out that Netflix offers my favorite TV show. I consider signing up for it, just for that. But is that worth it? Or should I just buy the movies on Amazon?

- **Purchase:** I decide to pay for a Netflix subscription.

- **Retention:** I continue to pay for Netflix (because I enjoy it… or because I forgot that I have a subscription).

- **Advocacy:** When my friends ask what shows I watch, I mention that I watch my favorite show on Netflix. It seems to have a decent selection of other shows, I tell them.

Improving *any* of these stages can impact the success of your product. Therefore, ask customers—current and potential—questions that address each part of the journey. What creates awareness? What turns awareness into consideration? Consideration into purchase? And so on. Look for the factors that influence each stage.

---

3   Read more about Jobs to be Done at https://medium.com/make-us-proud/jobs-to-be-done-framework-748c761797a8

USABILITY GUIDELINES

Product managers are expected to know some common usability principles. Memorize these so you don't make rookie mistakes.

The gold standard for usability heuristics comes from the Nielsen Norman Group.

10 Usability Heuristics for User Interface Design[4]

These are Jakob Nielsen's 10 general principles for interaction design. They are called "heuristics" because they are broad rules of thumb and not specific usability guidelines.

#1: Visibility of system status

The system should always keep users informed about what is going on, through appropriate feedback within a reasonable time.

#2: Match between system and the real world

The system should speak the users' language, with words, phrases, and concepts familiar to the user, rather than system-oriented terms. Follow real-world conventions, making information appear in a natural and logical order.

#3: User control and freedom

Users often choose system functions by mistake and will need a clearly marked "emergency exit" to leave the unwanted state without having to go through an extended dialogue. Support undo and redo.

#4: Consistency and standards

Users should not have to wonder whether different words, situations, or actions mean the same thing. Follow platform conventions.

#5: Error prevention

Even better than good error messages is a careful design which prevents a problem from occurring in the first place. Either eliminate error-prone conditions or check for them and present users with a confirmation option before they commit to the action.

#6: Recognition rather than recall

Minimize the user's memory load by making objects, actions, and options visible. The user should not have to remember information from one part of the dialogue to another. Instructions for use of the system should be visible or easily retrievable whenever appropriate.

#7: Flexibility and efficiency of use

Accelerators—unseen by the novice user—may often speed up the interaction for the expert user such that the system can cater to both inexperienced and experienced users. Allow users to tailor frequent actions.

#8: Aesthetic and minimalist design

Dialogues should not contain information which is irrelevant or rarely needed. Every extra unit of information in a dialogue competes with the relevant units of information and diminishes their relative visibility.

#9: Help users recognize, diagnose, and recover from errors

---

4   Reprinted with permission from https://www.nngroup.com/articles/ten-usability-heuristics

Error messages should be expressed in plain language (no codes), precisely indicate the problem, and constructively suggest a solution.

#10: Help and documentation

Even though it is better if the system can be used without documentation, it may be necessary to provide help and documentation. Any such information should be easy to search, focused on the user's task, list concrete steps to be carried out, and not be too large.

Beyond those 10 heuristics, here are some common guidelines to remember:

- **Limited attention:** Real users pay much less attention to your product's UI than you'd guess. People subconsciously ignore big flashy banners and anything else they think are ads. They won't read long paragraphs or even sentences of text. They can get interrupted and distracted at any moment. If the main call-to-action is not crystal clear, they'll give up.

- **Whitespace and proportions are important:** Whitespace and proportions make a huge, visceral impact on how people react to your product. Too little, and it will feel cramped and difficult; too much, and people will feel like the app is oversimplified and slow. It's almost impossible to get useful feedback on a design when these details are off because they create such a strong negative reaction.

- **Accessibility:** About 4% of the population is partially colorblind, and about 2% of the population has another visual disability.[5] Testing your product for screen readers and color blindness are easy ways to avoid excluding some of your users. Don't rely solely on color or images without alt-text for any important part of your UI. As a bonus, when you design for accessibility, people without disabilities often benefit from the design as well, a concept called "universal design."[6]

Consider reviewing your existing product with these guidelines in mind. Where do you follow them? Where do you break them?

USER RESEARCH

User research refers to a wide range of methods—not just usability tests, but also contextual interviews, surveys, card sorting, diary studies, beta programs, and many more.

Most user research (other than some surveys) is qualitative rather than quantitative.[7] That means it's useful for answering open-ended questions like, "What criteria do customers consider when they make a purchasing decision?" but not appropriate for numerical questions like, "What percentage of people care about the price?"

The outputs of user research are findings, recommendations, and new models.

TYPES OF USER RESEARCH

There are countless types of user research. Here are some of the more common methods.[8]

---

5   Specifically, about 8% of men and 0.5% of women are red-green colorblind (i.e., have difficulty distinguishing red and green). This trait is carried on the X chromosome and is a recessive trait.

6   A famous example of this is the vegetable peelers with wide comfortable handles from OXO. They were originally designed to help people with arthritis, but soon they learned that everyone loved comfortable handles.

7   Qualitative research generates descriptive data while quantitative research generates numerical data.

8   Focus groups are notably absent because they are not recommended for product research.

Field studies

- **What It Is:** A field study is when you visit your users in their natural habitats, such as their workplace (for business software) or their home (for personal software). During a field study, you observe people in their real context. You might, for example, see what their computer setup looks like and how frequently they get interrupted.

- **When It's Good For:** Field studies are great for early steps in the product life cycle and can be done even before you have a product. They're helpful for identifying and validating opportunities, especially for discovering user problems that are so ingrained that users don't even notice.

- **Beware:** Teams usually conduct field studies close to their office, which creates a location bias. If you have a global product, you may wish to travel to visit customers in other cities and countries.

Diary studies

- **What It Is:** Diary studies are when participants keep a log of their thoughts and behavior over a period of time. For example, you might run a diary study where people record each time they order food and how they decide what to get.

- **When It's Good For:** Diary studies are great for studying conditions that are either difficult to create in a session or to remember accurately after the fact. They can also be excellent for uncovering the meaning behind the metrics. For example, you might see that people frequently visit your product's dashboard page, and the diary study reveals that most people are going to the page to grab screen-shots for a slide deck.

- **Beware:** Running a diary study requires careful motivation of the participants so they don't drop out. Check in with them regularly and compensate them for their continued participation.

User interviews

- **What It Is:** Interviews are when you ask people questions directly. You can ask questions about their past behaviors, their preferences, what they care about, how they make decisions, or anything else you want to learn. It's best to plan out your questions in advance and make them as open-ended as possible. This can be done remotely over video calls with screen sharing.

- **When It's Useful:** User interviews are a great way to learn about users who are different from you. They work well early in the product life cycle before you have anything concrete to show. They can also be a way to validate a survey you want to send out; you can ask questions live and follow up if they misunderstand any of the questions or if any new questions come up.

- **Beware:** People are notoriously optimistic in interviews (e.g., "Of course I'd use that feature"). To work around this, ask about concrete past examples (e.g., "Walk me through the last time you created a dashboard").

Surveys

- **What It Is:** Surveys are a series of questions sent out to current or potential customers. When surveying potential customers, you can use an audience or panel services like SurveyMonkey Audience, or Google Surveys. These services have access to a diverse range of people, allowing you to ask simple screening questions to make sure people fit into your target group before they take the survey.

- **When It's Useful:** Surveys allow you to gather information about a large number of users and are great when you want to answer "how many" questions. For example, you can use a survey to discover what percentage of your customers watch YouTube regularly.

- **Beware:** Poorly worded surveys or those with a confusing set of options can easily skew the results. Test your surveys with a small number of respondents to make sure you're getting useful information back.

Usability tests and concept tests

- **What It Is:** In usability tests or concept tests, you place users in front of a prototype or live product, give them some context, ask them to "think out loud," and then observe what they do. You can give them specific tasks to complete or let them explore on their own.

- **When It's Useful:** With usability tests, you're looking for the details of where they stumble, and with concept tests you're looking to see if the overall concept resonates with them. They're great in the Design phase.

- **Beware:** Some products are hard to test with fake data. For example, an email client relies on users recognizing the names of senders. For these situations, you can create customized mocks by asking for their data in advance or create prototypes that work on live data.

To find participants for these tests, you can put an intercept pop-up on your site using a tool like Ethnio. You can also use UserTesting.com to recruit participants and have them run through the test asynchronously. Both of these approaches will help you recruit participants quickly so you can get results faster.

For consumer products, another popular approach is to visit a coffee shop, cafeteria, or bar, and ask random people if they'd be willing to try a prototype. This approach might lack some rigor (and create some bias, particularly if you're not careful), but it's better to get some feedback on your product than none.

Participatory design (co-design)

- **What It Is:** In participatory design, you have users draw or describe their ideal solution instead of just showing users concept mocks. For example, you might ask a participant to map out their notion of an ideal homepage or draw out how they would like a specific integration to work.

- **When It's Useful:** Participatory design is great not just for soliciting solution ideas but also for thoroughly understanding user needs when they use vague terms. For example, someone might ask for "integration with messenger," but that could mean different things. When you ask them to draw it out, you'll gain a better understanding: "Oh, you wanted to see the two tools side by side, and be able to drag and drop files between them." This method also helps uncover hidden opportunities that could be missed if you just showed the users a precreated design.

- **Beware:** Do not expect the customer to create the whole solution for you. Their design choices will illuminate their thought process, but might not take all of the constraints and use cases into account.

Card sorting

- **What It Is:** In card sorting, you give the participants cards with items that need to be organized and ask them first to put them into groups, and then to name the groups. For example, would people visiting a university website expect to find a campus map on the "Campus Life" page, or the "Visit Us" page? Card sorting can be done in person, or remotely, with online tools.

- **When It's Useful:** Card sorting is a research method specifically designed to understand the mental model of users. It's frequently used when deciding how to best organize site navigation.

- **Beware:** Limit the number of cards to avoid overwhelming users.

Beta program

- **What It Is:** A beta program is when you give a small number of users early opt-in access to new functionality in exchange for honest feedback. Beta programs let you validate ideas and get feedback before your official launch.

- **When It's Useful:** Beta programs are a great way to support incremental development because you can ship functionality to beta customers long before it's fully finished. For example, you might get customers set up with a custom script you run for each of them, rather than an in-app UI. Beta users are often open to using a less polished UI or reading a "getting started" document.

- **Beware:** Participants often have an initial burst of enthusiasm to try out the new functionality as soon as they get access, but this will wane over time. If you give access too early, any feedback will likely be on the obvious stuff that's missing rather than detailed feedback you really want.

How to start a beta program

First, figure out your goals and questions. You want to find out if customers use the new functionality, if they like it, and if they'd be disappointed to lose it (the product-market fit question). You might also have specific questions around UI or requirements.

> **The product-market fit question:** How disappointed would you be if you could no longer use this product?

Recruit beta participants who match your target market as closely as possible. A beta program usually has between 10 and 100 users. You can find beta participants by looking through your sales and support channels, reaching out through email, or by putting a link in your product. Clearly explain that they'll get early access in exchange for their honest feedback, and let them know of any potential risks.

Getting feedback

You will want multiple ways for users to give feedback—both ad hoc and structured. You can give participants an email address, feedback forms, or a feedback link in the product next to the new functionality. You might also want to reach out with a survey after they've used it for a period of time. You can use the survey to identify people you'd like to have a longer conversation with, or who might be good spokespeople at the launch.

Finally, actively communicate with your beta participants. Let them know when you've updated the functionality, and thank them as the launch date approaches. Also, be sure to inform them when you'll be shutting down the beta.

RECRUITING USER RESEARCH PARTICIPANTS

Ideally, you want to talk to people who are customers or potential customers. If your desired customer base is challenging to reach, you can also look for people who are good proxies for your target market. For example, talking to retired nurses rather than active ones, or salespeople at medium-sized companies rather than large-sized ones. You could also ask random people for feedback, but you'll need to think carefully about whether you believe their feedback will be similar to what your target audience would say.

If you'd like to talk to your own customers or potential customers, a great way is to put a prompt on your website using a tool like Ethnio or Intercom. To get feedback from random people, you can use a site like UserTesting or put up a booth in a coffee shop.

Many people will participate in short sessions for free, but if you aren't getting as many participants, consider offering incentives like gift cards or discounts.

USER RESEARCH MISTAKES TO AVOID

While research is a powerful tool, it can also waste time—or even lead you astray. This is particularly true the first few times you do product research. To make your research the most effective, watch out for the following mistakes.

Asking the wrong question

It's disappointing to finish your research only to find out that you asked the wrong questions. The trick to asking the *right* questions is to know in advance *how* you'll use the answers.

A great framework for this is a decision tree (pg 73) that lays out potential answers and what will happen based on each one. If you have skeptical stakeholders, you can even share the decision tree with them before you begin the research to ensure you're asking the right questions.

When you draw out the decision tree, you might sometimes see that all of the answers lead to the same decision. Imagine, for example, testing a product with a paper prototype, and making this mini-decision tree:

- **If it does well:** You'll move on to a higher fidelity prototype.

- **If it does badly:** It might be just because the prototype was low fidelity. Move on to a higher fidelity prototype for a better test.

What have you achieved with this simple prototype? In either scenario, you move on to a high-fidelity prototype. You might still choose to casually show the paper prototypes to some colleagues just to catch obvious issues, but save your more formal recruiting efforts for the high-fidelity prototype.

Other times, you might also see that your questions don't give you enough information to make a decision. You might want to ask how many hours they spend using your app each day, but you realize that to make a decision, you also need to know how much time they'd ideally like to spend on your app.

You might think your decision tree looks great, but then you learn that a stakeholder doesn't agree. For example, suppose your user research shows that people don't need support for old browsers, but the head of marketing explains that they want browser support to win over industry analysts, not end-users. In this situation, you'll need to rethink your decision tree in order to see if there's a different question that could lead the head of marketing to agree to deprecation.

Leading the witness

It's easy to accidentally skew the data with your wording or by inadvertently asking leading questions.

If you ask, "How would you share this?" people will spot the button labeled "share" instantly. But, if you ask, "How would you send this to a friend?", they might not find it so quickly.

Another variant of leading the witness is asking if they'd like a feature. Everyone likes features. Instead, ask how much they would be willing to pay for it, how often they think they'd use it, or what they would be willing to give up for it.

Too many participants for usability studies

The rule of thumb for usability studies is approximately five participants.[9] Above that, you hit diminishing returns for uncovering new issues, and you still don't have enough participants to answer quantitative questions.

When you interview too many participants, you not only waste time on the current project, but you might also scare your team away from future usability studies because they'll think testing is too time-consuming.

Not treating user researchers as partners

Some PMs think that user researchers only exist to run usability studies or to prove the PM's ideas are good. If you involve user researchers at the beginning of the product life cycle, however, they can prove to be valuable strategic partners who help you deliver more successful products.

Don't treat your researchers as someone you toss requirements to, and who just tosses back results. In a good partnership, there's a healthy balance of back and forth communication. You discuss trade-offs around various methodologies, recruiting criteria, and timing. You attend user sessions and discuss the patterns you noticed. You make sure you understand the priority of each finding and set aside time in the schedule to act on the high-priority recommendations.

---

9   For more information, see https://www.nngroup.com/articles/how-many-test-users/.

KEY TAKEAWAYS

- **Talk to users:** First-hand knowledge of real people is a baseline requirement for being a good PM. These conversations are how you'll build up expertise, gain credibility, and add unique value to your team. Set up your schedule so that you talk to users and potential users on a regular basis.

- **Translate what you see and hear into insights:** You can't take everything a customer says at face value. You need to examine and translate your observations into useful insights. People might ask for features that only solve a small part of their underlying problem. They might be overly optimistic that they'd buy a product before they see the price. Proper user research techniques can avoid common pitfalls.

- **User research is cheap:** Real-world customer behavior is full of surprises and user research is (relatively) cheap. Don't invest months of engineering time on assumptions you could have validated. There are a wide variety of user research approaches, not just usability sessions. Before assuming your question can't be answered with research, talk to a researcher.

- **Great products address real customer needs.** Customers might be incorrect about the best solution (e.g., a faster horse instead of a car), but can guide you to real underlying needs (e.g., faster transportation). Frameworks like Jobs to Be Done can help you identify real needs.

CHAPTER 5

DATA INSIGHT

UNDOUBTEDLY, CONVERSATIONS WITH users are incredibly valuable. They offer a depth of insight into their experiences and motivations; not just *what* they do, but *why*.

There's a catch, though—in fact, many catches.

Qualitative (descriptive) data from user research only samples from a few people. Usually, those people are only a rough approximation of your true user base: they speak your language, live near you, and have free time in the middle of the day to participate in research. There's often a huge gap between what people *say* they will do or how they behave when they're being watched, and what they *actually* do.

This is where *quantitative (numerical) data* comes into play. As a PM, you need to use quantitative data and metrics to learn what people actually do, identify new opportunities, and measure success.

RESPONSIBILITIES

LEARN YOUR COMPANY'S KEY SUCCESS METRICS

What does success mean to you? That's an interesting question for an individual—but it's also an interesting question for a company. And, as it turns out, companies (and teams) might define it in somewhat different ways.

When you're new to a team—whether junior or senior—you need to learn the relevant metrics. How does your company measure success? What about your product? What does good usage look like?

Ideally, your company has prioritized those metrics so you know which are the most strategically important. For some companies, the most important thing is user growth. For others, it's retention, revenue, time spent on the site, or winning customers in key industries.

Your company should have a dashboard that can show you the metrics over time. If it doesn't, please work with your team to create one! It's awfully hard to optimize metrics if you can't easily understand what they are (see "Create a dashboard for your team" on pg 51).

Consider what product work has moved those metrics. If you're new, it can be useful to discuss this with your team. What past changes have driven these metrics, positively or negatively? If answering this question is challenging, that can be a red flag that the team hasn't been paying much attention to metrics.

Think also about how your team's work and metrics connect to the company's metrics, and make sure your team understands that connection. For example, if you're working on the spam detection tool of an email system, your team might be optimizing around false negatives and positives, while the larger product is optimizing around user retention. What is the relationship between these? Will improving one improve the other?

LEARN HOW TO PULL DATA FOR YOURSELF

Speed of cycles is critical in data analysis. You need to have a hypothesis, test it, form a *new* hypothesis, then test that one as well, and keep iterating. If you need to wait for someone else to send you the data, it can take the process from 15 minutes to several days. That is why it's so important to learn how to pull your own data..

How you do this will depend on the company. Some companies have customizable dashboards, and each PM can create their own. That's great! But at other companies, you'll just use SQL. That's okay too.

In fact, even if you have access to a customizable dashboard, you might still find SQL very handy. It gives you more granular control in data analysis, and ultimately saves you a lot of time. Don't be intimidated if you have no technical background either; spend a day or two learning it, and you can learn the rest as you go.

CREATE A DASHBOARD FOR YOUR TEAM

Every product should have a dashboard, accessible to PMs and non-PMs. If you're designing this from scratch, or just revising it, here are some important things to keep in mind:

- **Show the Success Metrics:** Include graphs that show the most important success metrics for your product. These are often hard-to-move metrics, such as retention. You might not see these move with any particular launch, but you can observe the trends over time.

- **Look for the Precursors:** What drives the success metrics? For example, if a core success metric is time spent online, but that's driven by the number of users and the posts per users, you'll want to track those too. These will give you an early warning if a product change is particularly good or bad.

- **Show *How* People Are Using It:** Sometimes teams lose track of how people are actually using the product, and what is most important to people. Include metrics that help illuminate how people are actually using the product, such as the relative usage of various features. Even if these don't move often, they'll help you and your team stay grounded in the reality of how your product is being used. This can serve as a steady reminder to work on the parts of your product that will have the highest impact.

- **Reduce Noise:** Consider slicing or filtering metrics in ways that reduce variance and noise. For example, you might look at the number of users who comment, rather than the raw number of comments. If there's a high variance in the number and quality of new users you get each day (for example, because of press articles or being featured in an app store), you can set most of your graphs to filter out users who haven't passed a quality bar. This could be the people who finished setup, or who have used the app on at least three different days.

- **Normalize Metrics:** Consider normalizing metrics by dividing by the number of active users to get charts where the lines are horizontal unless there's a real behavior change. For example, the number of comments each day will be going up if your user base is growing, and it's difficult to tell by just looking at the graph whether or not people are commenting more. If you look at the number of comments divided by the number of active users, you'll be able to quickly see if people are commenting more.

- **Account for Seasonality:** Some products are used more during certain times of the week or year. If you don't account for this, it can be difficult to understand if a downward or upward trend is meaningful. One simple way to account for this is to overlay a dashed line from one year ago (or a week ago) to quickly spot seasonality bumps and dips.

- **Show 7 Day Averages:** Some products are inherently "spikey", where they might have momentary peaks in usage due to a popular post or some other event. To get a better handle on the trends, it can be useful to view a 7 (or 14, 28, etc) day average. This is also another way to adjust for products where usage is affected by the day of the week.

REVIEW YOUR TEAM'S METRICS REGULARLY

Your product's metrics should be reviewed on a regular basis. This helps you quickly identify any surprises in the metrics and promptly fix any issues. Some of the key questions to ask are:

- Have the graphs for any metrics increased or decreased relative to their prior trend? If so, investigate to find out what caused the change.

- Can you see the impact of any recent product or marketing changes in the metrics?

- Have any metrics crossed a threshold that's worth celebrating?[1]

- Are there any interesting long-term trends? Pay special attention to metrics that support or refute the product strategy.

Some teams find it helpful to set up a rotation system for reviewing the metrics. Each week, designate someone to review the metrics and follow up on any surprising changes. This ensures that people across your team are familiar with the metrics, and that the review actually gets done.

EXPLORE THE DATA ⚡

In the same way that you might run exploratory user research to discover new insights, you can explore the data your product gathers to discover new opportunities. Data can often be used in creative ways—but to do this, you need to understand what data is out there. Here's an example.

Once, at Google, my team wanted to use the user's IP address to relevant local results for searches like "pizza restaurants." My hunch was that this IP address location was accurate enough. But how could I prove it? We were reluctant to run an experiment immediately, since it wouldn't really tell us how predictive IP addresses were of a user's location. A lot of "bad location" guesses could be jarring to users.

---

1   The threshold itself might not be meaningful, but it helps team morale to celebrate milestones.

PAUSE FOR A MOMENT AND CONSIDER THIS SCENARIO FOR YOURSELF.

Imagine you work at Google. How do you prove that IP addresses match people's locations, when you don't actually know people's locations?

There are likely many answers, but here's how I tackled it.

First, I realized that a subset of users had, at some point, typed in a zip code (presumably their own) while searching for weather forecasts or movie times. I could confirm that their IP address's location roughly matched the zip code. So far, so good.

But IP addresses could still be miles away from their location, even if it's the right zip code. How do we determine if the IP address is *better* than the zip code? Again, imagine you're at Google tackling this same problem. What data might be helpful to you?

I realized that those same users *also* periodically searched for specific restaurants or stores. So the question was: when they searched for specific places, was it more likely to match the zip code or the IP address?

It turned out that the IP address was much better than the zip code, which means that it was likely quite accurate. I now had the confidence to start an experiment, knowing that we would rarely be wrong about their location. The experiment proved successful, and we launched this change.

All of this was only possible because I knew what data existed.

Get curious and explore the different types of data available at your company. This might be the Google Analytics dashboards, raw user logs, NPS reports, search logs—anything you have access to. Start with any questions you can think of, whether they're directly related to your projects or just something you're curious about. Look for anything surprising, and then try to dig in to find out what it means or what caused it. If you find interesting insights, make sure to share them with other people.

SHAPE YOUR COMPANY'S KEY SUCCESS METRICS ⚡⚡

Metrics aren't set in stone. As you advance in your career, you may need to help the whole company focus on the metrics that matter the most. If it looks like people are chasing the wrong metrics or confused about which should be the top priority, it's a sign that you can step up to help.

To shape the company's success metrics, you want to lead a cross-functional, collaborative process; it's important to get broad buy-in. Identify all the problems you see with the current success metrics, and invite people in roles across the company to share any problems they see, or any worries they have, with changing the metrics.

The frameworks at the end of this chapter provide some guidelines on how to choose good metrics.

See also: "Good metrics versus vanity metrics" on pg 56; "Pirate Metrics" on pg 56

P&L RESPONSIBILITY ⚡⚡

At some companies, the most senior PMs become responsible for their business unit's profits and losses (P&L). This means they have an extra layer of accountability that includes not only the product team, but the business teams such as sales and marketing as well. They're responsible not just for shipping excellent products, but also for ensuring that those products bring in enough revenue without generating too much cost.

When you have P&L responsibility, you'll work with someone from finance on a team budget. The budget covers the plans and targets for the year, usually on a quarterly or monthly basis. It will include costs such as how many people you're expecting to hire in each role, and how much you'll spend on advertising or other expenses. It also includes revenue that you'll forecast based on past revenue, seasonality, sales headcount, marketing, and product launches.[2]

It might seem impossible to get the forecast right, but luckily you don't have to. Ely Lerner, who ran a P&L at Yelp, shared his perspective:

> You probably never are going to forecast correctly, so the tip is to always be a step ahead of realizing when the plan is wrong. That gives you more time to correct it, and more time to communicate it. You'll want to have a conservative financial plan you share with Wall Street and a more aggressive internal target you rally your teams to try to stretch and go hit.

When you come up with your budget, especially at a public company, you'll need a narrative about why you're investing the way you are. For example, your strategy might be to maximize profit, or it could be to spend more in order to grow your market share. Either approach could work, but you'll need to convince investors that you're making the right choice.

Forecasting is important because the plans you set and your ability to hit them can directly impact the stock price, which in turn affects compensation and can even increase the risk of the activist investors taking control of the company.[3]

Each month or week, you'll report on the forecasts and analyze the drivers. If revenue is down or costs are up, you'll want to dig in to make sure you understand exactly why. Over time, you'll build up dashboards and models that help you quickly hone in on what part of the funnel is falling behind.

Driver analysis might seem like a lot of work, but as Sachin Rekhi, who ran a P&L at LinkedIn, shared, it can really improve your product intuition and make you a better PM:

> Now when you create initiatives, you're thinking about which driver the initiative is going to boost, and by how much. Of course, you are never accurate, but at the end of the quarter you would look at what you actually did and build your intuition for what features and changes in the product actually had some meaningful metric output.

If things aren't on track, you'll then work with teams to see what levers you can pull to get things back on track. You might shift budget from long-term bets to short-term drivers like advertising. You might have engineers build tooling that makes sales people more productive.

---

2   Seasonality is an important part of modeling. For example, many industries experience a decrease in the growth rate during the summer or a big dip during holidays. You'll want to compare your metrics to a baseline from the year before so you don't confuse seasonality for a metrics change that's more under your control.

3   Activist investors are outsiders who buy a significant stake in a company in order to influence how the company is run. They pressure the company to make changes that they think will increase the stock price.

GROWTH PRACTICES

USE BENCHMARKS TO MAKE SENSE OF DATA

Early in my career, the expectation that PMs would have memorized a variety of metrics about their product scared me. I couldn't understand why I would need to be able to recite information like how many users our product had, or what the growth rate was from memory. It reminded me of struggling to memorize important dates in history class. Sometimes it made me wonder if I was really cut out to be a PM.

My breakthrough was learning to use benchmarks to add context and make data meaningful. Benchmarks are points of reference, either industry standards or internal references based on past launches.

For example, venture capital firms have revenue and growth benchmarks in place that they use to determine if a product is doing well. These can be helpful for self-assessing how your product is doing.

While you're reviewing the data, find a reference point so you will know how to interpret the numbers you're looking at.

BUILD YOUR DATA INTUITION

Over time, you'll get better at spotting signals in noisy data. While it might look like magic, spotting signals is simply based upon recognizing patterns you've encountered in the past.

You can speed up the process of building up your intuition by observing other people analyzing data and identifying patterns. Sit in on experiment analysis meetings, or read past experiment write-ups. Try to turn the numbers and facts into a story that makes sense.

RUN BETTER EXPERIMENTS ⚡

Experiments can be useful, but that doesn't mean you should test every idea or solve every argument with an experiment. It's okay—even good—if some experiments fail. But experiments take time, and if too many are failing, you probably aren't using your team's time wisely.

Nundu Janakiram, Director of Product in Rider Experience at Uber, shared the importance of improving the success rate of your experiments:

> Good product managers learn from failure...but *great* product managers also fail less.
>
> Insightful user research allows you to be right more often. When you have a deep understanding of your customers' relationship to your product, you'll be able to run experiments more efficiently.
>
> Experiments can have a lot of hidden costs, and over-experimentation can stall decision-making and drag down your forward momentum. Avoid trying to resolve every internal debate with "Why don't we just test it?"
>
> Focus your experimentation energy on answering the most important questions that would allow you to move confidently forward in the product development process. Great PMs fail less because they are *efficient* with their learning; over time, these PMs will develop a more intuitive understanding of their product, and require fewer experiments to get successful results.

If one of your experiments fails, take the time to reflect on how you could have caught the problems earlier. Was the experiment well-designed and executed properly? Could you have validated the idea with a prototype before running a test?

CONCEPTS AND FRAMEWORKS

GOOD METRICS VERSUS VANITY METRICS

Good metrics give you real, actionable insight on how well your product is doing, and whether it's improving or not. Bad metrics are misleading and may be nothing more than "vanity metrics"—metrics that feel good but don't really matter for your company's success.

For instance, consider metrics like "total registered users" or "daily pageviews." At first glance, these metrics appear potentially useful. We probably *do* care about how many users we have, and how much traffic we're getting.

But are they actionable? When they increase, do they mean that the product has become more successful? (Think about this for a moment yourself, with the respect to metrics of "total registered users" and "daily pageviews.")

- **Total number of users:** This increases with time. It literally cannot decrease. So, surely, its increase does not mean that the product has become more successful.

- **Daily pageviews:** This *can* be meaningful, but it can also be arbitrarily inflated by just breaking up an article into multiple pages.

These metrics are vanity metrics because they can go up even when things are going badly. They don't necessarily help a team understand which changes are helping or hurting the business.

> Good metrics are those that are correlated with strategic, long-term success. They represent the product working the way customers and the business want it to work. Good metrics are specific enough to be actionable.

They are often cohorted (grouped) by week or month (like week one retention) and frequently are per-customer metrics (like average revenue per user, or ARPU). When these metrics improve, you can be more confident that they represent an actual improvement.

PIRATE METRICS

One of the most memorable sets of good metrics is what Dave McClure calls "Pirate Metrics" because they have the fun acronym AARRR.[4] These customer life cycle metrics are called "funnel metrics," a metaphor of a leaky funnel that drips water. The idea is that you begin by putting a lot of customers at the top, start losing some at each step, and the ones who make it to the bottom without "leaking out" generate actual revenue.

- **Acquisition:** New users coming to your product, such as monthly sign-ups or downloads.

---

4   For more information, see https://www.slideshare.net/dmc500hats/startup-metrics-for-pirates-long-version.

- **Activation:** Happy or successful users, represented by a product-specific metric. For example, Facebook might track "adding at least seven friends." SurveyMonkey might track "sending a survey that gets at least five responses." Typically, you'll review monthly metrics of what percentage of newly acquired users hits this "activation" stage.

- **Retention:** Users who come back to your product, tracked as metrics like daily active users (DAUs), monthly active users (MAUs), or the ratio of DAUs/MAUs. You can also look at usage metrics such as how many minutes users watched videos on YouTube.

- **Referral:** Recommending the product to other users, such as invites sent. Many companies also track the Net Promoter Score (NPS), calculated from responses to the survey question, "How likely are you to recommend this product?" This question can serve as a proxy for word-of-mouth recommendations.

- **Revenue:** Generating revenue; for example, subscription fees, purchasing a product or generating ad revenue. It's important to track the lifetime value (LTV) of a customer so you can compare that to the cost of acquiring a customer (CAC). The rule of thumb is that LTV:CAC should be at least 3:1. When a paying customer cancels a subscription, that is called "churn."

Observe that these metrics are tightly coupled with the Customer Journey framework (pg 41). Metrics along these lines are appropriate for a wide variety of products, but they may need to be tweaked slightly to be more relevant for your business.

A/B TESTING AND STATISTICS

A/B testing, also known as "split testing" or an "online experiment," is a live experiment conducted on your user base. A random sample of users sees one version, called a "variant," and the others see another variant. Then you compare to see which variant did better at achieving your goals, such as increasing clickthrough or conversion. Once the test is over, the variant that did better is usually ramped up to 100% of users.

By testing two random samples of users at the same time, you can be sure that any differences between the groups is due to the product change you made. If you instead launched a change to all users and tried to compare this month's dashboard to last month's dashboard, you wouldn't know what changes came from external factors like seasonality or a competitor's ad campaign.

Some A/B tests compare two alternatives against each other, such as whether a button should be blue or green. Others compare the way things are today (the control) against a change (the treatment), such as adding a search box to the top of the page.

> A/B testing is incredibly useful because it gives you real information on what people actually do, rather than what they say they do. It paints a much more accurate picture of the real impact of your launches.

Small changes, like what words you put on the signup button, can have a huge impact on important metrics like signups. On the other hand, A/B testing extends the project timeline and can confuse and frustrate users if they notice they're seeing different versions of the product. A/B testing should not be used indiscriminately—use it for changes in high-traffic, sensitive parts of the product that would have primarily short-term effects.[5]

WHAT YOU NEED TO KNOW ABOUT STATISTICS

The principle behind A/B testing is simple enough. Try two different things. Pick the better one. Easy!

The more complicated question is: How long do you run the experiment for? When can you be confident that Option 2 is *actually* better than Option 1? This is where an understanding of statistics comes in handy.

Imagine that you're trying to determine if a coin is "fair," that is, if it has an equal likelihood of heads and tails. After twenty flips, you get 60% heads. Is the coin unfair? Hard to say. If you flip 1000 times, however, and you get 60% heads, you can conclude that the coin is probably unfair.

The longer we run the experiment, the more our confidence in the result will increase. However, there is a trade-off. Experiments are time consuming, so we don't want to run them longer than necessary.

This is the same with running A/B tests. We need to run variants "A" and "B" long enough that we can be confident that in our answer, but not so long that we never make a decision and can't move forward and try other things.

So, how long should we run the experiment? How many people should see the "A" and "B" variants before we can make a decision? We want to run the experiment until we have "statistical significance" for your success metric, which means until it's *unlikely* that the difference in the metrics is due to random chance.

To figure out statistical significance, you have a choice of two calculations: the confidence interval or the p-value. Both of these calculations will give the same answer of whether a result is statistically significant, but the confidence interval gives you extra information about the range of possible values.

Confidence interval

Suppose we wanted to estimate the average height of students at a school. The more children we measure, the closer our calculation will be to the actual average. Suppose we measure 50 students at random and report that the 95% confidence interval (the standard confidence interval used by most companies) is 48 inches to 52 inches. This roughly means that there's a 95% chance that the actual average height—if we were to measure every single student—is between 48 inches and 52 inches.[6] However, there's still a 5% chance we're wrong, and the average height is higher or lower than this range.

Of course, product managers usually don't work with heights. They change parts of applications and ask, "Did it help or hurt? How much?"

If your experiment shows a 95% confidence interval for signups of 10% to 12%, this means that there's a 95% chance variant B increased signups between 10% and 12%. That's a win! If instead, it showed variant B signups at -12% to -10%, that would be a loss.

Often, our confidence intervals span negative and positive numbers, such as -4% to 3%. What does it mean when a confidence interval includes zero? It means that we don't know whether this change increased or

---

5   Onboarding and monetization flows are great for A/B testing because of how sensitive they are and how quickly you can learn if they work. Changes that aim to improve retention or brand sentiment are hard to measure with an A/B test.

6   Technically speaking, it means that 95% of confidence intervals constructed with the same number of samples would contain the true value. The rough definition is a lot easier to use in practical settings.

decreased the metric. Because the confidence interval covers zero, the change could be negative—up to a 4% loss—or positive—up to a 3% gain.

If you have reasons outside of the data to believe that your change is a good one (for example, customers in your beta group love it), then you might decide that you're okay with a loss of up to 4%, and decide to launch the change.

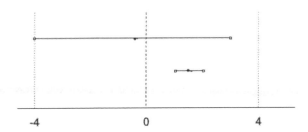

The top confidence interval could be a win, a loss, or neutral. As the experiment gathers more data, the confidence interval shrinks, and we can see the experiment is likely a 1-2% win.

The longer you run the experiment, the more the confidence interval will shrink (that is, our range has shrunk, and we have *more* clarity on the expected impact). If later it shows 1% to 2%, that means there's a 95% chance your experiment improved the metric between one and two percent. You could call that a win.

P-values

The other calculation you might hear about is the p-value, which is the probability of seeing these experiment results if your metric wasn't a win (i.e., if the metric was a loss or neutral). Most companies use 0.05 (5%) as the cut-off, which is equivalent to a 95% confidence interval.

The p-value and confidence interval are directly related. If the p-value is below 0.05, the lower end of the 95% confidence interval is above zero. Most PMs would prefer to see a confidence interval because it gives more information on the best and worst-case scenarios.

Beware of p-hacking

Using that 5% cut-off can get us into some trouble, if we're not careful.

Suppose we are A/B testing an app redesign and we find that, with 95% confidence, usage of the chat feature increased. That's almost certainly meaningful, right?

Well, yes and no. If we have 95% confidence that the impact was "real", there is still a 5% chance that the impact was just random—that is, uncorrelated with the redesign.

Now imagine that we examine the data to look at the potential impact on *dozens* of features—chat, user profiles, search, groups, events, exporting, and so on. If we tolerate a 5% chance of being wrong, odds are pretty good that *one*, out of dozens of features, will show an impact at the 95% confidence level.[7]

---

7   If this is still confusing, think about rolling a 20-sided die, labeled 1 to 20. I predict you'll get a 13. Pretty cool if I get it correct, right? But if I repeat this dozens of times, and get it right once or twice, it becomes distinctly less impressive.

This is what's known as p-hacking. It's fishing through data to find impacts or correlations. If you fish for long enough, you'll probably find something—just by randomness (see "P-Hacking, via xkcd" on pg 61).

What's the fix? Being more methodical.

First, decide what you're measuring in advance—register those "variables"—and don't look for too many possible impacts.

Second, if you *do* find an impact outside of what you registered, toss the data. That doesn't mean you have to *ignore* what you saw. Just toss it. Re-run the experiment from scratch, measuring that thing. If it still holds up, you should be good (probably!).

STATISTICS AND EXPERIMENTS

Now that you understand the statistics, what does that mean for running experiments?

- Run experiments longer for greater precision about the impact. If you're looking to be able to detect, say, a 1% improvement, you'll probably need to run a pretty long experiment. A 50% improvement would show up more quickly. Work with your data scientist to determine if you can feasibly detect the level of change you're looking for.

- Ignore metric changes that aren't statistically significant, especially if you did not pre-register them. There will always be metrics that look like they've improved or declined just based on random chance.

- The more experiments you run, or the more metrics you look at, the higher the odds that you'll see an anomalous result; a metric that looks like a statistically significant win or a loss but is actually neutral. This means you shouldn't run a lot of random experiments just to see what works; you'll lose the ability to confidently know which things worked.

- Local metrics, like clicks on the button, move more easily than key success metrics, like retention. Design your experiments so you can learn something valuable even when key success metrics are neutral.

KEY TAKEAWAYS

- **A product's key success metrics are manifestations of its strategy:** Some products prioritize gaining market share while others aim for profitability. Successful usage for some products is once a month, while for others, it's multiple times a day. Make sure the metrics you care about match up with your intended strategy.

- **Use data to complement user insights:** User research gives you a rich and detailed perspective, but it can miss real-world problems that happen infrequently or when people are distracted. Metrics and user data are excellent tools for learning how people actually behave in the real world.

- **Get hands-on with data:** Make sure your product has logging set up so you can gather data on how people use it, and then look at the data regularly. Explore the data to find product opportunities. Ask questions and follow your curiosity.

- **Use, but don't overuse experiments:** Experiments are great for detecting large expected changes, but you can't just throw hundreds of ideas into experiments and hope to spot a win. When you run too many random experiments, the chance of false positives goes up a lot.

Reprinted with permission from the always fabulous xkcd (https://xkcd.com/882/).

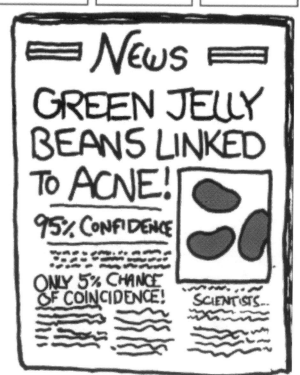

CHAPTER 6

ANALYTICAL PROBLEM SOLVING

THE GOOD THING about the Google APM program was that I got to take on opportunities outside of my comfort zone. The bad thing was that, well, I *had* to take on opportunities outside of my comfort zone.

And so was the case with my upcoming rotation. The Search team had a reputation for requiring strong analytical skills—skills that I wasn't so sure I had. I'd struggled with analytical interview questions in the past. In fact, I was still feeling a little burned by a recent consulting interview where I was asked to pull new revenue opportunities out of a stack of spreadsheets. Let's just say that did not go well.

Still, I proceeded with the rotation. The only failure is the failure to try, right? Let's hope!

It turns out that my fears were unfounded. Not only did I excel on the Search team, I became known specifically *for* my analytical skills. It wasn't that I became a spreadsheets whiz, or that I could immediately extract meaning from numbers.

Rather, it was my tenacity and pursuit of *understanding*. I followed my curiosity and never rested until I had a firm mental model of a program. I browsed thousands of random search queries to see where we should have been showing images, and then developed a framework for understanding why and how. I worked with diary studies to figure out what people really wanted when they searched for restaurants. I double checked the accuracy of hundreds of local listings once I realized that, even when the web address was correct, the phone number or physical address could be wrong.

Creating these mental models wasn't always a quick or solo activity; it was a process, often team-wide. At Asana, I created giant spreadsheets laying out the tradeoffs of each solution, and often they felt like a mess at first. But diligently, and with my teammates' help, I'd bring order to these spreadsheets, distilling them down to their deciding factors.

> Analytical skills aren't about sudden strokes of genius—bursts of insight—when faced with a problem, they're not about solving math equations in your head, and they definitely aren't about PMs blazing into the room to conquer the problem. Rather, they're about structured problem solving.

Great PMs have these skills, and know how to use them effectively. They detect when their team is stuck, clear away the noise, ask the right questions, come up with a framework for decision-making, gather the information to apply this structure, and drive good decisions. This is what analytical problem solving is all about.

RESPONSIBILITIES

IDENTIFY AND STRUCTURE AMBIGUOUS PROBLEMS

BRINGING CLARITY TO AMBIGUITY

French or German? Asana was locked in a contentious debate over which language to pick for its first translation. Does it look at the number of speakers worldwide? Or within its user base? Or perhaps where it wants to grow the most?

Lili Rachowin, a PM Lead at Asana, took charge of the decision-making process. She showed up to the hour-long review with a table of possible considerations—all the expected facts and numbers, along with some new items we hadn't considered. She argued that, with this being the *first* translation, the most important factor was the willingness among the respective customer base to tolerate translation mistakes. The team hadn't thought of that, but agreed. Her proposal was approved on the spot.

Rachowin brought clarity to the ambiguous problem.

Product managers continuously face ambiguous problems. They must learn to recognize when they have an ambiguous problem and how to apply structure to it. Without this skill, they might try to solve problems based on their own intuition, or push these problems onto other people because they feel stuck.

Consider these ambiguous problems:

- Should we delay the launch to include new features or to polish the product?

- Which metrics should we be trying to improve?

- Which user problem should we focus on?

- How can we increase revenue?

- How can we increase the usage of this feature?

- Do we build our own solution or should we buy one?

- Why did the graphs show a drop on a particular day?

At a high level, these and other ambiguous problem break down into two core types:

- **Exploratory problems:** We have a question or problem, and we don't have a good idea of the potential answers. "How can we improve revenue?"

- **Decision-making problems:** We have an idea of what the potential solutions could be, but we don't know which one is the best. "Which of these features should we launch first?"

Let's consider them both.

Exploratory problems

Although exploratory problems are, by definition, wide open, you can still apply structure. Structured brainstorming can help.

Think of a few ways to slice up the problem space, and then brainstorm solutions inside each slice. As a PM, it's usually your responsibility to set up the structure. You can then bring more people into the loop and let them share their thoughts on the current slices, add additional slices, or offer any other relevant ideas.

For example, with the, "How can we improve revenue?" problem, here are a few slices:

- **New versus existing customers:** Consider how to increase the number of paying customers versus how to encourage existing customers to pay more.

- **Size of bet:** Consider what small optimizations and big new initiatives you could make.

- **Revenue stream:** Consider how to increase subscription revenue versus how to increase advertising revenue.

- **Customer type:** Consider revenue improvements for each persona or user profile.

For the question, "Why did our metrics drop all of a sudden on this day?" here are a few ways to drill down:

- **Internal versus external changes:** Did we do something such as launching a feature or changing our ad spend? Or did something in the external world happen, such as an international holiday or a competitor announcing a new product?

- **Geographically:** Did we see a change in different countries?

- **Product line/product area:** Did we see a drop across all of our products (or all parts of our product), or was it localized?

- **Funnel:** Was the drop in only one part of the funnel?

- **Source:** Did we see a drop coming from a particular referral source?

- **Customer type:** Was a particular type of customer affected more than others?

Sometimes, simply brainstorming the slices will solve the problem. For example, in the metrics question, you can look at each slice and, eventually, you'll find the culprit. For the other cases, you've just transformed your exploratory problem into a decision-making problem.

Decision-making problems

Once you've got some options for solutions, you have a decision-making problem. As with exploratory problems, you want to try a few different ways of structuring the problem, and then evaluate which method seems the most helpful.

> The goal with ambiguous decision-making problems is to simplify the problem down to the core, important tradeoffs.

The main issue with an ambiguous problem is usually information overload. There are so many potential facts and tradeoffs that it's difficult to figure out what really matters.

One approach is to structure the options in a continuum across categories. You can then evaluate the decision at the category level rather than the individual solution level.

- Low risk versus high risk

- Low investment versus high investment

- Short-term benefit versus long-term benefit

- Growth focused versus revenue-focused

- Build versus buy

- … or any problem-specific categorization

If you just have two options, this approach will often illuminate a third, middle option that you might have missed.

For more approaches to structuring problems, see "Concepts and Frameworks" on pg 71.

LOOK INTO THE DATA YOURSELF

Great PMs are willing to get their hands dirty. They want to see the raw data for themselves. And the better their analytical skills are, the more likely they'll be able to spot something for themselves that other people missed. That's why great PMs don't delegate fact gathering to other people; they want to do this themselves.

A year before Lili Rachowin solved the problem of which language to launch first (see "Identify and structure ambiguous problems" on pg 64), she solved another problem by looking at the data herself. She had stepped in as the PM of a product as it was getting ready to launch. Nearly a dozen people were stuck arguing over the launch date for weeks. She opened up a spreadsheet, walked over to the finance department, and calculated how much money was being lost every week the launch was delayed. When people saw the results, the disagreements stopped.

HELP TRIAGE AND REPRODUCE BUGS

Once your product is launched, bug reports will start coming in. Some will indicate severe issues and others will be mild. Some impact many users and others just a few. Some will be easy to fix and others require more work. For some, the problem will be immediately obvious and others will be harder to diagnose.

As a PM, you'll consider all of these factors and decide what to do with the bug. Some of the bugs wouldn't be worth the time they would take to fix, and so you close them as "won't fix." Many of them will be slotted in to be worked on in the coming weeks or months. For the worst ones, you might ask an engineer to stop what they're working on and fix it. This process of prioritizing which bugs to fix and how quickly to fix them is called "bug triage."

To prioritize bugs, consider the following factors:

- **Damage to users:** Can this bug cause any large or lasting damage to users? Does it expose them to a security or privacy issue? Could they lose data?

- **Damage to company:** Can this bug cause any large or lasting damage to the company? Could it damage the company's reputation severely?

- **Impact on metrics:** Does this bug have a large impact on key company metrics? Does it hurt costs or revenue? Does it hurt activation, adoption, revenue, retention, or referrals? Is it causing a large number of support tickets?

- **Scale of impact:** How many users are affected by the bug or exposed to the bug? Does the bug disproportionately affect important customers (e.g., paying customers or large customers)? Will more or fewer users be affected in the future?

- **Workarounds:** Are there workarounds? Would a user discover the workaround on their own?

- **Ease of fixing:** Is the bug easy to fix? How long would it take to fix?

- **Now vs. later:** Is it timely to fix the bug now? Is it cheaper to fix the bug now than it would be later? Is there marketing planned around that part of the product?

- **Cost/benefit relative to other work:** How does the cost and benefit of fixing the bug compare to the cost and benefit of focusing on new feature work?

As part of the triage process, a good PM takes a first pass at the bugs to understand them, clarify them, and resolve them as quickly as possible. This is where analytical problem solving can come into play.

Perhaps you've seen a similar bug before and you have a guess about what the problem is and how the user can resolve it (for example, by turning off a particular chrome extension or requesting a new password). Otherwise, you can try to reproduce the bug and narrow down the circumstances in which it occurs (for example, only on one browser, or only when your shopping cart is empty). Depending on your technical skill, you might even look at logs to identify the error or crash.

The more detailed and specific you can get the steps to reproduce the problem, the faster the engineer will be able to fix it.

SYSTEMS THINKING ⚡

Imagine you're working on a new type of user-generated content, and an engineer asks you if it's critical for this type of content to show up in search. A few days can be saved if you skip it.

This might sound like a simple prioritization decision, but the implications can be much larger. The engineer didn't mention this, but if you say no to search, the feature will be built in an entirely different way that makes it much more expensive to add search later on. It also won't let the content show up in any dashboards or pick up any premium functionality. In an ideal world, the engineer would have explained the repercussions of the decision, but in this case, they wrongly assumed you already knew them.

> Systems thinking is the skill needed to see how different parts of a system (like a product or company) connect to each other, to ask the right questions, and to make decisions that account for how those interconnected parts will be affected.

People who are strong at systems thinking will play out scenarios in their minds to see all of the repercussions, and then adjust plans to optimize for overall success.

Some types of interconnectedness to think about can be found below:

- **Feedback loops:** Will the results of this also act as inputs in the next round?

- **Cannibalization:** If one product is successful, will it decrease the usage of another?

- **Funnel stages:** If you widened the top of the funnel to bring in more signups, could those users behave differently later in the funnel?

- **Product components and functionality:** What impact does this new functionality have on other components such as search, notifications, permissions, or onboarding? Are there implementation choices that affect what 'nice-to-have' behaviors you'll get for free?

- **Incentives:** Does success in one part of the product change user behaviors elsewhere?

- **UI components:** Will changes in this one place work everywhere the component is used?

- **Platforms:** Does this new functionality work the same on mobile, on desktop, and via the developer API?

- **Flexibility:** What changes become easier or more challenging in the future? Are you locking yourself in to certain decisions?

- **Resource requirements:** Will this cause scalability issues on the backend or for customer support?

- **User life cycle:** If you make a change, such as giving new users unlimited space, what impact will that have in the long run?

If this is an area where you need to improve, the best way is to get as many examples as possible. Ask a mentor or a coach to point out opportunities where you could have used more systems thinking.

Improving your systems-level thinking often means deepening your understanding of the underlying infra-structure—for example, by talking to the engineers on the infrastructure team. Ask questions about the options and their implications. Draw diagrams or create visual models to help you understand how every-thing connects. That will help you recognize the cases where product decisions seemed straightforward but actually have important side effects. While you're building up your understanding, you can create a safety net by specifically asking about the repercussions of your choices.

Another approach to systems thinking is to improve your ability to learn from past experiences. Rather than predicting all the things that might possibly happen in an interconnected system, you can keep checklists of the mistakes you and your teammates have made in the past and scan through them when building a new feature. You can sit in on experiment analysis meetings and read blog posts from other PMs to build up your internal library of possibilities to consider.

GROWTH PRACTICES

BE CURIOUS: PREDICT AND EXPLORE

Curiosity is a key element of problem-solving; not only does it help you notice the problems, but also guides you in figuring out the details that will help you solve them.

Start by predicting what you expect:

- If you're about to look at experiment results, make a quick estimation of what you think the numbers might be.

- If you're about to attend a meeting, try to guess what each person will say.

- If you're about to go to a training session, hypothesize what the advice will be.

This will help you notice when something is interesting and unexpected.

> If you don't make these predictions in advance, your brain could trick you into thinking that the answer was exactly what you expected. It's easy for "that makes sense" to feel like "that was expected," after the fact.

Once you notice something unexpected, take some time to explore it. Draft some questions and seek to answer them. This is where you'll start to expand your knowledge, which will help with future problem-solving.

DON'T JUST POINT OUT PROBLEMS

Some PMs take "constructive criticism" a little too far. This isn't necessarily out of cruelty. Sometimes it's because they take great pride in their ability to identify problems, to the point that they believe they're being helpful by pointing out everything that could possibly go wrong (particularly with other people's work). Needless to say, this is the wrong approach.

While it's important to be aware of problems, PMs need to find solutions to overcome these problems and find a way to keep teams moving forward. Also, remember that you don't get credit for having the "right" solution if you're not able to convince people to adopt it. This largely involves a shift in your mindset.

> Instead of assigning value to the problems you spotted, assign value to the good outcomes you drove. It's easy and not especially valuable to say, "Here are all the reasons that won't work." It's harder but much more useful to say, "I can find a way to make that work."

It's important to note that once you advance into leadership positions and are responsible for reviewing other people's work, this advice flips. You might just want to point out problems so that you encourage teams to take ownership over finding their own solutions.

ARTICULATE YOUR FRAMEWORKS ⚡

Frameworks are a product manager's secret weapon. You're already creating and using frameworks—they're just the logic you're using to make decisions—but you might not be articulating them.

If I were to ask you why you ordered your team's roadmap in a particular way, or why you made a specific product decision, you could think about it and then give me an answer. Perhaps you only considered one factor, like what the engineers wanted most, or you might be using a different ad-hoc framework for each decision. Nonetheless, as imperfect as they are, you *have* created frameworks.

> Articulating your frameworks is important because it shows people the logic and consistency behind your decisions. Writing them down gives you something concrete to improve upon.

This leads to many benefits, including:

- **Building credibility:** You will build credibility because people will understand the knowledge and critical thinking behind your decisions. They'll have more trust that you're making the right calls because they will understand the context behind every decision you make.

- **Less team frustration:** Your teammates are likely to be less frustrated when new information comes in that changes a decision. If they are only aware of the decision change, they might think that you hadn't thought through your original decision adequately. But when they see that the framework is consistent, they can anticipate the kinds of changes that might come up, and have a better understanding of why the initial decision had to change.

- **More constructive feedback:** You'll get more constructive feedback from people because they'll be able to spot missing information or incorrect assumptions within your frameworks.

- **Greater efficiency:** You will save time because your teammates can use your framework and answer some of their own questions rather than always having to come to you for answers. Sometimes, you'll even save time for yourself because you'll realize you can reuse a pre-existing framework rather than creating a new one from scratch.

- **Improved decision-making:** Your frameworks will improve as you articulate them. For example, you might be thinking that your new team needs an easy project to get started. You then explain that it's useful to have a trial run of working together (PMs, engineers, and designers) without needing a lot of executive buy-in, both to get to know each other and to learn the new codebase. All of these extra details help narrow down what kind of "simple" project is best. You might not have thought of them if you didn't take the time to articulate your framework.

Here's an easy way to articulate your framework: Whenever someone asks for your opinion or a decision, instead of just sharing it, also include the factors that would lead you to a different decision. For example, if someone asks which privacy setting should be the default, you could say:

> We should set the default to share full profile information because this feature is only available in our enterprise tier and profile information is not sensitive within a company.

If you later on decide to move the feature to another tier, or you learn that profile information *is* sensitive within a company, your team will understand why the decision changed.

In addition to communicating your own frameworks, you'll also want to identify the frameworks others are using. You can try to reverse engineer their frameworks or ask them directly how they're making decisions. This will sharpen your skill and expand your repertoire of possible problem-solving approaches.

OPTIMIZE ACROSS PRODUCTS AND OVER THE LONG TERM ⚡⚡

Consider this scenario: Your company offers a suite of products, and you are lead PM for one of them. Each product in this suite offers a consistent in-product dashboard, but you have an idea for a special dashboard that would be even better suited for your product. Should you do it?

Sometimes, yes. But proceed with caution. That mindset of "even better for *your* product" can be problematic. You need to think about what's best for the company, not just your product. Will people get confused by an inconsistent dashboard? Could it hurt the sales motion to have an outlier?

You also need to think long term. Who will maintain this "special" dashboard? Will it take longer to ramp up new teammates if your product works differently?

It is certainly normal for a junior PM to optimize around just their product. However, as they get more experience, they need to expand their perspective to optimize across *many* products—including those that aren't "under" them. They also need to take into consideration the future. What will be the best for the company, in the short and long term?

VISUALIZE HOW IT'S BUILT ⚡⚡

One day, I saw a surprising bug: a user's notifications were getting archived as soon as they arrived. The on-call engineer looked into it and was perplexed; the notifications didn't appear to be marked as archived. I thought back to how the notification system was built and remembered that there were two ways to archive notifications—individually, and by pressing "archive all." I suspected that the user's "last archived" date was somehow set to the future in our database. We looked, and that's exactly what had happened! We fixed the date and the problem was solved.

Problem-solving can often feel like a guessing game. How could you predict what decisions might have surprising side effects? How can you guess what's causing a bug? The most reliable way is to have a deep understanding of the underlying system and visualize building the solution yourself.

Familiarize yourself with what the records look like for the main objects in the database. What information is directly available on the record, what would need to be looked up separately, and what isn't there at all? The information that's directly available will be easy to use, while other information might be harder or slower to use. You might find all kinds of useful details precalculated and ready to use, for example, data on how active the user is or where they're located.

Learn about the components in the framework. This could involve UI components (such as color selectors or buttons) and infrastructure (such as Amazon's Elastic Search). Each component will be able to do some things easily, some things with more expensive customization, and some things not at all. If you can visualize which components you'd use to build a feature, you can predict what strengths and limitations come with it.

CONCEPTS AND FRAMEWORKS

THE 2X2 MATRIX

A 2x2 matrix is a very popular framework. It's incredibly simple, but works really well for evaluating options or organizing information.

A 2x2 is just a square divided into four quadrants, where each axis represents a dimension you care about. Potential solutions are slotted into the appropriate quadrant. The diagram highlights the tradeoffs and helps you uplevel the conversation from specific solutions to higher-level decision criteria. Sometimes a 2x2 even helps you find a "best of both worlds" solution.

Let's say your product is an online art gallery, and you want to make it easier for people to find art they might like. The designer comes up with a beautiful design with nine preset categories (contemporary, pop-art, impressionism...), each of which leads to a themed category page. The engineer feels that predefined categories are too limiting and wants to implement search across the comments on each piece of work in order to be more flexible and extensible. The designer pushes back, saying more users will benefit from browsing a list of recognizable categories than if they needed to think of their own search terms.

If you pull away from the specific solutions, then fundamentally, your decision criteria is around this: Do you want browsable or searchable? Do you want something more limited or something extensible?

You can lay these criteria and options out in a 2x2 to make the problem easier to reason about.

	Browsable	Searchable
Limited	Present categories	
Extensible		Search across comments

This diagram highlights the conflict and you *could* lead a discussion about whether it's more important to have a browsable or extensible solution. But, the diagram also prompts you to consider solutions that get the best of both worlds. User-generated tags would be both browsable and extensible!

	Browsable	Searchable
Limited	Present categories	
Extensible	Tags	Search across comments

RED/YELLOW/GREEN TABLES

If you have three or more decision-making criteria, you can create a table where the columns are the criteria and the rows are the options. The squares are filled in red, yellow, or green (or checks and x's, if you don't have colors), depending how well each option does on the category. You might be able to see that only one option has no red squares, or that every option that's good on cost is bad on long-term benefit.

	Browsable	Extensible	Inexpensive
Preset Categories	✓	✗	✓
Search	✗	✓	✗
Tags	✓	✓	✓

IF WE'RE OPTIMIZING FOR...

Another way to structure a problem is to identify which choice is the best for each potential optimization. This helps people to make decisions based on their values and goals rather than needing to understand each option.

If we're optimizing for...	The best choice is...
Launching as quickly as possible	Preset categories
Scalable discoverability	Tags
Incremental learning	Preset categories, then tags
Finding individual pieces	Search

DECISION TREE

When you have a complex problem, diagramming the problem via a decision tree can be useful. Each node in the tree represents a question, and the branches represent possible answers. This helps people understand your thought process and ensures that you've planned ahead for different possibilities.

In text, you can use a bulleted list with indentation to represent the tree:

- If the A/B test result is...
  - Positive
    - » If there are customer complaints…
      - + Interview customers and iterate
    - » If there are no customer complaints…
      - + Launch it
  - Negative
    - » Do not launch it
  - Neutral
    - » If there are customers who love it…
      - + If there are no complaints...
        - ◊ Launch it
    - » Otherwise…
      - + Do not launch it

EIGENQUESTIONS

When Shishir Mehrotra, now co-founder and CEO of Coda, was a PM at YouTube, there was intense debate that wasn't getting anywhere. The engineers wanted to link out to other websites when the user searched for TV shows that weren't available on YouTube. The business people disagreed. Should they link out or not?

As he searched for ways to solve the problem, Mehrotra realized that framing the debate around a different question could help. A few weeks earlier, he'd sat in as an observer on a product review of Google Product

Search, and heard the executives discussing product choices in terms of consistency vs. comprehensiveness. He realized that framing might cross-apply to his product as well.

At the next leadership team off-site, he kicked off a discussion with a new question: would the online video market be one that rewarded consistency or comprehensiveness? Unlike the earlier question, this new question could be resolved. After much discussion, they settled it; consistency was more important than comprehensiveness.

Surprisingly, not only did this decision answer the original question, it also resolved several other issues that hadn't seemed related previously. They ultimately decided that they would not link outside of YouTube for search results. They also removed the ability for creators to opt content out of different devices and removed all third-party embed players. They even decided to take back control of the YouTube iOS app from Apple.

Mehrotra named this kind of root question an "eigenquestion," a question whose answer likely answers subsequent questions as well.[1]

To use the eigenquestion methodology, follow these steps:

1. Diagram your questions and options with your team. Spend extra time making sure you've gotten all of the important questions out. Look outside to other teams or industries for alternate framings.

2. Walk through each question and ask, "If we decided this, which other questions would be answered?" Find the question that answers the most other questions. This is your eigenquestion.

3. With your team, list the range of options that could answer the eigenquestion, and identify the pros and cons of each one.

4. Align on a decision. Check in with your teammates on how they feel about the options. If people are uncomfortable with your proposed option, take the time to fully understand why.

5. Commit and determine accountability. Make sure you know who is responsible for communicating the decision and making it happen.

It may feel like this methodology is a long, even burdensome, process, but it can help you make more robust decisions that save time in the long term. If you start with the eigenquestion, you will not only answer that question, you'll answer a dozen subsequent questions as well.

FIVE WHYS

"Five Whys" is a useful framework to conduct a retrospective analysis of a problem. If you practice Five Whys across a range of problems, you'll hone your problem-solving skills, and learn to go beneath surface factors to identify the root cause.[2]

You can run a Five Whys for many different problems. For example, site downtime, missed OKRs, failed launches, cross-functional collaboration issues, or any other issue that's causing problems or frustration. The problem is usually a brief statement like, "The site was down for three hours," "the sales team wasn't told that the launch was happening this week," or "we missed the OKR to raise adoption by 30%."

To run a Five Whys:

---

1   Read more about eigenquestions at https://coda.io/d/Eigenquestions-The-Art-of-Framing-Problems_dQnxKKTYZ4r.

2   Read more about Five Whys at https://wavelength.asana.com/workstyle-ask-5-whys-to-get-to-the-root-of-any-problem/.

1. Schedule time with the people involved in the problem.

2. Explain that the goal is to learn about deeper systemic issues, and not to assign blame.

3. Create a detailed timeline of what happened. Timelines can be very illuminating as it gives people the full picture of what happened.

4. State the problem and ask, "Why did this problem happen?" Write down all the first-level answers.

5. Go back to each first-level answer, and ask why it happened or any related questions around why the problem wasn't caught or fixed sooner. For example, if a developer submitted code that crashed, why wasn't it caught by test cases.

6. Keep going deeper until you feel like you've uncovered the root cause. Often, a process failure is identified as the underlying issue.

7. Record the lessons learned and decide on appropriate action items to prevent similar problems in the future.

Be careful not to overreact with your solutions. If a problem has only happened once, adding a heavy process to prevent it might be worse for your team than doing nothing.

KEY TAKEAWAYS

- **Lead your team through effective decision-making:** As a PM, you don't need to solve every problem yourself, but you *do* play a key role in structuring the problem. When you frame a problem in a way that surfaces the underlying issues, your team will come up with better and more robust solutions.

- **Draw it out:** Tables and diagrams are surprisingly helpful for analyzing problems. If you're stuck, try organizing the pros and cons in a few different formats until you find one that resonates.

- **Pay attention to the whole system:** Most interesting problems have interconnected impact and require systems thinking. Make sure you understand the broader context. Don't oversimplify the problem into an isolated decision. Instead, make a list of possible repercussions and check your solutions against them.

- **Articulate your frameworks:** Share the thought process and structure behind your problem solving instead of just the solution. This helps people trust the solution you came to and enables them to make aligned decisions in the future.

CHAPTER 7

PRODUCT AND DESIGN SKILLS

I'VE HAD A TV remote where I couldn't find the power button in the dark (why was it not in the top corner?), and another that was so tiny it inevitably got lost in the couch cushions (thanks, Apple TV!). My library provides ebooks through an app that stalls for a second every time I flip the page. During tax season, I click on every tab and menu on my banking site to find where they put my tax forms. Some antivirus software cheerfully interrupts you every week to let you know that no problems were found.

> These decisions remind me of the importance of good product sense, and the pain when it's lacking.

Sometimes, product problems can be more serious. Confusing UI has caused people to tweet their search queries (or worse!) to the world. Social media algorithms can promote extremist content. The Galaxy Note 7 phone was prone to a teeny issue called "spontaneous combustion."

Most frequently, poor product choices mean people don't use the product at all. The video streaming app Quibi couldn't be watched on a TV nor could clips be shared on social media when it launched. Google Glass was a brand of smart glasses that couldn't overcome the "creepiness" factor.

Product and design sense is about so much more than making things look pretty. Building great products requires translating insights into good product decisions. It requires focusing on what's most important to a product's success.

RESPONSIBILITIES

DO PRODUCT DISCOVERY

Sometimes, you just want to *get stuff done*, and it can be tempting to jump right into designing solutions. I know the feeling. There might be executives or sales people who insist they know exactly what feature is missing. You might have engineers who are eagerly waiting for work.

But rushing to a solution without thoroughly understanding the problem can lead you astray. You can build something no one wants, and not build the thing that people actually *do* want.

Product discovery is a key piece of preventing these mistakes. During product discovery, you validate that users actually have the problems you think they do, and that they would actually value the solutions your team came up with.

While there are many ways to go about product discovery, one well-documented way is the GV Design Sprint.[1] A design sprint is a five-day structured process for product discovery.

- **Understand (pre-sprint):** Gather information about problems, opportunities, and goals from experts across the company.

- **Define (day 1):** Choose your problem or opportunity, goals, and success metrics.

- **Sketch (day 2):** Generate a wide range of potential solutions.

- **Decide (day 3):** Select a concept to prototype.

- **Prototype (day 4):** Prepare a testable prototype.

- **Validate (day 5):** Put the prototype in front of users and get feedback to validate, or invalidate the concept.

What you'll notice here is that the team spends a whole day thinking about which problems or opportunities could best help with the desired goal.

For more on product discovery, the book *Inspired* by Marty Cagan is an excellent guide.

ALWAYS BRING THINGS BACK TO THE GOALS

Connecting work back to the goals is one of the most important things that a PM does.

Think of your team's work as a spray of water from a hose trying to fill up a small bucket. Some people are spraying too wide and a bit off-center, so a lot of their work isn't filling up the bucket.

Some people may even be pointing at the wrong bucket. Even if they started spraying in the right direction, over time it may drift.

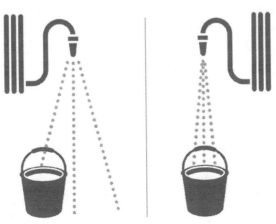

---

1   Learn more about the GV Design Sprint at https://www.gv.com/sprint/.

Refocusing people on the goals saves them time and achieves better, more reliable results.

Here are some examples of goals to clarify:

- Is the key success metric to get new users, increase engagement, or monetize?

- Does your new feature save people time or help them get better results?

- Are you trying to lure customers away from a competitor?

- Is there a specific use case you're trying to enable?

- Are you aiming to quickly validate an idea, or launch something fully polished?

- How much user backlash are you expecting and willing to tolerate?

If you get these wrong, you'll get the details wrong and optimize for the incorrect things.

Don't hide internal goals and constraints

Hank got harsh feedback on his proposed roadmap: the projects were much too small and didn't line up with the team's ambitious goals.

He felt like the feedback was unfair. He had done the best he could in the face of several constraints. One of the engineers was an intern who would only be around for 3 months, and another engineer was taking a long vacation. Plus, the team was switching to a new technology stack. How could he be expected to also tackle big ambitious projects during that quarter?

Hank wasn't wrong, but he also wasn't totally right. The mistake he made was leaving those internal goals and constraints out of the conversation about goals. He needed to share them as context for the roadmap decisions. When he kept them secret, he appeared to show poor judgment.

We all have to make compromises sometimes; that's understandable and doesn't make you a bad PM. But just as you might show the user data backing up certain decisions, it's important to explain the context behind these compromises.

DRIVE PRODUCT DECISIONS BY LAYING OUT YOUR INSIGHTS AND REASONING

It's a common interview question, but it's also a common real-life question. What do you do when someone disagrees with you? What if they're more senior—maybe even more knowledgeable and experienced—than you? Do you fight for what you believe is right, or concede to the "expert" (perhaps even your boss)?

This is a tough question, sometimes mired in politics and interpersonal relationships. But luckily, you typically don't need to choose between being stubborn and being a pushover; you can drive product decisions by showing the thought process behind your conclusions.

When you articulate your frameworks and show the intentionality behind your choices, people will either agree with you or move the conversation to a higher level about your insights and reasoning. If you disagree on insights, there's often a way to quickly learn or test which line of reasoning is correct.

PARTNER WITH YOUR DESIGNER TO COME UP WITH GREAT SOLUTIONS

Katie Guzman, PM Lead at Asana, joined the team in the middle of a major redesign. She agreed with nearly all the design choices, except for one that jumped out at her as being a little odd—the header took up too much space. The designer agreed, but none of his potential solutions were passing design review. She asked if she could take a stab, and with a little bit of subtle rearrangement, she came up with a design that worked for everyone.

The designer is usually responsible for the solution from a user experience perspective, but that doesn't mean that product managers don't need to be good at product design. Product managers are a designer's primary partner and often come up with key elements of the solution or key feedback that leads to better solutions.

> A PM shouldn't dictate a solution to the designer; rather, they should share their thoughts in a way that's respectful of the designer's role.[2]

As a PM, you're responsible for defining what success looks like and ensuring that the solution meets those criteria. This means that you can't sit back and quietly accept whatever solution the designer comes up with. Product design takes teamwork. Just like a PM expects teammates to sometimes catch missing corner cases or sub-optimal decisions in spec review, designers expect teammates to sometimes catch missing steps or suboptimal designs in design review.

It's important to build up your design sense so you can be a strong partner to your designer.

For more on how to work well with designers, including bringing them problems, not solutions, see "Working with designers" on pg 271.

DESIGN ETHICAL PRODUCTS

As a PM, you are the primary person who is in a position to ensure that both your team and company act ethically. If the product you're asked to build has the potential to harm people, you need to realize that and insist that the product changes.

This won't always be easy. Mikal Lewis shared with us that he has faced this challenge from both a career and product perspective:[3]

> I've faced this challenge as an African-American product leader. Modern work culture prioritizes great performance over good humans. However, being ethical and building ethical products means making a conscious choice that other things are more important to you than winning. Before you're faced with an ethical dilemma, ask yourself what values you won't compromise—even if it costs you your job.
>
> Over a long career, the probability that you'll face an ethical dilemma approaches one. This is doubly true for minority groups.

He challenges us to think about our values and which ones we wouldn't violate—even if it meant losing our job.

Well intentioned product choices can lead to unintended outcomes. The people designing Facebook's news feed wanted to promote interesting content, but accidentally built algorithms that favor polarizing or extremist content.

Sharon Lo, a PM for Ethics and Society at Microsoft, provides a perspective on how to build ethical products that centers on intentionality.

---

2   Note here how Guzman *asked* to give it a try. By doing that, she demonstrated respect for the designer's role, and made him more open to her suggestions too.

3   Mikal expanded on this at https://community.praxisproduct.com/2020/07/03/good-is-greater-than-great/.

> We've all seen the way technology has impacted society so quickly in the past decade. As PMs, we shape the products in technology. Are we crafting the world we want to live in?

How can you be intentional as a PM of whom or what may be affected and how they might be affected? Consider direct, indirect, and excluded users. Indirect users might include bystanders and people whose jobs are impacted by the product. Excluded users are people who can't use your product, for example, because of accessibility.

To understand the impact on these groups, see Microsoft's Harms Framework.[4] This will help ensure you consider the different types of unintended harms your product might create and mitigate those harms.

CATEGORY	TYPE OF HARM
Risk of injury	Physical or infrastructure damage
	Emotional or psychological distress
Denial of consequential services	Opportunity loss
	Economic loss
Infringement on human rights	Dignity loss
	Liberty loss
	Privacy loss
	Environmental impact
Erosion of social and democratic structures	Manipulation
	Social detriment

ADVOCATE FOR A BALANCED SOLUTION ⚡

Early in your career, you might fall into the trap of seeing PM and design as opposite ends of a seesaw. You end up in constant negotiations with your designer; they're asking for more time to polish up their designs, and you're asking for less time and faster shipping. Ultimately, you end up meeting somewhere in the middle. You might even think of this as a healthy balance.

Some people even go so far as to propose choosing extremes *as a negotiating tactic*. "Pick something further than what you want, so you'll get closer to what you actually want," they'll say.

But this attitude will end up holding you back. People will begin to lose trust in your judgment, and your designer might feel like they're constantly fighting with you and that you're not on the side of good design.

---

4   Explore the Harms Framework at https://docs.microsoft.com/en-us/azure/architecture/guide/responsible-innovation/harms-modeling/.

Instead, switch things around so that you always represent what you think is best overall. If you're previously been going with extremes, you can let people on your team know that you're changing your approach. Show that you have the judgment to know when more time should be invested in design, so that your team can trust you when you suggest the opposite.

All of these actions demonstrate to your designer that you are a good representative of their concerns, and that you're on their side. Your designer should feel like you're a great partner, not an adversary.

GIVE GREAT PRODUCT FEEDBACK ⚡⚡

As you advance in your career, reviewing other people's product decisions becomes a bigger part of your job.

Your goal should be to help the team create the best product and make the best trade offs. You want to share and explain your feedback so the team really understands what you're saying, acts on the feedback, and feels comfortable coming back to you for advice the next time.

Here are some things to keep in mind for great product feedback:

- **Timing:** Make sure the feedback you're giving is useful for the team at their current stage. If your feedback is that they need to throw away a lot of work and go back to the beginning, you'll need to plan out that conversation very carefully.

- **The type of feedback they're looking for:** If a team says they're looking for feedback on the interaction design, not the visual design, it's important to focus on that. If you do need to give a different kind of feedback, make sure the team understands why you're giving it.

- **Frameworks and rationale:** Instead of simply telling people what to do, explain to them the reasoning behind the change so they can figure it out for themselves next time.

- **Larger perspective:** It's very helpful to share feedback that comes from a context they might not know. For example, you may be able to share an insight from a leadership meeting that's relevant to the product choice.

- **Old ideas are often the best ideas:** One of the most demoralizing things you can say to a team is, "We tried that and it didn't work." Just because an idea didn't work in the past doesn't mean that a variation wouldn't work now. The idea might have been ahead of its time. You can point them to the lessons from past attempts, but don't shut the whole idea down.

- **Respect their expertise:** As an outsider, have the humility to know that you might not know as much as the immediate team does. Ask questions and provide information, but once you've done that, trust them to make the right decision as much as possible.

Giving good product feedback is one of the most leveraged ways to help create great products.

CREATE PRODUCT (AND/OR DESIGN) PRINCIPLES ⚡⚡

Product principles are a set of values that your company uses to guide designs, evaluate solutions, and resolve difficult tradeoffs. They require extensive collaboration and buy-in to create, but once you have them, they'll simplify many future decisions.

You'll know you need principles when teams repeatedly get into challenging philosophical disagreements, or you feel like you're getting pushback on things that seem obvious, such as consistency.

Before you create your own principles, you can first take a look at the design and product principles other companies have created. Design principles often involve universal design, consistency, tone of voice, and delight.[5] On the product side, common principles are created around user trust, innovation, and lean development.[6]

To get started, it's helpful to come up with many examples where principles could have helped teams make a choice. Those examples will highlight the difficult tradeoffs you need to resolve. There isn't much value in creating a list of generic principles that don't change how your team designs products.

Once you have the examples, identify what the core tradeoffs are. What were people valuing differently that led them to make different choices?

It's great to make the process collaborative, but in the end, make sure that the key stakeholders have fully bought into the principles. They'll need to reinforce the principles and ensure that they're being used to guide decisions.

GROWTH PRACTICES

PICK THE FASTEST AND BEST WAYS TO TEST HYPOTHESES

Validating your ideas and testing your hypotheses doesn't have to be expensive. The faster and more lightweight your test, the more tests you'll be able to run, and the faster you'll be able to iterate past bad ideas to the ones that will be impactful.

Here are a few ways to speed up hypothesis testing:

- **Test on people around you. Instead of recruiting real users, you can often run simple tests on the people around you:** your coworkers, friends, friendly customers, or people walking around your building. This works well for testing things like usability or copy (the text in your product), but keep an eye out for places where they might be different from your target audience.

- **Use a site like usertesting.com to recruit participants for you.** If you recruit people on your own, it will likely take at least a week to get all of the sessions scheduled, and you'll probably have a few frustrating cancelations. Using an online testing site can get you results that night. You'll need to prepare your test carefully, since you can't adjust the test between one participant and the next.

- **Set up a recruiting intercept on your product's website.** With a product like Ethn.io, you add code to your website once, and then can easily turn a recruiting pop-up on or off whenever you want to catch users who are actively on the website. Whenever you want to talk to real users, you can turn the intercept on and be talking to people in minutes.

- **Use low-fidelity prototypes.** Most concepts can be tested with simple marker-on-paper sketches. It's true that you won't get much useful usability feedback, but you might be surprised at how much you'll learn about the desirability of your idea.

---

5   Learn more about design principles at https://medium.muz.li/design-principles-behind-great-products-6ef13cd74ccf.

6   Learn more about product principles at https://www.productplan.com/product-principles/.

- **Use high-fidelity prototypes.** When you want to test the details of how your product works, you don't need to build it out first. Instead, you can create a high-fidelity prototype that looks just like the real app, but is not based on real production code. These prototypes can range from static click-through prototypes to chrome extensions that modify the real app.

- **Have an open-ended conversation with real users**. Instead of designing anything, you can sometimes learn a lot just from talking to people about their problems and their reaction to your potential solution. Try to dig deep to find any potential blockers. You can even ask them to draw their own versions of their ideal product. This works best as an early approach that's followed up with more structured research to protect against overly optimistic responses.

- **Invite stakeholders to the user sessions.** Instead of running sessions for weeks and then presenting formalized results to your stakeholders, invite them along to the sessions. They'll see the results with their own eyes and get a chance to quickly redirect the test if they don't think it's testing the right hypotheses.

- **Run a quick A/B test**. For simple text and design changes, it's sometimes faster to make a change in code than it is to run user tests. This approach is especially useful when you're testing a change that gives immediate feedback, such as testing whether a different email subject line increases email opens or testing whether moving a button gets it more clicks.

- **Run a "fake door" test**. A fake door test is when you create the entry-point for a new feature without building the feature itself. This lets you evaluate interest in the feature. For example, clicking on "Dashboards" might take the user to a page that says "Thank you for your interest. We will let you know when dashboards are available." Because people can get frustrated with fake door tests, it's best to run them for short amounts of time or with very carefully crafted landing pages.

- **Create a concierge MVP for a few customers.** Before building a full production-ready feature, you can often come up with a more manual, behind-the-scenes approach that works for a few users. For example, you could manually create dashboards with custom scripts for a few of your customers to learn if people are willing to pay for them.

- **Analyze existing data**. Instead of running an experiment, you can often test your hypotheses with existing data. For example, if you'd like to build a feature that only works when users have profile photos, you can first calculate how many users have profile photos. If the number is low, it might not be worth building your feature.

Look for the fastest and cheapest way to validate your hypotheses so that you'll be able to test most of your risky assumptions before investing too much time in them. Save the more expensive methods for the "big bets" where you need the extra precision and confidence.

DESIGN FOR STICKY USAGE

It would be nice if people just *used* the products they like, but in reality most people will not be proactive about using your product. Instead, you'll need to think carefully about the triggers that remind people to come back to your product. This is an area where you'll need to be especially careful about ethics: too much usage of your product isn't always good for the person using it.

Here are a few approaches to help bring people back to your product at the appropriate time:

- **Notifications**. The best kind of notifications let people know that something they were waiting for is available. Perhaps they were waiting for a coworker to complete a task or for their food to be delivered to their door. In these cases, people would be frustrated if you *didn't* notify them. People might also opt-in to reminders to use your product daily, for example with a meditation or meal-tracking app.

- **Product Updates**. Sometimes people stop using your product because it doesn't have all the functionality they need. Sending monthly update emails (with an unsubscribe option) is a great way to remind people about your product and entice them to try it again.

- **Visibility**. A visual reminder can be a powerful way to bring people back to your product. Consider downloadable apps that will show up on a user's home screen or entry points from other products. Integrations are a great way to increase visibility.

- **Gamification**. Techniques like "streaks" for using the product multiple days in a row can encourage people to start a habit, although they can also backfire when people accidentally break a streak.

Think carefully about how your product is meant to fit into people's lives, and then make it easy for people to use your product when they want it. If there aren't many good triggers to prompt people to use your app, consider if there are ways to add more.

BUILD PRODUCT MINDSET

Product mindset is a habitual approach where you start from problems, goals, and people's needs.

It's about asking yourself, "What problem are we trying to solve?" and, "What problem should we solve?" When you have a product mindset, you notice problems everywhere and you're able to connect those problems to bigger goals in order to figure out whether those problems really matter. You constantly analyze what your goals should be and prioritize accordingly.

Product mindset is a critical quality to possess as a product manager because you spend your days making lots of little decisions. If your mind doesn't automatically remind you to figure out your goals, you could end up making bad decisions. And if you're not thinking deeply about which problems to solve, you'll set bad goals.

If you find yourself rushing into execution before really considering and evaluating your goals, you're not demonstrating a product mindset. If you find yourself focusing on how exciting a solution or technology is without connecting it to the problem it solves, you're not showing a product mindset.

If product mindset isn't natural to you yet, you'll need to work to build this habit.

1. **Check for assumptions that might get in the way of having a product mindset.** Do you assume that you can't push back on the goals set by your boss? Do you think true innovation comes from a spark of creativity rather than a deliberate process? Are those assumptions holding you back?

2. **Set reminders for yourself.** You can create templates for documents and meeting agendas that start with goals. You can practice by asking yourself, "Is this problem worth solving?" for every problem for a week. Write, "What problem are we trying to solve?" on a sticky note and put it on your monitor where you'll see it all the time. With enough repetition, it will eventually become natural.

Developing your product mindset will help you make better decisions.

PRACTICE IDENTIFYING AND PRIORITIZING GOALS

Go through the following exercise with several products, both technical and non-technical. Choose products where you are not the target audience since those will stretch you more. Try it with your own product and with your competitor's products. The wider the variety, the more you'll learn.

If you want to improve the product mindset of your team, this is an exercise you can do with them, too. Again, you can use your own product, but it's also very useful to use other products.

Write down all of the business and customer goals you can think of

What's the *real* job that the product does for people?

Mikal Lewis, founder of Praxis Product Leadership, challenges people to think of the real purpose of wearing headphones in an office. It's not just to listen to music; it's also a polite way of signaling other people to not disturb you. Can you find any non-obvious goals for your product?

Do the goals change based on who built the product? For example, when a local government provides a service, they often have goals around providing equal access to everyone in the community that a for-profit company might not have.

Are there multiple users or customers with different goals? A parent buys a toy and a child plays with it. In a marketplace product, you need to attract both buyers and sellers.

When you think you have all of the goals, you can look at the marketing material for the product to see if they mention others you might have missed.

Prioritize the goals

Which goals are critical to the company's mission and success? Do any goals conflict with each other? If so, how should they be balanced against each other?

It can be tempting to say all of the goals are equally important, but that ignores important tradeoffs and strategic choices.

For example, a video streaming platform might care about having a delightful user experience, but that's much less important to their success than having compelling content. People won't come back to the app if there's nothing good to watch.

STAY CURRENT WITH WELL-DESIGNED PRODUCTS

Early web and app design makes us cringe now. Think: 3D text, Comic Sans, flashing banners, chaotic layouts, and the occasional website that beeps out a tune while you dash to kill your sound.

We've come a long way—mostly for the better, but certainly different.

In some cases, product design evolves like fashion, with one style entering as another exits.

In other cases, technological innovations clear the way for better designs. Search-as-you-type and continuous scrolling are popular now, but wouldn't have been feasible back when we were all on dial-up.

And still in other cases, new design patterns evolve because a few key players adopt one approach and the rest of the industry follows their lead. The usage of a heart icon to like/favorite something has become ubiquitous, and it's generally in everyone's best interest to adopt this same imagery.

Great designers around the world are constantly inventing new design patterns and better UI elements that you can incorporate into your own product. By using a wide variety of products, you'll build up your sense of what the best-of-breed patterns are and where standards are emerging. You'll also see the places where there are a few common options and you can form your own opinions on which work best.

Good design rarely requires reinventing the wheel. Most of the time, it's better to reuse a familiar pattern.

DEVELOP YOUR QUALITY BAR

Product managers are responsible for defining what success looks like, and a big part of that is determining the quality bar.

If your bar is set too low, you'll ship buggy or unpolished products that cause users to lose faith in it. You might notice the quality issues show up in the metrics, or they might slowly add up over time. Beyond the product implications, teammates won't want to work with you if they're not proud of the things your team ships.

If your bar is set too high, you'll invest too much in finding "the perfect" solution, leading to a bad return on investment. Users miss out on important functionality while they're waiting for you to perfect it, and your overall product improves more slowly than the competition. Your team might also be reluctant to iterate based on learnings because they've already sunk too much time into it before the launch.

> Your users' expectations set a baseline for the quality bar. If your product is less polished or has more bugs than the products they compare it to, it will feel low quality. As other products improve their quality, the acceptable quality bar for your product will rise as well.

Developing your quality bar includes two parts:

1. **Notice quality issues:** This includes things like UI elements that are a pixel off, designs that have usability issues, flows that will be difficult for new users to follow, and features that fail under edge cases. If you're having trouble spotting quality issues, try partnering with someone who's got a sharper eye, like a designer or user researcher.

2. **Choose which issues to fix, but keep cost in mind:** If all of the quality issues were free to fix, you would fix them all. When you're prioritizing quality issues, you don't want to skip fixing a very inexpensive issue, and you don't want the team to surprise you by spending two weeks fixing something you thought would only take minutes. You need to work closely with your designers and engineers and state your costing assumptions out loud.

Here's how a sample conversation might sound:

> Okay, we've just done a thorough team review and noticed these ten issues that I wrote down. Let's go through them and figure out which ones we want to fix before launch.
>
> We should fix all the typos because I'm assuming those will only take a few minutes; does that sound right?
>
> The drop target being small is pretty frustrating; is there any way we could fix it in less than a day? How about we spend an hour looking into it, and if it'll take longer than that, we don't fix it? Designer, does that seem reasonable?

> The error message when files are too big is not very helpful, but I know we don't have much control over that dialog, and I don't think many users will hit it. I'll look at the logs and customer tickets a few weeks after launch and we can see if it ends up being a problem.

For more on prioritization, see Chapter 17: Roadmapping and Prioritization (pg 193).

EXPAND YOUR PERSPECTIVE: CONSIDER MORE RADICAL SOLUTIONS

Early in your career, a lot of the solution space is constrained; you have a set team size, a designated amount of time, and obvious boundaries for what types of solutions you can suggest. As you advance in your career, however, you'll need to shift to seeing those things as flexible rather than fixed.

Here are some questions to consider:

- What types of solutions would be possible if you expanded your team size?

- What if you could move the deadline?

- What if you could form a partnership with another company or buy a ready-made solution?

- Could the problem be solved outside the product, such as via customer support or the sales team?

- What if you could change how the business model works?

- If you could wave a magic wand and build anything you want, what would it be?

As you move into product leadership, it's important to not only build the best product given the constraints but also to push on those constraints to see which ones are worth the tradeoffs.

CONCEPTS AND FRAMEWORKS

WIREFRAMES, PROTOTYPES, AND FLOWS

Wireframes and prototypes are great ways to share ideas and do early concept testing. Higher fidelity prototypes can be used for usability tests. A wireframe is a still drawing of a part of your product, while a prototype is an interactive model of your product. Most products can and should be tested as prototypes before any significant investment of engineering time.

A key concept in wireframing is "low fidelity." Low fidelity means that the mocks are not meant to be implemented exactly, but rather, they're symbolic of the actual design. Prototypes can be as simple as drawing with a marker on a piece of paper and simulating a "click" by swapping to a new piece of paper. When you draw a low-fidelity wireframe, include only the most important components that the user needs to see. The goal is for wireframing to be fast so you feel comfortable testing ideas and iterating on them.

It's important that your mocks look as low fidelity as they're intended to be, or else you might have engineers accidentally copying colors and spacing from your mock, or creating new components when they should have used existing ones. This is why some prototyping tools purposefully look like they were sketched by hand.

Please note: It is okay to make wireframes to illustrate an idea, but it is not okay to pressure your designer into going with your solution or expect them to just "pretty up" your wireframes. It is also not okay to take all of the fun work by handing over wireframes before the designer got a chance to explore on their own (unless they asked for your help).

Another key concept is "flows." This is the idea that you don't want to think only about static screenshots, but also about the full set of steps that a user will go through, from the very beginning (including empty states), through setup and configuration, to the actual usage. You can represent this with a flow diagram (screenshots connected by arrows), or with an interactive prototype.

It can be helpful to use a tool like Balsamiq, Framer, Sketch, InVision, or Figma to draw wireframes and prototypes. These tools have libraries or kits you can use to represent standard components so that you don't have to draw them yourself. The options for wireframing and prototyping tools are rapidly evolving, so do some research to find out what the latest and greatest ones are.

OPPORTUNITY SOLUTION TREES

As a new PM, when I was asked to build a very specific solution, it could feel discouraging. On one hand, I understood that I was junior and shouldn't expect as much leeway. On the other hand, it felt like the real "product" work was taken away from me; I was merely executing someone else's plan.

In reality, that wasn't quite right. Even when asked to build a specific solution, product discovery is essential.

A great mental model for product discovery is Teresa Torres's Opportunity Solution Tree.[7] This visualization helps you widen your perspective and imagine alternative solutions that could help you find a better way to achieve your goal.

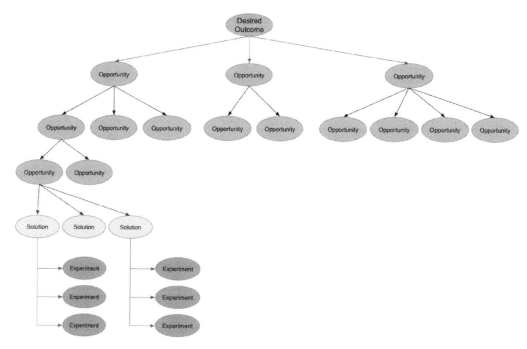

---

7   Learn more about Torres' opportunity solution tree at https://www.producttalk.org/opportunity-solution-tree/

For example, when your boss asks you to build a spreadsheet export feature, you can interview internal stakeholders (to learn about their goals for this feature) and customers (to understand their potential usage of it). You might learn that the goal is to close more deals by addressing the reporting requests, or it could be to get the senior managers at the customer's company more involved with the product by sending them summaries. Each of these opportunities can then lead to different solutions, such as building reporting directly into the product, building a PDF summary, or building integration with reporting software.

PRODUCT TEARDOWNS

Product teardowns can yield a number of benefits, including developing your domain knowledge, design sense, and creativity. In a product teardown, you get together with a few people to review another product. As Jens-Fabian Goetzmann explains:[8]

> Every Friday afternoon, the product management team and other interested folks from the design, research and analytics teams sit together for an hour and "tear down" an interesting mobile or web app. By "tear down," we don't mean "criticize", but rather investigate and reverse engineer the thinking and experience underlying a product. This gives us inspiration to improve our own product.

Try to notice all of the intentional decisions that went into the product so you can learn from them.

Depending on your goals, you can approach the session differently.

- **Domain Knowledge:** When you're trying to build your domain knowledge, product teardowns are a great way to become familiar with your competitors. You can see areas where they've offered different features than your product offers, or solved a problem differently, and then you can try to figure out which way works best based on those differences. You can look at their product reviews to validate your guesses about what customers would like, or not like, about the product.

- **Design Sense:** When you're trying to build your design sense, pay close attention to design patterns. Look at how the product handles navigation, error cases, empty states, alerts, and information architecture. What kind of iconography and labeling do they use? It can be especially helpful to teardown products that your customer base already uses and is familiar with since they will set the standard for what your customers expect.

- **Creativity:** When you're trying to build your creativity, look at a wide variety of products and brainstorm ways you can use their patterns in your product. Do they do something clever with onboarding or machine learning? What would your product look like if you tried to rebuild it like Spotify, Slack, or Waze?

It can be tempting to focus on what doesn't work well about the product, but you'll get much more out of it if you focus on what *does* work well, and look for inspiration.

---

8   Jens-Fabian elaborates on this at https://www.jefago.com/product-management/product-teardowns-at-yammer/.

BRAINSTORMING

Many people, when they think about brainstorming, picture a group of people crowded around a table, each shouting out ideas. Unfortunately, research shows that this method reduces the creativity and diversity of solutions.[9] Once one person has said an idea out loud, the rest of the ideas tend to converge around it.

This is not what brainstorming is—or at least what it should be. Brainstorming is a structured process that helps generate creative solutions and includes stakeholders.

Start with independent brainstorming before sharing as a group

To generate a variety of divergent ideas, give people time to write and draw ideas by themselves at the beginning of the meeting before sharing with the rest of the group. When possible, share the context and brainstorming "how might we..." prompt before the meeting so people can think about their ideas in advance if they want. Not everyone loves brainstorming under pressure!

After the independent brainstorm, ask people to share their ideas and leave room for discussion. This is the time when people can build on each other's ideas.

Invite people from multiple teams and roles

When you're setting up the brainstorming session, invite more than just PMs and your feature team. Consider designers, engineers, salespeople, product marketers, customer support representatives, executives, and anyone else who is a stakeholder or who might have a different perspective on the problem.

Inviting a variety of people offers the following benefits:

1. **Creativity:** People with different perspectives will often come up with creative, out-of-the-box ideas that will improve the overall solution.

2. **Listening:** Brainstorming is an efficient way to include and listen to many people at once. All of your stakeholders and partners get a chance to tell you what they think you should build, without your having the pressure to individually respond or explain why their ideas don't work. More than that, the solutions they suggest will often help you better understand what they are thinking and what they care about.

3. **Morale:** Brainstorming is fun. People enjoy being included, and it can also be a team bonding experience.

Set up the brainstorming with some structure

Unstructured brainstorm has its benefits, but it can also feel intimidating. Many people won't know where to get started, and might even preemptively nix their own ideas because they "aren't good enough." A little bit of structure or direction can make things fun and help you achieve more interesting results.

- **Crazy Eights:** Fold your paper into eight pieces, set the timer for eight minutes, and try to fill each square with a different idea before the time is up.

- **Brain Writing:** Each person writes/draws an idea on their piece of paper and then passes it to their right. In the next round, you look at what's already on the paper in front of you and build on top of it.

---

9   Learn more about this from the Harvard Business Review's article at https://hbr.org/2017/05/your-team-is-brain-storming-all-wrong.

- **Different Hats:** Ask people to come up with ideas based on different categories or constraints, such as one normal, one silly, one that's inexpensive to build, and one that's fancy. You can also use this to split the brainstorming by customer type or use case.

- **Random Combinations:** Write themes or constraints on flashcards and have each person or group pull two cards and come up with ideas that match the combination, such as "email" and "power users."

Kate Bennet, Director of Product at Lab Zero, has templates for sprint retrospectives that include several brainstorming activities:

> In some retros, I draw a sailboat on the board. The wind represents things that help us; the anchor, things that hinder us. A shark represents the team's fears, and a tropical island is the team's hopes or goals. I'll give everyone a stack of Post-It notes (or a link to an online whiteboard) and give them five minutes to put Post-Its on each part of the image. We found that by mixing it up and changing the format to meet the needs of the group, people get more interested and energized by the retro. They are then more likely to actually share things that matter to them.

Make sure to convey an attitude of being welcoming to good, bad, and wacky ideas. You want everyone to feel comfortable proposing ideas, and even the silly ideas might inspire great ones.

KEY TAKEAWAYS

- **Always start with the goals:** Taking a few minutes at the beginning of each piece of work to get everyone on the same page about why you're doing it and what you're hoping to accomplish can make a huge difference in your success. Frequently revisiting the goals not only keeps people on track, it helps morale as well!

- **Don't skip product discovery:** A huge number of failed or disappointing launches trace back to the untested assumption that users would want the thing being built. Even when an executive orders you to build something, at least run some cheap validation in parallel to starting the work.

- **Prioritize what matters:** There will always be a long list of potential feature work, but it's not all equally important. Take the user and data insights you discovered and use them to focus your team on the work that will be most critical to the product's success.

- **Consider potential harmful consequences:** As a PM you're responsible for the positive and negative impact of your product. While it may seem less "fun" to add protections and limitations, it's important to ensure your products don't cause harm.

- **Use great products:** The best way to improve your product sense is to use a lot of great products and pay attention to them. Even when your product sense is strong, keep using great products to stay on top of new patterns and best practices.

- **Creativity can be developed:** Many innovative product ideas come from cross-applying an idea from one domain to another. The broader your research, the greater the chance you'll find inspiration. Brainstorming with diverse groups of people is another way to expand your breadth of ideas.

CHAPTER 8

TECHNICAL SKILLS

PMS HAVE A touchy relationship with technical skills. Some PMs come from an engineering background and need to learn how not to step on their engineer's toes. Others have never written a line of code and are afraid they'll sound stupid if they ask questions.

Overall, PMs need to understand the technology behind their product enough to be an effective partner to their engineers in brainstorming, costing, problem solving, and representing the team. Beyond that, engineers often appreciate when PMs are willing and able to take on some easy or tedious coding tasks; it can help teams to hit their deadlines, ship with more polish, and build camaraderie.

RESPONSIBILITIES

PARTNER WITH ENGINEERS ON PRODUCT DECISIONS

Some PMs believe it's their job to have all the ideas and do all the product thinking. They'll go off with their designers and come up with a grand vision to present to the developers for implementation. If an engineer comes up with a proposal, they'll quickly dismiss it—either out of a lack of respect or because they're being territorial.

Instead, proactively share your product thinking with engineers. Include them in brainstorming meetings and ask them for their input. Engineers often become the source of innovative ideas because they know the technological possibilities.

Laika Kayani, Sr. Director at AI Platform Product Management at Lumiata, explained how she works with engineers to create great solutions:

> As a PM, I'm very specific about the outcome I'm looking to achieve for the customer. When we build a new machine learning model, we talk about whether we're optimizing for speed, cost, or performance and discuss options. One time, I worked with a customer who was hitting capacity issues with their ML models. One option would have been to simplify the ML features of the model all together. When I discussed the customer's goals with the engineers, we came up with a better solution where our

company hosted the infrastructure rather than the customer relying on an internal IT team to allocate additional capacity.

Working together often leads to better solutions than either of you could come up with on your own.

LEARN ABOUT HOW THE TECHNICAL INFRASTRUCTURE IMPACTS THE PRODUCT

You might not have a technical background, but you're probably a generally intelligent person. That, and a little bit of bravery, is really all you need to be successful with technical skills in your early career.

Find an engineer you feel comfortable with and ask them how the system works. They'll use words you probably don't understand, so ask them what those words mean. Ask them what the implications of the system are on the product, what kinds of things are easy to build, and what things are difficult.

As a PM, you'll have assumptions about what types of things can be built and approximately how long they would take. When you're caught by surprise, or you're told, "We can't do that—it's too difficult," ask for clarification so you can understand the details.

For more approaches on how to tackle something that's "too hard to build", see page 102. There are often alternative solutions that will accomplish your goals.

IF YOU KNOW HOW TO CODE, CONSIDER CONTRIBUTING TO HELP OUT

This advice is a bit of a double-edged sword. As you advance in your career, you don't want to pick up coding responsibilities that take away from your time to invest in strategic thinking. Early in your career, however, writing some code can be a quick way to earn credibility with your engineers and help your team.

The best types of tasks to pick up are those that your engineers don't really want to do. For example, many engineers shy away from frontend work like writing simple CSS. Often, the work they don't want to do is tedious, which is great because they can teach you how to do it once and then you can learn by doing it over and over again.

Stay away from any code that your engineers aren't excited to have your help on, and don't let your coding erode your humility. If your attempts to help out aren't appreciated, there are probably much better things for you to spend your time on.

GROWTH PRACTICES

CHECK IN WITH YOUR MANAGER AND ENGINEERS

The amount and type of technical skills that are needed and valued can vary from role to role and company to company.

It's a good idea to check with your manager and engineering partners as to what they feel might be useful. They can let you know if they think a coding class would be helpful, and if so, what language. Instead of coding, they might prefer you to just familiarize yourself with the specific technologies the team uses or to skip technical skills and focus your time elsewhere.

BUILD YOUR COSTING INTUITION ⚡

Early in your career, you want to tread lightly and avoid estimating engineering costs. Engineers are very sensitive to PMs suggesting that work could be done more quickly, so it's better to ask directly instead of assuming.

Once you've built up credibility and formed strong relationships with engineers, you can get a lot of product benefits by understanding engineering costs and being able to do rough costing on your own.

Before we go further, I want to reiterate:

> You can make a time estimate for your own benefit, but never sign your team up for anything. If you will be using a time estimate outside of just personal use, it's crucial that this estimate came from the engineers.

So, what can you do with your own estimates? A few options:

- **Sift through the solution space to figure out which solutions are likely, or unlikely, to be too costly.** This is great when you're working with a designer or a stakeholder because you can quickly flag ideas that might be expensive and come up with alternatives in the moment. That quick feedback can save a lot of iteration cycles. If you're going with this approach, it's a good practice to double check the cost of the original idea with an engineer later, to make sure you didn't dismiss an idea too quickly.

- **Catch misunderstandings or missing information early.** If you expected a change to take a few hours, but the engineer thinks it will take two weeks, one of you knows something the other doesn't. Perhaps you know about an existing component or a pre-calculated value that can be reused. Once you've been at the company for a while, or if you're bringing relevant information from your last company, it's not that uncommon for a PM to know something that can really speed up the technical implementation.

- **Take a first pass at prioritization (on a smaller scale) and roadmapping (at a larger scale).** Prioritization and roadmapping are all about cost vs. benefit, so the better your intuition on the cost, the more reasonable your first draft will be. As you're sharing your draft with engineering, you can include your rough costing estimate at the small/medium/large level of granularity (often called t-shirt sizing). Make sure to ask if any of your estimates are off.

How to Build Your Costing Intuition

To build your costing intuition, you need to understand how the work breaks down into component pieces, and then pattern match against how long similar pieces took to build. It's important to pattern match against work within the same company because things like the infrastructure, testing framework, and deployment schedule can have a big impact on how long things take.

The two biggest factors in cost are usually:

- **How much of the solution can be reused, and how much needs to be built from scratch.** For example, imagine you're adding a form to a dialog box and you want it to have a calendar picker and a color picker. If your product already has those pickers, it will probably be pretty cheap to build. If not, it will take longer and be more costly.

- **Performance.** If you want something that touches a lot of pieces of data–like counting up millions of records–that will usually be intolerably slow if built in a low-cost and straightforward way. It might even create stability issues. The same thing applies for a design that needs to look up a lot of data sequentially, such as finding all the actors in a movie, and then all the other movies those actors have been in. There are engineering techniques to make designs like that work fast, but it takes longer and is more costly to build them.

CONCEPTS AND FRAMEWORKS

TECHNICAL TERMS AND CONCEPTS

It's impossible to teach you everything there is to know about technology, but here is a quick crash course. Understanding this terminology will greatly help you when talking with your engineers.

API

API stands for Application Programming Interface. It's the equivalent of UI for computers communicating with each other.

There are internal APIs that different products and systems within your company use to talk with each other, and external APIs that can be used by developers outside of your company to connect to your product or build on top of it. Just like a person is limited by the UI (for example, the mobile version of an app might not have the same functionality as the web version), computers are limited by what APIs are available.

Companies with a wide variety of products often move to a **service-oriented architecture**, which is when the components and pieces of infrastructure are separated into isolated **services** that communicate over APIs, rather than being an interconnected tangle of code.

Implementing APIs
When talking about APIs, you might hear **CRUD** (pronounced like the word "crud"), which stands for Create, Read, Update, Delete, which are the four basic actions you can take on data. For example, a CRUD API on Twitter for tweets would let you create a new tweet, retrieve the text of a tweet (if you know its numeric ID), edit the tweet, or delete the tweet.[1] A CRUD API is usually the first API a product would provide, before building more special-purpose APIs, such as to pin a tweet to your profile.

Many APIs will either use **XML** or **JSON (JavaScript Object Notation)** to format the information they share. Both are text-based formats that are easy for computers to parse and understand. If you hear people talk about **JSON objects** or a **JSON Blob**, they're talking about a piece of data formatted in that easily shareable and usable structure.

For **authentication** (**auth**), APIs usually use **access tokens** instead of sending your username and password around on every request. Think of access tokens like getting a hand stamp after showing your ticket at a museum.

Client (also called frontend) and server (also called backend)

The **client** is the part of the product that runs on the user's device—for example, the mobile app or the website you see when a page loads. The **server** is the part of the product that runs on the company's comput-

---

1   Yes, I know you can't actually edit tweets. This is just an example.

ers or on cloud computing services like Amazon Web Services (AWS). Any data you can access from multiple devices is stored on the server, and the client only gets a temporary copy.

Things that can be done purely on the client side can be instant, while things that require a **round trip to the server** (the client sends a message to the server of what it wants, and the server sends back a response) often have a noticeable delay of a quarter of a second or more.

Mobile vs. web apps

On a mobile app, there's often a lot of content in the mobile client, which is why they take a while to download and you need to perform periodic app updates. Images and especially videos will make it take especially long; text doesn't make as much of a difference. After you open the app, you'll sometimes get a slow progress bar that says, "downloading new content." If you're using the app in airplane mode, that means you're using it without the server. If you fix a bug in your mobile app, you need to resubmit it to the app store and wait for people to download the update.

On a web app, the client code is downloaded from the server every time you reload the page. This is why you never need to update your web app. In a web app, if you notice a problem, you can often fix it for customers within minutes.

Optimizations

Need stuff to go faster? Here are some common approaches:

- There are often **background jobs** or **cron jobs** that run on the server. A job is an independent piece of code that runs separately from the rest of the server code, rather than in direct reaction to a client request. A cron job is a job that runs on a regular schedule (such as every ten minutes or every night) and might be used, for example, to send out a daily summary email. A background job runs in the background to **asynchronously** perform tasks that are too slow for the client to just wait. Background jobs might perform tasks for users, such as generating a big export file, or they might perform tasks for the system, such as when a profile name change takes a few minutes to propagate through the system.

- Somewhere in this system there might be a **cache** (pronounced "cash"), or multiple caches. One popular caching system is called **memcache**. A cache speeds things up by storing the results of expensive calculations. That's great, but they sometimes introduce bugs, and they can quickly drive certain server costs up.

- **Lazy loading** is a coding design pattern where you defer an expensive calculation until it's needed. For example, imagine you've had a product for a few years and now you want to remove curse words from all user-generated content. Instead of running a background job to update all the content (which could take months), you could remove the curse words only when someone tries to look at the content.

Also read about optimizing databases (pg 99).

Deployments and development, testing, staging, beta, and production servers

Engineers write code all day, but that code doesn't immediately go live for customers as soon as it's written. Instead, they test out the code in a sequence of isolated development environments to make sure that it performs as intended, functions well with all the recent changes that other engineers have made, and works with real data. **Deployment** is the process of getting the new code live for customers.

Engineers start with a **local sandbox** (also called the **development server** or **dev**) that runs on their own machine.[2] The sandbox environment might have a lot of differences from the real environment (for example, having just a tiny amount of fake data), but it's very quick to see how the code works and iterate on it. Each engineer has their own sandbox so everyone can write code at the same time. After an engineer types the code, they might have to **build** or **compile** the code, and that could take a while, depending on the computer language and the architecture of the codebase. Speeding up compile times can make a big difference in the speed of development, as it allows developers to more quickly test their code.

Part of writing code involves writing new **tests** that validate that the code works as expected. If the team uses **test-driven development** (TDD), they write each test *before* writing the associated code—the tests serve as a type of spec or acceptance criteria. For most other teams, the main purpose of the newly written tests is not to catch bugs, but rather to prevent future code from accidentally breaking this code.

Managing code

As the engineers write their code, they use a **version control system** such as **git** or **github** to keep track of their changes and get the new code that the rest of the engineers have written. The centralized copy of all the code is called the **master branch**.

Each engineer has a **local repository**, or a copy of all the code on their local machine. When they start working on a new feature, they'll often create a new, named **feature branch**. Each branch has its own changes and version history. Branches are helpful because if an engineer is halfway through a new feature and someone asks them to fix a bug in a different part, they can switch to a new branch to make the small fix while still saving all of their other work separately.

Committing code

As the engineer works, they **commit** the changes, which is basically saving the changes back to the version control system and updating the version history. Once everything is ready and they want to es**merge** their branch back into the master branch, they create a **Pull Request** (**PR**) or **change list**. The PR shows all the **diffs**, or changes (lines of code added, removed, or changed). If you know how to read code, it can sometimes be helpful to take a look at the PR—for example, to learn what an event is named in the logs.

The PR might now be sent off for a **code review**, which is when another engineer looks over the code to catch bugs or style mistakes. Many companies require code reviews prior to checking in code. If your team doesn't follow this practice yet, you might want to look into it. It's a good way to catch bugs, ensure good practices, train new people, and also help each person on the team understand the codebase more fully.

Once the PR is accepted, everyone else's changes from the master branch are **merged** into the local branch. If everyone was editing different lines of code, the merged code will automatically combine everyone's changes. If two people tried to edit the same line, it will send back a **merge conflict** and the engineer needs to look at it to manually fix it.

Validating code before deployment

The PR is then **pushed** to the **testing server** to run tests. The testing server is shared with all of the engineers, so if a lot of them submit code at the same time, there might be a long wait while tests run.

The testing server usually runs **unit tests** and **integration tests**. Unit tests are small isolated tests that automatically run through all the functionality of a component and check that the right results are returned. The

---

2   "Sandbox" can also refer to an isolated practice environment that customers can play around in to test out a product.

point of unit tests isn't really to check that the code you just wrote is correct; it's more to ensure that no one else makes a change that breaks your code. Integration tests are larger tests that run through flows and can ensure full use cases work.

If the company uses **continuous deployment**, code that passes tests automatically is merged back into the shared master branch and deployed to the next server in the sequence. It might either go directly to the **production server** (**prod**) that is used by real customers, to a **beta server** that internal employees or a small percentage of customers use, or to a **staging server** that is an exact copy of production to run **load tests**. Each company will have a set of rules for when the code is ready to go to the next server—for example, after a few hours, or when the production engineer says it's ready.

When the coding stops

If code is submitted that stops the shared master branch from compiling, this is referred to as **breaking the build**. This usually happens when an engineer skips the testing steps in an attempt to save time. No one can submit new code until the build is fixed.

Once the code goes live, that doesn't always mean that customers will start seeing the new functionality. Changes or new features can be gated behind a **feature flag**, which is a configuration setting that lets you toggle functionality on or off. Flags are often used as a part of A/B testing—each user randomly has the flag on or off. The code for using flags simply says, "If the flag is on, run this code; otherwise run that code."

Sometimes, companies will have a **code freeze**. This is when code stops automatically deploying to the next server. This is done to prevent new bugs during important times, such as when most people will be out of the office for a holiday, or when there's a big launch happening. During a code freeze, commits can be manually deployed individually (also called **cherry-picked**), such as to fix a single bug.

Product analytics and logging

Modern applications have rich **product analytics** and **log** almost everything that users do.

The things that are logged (such as when a person opens the app, hovers over the search button, clicks the search button, or clicks on a search result) are called **events**. The events aren't automatically logged; engineers must add a little bit of code for any action they want to log, which is also called adding **instrumentation**.

When an event is logged, a lot of information can be recorded, such as the name of the event, the time the event happened, the user ID of the person who did the event, the type of device they were on, and any other **metadata** you would want to slice and dice. For example, when someone presses the search button, you could also log how many words they had typed into the box.

After the events are logged, they often need to be processed before you can look at them. This usually happens overnight (via a cron job), so when you come in to work in the morning, you can look at data up to yesterday. There are privacy implications of looking at raw logs, so usually the data needs to be anonymized and aggregated before anyone looks at it.

SQL and databases

Databases are the systems that store data, like a supercharged spreadsheet for computers to use.[3] Just like there can be multiple sheets in a spreadsheet, there can be multiple **tables** in a database. Different database types are optimized to do different things quickly.

Your product will probably use a general-purpose database like **MySQL**, **Postgres**, or **MongoDB** for all of the important data your product has, such as user information and user-generated content.

For event logs and business analytics, your company might also use a special-purpose **data warehouse** like **Redshift**. The logs are moved into the data warehouse with a process called **ETL** (Extract, Transform, Load).

If your product provides search, you might also use **ElasticSearch.**

SQL

SQL (pronounced "sequel") stands for Structured Query Language. It is the computer language used to add, edit, and retrieve data from most databases. As a person, you can use SQL to interact directly with the database, but usually, you would only do that with logs databases, not production databases. For production databases, the server code generates the SQL query and sends it to the database.

In general, doing something in SQL is much faster than doing it in server code, but there are limits to what types of things SQL can do.

Optimizing databases

The information in a database is generally split across multiple tables to avoid duplication and needs to be recombined before it can be displayed by the product. For example, in a database storing posts and comments, one table might hold comments with its parent (post) ID, while another table stores the actual posts. When the program wants to show how many comments post 1234 has, it may need to perform the relatively slow operation of counting all the comments tied to post 1234.

To speed up the app, they could store a **denormalized** copy of the precalculated comment count in the posts table and try to keep it in sync with the correct count. Denormalization improves **read speeds** (the time it takes to view data) at the expense of slower **write speeds** (the time it takes to add or update data). It's widely used, but can lead to bugs and longer development time.

Algorithms and Data Structures

A **hash table** or **hash map** is a widely used coding technique (a data structure) that makes it very fast to map a **key** (any unique number, word, or phrase) to a **value**. Engineers figure out all kinds of clever ways to use hash tables to solve problems. For example, you ask your engineer if your idea for a feature would be too slow and they might reply, "No problem. I can use a hash table." Don't, however, suggest a hash table to your engineer; if you don't know what you're talking about you'll sound foolish.

Running time or **big O notation** is a way of describing the efficiency of an algorithm (in relation to the amount of data). It doesn't give an exact time; rather, it is essentially a mathematical function to describe how much slower the algorithm gets when the data gets large. For example, if you double the number of

---

3   You might also hear the term datastore. This is a more broad term, referring to any system that is storing data. A database is one type of datastore, but a datastore could also refer to file storage or other non-database storage systems.

contacts in your address book, does your filtering algorithm stay the same speed? Or does it take twice as long—or worse? The common runtimes you'll hear are:[4]

- **O(1) ("constant time"):** The algorithm stays roughly the same speed, no matter how much data you have.

- **O(log n) ("log n time"):** The algorithm gets a little slower as the dataset increases, but even doubling the data makes little difference. A 10x increase in the dataset might, for example, double the runtime.

- **O(n) ("linear time"):** The algorithm increases proportionally to the dataset size. So if your dataset increases 10x, the runtime might increase 10x too.

- **O(n log n) ("n log n time"):** The algorithm is a little worse than linear. A dataset increase of 10x might, for example, increase the runtime 11x. This is tolerable for real-life problems, and is actually how long sorting will typically take.

- **O(n^2) ("n squared"):** The algorithm is much worse than linear. If the dataset increases by 10x, you might get a 100x increase in the runtime. That's usually unacceptable for software, unless you know that you'll only be running it on very small amounts of data.

- **O(2^n) ("exponential"):** Eek. The algorithm is so, so, so much worse than linear; a 10x increase in data may cause a 1000x increase in runtime. A 20x increase would mean a 1,000,000 increase in runtime. See the problem? One would very rarely implement an algorithm like this in production software. It's just too slow.

Is O(n) faster than O(n^2)? Yes and no. On very small amounts of data, maybe not. But when your data gets sufficiently large, then yes. However, one O(n) algorithm could be much faster than another O(n) algorithm. Mathematicians probably won't like this, but you can think about big O as a somewhat handy-wavy description of how slow your algorithm gets when you have a ton of data. O(1) and O(log N) algorithms are usually great, and O(n) and O(n log n) is usually fine. O(n^2) or slower is usually unworkable. But it all depends on what you're doing![5]

---

4   These descriptions are a bit of a simplification. Imagine an algorithm which takes (100 + n) seconds to run on n pieces of data. With 5 pieces of data, the algorithm takes 105 seconds. On 10 pieces of data, it takes 110 seconds. So it has *not* actually doubled in time, even though the input size has doubled! However, the *slope* is linear. As n gets really big, doubling the data would actually roughly double the time.

5   I said *usually* fine. So what about searching for a contact in O(log N) time—is that okay? If you're searching in your phone's contact list for a person in O(log N) time [where N is how many contacts you have], that's probably fine. But if you're searching the entire internet for a person [where N is the number of pages on the internet], well, you'll be waiting a *long* time.

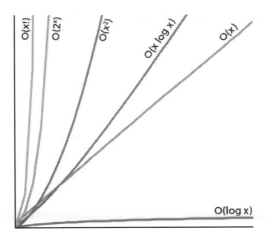

In the earlier graph, observe that the times might look somewhat similar when the data is small. But, when the data gets really big, the slower runtimes become really, really slow.

A few more terms

- Since clients and servers can be anywhere in the world, time zones make dates and times ambiguous. To fix this, the code usually stores and does calculations in **UTC time** (Coordinated Universal Time), and then adjusts for local time zones before displaying to users. UTC time almost matches up with Greenwich Mean Time (GMT, the time zone London, England is in) except it doesn't change for daylight savings time.

- **Swag** stands for Scientific Wild-Ass Guess and is another word for a cost estimate. The word swag is meant to convey that the estimate is just a guess. When using swags to build a timeline, you usually at least double them–perhaps even quadruple them–to account for the estimate being off and to account for all the other things that need to get done in a day, such as doing code reviews and writing tests.

- **UUID or GUID (pronounced as two syllables:** "goo ihd") stands for Universally Unique Identifier or Globally Unique Identifier. These are very large randomly-generated strings (for example, "712f58d0-0208-4fc4-b80f-fc4e960bfac2") that are typically used to give an "ID number" to objects in a database. They are handy because you can assume they are unique, without actually having to check if you've used that ID before. (Why don't you need to check? Because it's just phenomenally unlikely.)

- **Technical debt** is the concept that doing things the fast way now will create bugs, cause future work to take more time, or require additional engineering work in the future. When you borrow money—take out financial debt—you get the ability to buy something now, but you have to pay it back (with interest!) in the future. Technical debt works the same way; you can launch now, but you'll have to pay for it later. And, just like financial debt, there is a time for technical debt. But one should proceed carefully here because it can catch up to you.

WHAT DOES "THAT'S TOO HARD TO BUILD" ACTUALLY MEAN?

At many points in your career, an engineer will tell you that your idea is too hard to build. Don't let that be the end of the conversation. Dig deeper to figure out exactly what they mean. Ask why it's deemed too challenging, and what parts make it so.

There are three common responses: high expense, poor performance/scalability, and increased technical debt.

It would be expensive to build

"Hard" often means that it would take a long time to build.

- Perhaps the engineers are using a pre-built component that doesn't support the functionality you want, and they'd have to build their own component from scratch to support your idea.

- It might be that you're underestimating how many parts are needed to make your idea work.

- It could mean that they'd have to touch a part of the code base they're not familiar with, which would require ramp up time.

- Maybe it would require a data migration that would take weeks to run.

Once you understand which parts are expensive, you might be able to find alternatives that are much less expensive. The component might provide slightly different functionality that would still be acceptable. You might not need every part of your idea. Perhaps an engineer who's already familiar with the code base could help out. You might decide you don't need to migrate old data.

Another good follow-up question in these cases is, "How long do you think it would take?" If the work is important enough, you might decide it's worth it to take the extra time, or you could ask for more engineers on your team to help.

The performance would be very slow or have poor scalability

"Hard" sometimes means that the feature you're asking for requires calculations that take a long time or take up significant computer resources. For example, you have a list that contains millions of items, and you want to count up a subset of them. Or, maybe, you have a list that's thousands of items long and you want to compare each item to every other item.

There are several ways to handle performance concerns:

- Add limits. For example, you could show "99+" if the count goes past 99.

- Change the product to something that needs fewer calculations at a time. For example, you could do the comparison only after you've narrowed it down to one item.

- Invest more engineering time to build a system that can show the results quicker. For example, you could denormalize (pg 99), cache (pg 96), or pre-calculate the information.

Performance is very important, so if you can't find an alternative solution, you might need to cut the slow feature.

It would introduce technical debt that makes future projects take longer to build

"Hard" sometimes means that the solution would add undesirable complexity or be fragile and error-prone. For example, it could mean moving away from standard components, introducing new backend systems, or adding a corner case that needs to be remembered in the future.

Technical debt is challenging to work around. It makes your engineer's jobs more difficult and slows down future development. It's not good to argue against it, and it tends to be the least understandable. So, while it's still a good idea to ask which part adds debt, you may not understand the answer well enough to formulate alternatives.

As always, you can ask your engineers if they can devise alternatives that wouldn't have the same engineering debt. If they understand the problem space, they might come up with something spectacular.

If you still think it's important to build it, try seeing if the team can launch now, and invest in fixing the engineering debt later. You should only go with this approach if you can actually commit to investing the time later.

KEY TAKEAWAYS

- **Partnering is critical:** The most important technical skill is building a strong partnership with engineering. If you feel comfortable asking questions and you include engineers early on in the product life cycle, you can almost always learn the technical details you need on the job.

- **You don't need a technical background to learn your product's technology:** Develop your understanding of the technical infrastructure of your product to the extent that it impacts user-facing decisions. Don't let lack of confidence or embarrassment stop you from understanding the constraints. Ask questions.

- **Dig into "that's too hard":** When an engineer tells you that something is too hard to build, it can mean several different things. Learn which one it is, and take appropriate action from there.

- **Estimating costs is a skill you build over time:** Build up your judgment over time of how long different features take to build and which details can make a project longer or shorter. Use that judgment to consider and propose alternate solutions, but check with engineers in case you're missing something.

CHAPTER 9

WRITING PRODUCT DOCUMENTATION

FINALLY, WE GET to the part about product documentation! The one deliverable PMs are actually responsible for.

Careful, though.

PMs tend to expect too much from the document itself, and not enough from the thinking and collaboration that goes into writing it.

Whether you use a product specification (spec), Product Requirements Doc (PRD), lean product canvas, or product brief—all of which serve the same purpose—it's not a magic document. It's just a tool used to think through the important details, share your thoughts, solicit feedback, and improve the plan. And, like any tool, it can be misused.

This is why it's important to focus on the process and evolution, not just the final result. All of the product work you do throughout the product life cycle gets pulled together in the documentation. Transferring those ideas into writing gives you a chance to catch missing pieces and differing assumptions before they cause problems. Writing product documentation isn't about handing your perfect plan over to the team—it's about making the plan better!

USE THE DOCUMENTATION PROCESS TO CLARIFY YOUR THINKING

Don't think of the spec as something that's just for other people. Use the writing process to organize your thoughts, plan ahead, anticipate risks, and to clarify your thinking overall.

Spec templates can be especially helpful by reminding you of all the areas to think about. If you are using templates, however, be sure to remove irrelevant sections and boilerplates, or it will make your spec hard to read. Additionally, if you're writing the spec template, be very careful about the length and effort it takes to fill out. If the template becomes overwhelming, people will stop using it altogether.

OPTIMIZE FOR MAKING THE DOCUMENT EASY TO READ AND UNDERSTAND

The most important thing about a spec is that it gets read and understood. This, however, can actually be a significant challenge. In actuality, most people don't want to read specs.

Here are some tips:

- Use diagrams and pictures to illustrate concepts.

- Use bullet points so important information doesn't get skimmed over in a paragraph.

- Keep it short—move as much as possible to an appendix.

- Include information about alternatives considered and your reasoning.

- Highlight the controversial bits / the places you need the most feedback and alignment.

- Check in with your key partners for feedback on your spec format and if there are any changes they'd like.

If none of these approaches work, you might choose to meet with your teammates to discuss the important pieces, rather than assuming they read the document.

USE THE SPEC AS THE FOCAL POINT FOR FEEDBACK

Before the spec is finalized, you want to get feedback from all important stakeholders. If they have a problem with anything, you want to hear it now.

Ideally, you'll first share the spec with your closest partners, like your designer and engineer. If you're still at an early stage in your career, you might want to share it with your mentor or manager even earlier. Once your core partners have given their input, it makes sense to open up broader.

Depending on your company and personal preferences, you might want people to give feedback asynchronously in the document, or you might want them to ask questions in a meeting.

If you have a choice, asynchronously is nice because it lets you gather all the feedback before you start responding. You might find that two pieces of feedback conflict, or that there's one controversial area that needs further discussion. When you can read the feedback on your own time, it lets you better prepare for the next steps.

BE CLEAR WHEN THE SPEC STOPS BEING THE SOURCE OF TRUTH

For a while, the spec will be the source of truth. During that time, when any changes are made, the spec should automatically be updated accordingly.

At some point, it makes sense for "the source of truth" to move somewhere else, such as the designer's mocks, tickets filed, or the working code. When this happens, be sure to clearly mark that your spec is no longer being updated, and verify that all relevant parties are aware of the change.

It takes a moderate amount of effort to keep a clear source of truth. Often, there will be many places that link to the old spec—or one spec might be split into several smaller specs. It's a bit of work, but well worth the effort to avoid the frustrating situation of someone accidentally following outdated instructions.

FOCUS ON OUTCOMES

Product documentation is one of the few deliverables that PMs are actually responsible for, but don't get fooled: delivering a spec is not your job. PMs sometimes spend too much time making their specs perfect since these are one of the only things that are entirely within their control. Make sure you're *outcome*-focused rather than being *output*-focused. For example, ask, "Did we identify and address risks well? Was everyone aligned on the plan? Was the launch successful?"

EXAMPLE SPEC

A book is a product, and this book happens to be one that our readers are, by definition, familiar with. So, let's consider what a spec for this book might look like.

Following a template like the one below can help surface important details and ensure you're solving real problems that people actually care about.

Note the frequent use of headers and bullet points that make it easy to skim through. The "Use Cases" section lists the important scenarios or uses the product should enable. The "Key Trade-Offs & Decisions" section highlights the places where the PM considered alternatives to help readers understand the reasoning.

PROBLEMS

- Companies often build terrible products that could have been much better with improved PMing.

- PMs don't always know what it takes to PM well.

- The best PMs aren't always effective at managing their own career, so they don't always get to have as much influence as they should.

- Mentors aren't as effective as they could be because they spend so much of their mentoring time answering basic questions.

GOALS

- Better products in the world

  - **Success looks like:** People saying the book helped them build better products.

- Better PMs

  - **Success looks like:** The book sells well and earns good ratings from PMs and PM managers.

- PMs get the recognition and promotions they deserve

  - **Success looks like:** Amazon reviews saying the book helped them get a promotion.

- Mentors have more time for personalized mentoring

  - **Success looks like:** PM mentors recommend the book.

- Internationally relevant

  - **Success looks like:** Readers don't say that the book is too US-centric

USE CASES

In Jobs To Be Done format (see "Jobs To Be Done" on pg 40)

- When I'm early in my PM career, I want to

    - Learn PM skills, tips, and tricks, so I can

        » Be great at my job

        » Not embarrass myself by making a mistake

    - Understand the PM career ladder, so I can

        » Focus on the most important skills

        » Advance quickly

    - Learn how to set career goals, so I can

        » Make sure I'm getting the right experiences

        » Decide if I really want to be a people manager

        » Avoid the rat race

- When I'm having trouble earning a promotion, I want to

    - Clearly understand the expectations of the level, so I can

        » Diagnose what's going wrong

        » Focus on the most important activities

- When I've advanced to product leadership roles, I want to

    - Learn best practices for running a PM team, so I can

        » Set up my team for success

        » Help PMs on my team grow

    - Have documentation of what excellent PMing looks like, so I can

        » Show PMs on my team what they should focus on to grow

        » Focus my 1:1 time on personalized coaching

TIMELINE

1. Table of Contents (1 day)

2. Rough first pass (4 months)

3. In-depth interviews (2 months)

4. Finalize draft (3 months)

5. Feedback from beta readers and copy editing (2 months)

6.   Publishing (1 month)

DETAILED PROPOSAL

PM Skills

- 80% of the book
- Break down all PM skills, what they mean, and what to focus on at early, mid, and advanced career
- Group into Product, Execution, Strategic, Leadership, and Management
- Include real quotes wherever possible

Managing your career

- 20% of the book
- All of the things that it takes to succeed beyond just being good at your job
- Include interviews with successful PMs who took various paths to help people decide on their own career goals, and show what success looks like

KEY TRADE-OFFS & DECISIONS

How to group PM Skills

Every company groups these skills together differently. I decided to go with the organization that makes the most sense to me, and mitigate the risk by ensuring that the keywords people would look for show up in the table of contents. We'll look for feedback on this organization during the beta reads.

How to highlight information that's relevant for senior PMs and higher

We wanted to make sure that the book is helpful for senior PMs, and considered pulling all of the tips for senior PMs into a separate chapter rather than interweaving them in each skill section. I think it will be helpful for more junior PMs to see which skills they have yet to develop, as well as encourage senior PMs to scan the early career skills for anything they find useful. We'll look for feedback on this during the beta reads.

KEY TAKEAWAYS

- **The journey is more important than the destination:** Product documentation is just a tool used to think through the important details, share key decisions, solicit feedback, and improve the plan. The final deliverable isn't as valuable as the process you go through to write the documentation.

- **Don't replace judgment with templates:** Templates can help jog your memory about which areas to consider, but they're not a replacement for judgment. Don't get over-focused on picking the right template; instead, focus on understanding the purpose of each section of the template, and how it contributes to the desired outcome.

EXECUTION SKILLS

PROJECT MANAGEMENT

SCOPING AND INCREMENTAL DEVELOPMENT

PRODUCT LAUNCHES

GET THINGS DONE

PART D

EXECUTION SKILLS

D

EXECUTION SKILLS

EXECUTION SKILLS HELP you run and deliver your projects quickly, smoothly, and effectively. They help you get things done. In this section, we'll develop the skills for running a product development team and launching products.

- **Project Management** (pg 113) will teach us how to plan out a project and keep it on track. We'll learn about Agile and the best practices to improve your team's velocity.

- **Scoping and Incremental Development** (pg 126) will teach us how to split work into multiple launches to launch faster and more successfully. We'll learn about Minimum Viable Products (MVPs) and the importance of getting your product in front of real users.

- **Product Launches** (pg 136) will teach us how to prepare for launch day. We'll learn about picking the launch date, which details to cover in a launch checklist, and discuss different launch strategies.

- **Get Things Done** (pg 149) will teach us how to manage our time and overcome roadblocks. We'll learn the 4 D's framework and how to be effective on remote teams.

Execution skills are especially useful in the middle and end of the product life cycle.

CHAPTER 10

PROJECT MANAGEMENT SKILLS

MANY PMS CRINGE at the thought of project management. After years of explaining to our friends and family that we are *product* managers, not *project* managers, we might have built up some negative feelings. Luckily, there are modern approaches to project management that are lightweight and less tedious than traditional project management. But no matter how you approach it, it is critical to get it right.

Without good project management, products get delayed by duplicated work, dependencies, poor time allocation, people running out of work, distractions, and misunderstandings.

The PM's responsibility for project management varies a great deal from team to team. Sometimes the PM takes the lead, while other times, an engineer or dedicated project manager drives project management.

CONCEPTS AND FRAMEWORKS

Agile, Lean, Kanban, and Scrum are modern frameworks and philosophies that influence software development at most tech companies. If you've heard of Sprints, Product Backlog, or Daily Standups, you're already familiar with some of the concepts. Most modern teams use a few of these elements.[1]

Here is a quick overview of these approaches and the terms you might hear. Be warned that many people use the terms loosely or interchangeably.

PHILOSOPHIES

Lean

Lean is a philosophy used to maximize customer value while minimizing waste. It comes from practices developed at Toyota and was the philosophical underpinning of agile. Today, it's mostly used interchange-

---

1   In most of the book, we've put "Concepts and Frameworks" as the third section, after "Responsibilities" and "Growth Practices." But for this part, we felt it was important to describe the frameworks first, as you need this terminology to understand the Responsibilities and Growth Practices. It's a loss for consistency, but a win for comprehension.

ably with agile or to reference newer concepts, such as Lean MVP, which focuses on validating the product with customers before investing too heavily in building it out.

Agile

Agile is a philosophy and high-level methodology that is **flexible** and **iterative**. Agile is in contrast to the older Waterfall methodology, where decisions and deliverables from each stage in the process were locked in and "thrown over the waterfall" to the next stage.

With waterfall, PMs would write up and review long specification documents that detailed how every part of the product would work. Those would go through a heavy review and approval cycle. The document would then go to designers who would design every pixel of the flow, without making any changes to the initial requirements. Those designs would then go to the engineers who would code up the designs and requirements exactly. Finally, months or years later, customers would get the product. There was a lot of upfront work and not much encouragement to change things from earlier stages.

AGILE vs WATERFALL

Agile processes include the same stages as Waterfall, but the cycles are smaller and the lines between the stages are blurrier. With agile, a PM doesn't write out every detail of how the product works. Instead, they have a conversation or create a brief document about the requirements. The designer might make lightweight mockups to test with real users. That test might reveal that the requirements need to change. Engineers might start coding before designs are finalized and work side-by-side with designers to try out a few alternatives. The product is broken up into multiple small launches, each of which is shared with customers as early as possible so their feedback can influence future work.

Agile can be thought of as a spectrum. Most teams say they are "agile-ish." A team can become "more agile" by decreasing the size of the cycle (i.e., breaking work into more incremental milestones and launches) and replacing long formal documentation with in-the-moment collaboration.

Scrum

Scrum is a popular agile framework with specific roles, tools, and processes. Scrum has introduced or formalized the concepts of Backlog, Sprint, Daily Standups, and Retrospectives. Many teams use some or all of these concepts without necessarily calling it Scrum.

In Scrum, teams work in **sprints** of one to four weeks. At the start of each sprint, the team does **sprint planning** where they pull work from the **product backlog** into the **sprint backlog** and estimate how much work can be done in the next sprint.

During the sprint, team members pick work off the backlog and meet daily for a fifteen minute **standup** meeting where they share progress and help unblock each other. At the end of each sprint, the team has a **sprint review** on what was done and a **sprint retrospective** on how things went and could be improved.

Two key roles in Scrum are the **product owner** and **scrum master**. At many companies, the product manager will fill the role of product owner. If they are split, however, the PM is more focused on strategy while the product owner handles the day-to-day tactics. The tech lead will often fill the role of scrum master.

The product owner is responsible for managing the backlog, stakeholder management, and accepting work when it's complete. The scrum master is responsible for making sure Scrum is done well by setting up and running the meetings, unblocking people, and working with the product owner to make sure everything is ready for the start of a sprint.

Many teams pick and choose a few elements of Scrum or make their own adaptations to the framework. It's rare to find a team that implements Scrum exactly as laid out in The Scrum Guide™. Luckily, that adaptability is exactly what the creators of Scrum wanted![2]

Kanban

Kanban is another agile framework that's best known for the concept of the Kanban board.

A **Kanban board** is a visual way to organize work and workflows. The work is written onto **cards** that start in the first column and are moved as the work progresses. Each column represents a workflow stage such as Not Started, In Progress, In Review, and Done.

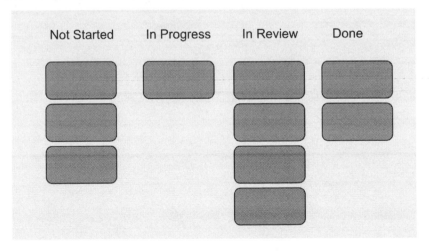

---

2   Read more at https://www.scrumguides.org/.

With a Kanban board, it's easy to see how much work is in each column so you can make sure things aren't getting stuck in one stage. In strict versions of Kanban, each stage has a limit to how many cards it can have—if you hit the limit, you need to focus on moving cards to the next stage before you can put more work in.

PRODUCT BACKLOG

A product backlog is the prioritized list of work for a product development team. It includes planned features, detailed requirements, bug fixes, infrastructural work, and research that needs to be done.

The work can be written as straightforward tasks, or it can be represented in a format called **User Stories**. The typical template for a user story is: "As a <who>, I want to <what>, so that <why>." For example, "As an administrator, I want to require two-factor authentication, so that I can increase security." This format helps ensure that the PM is handing over problems and requirements with context, rather than just solutions.

User stories can be grouped together into larger bodies of work called **epics**, which can then be grouped into an organizational layer called **initiatives**, which can then be grouped into a layer called **themes**. For example, the story from the previous paragraph could be part of an epic, "Launch improved administrator tools," which is part of the initiative, "Become enterprise-ready," which is part of the theme, "Every Fortune 500 company uses our products."

The tasks or stories usually have **cost estimates**—for example, in the format of **story points**. Story points are an abstract unit of cost; 1 point is the easiest possible work, 2 points is work that should take twice as long as a 1-point task, and it increases from there. Engineers (not PMs) set the cost estimates.

> ### BUT WHAT IS A "POINT"?
>
> It can be tricky at first for teams to wrap their minds around what's essentially a brand new "currency." After all, what does 1 point, 2 points, and 3 points really mean? If you're running into this issue, a fun technique is **planning poker**. In planning poker, each engineer estimates a story independently, and then everyone reveals their guesses at the same time (for example by showing their guess by holding up the appropriate number of fingers). People can then discuss their reasons for differing estimates until the team converges.

Just like the exchange rate between the euro and the dollar can change over time, the exchange rate between points and days can vary. At the end of each sprint, the team adds up the number of points completed to calculate the **velocity** and then can use that calculation to estimate how many points can be completed in the next sprint. If you know that half of your team will be out on vacation next sprint, you might expect to complete half as many points. If the team completes many fewer points than expected, that's something to discuss in the sprint retrospective.

You should work with the engineers to keep the tasks fairly small. Sometimes, PMs think so much about the big picture that their tasks become too big as well. If a task costs more than eight points (or longer than two weeks), the engineer's estimates can get wildly inaccurate. There's a simple fix: break up the task into smaller tasks.

It is the PM's responsibility to build and maintain the backlog. **Backlog grooming** (or **backlog refinement**) refers to keeping the backlog up-to-date, prioritized, and actionable. For example, the PM needs to make sure that the items at the top of the backlog have the necessary design work done and enough details so the work is ready to pick up.

HOW DESIGN AND DISCOVERY FIT IN

Agile is a great, lightweight approach to scheduling work, but there's a missing piece: When do designers do their work? Almost certainly, the design work will come before engineering, but how much before?

This depends on the team, but there are two main approaches—each with their pros and cons:

Designers work one sprint ahead of engineering.

The approach works if designing something takes less time than building it. It encourages tight collaboration between engineers and designers and makes it easy for the team to change direction without wasting a lot of design work. The downside is that this approach timeboxes design work into one sprint, which is not always desirable or feasible.

Engineering doesn't start until the Discovery and Design phases have gotten a large enough head start.

This approach works well when you want more time for discovery and design, but having design work done far ahead of time can make your team less nimble. Designers will make more decisions within their design tools without a deep understanding of the engineering costs, rather than playing with working code and iterating. Additionally, you'll need to figure out what the engineers do while they're waiting.

If you're starting a brand new team, the engineers might stay on their previous team until you're ready for them, or they can do engineering discovery work, such as prototyping new technologies. They might also be able to start on backend work that doesn't depend on the design.

If you already have a team, the PM and designer need to dual-track their work. This means they do discovery for the next project while supporting the engineers building the current project. It's up to the PM to ensure the schedules align so that everyone has important, actionable work. For example, you can have the engineers work on an additional release with lower priority features and polish, or give them time to reduce technical debt.

RESPONSIBILITIES

HAVE AN EXPLICIT CONVERSATION ABOUT YOUR PROJECT MANAGEMENT RESPONSIBILITIES

It's very common for PMs, engineers, and designers to have different expectations about the PM's role in the software development process or to have confusion around the process. You might have expected the engineering lead to run most of the project management, but they expected you to do it. When you join a new team, establish the expectations before work starts. Even at the same company, each team might distribute the work differently.

Once you've been on a team for a few weeks, check in with your teammates and ask them how the project management has been going, from their perspective. You don't want to be surprised through your manager or during your peer reviews that you're not living up to their expectations.

GROOM AND PRIORITIZE THE BACKLOG

Make sure your team always has high priority work in the backlog so they don't run out of things to do.

One area that sometimes causes confusion is when the engineers aren't clear what work is ready to pick up. For example, they might think that there are still open questions on one of the tasks. Or, perhaps the engineers were waiting for the designer to discuss the design; but meanwhile, the designer was waiting for the developer to pick up the work so that they can discuss it further. The easy fix for this is to come up with a clear standard to mark the state—such as "ready for engineering"—for each task.

CREATE MILESTONES AND CHECKPOINTS

Big projects need to be broken down into milestones and checkpoints. This allows you to assess how well the work is going and adjust it if needed. Beyond that, milestones are great for morale and creating a sense of accomplishment.

In general, it's very hard to estimate what percent of a big piece of work is done. The pareto principle states that the last 20% of the code takes 80% of the time. That's why milestones are so important—until the team hits a well-defined milestone, you won't have much of an idea how much work is left.

While milestones can be set however you like, they should ideally represent clear increments of internal, customer, or business value. For example, you can set a milestone for when the work is internally dogfoodable, or when the first external customer is using the code.

Once you have milestones, use them to motivate the team. Remind people of upcoming milestones and celebrate when they've been achieved.

WRITE GOOD STATUS REPORTS

Status reports are important because they're a major way that people outside of your immediate team learn about what your team is doing. When done well, they help you get both support and recognition.

A good status update keeps the audience in mind. What do they need to know? What will they be interested in? How do you make it informative, understandable, and fun to read?

Generally a status report will cover:

1. **Is the project on track?** It might feel scary to say your project is yellow or red, but it's much worse to say everything is going well when it's not. You'll look dishonest and lose trust.

2. **What's happened recently?** Focus on key accomplishments and important changes. This is a good place to celebrate the work the team has accomplished up to date.

3. **What's next?** Discuss the upcoming milestones or the next piece of work that will be tackled.

4. **Are there any issues or risks?** This helps give stakeholders an early warning of what might go wrong, and gives them the opportunity to help out if they can.

Ideally, status reports shouldn't take much time to write. See if you can align your status report with your other team processes so it doesn't create much additional work. A weekly cadence is typical. When sending your status report, don't be afraid to send it broadly to anyone who might be interested in the project, especially product leaders and cross-functional partners.

CHECK IN WITH YOUR TEAM MEMBERS

While sometimes there's just more work than expected, it's not the only reason people fall behind—or even necessarily the most common. They might fall behind because:

- They're stuck and spinning their wheels.

- They disagree with the work and don't want to do it.

- They're starting new work rather than finishing previously assigned tasks.

- They're refining and perfecting rather than sharing work as early as possible.

- They're prioritizing other obligations over the work you care about.

- The work is more involved than they had originally estimated.

In any case, as a PM, you're responsible for ensuring your team stays on track. One of the best tools for this is checking in with each team member regularly. When someone falls behind, figure out why—don't just make assumptions. Most of the issues can be addressed with a conversation or some extra clarifications.

SOLVING THE PROBLEM COLLABORATIVELY

Sair Buckle ran into this issue as a senior staff product manager when she recognized there was a clear slow down in velocity by a senior engineer. Instead of assuming he was simply falling behind in the work, she sent him a casual message to learn more about his planned approach.

This offered an open and safe space to raise concerns about the overall direction of the migration. He had been delaying work because he needed a forum to express his hesitations and he did not feel comfortable raising them independently with his new dev manager. Together, they took his recommendations to the dev manager to discuss opportunities for improvement.

Like Buckle did, it's important to approach these issues in a way that shows respect and consideration for your teammates. You can suggest another person with whom they can brainstorm if they get stuck, remind them of the importance of finishing work and sharing it, help prioritize their overall list of responsibilities, or assist in rescoping work.

Checking in early and often can be useful, but there isn't a one-size-fits-all strategy. Some people really appreciate a daily check-in and want your help staying on track, while others prefer not to be micromanaged. Ask people what works best for them.

ADJUST PLANS AS THINGS CHANGE

Recall the famous interview question: What do you do when your team falls behind schedule?

At a high level—both in interviews and in real life—you have three levers to pull:

- Add more people to the project

- Move the launch date

- Cut scope

There is, of course, no right or wrong answer. All of these are promising options given the right circumstances, and all can be terrible in the wrong circumstances.

Junior PMs often overlook the option of adding people because it requires making a case to product leadership. Don't ignore this option if your work is high priority for the company and you catch the problem early enough. Adding people can work if there is independent, parallelizable work that doesn't require a long ramp-up time. If it's the week before the launch, adding more people would probably delay you further.

Moving the launch date can have big implications. The financial plans of the company might have relied on a particular launch date. As the launch date moves, the cost of the project increases, which makes it harder for the project to have a good return on investment. And, of course, if you delay the launch, users have to wait longer for all the great things you built.

Cutting scope is usually the preferred approach. The product backlog should already have been sorted by priority order, so hopefully you can just drop the items lower on the list and have the most important work prioritized. Most projects have some scope that can be cut; however, you don't want to cut scope in a way that could affect the success of the project.

SHARE YOUR BEST PRACTICES ACROSS THE ORGANIZATION ⚡⚡

Once you reach the advanced levels of product management, you're expected to have influence across the organization, even if you're not a people manager. You've had a lot of experience running teams, and you're now well-positioned to recognize opportunities by observing how other teams are set up.

There are a lot of different ways to share your best practices, and the measure of success is that people actually learn from you and adopt your advice. It doesn't matter how many learning talks you give or how many guides you write if people aren't finding them valuable.

> The best way to share your best practices, especially as an IC, is usually to share what worked for you—but to do so in a collaborative way rather than a lecturing tone. Even if you have more seniority than the other PMs, they might get defensive and be less receptive to your advice if they sense a power dynamic.

For example, you might share the templates you use, or a list of advice you've written up for yourself. You can organize "best practice sharing" sessions where everyone gets a chance to share their advice. You can also offer to mentor people and let them come to you with questions.

GROWTH PRACTICES

BE AVAILABLE

If your engineer is blocked and needs to ask you a question, work stops until they get your answer. If you're frequently busy and take a while to respond, your engineers will get frustrated. On the flip side, if you're usually available, you'll have more opportunities to assist your team.

Ideally, the PM, designer, and engineers should all be near each other so they can call each other over whenever they want. You'll notice you get a lot more questions when you sit next to someone as opposed to when they send an email or walk over to you.

If you don't sit with your team, it can be helpful to occasionally walk by people's desks and ask how it's going (while being careful not to interrupt people's flow). If you work remotely, you can send a friendly chat during a time you think they're available. Sometimes, they'll have something on their minds, or you'll find out that they're stuck on something they didn't realize you could help with.

Beyond that, try to respond promptly to anyone, especially people on your feature team. Adopt "inbox zero," or another system, so you don't leave people waiting days for a response.

REDUCE DEPENDENCIES

A dependency is when one piece of work can't start until another finishes. Most project plans have numerous dependencies, for example building the backend before the frontend.

It can sometimes be strategic to take on a dependency. For instance, when Apple releases a new version of iOS with new API capabilities, they also want to have several products available on launch day that use those capabilities.

Keep in mind though that each dependency adds another way your project can be delayed. When the dependency is on another team, it adds a risk that is out of your control and extra communication overhead.

In many projects, a little bit of extra work can enable you to reduce or remove a dependency. For example, if building the frontend has a dependency on building the backend, you may be able to build a fake backend quickly. This enables the frontend team to start their work, while another team builds the real backend. Or, if your feature overlaps with work from another team, you can build your feature to work both with and without the other team's changes; this is a bit more work, but enables one team to launch before the other.

OPTIMIZE AROUND YOUR TEAM'S RESOURCES ⚡

Usually teams should work on the highest priority projects, but sometimes you can get better results by optimizing around people's availability.

Try to figure out which people are on the critical path, and plan around them.

Here are some examples:

- **Design constrained:** Pick engineering-heavy projects like investing in performance and scalability. Run earlier A/B tests.

- **PM constrained:** Pick straightforward projects that don't require as much discovery.

- **Engineering constrained:** Focus on strategic thinking.

Keep a few ideas for these types of projects in the product backlog so they'll be available when you need them.

IMPROVE YOUR TEAM'S PROCESSES ⚡

Team processes make a huge impact on how well the team executes.

Apply your product skills to assess how your processes are performing. Do people feel like they're moving as fast as they can? Are they happy with the quality of work they're producing? What are their biggest frustrations? What would it take to ship products 50% faster?

Once you know where the opportunities are, you can pick the processes you want to add or change. Sprint retrospectives and daily standups are a great place to start. Partner closely with the engineering and design leads to roll out the changes.

Here are a few more processes to consider.

Set up project management software

If your entire company consists of three people in a room together, you can probably get by with sticky notes on a whiteboard—it keeps the overhead low and makes for interesting room decor.

Once your company starts to grow, you'll need to start using a project management tool to keep track of who is doing what, and what their deadlines are. I'm obviously biased from working on the product for eight years, but I love Asana as a project management tool.

Project management software is important for several reasons:

- **Clarity:** Each person on the team knows what they're responsible for and when it's expected to get done. This reduces miscommunication and saves you from having to remind (aka nag) your teammates.

- **Everything in one place:** Conversations, clarifications, and designs are all kept attached to the task so people don't work based on an old plan. If you can't remember why a decision was made, you can look back at the conversation to see.

- **Delegation:** Instead of personally keeping track of how every task is doing, team members can keep their own tasks updated. This saves everyone's time.

- **Reducing work about work:** Since everyone is keeping their own tasks updated, this will eliminate the need for status update meetings. People won't receive a barrage of emails because they can look up information on their own, or have focused conversations about the work.

- **Facilitate remote work:** Remote work has become increasingly common in recent years. The good thing about project management software is that it's inherently online, and therefore accessible to anyone working remotely, whether temporarily or permanently. By contrast, the ol' sticky-note tactic leaves any remote workers in the dark.

Use demos as a forcing function

One of the tricks of great project management is to nudge people in effective ways. No one wants to feel micromanaged, but most people love showing off their best work.

Demos are a great example of a forcing function. To give a demo, your team needs to have working code (or a fairly complete design for a designer). If everyone knows that Friday is demos, they'll feel motivated to get their work into a demonstrable state by then. There's often a flurry of activity on Thursday night as people finish up the work that's been dragging on all week.

You can enhance the forcing function of demos by adding on extra guidelines. For example, you can set it up so that all demos are run on a shared beta server, so people need their code checked into beta (not just running on their local machine) if they want to demo.

Use special days to invest in areas that get overlooked

High-performing teams are often laser focused on delivering their product. This is usually a good thing, but it can mean that some important maintenance areas get overlooked:

- **Bugs:** Each individual bug might be low priority, but together they add up to a bad experience.

- **Polish:** Small bits of usability and design polish can really improve the quality of the product overall, as well as improve morale by ensuring everyone is proud of the product they work on.

- **Internal Tools:** Improving internal tools and processes can have a multiplier effect on the team's velocity.

Setting aside special days to work on one of these areas is a great way to make progress. Schedule a Bug Bash, Polish Week, or Grease Week for your team—or your whole department.[3]

One way to get the most out of these special days is to turn them into a fun competition. Keep a leaderboard of how many bugs each person fixes and have a variety of small prizes: most bugs fixed, oldest bug fixed, bug with the highest number of customer reports fixed, etc. You can also consider bringing in snacks, playing music, or having fun activities to get people excited.

SNIFF OUT RISKS AND MITIGATE THEM ⚡

As you gain general and domain experience, pay attention to what kinds of things cause problems. Is there an older part of the codebase that's prone to bugs? Do animations tend to have performance issues in different browsers? If you're new in an area, you can find a mentor who has more expertise and ask them what kinds of risks they look for. Ideally, the mentor can tell you a story about what went wrong, since those stories will help you remember and recall the risk when it comes up again.

For each risk, come up with a mitigation:

- Can you do something now to determine if the risk is a problem? Perhaps you can run a concept or usability test now.

- Can you set up a plan to handle the risk? For example, if stability is a risk, you should probably plan for a slow rollout in order to catch problems while they're small.

- Can you set up a fallback plan? Plan ahead with a decision tree about what you'll do if problems occur. For example, if you're worried about customer backlash, you can prepare a document with appropriate Q&A talking points.

Detecting risks early improves the quality of your product and the accuracy of your project timeline.

DRIVE QUALITY AND VELOCITY IMPROVEMENTS ACROSS PRODUCT TEAMS ⚡⚡

Are your product teams moving fast enough and delivering a big enough impact? Product leaders can do a lot to speed up team velocity and improve the product quality.

First, gather information. Look at team retrospectives, compare cost estimates to how long things actually took, compare launch targets to the actual results, and survey people about their feedback.

Here are a few problems you might discover.

- **Launches hit their dates but miss their targets:** Was the scope not ambitious enough? Did the team not pursue enough directions or give up too early? Was the quality not high enough? Each of these problem areas can be coached for future projects.

- **Launches miss their dates:** Were the estimates off? Did something slow down the team? Better estimating processes, larger teams, or infrastructure investments could help.

---

3   Polish Week is a week when teams focus on small customer-facing improvements and Grease Week is when teams focus on "greasing the wheels" with improvements to internal tools. You can learn more about these at https://blog. asana.com/2012/10/polish-week/ and https://blog.asana.com/2013/07/grease-week-at-asana/.

- **Teams spend a lot of time on other priorities instead of their main project:** Can you move to a culture where all work is scheduled and has attached goals or OKRs? As a product leader, you can guide them to reduce their commitments and be clear about which are the highest priority. If something like technical debt tends to get pushed off, ask the team to tackle it first before moving on to other work.

- **Process slows the team down:** If teams are going in the wrong direction for too long, you might need to add earlier checkpoints. If the teams are losing time preparing and waiting for a lot of reviews, you might want to remove earlier reviews and catch issues later. If teams are spending too long iterating, you might want to give clearer guidance on the amount of iteration expected.

- **Mismatch between your expectations and the skill level of the teams:** You can invest in training and mentorship, hire more skilled people, work on easier projects, take a more hands-on approach, or accept lower quality or velocity.

The investments you make here will have a multiplier effect on your teams.

CONSIDER PARTNERSHIPS AND ACQUISITIONS ⚡⚡

Early and mid-career PMs usually ignore partnerships and acquisitions as potential solutions for solving problems. Instead, they jump straight to internally building a new solution. By expanding your perspective, you can sometimes find a much better solution.

Ely Lerner, who's been responsible for integrating two acquired companies at Yelp, suggests partnering with your corporate development team and keeping them up to speed on the kinds of problem spaces you're thinking about. Meeting with potential partners can be valuable even if the partnership doesn't pan out, since they can give you new perspectives on the industry.

Acquisitions are notoriously high risk, high reward. Most acquisitions fail, but some of the most successful brands have flourished after acquisition: PayPal, YouTube, and Instagram, to name a few.

To successfully integrate an acquired company, Lerner shares two pieces of advice:

> First, see if you can implement something as a partnership before fully integrating the companies. Second, there's a lot of value in getting a bunch of fairly senior engineers who can serve as cultural ambassadors from your existing company, and dropping them into the acquired team on day zero. Since they're embedded, they can help with a gradual culture shift and avoid an us-versus-them thing.

KEY TAKEAWAYS

- **Choose the practices that work for your team:** Agile project management practices can seem overwhelming, but you don't need to use them all at once. Start with the ones your team is excited to try. When your team runs into issues, there's likely an agile practice that can help.

- **Don't assume someone else is responsible for project management:** The eng lead may drive a lot of the project management, but not always. Make sure you are clear on which parts the team expects you to own. If no one else is driving, you'll need to take the lead.

- **Keep your team fed:** Make sure there's important, actionable work ready for your team at all times. You'll need to plan ahead to make sure you have enough research done for design to get started and enough design done for engineering to get started. Talk to your teammates to make sure you're on the same page about whether work is ready to start.

CHAPTER 11

SCOPING AND INCREMENTAL DEVELOPMENT

WHEN I STARTED as a PM, I wanted my products to be perfect. I researched the customer problems and came up with a long list of features and details that would cover every need. My idealism quickly hit reality when I learned that I had exactly forty days of developer time to fill. It would take more than one hundred days to build everything on my list!

This was my introduction to scoping: the careful process of deciding what to include and exclude. Saying "yes" to one feature meant saying "no" to another. Should I include the work to show the count of comments on each blog post, or invest that time to make it easier to upload images? Did wiki pages need to be customizable, or could we cut a corner and use that time to improve page load times?

> These decisions felt difficult, but I later learned that I had it easy. The time was fixed; I only needed to decide how to fill it.

In my next role, I not only had to choose what work to include or exclude, but also how long to spend on the project before shipping. Without the firm guideline of forty days, I let my teams chip away towards perfection and tell me when they wanted to launch. Some of the projects shipped quickly, but one had been in progress for several quarters.

I had let engineers set the pace, and they were moving at a fine speed—or so I thought. I didn't realize at first that our prolonged development life cycle was a problem. In fact, it was only at my performance review that I realized that I needed this project to, well, *launch*.

In retrospect it makes sense; if the team wasn't shipping the work, it wasn't contributing any value. Once my team and I framed the question of what would it take to launch next quarter, we easily came up with a new approach and launched it quickly. Fixing the date made the new solution almost obvious.

This isn't to say that our approach—set a date, and then pick what you can launch—is the right approach in other scenarios. When I joined Asana, the product had been in development for years but not yet launched publicly. Launching immediately would be a mistake though, as a good launch would–or could—generate a surge in demand. The quality of our product on launch day mattered a lot more than whether it launched a month or two later.

We still needed to launch soon, but we would first prioritize the things that would damage our reputation if we got them wrong. We decided to fix up the visual design and build a mobile app. We knew people would have a lot of feature requests, but if people used the product enough to have requests, that would be a good problem to have.

> There are many different ways to slice up your releases, and some of them are much better than others. The best approaches allow you to learn and course-correct as you go, eventually landing on a product that fully solves end-to-end user needs. Doing this well can shave months off of your project timeline. Even more importantly, it can mean the difference between a product that users love and one that they won't use.

As a PM, you're responsible for scoping—determining the scope of what's included and excluded in a release. You need to decide which ideas should be tested first. You need to build up your judgment around which work can be skipped and which work is crucial. You need to convince your team to change plans based on what you learn from early releases.

CONCEPTS AND FRAMEWORKS

INCREMENTAL DEVELOPMENT

Incremental development is the approach of breaking a giant launch into multiple releases, and using what you learn from each release to guide the next. Instead of working for three years on a product and finding out on launch day whether people like it, you can show your work to customers much more frequently and learn the most critical feedback early.

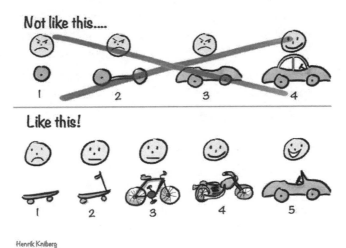

Henrik Kniberg

One of the most famous examples that illustrates this is Henrik Kniberg's skateboard metaphor:[1]

---

1   Henrik elaborates on this at https://blog.crisp.se/2016/01/25/henrikkniberg/making-sense-of-mvp.

- In the first example, the team split the work up into multiple releases, but the early releases of a tire and partial car weren't usable. The increments didn't deliver any customer value, and they didn't help the team learn.

- In the second example, the team delivers something functional with each release. The first release of a skateboard doesn't satisfy the customer, but the team can start getting useful information about what customers value. The next versions start to deliver customer value and give the team valuable information about what customers like and what planned functionality they don't actually need. In the end, instead of building the plain car they'd expected, they build a convertible that customers love.

Many product ideas do not deliver customer or business value in the first incarnation. In *Inspired*, Marty Cagan says "half of our ideas are just not going to work." Even the best PMs have a lot of ideas that don't end up having the impact they had hoped for. The difference is that great PMs validate their ideas early on so that they can discard bad ideas quickly and spend more time building things that will actually work.

MINIMUM VIABLE PRODUCT (MVP)

The definition of a minimum viable product from Eric Ries's book, *The Lean Startup,* is: that version of a new product which allows a team to collect the maximum amount of validated learning about customers with the least effort.[2]

MVPs can be early working prototypes of a product, but they don't have to be. You can set up an AdWords campaign or a button in your product that goes to a "coming soon" landing page to measure interest. You can fake the backend by having humans manually do the work.

Common mistakes with MVPs

When the concept of MVPs was introduced, it immediately took off. Unfortunately, the idea also spawned a lot of backlash from instances where MVPs were used incorrectly.

Low quality experiments: Burnt Pizza MVP

Des Traynor, co-founder of Intercom, shares the thought experiment of a team trying to learn if there's a market for pizza. To test it cheaply, they use a crummy pizza oven and the pizza comes out burned. If no one buys it, does that prove there's no market for pizza? No! It just proves there's no market for burnt pizza.

The same problem applies when teams add a new feature in a cheap way that slows down the product performance: they've only learned that users like fast products, nothing about the new feature.

Make sure your MVP is high enough quality and complete enough to meet your learning goals.

Leaving the product in an unpolished or unsustainable state

Some teams scope a lean MVP for learning, but then don't invest the extra work to make it a sellable and sustainable product. That's a quick way to frustrate your cross-functional partners.

For example, Google's short-lived Inbox product showed that consumers loved the new UI, but they couldn't migrate Gmail enterprise customers over without rebuilding many of Gmail's advanced features. As a result, it wasn't a sellable and sustainable product. They decided to scrap the product and integrate some of the

---

2   Read more about minimum viable products at http://www.startuplessonslearned.com/2009/08/minimum-viable-product-guide.html.

UI into Gmail, rather than maintaining two code bases. If the team had focused on sustainability from the beginning, they might have chosen an approach that built on top of Gmail's functionality.

TIME AND VALUE

Product improvements don't deliver value until they're shipped.

Let's say you've built a new product that will save people hours of tedious work every day. Before launch, when you're building and iterating on it, it's saving people zero hours.

Of course, the time you spend building and iterating on your products makes them better.

You can think of the decision about when to launch with a diagram like this:

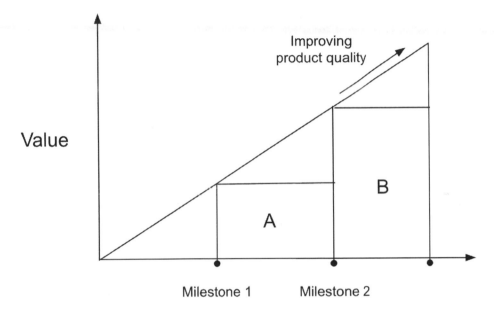

If you release at milestones 1 and 2, users get the value of area A + area B. If you wait until milestone 2, you only deliver the value of area B. The larger area A is, the more it's worth considering an early launch. If the product at milestone 1 delivers a lot of value already, or if there will be a long time before milestone 2, it's often better to launch early and iterate.

RESPONSIBILITIES

BREAK WORK INTO INCREMENTAL LAUNCHES AND VALIDATE EARLY

As a PM, you want to get the scope of your releases just right. If you bundle too many features together, people need to wait longer to use the great thing you've built. If you leave out important functionality, your launch can be unsuccessful and you might learn the wrong lesson about the overall viability of the idea.

Here are some different approaches for splitting a product into multiple releases:

- **By risk tolerance and friendliness:** Start by releasing to users who can tolerate the most bugs, missing functionality, and UI hurdles so you can start getting feedback before all the polish is added. For example, you could split the releases into team dogfooding, internal dogfooding, friendly customers beta program, experimenting on new users, experimenting on all users, and full launch. You could wait to build functionality such as onboarding and premium upsells until you start experiments on new users.

- **By complexity of need:** Start with the users who have the simplest needs, and build your way towards the more complex needs. For example, people who don't use a competitor's tool, then people who are comparison shopping, and finally people currently using a competitor. The first launch would just include the basics, but later releases could add functionality that advanced users need.

- **By customizability:** Start with fixed options that will meet a subset of use cases, and then add customization options. For example, a pre-generated report followed by a customizable report.

- **By customer type or use case:** List which requirements you need for each, then look for a list that's short and mostly a subset of things you need for your higher priority use case. Start with the shortest such list you can find. For example, you might build a product that's good for amateurs and then later expand it to work for professionals.

- **By length of engagement:** Start by building things people need in the first week, and then build things that are needed later on if the usage is high enough. For example, you might delay building summary emails or churn states until after the first launch.

- **By cost:** Look at the list of cost estimates and drill into anything that's particularly expensive. Check if there's an alternate slice that avoids the expensive work, especially in the early versions. For example, you might use a simple heuristic rather than a machine learning algorithm, or start with an existing component rather than a customized one.

One thing you should *not* do is **cut out polish**.

> A quick way to create discord with your designer is to try to scope out polish or leave it for a later release. Polish and delight are important for a user's first impression. Leaving out polish will result in a lower quality product. It's better to handle one use case well than many use cases poorly.

It's fine to have an open discussion with your designer about how much polish is valuable, but don't pull a bait-and-switch by saying you'll include polish and then cutting it when the timeline gets tight.

Don't scope too small

While it's important to keep the development cost of a release low and launch early to validate customer needs, those costs need to be balanced against the potential gains. Scoping too small can cause its own set of problems. Sometimes an extra few days or weeks of work makes all the difference in terms of usability, customer delight, and the success of the product. Sometimes it's much less expensive to build the full set of features while engineers are familiar with the code than it would be to have someone build the features a year later.

Instead of having a hard and fast rule to only include the work that is absolutely required for launch, take a look at the longer list of "nice to have" work with your design and engineering team, and evaluate the cost, the benefit, the risk of not including it at launch, and whether the cost changes if you decide to build it later. If you've designed your project schedule with appropriate buffer time, you might decide to add in a few extra "delighters" that make customers happy and increase your chances of success.

A PROBLEM WITH SCOPING

Noa Ganot saw the cost of scoping too small when working on which database versions her enterprise product would support. At first the product supported only the most popular versions with the idea that they could quickly add more support whenever a customer needed it.

Unfortunately, that meant that the sales team needed to ask each customer about their configuration instead of being able to confidently say that all configurations were supported. While this was acceptable early on, at some point this was no longer good enough. Some customers didn't even know which database version they had. By listening to the sales team, Ganot learned about the trouble this gap caused. She realized that this was a situation where scoping larger than the immediate customer need (supporting every database version, even those that hadn't been requested yet) would be worth the investment. Her team made the change and she saw the results in improved sales conversion.

DRIVE TEAM ALIGNMENT AROUND LEAN MVPS ⚡

If your team isn't currently bought into the idea of lean MVPs, you can work with them to introduce the idea. It often requires some learning, listening, and trust to convince a team to start with smaller scoped releases, or to build throwaway code for the purpose of testing.

Depending on your team's concerns, there are a few ways to address them.

- **Concern that the code might be left in a half-done state:** Find ways to commit to finishing up the code. Depending on your organization, this might be done by the OKRs you set, the way you communicate what "done" looks like, the launch dates you share, or what percentage of your users you roll out changes to. It's a good idea to start a list early of what additional work needs to be completed before the team can move onto something new.

- **Concern that leadership might pull people off projects after the MVP is done:** If leadership at your company has a history of pulling people off projects too soon, you might need to first work with those leaders to convince them the value of MVP development. Come to an agreement to keep your team until the work is either in a stable productionized state, or removed altogether.

- **Concern that they're wasting time building throwaway work:** Get them used to MVPs with no-code or very-low-code MVPs. You can also draw out a few possible options to show how the throwaway work is likely to save them time in many scenarios.

If the team agrees to lean MVPs in theory, but pushes for unnecessary scope creep, that could be a sign that you haven't been clear enough about what you're trying to learn from the MVP. Get crystal clear on your hypothesis and what risks you're trying to mitigate with the MVP. It might help to draw out a decision tree, so the team can see when the extra scope they want could be added.

INVEST IN SYSTEMS THAT SUPPORT INCREMENTAL DEVELOPMENT ⚡⚡

Incremental development works best when you have the infrastructure and components to create quick prototypes and cheap early versions. If every small idea you want to test requires the creation of many new components, data migrations, and heavy design reviews, it will be hard to convince your team to build prototypes and MVPs.

If design is the bottleneck, invest in a design system and reusable components. From the process side, you may want to institute "fast track" rules. For example, you could create a rule that any A/B test that uses all pre-existing components can skip design review or require a lower level of approval.

On the engineering side, there may be data model improvements or framework investments that will support the types of experimentation you'd like to do. Partner with the engineering team to see what it would take to make quick tests possible.

GROWTH PRACTICES

ACCEPT THAT YOU DON'T KNOW EXACTLY WHAT TO BUILD

Bicycle helmets are a good idea, right? If you hit your head during a bike fall, helmets reduce your risk of a fatality by at least 50%. So, other than perhaps messing up your hair, how could a helmet possibly backfire?

It turns out that the real world is a bit more complicated. When people wear a helmet, behavior changes. They bike a little faster, or perhaps in worse weather, or on a busier road, or take that turn a little more sharply. The cars around them, also, might not give them quite as much space.

They might also decide they'd rather drive than lug a helmet with them to their meeting—and thus there are more cars, fewer bikes, more pollution, less exercise, less understanding of *how* to handle bikes on the road, and so on. In fact, when Australia instituted a helmet law, the main effect was a notable decrease in cycling.[3] Whoops.

> SO YOU'RE SAYING HELMETS ARE BAD?!?
>
> No! We're not arguing against helmets. Not at all. A helmet likely saved the life—or at least the functioning brain— of my husband a few years ago.[4]
>
> However, it's nonetheless the case that what makes sense in isolation doesn't always translate perfectly to the real world. People are complicated, and so is the real world.

What does this mean for product development? It means that you need to have the humility to believe that ideas that seem great at first might not be great in practice. You need to treat your ideas as hypotheses.

---

3   From the book *Risk* by John Adams, 1995

4   Or, perhaps, if my husband weren't wearing a helmet, he wouldn't have been biking so quickly around a corner—and he never would have broken those bones *and* his helmet.

It's tempting to believe that you know exactly what customers need, especially if you've done a good job at the initial product discovery. But, people and products are complicated. The kind of feedback you get in the controlled setting of user research doesn't always match up to how people use (or don't use) your product in the real world.

We saw this one time at Asana during the development of custom fields. We had done extensive user research and had a list of must-have features. Yet one request popped up over and over again during our beta releases: color-coded fields. Early user research missed this because it wasn't the sort of thing users knew they needed until they really experienced the feature. Fortunately, this was quick to add; we did so and had a successful launch.

When you break your product into smaller launches, you get feedback earlier, which leads to more successful products.

USE YOUR JUDGMENT TO OPTIMIZE FOR THE RIGHT TIME FRAME ⚡

It doesn't always make sense to start with an MVP or scope the work as small as possible.

For example, it can be less expensive to make changes while you're working on a part of the code than months down the road. While the work is still active, you have full context on it; months later, you might need to refresh your understanding or get your development environment set up again. Incremental launches also create some overhead, so sometimes it's better not to split the work up as far as it will go. Additionally, sometimes increasing a project's length by 5 or 10% isn't that big of a deal.

As you advance in your career, you should break away from rigid rules on what should make it into a release. Instead, develop frameworks for when adding a bit more polish or functionality is justified. Consider the following:

- The cost of the work, in terms of how much time it adds to the project, what percentage of the overall time it is, and how it affects your milestones. If the cost is tiny and you'll still hit your deadline, the work might be worth considering.

- The customer and business benefit of the work. If the benefit is huge, especially if it might have a big influence on the success of the project, it's worth considering.

- The team morale benefit of the work. If someone on the team feels very strongly about the work and it's cheap enough, it might make sense to do it.

- The timeframe you want to optimize for (probably six months or a year). It's risky to slow down work right now for benefits that won't pay off for 18 months.

- The likelihood that the hypothesis will be validated. If there's a high chance the launch is a success, then by including the extra work you were just getting a head start. But if the whole project is thrown away, then you will have wasted more work than necessary.

REFINE AND SIMPLIFY YOUR HYPOTHESES ⚡

One of the things that gets in the way of tight scoping is when multiple problems and questions are tangled up together. The competing problems pull against each other so it's hard to feel confident in cutting anything.

When you untangle the problems and figure out which one is key, you unlock the ability to do effective tight scoping.

HYPOTHESIS REFINEMENT

When Sam Goertler was a PM at Asana, she was put in charge of the problem "customers say the product isn't easy enough to use." She worked with her team to refine that ambiguous and hard-to-action problem into the hypothesis, "if we maximize clarity for the project management use case, new user growth will increase." She then refined it to the tagline "Maximize Clarity," which made it easy for everyone to remember, apply, and share.

This refinement helped guide the team through many tough calls, such as design changes that optimized for project management over other use cases. Soon, all the team members were answering each other's questions with, "Which option maximizes clarity?"

ENCOURAGE MVP THINKING AND PUSH BACK AGAINST PERFECTIONISM IN YOUR ORG ⚡⚡

Most people don't see perfectionism as a real problem—so much so that it's seen as a joke or humblebrag to say that your greatest weakness is being a perfectionist.

On most product teams, however, perfectionism is a real problem. This obviously doesn't apply to mission-critical software like rocket launches or healthcare devices, but for most products, it's much better to launch with some gaps or bugs than to over-invest in the work.

Spending too much time on the work has many problems:

- Development time has a real cost—everyone's salaries. If you're at a startup, this eats into your runway and decreases the chances that the company will be successful.

- There's an opportunity cost to delaying a launch. Customers aren't getting value or paying for the value until you release the work.

- If you're not getting feedback from real customers, you're probably perfecting the wrong things. You might be tweaking the alignment on a UI that needs to be revamped entirely, or fixing a bug that few users will hit.

As a leader, it's your responsibility to make it safe to fail. Celebrate lessons learned. Praise tight scoping. Don't let people shame each other for making smart scoping choices. Protect the iteration time after an MVP launch so the team has time to use what they've learned. Ensure the team's goals or OKRs support incremental development. Point out where people could have spent *less* time on their work.

KEY TAKEAWAYS

- **Ship and learn as early as possible:** You're probably wrong about some of your product assumptions, so don't build too much into your first release. Start with the smallest valuable subset of the product and give it to real people (perhaps in a beta program) so you can get real feedback. That feedback can stop you from building unnecessary features and guide you towards the work that will really drive the product's success. Plus, the sooner you ship, the sooner customers and the business can start benefiting.

- **Don't ship something too small or low quality:** While scoping is important, it can go too far. Don't ship a burnt pizza and declare no one likes pizza. It's usually better to cut functionality or use cases than to cut polish.

- **Scoping well takes humility and bravery:** You need to be humble enough to believe that real customer feedback will improve your product. You need to be brave enough to release a product that you know isn't perfect. It might be emotionally easier to hold the launch until you've built and polished every feature, but you'll usually create better outcomes if you launch incrementally.

CHAPTER 12

PRODUCT LAUNCHES

A LAUNCH CAN feel halfway between a beautifully orchestrated symphony and that moment when the pinata breaks open, the kids rush at the goodies, and you just hope there are no lasting injuries.

On one hand, you have a series of partnerships, with lots of proactive communication and collaboration. Teams are working in sync with each other, with one team picking up where another team left off. Marketing is preparing the blog post, while design polishes up the final screenshots, and engineering is squashing the last few critical bugs.

But at the same time, it can feel frantic and rushed, with many late nights. Teams are trying to do their part and not let each other down, but cuts will nearly always have to be made. Perhaps engineering isn't able to get that feature done, and so marketing and sales have to tweak their work. You might discover a major issue at the last minute and have to face the gut wrenching decision of whether to move the launch date.

And somebody has to make sure that nothing gets left behind.[1]

A launch is a pinnacle moment for your execution skills. All eyes are on you, waiting to see if you can pull off something spectacular. Your first products might go out into the world with just a blog post and a help article. As you hone this skill, the complexity of your launches can grow, and someday you could be standing on a stage in front of an audience of customers, partners and journalists, announcing your latest product.

CONCEPTS AND FRAMEWORKS

LAUNCH REVIEW

After your team has been working for months and the code is finally done, can you go ahead and ship your new feature to customers? For most sizable features and products, you still have one more step: a meeting with senior management called the launch review.

The launch review is the meeting where you'll (hopefully) get the final approval to ship your product. It's a good idea to hold this meeting several days before your launch date, so you'll have time to address the

---

1   And by "someone", we mean you.

issues that inevitably come up. It's usually okay to take your product to launch review before it's 100% final, as long as you can clearly let the reviewers know which parts are still in progress.

If you've been working closely with the approvers and sharing demos and data along the way, the meeting might be an easy run-through of the product and a quick review of the launch plans and marketing material. The reviewers will likely catch a few small bugs and point out opportunities for improvement. You'll then work with your team to decide which bugs and ideas to squeeze in before launch.

When you work more independently, the launch review can have more surprises. If you've run an A/B test, this may be the meeting where you present your results and the reviewers decide if the results are strong enough to justify a launch. If your company has a large group of reviewers from different departments, you might learn belatedly that one of them has an issue with the launch. Sometimes you'll be dismayed to hear the entire premise and approach of your product questioned.

> No matter what happens, stay calm, and don't take it personally. Remember that the reviewers share the same goals as you—just with their own perspective. Everyone wants to launch great products quickly, and no one wants to waste work. Once it's clear that everyone shares the same customer and business goals, you can have a logical discussion about how to address the concerns and the tradeoffs involved.

It's a common mistake to overreact or underreact to executive feedback, so take the time to understand whether their feedback is just an idea, a strong suggestion, or an order. Even when the feedback is closer to a direct order, you'll still have the flexibility to explain the tradeoffs (perhaps they didn't realize their idea would add three weeks to the schedule) and propose alternate solutions.

LAUNCH CHECKLIST

One of the most common reasons for a failed launch is that something gets left behind. A launch checklist can be your savior. Start by considering these areas:

- **Rollout plan:** What is the launch date and time? Will it start with an A/B test, beta program, or will it go out slowly in a staged rollout?[2] Which systems need to be pushed and in which order? How long does each deployment take? When in the timeline does the marketing go live? Will you reserve a conference room on launch day (a "war room") so everyone can be available to handle any issues?

- **Product:** Has the product been thoroughly tested and been put through any necessary QA? Is there in-product onboarding? Is it available on all platforms? Is it internationalized? Has it gone through all the launch reviews? You will probably want to create a separate testing checklist to make sure you consider all the important flows and corner cases.

- **Logging:** Is all of the logging in place so you can analyze the success of the launch and learn how people are using the new functionality? Have you tested the logging to make sure it's working as expected?

---

2   A staged rollout is when you ramp up the percentage of users who get the new code slowly over a period of hours or days.

- **Infrastructure:** Have you reviewed the changes with all of the relevant infrastructure teams (security, stability, site reliability engineers, etc.)? Should you do a dark launch to test the stability?[3]

- **Other reviews:** Does this need any other reviews, such as from the legal or finance teams?

- **Marketing:** Are all of the go-to-market materials ready? How will potential users learn about the launch? Will there be a blog post, press release, email campaign, or larger launch event? Does the app store listing need to be updated? Is the positioning consistent with the launch goals?

- **Sales and Support Enablement:** Do they have the training they need? Is documentation updated? Do they need new collateral or videos? Do they need new internal tools?

- **Other systems:** Do any other internal systems need to be updated, such as billing systems?

- **Company communication:** Will you send out a launch announcement? Will there be a launch party?

Ideally, your team already has a standard launch checklist that you can use. If not, work with your team to create one yourself.

GO-TO-MARKET (GTM) STRATEGY

Launching a product involves a lot more than simply pushing your app to the app store. How will people know it's there? Why will they choose it over all the other apps?

A go-to-market strategy is the plan, usually owned by product marketing, of how to launch a product to customers. It focuses especially on how to reach customers and how to achieve a competitive advantage. Most of the GTM strategy is developed long before the actual launch, using the skills found in Chapter 16: Strategic Framework (pg 184).

As the launch approaches, you and your product marketer will work to finalize the messaging and plans.

Positioning Statement

You've heard these before: "It's Uber for photography", "It's Pinterest for meditation", "It's Khan Academy for cats." Those are positioning statements.

For product teams which need to align product, marketing, and brand, a positioning statement is an elevator pitch that articulates how you want customers to view your product. Unlike a mission statement, a positioning statement frames the product within a known category and against the competitive landscape.[4]

Here's a popular template created by Geoffrey Moore in *Crossing the Chasm*:

> **For** (target customer)
>
> **Who are dissatisfied with** (the current *market alternative*) / **Who** (statement of need or opportunity),
>
> **Our product is a** (new product category)
>
> **That provides** (key problem-solving capability).
>
> **Unlike** (the *product alternative*)
>
> **We have assembled** (key whole product features for your specific application / key differentiators).

---

3   A dark launch is when you run a new backend in parallel without connecting it to the frontend.

4   Look at that! We just wrote a positioning statement for positioning statements.

Positioning statements are important because potential customers and users aren't going to take the time to understand your full product vision. Instead, you want every customer touchpoint, from online ads, to in-product education, to keynote speeches to reinforce the same message. You want that message to be perfectly honed so the person who hears it says "Yes! I do have that problem and I do want that solution!"

Take the time to align with your extended team on a positioning statement before any launch materials get created. All of the other go-to-market materials, from ad copy, to sales talking points follow from that statement.

Promotion

How will people learn that your new product exists? If you work at Google or Facebook, the press will be eager to hear about each of your launches and you can usually cross-promote between products. For the rest of us, we need to dedicate special attention to promotion.

There are many ways (channels) to promote a product. Here are a few to consider:

- **Online ads** like search ads (search engine marketing or SEM) or social media ads. It's easy to track the cost and effectiveness of online ads since you'll know if someone clicked on the ad and whether they eventually became a customer. Which keywords will you target?

- **Public relations** (PR). Can you interest the press in writing an article about your launch? Which publications does your audience read?

- **Search engine optimization (SEO).** Many companies try to rank their webpages at the top of search results by providing widely useful content, such as StitchFix's fashion blog.

- **Blog posts, email campaigns and social media**. These channels help you reach your existing user base to tell them about new features or products. To get the best results, you'll want to have happy reference customers.

- **Events, conferences, and tradeshows**. For large launches, an event can help pull press and customers together to gain more attention and make a bigger splash.

- **Partnerships**. Launching with partners, especially for platform products, can make a big impact. It's hard for customers to imagine how a platform will benefit them until they see what partners have built on top of the platform.

- **Distribution**. Could your product be promoted by another company or come preinstalled with another product? This can be an expensive approach, but can lead to massive reach.

- **Sales**. Will you have a sales team following leads (potential customers) or reaching out to potential customers? What materials will they need to support a sale? How will you generate leads?

For most launches, you'll want to use a mixture of channels based on the customers you're targeting, the cost of the channel, and the effectiveness of the channel.

REFERENCE CUSTOMERS

Reference customers are happy customers who got early access to your new product and are willing to give testimonials about how wonderful it is. These customers can be quoted in your press release, featured in case studies, or even invited on stage during a launch event. They serve as social proof that your product works.

To develop reference customers, invite potential reference customers to a pre-launch beta of the new product and pay close attention to their feedback. Communicate frequently with them and invest in the relationship. You'll want to start with several potential reference customers, in case one of them ends up having unique requirements that you won't address before launch.

RESPONSIBILITIES

DON'T LAUNCH UNTIL THE PRODUCT IS READY

As the launch date approaches, the pressure mounts. Be careful: don't let your eagerness to launch cause you to ship a product that flops.

Drew Dillon, a product leadership consultant and former CPO, shares:

> A great product launch needs happy customer references. Execute a beta program and dedicate sprints to get to a target satisfaction level.

Running A/B tests or beta programs will give you a wealth of information you can use to predict success. If customers don't seem to be loving your product or the changes seem to be a loss, take some time to iterate and improve. It's better to push the launch date out by a few weeks than to release something you know won't succeed.

ENSURE NOTHING FALLS THROUGH THE CRACKS

There are too many moving parts during a launch to keep them all in your head. As you're working through the launch checklist with other people, take a "trust, but verify" approach. Make sure it's clear who is responsible for each piece and when it needs to be ready. You might want to set up regular meetings to check in on everyone's progress and make sure nothing has fallen through the cracks. The RACI/DACI framework (pg 237) can help make roles clear.

QUALITY ASSURANCE

Even if you have a QA or Test team (which not all companies do), you should be involved in creating the test plan and you should run through the most important flows yourself. You want to look beyond just software bugs to find anything that could hurt the user experience.

IT COULD HAVE BEEN BAD!

Natalia Baryshnikova, former Head of Product Management at SmartRecruiters, once did a roll out of her product for a big Australian company. Everything had passed QA, but she noticed the final screen said, "Congratulations, we're rooting for you!"

Having worked across different cultures, she knew colloquial phrases could be problematic and double checked with the customer. As it turns out, that phrase is a bit obscene in Australian slang, and it was a good thing she caught it!

Here are some approaches to quality assurance:

- **Team Review:** Sit down with the designers and engineers and slowly walk through the entire product and every corner case. The engineers should help guide the review to make sure all of the code paths are tested.

- **Internal dogfooding:** From the phrase "Eat your own dogfood," this is when your team uses the product while it's in development. Sometimes you need to get creative with how to get people to dogfood if it isn't a product they would normally use. For example, ordinary Googlers don't have much reason to run ads, so at various points, Google has given employees a small amount of money to put towards AdWords. Make sure to give people a clear place to share any bugs or feedback that they have.

- **Testing bash:** Invite a bunch of coworkers to help you test. You can assign each person a specific area to test, for example a certain browser or part of the app. You might want to bring snacks and have prizes for the most bugs found.

- **Testing scripts:** A step-by-step plan of each flow and corner case to test. You can invite your whole team to help brainstorm cases to include.

- **Run through it all yourself:** Always make sure you've tested the product yourself. You're the most familiar with how your product is supposed to work, so you'll be able to spot problems that everyone else missed.

Pay special attention to:

- **End-to-end flows with a beginner's mind:** During development, you often try out each piece independently. But sometimes, when they all fit together, something is still missing or goes wrong, especially from a usability perspective. Try to imagine you're a beginner with no product familiarity and walk through from end-to-end.

- **Each of the different flows:** If the product works differently for users who are logged in versus logged out, or for premium versus free, make sure to test each of those flows.

- **Common cases that don't get internal dogfooding:** Consider what parts the dogfooders will miss (e.g., new user signups, empty states, upgrade flows, or onboarding).

- **Corner cases:** The corner cases will be unique for each product. Consider the surprising states the user can get into, like having an empty name field or putting a lot of data into the system. Also, consider various error conditions like entering invalid input, or losing internet connectivity.

- **Design details:** Is the alignment and spacing correct? Are the images sharp? Are all of the hover states and animations working? Does the design match up with the mocks?

- **Devices:** For web apps, test them in different browsers and with different screen sizes. For mobile apps, test on each supported platform and size. Many at tech companies use Chrome on a Mac, but that's not true for all users or customers; make sure you're using Safari, Firefox and Edge as well.

- **Internationalization:** You'll generally want to test using German (to make sure long words don't display poorly), Japanese (to make sure double-byte characters can render), and Arabic (to make sure right-to-left languages display correctly). You'll also want to try entering accent marks and emojis to make sure they're stored and displayed correctly.

It's important to create a "we're all in this together" atmosphere towards bug finding and fixing. Even if you have a dedicated test team, the more eyes you have the better.

HANDLE ANY LAUNCH PROBLEMS

Imagine it's launch day, and something has gone wrong! The app crashes. The download button goes to an empty page. Users are writing angry tweets. Yikes!

Here are some best practices for handling launch problems:

- Take a deep breath. Make sure you're in the right mindset to problem-solve without assigning blame. You'll want your team focused on fixing the issue, not feeling defensive.

- Bring the key people into a room or video chat together to discuss the problem and potential solutions. Having other people to think through the problem with you can help prevent a hasty mistake. A shared room reduces miscommunications and helps you move quickly.

- Let your manager know. Proactive communication will do a lot to build trust, and they may be able to help you.

- Consider whether you should roll back the change. How bad are the problems? Can you roll it back without harming customers? Have marketing materials already gone out to customers who will be looking for the new changes? If you're rolling back the change, make sure you pause any future promotions such as in-product announcements or email blasts.

- Can you "cherry pick" a quick fix? Work with the engineers to see if there's anyway to bypass some of the standard processes to get a fix in quickly. Be careful though; many times skipping tests to push a quick fix for a small bug accidentally causes a larger bug. If your app is in an app store, you may be able to reach out to ask for quicker approval of your new release.

- Work with your marketing team on how to reply to customers. Make sure customer service representatives and social media managers have the new messaging.

- Once everything is settled, hold a retrospective or "5 Whys" (pg 74) to identify the root cause of what went wrong, and how you can prevent similar problems in the future.

Launches can be high-stress events, and it's up to you to stay calm and guide the team through any problems that arise.

CELEBRATE AND COMMUNICATE BACK TO THE COMPANY

After weeks or months of building a product and preparing for a launch, everyone will be eager to hear how the investment paid off. Even people who were not directly involved will want to know how things went and what it all means for the company.

Here are some ways to celebrate and inform people:

- **Launch announcement:** The day of the launch, send a company-wide message letting people know what was launched (screenshots help) and thanking all of the people who contributed to the launch (including cross-functional partners). If you're not sure who should be thanked, ask a point person from each team you worked with to gather their list. If you have any early data or anecdotes on how the launch is doing, share that as well.

- **Launch party:** This can be as simple as buying cupcakes and inviting people to a conference room (or delivering cookies to people who work from home). For larger launches, you might want a bigger event; talk to your team admin or facilities staff about how to set that up. To make it extra special, write up a toast or small speech to deliver to the team.

- **Post-launch updates:** Once you have real data on the success of the launch and have held a retrospective, send another announcement to share. If the news is good, make sure everyone knows about it. If the news is bad, include the key takeaways of what you learned and what it means for the future.

The key to these celebrations and communications is that most people at the company won't know how to feel about the launch unless you tell them. By properly celebrating, you can improve morale across the company. By honestly sharing launch outcomes, you can prevent people from forming incorrect stories or drawing false conclusions.

GROWTH PRACTICES

PARTNER WITH LAUNCH STAKEHOLDERS EARLY

The top complaint that launch partners have about working with PMs is that the PMs don't involve the partners early enough in the process. Partners need to know about upcoming launches so they can plan their own schedules and give early input. Ideally, you'll tell them about upcoming launches as soon as the product work is on your schedule.

The most effective way to work with stakeholders is to treat them like true partners, not a service. Make them part of your launch team, rather than treating them as an obstacle or a box you need to check. This increases the communication overhead, but makes them feel invested in the launch.

I didn't loop in stakeholders early enough, and now they've identified an issue that will block my launch!

Breathe. Don't panic. This can happen to anyone. Let them know you appreciate their concern.

To resolve the issue:

1. Bring the stakeholders up-to-date with the goals, context, and priority of the launch.

2. Work together to write down options from low risk to high risk, along with the pros and cons of each. Look for ways to mitigate the risk.

3. If you don't agree on an option, escalate the decision. Don't get emotional or defensive. Stay focused on uncovering what's best for users and the business.

4. Once you have a plan, send an update to stakeholders. Let them know what new information has come to light, what the new plan is, and that you'll come up with a plan to identify issues like these earlier next time.

Take heart that, assuming a healthy company culture, the "blocking" stakeholder has the same end goals as you: successful launch, successful product, and successful company. They might just have a different vision of how to achieve this.

USE LAUNCH REVIEWS AS A WAY TO EARN CREDIBILITY

By the time you get to the final launch review, you're probably feeling impatient to launch.

Be careful, because launch reviews can have a huge impact on your credibility. If you bring a buggy or sloppy product, it will reflect poorly on you.

You can make launch reviews work in your favor if you're well prepared. Instead of hiding bugs, shortcuts, and other problems, share them proactively. Tell the reviewer what you're planning to do about each of them. For the problems you don't intend to fix, explain why. If something new comes up during the review, state that you'll look into it and prioritize it appropriately.

REFINE THE WAY YOU THINK ABOUT LAUNCH DATES ⚡

As a PM, you'll often be asked for a launch date. This is not as simple as it sounds. There's no way you'll be 100% sure of the launch date.

If the code is all written and you're planning to launch on Tuesday, you'll be within a day or two most of the time. The extra day might come from a push that failed or a problem on another team blocking your launch. Occasionally you'll discover a severe bug that takes more than a week to fix.

If you're talking about a launch that's planned for three months from now, there's a lot more uncertainty.

I've seen all the following issues occur:

- Projects delayed months because the legacy code they touched was more complicated than the engineers had expected.

- One product looked great in design reviews, but when we tried it out with real user data we realized the design was confusing and spent an extra month improving it.

- One time, we built our new features on a new piece of infrastructure that never launched and we had to rewrite half the code.

- Another time, we paused work to move several engineers onto an urgent spam issue.

- One feature was a week away from launch when we noticed a data corruption issue that took a few weeks to repair.

In each of these cases, the specific delay came as a surprise. But in the bigger picture, it would have been *more* surprising if all of them had launched on time. Software launches are notoriously difficult to estimate.

> Instead of thinking about the launch date as a single day, think about it as a range of dates, from the earliest you might launch to the latest.

For each part of the range, make sure you have your team's full buy-in. Never commit your engineers to dates without their full agreement.

The lower end of the range should be the best case scenario, if nothing goes wrong. To come up with the date consider:

- Add in time before the engineering can start—for example, design time, and time learning new technology.

- Put a multiplier on the engineering estimates (e.g., one ideal day = two real days). Check with your engineers and other PMs to see what multiplier they recommend.

- Check for any planned vacations, offsites, or other non-working days.

- Add in time for running A/B tests or a beta program. You may also want to share the estimated A/B test start date when sharing your dates.

- Add on time for how long the deployment and any other post-code work takes (e.g., translations).

- Consider adding an extra 10 to 20% buffer on top of everything else. Yes, even in the lower end of the range. Good project managers should always assume that something will go wrong.

The middle of the range should be based on your estimate of an average number of things going wrong. Consider:

- What might you learn from user tests, A/B tests, or the beta program? How long would those things take to address?

- What types of problems could the engineering team have, and how much time would they add?

- What are the other risks, and how much time would they add to the project?

For the upper end of the range:

- Try to figure out the date by which you're 90 or 95% sure you'll have launched.

- For a multi-month project, this is usually at least two months after the lower end of the range.

- Everyone on the team should agree that if it goes past that date, something went really wrong.

When people ask for a launch date, try to share the range and some examples of what might cause the project to go beyond the best case. When communicated well, this can help build trust and credibility. It shows that your team is trying to move as fast as possible, but also that you've planned ahead for what could go wrong.

> If everything goes perfectly we'll launch at the beginning of May, but we might learn from the beta program that we need to build a new onboarding flow, which could move our date out as far as June.

Some people will insist on a date, rather than a range. The marketing team probably needs to know the lower end of the range so that the go-to-market materials are ready for launch day (although you should really share the whole range so they can plan for marketing across the year). The financial model should be conservative, so use the upper end of the range for the finance team.

TAKE RESPONSIBILITY FOR THE END-TO-END CUSTOMER EXPERIENCE ⚡

April Underwood likes to say, "Shipping code to production is not a launch. A launch is when customers actually understand what it is and why they need it."[5]

As a PM, you probably won't drive the areas outside of product, but you can still be an influential partner.

Here are some areas to consider:

- The marketing strategy and positioning

---

5   See the full Q&A on page 460.

- Pricing and packaging

- Onboarding materials

- Help center documentation

- Sales enablement materials such as talking points and demo environments

- Customer success materials

- External launch partners

- External consultants and contractors

- Advertising

- Distribution channels

All of these things impact your product, and thus are important to you—even if they aren't within your jurisdiction. Just as you keep teams like marketing and sales informed about your work, you'll want to be informed about their progress.

To be a good, influential partner, first meet with the people driving the decisions and learn about their approach and frameworks. Some people have set processes and timelines, and others might take a more ad-hoc approach. If they already have processes, find the most useful places for you to see work in progress and figure out when it's most helpful for you to give feedback. If they have a more ad-hoc approach, you might need to put together a timeline to ensure you have a chance to contribute feedback at an appropriate time.

When giving feedback, be respectful of your partner's expertise, while not underselling your own expertise in the product and problem space.

Simple things to check for are gaps or mistakes, such as:

- Does the marketing strategy assume features that won't be included at launch?

- Does the pricing and packaging cover all types of users?

- Are there corner cases that should be explained in the help documentation?

- Do the sales talking points include the key things customers have said they care about?

- Do any pages on the website need to be updated because of the product changes?

- Is the experience consistent, with the same terminology and imagery, across all of the customer touch points?

Beyond the basics, you can look for opportunities to improve the end-to-end customer experience. For example:

- Do you have marketing insights based on the user sessions you did?

- Do you have ideas for using launch partners or distribution channels to reach a wider audience?

- Are there ways to make the product easier to demo to customers?

Share your ideas with your partners, using your knowledge of their approach and frameworks to find a way that could work for them. If your ideas would require a radical change of approach, you'll need to plant the seeds of the idea early.

GET THE LAUNCH STRATEGY RIGHT ⚡⚡

When Nate Abbott launched Airbnb Experiences, he came face-to-face with the tradeoffs around launch strategies.

Airbnb Experiences was a pivotal launch for the company. They were expanding from home sharing to travel, and they needed to reposition themselves in the market. For that goal, a big public launch event was the best strategy. They threw a big party with journalists and shouted their message from the rooftops.

As the product lead, Abbott knew his role would be different in a marketing-led launch like this. He focused on two things:

1. Optimizing the product to best help the launch achieve its goals.

2. Covering every single logistic perfectly.

Being a great PM required setting aside his ego. The marketing message, not the product-market fit, would be center stage. Creating checklists and running a tight ship isn't glamorous, and in fact can feel quite uncomfortable at times.

Abbott shared how those priorities impacted the product:

> We didn't just roll out an entirely new booking system for experiences. We actually re-architected the entire homepage and the way people interact with search on Airbnb.
>
> Early on, we had debated having Experiences be a totally separate app, but instead we dedicated a huge amount of product and engineering resources to create an integrated search experience. I had standups with the team every day and a spreadsheet of the red flags that kept me up at night. One of those red flags was that we couldn't get the animation right on the header bar. I told the team, "if we don't have this by Sunday, I'm calling a hard stop." And one of our awesome engineers disappeared and four days later emerged with the perfect header.
>
> These details weren't critical for the *product*, but they were critical for the *launch*. They told the company narrative. The CEO could go up on stage and scroll the app itself to show homes and experiences together. The app told the story of the transformation around our trip platform that we really wanted to have.

A big marketing-led launch does have a lot of downsides, however. As Abbott shared:

> We kept the entire thing under wraps and did not do much market testing with our core market before we launched.
>
> We therefore missed some of the key signals—for example, how people were not into three day trips, and instead wanted bite sized afternoon experiences that would work in their existing schedule. It took us two months to adjust to those learnings after the launch.
>
> From a product perspective, I wish we could have done a slow rollout and tested with our existing user base. From the larger perspective however, the success of this launch was measured by whether we'd

changed the market's perception. In this case, the broader story worked, even if the product wasn't perfect. It was a successful transition for the company.

When deciding between a big marketing-led launch moment (where the date is set in advance and the product is kept under wraps) and a product-led slow rollout (where the product is launched incrementally without any big announcements and marketing materials only go out after the product team says the product is ready), the key is to think about your goals and target audience. When your goal is to deepen engagement with your current customer base, there's not much need for a big launch. When your goal is to enter a new market or change the company's market perception, a big launch is probably worth the cost

KEY TAKEAWAYS

- **Launching is a complex, cross-functional process:** As the PM, you'll need to make sure every team stays coordinated and on track. Templates are incredibly helpful to ensure you don't forget about a step.

- **Treat the launch date as a range:** It's impossible to accurately predict when a feature will launch, and guessing incorrectly can cause a lot of problems. Some teams need to know the earliest you might launch so they can prepare supporting materials, while other teams need to know the latest you might launch so they can create conservative financial models. Sharing a range from best case to worst case better conveys the information and helps you build credibility.

- **Take direct responsibility for the quality of the launch:** Even if there's a QA team, you need to try out the product, look for bugs, and make sure the whole thing works end to end. Even if there's a marketing team, you need to review the launch materials and make sure they're compelling. Even when you trust your engineers, you need to double check anything that could go wrong with the infrastructure. No excuses.

- **Treat cross-functional partners as part of the team:** It takes a lot more than product, design, and engineering to pull off a successful launch. Loop in other teams early, and be open to their influence. Help them feel invested in the launch and give them credit for their work.

CHAPTER 13

GET THINGS DONE

PICTURE JAKE. HE'S a new PM, fresh out of a top college with a great GPA and great projects. Maybe he even had a successful internship at your company.

He gets off to a great start, doing all the things he needs to do. You picture him moving on up, gaining more and more responsibility.

But then, perhaps six to twelve months in, he starts to falter. Your super responsible PM is falling behind schedule. The work he does is excellent, but there's so much he isn't doing and needs to.

What's gone wrong? Simply put: he's struggling to *get things done*. Fortunately, this is a skill one can develop.

CONCEPTS AND FRAMEWORKS

WHAT DOES IT MEAN TO BE A PERSON WHO GETS THINGS DONE?

Getting things done isn't about working nights and weekends. It's about *how* you work. How do you manage what you do, and what people around you do? How do you work with others? It means that you avoid the traps that can block things from getting done. People who get things done tend to share the following traits.

Action-oriented

- **Bad:** Getting caught up in analysis paralysis. Held back by fear of risks. Waiting for people to get back to you.

- **Good:** Knowing that *done* is better than *perfect*. Being enthusiastic and slightly impatient. Motivating your team to move forward, even when faced with incomplete information.

High capacity

- **Bad:** Not being able to make time for important work. Being a bottleneck for the team.

- **Good:** Knowing how to manage your own time. Prioritizing work. Working quickly. Sharing work early. Putting in enough hours (~50 hrs/week) to get important work done. Being able to effectively PM multiple teams.

Reliable

- **Bad:** Coworkers need to remind you to do things. People have to ask for status updates.

- **Good:** You do what you said you'd do. You stay on top of your inbox. You follow up on commitments and renegotiate them if you can't keep them. On long projects, you show consistent progress and proactively communicate status, risks, and setbacks.

Results-oriented

- **Bad:** Focused on the process like writing a spec or checking off tasks. Mostly does what they're told to do. Overly deferential to other functions, as in "legal won't let us".

- **Good:** Not considering your work done until you've gotten the results you were looking for. Finding scrappy ways around the processes or roadblocks that get in your way.[1]

It's true that working longer hours is necessary at times, and that working *more* can compensate somewhat for weaknesses in some of these attributes. But still, if you aren't action-oriented, reliable, high capacity, and results-oriented, you'll struggle to get things done, even *with* long hours.

PERSONAL PRODUCTIVITY SYSTEMS

"Getting things done" isn't just about your instincts or automatic behavior. Even if you are already tuned to work basically productively, there are strategies around *how* to be productive that can help you maximize this. Tracking your work and choosing work by priority are generally key aspects of any productivity system.

Getting Things Done

A great system for organizing your work is David Allen's *Getting Things Done* (GTD).[2] It has multiple components which can be picked up independently or all together.

1. **Capture all your to-dos and ideas in writing**. Our brains are terrible at remembering things, and it's stressful to try. Keep the number of places you capture ideas to a minimum.

2. **Process what you captured and clarify "next actions."** If an item takes less than two minutes to do, do it right then. Otherwise, clarify the next concrete step and move it to the "Next Actions" list. You can also schedule tasks for later on your calendar, or delegate them. Anything else goes to the "Someday/Maybe" list.

3. **Work through your next actions**. When you have time to work, look through your next actions list and pick something based on priority and the amount of energy you have.

4. **Weekly review**. Go through your lists and make sure everything is clarified, actionable, and where it is supposed to be.

---

1 Tech companies use the word "scrappy" to mean quick and resourceful, for example, finding clever alternate solutions to work around constraints.

2 Read more about Getting Things Done at https://gettingthingsdone.com/.

We strongly encourage you to read *Getting Things Done* for more details; there's a reason it's a popular book among PMs.

Set dates for work that is important but not urgent

If something is due tomorrow, it's relatively easy to clear out some time to get it done.

On the other hand, something like a small usability bug in the signup flow might be important to fix, but on any given day, it's okay to push it out another day. Unfortunately, those days tend to add up, and when you realize the bug has been sitting around for months, the cumulative impact adds up to something that's no longer small.

To get past this predicament, try this thought exercise: how long would be too long for this work to go undone?

Once you have a time span in mind, set a due date that's a day sooner than "definitely too long". Of course, you can work on it earlier, but if not, once you get to the date, treat it as urgent.

TIME MANAGEMENT

Every product manager feels like they don't have as much time as they want, and yet every day PMs find ways to keep their teams running on the current work, to prepare upcoming work, to invest in strategic thinking, and to run a few extra projects or processes on the side.

Time management is the biggest blocker PMs face as they advance. You can't reach the higher levels of leadership until you learn how to carve out time for strategy. As a people manager, even more of your time gets absorbed by 1:1s and other meetings.

So, what's the secret?

> It all comes down to accepting that we have more work to do than can actually be done, and then being intentional about what we choose to do.

Accept that you have more work to do than can actually be done

Acceptance is the first step in time management. If you insist on believing that you can get to every item on your to-do list if you simply work hard enough and smart enough, it will be too painful to prioritize what needs to be done.

Many PMs have gotten straight As throughout school, so it's hard to make the mental shift that taking a metaphorical B or C on some of your work is the right thing to do. But when your schedule is full, every piece of work you say yes to implicitly means saying no to something else.

Analyze your ideal vs. actual time allocation

For time management—as it is every problem we face in product management—it's a good idea to start with your goal. Once you know how you'd ideally spend your time, you can assess how you're actually spending your time and then come up with a plan to match your ideal.[3]

Consider categories like:

---

3   I expand on this at https://wavelength.asana.com/workstyle-time-management/.

- **Customer research:** Meeting with customers, watching user sessions, reading support emails, looking at usage data.

- **Working with the engineers and designers:** Brainstorming, problem solving, giving feedback.

- **Project responsibilities:** Writing specs, proposing OKRs, analyzing experiment data, prioritizing the backlog, project management.

- **Strategic thinking:** Working on the vision, planning the roadmap, exploring strategic ideas.

- **Recruiting:** Interviewing candidates, sourcing candidates, coffee chats with potential candidates, developing new interview questions.

- **Personal development:** Reading books and blog posts, attending or speaking at conferences, working with a coach.

- **Managing and mentoring:** 1:1s, writing reviews, leading training sessions.

- **Company commitments:** All hands, product team meetings, show and tells.

- **Being available for whatever comes up:** Being responsive to teammates, unblocking people, fighting fires, helping out.

These categories may well change over time, and that's okay.

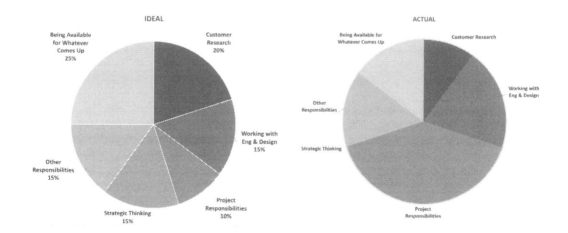

Once you've decided which categories to track, look at how you want to spend your time versus how you actually spend it:

1. **Make a pie chart of how you'd ideally spend your time**. Set aside at least 25% of your time to be available for the things that inevitably come up. At senior PM and above, set aside 15% for strategic thinking.

2. **Assess where your time actually goes**. You can spend a week and mark off time on your calendar along with a rough summary of how you spent that time. Take a look at recurring meetings too.

3. **Compare**. Once you've visualized both your ideal and actual pie charts, compare them to see where you need to make adjustments.

When you do the math on your ideal time allocation, you'll often find that your percentages add up to more than 100%. Here's where accepting that you can't do it all fits in. You'll need to make some compromises to get to a realistic plan. Adjust the allocations until you feel good about your pie chart.

The 4 D's: delete, defer, delegate, and diminish

When you don't have enough time for a responsibility, there are four ways to spend less time on it.

- **Delete:** Say no to the work. If you were assigned it, make sure to have a discussion rather than silently dropping the work.

- **Defer:** Set a reminder to complete the task on a specific date in the future. If you keep deferring the same work, take an honest look at whether it's a priority for you.

- **Delegate:** Hand the responsibility to someone else. You can work with your manager to find an appropriate person.

- **Diminish:** Reduce the time you spend on the responsibility. Shorten meetings or consolidate them. Where acceptable, stop at good instead of perfect.

This decision is a natural and necessary consequence of having too little time to do everything. Be thoughtful about your choice, but don't feel ashamed.

BIG ROCKS FIRST

Imagine you've got rocks of all sizes that you're trying to fit into a jar. If you put the smaller rocks in first and let them fill up the bottom, the bigger rocks won't fit on top. But if you put the bigger rocks in first, the smaller rocks can fill in the gaps between the big rocks and you can get them all in.

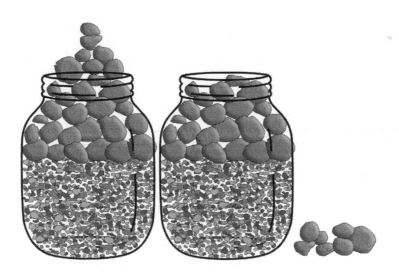

The same goes for your responsibilities and tasks. If you start each day with the small five-minute tasks and throw in a few meetings, it'll be really hard to find three consecutive hours for deep focused work.

Instead, when planning your week, start by scheduling time for your most important work. As a PM, it really helps to block that time off on your calendar so it doesn't get filled in with meetings. It also adds a little internal pressure to actually use that time for the important work. Once you've fit your big tasks in, you can fit your smaller ones in between.

Proactively blocking off time on your calendar for your most important work can help you get uninterrupted time to get into the flow and take control of your day.

Get out of the office to make space for uninterrupted work

If simply blocking the time off on your calendar isn't working, creating a little more physical space might help. You can go work from a coffee shop, or hide away in a different corner of your office. Try blocking your notifications, and pretend you're working off the grid, or actually invite your team to an offsite strategy session in the woods.[4] Set your out-of-office indicator.

If you're feeling guilty about ignoring your team for a day, try this thought exercise: would you take a Friday off work if your friend were getting married? If your team can handle you taking a vacation day or a sick day, they can certainly handle you taking a strategy day to invest in the future of the team.

BEATING PROCRASTINATION

Justin Rosenstein, one of the co-founders of Asana, wrote about his three-step process for beating procrastination:[5]

1. Face whatever I'm putting off.

2. Be honest with myself or a friend about why it's uncomfortable.

3. Identify one easy next step.

When you follow these steps, you'll find that, often, the next step is something easy that involves asking someone a question or looking something up. For example, if you're avoiding writing a spec, the next step might be something like "find the template" or "look at existing research."

The reason this works is that procrastination usually comes when something feels unclear and overwhelming. If you give yourself permission to look at the work without having to do it right then, you can usually break it down into pieces that aren't so scary.

RESPONSIBILITIES

HAVE A POINT OF VIEW

New PMs sometimes think their job is to get the right people into a room, and then to let them make a decision. Or they think they should escalate every important decision to someone above them. Neither of these is effective. As a PM, you're responsible for becoming the expert in your area, analyzing tradeoffs, and forming a point of view.

---

4   Read more about this at https://medium.com/building-asana/working-from-woods-35236950d100.

5   Rosenstein expands on this at https://www.linkedin.com/pulse/20140121123613-25056271-tasks-down-how-to-overcome-procrastination-by-facing-discomfort/.

Your point of view is one of the most valuable things you can add as a PM. You've taken the time and made the investment so that everyone else doesn't have to. If you don't have a strong point of view, you're pushing the responsibility for research and thinking onto someone else, and they probably have better things they could be doing with their time.

No matter how opinionated your coworkers are, they don't actually want to make the decision for you. They want you to understand their point of view, and they want to be able to trust you to make the decision that is best overall. The best outcome is when you can efficiently explain all of the different points of view and why you've come to the conclusion that you did.

Your point of view won't always be right, and that's okay. You'll learn from the times when your decisions get overturned or your recommendations don't get chosen.

FIND WAYS AROUND ROADBLOCKS

New PMs often hit a roadblock and just stop. Maybe an engineer said it couldn't be done. Perhaps the research team said they have no time to help. Maybe marketing said something more important came up. You might be used to following the rules and it doesn't occur to you that there are other ways to get things done.

In reality, PMs can do *a lot* to get past roadblocks. This often feels like, "You can do that? I didn't realize that was an option!"

FINDING A WORK AROUND

One PM, Victor, hit a roadblock after he built a new internal tool. The team that had requested the tool had gotten nervous and wanted more time before they started the pilot. Instead of delaying the pilot, Victor talked to dozens of teams across the company and found another team who *was* willing to pilot the new tool. That team loved the tool. Their recommendation convinced the original team to get onboard as well.

To get around a roadblock, consider these approaches:

- **Can you convince them to change the no to a yes?** Try setting up a face-to-face meeting with them. Sometimes, just explaining why it's important is enough. Perhaps you can help them reprioritize. If it's still a no, you can check with your manager if bringing in someone more senior might add some credibility and pressure to your request.

- **Is there a way to get it done without them?** Perhaps you can do it yourself or find another team to help. Maybe there are outside resources that can help.

- **Is there another way to achieve the goal?** Maybe the specific technical solution won't work, but the engineers can help find another solution that would.

- **Do you have personal relationships that can help?** Perhaps you know someone on the team that's saying no, and you can talk to them to get advice on next steps.

- **What's the next best option?** Are there ways to supplement that option to make it as good?

- **Is there any learning or validation you can do to move forward?** Maybe once you have more information you'll change people's minds or come up with a new idea.

- **Can you ask your boss for help?** It's best to fix the problem yourself, but asking your boss for help is much better than getting totally stuck by the roadblock.

When you overcome a roadblock, you help your team move forward so you can all achieve your goals.

KEEP OR RENEGOTIATE YOUR COMMITMENTS

When you tell someone you'll get something done, that's making a commitment. An important part of being reliable is doing what you say you'll do.

If you keep your commitments, you'll be seen as reliable and be valued for all you get done. If you don't, you create extra work for the people who need to check up on you and you'll lose credibility.

Write your commitments down in your productivity system. Add dates or reminders so you won't forget them. If you fall behind, let people know as soon as possible, and work out a new plan with them. Don't let the deadline go by without saying anything.

COMMUNICATE PROACTIVELY

Let stakeholders know as soon as something important changes or you hit an important milestone. Even if everything is going according to plan, you should still send regular updates so that they don't worry or don't need to ask.

Proactive communication is particularly important with your manager as it's one of the primary ways they'll assess your autonomy. If you're feeling micromanaged, that is often because you haven't been proactive enough with your communication.

RUN MULTIPLE TEAMS AT ONCE ⚡

Taking on multiple teams is a straightforward way to increase scope. You're responsible for more people, and with more teams, you can launch more products.

The biggest blocker to expanding your scope in this way is often emotional. You might worry that you're letting your current teammates down if you pick up more work and become less available. Talk about your fears with other PMs you trust.

DON'T BE A ROADBLOCK ⚡⚡

Have you ever worked with a product leader who seemed to slow you down? Maybe they kept sending you off on tangents to gather more data, or forced you to spend more time iterating when the work was already good enough. Maybe they kept you waiting forever on decisions so you were blocked and couldn't move forward, or maybe they were way too busy, but still needed to approve every last detail.

Don't be that kind of product leader.

When you move into leadership, it's your responsibility to keep teams moving quickly. Pay attention to how your feedback and requests might slow a team down. Encourage people to tell you when they're blocked, and prioritize unblocking them.

GROWTH PRACTICES

DON'T TREAT WORK LIKE SCHOOL

"I've clearly done this wrong. There's no good solution," complained a new PM one day to Josh Kaplan, former GPM at Dropbox. "That's okay," Josh replied, "You didn't fail; you just need to grapple with the tradeoffs now."

As a PM, you won't be handed discrete tasks. You need to figure out for yourself what needs to be done and how to do it. When you talk to other people, you can't assume they understand your assignment or the background context. There's no single right answer. You'll need to think deeply about the tradeoffs. Recognize that you're solving a brand new problem.

Focus on outcomes, not deliverables

In school, your grades were all about deliverables; if you did what you were supposed to do, you got an A. As a product manager, that's not how it works.

If you create a spec but people don't read and follow it, it doesn't matter how good the spec was in the first place. If your team launches by the deadline but you don't hit your success metrics, your job isn't done yet. Getting to the desired outcome might include a lot of work other than just handing over deliverables.

SHARE WORK EARLY

Nearly every PM learns this lesson the hard way.

It takes a lot of courage to share work before it's done and polished. It can also take a lot of humility to consider that your first approach might be going down the wrong path entirely. If you don't share your work early, though, you risk wasting days or weeks of work.

To make it easier to share work early:

- **Call it a draft**. You can put lots of extra qualifiers to emphasize that the work you're sharing isn't final. Try phrases like, "Here's a rough sketch," "I just jotted down some notes," and "Can you take a quick look at this early draft?"

- **Find a friendly mentor to take the first look**. You might not want to share your messy draft with the whole team, but perhaps your manager or a friend could take a look to let you know if you're on the right track.

- **Ask if it's on the right track**. Sometimes people will be afraid to tell you that there are major problems because they don't want to hurt your feelings or demoralize you. By asking explicitly, you make it easier for them to tell you.

- **Set rules for yourself**. If it helps, tell yourself you'll share whatever you have in three days, even if it's not done.

Keep in mind that the longer you wait, the greater pressure there is on the final deliverable—and the greater chance of it being significantly offbase.

PRIORITIZE BEING RESPONSIVE TO YOUR TEAM

In other roles, you might be able to put on headphones and ignore people all day while you're in flow. PMs don't have this luxury; they would slow down their team if they did that. Often, other people can't move forward without PM input.

If you're suffering from inbox overload, find a way to filter the important notifications that need your response from the rest.

- **Email:** Filter mailing lists, sent directly to you, from specific people.

- **Work Management:** at (@) mentions, assigned to you, due dates.

- **Chat:** Channel notifications, at (@) mentions, keywords.

If it's difficult to filter automatically, you can let your team know the best way to reach you, and encourage them to reach out when they need you. Sometimes, teammates notice that you're busy and try not to bother you, even when you'd like them to. Be sure to reinforce that they're your top priority and that you do have time for them.

BE INTENTIONAL ABOUT HOW YOU USE REAL-TIME AND ASYNCHRONOUS COMMUNICATION

Real-time communication is when everyone is in the conversation at the same time, like a face-to-face conversation or a meeting. Asynchronous (or async) communication is when one person sends a message, like a chat or email, and they're not sure when the other person will read it and reply. Each type can be valuable when used correctly.

Benefits of real-time communication:

- **It's easier:** you don't have to carefully plan out what you're going to say.

- **Fewer miscommunications:** you can convey tone and get feedback from the other person to avoid misunderstandings.

- **Faster resolution:** there's no time spent waiting for the other person to read and respond.

Benefits of async:

- **No scheduling hassle:** especially when a lot of people are involved, sometimes it's not feasible to find a time when everyone is free to have a discussion. Each person can read and respond when it's most convenient for them.

- **Written reference:** async conversations naturally create a reference of what was said. This can be great for tracking what decisions were made and why.

- **Usually more time efficient:** it's a lot faster to read an email and type up a quick response than to get pulled into a 30 minute meeting.

- **No flow interruption:** people can respond when they're ready, whereas real-time communication can often interrupt a person's flow and schedule with the meeting, phone call, or quick chat.

You can add a lot of value by switching real-time discussions to async, and vice versa. A recurring meeting might be better as an async check-in. An email thread that's going back and forth might be quickly resolved by a quick chat.

USE "TIMEBOXING" WHEN YOU NEED TO BALANCE HOW LONG TO SPEND ON SOMETHING

Timeboxing is a simple technique where you agree on the maximum amount of time you want to spend on something before you start working, and then you cut off the work if it takes longer than that. You can use it for any kind of task, from engineering work to decision-making.

Timeboxing works well because it lets you control the cost of work and therefore, your return on investment. It's much easier to be rational about how long to invest in a piece of work before it's started, especially because it avoids the sunk-cost fallacy. It helps codify the common goal of "we'll do it if it's cheap."

For example, you can timebox the amount of time you'll spend fixing a rare browser bug to three hours. The engineer will try to fix the bug for up to three hours, and after that, they'll move on to something else, even if the bug isn't fixed. Timeboxing avoids the unpleasant surprise of finding out an engineer is still working on the "easy" bug a week later.

MOVE FASTER

Pay attention to the times when you're slow to take action, and find the root cause.

Here are some common opportunities where PMs can be more action-oriented.

It doesn't seem like anyone is waiting for your decision

In practice, any uncertainty usually slows people down. This happens even when the uncertainty shouldn't directly affect what they're working on at the time. It's hard to work at full speed when you're worried that something might change, or you don't have a clear view of where you're going. So, even if people aren't blocked on you, it's still a good idea to drive to clarity quickly.

Creating fancy frameworks when simple judgment would do

I've seen PMs create a complex formula for prioritizing work and then spend a week reformulating it when the results didn't make sense. I've seen teams spend days trying to pick precise numbers to use for launch criteria.

In many cases, you can save a lot of time by allowing for judgment calls. If the ranking isn't quite right, move things around. Set rough guidelines for the launch criteria and have a conversation if the results are borderline. Loosen up your framework to catch the most important cases without being too precise on the other buckets.

Too much iteration

Some projects get stuck in the design phase. The designer shows their work to other designers, and then spends weeks trying to address every piece of internal feedback.

Regroup with your designer after they show their work to decide what feedback needs to be addressed. Help them see the balance between iteration and getting work in front of customers sooner. Support them in moving forward.

"TRUST, BUT VERIFY" DURING CROSS-FUNCTIONAL COLLABORATION

Cross-functional collaboration is a tricky part of product management. You're trying to get things done, but you're relying on someone else.

If you hand over some work to another team and then don't check back with them until launch day, chances are something will go wrong. Maybe one of the goals was misunderstood, or the work is running behind, or something urgent came up and they forgot about the work for your launch.

If you treat the other team like they're incompetent and try to micromanage them, they probably won't want to work with you again.

Instead, start from a place of mutual trust and respect, but set up some checkpoints where you can verify that things are going as expected.

LEARN HOW TO DELEGATE WELL ⚡

When done well, delegation can be a win-win. The work that feels tedious to you might be an exciting growth opportunity for someone else. You might be able to pass along responsibilities to more junior PMs, or even designers and engineers.

Hand over ownership of a full responsibility

You should try to hand over ownership of a full responsibility, rather than farming out individual tasks.

For example, instead of asking someone to add a few specific charts to a dashboard, tell them about your goals for the dashboard and the problems with the current one, and then put them in charge of the dashboard. You can share your ideas, but give them space to come up with even better approaches. Agree on some checkpoints so you can make sure they're on the right path.

They'll get the satisfaction of owning the dashboard rather than feeling like they're doing you a favor. You'll get better results and better morale.

Understand your reluctance to delegate

Sometimes, the biggest hurdle a PM faces to delegation isn't convincing someone else to take on the work, but rather convincing *yourself* that you can and should delegate this. If you're hesitating to delegate work, consider why. Some common reasons to be reluctant include:

- **It doesn't seem like anyone would want to do the work**. Reflect on what makes the work important and what skills it requires. Those will become part of your "pitch" for the work. Look at people across the company, not just within product teams, to see who might enjoy contributing or want to build those skills. Ask managers if anyone on their team would be a good match.

- **No one else can do it well enough**. Does it really need to be done well? If you stopped doing it, could your time be better spent doing something else? If you're sure it needs to be done well, consider training people on the skills needed, or hiring someone with the right skills.

- **You don't want to give it up**. If you really enjoy the work or the prestige of the responsibility, you need to make a choice. You don't have to delegate the work if you enjoy it and have enough time for it.

Not everything must be delegated, but most people are not delegating as much as they can or should. Be thoughtful about why something that could be delegated isn't.

Take responsibility for defining what success looks like, and delegate the solution to your designers and engineers

It's hard to get a lot done when your engineers ask you to figure out the wording for every error message in the product. Many PMs get stuck in this kind of tactical work, and it's a poor use of everyone's time. It wastes your time because you need to document extraneous, repetitive information. It wastes your teammates' time because they need to stop their work and wait for a response from you instead of making a reasonable guess.

As a PM, one of the best ways to delegate is to take responsibility for defining (and evaluating) success, and then asking your teammates to be responsible for coming up with a solution. For error messages, you might define success as all error messages using a specific component from the UI library and the text following the sentence structure of the existing error messages.

Teach your teammates how to answer questions on their own, including things like where to look up style guidelines and common components. If you don't already have a list of style guidelines and design principles, this might be the time to create them. If you're holding all the rules in your head, you're forcing yourself to be a bottleneck.

Finally, set up checkpoints to review the work to make sure it meets your definition of success. For example, you might ask them to show all of their new work at weekly demos or to let you know whenever new code is checked in. If the work doesn't meet your definition of success, reflect on whether you need a clearer definition of what success means, better training, or both.

DON'T TREAT RULES AS SET-IN-STONE ⚡

There's a myth many PMs implicitly believe that you're supposed to follow all the rules and processes. After all, rules are meant to be followed, right? As it turns out, no. Not always.

THANK YOU FOR BREAKING THE RULES

Noah Weiss, VP of Product at Slack, found himself in a tough spot when he wanted to offer free trials of the premium version of the product. His team's first attempt had failed: not only did offering a free trial on the first day not bring in more revenue, it confused users who had heard the product was free and scared them away. Their second attempt also failed: forcing all users into the trial *did* create huge revenue gains, but it was unacceptably negative for activation. The CEO told him unequivocally to cancel the project and not waste any more resources on it.

Weiss considered his situation, and came up with a promising solution. They could offer the free trial of premium only after someone had used the free product for a week. He believed this iteration would mitigate the downsides of the first two experiments while preserving the gains. He knew a way to run the experiment quickly, and his relationship and reputation with the CEO was strong. Weiss decided it was worth the risk, as all his research on other products showed that trials added a lot of value.

Weiss set up a small team to build out the third experiment. It was a huge success. The CEO thanked him in front of the company: "Thank you for persevering. Even though I said it wouldn't work and not to do it, that kind of grit and scrappiness is exactly what's gonna make us successful in the long run."

As a PM, you're measured by the outcomes you create. If you break a rule and something goes wrong, you will probably just be told not to do that again. As many people say, it's easier to ask for forgiveness than to get permission.

Use your judgment and ask your coworkers to learn which rules are bendable, and only do it when you feel confident that the benefit is worth the risk.[6]

GET YOUR TEAM EXCITED ABOUT WHAT COMES NEXT ⚡

When people are focused only on their current work, they often want to take the time to get it just right. It doesn't seem like there's any downside to taking an extra week to polish a corner case or do more research. It can be hard to get their buy-in to be more action-oriented because it seems like all risk and no reward.

When you're faced with this, it can help to spend time with your team envisioning the amazing long-term future you're building towards. This will help build up some enthusiasm for the work that comes next. When your teammates are excited about the next project, they'll start to share your eagerness to move more quickly, and they'll see the benefit in being more action-oriented.

SHARE YOUR MONTHLY PRIORITIES WITH YOUR TEAM ⚡⚡

As you advance in your career, it becomes harder for those around you to know what you're working on.

You can share a brief update on your priorities for each month (and how you did on last month's priorities) with the people on your team, your manager, and your cross-functional partners. This achieves a few goals:

- It helps people understand how busy you are so they'll have realistic expectations of how much time you're spending on the things they care about.

- It shares context with your team about what kinds of things you're working on.

- It lets you be a role model for others on your team; they can see what kinds of work you do and how much you do.

- It avoids the resentment or loss of credibility that can happen if people think you're not doing enough.

- It can improve your own morale by giving you space to acknowledge the work you do.

Some PMs send updates on the priorities as they go; others write a summary at the end of the month.

SET UP REGULAR WORKSHOP TIME TO OPTIMIZE YOUR SCHEDULE ⚡⚡

As a product leader, you might hit a point where 1:1s and ad-hoc meetings aren't enough to support your teams.

One way to scale is to set up pre-defined weekly "workshop" hours, where teams can sign up to bring product topics to you and the engineering and design leaders. This ensures the right people are in the room for product discussions and frees up your 1:1s to be more about personal development.

---

6   Obviously, don't break ethical, legal, or safety rules.

It often takes some iteration to make workshop hours effective for you and your team. Figure out who should attend and how often teams should bring their work. Consider using the Do/Try/Consider framework to make your feedback clear.[7]

CLEAR ROADBLOCKS FOR YOUR TEAM ⚡⚡

Once you've built relationships across the organization and earned credibility, you can use those relationships to clear roadblocks for your team.

When cross-functional collaboration seems to be getting stuck, try bringing it up semi-casually with the leader of that function to see if they're aware of the problem. They might be able to understand what's going wrong and help you fix the problem.

For example, one PM was frustrated because his data scientist was taking a long time to analyze the results of an experiment. The PM's manager talked to the head of data science and explained how important it was to get results quickly. The head of data science was able to redistribute some work and the PM got their analysis the next day.

To do this well, you want to ensure that the tone is one of collaborative problem solving and helping each other out, not tattling. If it seems like you're blaming the person on the other team, you might make things worse by creating animosity.

REMOTE WORK

In March 2020, many PMs found themselves facing a new reality as companies switched—abruptly—to work-from-home during the coronavirus pandemic. For Dian Rosanti, Senior VP of Product Management at Gojek, leading teams while remote was nothing new. Rosanti had been working with geographically dispersed teams for the past seven years and had built up a library of best practices. By thoughtfully adjusting to the new pressures of a pandemic and social isolation, she was able to help her team and herself stay effective, and share what she learned with other PMs.[8]

Here are Rosanti's best practices for remote work:

- **Manage Expectations:** Use a stakeholder management framework like RACI (pg 237) to let each person know how they're expected to contribute to a project. Ask people to share their working hours and the best ways to reach them for various types of conversations or requests. Have teams and individuals create an agreement for how quickly they will respond to questions (for example, within 48 hours).

- **Use work tracking software:** Rosanti uses Asana to document goals, meeting notes, key decisions, cross-functional communication, and portfolio tracking. This enables people across departments to stay in sync, see the current state, and recall past decisions. It also makes it easy to appreciate your teammates' work and course-correct if necessary, because it makes work visible.

- **Protect your time:** It's easy to lose your boundaries when working remotely. Meetings can creep in and leave you without enough continuous focus time for creative work. Consolidating meetings, holding async standups (people send their update to a chat room), and setting "no meeting" hours can help.

---

7   Read more about this on pg 299

8   Watch "Product Management in the Time of Corona" from GoTalk at https://www.youtube.com/watch?v=4MmJ1w3Z_yY

- **Reduce communication overload:** When teams move remote, the amount of emails and chats can get overwhelming. Set social norms to encourage mindfulness around how your message will affect others: default to BCC for FYI emails to minimize reply-all noise, don't reply if you don't have something important to add, send updates on a predictable schedule.

- **Ask people how they're doing outside of work:** When people work remotely there are fewer natural opportunities for serendipitous watercooler conversations. You can set aside the first few minutes of team meetings for casual conversations and ask people to share something personal in their check-ins. You might even set up an open zoom meeting where anyone on can drop in to chat and hang-out. It might feel strange to talk about your life outside of work, but it's a proven way to strengthen relationships.

- **Create space for unstructured communication and bonding:** A silly chat channel, like one for posting pictures of cats, for posting memes, or for typing random things in all capital letters, can be a great way to encourage team bonding.[9] It gives you a chance to get to know your coworkers and build community.

- **Meet in-person once a quarter if you can:** While remote team-bonding is improving, it's a good idea (barring any worldwide pandemics) to get the whole team together once a quarter. Simple things like eating lunch together or going on a walk for coffee help you see each other as real people and make future work easier. Otherwise, consider fun online team-building events, such as virtual cooking classes.

Even with all the best practices, working in a pandemic is not the same as ordinary remote work. Rosanti found that her team needed to revisit objectives and compress prioritization cycles to help the business adapt. From a personal perspective, she also emphasized the importance of managing one's time and energy: flexible schedules, frequency goals, putting everything on a calendar, and practicing gratitude helped her adjust to the isolation.[10]

---

9   #capital_hill was a delightful, surrealist chat room at Asana where we would debate whether a taco is a sandwich and other random ideas.

10   An example of frequency goals is committing to exercise three times a week, without setting a fixed time.

KEY TAKEAWAYS

- **Set up a system to keep track of your work:** Don't live out of your email inbox or memory. If you always choose your work based on the most recent or most urgent request, you'll underinvest in important work.

- **Be honest with yourself about how much time you actually have:** Once you accept that you can't do it all, it's much easier to delete, defer, delegate, or diminish the extra work. You'll feel better about sharing early work and doing the "quick and dirty" version.

- **Make time for the important work:** Block off time on your calendar to tackle your most important work. Don't let the small, urgent tasks crowd out the work you really need to do. It's hard to say no to that other work, but it's critical to ensure you're spending your time in the way that's most helpful to your team, your company, and yourself.

- **PMing is an active role:** PMing isn't about getting the right people into a room and letting them make decisions. As a PM you need to form your own opinion about what is right, and then overcome any obstacles in the way. If people disagree or block your progress, it's your responsibility to find a way forward. You need to figure out what needs to be done and do it.

- **Tell people before they ask:** It's not enough to just do the right things, you also need to let the people around you *know* that you're on top of everything so that they can relax and let you handle it. Respond to people quickly, even if it's just to tell them that you'll get back to them by the end of the week.

STRATEGIC SKILLS

PART E

STRATEGIC SKILLS

STRATEGIC SKILLS

STRATEGIC WORK IS critical for a PM to invest in because it sets the direction that a team heads in. It protects the value of product and execution work by making sure they fit into the larger picture. Knowing the long-term vision helps teams make better product decisions.

Without strategic thinking and vision, teams often get stuck in local maxima. They continue to improve their initial idea incrementally, but they don't realize that incremental changes will never deliver a big enough improvement.

In this section, we'll develop the skills to steer our teams in the right direction.

- **Product Strategy Overview** (pg 169) will teach us what strategy is and what it means to be strategic. We'll learn the three components of a product strategy and frameworks for creating a strategy.

- **Vision** (pg 179) will teach us how to create a compelling vision for our product. We'll learn about the "work backwards" framework and see how an ambitious vision can help teams succeed.

- **Strategic Framework** (pg 184) will teach us how to connect our vision to the business and market to create a winning product. We'll learn frameworks such as the 4 P's, 5 C's, and Porter's 5 forces.

- **Roadmapping and Prioritization** (pg 193) will teach us how to create a long-term roadmap for accomplishing our vision. We'll learn how to prioritize competing goals, how to gather feedback from customer-facing teams, and how to say 'no.'

- **Team Goals** (pg 206) will teach us how to create effective goals that motivate our teams. We'll learn about OKRs, counter metrics, and setting targets.

You'll use your strategic skills primarily during planning cycles, for example in preparation for the beginning of a year or before starting a new initiative.

CHAPTER 14

PRODUCT STRATEGY OVERVIEW

COMPANIES HAVE LIMITED resources, and the "best" products don't always win. It doesn't matter how fast you move if you're going in the wrong direction. It doesn't matter how well-designed your product is if people don't use it.

That's why, at some point in your career, you'll probably hear that you need to be more strategic. It might leave you wondering, "Now what?"

When I first got this feedback, it was a gut punch. If I'm bad at strategy, how can I ever be an amazing PM?

But I misunderstood something that was very, very important.

Strategic skills are not innate; I could learn them. I could dissect the key components—vision, strategic framework, and roadmap—and learn tangible practices to improve them. I could solicit input from key sources, follow trends, evaluate risks, and pull these together into a clearer direction for the product.

Saying "you need to be more strategic" isn't like saying, "you're bad at math and always will be." It's more like saying, "you don't know geometry and you should learn it." This is a skill that you can learn—and that's what this chapter, and this part, is about.

WHAT DOES IT MEAN TO BE STRATEGIC?

Being strategic is about deciding where you want the product to go and making a plan to get there. It's about understanding the industry, market, and trends to predict what will be important in the future. It's about creating a vision, setting ambitious goals, and convincing your team that you're heading in the right direction. It's about evaluating different approaches and picking the best one. It's about sharing ideas for the big opportunities your team should work on next. It's about laying out the steps that get your team from start to finish.

Early in your career, you usually work with the strategy that was created by your product leader. You probably have some kind of framework for how you're choosing projects and prioritizing work, but you haven't advocated for that framework or painted a bold picture of the long-term goal that your team is working towards. Typically, while you help craft the details of your team's goals, you don't set the direction.

As you advance in your career, you'll need to expand your strategic skills. You'll need to be able to identify and research new strategic opportunities. You'll be expected to create a vision for addressing those opportunities and define what success looks like in ways that go beyond the pre-existing plan. You should be able to create a long-term roadmap that shows how all of the work fits together to achieve ambitious results. You should also be able to communicate clearly to drive alignment on the strategy and ensure that everyone on the team understands what they're working towards.

STRATEGIC VS. NOT STRATEGIC

Since it can be difficult to understand what being strategic means, here are a few examples.

Vision

- **Not strategic:** Prioritizing projects based on the number of customer requests or the sales team ranking.

- **Strategic:** Painting an inspiring vision of what the product could be in two years and choosing projects that work towards that vision. Connecting the dots for stakeholders about how each project contributes to the larger goals they value.

Competitive framework

- **Not strategic:** Analyzing the features competitors have and using that to guide your roadmap.

- **Strategic:** Identifying a valuable customer segment that the competitor handles poorly and then prioritizing must-have projects to focus on winning over those customers.

Strategic framework

- **Not strategic:** People aren't quite sure why you're saying yes or no to various pieces of work or what you're optimizing for. Some people's pet ideas keep getting resurfaced and they're frustrated that you haven't explained why the team isn't working on them.

- **Strategic:** You've written up a clear, opinionated framework about which bets you're making and why.

Alignment with company strategy

- **Not strategic:** Choosing a direction based on what you've learned from customers in your own research.

- **Strategic:** Understanding the company's strategic direction, as well as the goals of other teams across the product and business, and using that to choose a direction that supports the bigger picture.

Systems thinking

- **Not strategic:** Making short-sighted decisions without noticing the long term or global implications. Inappropriately prioritizing the short term over the long term. Prioritizing the team over the company. Focusing on parts rather than the whole.

- **Strategic:** Spotting trends and connections to create better solutions. Considering how decisions will affect the bigger picture.

Long-term roadmapping

- **Not strategic:** Talking about a big idea vaguely, without a plan of how to get there.

- **Strategic:** Writing up a quarter-by-quarter plan of what work to take on, and in what order, to achieve the vision. Highlighting which new skills the team needs to develop and where a larger team size would be most valuable.

Execution

- **Not strategic:** The team always seems to be playing catch-up and can't find time for strategic work. Stuck doing incremental work. Not making progress on the long-term roadmap.

- **Strategic:** Making space for strategic work, even when it involves tough prioritization calls. Working with leadership to ensure the team has what it needs, whether that's more staffing or permission to drop non-strategic work.

Goal setting

- **Not strategic:** Setting goals based on launching a predetermined solution and hitting the targets that you expect the solution to achieve.

- **Strategic:** Rallying the team around a single key success metric. Setting ambitious targets that change how the team looks at problems and finding new solutions.

Planning ahead

- **Not strategic:** Focusing 100% on the upcoming launch and delivering it perfectly.

- **Strategic:** Once engineers have started working on the current launch, carving out time for researching, sketching, and forming opinions about what might come next.

Autonomy

- **Not strategic:** Working on the projects that your manager has asked you to work on.

- **Strategic:** Advocating to leadership which projects you believe the team should work on next. Advocating for new teams to be spun up.

Advocacy

- **Not strategic:** You know what your strategy is and even wrote it down somewhere, but the engineers and designers on your team (and your manager) couldn't say what it is if asked.

- **Strategic:** Everyone on the team can recite a similar explanation of the strategy and goals. Leaders across the company understand your strategy and why it's important.

If you're getting feedback that you're not strategic enough and can't figure out why, try showing the list to your manager and ask about the areas in need of focus.

WHAT IS A PRODUCT STRATEGY?

There's no standardized definition of what a product strategy is.

As you might imagine, this can create a lot of confusion. Many PMs think they have a strategy, and yet their manager keeps telling them they need to *create* a strategy. What's going on?

There are three separate components that can make up a strategy. When there's confusion, it's usually because one of them is missing.

The three components of a product strategy are the product vision, the strategic framework, and the road-map.

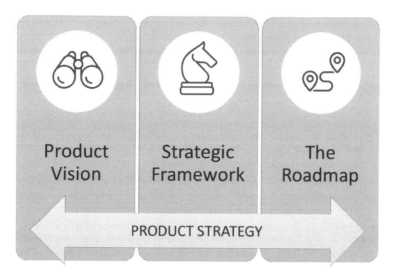

Often, the head of product or CEO creates a strategy for the entire company, directors create a more focused strategy for their group, and individual PMs create even more focused strategies for their teams. This section will describe what you need to know about each component and how to create your own product strategy.

THE PRODUCT VISION

The **product vision** is an inspiring description of the future we want to head towards. It could be high fidelity like a demo video, low fidelity like a storyboard, or even something as simple as a one-sentence vision statement.

A great product vision includes some specific details, insights, or opinions that bring the vision to life. The details will change over time, but the vision provides a North Star that the team and customers can get excited about.

Why have a product vision? The product vision inspires people and helps them quickly understand what they are working towards. It helps them understand how all of the individual pieces of work add up to something meaningful. Once they're bought into the vision, people will work hard to achieve it.

Chapter 15: Vision (pg 179) goes into this in more detail.

THE STRATEGIC FRAMEWORK

The **strategic framework** is like the spec for your strategy.

It includes the high-level framing, goals, and principles of the strategy. It describes the target market. It talks about what bets you're making and why.

The framework aligns people to the approach for achieving your vision. When done well, it helps people remember the important parts of the strategy—for example, with concise taglines and memorable names for important concepts.

Why have a strategic framework? When people understand the framework, they're empowered to make good, fast decisions on their own. Also, if the framework is clearly defined, any erroneous assumptions can be more easily identified and fixed.

Chapter 16: Strategic Framework (pg 184) goes into this in more detail.

THE ROADMAP

The **roadmap** is the prioritized, sequenced, and roughly-costed plan of work that leads to achieving the vision. The roadmap shows which steps come first and which key milestones come next. It gives a rough sense of the scale of the problem (e.g., will it take a year or ten years to achieve the vision?).

Why have a roadmap? The roadmap aligns people on the steps it will take to achieve the vision. The details of the roadmap will change over time, but the concreteness of the roadmap helps ground people on how much work is required and how many people need to be hired. The roadmap also provides a baseline against which to track progress, so that the team can assess if the current plan is working or needs to change.

Chapter 17: Roadmapping and Prioritization (pg 193) goes into this in more detail.

CREATING A PRODUCT STRATEGY

You don't need to own an entire product to create a product strategy. You can, and should, create a strategy for any scope that encompasses multiple launches. Smaller strategies should ladder up to the broader strategies.

Creating a product strategy should be a collaborative process. You want to focus on getting buy-in from all of the important stakeholders. After all, the point of a strategy is to align people in a common direction. That said, most stakeholders will not be deeply involved in the day-to-day creation of the strategy.

MAKING THE TIME

Many PMs get stuck feeling that they don't have enough time for strategic thinking. There's a ton of urgent work and they already feel like they're behind.

If you haven't already, go read Chapter 13: Time Management (pg 151).

The mindset shift

To make time for strategic work, a PM needs to make the mindset shift from "I'm a great PM for my team" to "I'm a great PM for my whole company."

You already show a small version of this mindset when you balance the needs of different members of your team. I never hear PMs say they can't make time for their designer because the engineers need them so much, or vice versa. No one likes to disappoint a teammate, but PMs know they need to support the whole team.

Imagine that your immediate team is one of your teammates, and the company is another teammate. You can't take the side of your team over what's best for the company. You need to support both.

Once you've made the mindset shift from being a great PM for your team to being a great PM for your company, making time should become much easier. You still won't *want* to drop work that would help your team, but it becomes an option you can consider against the tradeoffs.

Understand the importance of strategic work

Since making time is a tradeoff, you need to start by understanding how important strategic and visioning work is.

For many teams, visioning is critical. Imagine if the team at Apple had been so caught up in the day-to-day work of designing the new iPod that they didn't take a step back and realize they should be designing an iPhone instead.

You can always find incremental work to do by continuing along the current path. There will always be more customer requests to satisfy and more features to build. But, maybe there's a new direction that would deliver even more impact.

By the time your current project wraps up, it will be too late to pursue innovative new directions for the next cycle. If you want to reconsider the strategy, you need to start early enough.

What if the engineering lead says you can't spare any time for strategic work?

Here's the truth about your execution work: it will always expand to fit the amount of time you give it.

There are times you need to focus on execution, for example when a big launch is coming up. But, most of the time your team and the company will be better off if you make some time for strategic thinking.

Talk to your engineering lead and listen to their concerns. Once you know the concerns, you can handle them appropriately.

Some possible scenarios include:

- **They don't see the importance of strategic work**. If you can't convince them with your logic, you might need to put in a few extra hours to create a quick strategy draft on your own so that you can show them the value.

- **They want to stay engineering-driven, and not have a PM tell them what to do**. Include the engineers in the strategic work. You can frame the strategy as "these are your ideas; I'm just going to help put them together so the rest of the company can see the importance of our work."

- **They think you're currently underperforming as a PM.** Address those issues first. You might put in a few extra hours to create a light strategy without taking time away from your team.

- **They want a project manager, not a product manager.** This is a tricky situation. Work with your manager to align on expectations. Early on in your career this can still be a great opportunity, but you might need to look for other roles to continue growing.

Remember that strategy is an important piece of being an effective PM, and it's important that you prioritize it appropriately.

Consider quick approaches

Creating a strategy usually doesn't take as long as many people fear.

Here are some quick approaches that can work well when you have a small area that isn't too controversial or mission-critical:

- **Draft and Feedback:** Jot down a quick draft of the three strategy components and share that draft with your teammates. Having something in writing gives people something concrete to give feedback on and gets the ball rolling. If you keep it intentionally short and unpolished, you can avoid the situation where people wish they were looped in earlier.

- **Full-Day or Half-Day Strategy Retreat:** Gather teammates and stakeholders together to share ideas and discuss direction.

- **30% Time:** Over one-to-three weeks, spend a third of your time researching and brainstorming. At that point, you'll have one or more ideas for possible directions and can decide how much more time to invest.

The next section covers the approach for larger areas that are more critical or more controversial.

CREATING A LARGE STRATEGY

When your team is small, you can often get by with drafting a strategy alone and then asking the team for feedback.

When the stakes get higher, the team gets bigger, or controversy builds, then it's important to create the strategy collaboratively.

Here is a process for creating strategies from Asana's Head of Product, Alex Hood.

Step 1: Dive into lots of input

A strategy should not be designed in a vacuum.

Review the strategies and vision that this strategy will contribute to (for example, the company strategy). Does this strategy build upon or enhance the declared product strategy? At a minimum, it should tie to it directly. Better, it accelerates the overall product strategy.

Review pertinent insights from customers, tests run, competitive analysis, or any other sources. Go broad on getting inputs without burning too much time upfront.

Step 2: Kick it off

The kickoff sets the tone for the process. People might be nervous about creating a new strategy, but you can set them at ease.

Have the right stakeholders at the meeting. You can create a DACI chart (pg 237). Share summaries of what you learned by reviewing new insights. Share how this new strategy will layer into existing higher-level visions or strategies so that no one thinks you are reinventing the wheel. People will be more supportive of strategy work that enhances prior art.

Some questions to ask at the kickoff include:

- What strategic questions are top of mind?

- Are there examples of decisions where a better strategy would have helped?

- Is there anything timely coming up related to the strategy (e.g., an important milestone or decision)?

- What parts of the strategy would each person like to get involved with?

Establish a timeline with key objectives and check-ins.

Step 3: Checkpoint 1—key hypotheses

A product strategy entails several key hypotheses—the assumptions or assertions that drive your product decisions. For example, you might have hypotheses around a build-versus-buy decision, pricing strategy, market research, data analysis, or engineering framework.

Split these hypotheses into different workstreams (with owners and participants) so that individual teams can tackle them and report back.

At the first checkpoint, each team can present their hypothesis and the reasons they believe it. Then, come up with the most important set of key questions that are needed to validate or invalidate these hypotheses and discuss a plan how you'll figure out the answers. Keep your list small (two to seven at most). In your check-in, ask stakeholders for their thoughts and ensure people agree that you're asking the right questions.

Step 4: Checkpoint 2—draft strategies/bets

Once teams have researched each workstream, create a draft of the overarching strategies. For example, a hypothesis around freemium pricing might get solidified into a strategy to give away basic photo editing for free but charge for advanced photo filters.

Write down strong assertions. Take a stand and be controversial. Come up with several candidates for strategies. Get people to co-create, co-edit, break down, and build them up together.

As a final step, create an exercise where you winnow down the list. For example, you can let people vote on their top 30% favorite strategies. Set the context though—it isn't a democracy; their votes are input into your decision.

Beyond the core set of people working on the strategy, you'll also want to get feedback from the larger group of people who will be affected. Ask each stakeholder to be a representative of their team and to check with their team for feedback and buy-in. You don't want to get to the end of the process and learn that the engineering lead didn't let any other engineers know what was going on.

Step 5: Checkpoint 3—declare

At the final checkpoint, partner with the stakeholders to declare your final strategies. This is the time to ensure the strategies are well-understood and to finalize the wording.

Then, use the balance of your time to determine the "so what?". Come in with a list of what the team might/ will do differently because of these pointed strategic decisions. What new work will be started? Use your final check-in to declare and begin execution so that your strategies get traction at their first moment of inception. Starting right away will reassure the team that the effort they put into creating the strategy will have meaning, and it allows you to jump start initiatives without a pause.

You may have a set of people who need to review and approve the new strategy who might not have been involved in the process until this point. At the very least, this usually includes your manager and your manager's manager, but could consist of a broader executive committee. They can be included in this checkpoint, or you can present your strategy to them after it.

Step 6: Create artifacts

Even though your team might have started new work based on the strategy, the strategy isn't finished until it is thoroughly communicated.

Create and roll out a communication strategy for up, down, and across the organization. Create strong visuals, decks, recordings, or documents that people can learn from and refer to. Repeat yourself often and make sure that everyone who should care about the strategy hears about it more than once.

These artifacts help you communicate efficiently in the future. They'll be included in every team's deliverables or brainstorming sessions that impacts your work. Design them to be referenced and reused.

Step 7: Create a scoreboard

Broadcast how you'll be doing and how you'll be keeping score and keep it up to date. This serves as a role model for accountability.

HELP! EXECUTIVES WANT A SAY IN THE STRATEGY, BUT THEY WON'T JOIN MY MEETINGS.

Executives are busy people (see "Working with executives" on pg 276) and they don't always find large team meetings to be good uses of their time. Instead, you can give them dedicated time to share their thoughts.

Some executives are willing to give you a "brain dump" of all of their strategic thoughts before you get started. You can ask them over email, set up a meeting, or join their office hours.

Other executives prefer to give feedback on a draft of your strategy. This approach often works better because important disagreements can hide behind unspoken assumptions. When you take this approach, you'll need to balance how complete the draft is when you share it against how much of your team's work could be wasted if the executive gives feedback that sends you back to the drawing board.

Send the draft in advance, and then set up a 1:1 meeting. Some executives will respond to the draft in writing to avoid the meeting, and that's a fine outcome.

SHARE YOUR STRATEGY AND EVANGELIZE IT

After your strategy is approved, your job is only about half-way done. You need to come up with a communication plan to share and continually reinforce the strategy. You need to advocate for the strategy and get people excited about it.

The tech community often calls this kind of advocacy "evangelism" because you're "preaching" about your idea.

Some ideas for communicating the strategy and getting people excited about it include:

- Create an infomercial-like vision presentation.

- Share your vision and strategy at the team meeting.

- Present your vision to the company at an all-hands meeting.

- Put up posters with key strategic points or printouts from the vision.

- In speaking and writing, explicitly describe how decisions and feedback connect to the strategy.

- Answer people's questions by referring them back to the applicable part of the strategy.

PMs and product leaders almost always underestimate how much they need to remind people of the strategy. If you think you've communicated the strategy enough, try randomly quizzing some team members on it; you might be surprised at how much work it takes to make the strategy stick. If you feel like you're constantly repeating yourself, you're probably on the right track!

KEY TAKEAWAYS

- **Strategy is more important than feature work:** It doesn't matter how great your feature is if the product fails. It's no use for your team to work really hard if they're headed in the wrong direction. Many teams waste years on incremental work that doesn't make a big impact. If your team doesn't have a good strategy, creating one should be your top priority.

- **A complete product strategy has a vision, framework, and roadmap:** They work together to paint a picture of where you're heading, why you're going there, and how you'll get there. The vision inspires people. The framework explains the details. The roadmap shows what it will take to deliver.

- **Communicate your strategy until it sticks:** It takes a lot of communication and repetition to help people understand and remember the strategy. Don't assume people remember the relevant pieces of the strategy. Reference the key parts of the strategy in your everyday conversations with your team.

CHAPTER 15

VISION

WHEN LENNY RACHITSKY joined Airbnb, almost 50% of the guests who tried to book an Airbnb failed. They'd found a place where they wanted to stay, but too often they were either rejected or ignored by the host. It was clear this was a problem.

For a year, he and his team tried to attack the problem incrementally. They tried to convince hosts to accept more bookings with reminders and incentives. They tried experiments such as warning the host if they weren't responding quickly enough. Plenty of the experiments were successful, but overall, the team did not see significant improvements on the 50% failure rate.

Rachitsky describes what happened next:

> There was a point at which we kind of flipped the script and wondered, "What if we were to work back-wards from the ideal Airbnb? What would we do if we started Airbnb today?"
>
> We realized the ideal experience is you find a home, you book it, and you're done. You have a home as soon as you find it.
>
> The Instant Book feature actually existed from early on. Some hosts didn't care about approving the guests; they just wanted to accept. But only 5% of hosts were using Instant at that point.
>
> So, the bet we made was to just go big on Instant Book and try to morph the entire marketplace from what it was (less than 5% Instant Book) to all Instant Book. We set this really ambitious goal of 100% Instant Book. We're going to move everyone to instant booking; we realized that's the future of Airbnb.

That ambitious vision was incredibly successful. It helped the team realize they were going down the wrong path when trying to incrementally increase acceptance rate. The 100% target helped the team deprioritize all work that would become obsolete once hosts moved to Instant Book.

Getting to 100% Instant Book is a great target, but on its own, it's an abstract wish. Rachitsky also made the vision tangible: "I made an image of a guy walking through a minefield, where the mines are all the little things that go wrong when a host gets an Instant Booking they don't expect (and thus don't use Instant

Book). For example, guests booking on short notice, or planning to have a party, or bring their dog. Our strategy and roadmap was to defuse each of those mines. That really stuck in people's minds."

RESPONSIBILITIES

BRAINSTORM AN AMBITIOUS VISION ⚡

Get your team together and ask "If we could wave a magic wand, what would the ideal experience be?"

Great visions are often found when you step outside the box because they remove a constraint that everyone assumed was fixed. Sometimes, they'll remove a step in the customer journey, such as in Airbnb's Instant Book. Sometimes, they'll require new technical innovation, such as Apple's voicemail transcription. Sometimes, they'll require a giant investment in a new area, such Google's Street View cars. And, sometimes they'll require a change in societal norms, such as Lyft asking you to get in a car with a stranger.

Here are some questions that can help you create a more ambitious and ideal vision:

- If we were starting a new company from scratch, what would "ideal" look like?

- What's the slowest part, and how could we make it twice, or even ten times as fast?

- What's the most frustrating step, and how could we remove it?

- What would a delightful experience be?

- If a customer didn't understand any technical constraints, what magical thing would they ask for?

- What are some new cutting-edge technologies, inside or outside of our company? Could we use any of them to open up new possibilities?

- If our company was willing to spend any amount of money on this project, what kinds of new things would be possible?

- Who is *not* using our product? Why not? What would it take to win them over?

- How could we double the impact this product makes for our customers?

- What are the market trends, and where do we think the market will be in ten years?

- How are the expectations and habits of our users changing, and does that open up new possibilities?

Once you have a larger vision, you can work backwards to create a roadmap and then decide the first step. You could still choose to do the next obvious piece of incremental work, but you might discover a clever way to get higher impact and be closer to the vision with the same amount of effort.

MAKE YOUR VISION CONCRETE AND INSPIRING ⚡

Once you have an idea of the future you want to create, you need to put it into a format where other people will understand it and be inspired by it. You'll want to share it and see if it resonates with your team and potential customers.

As a rule, a good vision is like an infomercial.

Infomercials always start out with an emotional story about how terrible things are: jars are too difficult to open, my wardrobe is generic and dull, the blender is too annoying to clean. I might have never realized I had that problem before.

The infomercials tell me there is a better way. I can open jars on my own, adorn my t-shirts with rhinestones, and make a smoothie every morning. The spokesperson is so excited about the benefits of these amazing products that I become excited too!

Once we're hooked on the problem and benefit, the infomercial goes into the details to convince us the product will really work. They show us a regular person using the product and how delighted they are with it. They explain the technology that makes the product possible. They go over a handful of different use cases so that you can see how your entire family will benefit.

Depending on your personality, you might be thrilled to share a vision like this, or it might feel unbearably silly. It can be helpful to watch a variety of product leaders introducing their vision, until you find a style that works for you. Some people lean into the silliness and get a bit goofy. Others stay calm and confident. The important thing is to leave people feeling sufficiently inspired.[1]

GROWTH PRACTICES

CHAMPION NEW OPPORTUNITIES OUTSIDE OF YOUR SCOPE ⚡

PMs at the higher levels are expected to make an impact at the company level, not just on their own team. To have this larger impact, you need to discover and advocate for new opportunities.

Dare Obasanjo, a partner group program manager at Microsoft, was looking for ways to grow Bing ad revenue and found an opportunity in the browser strategy. He saw that the biggest driver of ad revenue was the number of searches, and the biggest driver of the number of searches was browser market share. People tend to stick with their browser's default search engine.

Having a popular browser was really important, but Microsoft's browser at the time suffered from compatibility issues and the core engine was so expensive to build that the team didn't have enough engineers to invest in the user experience. Obasanjo realized that Microsoft could solve all of those problems by using the open source Chromium browser engine.

Obasanjo started advocating for changing the browser strategy:

> I realized I should go talk to the browser team. We started those conversations and I spent a lot of time evangelizing to leaders at the company.
>
> Microsoft has a big email culture, so I would advocate in various discussions and those discussions would be forwarded to VPs and directors of engineering. When a company leader started a discussion on the topic, I'd reach out and ask to meet and talk. When we met I'd explain my rationale.

That advocacy influenced some leaders to evolve their perspectives and became part of the decision-making process that eventually led to Microsoft adopting Chromium in the Edge browser.

The insights that lead to new opportunities can come from anywhere, but they often spark from an idea that's tangentially related to your day job, as Obasanjo's did. He started from his area of expertise and followed the

---

1   Try searching YouTube for "<product name> keynote" for various products to find these videos.

thread to an opportunity outside of his scope. He painted a vision of how a change in strategy could solve problems and help the company achieve its goals. Then, he put in the work to champion that vision with company leaders and followed through to influence the change.

In addition to helping the company, championing new opportunities is a way to take your career growth into your own hands. When you discover a new, greenfield opportunity, often you'll be tapped as the person to lead the initiative. This can move you into leadership roles much faster than waiting to be promoted into a pre-existing initiative.

ORGANIZE COMPANY-WIDE VISION BRAINSTORMING DAYS ⚡⚡

A **vision brainstorming day** is a special day, kind of like a hackathon, where people share their ideas for the future vision of your product. Unlike a hackathon, people don't need working code—they can share their vision in whatever format they like.

You can adapt the day to work for you. Here are some tips based on past experiences:

- Invite people with innovative perspectives from across the organization. Often, people outside of the immediate product organization are better at seeing past constraints.

- Create prize categories based on the directions you'd like to encourage. You can have categories for best overall, most futuristic, biggest money-maker, customer favorite, etc.

- If you're having trouble getting people to participate, consider blocking off people's schedules for preparation, and not just demos. Or, you can make participation mandatory for a subset of people.

- Have people insert their visions into a shared deck for demos, and include which person is "up next" on each intro template slide. This greatly reduces the transition time between each demo.

- Follow up afterwards to see if you want to add any of the new ideas to the roadmap, or spin up any new teams.

Although the primary goal of a vision brainstorming day is to elicit innovative ideas and directions, it has other benefits too. It serves as a creative outlet, team-bonding event, and a strategic practice session. It can also help reinforce a culture of visionary thinking, as well as expose team members to multiple examples of what good vision can look like.

FRAMEWORKS

WORK BACKWARDS

Amazon popularized the framework of working backwards with their approach of starting with the press release. This approach can be extended to any size of work, from an individual feature, to a team charter, to a full product.

It might seem counterintuitive, but working backward can help you come up with much better solutions than working forward. When you work forward, you tend to be biased by what already exists, what seems easy, or what will help you hit your quarterly goals.

It's true that your idealistic vision might take years to achieve, but great companies stick around for decades. If you start taking the steps to work towards your ideal vision, you'll be in a much better place in a few years than if you go in the wrong direction quarter after quarter.

KEY TAKEAWAYS

- **Be ambitious and inspiring:** There's a time and a place for pragmatism, but the vision isn't that place. You can work backwards from your vision to a more pragmatic plan later. To be good at visioning, you need to push aside all the constraints and reasons why things will be hard, and figure out what the actual ideal experience would be. If you're not excited about your vision, it's not ready yet.

- **A great vision is like an infomercial:** Sell the pain, then sell the solution. Include the key details and insights that convince people that the solution will really work.

- **Find green-field opportunities to champion:** A great way to accelerate your career growth is to identify new opportunities that no one in your company is working on, and then to create a vision for those opportunities. That vision can influence the company direction, and you might even get a chance to lead the new initiative.

CHAPTER 16

STRATEGIC FRAMEWORK

YOU HAVE YOUR vision. Perhaps, to customers and to your team, you sell a world where medications are safe, trusted, and reliably taken. Where people don't wind up in the hospital because of bad medication interactions. Where people don't find themselves lost in search results, fretting about side effects that have negligible risk. Where people take the medications they're prescribed at the appropriate dosage, at the right interval—for as long as they need it.

That's your vision, and it's motivational and inspiring. But it isn't enough. You need to understand how that vision will be achieved.

The strategic framework explains the principles behind that vision. It helps connect the dots between feature ideas, team strategy, and company strategy.

The strategic framework can look very different from one strategy to another. You'll need to identify which principals, insights, or decisions are important drivers of the strategy. Then, depending on how complex and controversial your strategy is, you'll figure out how much explanation you need.

Sometimes, all that's needed is a few paragraphs with a simple explanation of the approach, such as "discover and remove each of the roadblocks a customer faces in this flow." Other times, the framework needs to include pages of explanation and diagrams to explain how all the pieces fit together.

One great example of a strategic framework is a memo sent by the CEO of Slack, *We Don't Sell Saddles Here.*[1] In it, Stewart Butterfield lays out that their vision is organizational transformation and dramatically improved communication. Their strategy, however, is not to toute how their features will help businesses. That's useless; people don't know they want Slack, so they won't care about the details.

Instead, their strategy is to sell innovation—the transformation Slack brings—and do an "exceptional, near-perfect job of execution." He lays out that, since people don't know they want Slack, there is no tolerance for flaws. They must be excellent.

By aligning your team behind a vision and a strategy, your team will not just be more motivated, but also more empowered to make more effective decisions. The strategy ensures that your team won't just be moving quickly; they'll also be moving in a direction that has a good chance of success. And, if there happens to be a flaw in your strategy, it'll be much easier to spot and fix when you have something concrete for your teammates to review.

RESPONSIBILITIES

LEARN YOUR BUSINESS, MARKET, AND INDUSTRY TO SPOT OPPORTUNITIES AND OBSTACLES ⚡

The best product doesn't always win.

TiVo created the first popular DVR (Digital Video Recorder), and its product was much better than the cable company DVRs. But, the cable companies bundled their DVRs with their cable subscriptions. TiVo couldn't compete with that distribution model.

Products need great distribution, a great business model, a great brand, and great competitive positioning to win. All these aspects should play into your strategy.

Here are some questions to consider as you're developing a product strategy.

Business:

- What is the overall company mission, vision, and strategy? Competitive positioning? Top priorities?

- Are any of the company's priorities new or shifting?

- Are there any key company milestones coming up, such as a big conference or a fundraising round?

- What does the company see as its strengths, weaknesses, opportunities, and threats? (See "SWOT Analysis" on pg 188)

- What are the different business teams within your company, and what are their goals?

- What is the company's business model?

- How does your team fit into all of the above?

Market and industry:

- Who are your target users? What identifies them? How do they behave? How do they choose products?

- Who are the competitors in your space? How are they similar to or different from you? What do they do well? Where do they leave an opportunity?

- How is your product currently viewed in the market?

- What are the different ways to slice up the market? How big are each of those slices? What are the requirements to go after the different slices?

- What are the trends that could affect your business?

- What opportunities or obstacles do the above research lead to?

If your team has a product marketer, partner with them to explore the business, market, and industry. Otherwise, you'll need to explore this on your own.

GET CRISP ON YOUR TARGET CUSTOMER AND PAIN POINTS ⚡

It helps to be very clear on who your target customer is and what their top pain points are. Small differences in how people understand the target customer can create big problems later on.

Mckenzie Lock saw this when she was head of product at a consumer-facing startup. When she started, some people thought their customers' top pain point was the amount of time it took to find the product they wanted. Lock and team had the strategic intuition that saving money was a more meaningful value proposition than saving time. This theory was supported by the data: one of their most popular features was real-time price notifications.

She and her team invested in user research to validate their intuition. One thing they tried was running Facebook Ads with different value propositions. They saw the ads focused on saving money converted better than the others. That research gave her the confidence to reorganize the company's product strategy around getting their customers the best deals.

Surprisingly, many companies don't have an accurate view of *why* customers are choosing their products. They might know what features are being used, but haven't connected that to the deeper problems the product solves for people.

To figure out which details matter, consider factors that would affect:

- Ad targeting

- Positioning and messaging

- Sales outreach

- Customer training

- The size of the potential customer base

- Feature prioritization.

For example, will you start with power users or basic users? Will you be upselling existing customers or gaining brand new ones? Which competitors do you think you can win customers from? Which use cases will be a good match, and which are out of scope?

How painful are the pain points you're going after? Does your solution feel 10x better for your target customers? It's no use to go after a huge market if you can't convince its customers that your product is worth the effort to switch to. It can be a good strategy to start with a smaller market that you know you can win, and expand from there.

You can narrow in on your target customer and their pain points by partnering with marketing, sales, customer success, solutions engineers, user research, user operations, and any other customer facing teams.

GROWTH PRACTICES

ADDRESS QUESTIONS AND TRADEOFFS IN YOUR STRATEGIC FRAMEWORK ⚡

The goal of a strategic framework is to create alignment. It needs to answer the questions that people are likely to challenge you with, and it needs to provide the context and guardrails to ensure your team doesn't go off track.

If you listen well, it can be easy to figure out which questions to address.

- Is your manager constantly asking about a pet project? Make sure the strategy explains why it's in or out.

- Does the head of sales always ask about expansion? If so, include a section on expansion.

- Is there a recurring debate over prioritization? Make sure the strategic framework addresses it.

- Is there another direction the team might have gone? Explain why you chose the one you did.

- What solutions are your team considering? The strategy should provide a philosophical framework that steers people towards the best ones.

Once you have the first draft, invest the time to simplify and clarify the strategy. If it feels complicated, keep upleveling until you get to the fundamentals. For each item, ask why, and then group things together that share a common "why."

ALIGN YOUR STRATEGY WITH THE BIGGER PICTURE ⚡

At most companies, there will be a hierarchy of strategies that mostly aligns with the org chart. Each feature area has a strategy that fits into the larger product strategy, which might in turn fit into the strategy for a product line, which fits into the divisional strategy, and ultimately into the company strategy.

Your strategy needs to align with all of the strategies above it and fit in well with all of the other strategies at the company. It's no good to focus your team on a strategy of winning an international market if your company strategy is to stay domestic.

Make sure you seek out the other strategies at the company. Some companies will keep this information in a centralized place, while at others you'll need to reach out to people to ask if there are any strategic documents or presentations you can see. Not every team will have a vision, strategic framework, *and* a roadmap, but most will have at least one or two of them. You can also ask various leaders directly about their strategy when you set up "getting to know you" meetings.

When you write your strategy, don't assume that other people will understand how your strategy fits into the bigger picture. Make the connection explicit. Use exact phrases from the higher level strategy. Explain the step-by-step reasoning of how your strategy serves the goals of the higher level strategy. If the company is focused on growing revenue and you want to prioritize user growth, you'll need to lay out the exact path that turns user growth into revenue.

CONCEPTS AND FRAMEWORKS

CUSTOMER PURCHASE DECISION-MAKING PROCESS

There are many frameworks to model the decision-making process, but two of the most common are AIDA and REAN.

AIDA models customer decisions as Attention (or Awareness) -> Interest -> Desire -> Action.

- **Attention:** You need to get the customer's attention somehow. A snappy email heading, perhaps? A snazzy ad? Or maybe a mention from a trusted friend or website?

- **Interest:** Now that you have the customer's attention, you need to get them interested in your offering. What are the advantages or benefits of your product?

- **Desire:** With the customer's interest piqued, you need to convince the customer that they want your product.

- **Action:** Finally, with the customer desiring your product, they take action to purchase the product.

REAN expands this to add on post-purchase behavior.

- **Reach:** The customer is aware of your product.

- **Engage:** The customer is engaged and considering your product.

- **Activate:** The customer takes action to purchase the product.

- **Nurture:** The customer has purchased the product, and it's now your responsibility to nurture this relationship.

You can use these frameworks to think about the market you want to go after and where you'll need to direct your attention. You might find that getting the customer's attention will be fairly easy, but the "action" part (getting the user to actually switch from your competitor to you) will be more difficult.

MARKETING MIX (4 PS)

The "Marketing Mix" (also called the 4 Ps) is a way to understand the different aspects of a product's approach to marketing.

- **Product:** This is, of course, the actual item being offered. It should cater to a customer's wants or needs.

- **Price:** The price will determine how many and what type of customers purchase the product. Pricing can be more complex for online products and services as compared to physical products. For example, an online storage service could have a one-month free trial, followed by monthly or yearly subscriptions (which are discounted for non-profits), with additional "a la carte" purchases for an automatic backup utility.

- **Promotion:** Promotion encompasses all forms of advertising, PR, word of mouth, and sales staff. For example, promotion for a kids' product could include freebies given out to influential bloggers.

- **Place:** A physical product's distribution ("place") can include things such as online sales through Amazon, opening their own stores like Apple, distribution in retail stores, and sales through their own website. Greater distribution is not always better; many companies prefer to control the sales experience by limiting the sales channels. For online products, "place" might just be a single website, or it might include bundling the product with another company's offerings.

For online products, promotion can become very complex. A lot of products are competing for the customer's attention, and advertising is often insufficient to drive sales.

SWOT ANALYSIS

SWOT analysis is a structure to analyze companies and products.

- **Strengths:** Strengths are the *internal* factors that benefit a product. This can include anything about the costs, product features, company culture, reputation, infrastructure, or other aspects. For example, in considering launching the Kindle, one of Amazon's strengths would be that it is already the place where customers buy books online.

- **Weaknesses:** Weaknesses are *internal* factors that introduce challenges for a product. For example, since Amazon had not created a physical device prior to the Kindle, a weakness might be that it doesn't have experience with manufacturing.

- **Opportunities:** Opportunities have an *external* focus and relate to factors such as market growth, technology changes, competition, and legal regulations. For example, people growing comfortable with purchasing music online created an opportunity for people to buy eBooks online as well.

- **Threats:** Threats are the *external* challenges a product faces. For example, the publishers' digital rights contracts posed a threat to licensing content for the Kindle.

The following matrix represents the SWOT structure:

	GOOD	**BAD**
INTERNAL	strengths	weaknesses
EXTERNAL	opportunities	threats

This framework can help decide not only whether you should pursue an opportunity but also what strategies would further that pursuit.

THE FIVE CS (SITUATIONAL ANALYSIS)

The Five Cs provide an overview of the environment for a product or decision.

- **Company:** This encompasses all aspects of a company, including its products, culture, strategy, brand reputation, strengths, weaknesses, and infrastructure.

- **Competitors:** Competitors include direct competitors, potential competitors, and substitute products. For each of these, a discussion could encompass market share, trade-offs, positioning, mission, and potential future decisions.

- **Customers:** This includes aspects such as demographics, purchase behavior, market size, distribution channels, and customer needs and wants.

- **Collaborators:** Collaborators include suppliers, distributors, and partnerships. A discussion here might include what makes particular collaborators valuable and how they enable success.

- **Climate:** Climate includes aspects such as regulations, technology changes, economic environment, and cultural trends. A hostile climate can kill a business decision, while a positive one can greatly facilitate success.

This framework can guide discussions on whether you should launch a product and what the strategy should be.

PORTER'S 5 FORCES

Porter's 5 Forces is a framework for industry analysis.

This industry analysis can be useful for understanding a company's decision.

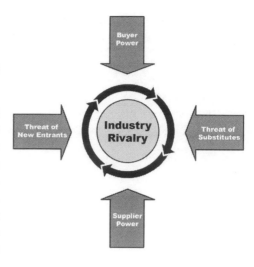

- **Industry Rivalry (Rivalry Among Existing Competitors):** More competitors generally leads to more heated competition, as does more direct competition. If many companies make the same product and they are not strongly differentiated, this will generally drive down prices for everyone. Many things can influence rivalry, such as market growth (growing markets enable competitors to expand without fighting with each other for market share) and high costs to exit the market (companies are reluctant to leave).

- **Buyer Power:** If a company or industry has relatively few buyers (for example, only the government and big banks), or some buyers have a very disproportionate share of revenue, these buyers will wield considerable power. This power allows them to affect prices, feature sets, delivery timelines, and other aspects.

- **Supplier Power:** Like buyers, suppliers gain influence over a company if the company is heavily dependent on them. This commonly happens if a company has a component that it exclusively (or almost exclusively) purchases from a single source.

- **Threat of Substitutes:** Competition exists not just from direct competitors, but also from substitute products. For example, even if Amazon were the only seller of electronic books (and therefore there was no direct competition), the prices of e-books would still be influenced by "competition" from physical books.

- **Threat of New Entrants:** With few barriers to entry in an industry, companies are constantly vulnerable to competition. If they price their goods too high, another company will enter the market and capture market share. Barriers to entry can include things such as proprietary technology, massive economies of scale, strong brands, or anything that's very difficult to do.

Consider, for example, the PC market. Buyers have considerable power, as many sales come from just a few retailers. Suppliers also have considerable power since there are limited manufacturers of certain components and high switching costs in changing manufacturers. On the positive side, there is some differentiation between competitors and limited substitutes. The market has moderate barriers to entry (branding, etc.). There are worse markets to be in, but there are also many better markets.

This framework could be useful in discussing whether or not you should enter a specific market. What's the industry like? If it's hyper-competitive, you might choose to avoid it.

PRICING MODELS

People generally use any or all of the following to price a product:

- **Cost-Plus Pricing:** Examine the costs of your product and set your price a little higher than that. This is tricky because there are generally fixed costs and marginal costs, so it's difficult to assess the cost per unit. Additionally, many online services don't have direct costs, and the costs don't determine whether this is a *reasonable* price. However, the cost of your product does suggest a minimum price (presuming you want to make a profit) and indicates something about your competitor's prices.

- **Value Pricing:** Some products have a clear and direct value to the customer. In those cases, you might be able to estimate how much money/time you are saving (or gaining for) the customer and price accordingly. This will suggest a maximum price.

- **Competitive Pricing:** A great number of products are priced by just looking at the competitors' prices. This is partially rational (because your customers might otherwise select your competitors) and partially due to laziness (because people don't know how else to price a product). Pricing lower than your competitors is not necessarily a good thing; it can signal lower quality to customers, and it might start a price war. However, competitive pricing can still be a starting point from which you decide to price higher if your product is positioned as a premium product.

- **Experimental Pricing:** In some cases, it's possible for a company to experiment with different prices and then correlate price with sales volume. Proceed with caution here, though; inconsistent pricing can frustrate or anger customers.

A thorough company might use cost-based pricing, value pricing, and competitive pricing to triangulate on a good price, and then tweak it slightly with experiments.

With these general approaches in mind, there are a number of pricing models to consider:

- **Free, Ad-Supported:** Many startups try this approach, but few succeed. Advertising alone is rarely enough to support a company, unless there is something unique about your product which makes advertising particularly effective.

- **Freemium:** In a freemium model, a basic level of the product is free but a premium version is paid. This can be good for attracting customers. However, you have to keep a close eye on your costs for supporting these free users, as well as on your conversion rate.

- **Tiered:** A company might offer multiple levels of pricing, segmented by volume, customer type, or features. You don't want to go overboard, though; too many tiers can be overwhelming for customers.

- **À La Carte:** A company can price each feature or service separately, letting the customer choose exactly which "upgrades" they would like. This can often lead to customers paying more than they would have for a bundled suite of features. Some customers will like this flexibility but others will be overwhelmed by it. The support costs of dealing with so many different suites of features can also be challenging. Mobile Apps often go this direction—paying for the initial download and/or for in-app add-ons.

- **Subscriptions:** Many services offer subscriptions to their product or service, particularly in the case of web applications. Some products are simultaneously available for purchase and as a subscription. This enables products to capture customers who only need temporary usage and may not be willing to make the upfront investment in a full purchase.

- **Free Trial:** Short-term trials can be a good way to let customers experiment with a product before the purchase, as a way to "hook" them. Trials can be bounded by time, number of uses, or particular features (e.g., you can import but not export). You have to be careful to ensure a good enough experience that customers will enjoy the product but not so good that they don't desire to upgrade.

- **Razor Blade Model:** A company can sell one component (e.g., razors) at, near, or below costs with the expectation that an add-on component (e.g., razor blades) will bring in additional revenue. This can work very well if the customer can only buy these add-on components from you. If there are other competitors with compatible add-ons, then you run the risk of customers purchasing the product from you cheaply and then the add-ons from your competitor.

A pricing model could use a combination of many of these attributes. For example, a company could offer subscriptions to its service, priced differently depending on the size of the customer's business, with additional upgrades purchased à la carte.

If you're having trouble creating a pricing model, you can also hire a pricing consulting firm. These companies have extensive experience with pricing and can help you choose the right packaging, pricing, and discounting model to optimize revenue. Neeraj Mathur, VP of Products at ForUsAll, shared the two scenarios where a pricing consultant is especially useful:

> When you are at a very small company where no one has done pricing before, a consultant can bring a wider understanding of the market and options. When you're at a large company, a consultant can bring the "leave no stone unturned" mentality that will help find opportunities to optimize price and cost, such as connecting you to cheaper sources of materials.

KEY TAKEAWAYS

- **The best product doesn't always win:** It's not enough to focus on building something that customers love. To succeed, you also need to consider the market, pricing, competitive environment, macro environment, company goals, and other business factors. This is where all of your business skills come into play.

- **Focus on tradeoffs and principles:** The most useful part of many strategies are the opinionated stances they take on tradeoffs. The strategy needs to highlight the contrast between the chosen path and potential alternatives. Ideally, most tough product choices can be decided by looking back at the strategy.

- **Connect the dots:** People feel more motivated and do better work when they understand how their work is strategic, important, and connected to the company's mission. The strategic framework explains how the team's work connects to the bigger picture.

CHAPTER 17

ROADMAPPING AND PRIORITIZATION

YOU'RE SETTING OFF on a long road trip across the country or continent. You pack your bags, prep some snacks and drinks for the ride, load your family and friends in the car, and you're off. Or are you?

In the days of Google Maps, Waze and other mapping apps, it's true that you don't actually need to plan your route. Just punch in your far-off destination and it will indeed route you there—and efficiently, too. Yay.

But what this approach misses is *your* goals and priorities. It's optimized solely around getting you to the final place destination as fast as possible. It didn't consider that you'd like to camp for a few days in a national park, or see the ocean, or visit your friend in Chicago along the way.

It also missed your constraints. You need regular cell and WiFi access, so you don't want to drive anywhere too secluded. You'll also need to stop somewhere to sleep each night—and some of those places might need reservations.

It turns out that just blindly setting off toward the final destination (or what you *believe* the final destination to be), doesn't perform well against your priorities at all. You can go without it for a short trip, but for a longer trip, you need a *roadmap* that takes into account your goals, constraints, and priorities.

> A product roadmap is much the same. Driving toward the final product might get you there eventually, but "there" might not be the right place at all. And it's often essential, particularly for a bigger project, to make a number of "stops" along the way.

As a PM, you're responsible for deciding what work your team will pick up, and in what order. You'll need to balance competing priorities and connect your plans to your strategy and vision to ensure you're headed in the right direction and can achieve your goals. This is what your roadmap does.

RESPONSIBILITIES

PRIORITIZE AND SEQUENCE WORK

Creating a roadmap is basically scoping (pg 126) at a larger scale. Instead of figuring out the incremental releases within a project, you're ordering work across multiple projects and a larger period of time.

Despite the proliferation of prioritization frameworks, there is no single objectively correct way to prioritize work. Prioritization is about tradeoffs, and it requires sound judgment.

It can be useful to create a table of the factors you're considering, and even to give each factor a weight. But don't blindly rely on the score. When you do this, you can wind up pursuing the wrong path, or wasting hours trying to refine your calculations until it gives the results you want. The tradeoffs between options are real, and purely quantitative calculations can miss that.

With all of those caveats, here are some factors to consider. They can be further subdivided, or grouped together to help highlight the differences. At the simplest, you could look at cost/benefit analysis.

Estimated benefits:

- **Dissatisfiers / Satisfiers / Delighters (The Kano Model):** How unhappy are people if the functionality is missing, and how happy are they when it's there? Make sure you first provide the table-stakes features, and only then invest more in the areas where you haven't hit diminishing returns.

- **Size of user benefit:** Sometimes you can directly measure a customer benefit like "seconds saved" or "money earned." Other times, you can estimate it at small, medium, or large, based on customer requests and what you've learned from in-person interviews.

- **Number of users who benefit:** What percent of the user base benefits? To estimate the number of users impacted, you can measure how many users visit the part of your product where the new entry point would be; it might be much smaller than you assumed.

- **Type of users who benefit:** How important are the users who benefit? Sometimes, a small slice of the user base contributes disproportionately to revenue and growth.

- **Completeness of use case:** Satisfying a use case completely is significantly more valuable than *almost* satisfying a use case. If your product is excellent for a single use case, people will use it more frequently than if it is just okay for many use cases.

- **Size of business benefit:** How much money is it estimated to bring in? Will it cut down on support costs? Does it help complete a marketing story?

- **Size of internal benefit:** Will it reduce future engineering cost? Will it improve team morale? Will it help the team learn something important?

- **Progress towards vision:** Is this an important part of the long-term vision?

- **Risk/certainty of success:** Is this a risky bet? Or is it well validated and likely to deliver the expected impact?

Estimated cost and constraints:

- **Size of engineering (and design, product, research) work:** What is the estimated number of days or weeks that the work will take to complete?

- **Team capacity and skills:** Has the team done work like this before? Will you have the right people to do this work well?

- **Within-team dependencies:** Are there other pieces of work that need to be completed first? Are there pieces of work that should be done at the same time to avoid switching costs?

- **Costing risk:** What's the chance that this work could be much more costly than originally estimated? Are there significant unknowns? Are there cross-team dependencies?

- **Other risks:** Could this work introduce security, scalability, performance, or brand risk? Is it a complex project where a lot could go wrong?

When you look at your final prioritization, make sure that you're tackling enough important work and not just "snacking" on the low cost/low benefit work.[1]

ENSURE YOUR WORK ALIGNS WITH THE STRATEGY ⚡

TAKING A STEP BACK

Adriana was a senior PM at an enterprise company when a customer asked for some new APIs. The APIs would have been cheap to build and would have strengthened the customer relationship, but Adriana took a step back to see how the work connected to the strategy.

She knew that revenue was the top strategic goal, and saw this API would not help revenue. Digging deeper, she realized it would actually hurt revenue because it would compete with a new product that was launching soon. Instead of building the API, she demoed the new product for the customer, and they loved it. By focusing on the strategy, Adriana avoided accidentally hurting sales for the new product.

As you plan your work, connect each project to the strategy explicitly.

> If a part of your work doesn't connect, treat it seriously. Do not plow ahead on the part of the strategy that doesn't connect; you'd be investing effort in something that the company doesn't think is valuable, and it will hold back your career.

Instead, see if there's a way to connect the dots from the goals you care about to the strategic goals. If not, discuss it with your manager and see if the strategy needs to be updated.

---

1   For more about the dangers of snacking on easy, low-impact work, you can read https://www.intercom.com/blog/first-rule-prioritization-no-snacking/

CREATE A LONG-TERM ROADMAP FOR YOUR TEAM ⚡

There's a great deal of debate in the tech community about long-term roadmaps. Some people worry that they'll be locked into dates, feature sets, or solutions that don't make sense. They worry it will prevent them from adapting and learning on the go.

Those are valid concerns, as these issues can happen when roadmaps are used poorly. Luckily, there are ways to create and use roadmaps that avoid those problems and create huge benefits.

Roadmaps are important for a lot of reasons:

- **Seeing the bigger picture:** Roadmaps offer a bigger picture that let you double check that all of your small decisions add up to something important and impactful. For example, you might realize that at your current pace, you won't be able to catch up with competitors before your startup runs out of funding.

- **Planning:** Roadmaps let you plan ahead for the resources you need. For example, you might realize that you'll need to hire another data scientist in the next six months.

- **Advocating for resources:** A convincing roadmap can help you advocate for getting a large enough team. When you ask for more people, leaders will want to know what you'll achieve with them.

- **Supporting partner teams:** Teams like marketing often need a headstart on big launches. Sales teams will set their targets based on the launches they're expecting. If you don't share your roadmap with partners, they'll make their own guesses, which may be much less accurate.

- **Starting important discussions:** For example, you might have assumed that applying machine learning to your product was low priority and put it far out on the roadmap. But when you showed it to your team, they were able to point out why it's important to start investing sooner in this.

- **Future-proof decisions:** By showing people what changes are coming, they can make sure to account for them in their current work. For example, if you expect to rewrite part of the app soon, people will know not to invest too much time polishing the old version.

- **Motivate the team:** People move faster when they're excited about what's coming next.

- **Recruiting:** People like to join teams when they're excited about the things they'd work on. When you can talk about what's on the roadmap, it becomes easier to recruit and close candidates.

Here are some tips to avoid the pitfalls of roadmaps:

- **Don't treat your roadmap as set-in-stone. Make sure the documentation reflects that uncertainty.** Invest in setting expectations upfront, so you avoid undue pressure later. For example, your time buckets can be "now, next, later," or, "this quarter, next six months, next year," to reflect time uncertainty. The items can be written as problems to be worked on, rather than specific solutions. You can point out the milestones when you're expecting to learn more and solidify future plans. Be explicit on the roadmap that these are estimates, rather than firm commitments, and that plans will change as you learn new information.

- **Revisit the roadmap regularly, particularly when new information comes in.** Just because you set your GPS, that doesn't mean you have to plow ahead when a road is closed. Depending on how fast your environment changes, you might want to revisit your roadmap every three to six months, and, of course, whenever there's major new information (which could be anything from a launch that didn't achieve its goals to a competitor making a big announcement).

- **Double check how people are using your roadmap to make sure it matches your level of certainty.** At many companies, people will understand that the roadmap isn't fixed. At others, you might need to hide the details to prevent salespeople from pre-selling features that you're not committed to. Design your roadmap with the audience in mind.

- **Group the roadmap by theme, initiative, or goal.** You can group into rows, or use colors. This lets people understand the roadmap at multiple levels of detail, and highlights the reason for undertaking the work.

- **Work with experienced engineers to roughly cost the size of investments.** You don't need detailed costs, but you must have a discussion about the tradeoffs and choices that would have the biggest impact on costs. Teams can later choose to take a different approach, but they should have a discussion with you if they're expecting to spend a lot more time on an investment.

- **Align your roadmap with your strategy.** Does the planned work match up with the goals? Are there any parts of your strategy which are being missed? Does this roadmap get your team to where you need them fast enough? If you're not sure what "fast enough" is, work with your manager and business teams to understand the broader company constraints.

- **Compare your sprint backlog to your roadmap.** If they are diverging, that's a good time to reflect, decide if you want to change anything, and communicate how things are going.

Roadmaps can be powerful tools—when used appropriately.

GROWTH PRACTICES

DON'T OVERLOOK THE OBVIOUS WINS

PMs tend to be lured by fancy new functionality, but the biggest wins are often obvious and even boring. If you can reliably find the cheap changes that bring big wins, you'll quickly become a top-notch PM.

I've seen PMs score big wins through simple improvements like:

- Changing the default setting from off to on.

- Fixing bugs in onboarding flows.

- Optimizing the very top of the funnel—for example, A/B testing the text and images on the signup page.

- Optimizing monetization pages.

- Optimizing emails and notifications.

- Internationalizing.

These fixes might not look "cool," but if they bump up your metrics and help customers, that's what really matters.

LEARN HOW TO SAY "NO"

Saying "no" is hard, and it's not a skill most of us practice regularly before becoming a PM. We're generally told what to do by those with power—our parents, our teachers, our bosses—and we don't really have the freedom to say no to them.

Cultural expectations can make it even harder.

Kunwardeep Singh, a senior product manager at Chegg, was born and raised in New Delhi. He states:

> Culturally, we were taught it's very rude or harsh to say 'no' to elders. In my early product days, I thought the business people knew more than me and I was supposed to say 'yes' to their product requests. That led to a lot of scope creep and misalignment between teams. I had to learn that saying 'no' is not offensive; it's not something bad. I'd ask myself after meetings why I'd said 'yes' and learned my own way of saying 'no' that worked for me.

Here are some tips on how to say no:

- **Let your roadmap say "no" for you.** Create a visual roadmap for the next quarter or year and fill it with the planned projects. When someone asks for new work, you can show the roadmap and discuss what would need to be removed to make space. The visual of the roadmap helps you and them understand that you can't say "yes" for free.

Jan	Feb	Mar	Apr
Project A	Project B		Project C

- **Reframe no as a good thing.** Instead of thinking that you're letting people down when you push back on their requests, frame it as helping people. You're helping your team by not signing them up for too much work. You're helping the requestor by letting them find alternatives and plan accordingly. You're making decisions that are in the best interests of customers and the business.

- **Make people feel good about your no.** Being good at saying no doesn't mean that you make people feel shut down. Often, when you want to say no to a specific product request, there are many parts that you can say yes to. You can agree and empathize with the problem they're pointing out, and then share your alternate plans for a solution. You can thank them for a good idea while showing them the roadmap of work that needs to come first. You can ask them to explain their reasoning and then say, "Here's how I've been thinking about it."

- **Learn from people who are good at saying no.** Each company will have its own nuances to how people say no. Watch if people are blunt or gentle. Ask them how they knew what to say. Keep an eye on what works well and what doesn't.

- **Reflect on times you wished you'd said no.** Ask yourself why you said yes and what you would say if you could go back in time. What would have made it easier for you to say no? You might find that feeling more confident in your customer research or having a more tangible plan for your team would have made it easier.

- **Set up principles to make saying no easier**. It's much easier to say no if you can point to a company-wide principle that explains the decision. For enterprise companies, it's helpful to have clear guidelines about when the product team will build a feature that only one customer is requesting.

Michelle Thong, Senior Product Manager for Nava Public Benefit Corporation, has found that, in government services, it can be particularly hard to say no. While companies can pick and choose their target customers, the government needs to serve everyone. Thong saw that government departments would sign up for many more projects than they actually had time to complete.

To help them accept the need to prioritize and cut some work, she had them write all of their projects, products, and services on a wall so they could see how much there was. When they saw it written down, they realized they couldn't do it all. She then had them slot projects into the next four quarters so the department could focus on the work that could be accomplished in a year.

DON'T PANIC WHEN EXECUTIVES TORPEDO YOUR ROADMAP

A CHANGE TO THE ROADMAP

Tara had spent months researching customer problems and putting together a roadmap that would deliver the optimal customer benefit. Suddenly, the head of marketing stepped in and insisted they add a handful of splashy features to round out the marketing story.

Tara pulled out customer quotes, ticket counts, and metrics to show that the features on her roadmap had a higher impact, but the head of marketing wouldn't budge. How could executives be so unreasonable?

Many PMs face similar situations, but it's rare that the executive is actually unreasonable. It's much more likely that the PM was too much in a bubble and didn't fully understand or respect the executive's point of view.

In the example above, did you see how Tara took the narrow view of "customer benefit" and dismissed the value of a complete marketing story?

This is not to say that the executive is always right, but if you want a chance of controlling your own roadmap, you need to show executives that you understand the broader picture.

- First, **back up to the shared goals**. If you need to, you can go all the way back to the company's mission statement, and try to find more specific goals you all agree on. Tara and her head of marketing agreed on the importance of a successful launch, which would bring in 20% more premium customers.

- Then, **find the highest level goal or assumption where you disagree**. Ask questions and get the executives to explain their point of view. Often, they'll have extra context or a different perspective that they didn't realize you were unaware of. Take a stance of humility here—if you've already assumed the executive is unreasonable, it will be harder for you to be open to their point of view.

In this case, the head of marketing had a draft of market analysis that Tara hadn't seen yet, and believed the current offering wouldn't bring in enough new customers. Once Tara understood that, she decided to work with marketing on a test of the marketing message with and without the splashy features to estimate the impact. They could move forward when they had better data.

If there's still a disagreement, you have a few options:

- **Discuss what percent of the roadmap should go to each goal**. You might find that everyone agrees that 10% is a reasonable amount of time to spend on splashy marketing features.

- **Highlight the tradeoffs**. You can put together a few roadmap options to make it clear what will get pushed out if you take on the extra work. When they see the alternative, they might realize it's not worth it.

- **Bring leaders with conflicting points of view into a room together**. Instead of serving as an intermediary, let the leaders talk to each other and hear the concerns directly from each other (while still guiding the conversation and forming a point of view). They'll have more shared context and more experience resolving conflicts at that level.

- **Test the assumptions**. Often, there's a quick test or data analysis that can help resolve differences.

- **Set up check-in milestones**. If there's no quick test and you need to take on the executive's project, you can still set up intermediate milestones to validate the work as you progress.

As you discuss and debate, assume the other party is acting in good faith. You probably share the same highest level goals, so now you need to figure out whether you disagree due to different information, different priorities, or something else.

PRIORITIZE COMPETING GOALS WITH A BALANCED PORTFOLIO ⚡

Early in my career, I prioritized work in a single stack-ranked list. It included new functionality that would work towards our vision, ideas for iteration on past features, small customer requests, and a backlog of long-term engineering investments we wanted to make. We calculated the cost and benefit of each... and the new functionality won every time.

Each individual prioritization made sense, but, taken together, the quality of our product was declining.

At some point, while working on strategy, every PM faces a scenario like this.

> The trick to managing these trade-offs is to treat your strategy and roadmap like a balanced portfolio. Decide at a higher level what percentage you want to invest in each goal.

You might decide that your team should focus 80% on user growth and 20% on revenue. Or, you may split your roadmap to be 30% on customer requests, 50% on big bets, and 20% on engineering debt. One common split that Google made famous is 70/20/10: 70% on sustaining the core business, 20% on related projects, and 10% on blue-sky big bets.

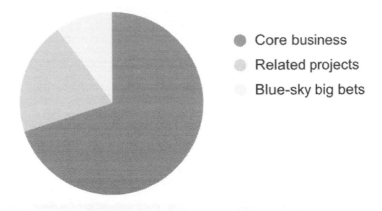

- ● Core business
- ● Related projects
- ● Blue-sky big bets

Once you have your buckets, you can prioritize potential work within each bucket, without having to compare items across buckets.

When you pick the percentages, you don't need to be too precise with the exact numbers. What you'll find is that when you present a percentage to your stakeholders, they will have an immediate reaction around which buckets seem too big or too small. As you iterate, you'll find there's some split that feels right to you and your partners based on their relative importance and the minimum investment that would be feasible. If you can't agree, that usually means there's deeper strategic misalignment on the relative priorities.

There are a few ways to implement the percentages:

- **Team size:** Allocate headcount to teams based on the percentages, and give each team one bucket. The benefit of this approach is that each team is empowered to own a priority and if the work from one bucket takes longer than expected, it won't crowd out work from another one. The downside of this approach is that if one of the buckets is less exciting (like engineering debt), the team that is assigned to it may suffer from poor morale.

- **Estimated cost on roadmap/backlog:** Put projects on the roadmap so that the estimated costs of projects from each bucket matches the desired percentage. The benefit of this approach is that it works with any sized team, and gives the team flexibility in how they order the work. The downside is that teams might push unpleasant work to the end of the schedule and run out of time to complete it.

- **Fixed order on roadmap:** This is similar to the method above, but enforces that the team picks up the high priority unpleasant work first. It's a little less empowering, but works well if the team has failed to meet their commitments before, or if another team has a dependency on the work.

- **Goals:** Ask the team to set goals for each bucket; review them to make sure that they roughly match the investment for each bucket, are what you want, and are achievable. This can, and should, be combined with the other approaches, to reinforce the connection between the strategy, goals, and actual work.

You need to find the solution that works for each team—and it might vary across teams or over time.

CONCEPTS AND FRAMEWORKS

RETURN ON INVESTMENT

This is a simple concept, but PMs sometimes forget to use it.

> When creating a roadmap, you need to consider both the expected benefits and the expected costs of the work. The ratio of these is called the return on investment.

If you have one project that you think will bring in $1 million in revenue and another that will bring in $5 million, it might seem like the second project is the clear choice. But, if the $1 million project takes a week and the $5 million project takes a few months, the obvious choice might not be right.

Similarly, if you have a project that you're very confident will bring in $1 million in revenue with 1 month of work, that could be a better choice than a project that might bring in $2 million in revenue in a month, but could also take six months. This is one of the reasons estimating costs and timelines is important.

Many projects don't have a revenue projection, but the same thought process applies. Would the project still feel worth it if it took five times as long as you expect? Software estimates are notoriously inaccurate, but over time you'll develop an intuition for which projects have higher variance.

OUTCOME-BASED ROADMAPS

The idea behind an outcome-based roadmap is that instead of sharing a roadmap that says which features you'll build in each timeframe, the roadmap says what outcomes you'll achieve in each timeframe. For example, instead of saying "build new calendar view," the roadmap would say, "reduce time-to-schedule-an-event by 20%," or, "build new calendar view to reduce time-to-schedule-an-event by 20%."

What's great about outcome-based roadmaps is that they keep the team focused on the results that matter, and can prevent stakeholders from thinking that the product team is committing to a specific solution. They emphasize the reasons and goals behind the work. This is particularly important if your team doesn't have a strategic framework or OKRs (pg 211).

> An outcome-based roadmap is a way to move in the right direction; they help ensure the team doesn't think just shipping features constitutes success.

The confusion around outcome-based roadmaps tends to be whether they can or should reference solutions at all.

Ignore solutions

As an extreme approach, you could ignore solutions and create your roadmap solely around the goals you'd like to achieve.

A roadmap that only includes goals could work if you're creating a roadmap that someone else is responsible for delivering, as long as they have a chance to consider solutions and costs with their engineers before agreeing to it. It gives them the most autonomy over what to build.

You can also use this approach if partners and leaders at the company don't need more granular timeframes than now/next/later.

This extreme has some large downsides. If you haven't thought about solutions, it will be hard to know if those goals are achievable at all, let alone in a given timeframe. It also doesn't give partners the ability to plan their own workloads.

Consider solutions but don't put them on the roadmap

A less extreme approach is for the product team to think about what features they might build for each outcome, but not write the solutions on the roadmap. The roadmap that is shared across the company only includes the outcomes. Those outside the team won't get overly attached to specific solutions, but the team benefits from the planning and has a more realistic chance of achieving the results.

If your team has earned trust that they can deliver, or if stakeholders aren't that interested in the details, this can be an effective approach. This approach works especially well for growth or monetization teams where the specific optimizations don't really matter, and the solutions really are likely to change based on how each experiment goes.

Include outcomes and solutions

The most general purpose approach is to start with a traditional feature-based roadmap and add high-level goals, outcomes, and a caveat that the solutions might change. With this approach, if the solutions change in a way that will affect partner teams (for example, changing from a big launch of a brand new calendar view to a small bug fix in the existing product), you'll want to communicate that change broadly so that people don't make plans around the original solution.

This approach works best when the high-level shape of the solutions matters to the company, for example, when there's a lot of partnership work. It's also the easiest approach to switch to if you currently use feature-based roadmaps. The other approaches require more executive buy-in and change management. Company leaders usually need to have an idea of what the product teams are working on, and, often, an outcome is too abstract for their purposes.

VOICE OF THE CUSTOMER

For most of my career, when it came time to create a product roadmap, I worked with customer-facing and business teams—of which there were many—independently. I'd gather the lists of their top requests, and then use my own judgment and understanding of company strategy to decide how to merge the lists. I spent a lot of energy explaining to the support team why I hadn't prioritized a revamp of the scripts they depended on, or I'd wonder if I'd been overly influenced by our charismatic salespeople.

One day, Asana's Head of Business, Chris Farinacci, excitedly shared an idea with me: What if the *business leaders* took ownership for collecting and ranking the priorities from the customer-facing and business teams into a single list? The business leaders were much closer to the business strategy and would know how to weigh the feedback coming in from each channel. I wouldn't be obligated to follow the ranked list when setting the roadmap—I could still use my discretion—but, we'd be aligned on the top customer and market needs.

And thus, the "Voice of the Customer" process was born.[2] It's had a huge influence on both the success of the work we tackled, and on cross-functional trust and morale.

---

2   Read more about the Voice of the Customer process at https://www.codementor.io/blog/how-to-build-a-product-roadmap-the-asana-way-2kvo8z70dm

How to Start

If you want to start a Voice of the Customer process for your product, the first step is to pair with the top customer or business leader for the product, as that person will be the one owning it. The primary benefit for them is that they get more strategic control over how product teams interpret the needs coming from business teams, since they decide the ranking of the final "Voice of the Customer" list. A secondary benefit is team morale and accountability. Each person on the business team will be able to see how their top priorities were merged into the ranking and know that those choices were made by people close to them within the organization.

Once the business leader is on-board and has picked a person to run the process, you'll want to work closely with that person to make sure the results you get are as useful as possible.

Here are some tips:

- Coordinate the timing, so that the product teams will get the final list of requests in time for their planning cycles.

- Make sure the person running the process is excellent at speaking to both business teams and product teams, and can translate between the two. You may want to suggest specific people with whom you've worked well in the past.

- Work with the person running the process on requests that are too solution-oriented or don't dig deeply enough to address the customer need. Share techniques you've used in the past, and give examples to show why the existing framing is misleading.

- Ask to see not just the final list, but also the earlier steps. This includes the individual lists from each team, the calculated ranking, and the changes made by business leadership. Ask questions when anything is unexpected.

- Double check that the list includes all of the business team's top priorities. Sometimes work that benefits future customers (like entering a new market) or internal teams (like billing infrastructure improvements) are high priority but get missed on the lists.

- Once you've made product plans, communicate to the company how those plans connect to the prioritized Voice of the Customer list. Let people see how many of their top priorities you're tackling, so that they can gain trust in the product plans and feel satisfied that their investment in the process was worth it.

- Be patient with difficulties. As a product person, sometimes it's hard to remember that not everyone else has the same skills of prioritization, surfacing underlying needs, and connecting those needs to product work. I've been shocked on many occasions when a customer-facing person casually brings up a brand new top priority at the end of a meeting because they didn't realize it was relevant earlier.

It might feel strange to hand this responsibility to another person, but doing so can greatly improve the relationship between product and business teams. Over time, people on the business teams will get better at translating customer feedback into useful product insights, and you'll be able to rely on them as helpful partners. In the bigger picture, you're not handing over much control, since you'll still be able to use your discretion to set the roadmap.

KEY TAKEAWAYS

- **Make a long-term roadmap, even though it will change:** Some people are afraid they'll be locked into a long-term roadmap, but proper communication can prevent that. A roadmap is critical because it lets you see if your plans will get you where you want to go fast enough. It gives you and your company the information you need for long-term planning, including hiring more people or adjusting financial plans.

- **Ordering and prioritizing work takes real judgment:** Don't expect a magic formula to do the hard work for you. The cost and benefit of each piece of work is an important input, but you'll also need to consider the overall balance of investments and any dependencies or synergies between different projects, as well as the perspectives of customer-facing teams.

- **Treat your roadmap as a balanced portfolio:** You don't need to compare apples to oranges, such as trying to figure out whether new features or eng debt is more important. Instead, when work goes after competing goals or has differing risk/reward profiles, consider what percentage of your portfolio you want invested in each.

- **Double check that your roadmap matches your vision and strategic framework:** Your roadmap is how you make progress towards your vision. When they don't match up, something is wrong. Perhaps your strategic framework ignored important infrastructural investments or cross-team commitments, or maybe you need to say "no" to non-strategic work.

CHAPTER 18

TEAM GOALS

IMAGINE THIS: IT'S the end of the quarter, and one of your engineers runs up to you, thrilled to share her work. It took several weeks, but she rebuilt the text editor and now it can handle bulleted lists and emojis.

That's great—you wanted those improvements—but… what about the monetization experiment she was supposed to be working on? Revenue hasn't been doing well and the company really needs a win. "No problem," she tells you, she'll get started on it next week after the hackathon.

Next week?! How can she be so calm about this? Why did she think it was okay to work on her own project instead of the one on the roadmap? It turns out she'd heard about the new company initiative to add customer delight and wanted to help out. She hadn't realized her work on the monetization experiment was more important.

People commonly run into problems by going after the wrong goals.

Once, I found myself stuck in a surprising disagreement with a designer over whether we needed two more weeks to polish the designs. Neither of us could understand the other person's point of view until we realized that we had conflicting goals: I was trying to start a small beta program to validate the customer need, and she was thinking about getting the visuals up to our quality bar for a full launch.

Another time, our growth team set a goal to increase adoption by 5% and spent the quarter working on an ambitious experiment that ultimately failed. When we talked to growth PMs at other companies we realized our mistake; we were putting all of our eggs in one basket and not iterating quickly enough. The next quarter we set a goal to run ten experiments and saw much more success.

> As a PM, it's easy to incorrectly assume that the "right work" is obvious to everyone. PMs think about roadmaps and strategy all day long. The designers and engineers on your team, however, might have looked at the roadmap during a strategy presentation months ago and forgotten most of it. You need a tool to pull the long-term strategy and roadmap into something more tangible that drives day-to-day decisions.

Team goals are that tool.

Once they are written down, shared, and approved, team goals (also called OKRs or commitments) become the guiding light for the team. In a healthy team culture, people *really* want to hit their goals and will work hard to achieve them. Goals align the team towards a shared measurement of success.

The importance of setting team goals

Creating team goals and sharing them with the rest of the company is a well established best practice. The benefits include:

- Forcing teams to be thoughtful about the purpose of their work.

- Supporting cross-team communication, coordination, and alignment. Goals represent a shared set of priorities and are one of the fastest ways to understand what people are working on.

- Creating an anchor point for reflection and learning. If you don't write down your intentions, you can't tell when you're exceeding or missing them.

- Helping teams make better tradeoffs and decisions.

- Creating the nudge that many people need to finish up work and ship it, rather than iterating endlessly.

- Enabling product leaders to ensure teams are working towards strategically valuable outcomes.

- Establishing clear expectations of what success looks like.

As Yogi Berra said, "If you don't know where you're going, you'll end up somewhere else."

RESPONSIBILITIES

CREATE TEAM GOALS

As a PM, you need to ensure that your team creates good goals that are aligned with the strategy and road-map. This should be a collaborative process, with the team feeling like they committed themselves to the goals they want to achieve; they should not feel that you imposed goals upon them.

Anything people on your team spend a substantial amount of time on should contribute to a goal.

That includes the planned product work and engineering investments, plus any responsibilities that are likely to require work (such as "keep the site up"). You don't usually create goals for internal responsibilities that everyone is expected to do, such as interviews or on-call rotations, unless you're asking for a shift in this work (more interviews, etc.).

The standard advice for goals is that they should be S.M.A.R.T.: Specific, Measurable, Achievable, Relevant, and Time-Bound.

- **Specific:** What are you planning to do, and what will the impact be if it is successful? Be sure that your goal isn't purely to launch; include outcomes like overall user engagement, engagement with the feature, or even internal stakeholder satisfaction.

- **Measurable:** How will you know if you hit the goal or not? What are the concrete criteria for success? You can add multiple criteria to help your team know what's important.

- **Achievable:** You want the goal to be ambitious, but achievable. This also applies to the set of goals your team is signing up for. Did you sign up for too much work?

- **Relevant:** Does the goal contribute to your team or company strategy? If you hit the goal, would you feel good about how your team is doing? Is it clear in the wording of the goal *why* you're doing it?

- **Time-bound:** Goals should always be tied to dates. The dates could be the end of the quarter, or could be the launch date.

If possible, work some flexibility into your goals or the grading process. The spirit of the goal is more important than the actual wording of the goal. It's silly to get hung up on wording and technicalities, as long as everyone is on the same page about the intention.

Good goals and bad goals

Let's dig into some examples to see how SMART goals work in practice.

Internal launch

- **Bad:** Create an internal product dashboard (due end of quarter).

- **Good:** Create an internal product dashboard that effectively replaces the legacy script, so that we can remove the legacy script next quarter and improve development speed. Measured by survey of Ops team (due end-of-quarter).

Stability and security

- **Bad:** App is stable and secure.

- **Good:** Achieve 99.9% uptime and no security breaches during Q1.

Growth teams

- **Bad:** Double the user growth rate (due end-of-quarter).

- **Good:** Run 10 experiments focused on increasing user growth rate, with at least one statistically significant win (due end-of-quarter).

Feature launch

- **Bad:** Launch <feature name> (due end-of-quarter).

- **Good:** Launch <feature name> by end-of-quarter, resulting in a 5 point NPS increase measured one month after launch.[1]

A good goal keeps the team focused on the right work. By planning ahead you can make sure that everyone on the team has the same definition of success.

---

1   Net Promoter Score, calculated from responses to the survey question, "How likely are you to recommend this product?"

ENSURE THE GOALS ARE MET

Have you ever suddenly realized, a week before the quarter ends, that you had a goal you forgot about? Maybe it was to create new product documentation or give a public presentation. Perhaps there was some eng debt your team intended to tackle but didn't get to. It's not a good feeling.

When you create your goals, set up a cadence of when you'll check in on the goals. Some goals might be discussed at every team meeting, while others just need to be considered once a month. Set reminders so you don't forget.

When your team starts to fall behind on a goal or it looks like you won't achieve it, there's a lot you can do to help. First, let your manager and other stakeholders know. Then, consider your options.

Here are a few ways to get a goal back on track:

- Talk to your teammates or other PMs to brainstorm solutions. Two brains are better than one.

- Reallocate within your team. Is there a lower priority project that can be paused so you have more people working on the problem?

- Clear away other responsibilities. You can help your teammates ask for a reduced interview load or reduction in other activities to help them focus on the goal that's falling behind.

- Ask for more resources. You might be able to borrow people from another team, hand part of the work to another team, get a contractor, or purchase third party software to help.

If it doesn't look like those approaches will work, see if you can renegotiate the goal to something more realistic.

GROWTH PRACTICES

INCLUDE COUNTER METRICS IN YOUR GOALS

Let's say your team's goal is to increase new user signups. If that's your only metric of success, you could easily hit your goal in a way that's bad for users and the company.

Imagine you offered people $50 to sign up. Signups would sky-rocket, but many of those people only signed up for the free money and won't return. The leadership team is unlikely to be pleased. What they really wanted was for you to increase signups *without* hurting the customer acquisition cost (CAC) or decreasing retention.

> Counter metrics are health metrics that you want to keep an eye on to ensure you haven't created unwanted side effects, such as CAC and retention in the scenario above. The best counter metrics will be specific to the goal you have and the types of solutions you're considering.

For example, let's say Zoom wanted to improve video quality to increase overall retention. Since the approaches to improve video quality might increase bandwidth which could be a problem, they might want to look at bandwidth usage as a counter metric, or perhaps retention of customers who have lower bandwidth connection. They'd then write the goal as "improve video quality by X% without increasing bandwidth usage."

To come up with counter metrics, ask yourself, "Is there a way we could hit this goal but it would be bad for users or the company?"

USE GOALS TO MOTIVATE YOUR TEAM ⚡

When done well, goals can be highly motivational. Most people like to hit their goals and will work extra hard if they think it will make a difference. It feels good to accomplish something you said you would. On the other hand, it can feel frustrating to put a lot of work into something that isn't related to a goal. And, if someone thinks they have no chance of achieving a goal, they might stop working on it entirely.

You can use that bit of human psychology to encourage the kinds of behaviors you want.

As you shape your goals with your team, here are some things to consider:

- **Paying attention to the incentives which your goals create**. If people are trying really hard to hit the goals, will they try to cut corners? Try to include criteria that align incentives in the right way. For example, you might want to specify that there are no P0 bugs in the week after launch.

- **Grouping together small pieces of work into a single goal**. For example, if your team is going to run ten experiments, you can create one combined goal for all of them. This can help your team focus on the larger impact rather than getting caught up in a single experiment.

- **Breaking large projects into multiple goals**. For example, if you can't set a launch date until you've validated the solution with a beta program, you can create one goal around the beta program, and wait to create the launch goal until after you've hit the beta goal. This creates intermediate milestones to celebrate.

- **Creating separate goals for different types of work**. Designers love to "clean up as they go," redesigning bits of the product near the new features they design. Engineers can get frustrated by what they perceive as a distraction from the main goal. An easy fix is to align the team around an additional goal to make some number of design improvements over the quarter. That will help all of the work feel meaningful.

Keep in mind that the scope of your goals should reflect your team's preferences. Some people like to have really ambitious goals to keep themselves motivated, while others prefer more modest and achievable ones because they hate to fail. Don't assume everyone shares your preferences, or that everyone thinks about goals the same way.

PICKING TARGETS ⚡

We know goals need to be measurable, but how do you decide where to set the target? Should you aim for a 10% lift, or a 100% lift?

On one hand, you might be tempted to set a very low target so that your team can easily beat it and exceed expectations—underpromise and overdeliver. On the other hand, you might want to set a big ambitious goal to motivate the team to achieve more.

When you set targets, you want to consider what the company needs from your team, what your team can achieve, and how the targets will impact decision-making.

What the company needs from your team

PMs aren't always proactively told what the company needs from them. Important information (like when the next fundraising round is, what growth rate investors are expecting, or how the monthly finances are doing) is often kept at the leadership level.

If you're not sure, ask!

What's achievable

To figure out what's achievable, you'll generally want to compare your planned work to a known baseline.

If you're planning a redesign, look to see how the last redesign impacted metrics, and start from there. If you're working on improving the retention rate, see what other work has made a difference, and make an educated guess about where this work might land.

Just as engineers get better at estimating costs over time, PMs get better at estimating impact.

How targets impact decision-making

At the end of the day, you'll need to decide whether you want to err on the side of too low or too high.

If you set a high target, you can encourage your team to think of innovative new solutions and make it clear that the team can only succeed if they prioritize this goal. You might also be able to ask for extra resources to achieve your ambitious target. But, if you miss the target, people might be demoralized and you might lose credibility in the organization.

If you set a low target, you manage people's expectations and you have the chance to really impress them if you exceed the target. But, depending on their personalities, your teammates might not work as hard once they've hit the target.

CONCEPTS AND FRAMEWORKS

OKRS

A popular format for setting goals is Objectives and Key Results, commonly called OKRs.[2]

When you write an OKR, the **objective** is your goal or intent. These are often written in the style of a mission statement and might not include specific numeric targets. An example of an objective could be things like "improve the new user experience," "successfully launch Version 2 of the product," or "achieve 90% revenue growth."

To avoid confusion about how likely it is that you'll hit the objective, you can label objectives as "aspirational" when they represent an aggressive target that the team is aiming for but likely will not hit, or "committed" when the team is committing to the result and expected to hit 100% of it. When objectives aren't labeled, many companies expect the team to hit about 70% of their objectives.

Each objective has three to five **key results**, which are the measurable milestones that contribute to the objective. Key results might look like "improve the onboarding completion rate from 50% to 75% by October 1st," "launch an experiment every sprint," or "maintain 99.99% uptime in Q1."

---

2   For in-depth information on OKRs, check out https://www.whatmatters.com/

Many companies create OKRs at multiple levels in the organization. The OKRs at each level can contribute to the OKRs at the level above. In effect, the team objectives are often the key results for the next-higher level of OKRs.

At the end of each quarter, teams grade their OKRs quantitatively (such as from 0.0 to 1.0) and share the results with their broader group. The grading could be a simple weighted average, a judgment call, or a more complex formula defined when the OKR was first created.

KEY TAKEAWAYS

- **Use team goals to drive cross-team alignment and reinforce strategy:** When you work with other teams, paired goals can help ensure you're on the same page about the priority of the shared work. When making tough trade offs, consider how they'll impact your team goals, and in turn, your team's progress toward the vision.

- **Success is more than just launching something new:** Goals create a focal point for reflecting on how your work went and how you can improve in the future. Make sure your goals capture the positive benefit you're aiming for, rather than creating bad incentives to launch at all costs.

LEADERSHIP SKILLS

PART F

LEADERSHIP SKILLS

IF YOUR TEAMMATES were robots, leadership would be a lot easier. They would do what they're told, wouldn't get offended, and would methodically evaluate all options. But we don't get robots. We get people.

Real people have emotions. Real people take shortcuts. Real people work better when they're motivated. And, as invincible as you might feel, you're a real person too. Leadership skills include managing your own mindset.

- **Personal Mindset** (pg 217) will teach us how to overcome the mental traps that can hold great PMs back. We'll learn about growth mindset, maturity, egolessness, and impostor syndrome.

- **Collaboration** (pg 224) will teach us how to work well with teammates and partners. We'll learn about resolving conflicts, psychological safety, and personality differences.

- **Influencing without Authority** (pg 231) is just what it sounds like. We'll learn stakeholder management and how to drive decisions.

- **Communication** (pg 239) will teach us how to avoid miscommunication. We'll learn best practices for written conversation, live conversations, meetings, and presentations.

- **Motivation and Inspiration** (pg 247) will teach us how to keep our teams motivated. We'll learn about intrinsic vs. extrinsic motivation and what to do during crunch time.

- **Ownership Mentality** (pg 253) will teach us how to take full responsibility for our teams and products. We'll learn about filling in the whitespace and contributing beyond your product team.

- **Mentoring** (pg 259) will teach us how to mentor others. We'll learn about apprenticeship, sponsorship, and giving feedback.

- **Working with Other Departments** (pg 271) will dive deep into working with designers, engineers, and executives. We'll learn what they care about and how to build trust with them.

The ideas in these chapters are highly influenced by the culture at US tech companies. Great leadership can look very different in other cultures. The book *The Culture Map* by Erin Meyer shines a light on cultural differences.

CHAPTER 19

PERSONAL MINDSET

PATRICK WASN'T QUITE sure what he was getting himself into with his first PM job, but he was confident he could figure it out. Things had generally come easily to him.

His first project was to improve the poorly utilized metrics dashboard. Easy enough; the problems were clear to him. There was a new dashboard startup that all his PM friends were talking about, and he was sure that things would get better if his team moved their dashboard to the new technology.

Some of his more experienced teammates warned against relying on an external provider, but he brushed those concerns aside; they were just too risk averse. Didn't the company always say they wanted people who took big risks? He wrote up plans for the first version and the engineers got started.

The first launch went well, but a few months later he got an email from the startup—they were shutting down. Their new dashboard would stop working in three months, and the team would have to rebuild it again. This was a disaster. That night, Patrick woke up in the middle of the night, mad at the startup and feeling sorry for himself.

He wasn't a bad guy. In a lot of ways, his mindset was pretty typical of new PMs, many of whom come in projecting confidence (while others are much the opposite). Nonetheless, without some significant course correction, he wasn't going to be able to learn from his mistakes. He needed to practice being a good leader, not just for others, but for himself too.

RESPONSIBILITIES

GROWTH MINDSET

In Satya Nadella's first six years as CEO of Microsoft, he transformed the company culture and added more than a trillion dollars to the company's valuation. How did he do it? By embracing the philosophy of growth mindset.[1] Satya explains, "We went from a culture of know-it-alls to a culture of learn-it-alls."

---

1   Read more about this transformation at https://qz.com/work/1539071/how-microsoft-ceo-satya-nadella-rebuilt-the-company-culture/.

A "growth mindset" means you believe your talents can be developed over time, with effort and persistence. People with a fixed mindset, by contrast, believe they are pretty much stuck with their talents (or lack thereof).

To understand the difference, imagine a task that you excelled in. This could be anything. Perhaps this is taking a math test as a kid, or making super cool car-shaped cake for a kid's birthday, or a triathlon, or a presentation to execs. How do you think about it?

- **Growth Mindset:** "I worked really hard. I studied a lot and I paid attention to what I was doing / I watched a zillion tutorials and worked slowly and carefully / I trained hard and made sure I slept well / I did my research about how to speak to the execs / If I seek out more feedback I'm sure I can do even better next time."

- **Fixed Mindset:** "I'm good at this stuff. Math is easy for me / I'm good with my hands / I'm athletic / I'm a good public speaker / I've mastered this so I don't need to work on it anymore."

Observe how the growth mindset's explanations are choices. They are things you can *do*. The fixed mindset, by contrast, is just stuff you *are*. If you did well, it's because you *are* good at it. If you did poorly, it's because you're bad at it.

Carol Dweck, who originated the term, discovered that people who have more of a growth mindset are more successful than those with less. And, fittingly, she discovered that people can develop a growth mindset.[2]

A growth mindset is important for two reasons:

1. It encourages people to invest in the work that will make them succeed.

2. It encourages intellectual humility and continuous learning.

Those with a fixed mindset (or, perhaps more accurately, who haven't *developed their growth mindset yet*) might avoid challenges or hard work. If getting a math problem wrong means you're bad at math, it's natural to prefer the easy problems that you won't get wrong.

To improve your growth mindset, pay attention to situations that trigger your fixed mindset. You can reframe "I can't do it" to "I can't do it… yet." You can talk back to the inner-voice that says you need to appear right at all costs.

Focus on this with your team, too. Develop their growth mindset by emphasizing and celebrating learning. It's okay to compliment someone's talents, but also praise their hard work and effort.

PUT ASIDE YOUR EGO

There's one surprising description that came up again and again in conversations about what makes a great PM: "ego-less." It's surprising, because if you've ever met a PM, we tend to have big egos. In a sense, you have to think a lot of yourself to feel like you have any place in leading a team. Plus, we get a fancy title and many of us enjoy getting credit for our accomplishments.

The thing is, a person's ego often gets in the way of great product management. If you hoard the praise for your work instead of redirecting it, you've missed out on a key opportunity to motivate your teammates. If you think you're too good to waste your time wading through data or attending to the details of project management, your team will suffer. If you reject a good idea just because it's not *your* idea, you'll get worse results. If you're too self-centered, you'll be deemed "difficult to manage" and it will hold you back.

---

2   Mindset: The New Psychology of Success

Instead, you need to shine a light on the accomplishments of your teammates. Be willing to step in wherever needed to ship great products, even if that means tedious data parsing or filling in for a QA gap. Welcome feedback and even criticism. Own up to your mistakes.

> Pretend, for a moment, that you don't care about being right, having the best idea, or landing that killer promotion. Do what's best for your team. **Put aside your ego**.

Putting aside your ego doesn't mean you won't be recognized for the great work you do. In fact, when you're the person standing up and calling attention to the accomplishments of other people on your team, people will see you as a leader, because that's how leaders act. That said, you can (and should) let your manager know about the good work you're doing (see pg 383) so that more invisible parts of your contribution are understood.

Intellectual humility

There's an apparent paradox with the best PMs: they're incredibly smart, and yet they're always open to the idea that they might be wrong. This trait is called intellectual humility, and it's a key to great PMing.

A PM with excellent product sense might have the fully-formed, best idea 60% of the time, but if they're stubborn and arrogant, they'll miss better ideas or iterations 40% of the time. Along the way, they've probably alienated their coworkers and stifled their creativity.

Another PM might start with the best idea much less often, but because they're less sure that they must be right, they question their ideas and solicit other good ideas from their teammates. They listen closely to feedback instead of reflexively defending their initial idea. By generating more ideas and feedback, they'll come up with much better results. As an added bonus, their teammates feel more engaged, which improves their future output.[3]

> Intellectual humility is closely associated with a growth mindset; you believe there could always be more to learn, even when things are going well. Intellectual humility is not only good for your team, but also for you.

Ironically, the more you read and study about a subject, the harder it is to maintain intellectual humility. After taking a course that teaches you the "best" framework, it's tempting to believe that the answer that got you an A+ on the test *must* be right in the real world. Those tests and frameworks (even the ones in this book) are, of course, oversimplified.

Luckily, a "fake it till you make it" approach can work with intellectual humility, as long as you can overcome the part of your ego that says, "I need credit for all the good ideas." You can humor the people around you by entertaining the idea that you might be wrong, listening to their feedback, and exploring alternatives, even if you don't initially believe your idea has any room for improvement. It can help to know the people around you will think *more* of you when you're not overly attached to your own ideas. Over time, the realities of running teams and shipping products will help make that humility more authentic.

---

3   This is one of many reasons why it's important to have a "no jerks" policy for hiring. A jerk might be good by themselves, but they also affect the morale of their coworkers. An employee who brings down their team is not a good employee.

MATURITY

Maturity is important in a leader; it helps people to see you as responsible and wise. Maturity builds trust and attracts respect.

To lead a team effectively, you need to not just *be* mature; you also need to *demonstrate* maturity. Focus on these personal qualities:[4]

- **Respect for expertise:** Experience isn't everything, but you shouldn't act like you know it all after trying something once. Aim to build mastery and pay attention to how your skills grow with repetition.

- **Awareness of context (and when you might be missing context):** Don't come charging into a new situation and assume you found the perfect solution that everyone else missed. Ask questions and show humility. Make sure you learn the goals and constraints.

- **Seeing the nuance:** Make sure you don't overlook important complexity. While junior PMs might tackle problems with black and white answers, as you advance, most situations will have complex trade-offs.

- **Restraint:** Great leaders don't act impulsively. They'll let other people speak first and don't interrupt. Instead of jumping into action reactively, they'll let some things work themselves out.

- **Diplomacy:** You need to be able to get alignment and buy-in without causing tension. This is especially important when working with cross-functional stakeholders.

- **Judgment:** As Ashley Fidler says, "Judgment is making an appropriate plan for the situation and developing a sense of what's going to work."

- **Fostering a healthy culture:** As a leader, you take responsibility for how your actions affect other people. If you complain, gossip, or reinforce an "us vs. them" culture, you might be stirring up trouble.

- **Discretion:** The higher you advance in a company, the more sensitive information you have access to. Don't share sensitive information, and don't brag about knowing confidential information.

- **Socially appropriate behavior:** Pay attention to social norms. Don't be a jerk on company mailing lists or chat channels, even random or miscellaneous ones. Avoid heavy drinking at work events.

- **Controlling your emotions:** Crying, yelling, moping, or showing over-the-top enthusiastic happiness can cause people to unconsciously assume you're less competent than you are. This doesn't mean you can't show *any* emotion though. It's okay to be sad, stressed, excited, or frustrated; you just want to seem balanced here.

- **Admit your mistakes.** The more power and influence you have, the more complex your choices are—and the more chances you have to be wrong. Have the courage to admit your mistakes. It makes you look stronger, not weaker.

- **Change your mind.** Digging in your heels and insisting that you're right doesn't help your team, your company, or yourself. It just makes you look childish. Change your mind with better information, and strike compromises when it's appropriate.

---

4   John Cutler kicked off a great conversation with this tweet: https://twitter.com/johncutlefish/status/1221196549771808768

Be aware, also, that the *perception* of maturity can be susceptible to bias. In tech companies where most engineers wear shorts and t-shirts, many young women feel the need to wear blazers to be taken seriously (something I've heard from many female leaders and used to do myself); that sort of thing should not be necessary.

If you're mentoring a PM, please avoid the vague feedback that they need to be more mature. Even if you have good intentions, it can feel biased and can make people feel unwelcome—like you're blaming them for being young (and, possibly, female). Plus, it's not actionable.

Instead, reflect on your impressions and get specific about the behaviors you saw and what qualities you'd like to see. Make sure your feedback is fair and unbiased before you share it.

EQUANIMITY

Equanimity is keeping calm under pressure. When things go wrong, the PM needs to stay calm and think rationally.

I used to pride myself on working through my stress. As the work piled up, I'd run from team to team making quick decisions and giving orders. Taking a break would have felt like giving in. Luckily, a coworker pulled me aside and kindly told me that the team could tell I was stressed, and I was making them miserable. *That* was a wake-up call!

Your mood contributes to the team's morale. Try to notice when you're stressed, and take a break. In the long term, sleeping well, eating well, exercising, and practicing mindful meditation can all help.

When you stay calm, it makes you look like a confident and competent leader. It signals to people that you've got everything under control and are ready for the next challenge, which helps them focus on their own work.

GROWTH PRACTICES

DON'T LET IMPOSTOR SYNDROME HOLD YOU BACK

Impostor syndrome is that voice in your head that tells you, "I don't deserve to be where I am. I got lucky and, sooner or later, people are going to realize that I'm unqualified." Not everyone hears this voice, but it is very, very common, even among the most successful people.

The most important tip for dealing with impostor syndrome is to understand that it is common and realize that just because you *feel* like an impostor, doesn't mean you *are* one. Beyond that, working with a trusted mentor can help.

Be careful not to let impostor syndrome hold you back. Watch situations like these:

- Not asking important questions for fear of looking stupid.

- Not applying for promotions or roles that you're ready for.

- Declining an invitation to speak at a conference because you're not sure you have enough to say of value, particularly in comparison to the other "more impressive" speakers.

- Getting sleep deprived due to excessive work hours spent trying to get things perfect.

If you're mentoring someone with impostor syndrome, check out "Mentoring someone with impostor syndrome" on pg 269 for advice on how to overcome it.

BUILD INTERNAL STRENGTH AND CONFIDENCE ⚡

In some jobs, there is a "right answer." The code works, the patient is cured, the students learn, and so on. You do your job well and everyone around you is happy. It's very satisfying.

With product management, especially as you take on more complex and ambiguous work, there's no clear right answer. You'll make tough decisions with lots of tradeoffs and risk assessments, and you might never learn whether the opposite choice would have been better. Often, someone will be unhappy with your choice. As you advance, you'll hear more complaints and less praise, even if you're great at your work.[5] When things go badly, you take the blame; when things go well, you pass all the credit along to your team. That's the nature of the job.

On top of all of that, as you advance, you'll have more responsibilities to handle with less free time. You'll need to get comfortable with doing the quick-and-dirty approach (aka rapid prototyping) for most things, even when you know you could have put together something better with more time.

The best advice on this is to realize that ambiguity is a natural part of the job. When you see situations where you can't make everyone happy or polish things to perfection, reframe it as a sign that you're working on difficult and important problems.

CONCEPTS AND FRAMEWORKS

THE DRAMA TRIANGLE AND SHIFTING ABOVE THE LINE

The Conscious Leadership Group has books, videos, and live training that are closely related to building a growth mindset. They use a metaphor of a line to describe the difference between being below the line (closed, defensive, and committed to being right) and above the line (open, curious, and committed to learning).[6]

When you're angry with a coworker for messing something up, forcing you to rush in to save the day, you're looking at things from a below-the-line perspective. It's natural to then enter into the "drama triangle," where we tell ourselves a story where each person plays the role of hero, victim, or villain. In this mindset we're fixated on assigning blame or being right. It's not necessarily a bad thing to spend some time in this mindset; it's just not a useful place to solve problems or make progress.

> It's okay to spend some time below the line. We need to work through our own feelings, too. In fact, even exaggerating the goodness or badness of the players of the drama triangle can be helpful. It can help us to vent, as well as to identify the patterns of the drama triangle.

But, when you're ready to solve problems, it helps to shift above the line.[7]

---

5   Think about the last time Facebook or Gmail did a "redesign." Almost universally, people grumble! Now, perhaps the design just gets worse and worse every year (and some probably argue it does). Or, perhaps, redesigns come with compromises and you just can't make everyone happy.

6   For more about the Conscious Leadership Group, see their website at https://conscious.is/

7   Consider, though, whether you're really willing to shift, or if you're still attached to being right.

Once you're above the line, you can reflect on the original conflict. You might ask yourself, "In what ways should they have acted the way they did?" Or, "In what ways should I have done something different?" This will help you learn from your experiences and find good solutions.

KEY TAKEAWAYS

- **Your mood and mindset affect your team:** When you're stressed, your team notices. When you fixate on who's right or wrong, it's harder to solve problems. If you doubt yourself, you might not ask the important questions. If you're overly-confident in your knowledge, you might not learn new information. Invest in yourself.

- **Maturity is mostly about slowing down, paying attention, and respecting other people:** While accusations of immaturity often carry some bias, maturity is a real leadership skill that doesn't just mean "grow older." Ask a trusted mentor for honest feedback.

- **Everyone has doubts sometimes:** PMs are responsible for the toughest decisions that have no right answers. There's often no way to know you made the right choice, and you won't get much praise for your work. That doesn't mean you're making a mistake or are unqualified, it just means the work is hard. The more senior you get, the more of these hard problems you'll face; think of it as a sign that you're advancing!

COLLABORATION

BY THE TIME Maya joined the team, the situation with Kim had gotten out of hand. Simply put, the other PMs hated working with her.

Kim was complex. A lot of bad mixed with a lot of good. She had razor-sharp product sense… but that tended to turn into razor-sharp criticism. She was action-oriented and tried to help other teams… but she did so by pushing the point-person aside. Her engineers loved her… but she drove a highly talented designer to quit. Ultimately, her attitude was getting in the way of not only her own promotion, but the company's success as well.

Maya, too, felt taken aback by the way Kim questioned her decisions and dismissed her input. Other PMs apparently handled Kim with an effective—but not necessarily healthy—approach: avoidance. They didn't invite her to meetings, didn't share their work with her, and so on.

That wouldn't work for Maya or her team. They needed to collaborate closely with Kim's team. Maya committed herself to developing a healthy relationship with Kim.

Maya reached out to Kim for a friendly chat. During that chat, Maya realized that Kim had been burned by sloppy decision-making in the past and had trouble trusting new coworkers. Kim really cared about her team and wanted to protect them from any mistakes.

With that deeper understanding, Maya was able to intentionally build trust and develop an effective working relationship with Kim. Maya showed her work early and explained her reasoning. When Kim shared negative feedback about Maya's project, Maya thanked her for it and asked follow-up questions to understand the concerns. They took time for regular coffee chats, and even the occasional lunch. When Kim's big project launched, Maya bought her a pack of her favorite candy to celebrate.

What Maya understood—and the other PMs didn't—is that it's not sufficient to say "well, it's *their* fault." It takes two to tango, but if the dance of collaboration isn't working, it's your responsibility to fix it. No matter how stubborn, grumpy, or unreliable the other person is, a PM is expected to find a way to work together smoothly.

RESPONSIBILITIES

TREAT PEOPLE LIKE PARTNERS

Almost all collaboration skills come down to the mindset of treating everyone you work with like equal and valuable partners—like they're a member of the team. That includes your engineers, designers, user researchers, data scientists, security and infrastructure, sales and support people, marketing, and even legal and finance teams.

When people feel like they're a member of the team, they'll work with you to help the team succeed. If you treat people like obstacles or servants they'll redirect their energy towards other teams where they feel included.

Here are some ways to treat people like partners:

- Include people early in the product life cycle and give them a chance to influence the direction.

- Learn about their concerns and take them seriously.

- Include them in your core team meetings or create regular partner meetings.

- Say "our launch" instead of "my launch."

- Invite them to launch celebrations.

If you notice your "partners" frequently becoming frustrated at your team, that can be a sign that they haven't felt treated as a partner. Review the list above, broach the issue with them, ask how you can improve.

CREATE PSYCHOLOGICAL SAFETY

> Studies have shown that one of the most important factors in high performing teams is psychological safety: the belief that you won't be punished or shamed for making a mistake.

Many PMs accidentally reduce the feeling of psychological safety on their team. PMs love to point out problems and make suggestions (it's often easier than pointing out the good stuff), but sometimes it feels condescending, or like one-upmanship. They might be too quick to shut down ideas, or let retrospectives turn into a blame game.

Check in with your team to see how well your team is doing on psychological safety (perhaps anonymously), and if there's a problem, address it. If you've been letting your bad moods bring the rest of the team down, stop it.

RESOLVE CONFLICTS PEACEFULLY

Conflict is part of work. If you've never gotten into a conflict, then you either haven't worked on anything important and complex, or you're just so good at managing conflicts that they don't feel like conflicts to you.

Conflicts arise because people have different goals, preferences, and ideas of how to solve problems. People who are great at collaboration catch those differences early and work with the other person to resolve them in a way that works for everyone.

- Find the higher-level places where you agree and work down from there.

- Assume other people are competent and have good intentions.

- Don't let things fester.

- Don't accuse or blame.[1]

If necessary, you might even send in your mentor or manager to help diffuse the situation. You don't want to be perceived as someone who "tattles" whenever there's an issue, but it's better than letting an issue drag on and completely burning the bridge.

ASK PRICKLY PEOPLE TO MENTOR YOU

One great trick for moving people from adversaries to allies comes from Niffer Nan. She once worked with a new engineering lead who seemed to block her at every turn and generally acted like he didn't respect her.

Instead of getting defensive, she asked him to ramp her up on technical aspects of the new area and regularly asked for his advice. He took her under his wing and became one of her biggest advocates.

People generally love to be respected as experts, and this approach can quickly defuse a power struggle.

GROWTH PRACTICES

MAKE TIME TO BOND WITH COWORKERS

It's easier to work with people when you see them as real people, and even easier to work with them when you like them. When you build a foundation of friendliness or friendship, it creates a buffer that protects the relationship from mistakes and misunderstanding. When you feel like you're working with friends, work becomes more fun and less stressful.

When you work in the same office as your coworkers, you can grab lunch together or go for coffee in the afternoon. You can walk by one another in common areas and stop to chat. If you feel up for it, you can even hang out outside of work and engage in activities like board game nights, soccer teams, meeting up as a group for a movie, or team dinners.

When you work remotely, it's still possible to bond. Take the first few minutes of meetings to ask them how their weekend was. Create a chat channel to share silly memes. Host a "video happy hour" at the end of the workweek to relax and chat. Set aside some fun time during the time you're all in town together, or go to a conference together. See also: "Remote Work" on pg 163

Many companies have some budget for "morale events" or "offsites" like a sushi-making class, pottery lessons, or indoor skydiving. See if you can organize something for your team once a quarter. Events where people are learning to do something new, or where there's a little bit of competition tend to be favorites.[2]

---

1   The book *Nonviolent Communication* by Marshall Rosenberg dives into this topic.

2   As you set up events, be mindful of your team's needs and lifestyles. If your events are all after work, this could be difficult for those with young children. Similarly, a rock climbing offsite might not be the best choice if some of your teammates have physical limitations. If you buy team t-shirts, consider whether they actually fit your teammates comfortably. It is extremely unfortunate when a morale-boosting activity actually makes people feel excluded, forgotten about, or burdened.

The people you work with today can be the foundation of your network in the future. Some of your coworkers might start their own company one day, or they might be the people you recruit to join yours.

Don't forget to connect with people on LinkedIn and share personal email addresses when you leave!

OPTIMIZE FOR LONG-TERM RELATIONSHIPS

You don't just want to achieve the best results on the current project, you want to achieve great results over time.

When you take this perspective, it's easier to invest in relationships and compromise. You might disagree with your designer or engineer, but decide that it's not important enough to fight over. You might hesitate to let a teammate stretch into a responsibility you know you could do better, but in the long run, it will be good to build their skills.

This advice can apply even in extreme cases. You might have the idea that you can push your team really hard to deliver outstanding results or save the team from a disaster, but the damage to your reputation might not be recoverable.

CONCEPTS AND FRAMEWORKS

There are a variety of approaches to assessing one's personality, each with its own pros and cons.

Fundamentally, these assessments each seek to distill us down to core traits or bucket us in some fashion. The reality, however, is more complicated.

Most people, for example, aren't cleanly extroverted or introverted, but rather are somewhat in the middle. Or perhaps they report being high on some attribute, but they are judging themselves relative to a skewed sample. Or they exhibit one trait at work, but another at home.

This is all terribly messy. Embrace it!

Despite their inherent inaccuracy, personality assessments have value. They encourage us to think more deeply about ourselves and our teammates, and understand how people are different.

Consider, for example, the Myers-Briggs (MBTI) assessment. True, its validity is very much debated among psychologists (so much so that it will be conspicuously absent from this section—sorry, MBTI fans!). But it can nonetheless introduce the extrovert to the idea that, although they are energized by going to a team morale event, another person might need some quiet space to recharge after that.

We present the frameworks here in that light. No, none of these are The One True Answer. But there is utility to be gleaned from each.

THE BIG 5

The Big 5 doesn't attempt to put you into a little bucket. Perhaps that's for the best.

Rather, you are rated from low to high on five attributes, each of which is independent of the rest. These are believed by many researchers to be the core building blocks of personality.

- **Conscientiousness:** This is about impulse control, self-discipline, and following through. Conscientiousness is generally a positive trait, for product management and many other roles. A person who scores low might be unreliable, might procrastinate, or fail to be organized about their work.

- **Extraversion:** While many extraverts are chatty and highly social, this doesn't have to be the case. Extraversion and its counterpart—introversion—refer to how you get your energy. Do you leave a party with your friends feeling energized? Or do you feel drained and like you need a night off to recharge? Successful PMs can be either introverted or extraverted—or anywhere in between.

- **Agreeableness:** Agreeable individuals tend to value getting along with others, and they take into account other people's feelings and they exhibit more prosocial behavior. A person low on agreeableness can be seen as argumentative, uncooperative, competitive—or just somewhat obnoxious. High agreeableness can make you more likable, but when it gets very high, it can also be seen as lacking leadership.

- **Neuroticism (or Emotional Instability):** This is essentially a measure of how strong your emotional reactions are. A person who shows high neuroticism gets stressed, sad, or angry easily. A very high score here could pose an issue in one's career. A low score indicates that you're more emotionally stable and relaxed.

- **Openness to Experience:** High scorers here are more open to unconventional ideas. They are often imaginative and flexible, and readily try new approaches. Sounds good, right? Unfortunately, they can also be seen as unpredictable, or they can take *too* many risks. A "less open" person might be less willing to dive into new ideas, but their skepticism and pragmatism can also offer benefits.

We wish we could offer a platitude like "no trait is inherently good or bad," but that's not really accurate—at least not for PMing. Realistically, high conscientiousness is probably better than low conscientiousness; low neuroticism is probably better than high neuroticism.

What we can say is that even the "good traits" have downsides in the extremes, and you can find very successful leaders at any level of these traits.

You can have a weakness; everyone does. What's important is that you consider what traits might hold you back, and consider how to mitigate or manage them.

THE ENNEAGRAM

The Golden Rule—do unto others as you would have them do unto you—is wrong. It assumes that everyone wants to be treated the same way, and that's just isn't the case.

At my first leadership training course, I was *shocked* to learn that many people like to plan out what they say in advance, instead of thinking while they talk. I'd assumed everyone was like me and would jump into the conversation. I realized I'd been accidentally excluding some people.

This made me eager to learn more ways that my assumptions about other people could be wrong.

The model I've found most useful at work, and personally, is the Enneagram.[3] It identifies and defines nine personality types, each stemming from a different core desire and fear.

---

3   Read more about Enneagram types at https://en.wikipedia.org/wiki/Enneagram_of_Personality

You don't need to believe that the enneagram system is "true" to get a lot of value from it. Just learning about some different ways that people look at the world can help you understand your coworkers better.

You may want to ask your coworkers which type they think they are and then look up information on how to work with people of their type. It can help you stop accidentally hitting people's buttons and learn to better appreciate their strengths.

Here's a brief description of the types.[4] Note that people are often not 100% any one type.

Type 1: The Reformer

Also called the perfectionist, people who are type 1 have high standards. They can have trouble accepting that done is better than perfect. They are often willing to put in extra effort to get their work to their own quality bar. Appreciate their integrity and don't take it personally if they are overly critical.

Type 2: The Helper

People who are type 2 are empathetic and relationship-oriented. They might have trouble saying no. They are often motivated to help the people around them. Take the time to form genuine relationships with them and acknowledge the ways they help you.

Type 3: The Achiever

Also called the performer, people who are type 3 are productive and ambitious. They might be impatient or overly competitive. They tend to be motivated by hitting goals and getting results. They thrive on all kinds of appreciation and recognition.

Type 4: The Individualist

People who are type 4 see themselves as unique and different. They can have trouble when they need to do mundane work. They tend to be motivated by work that has a higher purpose or achieves excellence. Appreciate their creativity and help them see the meaning and purpose behind their work.

Type 5: The Investigator

Also known as the observer, people who are type 5 are thoughtful and strategic. They can face challenges from isolating themselves. They tend to be motivated by deeply understanding complex systems. Give them time to think things over and reach out to them for their thoughts.

Type 6: The Loyal Skeptic

People who are type 6 anticipate problems and create solutions. They can face challenges from being overly suspicious or when the rules change. They're motivated by being prepared and love to question everything. Share information with them early and often, and don't get offended by their questioning.

Type 7: The Enthusiast

People who are type 7 are imaginative and optimistic. They can have trouble staying focused and following through. They're motivated by exploring new ideas. Give them space to brainstorm and share their ideas.

---

4   A full description of the enneagram goes beyond the scope of this book. You can learn more at https://www.ennea-gramworldwide.com/, https://theennneagramatwork.com/, and https://www.enneagraminstitute.com/.

Type 8: The Challenger

Also known as the protector, people who are type 8 are decisive and resourceful. They can lean towards aggressiveness and run into trouble creating conflicts. They're motivated by moving fast and having autonomy. Don't shy away from their directness, and when they challenge you, see it as an attempt to suss out trouble in advance.

Type 9: The Peacemaker

Also known as the mediator, people who are type 9 seek harmony and bring people together. They can face challenges from complacency and procrastination. They're great at leading people to resolve controversial decisions peacefully. Take the time to form a rapport with them. Don't try to rush them, instead encourage them to share their own needs.

KEY TAKEAWAYS

- **Good relationships make your job easier and get you better outcomes in the long run:** You'll work with the same people many times throughout your career, so it's shortsighted to prioritize the current project over your relationship. Invest in your relationships. When you disagree, do so respectfully.

- **To resolve conflicts, start with the goals you share:** At work, you'll always at least share a common company mission with your coworkers. By reaffirming your common goal, you can work your way to the heart of the conflict without feeling like you're on opposite teams.

- **Not everybody is motivated by the same things as you:** People with different personality types aren't better or worse, they're just different. Don't assume that people have bad intentions or don't have ideas to share just because they interact differently than you. Keep an open mind and treat people the way *they* would like to be treated.

CHAPTER 21

INFLUENCING WITHOUT AUTHORITY

TO THOSE OUTSIDE of tech, the product manager role can be very confusing. "What do you mean the engineers don't report to you?", they exclaim. "Can't you just tell them what to do?"

To be fair, I was similarly confused at first. I imagined that without the authority to tell my teammates what to do, they might just refuse to do any work and spend the day playing solitaire instead. I quickly learned that my fears were unfounded. My teammates were just as eager as I was to launch great products that delighted customers and helped our company succeed. And, while playing solitaire all day might be tempting, they did still have their own boss keeping them accountable.

What I learned is that I shared most of the same high-level goals as my teammates and partners. They *wanted* me to learn about our customers, think through product decisions, and propose the directions that would make our product successful… after thoroughly understanding their constraints and concerns. They didn't *have* to listen to me, but I could make them *want* to listen.

That is the essence of influencing without authority, and it's a core part of the PM's job—whether that PM is an intern, a fresh grad, or a very senior PM.

- You can't make the senior engineer take her time to build a feature, just because you said so.

- You can't make the legal team agree to extra risk, just to ship your product.

- You can't make the designer change the button text, just because that's your opinion.

And if you *try* to order everyone around, the relationship will quickly become dysfunctional, if not non-existent.

Instead...

- Maybe you can bring the senior engineer along on a customer visit, so she can see for herself how much the feature would delight customers?

- Maybe you can include the lawyers in team meetings at the beginning of the project so they feel like part of your team and then want to help with the launch?

- Maybe you can share your facts and frameworks with the designer, so your opinion isn't "just an opinion"?

Everything you achieve happens because you persuaded someone else to go along with your plan. You convince teammates to go along with your product decisions. You convince executives to fund your team and approve your launches. None of them are going to do something just because you said so.

Luckily, there are many ways to exert your influence even when people don't report to you. In fact, you'll find you use these same skills even when people *do* report directly to you. Ordering people around isn't a healthy way to accomplish your goals.

True leadership is when people *want* to follow.

RESPONSIBILITIES

BUILD RELATIONSHIPS

Many cultures have a complicated view of relationship-building. Friendships? Sure, that's good. Networking? Eek. That seems shallow, perhaps even seedy—like something a salesperson would do to manipulate others. Connections? Well, that's just unfair!

In reality, these are all different aspects of the same concept: *relationships*. It's easy, particularly earlier in your career, to assume that the best idea should just win, and it shouldn't matter who you know.

In reality, people just don't have enough time, energy, and trust to treat everyone as well as they treat the people they know and like. That doesn't mean they'll treat strangers poorly, but they might roll out the red carpet for friends.

> Good work relationships make everything easier. Teammates who trust you won't make you spend as much time justifying your decisions. Partners are more willing to assist you or take on risk. Mentors will take the time to share advice with you, and hiring managers will bring you onto their teams.

I first learned how much relationships mattered during a big launch at Google. I had followed the launch checklist and filled out the forms to get approval from each of the partner teams. One infrastructure team let me know that I'd have to wait a month for my change to roll out through all the systems; my launch was going to be delayed!

I shared the bad news with my manager who told me, "Oh I know someone on that team, I'll talk to them!" Lo and behold, the infrastructure team was able to fast track our changes and we made our date. I hadn't even known that fast tracking was a possibility.

Building those work relationships is simple. You don't need to be best friends—just friendly and respectful to colleagues. If you're already working with someone, invite them for a "getting to know you" conversation over coffee or tea—or just a walk around campus. If you'd like to expand the number of people you know across your organization, consider joining a group or extracurricular, such as a diversity and inclusion group, sports team, or another shared interest group.

EARN CREDIBILITY

Credibility is key for product managers. People are open to our influence if they trust our judgment. They need to believe that when we ask them to do something, we know what we're talking about, and that it's in their best interest as well.

Credibility also helps you earn autonomy. No matter how good you are at your job, you won't get more responsibility or more permission to work independently if people don't trust you. They'd worry that they'd have to clean up your messes.

It takes time to build credibility. More than anything else, your reputation as a PM will come from working on great products and having successful launches. But, beyond just doing your job well, there are ways to build credibility faster:

- **Articulate your frameworks:** When people understand the reasoning behind your decisions, they feel reassured that your decision-making process is sound.

- **Strike the sweet spot of confidence:** If you don't seem to trust yourself, other people won't trust you either. On the other hand, if you act more confident than warranted, you'll lose credibility.

- **Do what you said you'd do (and make sure they know it):** Reliability is a great way to earn credibility. Write down your plans and celebrate when you achieve them.

Note that credibility is relative to your level. Just because you're junior doesn't mean you can't have credibility—you can, but it's relative to the expectations of a junior PM. Likewise, very senior PMs can sometimes lack credibility, if they aren't meeting—or exceeding—the expectations of that level.

DRIVE DECISIONS

A top complaint engineering managers have about their PMs is that the PM doesn't drive decisions well. They talk about PMs who bubble every decision up to the CEO, or who get people together into a room but don't steer the conversation. They're bothered by PMs who let decisions linger unresolved for days or weeks, or who act unilaterally and exclude their teammates.

There are a few key elements to driving decisions well.

Take responsibility for making the decision

Great PMs are proactive about identifying places where a decision needs to be made. They don't procrastinate on decisions or hope someone else will take the lead.

Even when other people have more expertise, the PM should play an active role and form their own point of view.

> Listen to the experts, write out the arguments on a whiteboard, and look for missing information or contradictions. Do your own research if necessary. Identify the criteria that different people are using to arrive at decisions, and then drive a discussion on how the criteria should be weighed against each other.

It's important to take the time to learn what other people know and think. If they know something you don't, it won't make sense for them to trust you with the decision. You want people to feel like you're all on the same team working towards shared goals.

You're responsible for understanding and synthesizing all of the different points of view. You'll need that to have the courage to make tough calls.

Assert your decisions tactfully

Decision-making by consensus sounds nice and egalitarian, but in practice it's terrible. When you insist on discussing until everyone agrees, discussions often persist well beyond the point of diminishing returns. People argue until exhaustion. The winner is whoever can argue the longest, regardless of the merits of their side.

Instead, you need to judge when the discussion has gone on long enough, and then assert your decisions. If you're too indirect, people might not realize that you're stating a decision rather than just sharing an idea. If you're too assertive, it might sound dictatorial.

Here's an approach that balances both sides:

> In service of moving fast, I'd like to make a decision here. This is a product decision and falls to the PM, so I'd like to move forward with *(insert decision here)*. Does that sound okay to everyone, or would anyone like to escalate?

This approach works because it:

- Emphasizes the importance of making a decision rather than continuing to discuss

- Clarifies why you should be the person to make the decision

- Makes it clear that this is a decision, not just an idea

- Avoids sounding dictatorial by checking if it's okay, and giving people an option to disagree

- Discourages unimportant disagreement by raising the stakes from "continue to argue with me" to "escalate to our bosses"

If you worry there are some lingering hurt feelings after this, you can pull these people aside to chat one-on-one. The purpose of this is to smooth things over with the person and let them know you heard them, and not to resurface their opposition.

Move quickly

Wasting too much time making a decision is often worse than making the wrong decision. There's a trap called analysis paralysis, which is when you get stuck overthinking and overanalyzing and never make a decision.

Great PMs need to make decisions with incomplete information. They show good judgment in moving faster on decisions that are easier to reverse. They understand that unresolved decisions take a toll on the team.

Sometimes, you'll need to escalate to make sure the decision is resolved quickly enough.

Before you escalate, make sure you've done your homework:

1. Clarify the decision that needs to be made.

2. Determine the tradeoffs and the conflicting goals.

3. Try to drive agreement on which goals are more important.

The best way to escalate is to ask for a decision on which goal is more important, not the specifics of the solution. This approach works not only because the person you escalate to knows more about how the goals should be prioritized, but they usually are not close enough to the details to be the expert on the specific decision. They can provide context for you, and with that context, you'll be able to make a good decision.

GROWTH PRACTICES

CHOOSE THE RIGHT TIME TO SHARE YOUR IDEAS

A good idea can have a huge impact at the right time, but can be seen as an annoyance at the wrong time.

Pay attention to the planning cycles and product life cycle to get the timing right.

For example, if you want to pitch an idea that would involve spinning up a new team, you probably don't want to do this just before your company's busy season. You might have more success right before new grad engineers join at the end of the summer, or when a big project is finishing up.

Or, if you want the marketing team to take on some extra work, find out when they do their planning and pitch your idea to them at that time.

INCLUDE PEOPLE IN THE CREATION TO GET THEIR BUY-IN

There's a psychological effect where people are more attached to things they create themselves. You can use this to your advantage by including your stakeholders in the creation of products, processes, and plans.

Here are some tips for including teammates, while still retaining enough influence over the final decision:

- **Hold an early kickoff meeting**. People enjoy being included early because they get to shape the direction, and it won't be too late to include any of their ideas. You don't need to commit to any decisions early on, so you still have time to regroup if the ideas are very different from what you were expecting.

- **Structure the meetings to get the kind of input you want**. Organize the questions and topics to help guide people to the types of feedback and solutions you want.

- **Host a brainstorming session**. Brainstorming is a great way to solicit ideas without being obligated to use them. See "Brainstorming" on pg 90 for tips on how to run a great brainstorming session.

- **Allow other people to get the credit**. It might be tempting to share your ideas first so you get the credit for them, but you'll have more influence if you allow other people to feel like they thought of the ideas themselves.

- **Draft the solution by yourself, or in a much smaller group**. Once you've received input from everyone, it is usually more efficient to come up with the actual solution draft on your own or with a small group. Make sure to draw as many connections to other people's contributions as possible.

- **Frame it as a team solution**. Throughout the process, make sure to refer to the solution as belonging to the whole team, not just yourself. Use words like "our" instead of "my," and help everyone feel ownership and pride in the overall success.

Remember that, at their core, nearly everyone wants to feel important and impactful. Leverage this by giving people an opportunity to feel this way.

BUILD CROSS-DEPARTMENTAL TRUST ⚡

Product teams can get a bit elitist and dismissive of other departments like sales, support, or marketing. This breeds distrust; people in those departments think that product teams don't really understand how the business is run.

As you advance in your career, it becomes even more important to understand and represent the whole company, not just your team. You'll need to earn the trust of the executive team, and earning the trust of the department leads who report to those executives is a good way to do that.

If you invest the time to learn about other departments and understand their concerns, they'll see you as an ally and be less skeptical of your solutions. Ask them what's most important to them. See if they have any concerns about how they've worked with product managers in the past. Then, share what your team is working on. You can even hold Q&A sessions or present what your team is working on at their all-hands.

CONCEPTS AND FRAMEWORKS

STAKEHOLDER MANAGEMENT

Few words strike fear into the hearts of PMs like "Stakeholder Management." You need to deal with many people with different contexts, goals, experiences, and risk tolerance—each of whom can block your progress. Somehow, you're supposed to make them all happy and keep them all informed, on top of your day-to-day work.

A structured approach can help.

Step 1: Deeply understand your stakeholders and their goals

Start by understanding where each of the stakeholders are coming from. Learn as much as you can about their priorities, goals, and fears.

People managers and executives often care about goals that go beyond the product. They'll care about the potential impact on recruiting, morale, or financials. People who work in operations have their own sets of concerns that come from managing a large team of sales or support people.

If their goals or concerns don't make sense to you, ask yourself, "What would I have to believe to come to those same concerns? Under what circumstances would they be right?" This often directly points to data analysis or user tests that can validate the assumptions.

Later in the process, when you're trying to make a decision, bring the conversation back to the goals that you learned in this step.

Step 2: Clarify the decision-maker and other roles

It can feel scary to clarify who is the decision-maker when you worry that multiple people believe they hold that responsibility. But in practice, this is a critical step, and it's always better to bring it out into the open.

In addition to the one decision-maker, it is also essential to determine the roles of the other members in the group. Are there other people who can give blocking feedback? Are the rest of the people just advisors? You can formalize this with the DACI/RACI model:

- **Driver / Responsible:** The person or people running the process

- **Accountable / Approver:** The final decision-maker, or the person who must agree to the final decision

- **Consulted:** People who are included in the decision-making process, with two-way communication

- **Informed:** People who are kept up-to-date on progress, with one-way communication

There may be some negotiations involved during this step. People who you want to keep informed might prefer to be consulted. It helps to get advice from your manager or a PM who's been at the company for a long time; they'll know which people are really important to include and how much inclusion is expected at the company.

Step 3: Explain the process and communication plan

One of the big ways stakeholder management goes astray is when people aren't sure about the timeline and when they'll get updates. By laying out a plan, you earn trust and save yourself from lots of questions.

When you have a long-running process, you'll want to make sure you have a plan for status updates. Let people know when to expect them, for example, weekly or bi-weekly. When you are reliable with communication, it takes the burden of tracking the status off of them. If anything major changes in the plan, be sure to update people promptly.

See "Write good status reports" on pg 118 for tips on how to write a good status report.

Step 4: Make each stakeholder feel heard

After uncertainty, the next biggest problem with stakeholder management is when people don't feel heard. And yes, feeling heard is different than being heard; you need to reflect what you've heard back to the stakeholder until they believe you fully understand them.[1]

A nice way to do this is to go around the room and ask each person for their thoughts, while you take notes and project them. Let people see that you're capturing their points, and let them confirm that you wrote them down accurately.

Miscommunication is common in stakeholder management, because stakeholders come from outside of the team and have less shared context. You might use a word differently than they do. It can help to reflect what you heard in your own words to ensure you've understood correctly.

---

1   If you're a person inclined to debate or "play devil's advocate," you might have run across this before. Someone makes a suggestion, and you tell them all the issues. Did you hear them? Sure. You couldn't have critiqued the idea if you didn't hear them. But do they feel heard? Not necessarily. Feeling heard is different than being heard.

KEY TAKEAWAYS

- **Learn what people care about before you try to influence them:** People are only open to your influence if they believe you understand them and care about their needs. Learn about their job, goals, and worries. Reflect back to them. This is the foundation on which you'll convince them that your ideas are good for them as well.

- **Listen to your teammates, but don't always wait for consensus:** Including your teammates in product decisions is great, but sometimes you need to step up and make a decision, even when there's still disagreement. Sometimes, you'll really need full buy-in from everyone, but often you can encourage people to defer to you for the sake of speed.

- **Timing Matters:** Teams have planning cycles, and it's a lot easier to convince a team to consider something new when you catch them in the right part of the cycle. Sometimes you'll seed an idea early and nurture it over months or years before people feel open to it. Don't lose hope just because you get an early "no."

CHAPTER 22

COMMUNICATION

TEN MINUTES INTO my first meeting with the CTO, he just walked out. "If that's how you feel, I think we're done here," he said, metaphorically slamming the door behind him. Ouch.

This would have been a huge consulting project for me, revamping a massive company's hiring process. I (Gayle) had done some initial "evaluation" work to assess fit, which involved reviewing a set of hiring packets and presenting my recommendations. All went well—until this final step of the approval process.

Fundamentally, the exec and I disagreed on what—to him—was a major philosophical point. A hiring manager was trying to rationalize hiring an experienced engineer with no degree, and I didn't understand the concern. I wrote a comment to the effect of "Why is this such a big deal? The candidate has 20 years of experience. Any degree at this point is largely irrelevant."

The CTO disagreed and challenged me on my perspective.

"Would Google do this?" he asked.

"Yes, I believe so," I responded. (In fact, I knew so. I had plenty of degree-less coworkers there.)

"No they wouldn't." He scoffed. This is when he stated his earlier line and left. And that was it for our meeting.

But did it have to be? And, more importantly, was it salvageable?

His employees—who apparently sided with me (and were used to his storming out)—offered some advice. He looks up to companies like Google; if you're right that they don't require degrees, show him that. Stand your ground, but back what you're saying with data.

Ultimately, this salvaged the project, and it's what I should have done from the beginning.

The hiring manager's rationalization was a clue that I'd missed: some key decision maker must really value degrees. That issue needed to be confronted head-on, rather than via my little offhand remark. Moreover, the way to influence the CTO wasn't by showing degrees weren't that important; it was to appeal to his desire to "be like Google."

There was no miscommunication—we were quite clear about what we each believed—but there was a communication error nonetheless.

"Communication" is much more than just making your thoughts comprehensible. It is about understanding what your audience values, and picking up on the clues in their words and behavior. It's about tailoring what you say to them, and being proactive in addressing potential disconnects. It's about persuading by leveraging their values, rather than your own.

RESPONSIBILITIES

LEARN WHAT YOUR AUDIENCE THINKS AND CARES ABOUT

Imagine you could give people a magic potion that would let them see inside your brain and know everything you know, and read all your thoughts. Would that be the perfect communication tool?

No!

Communication isn't about transferring your thoughts over to someone else; in fact, it's almost the opposite. Clear communication is about understanding what other people think, and figuring out how to close the gap between their state of mind and yours.

For example, imagine you're trying to convince the executive team to invest in a new product your team wants to build. You provide plenty of evidence to show it would bring in a lot of revenue, but your idea is shot down. How could that happen?

The problem might just be that you didn't understand the executive team's goals and worries. This means that the data you gathered, despite the thoroughness, was ultimately irrelevant to them. Instead of revenue, they might be more focused on user growth. Or they might not have the right kind of salesperson to sell your product.

Effective communication directly addresses the goals and worries of the audience.

Try to build a mental model of the people you're talking to. Guess where they'll agree and where they'll be more skeptical. Try to predict their concerns and the questions they may ask you. If you're not sure, ask them!

GET CLEAR ABOUT WHAT YOU WANT TO SAY

Clear communication starts with clear thinking. If you're confused about what you're trying to say, other people will be too.

These approaches can help you clarify your thinking:

- Draw diagrams and create tables.

- Try organizing your thoughts in a few different ways—by category, by cause and effect, by priority, or by question.

- Try breaking your ideas down into smaller pieces to make them simpler.

- Look for the most important points.

- Sleep on it.

It's often helpful to distill your thoughts down to three key points. If this is tricky, that might be a sign that you aren't clear enough about your argument.

GROWTH PRACTICES

TAILOR YOUR COMMUNICATION FOR YOUR AUDIENCE AND GOALS

Before you start, make sure you know why you're speaking up, writing a message, or giving a presentation. What kind of a response do you want?

If your boss tells you that you need to send out a message, make sure to figure out what your goals should be. If you don't ask, you might guess incorrectly.

The details here can matter. For example, if the goal of your status update is to help everyone feel proud of the work your team has done, you might end it with "Give Amy, Bob, and Charles a high five next time you see them!" If your main goal was to encourage people across the company to test the product you might start it with "Last chance to give feedback before the launch!"

What information can you give the audience to make it as easy as possible for them to give you a good response?

- Do you need to change their mind about something, or address one of their worries?

- Do they need to see how your idea connects to their goals? Can you start from an idea they believe in and show them step-by-step how it leads to your conclusion?

- Would a template or specific instructions help them? For example, "share the five features that you think would most reduce ticket count."

- Might they feel defensive, micro-managed, criticized, or disrespected? Can you frame the message more carefully?

As you write your message, keep in mind that your message will probably not be read carefully. People will skim it—so make it skimmable! Use bullets, bold fonts (don't get excessive here, though!), headlines, and so on.

CATCH MISCOMMUNICATIONS AS THEY HAPPEN

Miscommunication can happen to anyone, but some people get caught by it a lot. Anyone might misread a word or get caught by surprise when a coworker has a different definition, and that's to be expected. But some people don't catch the problems in the moment, which leads to a lot of frustration.

People who don't notice their miscommunication tend to hear what they want to hear or what they expect to hear. They miss the clues.

Good communicators predict how the people around them will behave and notice any surprises. Anna Marie Clifton explains: "When someone replies differently than I expected, that's a clue that I don't understand them very well or one of us doesn't understand what's being communicated."

Here are some more techniques for reducing miscommunication:

- Pay attention to non-verbal signals like tone, facial expressions, and body language to see if people agree, disagree, or are confused.

- Don't overlook strange questions or wording, since it might be a sign of a misunderstanding.

- Try to predict how people will act and pay attention to when they act differently.

- Double check if someone seems fine with a change you expected them to protest.

- Define the key terminology you use in a shared glossary.

- Reflect back what you heard in different words.

- Follow up on verbal agreements in writing.

If you find that you're being misunderstood frequently, seek out the advice of a trusted colleague or mentor. Perhaps you use unusual phrasing, or just that tone is poorly conveyed in writing.

REDIRECT CONVERSATIONS TO THE RIGHT ISSUES

The next time you get in a conversation that doesn't seem to be going anywhere, take a step back and see if you're arguing about the wrong thing.

Let's say you're debating the placement of a button with your designer: you want the button to be visible all the time but the designer wants it to only appear when the user hovers. This might sound like a conversation about visuals and clutter, but it really ought to be a conversation about the target audience and their discoverability needs.

Sometimes, tiny disagreements represent much deeper unresolved issues. An engineer might dig in her heels on a small visual change when the real issue is that she feels like she has wasted her time because an executive has been changing his mind on previously approved designs.

Ask yourself "what is this conversation really about?" and redirect the conversation to the more fundamental issues.

CONCEPTS AND FRAMEWORKS

BEST PRACTICES FOR WRITTEN COMMUNICATION

Use a good opening

- **Do** use a clear subject line for emails including keywords that accurately describe the contents and helps people judge how soon they need to read it, eg. "When is the next product review?"

- **Don't** write mysterious subject lines like "You'll never guess what's coming next…" It sounds spammy.

- **Don't** start chats with "Hi" or "Can I ask a question?" Just ask the question. If you need, you can say "Is your screen private now?" or, "I've got a timely question, are you around right now?"

Keep it short and scannable

- **Do** use bullet points to make sure separate ideas don't get lost in a paragraph.

- **Do** use headings and other kinds of formatting and labels to help people understand and navigate your writing.

- **Do** provide a tl;dr or executive summary at the top.[1]

- **Don't** leave non-critical details or extra explanations in the main flow. You can include them in an appendix or follow-up comment.

- **Do** use pictures, prototypes, or diagrams to reinforce the important ideas.

- **Do** use emojis and humor to encourage people to read what you wrote, depending on your company culture. Tone is often poorly conveyed by writing, and a simple :) can actually help.

- **Don't** let humor get in the way of the meaning of what you wrote.

Make the call to action clear

- **Do** be explicit about what you want people to do, and by when.

- **Do** assign tasks or invite people to an event on their calendar to make sure they don't miss the action they're supposed to take, depending on your company culture.

- **Do** tell people exactly where to give you feedback, for example as comments in the document or in a private message.

- **Do** create templates or forms to make sure you get a response in the format you need.

- **Don't** hide a request at the bottom of a long email. Place it at the beginning and then ask people to read on for details.

Know when to move to a live conversation

- **Do** move to a live conversation if people are starting to type novel-length emails to one another, are misunderstanding each other, or are arguing.

- **Do** move to a live conversation when it's taking you a long time to figure out how to type up what you want to say, especially when you're worried about how to get the tone right.

- **Do** use chat or walk to someone's desk when you need a quick response, for example if the site is down or if your coworker might head home before they see your message.

- **Don't** send a chat or email if you wouldn't want it to show up on the front page of a newspaper. Obviously don't do illegal or unethical things anywhere, but written communication is prone to being taken out of context.

Hone your skills

- **Do** ask a mentor to review important communication before you send it out.

- **Do** workshop your writing after-the-fact if something goes wrong.

---

1   Tl;dr stands for "too long; didn't read," but it's sort of a synonym for "summary."

Written communication is asynchronous—the writer can write and send their message on their own time, and the reader can read the message at their own convenience. When that time delay is acceptable, written communication is a great way to be respectful of people's time, with the added benefit that you'll keep a record of what you said.

BEST PRACTICES FOR LIVE CONVERSATIONS

Be respectful of people's flow state

- **Don't** walk up to someone's desk and interrupt them when they're in the middle of something important.

- **Do** look at the other person's calendar and try not to schedule a meeting that would break up a large chunk of time.

Don't ramble

- **Do** figure out what you want to say before you say it, in most cases.

- **Do** think out loud when you're mentoring people to show them your thought process.

Some people love tossing ideas back and forth in a spontaneous conversation, while others consider it a big interruption. Get to know your teammates to learn what works for each of them.

BEST PRACTICES FOR RUNNING MEETINGS

Have goals and an agenda for each meeting

- **Do** send out the agenda in advance

- **Do** create more formal agendas with time slots for each topic when your meeting will have a lot of people.

- **Don't** let the meeting run over. Schedule a follow-up meeting if you need.

Assign a note taker

- **Do** have someone take notes during the meeting

- **Don't** distribute the responsibility unfairly. Set up a rotation so that you won't end up in a situation where some people are disproportionately burdened by notetaking.[2]

Match the meeting format to the goals

- **Do** keep decision-making meetings small. Six people or fewer is best.

- **Do** consider splitting people into groups to make larger meetings more effective.

Ensure everyone has a chance to share their thoughts

- **Do** send information before the meeting so people can prepare their thoughts in advance

- **Don't** assume that everyone is comfortable jumping into a conversation.

---

2   Many women recount stories of being expected to be the "secretary" for their group. The notetaking falls on them and just continues to. You should therefore be particularly conscious of specific people, or groups of people, doing the bulk of notetaking.

- **Do** proactively ask each person to share any questions or concerns, for example by going around the room.

Avoid meetings if you don't need them

- **Don't** have a meeting if you could just share information asynchronously.

- **Do** try to make meetings 30 minutes instead of 60 minutes when possible.

Keep in mind the costs of a meeting. A 10-person one-hour meeting may cost the company a few thousands dollars in time. Was that worth it?

BEST PRACTICES FOR PRESENTATIONS

Get comfortable

- **Do** find a public speaking role model. Not every style works for every person, so you want to find someone you'd feel comfortable and authentic emulating. You can browse through Ted Talks to find a variety of great speakers.[3]

- **Do** chit-chat with the audience to get comfortable before your presentation. Some friendly conversation about your weekend plans can help you feel like you're presenting to friends rather than strangers and scary executives.

- **Do** show up early to make sure the audio and video is working correctly.

- **Do** practice before important presentations.

Be clear

- **Do** be clear about the implications and takeaways of the information you're presenting. Imagine someone is standing there asking "so what?" after each thing you say. It might be obvious to you why it matters that, say, people use your product mostly in the morning, but spell it out for the audience.

- **Do** check in with people to make sure your presentation speed and content is working for them. When you're presenting to a small group, you can plan a short version of your presentation and then have backup slides to dig into the details and explanations if anyone wants to know more. For presentations to a large audience, you can do a dry run for a smaller group and ask them for feedback.

- **Don't** bury the lede. It might be tempting to hide your final recommendation until the end to build up suspense, but don't. It's difficult for your audience to follow along, absorb the information, and ask the right questions if they don't know what it's building up to.

Keep people engaged

- **Do** show some energy and try to look like you're having fun. Giving a presentation is a privilege. When you sound passionate about the work you're presenting, your audience will rarely be bored.

- **Don't** fill your slides up with text or read off your slides, especially when the presentation is meant to be entertaining. You can use speaker notes to remind yourself what you want to say, but if you're just reading off your slides, people will have a hard time staying focused. Instead, try using your slides mostly for images and a few keywords.

---

3   Browse TED talks at https://www.ted.com/.

- **Do** share examples, quotes, and anecdotes. Stories help people understand and remember the points you make. When you speak abstractly, people might not know how to interpret what you say, so the concrete examples help.

- **Don't** be afraid to be funny. People sometimes tune out during long presentations, but humor can draw their attention back in.

Most people are nervous about giving presentations, but it gets easier each time. If you'd like to gain presentation experience quickly, consider joining your local Toastmasters club.[4]

KEY TAKEAWAYS

- **Close the gap between their state of mind and yours:** To communicate well, you need to form a clear model of what the other people know and think. Try to anticipate their questions. Think about what information or support they'll need to come over to your way of thinking.

- **Keep your goals in mind:** Your communication should always have a purpose. If there's an action you want people to take, make sure your communication makes that clear and easy.

- **Be respectful of people's time:** A large meeting or presentation can easily take up dozens or hundreds of hours of people's combined time! Plan ahead, have an agenda, and skip or shorten the meeting if possible. The same applies to long emails. At a smaller scale, just interrupting someone when they're "in the zone" can break their flow and slow down their work.

---

4   For any college students reading this: Consider opportunities to join your school's debate team, or to start teaching as a TA.

CHAPTER 23

MOTIVATION AND INSPIRATION

STEVE WAS PROBABLY the twentieth person to tell me about foam rollers. He actually gasped a little when I told him I hadn't used them. "I don't know how I would live without my foam roller!", he said.

The first nineteen-ish people extolled the virtues to me of how they would ease my chronic shoulder pain—how the rolling helps with this and the pressure helps with that. And it's not that I didn't believe them; it just never rose to the top of my list.

But Steve's personal story and enthusiasm popped the importance up a few levels on the stack. I bought one that day.

Truth be told, Steve is actually Dr. Steve. My doctor. He *could have* given me a chart of reasons and details and benefits. But what he grasped, perhaps from years in the medical profession trying to get resistant patients to change their behavior, is that reasons aren't always enough to motivate. To motivate—as a doctor or a leader must—sometimes you need to *inspire*.

> Some leaders who are great at motivating and inspiring others are outspoken and charismatic. Others are authentic and personal. Some speak so rarely that everyone quiets down and leans in when they have something to say.

If you think about the times people have gotten you excited about an idea, you're likely to notice a variety of styles. To be a great leader, you don't need to match a particular style, but you do need a way to make the people around you *want* to follow.

RESPONSIBILITIES

KEEP YOUR TEAMMATES MOTIVATED

People are not robots. You'll get more out of your team if you figure out how to motivate and inspire them. They're more likely to work harder if they care about the work and they think it will help out teammates they care about. Morale matters.

There are many ways to motivate people, and what motivates one person won't always motivate another. Some people are driven by the purpose and impact of their work, some are more excited by gaining skills and mastery, and others are more inspired by trying to beat the competition. Understanding what motivates different people on your team will help you create a successful team.

If you're not sure what motivates someone, you can ask them questions such as: What brought you to this company? What's your favorite part of your job? What are you excited about?

INSPIRE EXECUTIVES AND PEOPLE ACROSS THE COMPANY TO BELIEVE IN YOUR TEAM'S WORK ⚡

The team you're responsible for represents a major investment for the company.

When people believe that your team is on the right track to deliver a huge impact, a lot of good things happen. It becomes much easier to advocate for the resources you need. You and your team get the recognition you deserve. People across the company feel excited about the future of the company, and employee retention improves.

The best tools you have for inspiration are your vision, your track record, and your enthusiasm. Reinforce the higher purpose of your team's work and successes to the rest of the company. Volunteer to be a guest presenter at the team meetings of other functions or divisions. Share your elevator pitch with executives if you ever meet them serendipitously, or request a brief meeting if you don't run into them organically.

RECRUIT PEOPLE TO YOUR TEAM ⚡⚡

As you advance, you become responsible for attracting engineers, designers, and PMs to your team. At a small company, this might involve pitching external candidates. At a large company, you might focus on convincing internal people to transfer to your team.

Keep your eyes open for people you'd want to work with, and then talk to them about your team. Share your vision and try to get them excited about it. Let them know why you picked them and why you think they'd be a great match. Learn about what they care about and make sure they know everything that might convince them to join.

For more information on pitching external candidates, see pg 316.

GROWTH PRACTICES

BUILD UP YOUR INTERNAL CONVICTION

The best way to inspire others is to truly believe in what you're doing, and to truly believe that what you're motivating other people to do is good for them.

Some people are too humble to see how wonderful their work is. Try thinking about why you've chosen the team you're on and the work you're doing, or at least why you haven't switched to another team. Pretend you're a visionary leader and think of what they would say to inspire people about your work. Try asking teammates or mentors that you find inspiring how they would talk about your team.

> Remember that growth is multifaceted. Just because your work has some problems or down-sides doesn't mean that there aren't positives that outweigh those downsides. For a moment, you'll have to take off the PM hat that's always looking for risks.

If you truly can't build up your internal conviction, that might be a sign that you should move to a new team or product.

USE MOTIVATION TO HIT DEADLINES, BUT SPARINGLY

There are times when you realize you're going to miss your deadline unless everyone chips in and works extra hard. You can motivate your team to rise up to the challenge, but you need to do it sparingly or you'll create resentment and burnout that outweighs the benefits. Expect your team to need time to recuperate afterwards: you're borrowing energy from the future and you'll need to repay it.

Get clear on the reasons it's worth it to work harder now

Your teammates will be angry if they think you're just trying to make yourself look good, but they might be convinced by how much the launch will help customers, how much revenue will be lost during a delay, following through on their commitments, or meeting an external constraint (like a conference date).

If you can, connect those reasons to the bigger picture. Are there financial plans, fundraising milestones, or competitive pressure that make the urgency real? The more compelling the reasons are, the more likely it is that your team will decide they want to put in the effort.

You should also double check that it actually makes sense to push harder. Does the launch date really matter? Could you cut scope instead? It might be better to just reflect on what went wrong and fix it for next time.

Ask in the right way

The way you make the request can influence the outcome.

Be honest about the problem. If it's partially your fault that the team fell behind, acknowledge that. You can frame the problem as new information so it doesn't sound like you're blaming anyone. For example, "We learned the authentication system had more complexities than expected." Share what you're doing to make sure it doesn't happen again.

Treat your teammates as partners in problem solving and try to come up with solutions collaboratively. Reinforce that the launch belongs to the team and is everyone's responsibility. For example you might say, "I've been looking for ways to make the launch successful and so far it looks like coming in on the weekend is the best solution. Does anyone have other ideas?"

Look for ways to make the extra work fun

Many people find that their fondest memories of a team are the times they all had to work extra hard together. Done well, it can turn into a bonding experience.

Here are some ideas to make late nights or weekends more fun:

- Order food to eat together—dinner, or just some fun treats

- Create a friendly competition

- Give out something memorable like a t-shirt or stickers

- Play music (if the engineers on your team like that)

- Head out to something fun afterwards

- Match people to the things they're interested in

I would encourage you to work alongside your team, even if PM work isn't a blocker for the launch. When you ask engineers to stay late, but you're not making the same sacrifice, it often leads to resentment.

CONCEPTS AND FRAMEWORKS

INTRINSIC VS EXTRINSIC MOTIVATION

Consider this scenario:

A STORY OF TWO FAVORS

Your friend Shana comes to you asking a favor. Could you spare a few hours this weekend to help her move? She knows it's an inconvenience, and so she'll pay you $20.

You do the math in your head. $20 for several hours of work? "No, thanks," you say.

She expresses her surprise. You helped Kari last month—and Kari didn't even pay you!

"Fine," Shana replies. "How about I don't pay you? Is that better?"

No, it's not better. What went wrong?

The problem here is *motivation*. There are two types of motivation, and they are not equally effective. **Extrinsic motivation** is when someone is motivated by external factors like rewards or punishments. **Intrinsic motivation** is when someone is motivated to perform an activity because it's personally rewarding, such as because they find it fun, feel connected to the purpose, or enjoy the challenge.

Intrinsic motivation is more effective than extrinsic motivation for any work requiring creativity. People who are internally driven to do their work will be more persistent, resilient, and creative. Extrinsic motivation is only recommended for non-creative work where people don't start with much intrinsic motivation, such as sourcing and batch-emailing candidates—but, even there, you have to make sure that the extrinsic motivation is sufficient.

A surprising finding from behavioral economists is that external motivators (like rewards and punishments) can easily replace internal motivation with external motivation. Worse, the internal motivation doesn't return when the rewards stop.

This was precisely the issue with Shana. Her extrinsic motivator pushed out your intrinsic motivation to be helpful, and wasn't sufficient for the task either. Whoops.

In his book *Drive: The Surprising Truth About What Motivates Us*, Daniel H. Pink shares a few examples:

- When children were told they'd get a reward for drawing, they chose to draw less in their free time than students who weren't told they'd be rewarded; the reward had turned play into work.

- When parents were charged a fee for picking their child up late from daycare, late pickups increased; they lost the internal motivation of guilt.

- When likely donors were offered a small payment to donate blood, they were much less likely to donate; it tainted an altruistic act.

As a leader, you need to be careful about accidentally demotivating your teammates with external motivations. A reward for fixing bugs, a promised bonus for shipping, or even excessive conversations about compensation can all reduce people's intrinsic motivation.

> There's a workaround. Surprise rewards that people don't expect beforehand don't seem to hurt intrinsic motivation. The time-honored PM trick of surprising the team with donuts is still a great way to motivate people.

In Pink's research, he found that there are three things that increase intrinsic motivation: autonomy, mastery, and purpose.

Autonomy

When people have self-direction rather than being micromanaged, they naturally feel more motivation. When it feels like someone else is steering the ship, it's hard to feel pride of ownership and motivation.

Here are some ways to foster autonomy:

- Tell people what to do (the results you want), but not how to do it.

- Treat people like you're all equal teammates. Stay late if other teammates need to stay late. Ask how you can help rather than blaming people for making mistakes.

- Include all team members in setting goals, creating a strategy, and planning.

- Run hackathons where people can work on whatever they want.

Mastery

People thrive on a sense of progress. They love to see that they are getting better, developing skills, learning, and tackling bigger problems.

To foster mastery:

- Set goals as a team and review progress together.

- Hold retrospectives and talk about what you want to do better next time.

- Let people work on projects where they're excited about the intellectual challenge.

- Recognize people's skills and offer them new opportunities to use them—for example, encouraging people-oriented teammates to plan team offsites.

Purpose

Purpose is the sense that the work is in the service of something larger than oneself. People are driven to accomplish something meaningful.

To reinforce a sense of purpose:

- Create a vision for your team. See Chapter 15: Vision (pg 179).

- Take every opportunity to remind people of how their work connects to the larger purpose. Expect people to forget the vision and strategy, and need reminding. Repeat, repeat, repeat.

- Let your own enthusiasm for the work shine through.

- Bring your engineers and designers along to meet customers in person.

One important type of purpose that drives some people is the affiliation motivation: being motivated by a sense of belonging. People who are motivated by affiliation want warm interpersonal relationships and strong bonds. They work hard because they want to support their team.

To support an affiliation motivation:

- Provide opportunities for team bonding like offsites or dinners.

- Celebrate milestones, such as launches, with a work party.

- Create team rituals like dressing up in a certain color on Fridays, keeping snacks at the newest team-mate's desk, or ending meetings with a team cheer.[1]

Remember: Happy teammates are productive teammates.

KEY TAKEAWAYS

- **Find ways to increase your teammates' feelings of autonomy, mastery, and purpose:** Even if it slows you down in the short term, you'll achieve much more as a team when people have the freedom to make important decisions, can take the time to perfect some of their skills, and understand the team's strategy and vision.

- **First be inspired, then inspire others:** The best form of inspiration is your own, genuine excitement. Even if you're not working on your top-choice project, take the time to understand the goals of the project and the pain points it will solve for users. If you're still stuck, talk to product leadership about why *they're* excited.

- **Teams can sprint to hit important deadlines, but it's costly:** The more they feel truly motivated, the more successful you'll be. Own up to your own mistakes that contributed to the need to sprint. Look for ways to make it a fun bonding experience.

---

1   Someone at Asana started a team cheer as a joke, and the practice quickly spread.

CHAPTER 24

OWNERSHIP MENTALITY

IF YOU EVER had a group project in college, you probably know this story. You get assigned to a team of three or four others—or maybe you pick them from the limited options.

Two weeks into the project, Chen has gone missing. You see him in class (it's hard to miss him when he stumbles in ten minutes late, clutching a Starbucks cup), but somehow he's never at the team meetings. Bethany at least is honest. Between swim practice and her campus job, she just can't do much. "I'm cool with whatever," she says—as though that's generous. Aarti tries to help, but it's clear she's a little lost. You find a small, isolated piece to hand off to her, and hope for the best.

So it's come down to just you and your buddy Tobin. This is unfortunate, but what are you going to do? Complain to the professor? "Not my problem," she'll say, "Figure it out."

Maybe the professor truly doesn't care. Maybe she feels there's no good way to get involved. Or maybe she figures that this is good preparation for the real world. In school and at work, you have to *figure it out*.

This is what an ownership mentality is. And it's as important in the real world as it is in school.

You need to take full responsibility for leading your team to success. You need to be willing to get your hands dirty and do whatever it takes, even if those tasks aren't included in your job description. You need to step up and take the lead so that other people can focus on their own work. Acting like an owner not only helps your team; it also shows that you're ready for expanded responsibilities.

RESPONSIBILITIES

FILL IN THE WHITESPACE

Early in his career, Sage Kitamorn worked on a product that had dedicated testers, but no strategy on how to turn the discipline of testing into quality. No one in the organization thought it was their responsibility.

Kitamorn saw the gap and stepped up:

> I decided to author a checklist of how we could determine that a build was good. I worked with the testers to build reusable scripts and ensure we covered all of the flows. At first, I wondered whether I was overstepping, but soon the whole team saw the benefit of higher quality. As a PM, it was my role to do whatever was needed to create a great product.

Product management is fundamentally a "whitespace" role. If there's something that needs to be done and no one else is doing it, the PM needs to take responsibility for it. Sometimes the gap is obvious, for example when there's no user researcher. Other times it looks like someone else should be filling the gap, but they don't realize they're supposed to, don't have time to, or don't have the skills to.

It can be a delicate situation when you step up to fill in a gap that should have been owned by someone else. Ideally, you can turn it into a partnership by aligning on goals. If not, you'll need to decide if the issue is important enough to risk ruffling feathers. If you're not sure, check with your manager.

TAKE RESPONSIBILITY FOR THE FULL CUSTOMER EXPERIENCE

Your title might be *product* manager, but you need to take responsibility for making sure all of your non-product partner teams are successful too. That doesn't mean you don't trust the other teams or that you'll micromanage them, but you should set up checkpoints to make sure everyone has what they need to keep everything on track.

- When you work with product marketing, make sure the messages match the benefits and target audience you were going after, and that all of the supporting material is ready for the launch date.

- If you work with salespeople, you'll want to understand how they sell your product and to ensure they have everything they need to do it effectively. This could be talking points, demo scripts, or features that help make a demo more compelling.

As you advance in your career, you'll want to expand your understanding of the factors that tie into product work. For example, you might need to learn how data scientists are allocated so that you can ensure your team gets the support it needs.

PROACTIVELY SHARE YOUR TEAM'S PROGRESS, CHALLENGES AND ACCOMPLISHMENTS

As the PM, you're responsible for making sure stakeholders know how your team is doing. If things are going well, they can celebrate with you; if they're going badly, they can help.

As Jules Walter, who led monetization at Slack, shared:

> A lot of people are afraid to tell leaders when something is hard, even though the work actually is hard. If you don't educate executives on the challenges, your team won't get the full resources they need or recognition they deserve.

Recognition is important for more than just your ego. If leaders don't know about your team's good work, they won't take it into account when allocating projects and resources.

But, if you share your team's accomplishments with leadership, you'll be trusted with more important work and more autonomy in the future.

Additionally, your team's morale will get a boost from this recognition. Your teammates will feel more motivated knowing that their hard work is appreciated—leading them to accomplish more in the future.

GROWTH PRACTICES

FIND THE ANSWERS FOR OTHER PEOPLE

When you're new on a team, people will ask you many questions that you won't know the answer to. It can be tempting to just tell that person how they can answer the question for themselves: which engineer to speak to, where to look in the documentation, and so on. After all, that will save time, won't it? Plus, they'll learn how to find the answers themselves.

When you're in a senior position mentoring someone, it makes sense to encourage them to find the answers for themselves. However, that isn't appropriate when a peer comes to you as the PM of a team. The PM is supposed to be the cross-functional point-of-contact. A different way of looking at those questions is to see them as a signal. Someone asked you the question because they thought it was important and they thought you would know the answer.

Instead, use this phrase that Dare Obasanjo recommends: "I don't have the answer but I'll look into it and get back to you." It lets you keep your position of leadership and as the point person even though you don't have the answer yet.

DIG INTO THE DETAILS YOURSELF

As a PM, you get a lot of data in summary form. The head of operations might hand you a list of the top ten customer complaints. You might run some data analysis on the most used features. Those summaries, however, don't always tell the full story.

As the PM, you should drill into the data to double check the conclusions and make sure you're not taking anything for granted. You need to understand the data so you can defend it and form your own opinions about it.

Beth Grant, a manager on Apple's Maps Data team, shared a story about when digging into the details made a big difference:

> We were creating the buildings layer for Maps, and we found that the operations side of reviewing the computer-annotated images was taking much too long. From previous experience, we knew the editing effort should be 10x less than what we were seeing, and we wondered if we needed to improve the computer-created buildings.
>
> We decided to dig into the details and see exactly what kind of changes they were making. What we found was that we had a bug in the editor instructions instead of in the software. When we reviewed a few samples of editor work, we realized that many of the edits weren't going to make a visible impact. For example, a huge portion of the recorded edits were spent zoomed way in to nudge a corner of a building a couple of centimeters—a distance not even perceivable in the end product. It totally reframed our next steps. Instead of updating the computer algorithms, we were able to change the instructions to editors to reduce low-impact edits.

Sometimes PMs get scared away from looking at the data when they think it would take a long time to look at all of it. Grant, however, knew she only needed to dig into a sample of the data to gain a lot of insight. If she hadn't double checked the details, she might have wasted her team's time on an unnecessary software fix, instead of implementing the operational fix that was better for everyone.

CONTRIBUTE TO THE BROADER PM TEAM AND COMPANY AT LARGE ⚡

As you advance through your career, you move from taking responsibility for your feature team's success to taking responsibility for the entire product, and even company's success. Your ownership mentality expands in scope.

This expansion is especially important if you're interested in people management. As you move up the management ladder, you're expected to contribute more and more to the broader organization as your direct work on the product decreases. Even as an IC, the most senior levels include an expectation of driving impact beyond your immediate team.

Here are a few examples of the ways you might contribute:

- **Repurpose what you've learned into materials for your peers**. You could share a template you designed, set up training for something you learned, or put together a process to remove an annoyance. You don't need any permission to do this; just send something out to the other PMs, and ask them to let you know if they find it helpful.

- **Volunteer for tedious work that gets you access to higher level meetings**. Executive meetings give you important insight into how the company leaders think. You usually won't be allowed into these meetings, but sometimes you can find a way in by volunteering to take notes or prepare data.

- **Pick up some strategic exploration work that no one else is exploring**. One of the best ways to become a leader of a new team is to be the person who identifies the need and does the original exploration. For example, you could research how to take on a competitor or go after a new audience.

- **Pick up grunt work that leaders really need someone to do**. This can be nuanced since you don't want to put a lot of time into something that isn't appreciated. Wait for something that's been clearly identified as valuable.

- **Work with a team you're considering transferring to**. Sometimes you can take on a small project with the potential team. You get to learn if you'd really like it and they get to see what you're capable of.

- **Lead a PM team or cross-functional process and improve it**. Volunteer to lead hackathons, organize product review meetings, run an onboarding session, or take on another responsibility that impacts a large number of people. Put on your "product discovery hat" and see how you can make it even better.

It does take extra time and effort to pick up extra work, but these internal contributions can have a multiplier effect on your impact. Making your teammates more effective is an incredibly leveraged way to increase your value.

CONCEPTS AND FRAMEWORKS

WHAT DOES IT MEAN TO ACT LIKE AN OWNER

One day, William was surprised to overhear the VP of product chatting with William's manager about his project: the new site navigation. His manager was describing the project, talking about the progress and challenges. Why wasn't the VP talking directly to William?

The problem was that the VP didn't see William as the leader of the team. That meant that, not only did his manager need to waste time answering questions about the navigation project, but the answers weren't even fully up-to-date. Even worse, William was missing out on hearing useful feedback directly from the VP. If William had made it clear he was responsible for the navigation project, the VP might have come directly to him.

Here are some examples of what showing ownership looks like:

Taking responsibility for all of the components that drive success

- **Not showing ownership:** Focusing on getting your own responsibilities done, without also ensuring that everything else is being taken care of.

- **Not showing ownership:** Pushing bad outcomes onto other people and claiming that they weren't your fault.

- **Showing ownership:** Double checking that all of the teams involved in a launch are on top of their responsibilities.

- **Showing ownership:** Reflecting on what you can learn and how you can personally drive better outcomes after each experience, even if the problems seem, at a surface level, to be someone else's fault.

- **Showing ownership:** Taking pride in your product and staying motivated to go after quality even if it takes a long time.

Identifying what needs to be done and doing it

- **Not showing ownership:** Making excuses that you followed the rules and did everything you were supposed to do.

- **Not showing ownership:** Waiting for someone else to give you instructions. Expecting someone else to take the lead.

- **Not showing ownership:** Quietly accepting decisions that you think aren't right. Following consensus without forming your own opinion.

- **Showing ownership:** Not expecting the playbook to be complete. Using your own judgment for ways you can help. Filling the whitespace.

Being the primary representative for your team

- **Not showing ownership:** Frequently redirecting questions about your team to other people.

- **Showing ownership:** Learning how to answer questions from stakeholders or going to find the answer yourself.

- **Showing ownership:** Proactively sending status updates about how your team is doing so other people don't have to ask.

When you act like an owner you signal to the people around you that you've got everything under control and they can rely on you.

KEY TAKEAWAYS

- **As a PM, there's nothing that's "not your job":** It's your responsibility to launch successful products that work across the entire customer experience. If there's a gap, either because no one has the appropriate role, or because the most appropriate person isn't doing a good enough job, it's your responsibility to make sure that gap gets filled. Be kind and diplomatic, but don't let your product fail.

- **If people don't see you as the leader of your team, you'll be overlooked:** When executives or other people at the company have questions, opportunities, ideas, or feedback for your team, they'll want to talk to someone who shows an ownership mentality—someone who will do the work to answer their questions or ensure their information gets to the right place. If they don't believe you're that person, you'll be left out of valuable conversations and end up hearing important context second-hand.

- **Taking ownership over product-team or company-wide processes is a good way to show you're ready for expanded responsibilities:** The advanced levels of product management involve broader responsibility to the entire organization. Activities that help the organization (instead of just your feature team) might seem like extra work or a distraction, but they're important for your career.

CHAPTER 25

MENTORING

CONGRATS! YOU LAND your dream job as a PM Lead at *Shoeless Socks*, a personalized sock subscription service. You walk into your first day excited to revolutionize the exciting world of sock delivery!

Your CEO pulls you aside and informs you that, due to some mix of circumstances around people traveling, a lack of experienced PMs, and an odd company culture, there's no one around to guide you. "No worries," she says. "You can figure it out."

Suddenly, the winding road ahead has grown spikes and roadblocks.

On Day 1, instead of an hour discussion about the team's priorities, you spent four hours trying to find the team's strategy documents. On Day 2, you prioritized the incoming bugs—only to learn that you were working off of an outdated list. It feels like your days and weeks are spent doing things wrong, or reinventing the wheel, or just trying to figure out *how* to do something.

By the end of your first month, you are exhausted and frustrated from all the senseless mistakes and inefficiencies. It didn't have to be this way!

By the end of your first year, you have likely quit—or, perhaps, changed things around so that this doesn't happen to the next PM.

Even for experienced PMs, a small amount of onboarding can be a huge multiplier on their productivity. Being able to ask a few questions saves hours of time. Regular feedback keeps them on the right path. If the mentor is particularly good, the mentee's trajectory can be transformed by being focused on the most important areas to develop.

> Mentoring takes time, but is incredibly impactful. Improving the quality and effectiveness of other PMs is one of the strongest ways to contribute to your company's overall success. When you become a mentor, you expand your influence beyond the teams you directly PM, to all of the teams that your mentees lead as well.

While mentoring is an important skill for all PMs, it's especially important for people managers and those who would like to become managers. Mentoring an intern or an APM is a great stepping stone to a management role. Sure, the intern is effectively a guinea pig for the employee's management skills. But the intern gets a dedicated resource, there to offer guidance and advice. And the mentor gets to learn a key aspect of management, without undue responsibility for someone's long-term career. It's a win-win.

Finding people to mentor

The easiest way to start mentoring is to volunteer. You can let your manager know you'd love to onboard a new hire or mentor a summer intern.

If that doesn't work, you can find your own mentees. Keep an eye out for people who are asking for help and offer to answer any questions they have. You don't need to limit yourself to PMs. If your teammates are interested in learning more about product management, you can let them shadow you on PM work.

See also: Chapter 29: Coaching and Development (pg 302)

RESPONSIBILITIES

TEACH YOUR MENTEE ABOUT THE COMPANY AND PRODUCT

When you mentor someone on your team, you want to make sure they learn the information that will help them succeed.

If possible, write up an onboarding document. You can link to material to read or watch, so you can make better use of your face-to-face time.

Here are some things to cover when you mentor someone who's new to your team:

- **Company and team purpose:** Make sure they know the mission, vision, and goals. Let them know the top priorities so they'll have the context they need.

- **Customer insights:** What are the fundamental insights they should know to start? Did anything surprise you back when you were new? Anything that might embarrass them to get wrong?

- **Product demo:** Even if your mentee used the product before they joined the company, chances are they are only familiar with a fraction of its functionality. As you show them the product, talk about the product-related decisions that were made and why.

- **Marketing/competitive landscape:** What should they know about the target audience or key competitors? How is the product positioned? What do you admire about different competitors or what worries you? What are the hot markets that the company is trying to expand into?

- **Tools and communication channels:** What dashboards and tools do people at the company use? What software do you have installed? Are there webpages you've bookmarked? What mailing lists, groups, or chat channels are you on?

- **Processes and workarounds:** What processes does the team follow? Are there templates or training? Are there steps that can be skipped or any workarounds that people commonly use? Are there unspoken rules?

- **The scoop on key people:** Which people are important to know? How do you get on their good sides and avoid their bad sides? Is there anything special to know about working with them, such as the best way to reach out to them? Which people are regarded as the best mentors and managers?

- **Any traps or pitfalls:** Is there anything that tends to trip people up? Any mistakes that they should avoid? Anything you personally got caught by that you can warn your mentee about?

- **The fun stuff:** Share the things that make work enjoyable. Is there a secret stash of chocolate in one of the rooms? A quiet place to work with a great view? A chat channel where people share funny memes?

Beyond the information that people need when they're new, you'll also want to continually share context with your mentee. Mentees appreciate when you share the highlights of strategic or higher-level meetings.

MENTOR THROUGH APPRENTICESHIP

As important as sharing knowledge is, the best way to mentor someone is through on-the-job training. A huge part of being a PM is handling the unexpected, so you need to get into the real work to see how it's done.

Here are some techniques:

- **Shadowing:** Invite them to watch you work in a variety of circumstances. They can join your meetings. They can sit next to you while you process your inbox. They can watch as you go over new prototypes with your designer. You can call them over to show them how you use data tools. If their desk can be put next to yours, there will be many opportunities for serendipitous shadowing.

- **Pairing on your work:** Include them in your active work. Talk through your decisions and ask them for their thoughts. Whiteboard together. Let them take the lead on some parts and redirect them as necessary. This is especially powerful when you include them on work that's more advanced or strategic than what they'd normally be responsible for; it will demystify what the next level looks like.

- **Pairing on their work:** Help them think through their decisions. Review their writing before it's shared more broadly. Let them rehearse presentations in front of you.

- **Reverse shadowing:** Watch them in meetings or presentations and take notes to share with them later. Point out the things they did well, anything they need to improve on, and what the next level would look like.

- **Be available:** A key differentiator between successful and unsuccessful mentors is how available they make themselves to their mentees. Schedule regular 1:1s so they can ask you any questions that are on their mind. If they don't ask you a lot of questions, check in with them proactively and reassure them that they're never bothering you with their questions.

On-the-job training like this is so valuable because you've developed expertise and approaches that aren't always easy to articulate. They can absorb this by watching you.

GIVE YOUR MENTEE FEEDBACK TO HELP THEM GROW ⚡

As a mentor, you have a unique perspective on your mentee's strengths and weaknesses.

Set up a cadence to give feedback and coaching regularly. For very junior PMs, you might want to debrief with them after each of their important meetings. As they get more senior, you might want to set aside a portion of each 1:1 or every fourth 1:1 to discuss their growth opportunities, not just tactical matters. Starting this habit early makes it easier if you ever have to share negative feedback.

As you think about which feedback to share and emphasize, focus on the top priorities that will help them grow and get to the next level. Make sure they have a clear and inspiring view of what growth looks like.

Your instinct might be to tell a mentee to just keep up the good work. But, if someone is meeting and exceeding expectations at their current level, it's time to start coaching them for a promotion. Reinforce that they're doing great, but also share the feedback you'd have for them if they were a level higher. Not only does this help them grow faster, it prevents them from feeling like it's unfair that they weren't promoted yet.

GATHER PEER FEEDBACK FOR YOUR MENTEE ⚡

Peer feedback helps both the mentor and mentee see multiple perspectives. Feedback is more powerful and more difficult to dismiss if you hear it from multiple people.

Many companies have official peer review cycles, but they might not be frequent enough for what your mentee needs. You can gather peer feedback unofficially, such as by meeting occasionally with their main partners, or asking for written feedback.

Be aware that many people don't like to write anything negative, so you'll sometimes miss problems if you're not careful. It can help to include an explicit multiple choice question such as "Are they on track to succeed? Yes, Yes with caveats, or No?" It can also help to let them answer anonymously, or to meet with them in person so you can read their body language.

There are a few ways to share the peer feedback with your mentee. You can share it directly. You can pick out key quotes (while being sure to respect the anonymity expectations you set up). You'll also want to share your interpretation of the feedback (perhaps after letting them self-identify the themes) so they don't focus on the wrong things.

BE A SPONSOR, NOT JUST A MENTOR ⚡⚡

To have a significant impact on someone's career, you need to do more than just advise them. You need to use your influence to help them get the recognition and opportunities they deserve.

Help your mentees get visibility for their good work. Share their accomplishments with company leaders. Celebrate their successes publicly and let everyone know about their contributions. Consider sending a note to their manager praising the things they've done especially well.

Find good career opportunities for your mentee. You can pass along invitations to speak at conferences. Recommend your mentees for important projects. Lend your credibility to your mentees.

As a people manager, sponsorship is even more important. It can look like hiring someone you believe in, promoting them, assigning them to important projects, putting them on stage at a conference, or giving them other career opportunities. Great sponsorship as a manager is often about recognizing that someone is ready for a big opportunity before they do, and encouraging them to take it.

GROWTH PRACTICES

GET COMFORTABLE GIVING EASY DEVELOPMENTAL FEEDBACK

Make sure you're sharing the following types of feedback on a regular basis.

Positive feedback

Positive feedback is fun to share and helps in multiple ways:

- Improves confidence

- Helps people feel appreciated

- Gives them more insight on what areas of their work was valuable and why

- "Catch them behaving" reinforces the behaviors you want to see more of

- Strengthens the relationships so it will be easier to point out problems when you need to

Some PMs will claim that they just like to hear constructive feedback and don't care about positive feedback. In practice though, they'll start to get demoralized or disconnected from you if you give mostly constructive feedback. Aim to give much more positive feedback than constructive feedback.

The more specific you can be with your positive feedback, the better the person will absorb it:

- **Basic:** "Great job with the launch!"

- **Intermediate:** "Great work catching that problem with your thorough testing!"

- **Advanced:** "Great work catching that problem with your thorough testing! Those test scripts you put together are a great example of good execution. Our customer support team is really going to appreciate that you saved them all of those tickets."

Small corrections

Small corrections are the "learning on the job" type of feedback that's expected whenever someone is trying something new or taking on a stretch project. For example, maybe they sent out a status update that was too long and difficult to read. Maybe they answered an executive's question in a confusing way.

To make the most of small corrections:

- Give small corrections in the moment (or as soon afterwards as you can share it privately).

- If your mentee likes to get a lot of feedback, try sharing "Five things you did well and two things you could have done better" on a regular basis.

- Ask "How do you think that went?" to open up the conversation. It gives them a chance to reflect and start to notice problems on their own, which is the first step to fixing them.

- If your mentee feels it went great but you noticed problems, you can point them out gently: "Did you notice that the salesperson seemed frustrated? What do you think she was getting at with those questions?"

- When possible, point your mentee to examples of the skill done well.

- Be careful not to overwhelm or distract them with small corrections when there's something more important they should be focusing on.

Remember that having a positive relationship with your mentee will make offering corrections like this much easier.

"Next level" feedback

"Keep doing what you're doing" is a dissatisfying answer for an overachiever.

Even when someone is on a good track and just needs more time to see their work through to get to the next promotion, there's still something they could be doing even better.

Instead, imagine they've been promoted to a higher level and the expectations are even higher. What would that look like? What feedback would you have for them at that point? It might be that they could do the same quality of work faster, or be able to anticipate problems sooner, or set a more ambitious goal.

Make sure your tone sounds inspiring and sends the message that they're doing well. "That presentation was great; you've got really strong communication skills for an APM! If you want to think about what the next level looks like, see if you could tighten it up to deliver the same amount of signal in half the time."

GIVING NEGATIVE FEEDBACK ⚡⚡

Sometimes, you'll notice performance issues that go beyond simply "learning on the job" and need to be corrected. Your goal is to give the information they need while preserving the relationship, and then to maximize the chance that they follow through and improve.

Depending on the severity of the issue, how early you caught it, and how strong your relationship is with the person, there are a few levels of formality you can use. For any serious issues, make sure to work with your manager first.

Don't use a feedback sandwich

You might have heard the advice to deliver criticism via a "feedback sandwich": first something positive, then the criticism, then another positive.[1]

At first glance, it seems useful; in practice it tends to be damaging. This doesn't mean something along those lines can't ever be helpful; just that, more often than not, it backfires to wrap up criticism with some cheap compliments.[2]

Consider this bit of feedback:

> Hey Brian, about that presentation. I loved the funny story you told at the beginning. It didn't seem like you were very prepared though: you hadn't pulled the usage data or looked at the error rate and that made it difficult to make a decision. We came to a good decision at the end, though. Thanks for running the meeting!

What is Brian supposed to take away from that? You'd like him to hear, "Hey, please be more prepared." But in practice, one of two things might happen:

1. He actually hears the criticism (great!), but he's ignored the positive stuff; the compliment was only given to facilitate criticism. So your positivity accomplished very little, other than making you seem sort of fake.

2. The positive stuff drowns out the negative feedback. He doesn't realize that this was actually important feedback, as people often overemphasize the first and last things they hear in a conversation.

---

1   Some more colorful terms include the "BS sandwich" or the "sh*t sandwich"—not that we're endorsing those terms.

2   A great article with more context (and links to data) is Adam Grant's "Stop Serving the Feedback Sandwich". https://www.linkedin.com/pulse/stop-serving-feedback-sandwich-adam-grant/

If you employ the feedback sandwich frequently, Brian *will* indeed learn from it—but not what you want him to learn. He'll learn that your compliments are a mere gateway to criticism. Next time you give him a compliment, he'll be bracing himself for what he did wrong.

There are better approaches.

Handling a first offense

The first time you notice a problem, you can take a lightweight approach:

1. Point out the problem factually.

2. Ask them about it, giving them the benefit of the doubt.

3. Reinforce that it's important.

4. Make sure they come up with a plan to address the problem.

Here's an example of what that might look like.

> **Mentor**: Hey Brian, I noticed you hadn't prepared the usage data or looked at the error rate before the meeting today. What's up with that?

Occasionally they'll give a great answer where they take responsibility on their own:

> **Brian**: Oh yeah, I feel awful about that. I'd meant to do it this morning but we found a P0 bug in production and I spent the whole morning helping the engineers fix it. I'll make sure not to save that until the last minute next time.
>
> **Mentor**: Awesome, it's important to be prepared for those meetings. Thanks for being on top of it!

More typically, they'll need a bit of support to come up with a plan:

> **Brian**: Oh yeah. I'd meant to do it this morning but we found a P0 bug in production and I spent the whole morning helping the engineers fix it.
>
> **Mentor**: Ah, that happens sometimes. But it is really important to be prepared for executive meetings so we don't waste their time and damage our credibility. What are your thoughts on how to make sure it doesn't happen again?
>
> **Brian**: Oh! I hadn't realized it was a big deal. I guess I can postpone the meeting if a last-minute emergency comes up.
>
> **Mentor**: Postponing could delay your whole schedule. What about preparing the data a few days in advance?
>
> **Brian**: That's a good idea, I'll do that, thanks!

Addressing a pattern

If the problem becomes a pattern that's affecting their performance, you may want to take a more formal approach. As with all negative feedback, make sure you deliver it in private.

Here's an example of a formal approach:

1. Ask if you can give them some feedback

2. Describe the issue and share two examples. Keep it factual, and explain the implications of the issue.

3. Reinforce your positive intention for giving the feedback

4. Invite them to share what they think

5. Come up with a solution and plan to follow up

Here's an example of what that might look like.

> **Mentor**: Hi Brian, I wanted to give you some feedback. Is now a good time?
>
> **Brian**: Sure.
>
> **Mentor**: I've noticed a problem where you're not prepared for meetings. Two weeks ago, you didn't have the usage data at the executive presentation, and yesterday there was no agenda for the cross-functional partners meeting. When you're not prepared, it wastes people's time and shows a gap in execution skills. I'm sharing this because I believe in you and want you to succeed. What do you think?
>
> **Brian**: I thought I didn't need an agenda since it was the second partners meeting.
>
> **Mentor**: Sending an agenda is important so that you can make sure the right people attend, and to make sure the meeting is a good use of everyone's time. We ran out of time on the sales update and didn't get a chance to discuss partnerships, which means you needed a follow-up meeting which could have been avoided.
>
> **Brian**: That makes sense
>
> **Mentor**: Alright, let's come up with a game plan for moving forward. What do you think would work?
>
> **Brian**: Maybe I could check in with you before my meetings to make sure I've done enough preparation?
>
> **Mentor**: That works for me. When's your next meeting?
>
> **Brian**: Friday
>
> **Mentor**: Okay, we can review your preparation at our 1:1 on Thursday. See you there!

For more help, the coaching group SNP gives training on delivering hard feedback.[3]

GET FEEDBACK ON YOUR MENTORING

Getting feedback on your mentoring is important for two reasons. First, it gives you the information you need to improve. Second, it helps you get recognition for the good mentoring you've done.

Mentorship happens in private, and so it's usually invisible to your manager and the promotion committee unless you work to make it visible. If you catch problems before they happen, your manager might not realize you did anything.

Talk to your manager about the challenges your mentee is facing and ask for feedback on how you've approached them. Get written feedback from your mentees that you can use in the performance review

---

3   SNP can be found at https://snpnet.com

cycle. Most mentees are reluctant to share critical feedback, so you might need your manager to collect anonymous feedback to get the full picture.

GUIDE YOUR MENTEES TO FIGURE OUT SOLUTIONS ON THEIR OWN

As a mentor, you should help your mentees figure out solutions on their own, rather than just giving advice or telling them what to do. Ask questions instead of giving the answer.

Your role is to help your mentee become independent. They need to learn how to build up their own mental models and frameworks, as well as break away from the school-mindset that there's a single right answer. They need to learn how to solve problems on their own.

You might find it difficult not to blurt out the "right" answer when someone comes and asks for advice. Here are some tips.

- Practice asking "what have you tried?", "what are you leaning towards?" or "What do you think we should do?" before sharing any of your own thoughts.

- Loosen your belief that you know the only right answer. Try to foster a mindset of curiosity.

- Ask broad, open-ended questions that illuminate your thought process like "What factors are you considering for prioritization?", "What are the tradeoffs?", "What has worked for you before?", "Where could you find that data?" or "How do you think they would react to that?"

- Silence is your friend. Let them have as long as they need to answer.

- Stay one level more abstract than the solution you have in mind. For example, ask "Is there a way you could make the information more easily digestible?", instead of "Should you add a graph?"

- If you really want to jump in with advice, first ask "Would you like to hear what I would do in that situation?" Give them autonomy over whether to take the advice, or not.

It's normal that you'll sometimes slip up and jump right into giving advice. Pay attention to those times and reflect on what happened, and over time you'll find it becomes easier.

REFINE THE WAY YOU GIVE DEVELOPMENTAL FEEDBACK

When you give someone developmental feedback, you help cut through the noise and show them what to focus on. You give them an outside perspective to shine a spotlight on what they're doing well and what needs improvement.

Here are some practices to improve how you give developmental feedback.

- **Get into the mindset that you're on their side**. If they don't believe that you're on their side, they'll reject your feedback. Make sure you're not giving feedback to criticize or complain; you're giving it because you want to see them succeed.

- **Give feedback privately**. This should be obvious, but don't give someone feedback in front of other people.

- **Be explicit about the message they should take away from your feedback.** Americans, for example, tend to downplay feedback when they have to deliver negative comments (leading American listeners to subconsciously "play up" negative feedback). This sort of adjustment—or lack thereof—can lead people to wildly misinterpret the message in either direction. Tell them if they should feel good about the feedback or if it's a serious issue.

- **Speak objectively.** Rather than using judgements and opinions, share the facts you saw and the feelings you had. You can use "The story I'm telling myself…" to introduce assumptions or guesses. This helps defuse defensiveness.

- **Be specific and share the implication.** For both positive and negative feedback, it helps to give specific examples and explain why those examples are good or bad. Reinforce the outcomes that happened because of their behavior.

For more details on how to give each type of feedback, see "Get comfortable giving easy developmental feedback" on pg 262.

CONCEPTS AND FRAMEWORKS

REVIEWING AND CRITIQUING WORK

Despite how much "critique" sounds like "criticism," you're not supposed to simply point out everything you don't like. A critique is about analyzing the work and assessing how well it achieves its goals. The term is often used for giving feedback on designs, but the concept also applies to reviewing specs, presentations, or any other work someone produces.

One of the best ways to mentor is through the feedback you give people on their work. By explaining the reasoning behind your feedback, you can help your mentees build their mental models and frameworks.

Here are some ways to give feedback on work to the people you mentor:

- **Double check their goals.** A critique needs to assess the work against the goals, so you want to make sure you're on the same page. Even if the goals seem obvious, the act of asking reinforces that the person is expected to be intentional.

- **Use "I like", "I wish", and "I wonder."** Using this framing helps you share your feedback without making people feel defensive. For example, "I wonder if this will be discoverable enough for our goals with just an icon."

- **Include positive reinforcement.** Let them know which parts are working well, and praise the places they've done something especially good.

- **Make it a teaching moment.** Share stories or context that will help the person absorb the lesson better. Explain your framework and reasoning. Allow space for discussion if they disagree or have questions.

- **Point out where they could do less.** Critique can have the unintended side effect of pushing people to pursue perfection. It's just as important to point out where they could have moved faster by cutting corners or calling it good enough.

- **Give them space to make their own mistakes**. When possible, give them space to make their own decisions and learn on their own. Instead of pressuring them into your solution, suggest checkpoints and ways for them to validate if their idea will work.

- **Pay attention to patterns of mistakes**. The patterns of mistakes can show you where you need to invest in more training or guidance.

For more on giving feedback on product work, see "Give great product feedback" on pg 81.

MENTORING SOMEONE WITH IMPOSTOR SYNDROME

Impostor syndrome (pg 221) is when someone thinks they got their success by luck or accident, and are afraid of being exposed as a fraud. Mentors play an important role here since people might not notice it for themselves.[4]

You might suspect that a mentee has impostor syndrome if they don't seem confident, they downplay their good work, seem reluctant to take on opportunities that you feel they're capable of, or spend too long perfecting work that is already good enough.

Here are some tips that may help:

- Introduce them to the concept of impostor syndrome and let them know that many—probably most— successful people have felt it. Just having a label for this can help someone understand that "I feel unqualified" isn't necessarily indicative of "I am unqualified."

- Help them see their strengths and the good work they've done. Point out the choices they made that not every PM would have made. Solicit peer feedback so they can hear directly from their coworkers what they're doing well.

- Set honest expectations. Give them context on what kinds of mistakes are normal and what information you expect them to learn, rather than already know.

- Shine a light on the ways their lack of confidence is holding them back. Point out when they undersell the research they did or waste time over-preparing.

- Help them find ways to quickly validate or invalidate their fears, such as sharing early drafts of their work with a trusted mentor.

- Model a willingness to admit what you don't know. Ensure that your work culture makes it safe to ask questions and learn. See "Create Psychological Safety" on pg 225.

- Be open with them about where their *actual* growth opportunities are.

Remember that impostor syndrome is extremely common, at all levels of experience.

---

4   It's particularly difficult to notice one's own impostor syndrome in the more "severe" cases. These people know that they feel unqualified, but they blame that on *being* unqualified. They don't think "I'm qualified, but I feel unqualified, so I must have impostor syndrome." No, they just think "I'm unqualified."

KEY TAKEAWAYS

- **Great mentors provide information, apprenticeship, and feedback:** Some things people learn best by being told, some they learn best by watching, some by doing, and some by hearing how they did. Don't limit yourself to just one or two of these techniques.

- **If you're uncomfortable providing feedback, plan ahead:** There are lots of handy phrases, templates, and approaches that make it easier to share feedback. Set up a plan for how you'll give feedback early in the relationship, so you're ready when you have tough feedback to share.

- **To develop their skills, help your mentee figure out solutions on their own:** To become independent, PMs need to learn how to find their own solutions. Instead of always rushing in with your advice, hold space for your mentee to think through their options.

CHAPTER 26

WORKING WITH OTHER DEPARTMENTS

PRODUCT MANAGERS ARE often called the "CEOs of product"—an analogy which has various issues. However, one big truth to it is that, like being a CEO, product management is a hugely cross-functional role. As a PM, you work with everyone across the company, and your skill at working with different types of people will be a big factor in how successful you are.

PMs who are unsuccessful working with other roles will usually find that their career stagnates. If engineers and designers don't like working with you, you'll struggle to recruit and retain team members. If execs don't like working with you, well, they will hardly want you to move up, would they? That would mean seeing *more* of you—and giving you more influence.

But this isn't just a likability contest (likability is a necessary, but not sufficient condition). Working effectively with an engineer, designer, or exec is about how you create excellent work using the best skills and insights from each of you.

While much of how you treat a person is the same across positions—people are people, after all—we have some specific advice to offer on working with designers, engineers, and executives.

WORKING WITH DESIGNERS

Product designers are generally responsible for solving problems from a user experience perspective. In a healthy relationship, PMs and designers are tight partners who share ideas and feedback, and ultimately trust each other's judgement and are willing to accept each other's decisions.

When the relationship isn't as healthy, things can get pretty ugly. The common complaints designers have about PMs include:[1]

---

1   For more on this, Laura Klein conducted an excellent survey: https://www.usersknow.com/blog/2019/9/12/product-team-mistakes-part-1-communicating-company-amp-user-needs

- **Focusing on the business value instead of the customer value.** Optimizing for metrics can be good, to a point. But, many metrics that can be measured in an experiment overlook the long-term harm of a poor user experience. Beyond that, designers tend to be more motivated by helping people than hitting numerical goals.

- **Treating the designer like a pixel monkey.** Designers don't like to be handed wireframes and told to "make it pretty." They want to hear about the problem, not be handed a solution.

- **Relying on personal preference.** A good design isn't about whether you (or an executive) like the colors; it's about whether the design meets its goals and works for real users.

- **Not contributing enough.** Each designer has some expectation of what the PM should be providing, and unfortunately that doesn't always match the PM's expectations.

- **Not understanding the product deeply.** Designers rely on PMs to understand how a change in one part of the product might affect other parts. Missing this can cause big mistakes or frustrating conversations.

- **Not valuing good design.** The details matter in good design. Consistency matters. PMs who treat the details as optional or cut design work at the last minute to hit a launch date are showing they don't value design.

Fortunately, there are techniques to encourage a strong, positive relationship.

HAVE A DIRECT CONVERSATION ABOUT WORKING TOGETHER

Because the roles of PM and designer have so much overlap and work closely together, it's important to have a direct conversation with each designer you work with about how you'd both like to collaborate. Ask what they appreciate or expect from a PM, and share what you'd like or expect from a designer. The relationship can vary a lot, especially based on how experienced the designer is.

Here are a few topics you might want to cover:

- Do you set up daily check-ins to go over designs, or will the designer reach out proactively when they're ready for feedback? Can you see their progress on a regular cadence?

- Do they like to start with a group brainstorm, or would they rather have time to think about the problem independently first?

- How would they like you to share your ideas with them? Are they okay if you draw some wireframes?

- What level of detail do they like in setting up the problem and constraints?

- Will they show you different directions that they've considered?

- When should designs use realistic customer data and when is it okay to use *lorem ipsum* placeholder text?

- How early in the process will the designer consider onboarding and empty states?

- Will the designer set and share their own dates?

This conversation might feel a little uncomfortable when you're not used to speaking so directly, but it will avoid discovering misaligned expectations later in your relationship.

TREAT YOUR DESIGNER LIKE A PARTNER

The PM/designer relationship works best when you treat your designer like a trusted partner instead of a resource.

As much as possible, share full context with your designer and include them in goal setting and strategy. Give them a voice when making decisions that affect the design, even if your company culture doesn't require you to do so. Ask them for feedback on your spec or for their thoughts on how to solve challenging problems. Invite them to relevant meetings, and let them present their own designs.

When disagreements happen, listen to their point of view. Try to come to solutions that work for everyone, but also be willing to defer to them in their areas of expertise.

Above all, invest in understanding each other's reasoning. Explain why you're making decisions and seek to understand their goals and frameworks.

BRING YOUR DESIGNER PROBLEMS, NOT SOLUTIONS

As a PM, you're responsible for defining the problem and ensuring the solution is successful. It's not your role to insist on a specific solution.

Defining the problem takes real work. Customers or internal stakeholders will often ask for specific solutions in their feature requests. The idea that comes to you in the shower is often a solution. You need to analyze the requests and ideas to determine the true pain points and goals. In addition to the customer pain points, you'll also need to set the context and requirements, such as timeframes, engineering constraints, learning goals, and different cases to design for.

Generally, it is okay to make wireframes to illustrate an idea, but it is not okay to pressure your designer into going with your solution or expect them to just "pretty up" your wireframes. Usually you should let the designer explore on their own before you share your own ideas.

If you and your designer disagree on the right solution, make sure to frame your disagreement in terms of the problem. Give feedback in terms of goals and principles instead of solutions. Leave space for the designer to come up with another solution that will meet all the requirements.

If you want to work at a company that has great designers, you need to create an environment where they want to work. Skilled designers want to explore tough problems, come up with creative solutions, and ship a polished product they can feel proud of. If you take away their autonomy, they will not want to work with you.

SPEAK IN TERMS OF USER BENEFIT, NOT BUSINESS BENEFIT

As Julie Zhuo points out in "How to Work with Designers", designers generally think about things from the perspective of the user and are motivated by how their work will help people.[2] PMs usually share the same customer-centric goals, but we often use language that focuses on metrics or business success and can sound heartless or even selfish to designers.

Designers sometimes think that PMs care more about hitting short-term metric goals in order to look good to company leadership than actually creating something that helps users.

As much as possible, frame things in terms of customer benefits instead of business benefits when you're speaking with designers. For example, instead of saying "we need to increase revenue" you can say "we need to be sure that people who want the premium version can find it."

---

2   Read Julie's post at https://medium.com/the-year-of-the-looking-glass/how-to-work-with-designers-6c975dede146

SET YOUR QUALITY BAR HIGH AND DON'T PULL A BAIT-AND-SWITCH

A quick way to lose the trust of your designer is to ship low-quality work. One way this happens is when the PM has agreed to the designs, but as the engineering work falls behind schedule, the PM then insists that the design needs to be cut. Or the PM states that the design work will be done in a "V2" that never comes.

The fair way to handle this situation is to be open about scoping concerns while designs are being made, and include the designer in decisions about changing scope. Consider cutting use cases or functionality instead of design polish. Don't say you'll do design work after launch if you can't guarantee it will actually happen.

It's common that PM and designer quality bars might be slightly different, but if they're far enough apart that it's causing repeated problems, this might be a topic for PM and design leadership to align on.

INVEST APPROPRIATELY IN DESIGN DEBT AND DESIGN SYSTEMS IMPROVEMENTS

Just like engineering infrastructure sometimes hits scaling limits or falls out of date, the design system can get cluttered with new functionality or start to look dated as design trends advance.

As Laura Klein found in her survey of designers, a main area of tension between PMs and designers is how much of the product to change at once.[3] PMs feel like designers often want to bundle major design changes with a small feature. Designers feel like PMs only want to add features and don't care about improving the design.

If the design improvements are small, it can make sense to combine the projects and improve the design as part of the new feature work. Some teams like to always set aside some buffer time on their projects so they can improve the design as they go.

Other times, it works better to split the work into two separate projects: one to launch the new features with the original goals, and another to improve the design, with its own success criteria. This helps the team feel like the design work is real, valuable work, rather than scope creep. If the design work is high enough priority, it can be sequenced before the new functionality.

Speak with your designers about what "design debt" they'd like to invest in fixing while you're building the roadmap. You can think about what percentage of time is appropriate to invest, and then let the designer prioritize the work that goes into that bucket.

WORKING WITH ENGINEERS

Engineers are responsible for creating technical solutions and maintaining them over time. In a healthy relationship, PMs and engineers are partners who work together to come up with innovative solutions that are fast, scalable, and don't slow down future development.

TREAT YOUR ENGINEERS LIKE PARTNERS

The most important rule for working with engineers is to treat them as respected partners. Include them throughout the product process, starting with early product discovery if possible. Share the full context with them so they can understand the purpose and reasoning behind the work. Invite them to visit customers or attend user research sessions so they can have first-hand experience with users. Ask them to share their ideas, and treat their concerns seriously.

---

3   Read more about this survey at https://www.usersknow.com/blog/2019/10/8/product-team-mistakes-part-2-select-ing-estimating-and-prioritizing-features

Don't treat your engineers like "code monkeys" who aren't allowed to have any product opinions. Don't assume they're lazy when they push back against work. Instead, seek to understand their reasons. If the reasons are technical, make sure you understand them deeply enough to recognize what solutions could work. If the reasons are around the product choices, take the time to discuss and come to a shared understanding; you might need to share more context to help show how you came to the decisions you made.

Engineers do their best work when they understand what they're building and why.

Understand and respect technical constraints

When engineers push back on a design for technical reasons, they usually have a good reason. If you ignore their concerns, they'll quickly lose respect for you.

You don't need to be an expert in computer science to understand technical constraints. Use your product knowledge to drive the conversation. For example, you can point out other parts of the product, or other products, that do what you wanted, and ask about what makes those different.

For more information on working with technical constraints, look at Chapter 8: Technical Skills (pg 92).

Never commit to dates for your engineers

If your team needs to commit to dates, your engineers need to agree to them. Ideally, your engineers independently calculate the dates they believe they can commit to, and you add some buffer on top of that.

Choosing dates for your engineers is disrespectful; it implies that they can work as fast as you want if you just tell them to. It takes away their autonomy.

Many PMs underestimate how long engineering takes in the real world. Beyond just coding the work, engineers need to write tests, set up infrastructure, and manage the deployment schedules. Even writing the code can take longer than you'd expect because they need to account for different corner cases and connect to the different parts of the system.

Respect their process

Engineering is creative problem solving. There's not a direct relationship between hours spent at the computer and speed to completing the project.

Most of the work happens in a state of flow. Any interruptions, such as stopping by their desk to ask a question or scheduling a meeting in the middle of a big working block, can force them to context switch and take a long time to regain productivity. Avoid this whenever possible.

On the other hand, productivity can happen in spurts. Sometimes, the engineer needs to take a walk around the block. Don't get frustrated with your engineer because it looks like they're goofing off—they might need the mental break to come back refreshed.

Relatedly, don't come storming in as a new PM and change engineering processes like sprint schedules or standups unilaterally. Work with the engineers to come up with process improvements collaboratively.

Avoid wasting their work

Imagine you spent all week working on a presentation and then you find out the presentation is canceled. You'd feel frustrated that all your work was wasted. Unfortunately, this happens to engineers more than it should. They finish building something only to learn that the design or requirements are changing and they have to start all over again.

Make sure you're clear about what product decisions are finalized, and which ones might change. If things might change after a beta program or an A/B test, let the engineers know. They might be able to take short-cuts or build in a more flexible way if they anticipate changes.

As much as possible, try to solidify the plans before engineering work starts. Run usability studies on proto-types. Ask important stakeholders for early feedback. Avoid last minute surprises.

WORKING WITH EXECUTIVES

Executives can be intimidating, but as you work with them, you'll understand them better and feel more comfortable around them.

Keep in mind the following points about executives:

- **They have very limited time**. Executives tend to be abrupt and direct. They might not explain them-selves. They can be impatient when they feel like someone is wasting their time. They might make you skip around in your presentation, or derail the entire agenda to talk about the points they think are important. They can't afford to waste time.

- **They rely heavily on trust**. To save time, executives prefer to rely on people they already trust, such as other managers. They'll quickly decide how much they trust you. If you don't sound confident in what you're saying, or if you've made sloppy mistakes, you'll quickly lose their trust.

- **They're focused on big goals**. Unless your project has the potential for a big upside, it's not that important to them. They might encourage you to think much bigger and go after wild ideas, even if pursuing those ideas doesn't seem practical for your team.

- **They're looking at the big picture.** Your work is just a tiny piece of a big puzzle. They care about opti-mizing across all projects more than just within your project. This is why they'll insist on consistency, shared infrastructure, and future-proof data models.

- **They know a lot of context you don't**. They're privy to how the business is doing across all depart-ments. They know what initiatives are on the horizon. They might have secret information about competitive threats, acquisitions, or big deals coming through the pipeline. They know what the board members are worried about. Sometimes their ideas seem random but are connected to that context.

- **Their job involves making difficult decisions**. Executives know that they can't please everyone. They care about your morale, but they're not afraid to disappoint you. This might desensitize them to bad behavior and lead them to act rudely when they're frustrated.

- **They don't want you to just blindly follow orders**. It might sound like they do, but usually that's a miscommunication. Executives presume that they'll be correct, but they want you to understand their goals and concerns and come up with a better solution if one exists.

The relationship between PMs and executives is parallel in many ways to the relationship between engi-neers and PMs. In both cases, one person has broader context, while the other person is closer to the work and getting things done. If you imagine how you'd like engineers to work with you, a lot of that will apply to you working with executives.[4]

WORK FOR FOUNDERS AND EXECUTIVES THAT YOU RESPECT

Founders and executives shape the culture and direction of a company.

If you don't believe in them or are not aligned with their approaches, you'll be fighting an uphill battle. You might be protected for a while if you have an excellent manager, but you'll be at risk if that manager leaves or is blocked by the people above them. It's unlikely that you'll see a lot of career advancement, and it probably will not be worth the emotional stress.

A particularly important example of this is with the head of product (or with the founders if you're the head of product) at a startup. Many PMs are caught by surprise at how involved the head of product can be with every design decision. If you fundamentally respect them, this can be handled with some discussion, gentle nudging, and letting them think that things were their idea. If you don't respect them, it will be infuriating and you might hit a stalemate.

SEEK TO UNDERSTAND

It's surprisingly common for people to brush off ideas from executives. They might assume that the executive is out of touch with reality or too attached to their own ideas. Sometimes, the PM will claim that the executives don't understand product best practices.

Even if there are elements of truth to those thoughts, you're doing yourself a disservice if you think of your executives as pointless obstacles in your way. Their ideas might seem strange, but that's often because they're viewing things from a much larger perspective than you are. Even when their ideas aren't directly relevant to the work at hand, it's often a valuable insight into the bigger picture.

UNDERSTANDING AN EXEC

Noah Weiss, VP of Product at Slack, had worked with his team to come up with a massive end-to-end overhaul of the customer experience that touched the home page, product positioning, team creation screens and onboarding flows. He warned the CEO, Stewart Butterfield, that this ambitious plan would take time: "We're not going to see results as quickly with this plan. The curve is not going to bend as quickly."

Butterfield replied enigmatically: "You're thinking about it backwards. If you bend the culture curve, the growth curve will follow."

Weiss wasn't sure what that meant, but the meeting was over so he put it aside. Maybe it just sounded profound but wasn't.

Then, the next morning, Weiss had an "aha" moment and understood what Butterfield had meant! To take on a project of this size, he'd have to change the whole culture of how they build product. "If we didn't change the culture, we couldn't take on this bet. And if we couldn't take on this bet, we certainly couldn't hit our growth goal at the end of the year."

---

4   This does NOT mean to treat your engineers like you're above them. This analogy is just to help you build empathy for the executive's point of view.

> Focusing on the culture change turned out to be energizing for the team. Everyone had wanted to do more prototyping, more user testing, and to focus on a cohesive experience, but they hadn't felt like they had permission before. Now, they effectively had a mandate. It was so successful that the approach spread across teams at Slack.

When you hear ideas from executives, take the opportunity to dig deeper. If you don't agree with the idea, talk to the executive from the mindset of "I'm probably missing something. Can you explain where my reasoning is wrong here?"

VALIDATE IDEAS FROM EXECUTIVES

Executives often feel strongly about surprising ideas. Rather than brushing off the idea or blindly charging ahead with it, take the middle ground of finding a way to validate it.

It's worth it to try to do a little validation, even if you're dead set against the idea. One of you is wrong—and it could be you.

Even if you like the idea, you should still do validation, just like you would for any idea your team had. An executive liking an idea isn't sufficient reason to make a multi-month investment without testing the concept in front of real people. It's your responsibility to ship successful products, and you don't get absolved of that responsibility just because an executive asked for the project.

BE PREPARED FOR YOUR MEETINGS WITH EXECUTIVES

Executives can be quick to judge. You don't want to get on their bad side by showing up unprepared.

Before you present your work to an executive, consider reviewing it with your manager or a mentor. Plan out what you want to say and anticipate possible questions. Look for careless mistakes. Make sure you've looked into any important data that's readily available.

If possible, send them your material in advance and ask them if they have any questions. That will give you time to look up the answers rather than being put on the spot during the meeting. If they do ask you a question where you don't know the answer, let them know: "I'll look into that and get back to you."

PROTECT YOUR TEAM FROM THRASH

Sometimes, executives will stop you in the hall and ask you to start working on something. Usually, they don't actually intend for your team to drop everything and work on the new idea. Even if that is their intention, as a PM, it's your responsibility to figure out if that is the right decision.

The executive is usually thinking about the urgency and priority of the new work. It's your job to think about the opportunity cost of stopping the current work. Context switching is costly and teams feel demoralized if they don't get to ship what they've been working on.

Most of the time, you'll be able to move the ideas to be considered in the next planning cycle, or to start after the current project finishes. But, sometimes you'll find that the executive is right and it's worth pausing the current work to take advantage of a new insight or opportunity.

Once you've figured out what you feel is the right decision, loop back with the executive to let them know. They might be totally fine that you've put the idea on the list of things to consider for next quarter, or they might come back with more reasons to do it sooner.

DON'T USE "BECAUSE THE EXECUTIVE SAID SO" AS YOUR REASON

When I was a new PM, I once told my team we needed to add a new feature because the VP had told us to. I thought this was inspirational; how often would we get a chance to build something that the VP cared about? Apparently, my engineers didn't think so, and word got around to my manager. My manager sat me down and explained why that's a bad approach.

In modern tech companies (especially in the US), hierarchy isn't seen as a good enough reason to do something. Employees don't assume that the highest up person knows more than they do about their specific work.

> For morale and engagement, it's important for each person to understand the purpose of their work. They can't understand the purpose of their work if the only justification they've been given is that an executive wanted it.

Instead, make sure that you personally understand the reasons the executive cared about the work, and share those reasons with your team. You don't even have to mention that an executive asked for the work, unless you think that will motivate your team in a positive way.

DON'T THROW AWAY THEIR IDEAS; BUILD ON THEM

Executives usually get to where they are by being good at their job. They can't always articulate their reasoning, but they have strong hunches that have often been right.

If you come in and tell them that they're wrong, they probably won't believe you. They'll think that *you* are being stubborn by not considering their ideas.

To avoid this, don't frame things as "their idea" vs. "your idea." Instead, frame your idea as something that builds on top of theirs. This neatly steps around issues of ego or defensiveness and helps you move forward collaboratively.

If they've written a product strategy that you disagree with, see how much of it you can reuse in your new version. Perhaps...

- … their old strategy becomes "Part 8" of a 10-part plan, after hitting a few important earlier milestones.

- … you can keep the features the same and regroup them, or keep the groupings the same and put in new features.

- … some sentences from the intro can be reused directly. You can tell them you loved the strategy and just reorganized it and filled it out a little bit.

If they've given you a terrible idea during design review, mock up that idea and a few more good ones. You can show them what you liked and didn't like about their idea, and then give it credit for inspiring you to think of even more good solutions. For example: "I loved the idea of making it more visual, so I tried your idea of using photography in the background, and then also tried adding some illustrations on top."

If they've got a meeting or process that doesn't work, frame your suggestions as small adjustments on top of what they've already put together, even if your changes are actually large. It's even better if you can volunteer to be responsible for those adjustments rather than asking them to take it on.

One of my direct reports successfully used this approach with me:

> I love that you've put together a weekly team meeting. Now that people have so many topics, I'm thinking it might be even better if we put together an agenda in advance. If you'd like I can take care of gathering the topics.

I was incredibly thankful for his initiative, and his framing made it easier for me to accept the help.

KEY TAKEAWAYS

- **Treat your coworkers like partners, not resources:** It takes people of all departments and disciplines to create a successful product and company. Especially for design and engineering, but also for roles like user research, data science, and marketing, you'll get better results if you include them in decisions and value their opinions.

- **Invest in understanding other people's jobs:** The more you learn about your coworkers responsibilities, processes, goals, and worries, the better you'll be able to collaborate with them. Many PMs make mistakes because they didn't understand where the other person was coming from.

- **Directives from executives are just a starting point:** When an executive tells you to build a feature, that's not permission to skip product best practices. Don't dismiss the idea or rush ahead to implement it. Just like you wouldn't take a customer request at face value, you should investigate the executive request to understand the underlying need.

PEOPLE MANAGEMENT SKILLS

PART G

PEOPLE MANAGEMENT SKILLS

THE PM CAREER ladder splits into management and individual contributor (IC) tracks at the higher levels. While ICs build products by influencing designers and developers, PM Managers build products by influencing and developing the PMs on their team.

In these chapters, we'll learn the skills to develop great PMs, to build great teams, and to create great product organizations.

- **Becoming a People Manager** (pg 285) will help us understand whether we'd want to go into management, and if so, how to make the move. We'll learn about some surprising aspects of the role and how companies choose who to make a new manager.

- **New Leadership Skills for PM Managers** (pg 293) will teach us how to adapt to a position of authority. We'll learn about reviewing work, holding people accountable, communicating strategy, and being a member of the leadership team.

- **Coaching and Development** (pg 302) will teach us how to help the people on our team develop their skills and grow. We'll learn about personal development plans, assigning projects, and performance reviews.

- **Building a Team** (pg 313) will teach us how to hire great PMs. We'll learn about designing an interview process, pitching candidates, and sourcing.

- **Organizational Excellence** (pg 328) will teach us how to design a well-functioning product organization. We'll learn about product processes, team culture, and org design.

These chapters only skim the surface of people management. To learn more, we recommend *The Making of a Manager* (by Julie Zhuo), *The Manager's Path* (by Camille Fournier), and *High Output Management* (by Andrew S. Grove).

CHAPTER 27

BECOMING A PEOPLE MANAGER

"YOU'RE A PRODUCT manager? How many people do you manage?" I'd heard the question so many times that I had my answer down pat. "I manage the *product*, not the *people*." I would reply.

Still, that question affected me. It subtly implied that managing people was the real marker of success. Was I on the wrong track? I loved my product and the impact I was having at Asana, but should I switch to one of the fast-growing companies with high turnover that made people into managers after a year or two? Was I a worse PM than my friends who'd chosen that path?

I felt a lot of external pressure to move into people management quickly, but in retrospect, I'm very glad I didn't give in. I did eventually move into people management, but the extra years I spent as an IC (individual contributor) were some of the most fun, impactful, and rewarding years of my career. As the company grew, becoming a people manager became the most impactful way for me to scale my impact—but the role does come with tradeoffs.

DO YOU REALLY WANT TO BE A PEOPLE MANAGER?

When you're just starting out, it's easy to think that managers are "in charge". And they are—to some extent. They do generally have some additional authority to make decisions, and to hire and—if needed—fire.

But as they say: "with great power comes great responsibility."

When you step into a management role, you become *more* accountable to other people for the decisions you make. You have to appeal to your engineers, your reports, and to more senior management. Your reports don't magically obey you, and even if they did, leveraging your power over them usually backfires.

This is all to say that people management is a complex role—loved by some, but not all. Be cautious about whether you truly want to make this transition; it's so easy to get caught up in the "prestige" associated with it—and don't be afraid to exit if it's not for you. But if it's the right fit, or you just want to try it out, go for it!

REASONS YOU MIGHT NOT WANT TO BE A PEOPLE MANAGER

People management can be emotionally draining

The decisions you make as a people manager can weigh heavily on you. Unlike product decisions, it's no longer "just software." You are responsible for people's livelihood now. You're responsible for judging people's performance and deciding who gets a raise and who doesn't. You might be in a situation where you need to fire someone.

These are all extremely difficult decisions that matter. It's relatively easy to treat a failed A/B test as a learning experience, but it's much more difficult to think of failures with your reports that way.

People management can be isolating

People treat managers differently, especially if they didn't know the person before they became a manager. You might find that you're not welcomed into the team the same way an IC would be. You might not be invited to outside-of-work events, or if you are, people might be more reserved in the way they talk to you. This makes work less fun, especially if there aren't other managers you can bond with.

You can't be entirely honest

As a people manager, you'll often learn secret or private information that you can't share with other people. For example, if you learn that someone will be leaving the company in a few weeks, you might need to reassign work without providing an explanation, or even hinting at the reason.

Sometimes you'll need to enforce a policy change you disagree with. As a manager, it's inappropriate to complain to your reports about the change; whether you agree with it or not, it will be your responsibility to roll it out successfully to your team. You can discuss your disagreement with your own manager, but to your team you'll need to support the company's decisions.

You need to get work done through other people

PMs already get work done through other people, but it's even more challenging when you need to rely on others to do work that you *know* you could do yourself. Most of the time, you know you could do the work faster and better than the people on your team, but you need to hold back and coach them rather than just telling them what to do. You need to give them space to do things their own way and make their own mistakes.

You have to disappoint people

Success as a manager isn't just about making the people who report to you happy. Your responsibility is to deliver excellent results and help the company succeed. Sometimes, what's best for the company isn't necessarily what's best for your reports. Sometimes what one report wants will conflict with another.

You might have to make tough calls about allocating people to projects or distributing stretch opportunities. You'll need to evaluate people and tell them when they're not meeting expectations. You might not be able to give people the raises they want (or even the raises you want to give them). You might need to add processes that improve product quality but slow teams down.

You need to put in a lot of hours and have a lot of meetings

When you're a PM, you get more and more efficient as you gain experience and improve your skills. Specs that used to take a week now take two hours. Some decisions take minutes instead of days. You catch usability problems immediately instead of after a usability test. Your work-life balance improves, and you can use the extra time to tackle new challenges.

People management isn't quite as scalable in that way. Sure, you'll get faster at making decisions and more efficient at resolving prickly situations. But, no matter how good you get as a manager, you can't make a 30 minute weekly 1:1 meeting take less time—and you'll need to have one of those with each of the people who report to you. You'll need to attend other people's meetings to gain cross-company context and share what your team is doing. If your team is hiring, you'll spend hours each week interviewing candidates. A substantial portion of your calendar will be filled up with meetings that don't get faster as you improve. In some ways, the quality of your work is directly correlated with the amount of time you put in.

You are responsible for process

Most PMs do not like process. They tend to prefer autonomy over rules. As a manager, you'll be responsible for setting up processes and getting your organization running smoothly. And, the higher you move up the organizational hierarchy, the more that spearheading processes becomes a fundamental part of your job.

Some PMs are eager to move into management because they want to leave day-to-day execution behind. In reality, execution is still a major part of your job. You just shift from helping a single team execute well to ensuring several teams execute well.

Recruiting becomes a big part of your job

If you grumble about how much time interviews take or you don't like talking to potential candidates, you might be disappointed to learn how much time managers put into recruiting. Some people love recruiting, but many do not.

At a growing company, you'll probably spend at least eight hours per week on recruiting. People who are great at building their team might have coffee chats every day of the week. You spend a lot of time pitching candidates, most of whom don't work out. You might travel for job fairs or to speak at conferences, in the hopes of finding someone good.

You don't need to be a manager to mentor people

People commonly say they want to become a manager because they love to mentor people. If you truly love to mentor people, you can do it without becoming a manager. In fact, many people hire leadership coaches who mentor them without a reporting structure.

In many ways, it's better to mentor people without being their manager. You'll be able to stay 100% focused on helping them grow without conflicting business interests. When you give feedback, it's easier to be supportive rather than judgmental.

If you want the "try before you buy" experience of management, see if you can officially mentor an intern or APM. These mentorship relationships are a great way to help you decide if you might like being a manager.

You'll usually be the person's main point of contact and will be responsible for helping create growth plans, giving performance feedback, and writing reviews.[1]

Becoming a manager is not always the best way to advance your career

In general, the company matters more than the role when it comes to advancing your career. If you don't want to be a manager, you can still advance in your career as a senior or principal PM. You can also consider coaching, consulting, and venture capital roles.

When you're at a great company you can learn best practices from your coworkers and ship products that have a big impact. You'll often build a stronger reputation, which opens up more options for you in the future.

You don't need to become a manager to make a huge salary

If salary is your top concern, you're generally better off taking an IC role at a big tech company than a manager role at a smaller company. Take a look at tools like levels.fyi to see salary ranges at different companies.

REASONS YOU MIGHT WANT TO BE A PEOPLE MANAGER

You can have a bigger impact

One of the main reasons to become a manager is that you can make a bigger impact with a team of people than you can by yourself.

Most products are built by teams of dozens or hundreds of engineers. To be responsible for a product of that size, you'd need to be a manager, or even a manager of managers.

You have more strategic influence

As a manager, you're responsible for setting the overarching vision and strategy to guide the teams under you.

Moreover, as a manager, you'll get to contribute to the strategies next to and above yours. You'll be invited to higher-level meetings where you can share your thoughts on the direction of the company. You'll be included in higher level decisions.

It expands your perspective

When you've never been a manager, their behavior can seem perplexing, or even incompetent. It can be hard to work with managers because you don't have a clear mental model of what they care about or how they make decisions.

Once you become a manager, you see the other side. You'll have experiences and gain context that helps you understand their perplexing behavior. When you face those same situations, you'll see the extra constraints, goals, and other information that make "the right way" not so right at all. That expanded perspective can help you make better decisions.

---

1   Note that different companies treat the internship process differently. However, at many companies, an intern's "mentor" essentially acts as their manager.

It can be very rewarding to support people and build a well-functioning team

Management is fundamentally a people-oriented job. You support people and help them grow. You bring people together and find ways to make the most of their skills. You convince talented people to join your team. You look for opportunities to help your teams create better outcomes.

Building strong teams is important and impactful.

It takes time to build people management skills, so it helps to start early

If you've already mentored an intern or APM and are confident that you want to be a manager someday, you might lean towards people management earlier in your career.

Unlike product skills, you don't get to exercise people management skills on a predictable timeline. People will need to be hired, fired, coached, and promoted on their own schedule. It takes years to build up a breadth of experiences. Over time, people management problems will feel like a routine part of your job, and you'll know how to handle them with confidence.

HOW TO BECOME A PEOPLE MANAGER

There are three things that need to come together at the right time for you to become a people manager.

THE ORGANIZATION HAS A NEED FOR A NEW MANAGER

Companies don't make people managers just to reward them for a job well done. They only add managers when they have people who need to be managed.

Joining a rapidly growing team increases your chances of becoming a manager quickly. Eventually they'll need more people to manage those PMs. Another opportunity occurs when an existing manager departs, but you probably can't predict when that will happen.

YOU ARE SENIOR ENOUGH AND PERFORMING WELL ENOUGH

Most companies have a minimum level where people become eligible to be a manager. Once you reach that level, you also need to be a top performer.

The exact bar for becoming a manager will be context dependent. If the PM team desperately needs a new manager, the bar could be lower. If there are very senior IC PMs on the team, the bar may be higher.

A common frustration among managers is when PMs who don't hit the bar want to become people managers. It's frustrating because those PMs often ignore feedback on how they need to improve, based on the mistaken assumption that PM skills aren't important for managers.

For example, a PM might say they don't need to improve their execution skills because they'll just have a direct report handle the execution for them. That's not a correct assumption. Managers require even stronger execution skills than IC PMs because they need to orchestrate delivery across several product teams and manage their increased workload.

Managers continue to use product, execution, strategic, and leadership skills once they have direct reports. At many companies, front-line managers still directly PM a feature team, in addition to their new management responsibilities. If one of their direct reports is out on leave, the manager will be expected to step in. Managers also use higher-level versions of those skills to drive success across all of the teams that report to them. Moreover, if a PM isn't excelling in their role, there's little reason to trust that they could teach others to excel.

LEADERSHIP THINKS YOU WOULD BE INTERESTED IN (AND GOOD AT) PEOPLE MANAGEMENT

You shouldn't simply assume that your manager will notice your great work and reward you with a management role. Instead, diplomatically let your manager know that you're interested in becoming a people manager and ask if you have any skill gaps you should work on filling.

Diplomacy matters here. You don't want to irritate the person you'll need as your advocate. An easy approach is to frame the conversation with your manager as future-looking: "I'd love to become a people manager eventually. What skills do I need to develop so I'll be ready when the opportunity arises? Can we brainstorm on some ways for me to build those skills?" Don't turn the conversation into an argument about how you think you do have those skills.

You may also want to have this conversation with your manager's peers. They'll have a more impartial perspective than your manager. By asking them for mentorship and acting on their suggestions, you'll be strengthening your relationship and turning them into advocates.

Here are a few ways to show you might be a good manager:

- **Mentor interns and APMs**. Treat it as an interview for management. Prioritize your reports, coach them, advocate for them, and ensure that they would be happy to be mentored by you again. If they do have performance problems, be sure to partner with your manager on the issues.

- **Earn the respect of other PMs**. When leadership is picking who will become the next manager, they'll pay attention to which person other PMs would be willing to report to.

- **Earn the respect of your manager's peers and other leaders at the company**. Whether a promotion decision lies ultimately with your manager or a committee, the opinion of other leaders matters. If they don't want to work with you, they could block your promotion.

- **Resolve conflicts on your own**. Managers often need to help their reports resolve conflicts. The best way to show you have this skill is to resolve your own conflicts without needing assistance.

If you're hesitant to introduce this conversation to your manager or manager's peers, consider why. It might be that you truly aren't ready yet; after all, no one is *actually* born ready. But it might also be that impostor syndrome is holding you back (pg 221).

COMMON TRAITS OF PEOPLE MANAGERS

When leadership is considering promoting someone into people management, there are a few traits they may look for.

- Steps up to help
- High capacity
- Proactive
- Flexible

- Knows how to get things done
- Gets good work out of their teammates
- Good at time management
- Good relationship with manager

- Respected by leaders across the company
- Easy to manage
- Few interpersonal conflicts
- Solves problems on their own
- Calm under pressure
- Willing to make tough calls
- Excellent judgement
- Shows discretion
- Strong communication skills

- Comfortable with executives
- Passes credit to others
- Celebrates their teammates
- Secure in their own skills
- Enjoys recruiting
- Enjoys mentoring
- Known as a good mentor
- Tolerant of people who are learning
- Teammates look to them as a leader

Overall, they're looking for someone who will help them scale. Someone who will effectively take over a portion of the team to save the leader time and energy.

MYTHS ABOUT BECOMING A PEOPLE MANAGER

Here are a few ways that are NOT how people become people managers.

- **Being at the company the longest**. Management isn't a queue where the people who have been waiting the longest are next in line to become a manager. It's about being the best candidate, not the one with the most tenure.

- **Interviewing**. Most companies don't interview people for internal promotions to management. Instead, what usually happens is that your manager or their manager picks the person they believe would be the best candidate and offers them the role. They only open the role to external candidates after they've decided not to go with an internal promotion. Some companies, however, *do* have policies that allow people to apply for internal management roles.

- **Outshining your manager**. You're not competing with your manager for their job. You could be promoted to be your manager's peer or to fill your manager's spot when they leave, but even in those situations, your manager's recommendation makes a difference.

Remember that to be promoted, people must *want* to promote you. You need to stand out from the crowd because you're great, not because you've pushed away the others.

MANAGING YOUR FORMER PEERS

When you first become a people manager, you might end up managing people who used to be your peers. That can be a bit awkward for everyone involved, so remember to be tactful in your transition.

This could be a sensitive time for your old teammates. They might have wanted to become a manager and could think it's unfair that you were chosen over them. They may not see you as more senior, and they might let you know it.

Don't let that hurt your confidence. You were selected for a reason.

Try the following to help the transition go more smoothly:

- You don't need to put on a show that you're the big boss now. It's okay to treat your old teammates mostly like peers, especially at first.

- If you are planning to change the way you interact with them, take extra care to explain the change so it doesn't feel like a power play.

- At the same time, you need to set clear boundaries and not tolerate any disrespect. If they ignore your requests, you'll need to address it immediately.

- Get a full handoff from their old manager to understand their personal development plan, how they're progressing, and any important information about their past performance. Are they close to a raise or a promotion? Get copies of past reviews.

- Have a conversation about their career goals in the first month. This helps establish your new role and ensures you won't put it off until it's too late.

Most of the time though, PMs assume this will be more awkward than it is. Your peers will usually recognize that you deserve this promotion, and they'll be happy for you.

KEY TAKEAWAYS

- **People management can be a lot less fun than it seems:** PMs tend to be ambitious and latch on to people management as a prominent milestone, but it's not the only way to have a successful PM career. You might feel more satisfied and get less burned out if you stay in an IC role for longer.

- **You need to be an experienced, successful PM to be eligible to become a manager:** Many PMs start focusing on moving into management roles way too early in their careers, which distracts them from the skills they actually need to be building. Don't neglect your PM skills.

- **Let your manager know if you're interested in people management:** Don't assume your manager knows what you want. Open up a forward-looking conversation so you'll be on their radar and will start to get useful feedback.

CHAPTER 28

NEW LEADERSHIP SKILLS

"WHAT GOT YOU here won't get you there." It's a common refrain we heard from product executives about the move into management.[1]

Priyanka was a well-loved, results-oriented, hard-working PM who cared about all of the people on her team and worked hand-in-hand with them to solve any problem that came up. She seemed like an obvious choice for management, but soon ran into issues.

As a PM, she was willing to do whatever it took to ship a successful product. She looked into every detail, joined every user session, and triaged every bug. As a manager, she tried to stay as closely involved, but got complaints about micromanaging. The better PMs tried to switch to other teams where they'd have more autonomy.

Things weren't any better with the PMs who were struggling. As a PM, she was careful to never blame her teammates when things went wrong. As a manager, she didn't hold people accountable; after all, weren't they all in this together? Unfortunately, at review time, they were quite surprised to hear they were missing expectations.

There were more problems when she worked with other company leaders. People loved the way she advocated for her team when she was a PM. At the leadership strategy session, however, she was called myopic for protesting an important pivot that would cancel one of her team's projects.

In many ways, success as a PM manager is the same as success for an IC PM—shipping great products by leading a team of people. As a PM manager, you're just working through one more layer of people. The leadership skills from Part F (pg 214) are as important as ever.

In a few ways though, as Priyanka learned, people management requires new, different leadership skills. Your official role changes your relationship with coworkers. Your scope expands to more teams, more strategy and a longer time horizon. To succeed in your new role, you'll need to develop your reports to take over your old responsibilities so that you can continue to expand even more.

---

1   Including in this excellent post: https://www.reforge.com/blog/crossing-the-canyon-product-manager-to-product-leader

RESPONSIBILITIES

SEE YOURSELF AS A MEMBER OF THE LEADERSHIP TEAM ⚡

As a people manager, it can be tempting to direct your attention downward and focus on being the best possible manager for your reports. You'll remember all of your own past managers and what you liked and didn't like and want to make your reports love you. You'll want to shelter them from unpleasant directives, defend them in conflicts, and never change plans on them when they're in the middle of a project.

That might sound nice in theory, but there's much more to management than getting stellar reviews from your reports. As a manager, you need to work with other leaders to create great outcomes across the entire company. You are more accountable to the teams above you than the teams below you.

Sometimes you will need to change plans on people and waste their work. Sometimes you'll ask one of your teams to set aside their own goals to help another team. You might need to defend a company policy to your reports, even if you personally disagree with it.

To succeed, you'll need to invest in your relationship with other leaders at the company. If you've found yourself in conflict with one of them in the past, now is the time to be the bigger person and step up to resolve it, for the good of both of your teams.

You speak on behalf of the company

When you are a manager, you're in a position of authority and your words carry more weight than they did before.

Imagine you're attending a meeting of your company's employee group for women. People are discussing that the new member of the executive team is a man. "I'm not surprised," you say, "This company only promotes men." As an IC, that comment would just be a complaint about the company's past behavior. As a manager, however, people in the room might construe it as an admission of discrimination. One of your reports, who was in the room, might sue the company stating that her boss told her only men could be promoted.

This isn't saying you should condone bad behavior, but you shouldn't speak carelessly around ICs, especially those who report to you. Even friendly teasing that was fine between peers can become scary when it comes from the person who determines your paycheck.

HOLD PEOPLE ACCOUNTABLE ⚡

As a manager, you need to foster accountability in your team. This means ensuring your reports follow through on their commitments, and if they miss their commitments, they explain why and take steps to do better next time. This doesn't mean that people need to be punished for missing a launch date; rather, that mistakes are taken seriously and learned from so that things can run more smoothly the next time.

The Five Whys process (pg 74) is a great way to foster accountability on your team. When OKRs are missed or other problems pop up, you can ask the PM to run a Five Whys and report back to you with what they learned, and what steps they're taking to avoid the problem in the future. The formalized steps help keep the conversation away from unproductive blame and towards future learning.

More generally, you can ask people to explain their actions and thought processes. Set up processes to ensure people do retrospectives for launches. Follow up with people when you notice something surprising. Ask people whether they are on track to hit each of their goals. If they are off track, ask what their plan is for getting back on schedule.

SET STRATEGY FOR YOUR TEAM ⚡⚡

As a manager, you'll rely on other people to execute your strategy. You need to find a way to divide the components of your strategy so multiple PMs can work on it at the same time. Here are some tips for approaching strategy as a manager:

- Write your strategy in a way that connects the dots between the company's higher-level strategy and the strategies for the teams under you. For example, if the company has ten priorities, you might own one of those priorities and write a strategy for it. You could then break it down into five initiatives and assign each initiative to a team.

- Be intentional about how teams will build on your strategy. Create clear places for them to carve out their own strategic approach while staying aligned with your intentions.

- Treat your reports like stakeholders in your strategy. Give them a chance to give their input before it's finalized. Reinforce that anything they intend to work on will need to connect to the strategy, so they should speak up if anything is missing.

- Be clear about prioritization, especially with peers and your own manager. If high priority work is falling behind, you might be able to reallocate resources from lower priority work on another one of your teams. Ensure teams clearly understand what work is high priority and why.

For more on strategy, read Part E: Strategic Skills (pg 166).

KEEP YOUR TEAMS CONNECTED TO THE STRATEGY ⚡⚡

Creating a strategy isn't enough. You need to ensure that strategy is understood and followed. Small misunderstandings can cause big problems: wasted work, missed priorities, misaligned product decisions, and decreased morale.

You'll need to repeat the strategy more often than you'd think. Take every opportunity to connect things back to the strategy. State what part of the strategy you're using when you make decisions. Remind teams how their project connects to the strategy. Talk about the strategic impact when you celebrate wins.

OKRs (pg 211) are a powerful tool to connect strategy to execution. Review each team's OKRs and don't settle until you're happy with them. You'll want to ensure that they are ambitious enough to make good progress towards the company's larger goals that you're responsible for.

REVIEW AND APPROVE WORK ⚡⚡

Early in your career, you brought your work to someone else for approval. Now, you're on the other side. *You're* the one who's responsible for ensuring the quality of your team's products.

You'll need to empower your team and ensure quality. The PMs who report to you are experts in their area and are much closer to the research, customers, and problems than you are. On the other hand, you probably have more experience, judgment, and bigger-picture context.

As a manager you'll review more work than you did as an IC—not just designs and working products, but also early specs and strategies as well. The best practices you learned while giving feedback to designers and engineers still apply:

- Set goals and define what success looks like. Your team is responsible for the solution.

- Frame your feedback in terms of principles rather than personal preference.

- Review the work to ensure it meets the success criteria.

Be aware that as a manager, your words carry more weight. People may feel less comfortable pushing back on your ideas or may accidentally interpret a casual comment as a direct order. The Do, Try, Consider Framework (pg 299) can help clarify intentions.

OBSOLETE YOURSELF ⚡⚡

Delegating is always an important skill, but as an IC, there are limits to how much you can delegate without getting into the territory of not doing your job. As a manager, the more you can delegate effectively, the more you can focus on higher-level responsibilities.

The advice in "Learn how to delegate well" on pg 160 applies here, but now you have even more flexibility.

Make sure to consider these options:

1. Coach and train your reports to grow into bigger responsibilities.

2. Hire new people who are capable of owning those responsibilities.

3. Become more tolerant of "mistakes."

Many leaders hold on to responsibilities for too long because they don't feel like they can trust anyone else to do a good enough job. By hoarding responsibilities, they become a bottleneck and slow down dozens, or even hundreds of people. Start by delegating the types of work where a mistake would be tolerable or reversible.

GROWTH PRACTICES

BUILD UP A SUPPORT NETWORK ⚡

Management can be isolating; your reports see you as "the boss" and your manager expects you to be independent. You might be surprised that you're no longer invited to hang out on the weekend, and that people are more cautious when speaking with you. You can't talk as openly about the challenges you're facing since they're often private.

Management is also emotionally taxing. Your reports might cry in 1:1s. They might be mad at you when they don't get allocated to the projects they want or don't get the raises they thought they deserved. You'll hear about the difficult situations people are facing in their personal lives. You'll feel responsible for the people on your team, and it might sometimes keep you up at night.

By intentionally seeking out mentors and peers to connect with, you won't be alone when you need help or empathy. Look for people with whom you can speak openly—for example, other managers at your company or a professional coach. You might also want to find people who are facing the same types of challenges as you, some who are a little ahead of you, and some who are much more experienced.

MAINTAIN AUTHENTICITY ⚡

You don't have to put on a big show about being the boss when you become a manager.

You'll be able to build up trust and have the most impact with the people who report to you if they feel like you're authentic and they can connect with you. One way to do this is to be open about your own failings and struggles.

SET HEALTHY BOUNDARIES ⚡

Some managers get so caught up in the idea of being a good and supportive boss that they fail to set important, healthy boundaries. They'll listen to an employee complaining about a new policy for hours or blame themselves when that employee ignores their feedback. They might make excuses for rudeness or disrespect.

This kind of permissiveness tends to backfire. First, it takes away your time and energy that could be better spent elsewhere. Second, it encourages bad behavior in your direct reports that will eventually limit their career growth.

> If you find yourself upset with one of your reports, that's a sign that you need to set boundaries.

You can limit the time you spend discussing a topic and end meetings that cross your boundaries. You can give your reports feedback that they're not taking responsibility for their own problems, pushing back on policies too much, being disrespectful, or that they're not taking feedback well.

It can feel uncomfortable, at first, to stand up for yourself in this way. It may help to imagine you were setting the boundaries for someone else on your team, not just yourself. You can also write and share a list of cultural expectations so that you have something official to help you feel justified in enforcing the boundaries.

AVOID MICROMANAGING ⚡

Just because you're accountable for the work doesn't mean you should start micromanaging. Great PMs do not want to be micromanaged, so if you want to build a strong team, you need to give people autonomy.

As a manager, it helps to reflect on where you can tolerate mistakes or solutions that are different from what you would have done. If the answer is "nowhere," then you'll be forced to micromanage.

Instead, consider letting your team learn things for themselves:

- Usability tests and small A/B tests are safe places to experiment.
- Work that's validated by a usability or A/B test can usually go out without too much extra review.
- For easily reversible changes, you can measure the success after launch to see if changes are necessary.
- Often a range of solutions could be acceptable, rather than requiring the absolute best one.

If you get stuck, remember that it's okay to tell them *what* the solution needs to achieve, just not *how* to do it.

BE INTENTIONAL ABOUT VELOCITY

As a manager, many of your decisions can affect the velocity of people on your teams.

You can increase velocity by hiring talented people, training them well, setting up product principles, creating a design system, and validating ideas early.

If you send a team back to iterate more before moving forward, that decreases velocity. That can be okay—after all, it doesn't matter how fast you go if you're heading in the wrong direction.

However, you need to be mindful of the delays you cause when you ask for more iteration. Only ask for this when you think the improvement will be worth the delay.

ENSURE THAT YOUR REPORTS FEEL FULL OWNERSHIP OVER THEIR WORK

You want to ensure that the people on your team feel full ownership and responsibility over their work, even if you're the one who is ultimately accountable. You won't be able to scale your influence without it.

Adam Thomas, a principal at Approaching One and product leader, puts it this way:

> You have no way of being more knowledgeable than the PMs on your team, so any traditional advice about the work itself is generally useless. Your job is to help them make better/faster decisions and step out of the way.

One way to put this into action is with the way you frame your questions. Presume that they are aware and on top of things. Instead of asking "You should find out how our competitors handle this," ask, "How do our competitors handle this?"

Ask questions to validate their assumptions. For example, you might ask, "How many people used that feature?" if you think it's important for the decision, or "Did that analysis slice by active and inactive accounts?" if you think they might have mistakenly not excluded inactive accounts.

As much as possible, treat your reports like the owners of the problem and yourself as an advisor. Even when you do know more than they do, don't let them rely on your knowledge rather than building up their own.

LOOK OUT FOR DECISIONS WITH BROAD OR LONG-TERM IMPACT

You need to step in when the fallout from a decision goes beyond the scope the team is responsible for. In these cases, you might need to ask for extra validation. In extreme cases, you might need to veto a decision.

Here are a few situations where the decision might go beyond the scope of the team:

- **Hard to reverse:** Could the decision impact the company's reputation? Would it be so expensive to change after launch that the team couldn't change it on their own without missing their other goals?

- **Long-term costs:** Most teams can plan three months out, but beyond that, they can't judge the feasibility of future plans. For example, they might say that they can rewrite a solution to be more scalable in a year, but you know the scalability will be needed sooner.

- **Cross-team impact:** When the decisions of one team impact another team, you might need to moderate. This is common when there are dependencies.

- **Consistency:** Each team might make decisions that make sense in isolation but add up to an inconsistent and confusing experience for users. Engineers might want to build their own infrastructure to optimize for their own use, but from a higher-level perspective, that's not the best use of engineering time.

Again, empowering your teams and delegating to them is valuable. But, there's also a time and place to step in.

INTENTIONALLY CREATE TRANSPARENCY ⚡⚡

The world of management can be very secretive. You work privately with your reports on their areas for growth. You attend confidential executive meetings. You learn about new initiatives and priorities. Much of your time is spent on work you can't talk about openly.

This secrecy has a few downsides. Your reports might assume you don't do much, and that can erode their respect for you. Additionally, when the secrecy involves useful context for decision-making, the team might make uninformed decisions or be confused by the requests they're getting. It's useful to counteract this secrecy by intentionally creating transparency:

- **Send out a list of your monthly priorities.** This can be high-level bullet points that are appropriately anonymized to maintain privacy. Often, just showing how many different things you're working on can earn credibility. The list helps people reach out to you at the start of an initiative, when there's still time for them to have an influence. It's also helpful to show what things you're not working on.

- **Talk to your reports about what's on your mind.** What keeps you up at night? What are you excited about? As much as possible, let them learn from you.

- **Include your reports on your work, whenever possible.** If you're working on strategy, ask your reports for their input and feedback. If you're going to give a high-stakes presentation, do a dry run in front of your team. They'll get a peek into your world and learn a lot from the example you set.

- **Share context from your higher-level meetings to your team.** One easy way to do this is to schedule your team meeting soon after your manager's team meeting so the information is fresh in your mind. Of course, respect confidentiality, but a lot of content from those meetings are relevant and not confidential.

Transparency can't always be offered, but when it can, it builds trust, respect, and a sense of fairness.

CONCEPTS AND FRAMEWORKS

THE "DO, TRY, CONSIDER" FRAMEWORK FOR PRODUCT FEEDBACK

Asana's "Do, Try, Consider" framework is a great way to empower your team while ensuring consistent and high-quality results. It gives approvers a clear way to share mandatory and non-mandatory feedback without being misunderstood.[2]

---

2   I also write about this at https://medium.com/@jackiebo/do-try-consider-how-we-give-product-feedback-at-asana-db9bc754cc4a

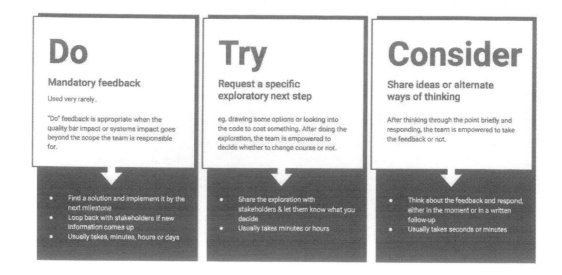

With this framework, when you give feedback, you clearly state if it is a "do," "try," or "consider." Each type of feedback has clear expectations around the intention of the feedback and how the team should respond.

- **Do:** Mandatory feedback. Teams try to find a solution and implement it by the next milestone. They'll loop back with stakeholders to let them know it's done or if any surprises came up. Use sparingly.

- **Try:** Request a specific exploratory next step like drawing some options or looking into the code to cost something. After doing the exploration and sharing it with the stakeholders, the team is empowered to decide whether they need to change course or not.

- **Consider:** Share ideas or alternate ways of thinking about a problem. After thinking through the point briefly and responding, the team is empowered to take the feedback or not.

To use this framework with your team, first introduce the concepts, and then be sure to tell them when you're using it. It might take a few examples before people really understand the type of response you're expecting. Soon the vocabulary will become second nature.

EDITING FRAMEWORK

Shreyas Doshi, a product leader who has previously worked at Stripe, Google, Twitter, and other companies, explains that one of the most important changes that a person must make when becoming a manager is shifting from creating work to editing work.

The first part of being a good editor is *recognizing* that your job has shifted from creator to editor. As a product leader, you need to create a strong team of PMs who can self-manage, and to do that you need to give them room to exercise their judgment. That will be the only way you can scale your impact.

Switching to an editor mindset can be especially hard for managers who feel like they need to prove they deserve the job. They might feel like criticizing the decisions of people on their team validates their own skills. Instead, you want to approach the situation with curiosity, such as, "Tell me what problem you're trying to solve with this."

The next part is to apply editing to all granularities, from product strategy down to pixels. To do this, you'll need to set expectations with your team that you intend to edit their work. You intend to offer suitable opinions on the work and evaluate the success of the work. Many PMs don't know what their manager's job really is; you'll need to explain what success looks like for you so they'll understand why you are editing their work. Be clear on which things you want to edit thoroughly versus which are optional to edit thoroughly. Beyond creating clarity, this signals which projects are the most important and where the PM should be spending the most time.

Finally, when it comes time for the actual editing, follow these steps:

1. **Listen and ask questions:** Improve your understanding before opining on things.

2. **Reframe problems:** Is the PM thinking too small? Are they worried about an impediment that you know can be resolved? Are they focused on the wrong problem?

3. **Explore alternatives:** Ask which alternatives they've considered and discuss them. If they've missed something in their evaluation of the options, let them know. If they haven't considered alternatives, ask them to.

4. **Direct or delegate decisions:** Be clear on which of your feedback is input for them to consider, which are strong suggestions, and which are non-negotiable.

By following these steps, you give your team the space and direction they need to deliver great work.

KEY TAKEAWAYS

- **Your team is the leadership team:** As a manager, your primary responsibility is to the broader company, not the people who report to you. Most of the time what's best for your team *is* best for the company, but you can't let fear of upsetting a report prevent you from doing the right thing.

- **Lead through strategy:** The primary way you direct your team should be through the strategy you set. If you focus on setting up the right vision, goals, and principles, you can then empower teams to execute. This keeps you out of micromanagement.

- **Shift from creator to editor:** Recognize that it is no longer your job to make decisions, but rather to set up the context and review the work. The PMs on your team are now the owners of their work. Be clear when your feedback is mandatory or not. Give them the space to exercise their judgment.

- **Obsolete yourself:** The best way to advance as a manager is to coach and train your reports to take on more and more of your current responsibilities. As they grow into your current role, that frees you up to work on higher level responsibilities.

CHAPTER 29

COACHING AND DEVELOPMENT

PHIL JACKSON IS considered one the greatest basketball coaches of all time. He led teams with players like Dennis Rodman, Kobe Bryant, and Shaquille O'Neal to 11 NBA Championships.[1]

Coaching famous basketball players isn't easy. The players are already among the best in the world—a fact their adoring fans remind them of every day. They depend on their teams, but they also want to be recognized for personal greatness. Their sport, like many sports, often celebrates aggression and competitiveness. Tempers run high and often lead to unnecessary fouls and poor teamwork.

For Jackson, coaching these stars meant fighting through the egos that often come with excellence. He had to not only identify how to improve on greatness, but also motivate them to follow his advice. At times, the latter was the trickiest piece.

With O'Neal, Jackson realized the biggest impediment was distraction. Jackson said, "Look, if you listen to me, you'll be MVP. You listen to me, you will win a championship." When Shaq agreed, Jackson instructed him to stop putting out rap albums, limit his commercials, and do everything he's told. Focusing on the game led Shaq to his best years of basketball.[2]

When it came time to coach Bryant on his relationships with teammates, Jackson leveraged Bryant's goal of becoming team captain. "How do you relate to your teammates?", Jackson asked. Bryant said he didn't. "That's not going to work out very well then." The message got through.[3]

> This is what coaching and development means. It's understanding what it takes to create a winning team. It's understanding people's goals and building trust so they'll be receptive to your coaching. It's picking the right combination of feedback, practices, and instruction to grow people into the skills they need to expand their responsibilities and be successful.

1   Phil Jackson wrote three books about his coaching career: Eleven Rings, Sacred Hoops, and The Last Season

2   More on this conversation at https://bleacherreport.com/articles/2892349-shaquille-oneal-says-phil-jackson-told-him-no-more-albums-limit-commercials

3   Read more about Bryant and Jackson's relationship at https://www.sportscasting.com/kobe-bryants-relationship-with-phil-jackson-transcended-basketball/

The skills in Chapter 25: Mentoring (pg 259) are an important foundation for coaching and development. As a manager, however, you have additional responsibilities. Coaching is not just about developing people in all the ways they want to grow; it also involves guiding them on which ways they *need* to grow and evaluating how they are doing.

RESPONSIBILITIES

SET EXPECTATIONS ⚡

PMing is a "figure out what needs to be done, and then do it" kind of role, so it's hard to set clear expectations. It sometimes feels like setting expectations would require figuring out what needs to be done for your reports.

The way around this is to set expectations around outcomes. You can start with the obvious ones: "your team will launch the work and hit the goals." You can also add expectations for what will go wrong to help people see where the opportunity for "exceeds expectations" lies. As much as you can, set expectations around specific PM skills. For example, if you have a career ladder, you can set expectations that they'll meet the criteria in a certain bucket by a certain time.

LOOK AT THEIR WORK, EVEN IF YOU'RE NOT THE APPROVER ⚡

PMs create documents, give presentations, send emails, and run meetings. They're also responsible for the designs, launch plans, and overall quality of their products. Looking at the work itself is an important way to form your own opinions of how your reports are performing and where they might need to improve.

It's easy to look at the work when you're officially responsible for approving it, but for other work, you'll need to have a plan. PMs sometimes bristle at the idea of showing you all of their work because they're afraid of being micromanaged, or they might just get busy and forget.

It's important to set expectations around your involvement from the beginning. Start with more oversight before giving more independence, rather than trying to add oversight once things go wrong. Removing independence after a project is underway will always feel like a demotion, so it should be reserved for the time when they actually underperformed.

Be specific about what work they should show you and what decisions they should run by you. Do you want them to forward you relevant conversations with "FYI" to keep you in the loop? Discuss what it will take for them to earn more independence; is there a particular timeline or milestone?

If possible, set up an organizational structure where you *should* be looking at their work. For example, could the PM manager be the approver for their PM's work?

CO-CREATE PERSONAL DEVELOPMENT PLANS ⚡

Work with your reports to create a personal development plan for each of them. It should cover their career goals, their strengths, their challenges, and what they want to work on.

Approach this as follows:

1. Have them write down their goals and self-assess their skills. All of this is key information in understanding what success looks like to them, so you can find matches between their interests and what the business needs.

2. Once you've seen their goals and self-assessment, compare it to your own assessment of their skills and what they need to do in order to advance.

3. Pick the top two to four areas for them to focus on; more than that would only end up being distracting.

4. Work with your report to come up with a plan; what are the milestones or deliverables, and how will you be able to measure progress? This discussion helps you and your reports align on what success looks like.

Check in regularly and make sure there's alignment between how they think they're doing, how you think they're doing, and how their goals match to their actual career progress. You should believe that if they hit their goals, they'd be on track for a salary increase or a promotion (or getting out of a more dire situation). If not, then consider what it *would* take, and work with them to update the plan to help them get there.

FIND OPPORTUNITIES FOR YOUR REPORTS TO STRETCH THEIR SKILLS ⚡

As a manager, you can help connect people to good opportunities. Recommend them for responsibilities that will allow them to grow. Hand over opportunities that come to you. Ask other managers if they have work that would be good for them. Put them in charge of things that stretch their abilities slightly, and let them know that you trust them and support them.

SCOPE PROJECTS BASED ON EXPERIENCE LEVEL ⚡⚡

Choosing a project is much more than just deciding what feature they're going to work on; you'll need to give them context and set guidelines for what you expect. In many cases, the exact same work can be scoped up or down to fit varying levels of experience and skill, just by changing those guidelines.

When deciding how much guidance versus freedom to give, it's better to start on the more restrictive side and loosen up the reins as they earn your trust. It's easy to loosen up; people feel great when you give them more autonomy. It's much harder to take away their freedom because they'll feel demoralized and may even ignore your attempts to rein them in. It helps to explain this framework from the start so that they won't worry that you'll micromanage them forever.

Here are some guidelines for setting up projects appropriately.

Intern	Full guidance with carefully crafted spots for them to fill in, for example "Interview these 3 stakeholders to learn their requirements." Discuss each piece of work before they start it and check in frequently. Make sure the project can be fully completed by the end of their internship with time to spare, and that it's okay if the project fails. The project should not be controversial.

1st year APM	Share the full background context, including the motivations for the project, key areas to research, and potential avenues to explore. Give very clear deliverables broken down step-by-step (e.g., "research", "spec", "review meeting") and an expected timeline. Check in frequently. Avoid projects where controversies will likely need to be escalated. Choose projects where it's okay if the project is delayed substantially or doesn't achieve its goals.
2nd year APM	Share the full background context and reference the steps you expect them to take, but you can allow them to generate the timeline and then check it. Encourage them to reach out to you when they need your assistance. Warn them of controversial areas and support them through these areas. Choose projects where there's some room for error.
More experienced PMs	Frame the problem, goals, and any constraints. Then let them figure out the "how." Continue to match the size, complexity, and criticalness of the project to the amount of trust they've earned.

It's great when you can perfectly match a project to the skills of a person so the work is just a slight stretch for them. Sometimes, you don't have that luxury because there's important work that needs to be done and there are no other options for who can do it.

If you need to scale a complex project down, here are some approaches:

- Be transparent that the project is a larger scope than you'd have liked for them. This will help them understand why it seems like they have less autonomy than usual.

- Put them in charge of a single phase of the project, such as running the beta program or taking the project from beta to official launch.

- Set clear expectations for the most complex parts that they will draft the work, with final approval from you.

- Have more frequent check-ins and working sessions where you can help guide the work.

When in doubt, start with a smaller scope. You can always expand it later.

GROWTH PRACTICES

BUILD A STRONG RELATIONSHIP WITH YOUR REPORTS ⚡

There's a common saying, "People don't quit their job; they quit their manager." Your relationship with your reports is a critical factor in their effectiveness and engagement.

To create a strong relationship, always ground yourself in positive intentions. Come from a place of believing in your report and being on their side. This doesn't mean you should overlook their problems or defend poor job performance, but rather, your intention in talking to them should be aimed at helping them to succeed, and not as a way to vent your frustrations.

Make sure you prioritize coaching your reports. You should see coaching them as your primary responsibility, not a distraction or random obligation. Have regular one-on-one meetings (1:1s) and avoid canceling them or arriving late. In fact, skipping 1:1s is widely seen as symbolic of poor management, regardless of the circumstances.

SET ASIDE DEDICATED TIME FOR COACHING ⚡

It's easy for 1:1s to end up focusing on tactical problems and nothing else.

One approach is to set aside every fourth 1:1 for coaching. You could also spend some time in each 1:1 on coaching topics.

It helps to be clear that you're coaching them so that your reports can notice and appreciate it. If you coach subtly, you might be surprised to hear that your reports don't think they're getting enough coaching from you. One tip is to come up with names or catchy phrases for the frameworks and approaches you share. This helps people feel like they're learning something substantial.

MAKE IT THEIR RESPONSIBILITY TO COMMUNICATE PROACTIVELY WITH YOU ⚡

PMs work autonomously, which makes them particularly difficult to manage. It's hard to be aware of all the work they're doing or how well they're doing it. It can also be challenging to insert yourself to course-correct or coach as needed.

To manage effectively, you'll need your reports to take the lead on communication. Emphasize that it's their responsibility to communicate transparently and build trust. Kate Matsudaira, an engineering manager describes it in this way:

> This implies an implicit contract: I will give you autonomy and independence, but it is your responsibility to share status and information with me.[4]

You can ask your reports to share their work with you using this template:

> Here's what's happening <the current challenge>. Here's how I <handled it/am handling it/am thinking of handing it>. Do you have any thoughts?

This template lets your reports maintain their autonomy and ownership over the situation while helping you understand the complexity of the work and giving you an opening to mentor.

SOLICIT FEEDBACK FROM YOUR REPORTS' PEERS AND PARTNERS ⚡

To get a full picture of how well your reports are doing, and to find the most important growth areas for them, you'll need to get feedback from the people they work with.

Peer feedback, or 360 feedback, is incredibly useful, but you don't want to rely solely on the infrequent official review cycles. Instead, you should meet face-to-face with the key partners of your reports and check in with them every few months. Those meetings can help you interpret nuances that might get lost in written feedback.

---

4   Read the full article at Chapter 51: The Paradox of Autonomy and Recognition (pg 496)

PMs tend to take direct quotes from their peers very seriously, so peer feedback can be a very helpful tool. They might not believe you when you tell them that their collaboration style is a problem, but they'd be less likely to dismiss quotes of what their teammates have said.

A scalable source of information is other managers. Sync with them to find out if any of their reports have said anything (good or bad) about any people on your team. If you learn something this way, you'll need to follow up diplomatically, since the feedback is second hand.

CREATE PLANS TO COUNTERACT IMPLICIT BIAS ⚡

Implicit bias refers to the subconscious assumptions that everyone makes. If left unexamined, these biases can result in actual unfairness.

Few people—hopefully—would aim to be biased, but it can happen without realizing it. For example, in an attempt to increase diversity, a major tech company established a rule that every interview loop must be at least 40% female. That sounds like a nice idea, but, in many roles, only 20% of their employees were female. The net result is that the women get pulled off of their "real" work and into recruiting an awful lot. And, to make matters worse, promotions didn't value the recruiting tasks as highly as the other work, leaving women with fewer accomplishments. Good intentions, bad results.

> ### AN EXERCISE FOR THE READER
>
> Close your eyes and imagine a successful PM leader pitching a new product in front of an excited audience. What did the PM look like? If you don't know enough great leaders of different races and genders, you might accidentally overlook talented people who don't fit your model of what a great PM looks like.

It's especially important to watch out for bias when it comes to coaching and development. Many times, implicit bias shows up not as being unduly harsh to an underrepresented group, but rather as giving people who look like you the benefit of the doubt and second chances. Try to extend those privileges to everyone.

Consider whether you're applying your expectations consistently. Are you judging some people on potential and others on accomplishments? Does poor collaboration feel like a minor issue for some people but a major issue for others?

Also consider whether your expectations are actually *appropriate* expectations. Expectations can be applied consistently, but still create bias. For example:

- A hiring manager strongly prefers those who learned to code early in life, seeing it as a sign of passion. Guess who is more likely to have learned to code early? Younger candidates, as well as candidates from wealthier families.

- A hiring manager frowns upon gaps in their candidates' resumes. Guess who is likely to have gaps? Women (due to pregnancy and childbirth), as well as those who have faced serious medical problems (among themselves or their family).

- A manager values confidence in their employees, and prefers to send the more confident ones into meeting with execs. But how does he judge confidence? The manager didn't realize it, but he was associating a deeper, louder voice as being more confident. His male employees tended to project great confidence, and thus landed these high-profile tasks.

All of these expectations ultimately create bias, even though this wasn't intended. Be sure your expectations are not just *applied* fairly, but are *actually* fair.

In addition to your expectations, review what stretch opportunities you offer, as these are an important area for development. Mekka Okereke, an engineering director at Google, suggests making a spreadsheet of which stretch opportunities you give each report along with their self-identified categories like race and gender. Then, review the spreadsheet and see how the stretch opportunities have been distributed. Does it match with your expectations? If not, you should work to close the gap.[5]

Implicit bias is a complex and ambiguous topic, but an important one. We've only offered a taste here. We fully encourage you to research this more and/or reach out to consultants who offer further training in this area. Note that anyone can have implicit bias—even against their own "group."

CONCEPTS AND FRAMEWORKS

COMPENSATION AND PROMOTIONS

As a manager, it's your responsibility to learn how compensation and promotions work at your company. Ask around to learn both the official and unspoken rules, so you can help guide your reports through the processes. If you can, buddy up with another manager in a similar position and who has been at the company longer than you have.

The processes and guidelines will vary from company to company, but here are some things to look out for:

- How are the decisions made? How much influence does the manager have in the decision? Are manager recommendations often accepted or bumped down?

- What factors are most influential? How much do peer reviews matter? How much does visibility amongst managers matter? How much do big launches or launch results matter? What kind of "proof points" are needed?

- What are the constraints? Are there quotas, budgets, minimum-time-in-role guidelines, or other factors? How flexible are those constraints and what are the best ways of advocating for an exception?

- What are the norms? What percentage of employees typically get promotions or compensation increases each year, and what frequency is typical? What sizes are typical? How is compensation balanced between salary and equity? How frequently are refresher grants given?

- Will other managers share information about how their reports are leveled and compensated to help you calibrate?

- Is there any documentation around leveling or guidelines? Does your company have good competitive information about compensation? Can the recruiting team help you understand market rates?

Overall, compensation is a bit of an art and a bit of a science. It takes a lot of experience to feel calibrated on the appropriate size and frequency of raises.

Here are some of the factors to consider:

---

5 Okereke explains this process at https://twitter.com/mekkaokereke/status/1218947464377450496.

- **Market Rate:** How much would you pay to hire this person again? How much would you give as a counteroffer if they said they loved being on your team but received a higher offer from another company? How much would they be paid at a company similar to yours?

- **Signal:** What signal do you want to send to this person about their performance and value? Perhaps they're paid well relative to the market rate, but you still want to give small raises to indicate how much you value them and to represent their increasing value to the company.

- **Timing and size of increase:** People's value and skills improve continuously, but raises are only given at discrete times. Sometimes it's better to give large increases less often (so the amount feels more substantial). Other times, it's better to give multiple smaller increases (so they can feel the continual progress).

- **Calibration:** Where does this person stand in comparison to other people on the team? Are the highest value people being paid the most? Unfortunately, it's difficult to get this perfectly aligned, but you can aim to move in the right direction.[6] If you have a budget, you'll want to be sure to allocate more of the budget to your top performers, rather than spreading it evenly.

Every once in a while, a manager approaches compensation like they're negotiating at a street market; they want to pay as little as they can get away with. And when they do that, they typically regret it. The employee will figure out eventually they're underpaid, and you'll lose your star performers—costing you more money in the end.

MANAGING UNDERPERFORMANCE

Not everything in management is sunshine and roses. At some point, you'll probably be faced with a PM who is missing some of the expectations for the job.

This could be for many reasons:

- Everyone on the team might love them, but they're unable to drive decisions and leave the team spinning in circles.

- They could be a "brilliant jerk," who has great ideas but makes the people around them want to quit.

- They might seem like they have a lot of potential, but they won't listen to your feedback or follow processes.

- They might be trying really hard but not improving in their handling of complex problems.

- They could have been an amazing employee a year ago but became disengaged over the past several months.

It's useful to first reflect on what the root cause of the situation might be. Then, ask the following questions.

Do I believe I can turn this around?

Bad situations *can* be salvaged, but trust your gut. If you truly believe that this is all some big misunderstanding and your report is eager to fix the problem, you've got a good chance of getting things back on track. If you're holding on because you don't want to admit failure, you're just prolonging a painful situation.

---

6   People might have been hired at higher compensation based on market conditions or because they interviewed well. People's performance can fluctuate over time. Most companies will not decrease a person's compensation.

Sometimes, you'll feel like a hypothetical manager in a hypothetical alternate universe could save the situation. Perhaps you'd be able to fix things if you could turn back time and start over, but things have gone on too long to fix now. You'll build your management skills over time, but for now, you need to be realistic about where you are.

Have I given clear feedback on the problem?

Being crystal clear about severe problems has two benefits. First, you ensure there are no misunderstandings. Second, you can reassure other people on the team that they would know if they were at risk of being fired.

Firing one employee can impact the feeling of security that other employees have, particularly if it *feels* like the firing is the result of one bad decision or conflict. Whenever an employee is fired, other employees start to wonder if they could be next. By using clear language and giving people early warning, you can reassure other teammates that they won't be caught by surprise if they ever run into issues.

Hopefully, it shouldn't be a total surprise that things aren't going well, although perhaps the employee didn't realize that it'd gotten to *that* point yet. It's useful to be explicit that, yes, it has gotten there.

Here's an example of how to word it:

> Your current performance is not meeting expectations for this role. We need to see major improvements in the next 30 days or you won't be able to stay in this role at the company.

You can then work on a plan for the improvements you need to see and how to get there.

Do they really want to improve?

The only way performance problems get resolved is if the person really wants to improve.

Often, underperformance is a symptom of the employee already being disengaged. Talk to them and see if you can figure out what's behind that disengagement. Is there a root cause that's solvable?

> If they don't want to improve, they won't. By the time you feel that they're missing expectations, you've probably already given them feedback several times.[7] They might deny the problem or feel defensive. They might externalize the problem and try to put the blame onto someone else. In these cases, it's unlikely things will get better and you should arrange a departure quickly.

On the other hand, if they hear your feedback and jump into action, taking full responsibility for the problem, that's a good sign. If they appreciate your feedback and start planning how to address it, they might be able to turn the situation around.

Is there a different role where they'd be likely to succeed?

Sometimes underperformance comes when there's a mismatch with the current role. You don't want to pass a problem on to someone else, but if you truly believe they would thrive in another role, it can make sense to work on that transfer, rather than losing them entirely.

---

7   If you haven't given them this feedback several times, why not? That's a red flag for your management skills.

Perhaps they'd do better with a different set of people, or as part of a team with a different culture. Maybe they would improve with a mentor they have more in common with. If you move them within the PM team, you also have the benefit of starting them fresh on a project with tighter expectations so you can get things off on the right foot.

Where is your time and energy best spent?

As a manager, it can be tempting to spend your time and energy trying to save an underperforming report. Unfortunately, that usually means taking that valuable attention away from your other reports who might benefit more. It will be more impactful to put your time into your best people.

Imagine the best-case scenario where your extra energy helps get the person back on track. Are they now one of the best people on your team? Are they better than the replacement you could hire?

Dealing with someone who is underperforming is a drain. It won't only be tough on you, but also on that person's teammates. Most managers say that they waited too long to fire an underperformer.

Now what? (How to let go)

Perhaps it's come to the point where you've realized that, for whatever reason, your struggling employee must move on. What do you do?

In the US, Europe, and many other areas, firing an employee has significant legal complications.[8] Doing the wrong thing can open you up to lawsuits.

This is where you need to get others involved, often your manager and the HR department. Larger companies have likely established a procedure for this, and it's important that you discover what it is.

This procedure might involve a Performance Improvement Plan (PIP) and legal documentation. At a very small company, it might be much more informal—a conversation, some severance, and they're on their way.

These policies can vary greatly across companies, due to company culture and legal restrictions. Don't fire until you understand how to do so. And, ideally, you should have been gathering this information much earlier.

---

8   If the employee was hired in the US, their paperwork likely says that they are "at-will" and specifically indicates that the employee can be terminated for essentially any reason at essentially any time. While that's technically true, that doesn't preclude the worker for suing you for some (actual or perceived) wrongdoing. This is why the legal implications are complex.

KEY TAKEAWAYS

- **Build a strong relationship with your reports:** Make sure they believe that you have their best interests at heart. Don't skip 1:1s. You can't coach someone who doesn't trust you.

- **Managing PMs is especially difficult because of how autonomous they are:** You won't know how well your reports are doing unless you seek out that information and encourage them to share their challenges with you.

- **Make sure your reports are clear on the top areas they need to develop to achieve their goals:** People aren't especially great at hearing developmental feedback. Learn what your reports want to achieve, match that against business needs, and then ensure they understand which areas are the most important to focus on. This is especially important if they are underperforming.

- **Match people to projects that will develop their skills:** The main way PMs grow is through the work they do. When possible, match people to the teams or projects that will be a small to moderate stretch for them.

- **Get your reports the compensation and promotions they deserve:** It takes real work to advocate for your reports and ensure they get the recognition they deserve. Take the time to learn the system and search for the information you need to make your case.

CHAPTER 30

BUILDING A TEAM

AT LEAST I could appreciate the irony in the situation. Here I was, having conducted dozens of interviewer trainings, yet my own process just felt too chaotic and random. I (Gayle) certainly didn't seem to be following the advice I'd doled out to thousands of people.

My phone screens especially seemed inefficient. In some cases, I'd discover minutes in that they didn't hit basic qualifications; why am I not discovering this *before* the phone call? Even with the good candidates, I wasn't sure if I was appropriately evaluating them vs. being biased by those I "clicked" with.

In my defense, this wasn't exactly a dev or PM job—my specialities. No, instead, I was hiring a nanny for my two sons. But it's all the same, right? (Sort of.)

As I'd instructed thousands of attendees at my trainings: "All interviewing, of any type, is about two things: signal and the candidate experience." Yes, my nanny interview process needed to look at least a bit more like a tech hiring process.

I fixed up and formalized my process. From now on, candidates got a screening questionnaire and a write-up about us and the job. If there was a mutual fit, we'd hop on the phone for a structured call evaluating communication, problem solving, and design.

Okay, I'm half-joking about the "problem solving and design" signals—but only half. Coincidentally, the signals I needed to assess *were* somewhat parallel:

- **Communication:** Can you communicate fluently in Spanish and English?

- **Problem solving:** How will you handle behavioral challenges and discipline?

- **Design:** Can you create fun activities to do with my kids so that they don't just do LEGOs all day?

The onsite interviews? Those were a different story. I like to step out of the way to see how the nanny and my kids connect. And, for better or worse, that gave my six year old the opportunity to step right into my shoes.

"Please read this to me," my son said, handing the surprised candidate a book moments after her arrival.

Halfway through the book, he announced that she can stop reading, because it was time to do art. Apparently, she'd passed the reading assessment, but he wanted to make sure they had time for the art assessment and running assessment. If only all interviewers kept to such a rigorous schedule!

"Well, what did you think?" I asked him after she left. He thought for a moment, "I'd give her a 7 out of 10." Evidently, he'd invented a numerical grading system too.

Perhaps he'd listened in to too many of my work calls, but what he intuitively understood was that interviewing is not just about figuring out if you like the candidate. It's about assessing what you need—separating what's trainable from what's not—and then assessing candidates based on those signals. Structure will help you do these things.

RESPONSIBILITIES

FIND AND ATTRACT CANDIDATES ⚡

The recruiting process has a funnel that's almost exactly like the marketing funnel, except instead of going from awareness to purchase, it goes from awareness to hire.

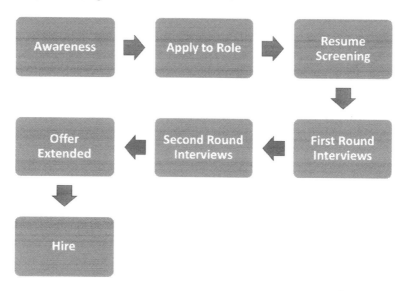

A company can focus on improving the conversion rate between each stage, but even in a well-running funnel, you need to put a lot of time and energy in. It takes on average 55 well-qualified candidates to hire a single PM.[1] If you get a response rate of 20%, you might need to reach out to 275 people to hire one PM.

When you're recruiting, consider approaches that help you find good people, and those that help good people find you. For the first category, you can search job sites, ask for referrals, attend career fairs, and reach out to people you admire. For the second category, you can build your own reputation through writing, networking, hosting events, or speaking at conferences.

---

1   The qualified-candidate-per-hire for product manager comes from https://resources.workable.com/blog/qualified-candidates-recruiting-metrics. The same site provides other statistics too.

EVALUATE CANDIDATES FAIRLY AND EFFECTIVELY ⚡

As a hiring manager, you need to decide what you're looking for, and come up with a process to measure those qualities. You need to decide on your risk tolerance since hiring someone bad is very expensive, but sometimes taking a risk can pay off.

You need to ask, prompt, and evaluate questions consistently across candidates to get a clear, calibrated signal. It takes practice to get beneath the surface of rehearsed answers.

Interview processes are covered in more detail in "Designing a PM interview process" on pg 321.

GROWTH PRACTICES

SOURCE AND REFER A LOT OF CANDIDATES ⚡

Referrals—when an employee suggests a friend, past colleague or other connection—are great. They offer extra bits of information on the candidate, and with potentially little effort on your part. What could be better?

Unfortunately, you can't rely exclusively on referrals for long. You just won't get enough candidates, and you'll miss out on so many great ones.

It turns out that many PMs are happy enough at their current job, but willing to make a switch for a great opportunity. Your job is to convince these "passive" candidates that your role is a great opportunity for them. If you reach out to a person when they're starting to feel antsy, you might be able to hire them before they're officially on the market. When you reach out to people you don't know, it's called sourcing.

Recruiting is a numbers game, and personal outreach works.

Many people will agree to a casual introductory coffee chat, even when they're not actively looking for a new job. With practice, you can generate active candidates out of those chats. Try setting a target for how many introductory meetings you want to have every week.

While you can't automate your meetings, there are ways to optimize outreach. You can use templates, mail merge, or let recruiters send messages from your email address. If recruiters are sending on your behalf, make sure you approve the message and double check the lists to make sure they don't accidentally reach out to someone you know.

If your network isn't very diverse, you can intentionally dedicate some sourcing time towards underrepresented candidates by, for example, reaching out to groups like SWE (Society of Women Engineers) or NSBE (National Society of Black Engineers).

Templates

If you're feeling shy about reaching out to people, here are some templates you can start from. Adapt them to match your voice:

- Hi, remember me from [place we met]? I'm a PM at [company] now and I love it. We're hiring, and I thought of you because [reason]. Would you be interested in chatting [or grabbing coffee] to learn more?

- Hi, I'm a PM at [company] now and we're hiring for [role]. I saw [relevant thing they put online] and thought you might be a great match. Would you be interested in chatting [or grabbing coffee] to learn more?

- Hi, we're hiring [role] at my company and I thought you'd be great for it. I know you might be totally happy at [their company], but I thought I'd take a chance and reach out.

- Hi, we're hiring [role] at my company and I thought you might know some people who could be great for it. Can you think of anyone I might be able to reach out to?

- Hi, just checking if you saw my message. No worries if you're not interested, just wanted to make sure it didn't get lost in your inbox.

It's great to cast a wide net, but also be sure the role is relevant to the candidate. Don't reach out to a senior PM about an entry-level job.

LEARN HOW TO SUCCESSFULLY PITCH CANDIDATES ⚡⚡

As a manager, you need to convince people to join your team. This is basically a sales pitch, where the thing you're selling is the role. This can happen early on, when you convince a passive candidate to interview, or at the end of the interview process, when you try to convince someone to accept your offer.

Many PMs start out uncomfortable with the idea of pitching. They might have an image of pitching that sounds "sales-y", inauthentic, or boastful. Luckily, good pitches aren't like that.

In a good pitch, you learn what someone cares about and then talk to them about how the role matches. You let your genuine enthusiasm shine through. You can be honest about the downsides of the role while sharing why they weren't dealbreakers for you.

Here's an example of what a good pitch could sound like.

> **Employee:** Thanks for talking to me today. I know you're not actively looking, but I'd love to learn a little about you and what you'd be looking for in your ideal role.
>
> **Candidate:** Well, I love my job, but I sometimes think I'd learn more and have more impact at a smaller company.
>
> **Employee:** That makes a lot of sense, and is a big part of the reason I came here, too. I love that I get to meet our customers and hear directly from them how much our product has helped them. And, we only have three PMs so each person owns a large part of the product. In terms of learning, we have regular learning-lunches, but I think where I've learned the most is in the weekly Q&As with the founders.
>
> …
>
> **Employee:** Is there anything else I can tell you about the team?
>
> …
>
> **Employee:** How are you thinking about this role compared to your other options?
>
> **Candidate:** I like it, but I'm wondering if I'd rather work on a consumer product that my friends and family use.

> **Employee:** That makes sense. The way I think about it is that our customers are really under-served, and so we're able to make a big difference in their lives. If we weren't building this product, they'd be stuck with a much worse alternative. I love getting to have that kind of impact.

During these chats, you might end up getting some signal (pg 323) that the candidate *isn't* a great match for the role. It's okay to be honest when the role doesn't seem like a fit. In fact, being candid about the reasons *not* to take the job can be an effective technique because it shows that you're willing to be honest. It's much better for them to turn down the role than to accept it and leave three months later when they realize they were misled.

PUT A PERSONAL TOUCH INTO CLOSING CANDIDATES ⚡⚡

When it comes to closing candidates, the best approaches are personal. You need to understand what each candidate values.

Compensation is obviously a huge factor, but there are many other things people take into consideration when making their decision. They care about the company's chances for success, how fast the company is growing, and how they feel they can learn and grow. They also look at how interested they are in the product, whether they like the team, and how they'll fit in.

One of the most effective things you can do for closing a candidate is to reach out personally and have other team members reach out as well. Let them know that you liked them and want to work with them. You might even invite them to spend more time with the team or send a personalized gift based on an interest they mentioned during the interview.

When it comes down to it, the people you work with on a day-to-day basis have a huge impact on your happiness. It helps to let them get to know you and your team so they can get a sense of how much they'd enjoy working with you.

CONCEPTS AND FRAMEWORKS

PM ARCHETYPES: BUILDERS, TUNERS, AND INNOVATORS

Sachin Rekhi, the founder and CEO of Notejoy, developed a set of three PM archetypes that can be helpful when building a team.[2]

Builders

- **Description:** Builders drive the roadmap for an existing product in order to build ever more useful, usable, and delightful experiences. They love solving real problems for real people. Traditional feature PMs are often builders.

- **Super powers:** Customer empathy, ruthless prioritization, and sweat the details.

---

2   https://www.sachinrekhi.com/3-types-of-product-managers-builders-tuners-innovators

Tuners

- **Description:** Tuners have an unwavering focus on a specific north star metric and do everything in their power to move that metric. They love seeing the measurable impact of their work. Growth and monetization PMs are often tuners.

- **Super powers:** Analytical ninja, hypothesis-driven, and relish moving the needle.

Innovators

- **Description:** Innovators are tasked with the challenging job of finding product/market fit for a brand new product. They take a hypothesis-driven approach to validate and iterate on practically every dimension of their product strategy. They love being on the cutting edge of new technologies. PMs at new startups and on new product development teams are often innovators.

- **Super Powers:** Product intuition, market understanding, and comfortable with ambiguity.

Different teams will need different types of PMs. When you start the hiring process, think about which archetype will best fit your needs.

OPTIMIZING FOR SIGNAL AND THE CANDIDATE EXPERIENCE

Interviewing—not just for PMs, but for *any* role—boils down to two goals: signal and candidate experience. That is, when we think about how many interviews to do, which employees should interview, what questions to ask, and what processes to put in place, we want to optimize for signal and for the candidate experience.

Signal

Signal is the information that we learn about the candidate—the *adjectives*, more so than *facts*. "Signal" might be that they show initiative, have strong work ethic, or are insightful about users. Notice that all of these things exist on a spectrum; signal is rarely a binary attribute.

We extract signal by analyzing the candidate's work experience, their responses to questions, and the way that they act, and other "facts." We look at what they did or said, and ask ourselves (and often them), *why?* We go deep to learn the signal:

1. What happened?

2. Why did it happen?

3. What does this say about them?

4. What does this predict about their job performance?

Let's see this in an example.

> ### CULTURAL VALUES CONFLICT
>
> Ravi, a PM candidate, explains why his team decided to automatically import the user's contacts, even though that worsened the candidate experience—and arguably jeopardized their privacy too.
>
> "Frankly, it was about money," Ravi tells you. "Importing contacts would increase revenue by 10%."

You wince. This approach flies in the face of your company's core values, of which #1 is privacy and #2 is the user experience. Maybe Ravi isn't such a good fit?

But then, you remember to dig a little deeper. Yes, the "fact" is that he prioritized money, at the expense of privacy and the candidate experience. (That's question #1 above: What happened?)

You ask Ravi why he decided to do that, and he explains that his company's first priority at that time was increasing revenue. He goes on to tell you that he expressed concerns about this singular focus to executives, but the directive was clear: given the company's financial situation, revenue was #1. (This addresses question #2: Why did it happen?)

Now, your takeaway is a bit different. The "signal" is not "this candidate puts money ahead of the user." Rather, it's that the candidate will make decisions based on the company's priorities and also advocate for what he believes is right. (Question #3: "What does this say about them?")

What does this predict about their job performance? (Question #4) It predicts that they're likely to respect your company's prioritization of the user.

(However, it might still be good to assess, in product design questions, their ability to *actually* follow through with that.)

Note how what started off as "candidate won't prioritize the user" morphed into "this candidate can prioritize the user."

Probing deeper is a very important skill, both in your interviews and in debriefs. We rarely want to take a candidate's first response as-is. We need to ask follow-up questions to understand why they did this so that we can then assess what it says about them.

As you construct your interview process, or reflect on whom you want to hire, think about the signal. What are the core signals you'd like to assess? These items might include traits like "data analysis" or "stakeholder management."

Generally, it's useful to have a list of five to seven core signals. If your list gets much longer than that, you'll have trouble finding a candidate who can fit those—or you'll have to drop your standards on some of the criteria.

The Candidate Experience

The candidate experience is about how the candidate experiences (i.e., reacts to, interprets, feels about) the company, the people, and the interview process as a whole. In a sense, it's the flip side of signal. Whereas signal is what the company learns about the candidate, the "candidate experience" is what the candidate learns about the company.

Certainly, happiness—whether the candidate liked the people and the process—is a big piece of this, but it's not the entirety. For example, if the candidate thinks their interviewers were kind but unskilled, that's not really a "good experience." The candidate will not walk away saying, "this is a company I want to work for."

The candidate experience impacts:

- **Offer Acceptance:** Candidates who have a positive experience are more likely to accept an offer. It's no use identifying fabulous candidates if they then decline your offer.

- **Word of Mouth:** If you're a large name-brand company, social media and the news just *love* stories about "my terrible interview at ___." If you're a smaller company, you might be less likely to wind up in the news, but any negative stories can stick around on search results for a long time, just waiting to push away your future candidates. You want your candidates, *especially* the ones you don't hire, to walk away with good things to say about their experience.[3]

- **Signal:** People do their best when they feel happy and supported. When they feel unhappy, they are less creative, make more mistakes, and hide their thoughts. You will be more able to evaluate candidates when they're having a positive experience. Bad experiences create false negatives.

A good experience means that candidates walk away saying that the people, process, and questions were organized, fair, and likable. These aspects can overlap. For example, a lack of transparency in the process can make the process seem unfair *and* disorganized.[4]

Evaluate your interviewers, questions, and process with these elements in mind:

- **Organization.** The process should be structured and a reasonable length (not too long or too short). Recruiters/managers are responsive. Interviewers should be prepared for their interviews. There is transparency about the process and expectations, and everyone does what they say they will do.

- **Fairness.** The questions feel relevant and are at an appropriate level of complexity. There were no big surprises; the candidate knew what would happen during the day. The candidate feels like they got a reasonable chance to showcase their skills. The questions were appropriate for the candidate and didn't feel too junior or too senior.

- **Likability.** Interviewers were welcoming and kind. They supported the candidate, offering help and guidance as needed. The candidate wasn't rushed, and got a chance to think. The candidate walked away understanding the role, the company, and the team. The interviewers were prepared. The interviewers were engaged and showed active listening; they didn't get distracted by their computer or phone.

The candidate experience extends to rejections as well. No one wants to hear that they were a poor communicator, and if you're telling someone they weren't technical enough for the role, it had better be unarguable. If recruiters will be giving feedback after the interview, stick to facts such as which interviews they scored lower on, rather than comments about their abilities.[5]

WHAT MAKES A GOOD PROCESS

An effective process builds the right team at a reasonable cost. More specifically, this means:

- **Minimal False Positives:** A false positive is an incorrect "yes"; in the case of hiring, this means a bad hire. Fewer false positives means that we've built a team of good employees.

---

3   The ones you hire are your employees, and somewhat less likely to post negative things online about your company. In that sense, the candidates who aren't hired (either because you didn't extend and offer or they didn't accept the offer) are the ones who form the "word of mouth."

4   In fact, when a company isn't explicit about how the interview process works, it's often *because* they are disorganized. They don't tell the candidate what to expect during the process because the company doesn't know yet; they're just figuring it out on the fly. And that is not a good thing.

5   Most companies do not give any feedback after interviews, but most candidates really appreciate feedback when it's a gap they can work on.

- **Minimal False Negatives:** A false negative is an incorrect "no"; in the case of hiring, this means we rejected a good candidate. Fewer false negatives means that the people we rejected were indeed bad candidates (or, put another way, we notice the good candidates and hire them).

- **Cost Effective:** A process should not only hire the right person, but it shouldn't be excessively time consuming for the company. Cost effectiveness is determined in part by our process: How long does it take? Who is involved? How often do candidates pass different stages of their process?[6] The other big piece of cost effectiveness is false negatives—rejecting good people means that we take longer to hire.

- **Short Term and Long Term:** Hires aren't just about who is a good fit *right now*; they're also about how you want to build the company or team for the future. Consider how your team's needs will evolve, and the makeup of the team. What skills and backgrounds do you need now, and down the road? If you want to build a diverse team—and hopefully you do—this isn't something you can just postpone until some "later" point.

In the previous section, we discussed the goals of signal and candidate experience. Better signal improves false negatives and false positives, and, therefore, cost effectiveness too. A better candidate experience primarily impacts cost effectiveness; if candidates don't like us or our process, it will take longer to find someone who accepts our offer.

Many companies will say that false negatives are better than false positives, and they design their process accordingly. That is, they would rather their process errs toward rejecting good candidates than accepting bad ones. Generally, the harder (or riskier, or more disruptive) it is to fire an underperforming employee, the more cautious you will want to be about false positives.

DESIGNING A PM INTERVIEW PROCESS

If your company doesn't already have a great process for interviewing PMs, you might need to set one up.

In general, you'll need to consider how each step of the process affects false positives, false negatives, and the amount of time your team spends on interviewing. You'll want to think about what the core signals are, and how you'll create a good candidate experience.

Your interview process can be a competitive advantage, if done well. It can enable your team to recognize and hire talented PMs that other companies missed.

Here are some guidelines on how to design a PM interview process.

Align on what you're looking for in a PM

Product management is fundamentally a whitespace role, so the skills you need will depend on the strengths and gaps on your existing team. It's important to discuss your goals so you can recruit the kind of PM you need.

Include the people who will be interviewing and working with the PM, so that everyone will be aligned. PMs do best when the people on their team really want them there, so it's important to have buy-in.

Here are some questions to consider:

---

6   I (Gayle) once was consulting (to optimize the hiring process) for a company where 90% of their candidates passed the phone screen, after which the successful candidates did a five hour onsite interview. Essentially, they spent one hour on the phone to save themselves, on average, 30 minutes later. Their process would be "cheaper" if they skipped the phone screen entirely!

- Do you want a very senior PM who will drive the processes, strategy, and roadmap across a wide scope, or do you want someone earlier in their career who will partner with the founder or another PM?

- Do you need someone with great design taste, really keen business insights, strong analytical skills, visionary strategy, or deep technical expertise? Which of those are most important to your team?

- Do you need someone who can hit the ground running with industry expertise, or do you have the time to invest in ramping up a generalist?

- Are there any specific gaps on your team that you're hoping the PM will fill?

- Are there any soft skills that are especially important for succeeding in your company's culture (e.g., making space for introverts, debating ideas on the fly, being passionate about a particular type of problem)?

- Which PM archetype (pg 317) would you like to hire?

- Which requirements can you be flexible on?

Be careful about putting too many things on your list. The more attributes you look for, the more your candidate pool shrinks. Something has to give. Usually, that will either be your time or your standards.

Identify qualities that are hard to teach (and therefore need to be assessed in the interview)

Managers, ask yourself a question: What's a reasonable "ramp up" time for a new employee? That is, when you hire a new PM, they certainly won't be productive in the first week. How long should it take for them to be really up and running?[7]

Most people say something in the range of four to twelve weeks. Great!

This means that if there is an important skill, but you can train someone on it in *less* than a month or two, then there's no need to look for this in a candidate. Broaden your pool, hire a better candidate, and *train* them (pg 260).

If a candidate has never run an A/B test, but has strong analytical skills, they can learn the basics quickly. They might not immediately see that the control side rules out differences based on seasonality, but that's an easy concept to learn. If they haven't heard of a minimum viable product, but they're good with prioritization, they'll figure it out. Don't hire on what you can train!

One interesting implication of this is that a job opening should rarely require "basic skills." If a skill is basic, it's usually learnable. Therefore, it shouldn't be required for the job; just teach the new employee the skill. If your interview questions build on the basics, let candidates know in advance which concepts you'll be covering so they can learn them before the interview. You'll get better signal when you give candidates a chance to be prepared.[8]

On the other hand, mindsets and what types of information a person notices can't be picked up quickly on the job. A person could develop these over time if they wanted to, but as a hiring manager, I wouldn't count on them improving quickly if they don't already have them. This includes customer empathy, awareness of good design, product intuition, product mindset, learning mindset, perseverance, collaborating well with

---

7   Yes, you should ask yourself this question with each job opening!

8   There is one caveat here. Sometimes, the lack of the skill isn't a problem, in and of itself. But the fact that *this* candidate lacks it, given their background, could be a red flag. For example, you could be concerned if a senior PM didn't know what an A/B test was, even though they could learn it. What other basic knowledge are they missing?

people, effective communication, being detail-oriented, and grasping complex concepts quickly. If you need employees with these traits, you'll want to assess them during the interview.

In the middle are a bunch of skills that can be honed with on-the-job experience, but they take time and mentorship. These are skills where you could read a book to pick up the basic tips, but there are so many nuances and complexities that you won't be able to figure out which tip to apply until you've been through it a few times. There are also skills where it's easy to learn what you "should" do, but it's scary enough that most people won't do it until they've been burned a few times (like learning to show your work early). This includes a lot of the PM processes; working with engineers and designers in a sprint cadence, writing specs, leading cross functional meetings, and pulling ideas together into a compelling strategy.

If you've got experienced PMs eager to mentor, you can build a great team by adding in high potential people who have less PM experience, such as new grads or people who want to transition to product management.

Put together an interview process that tests for all of the skills, experiences, and traits that you're looking for

Map out each requirement to the interview steps where you'll get some signal on it. Some requirements are important enough to assess in multiple places.

For example

Signal	Where to assess
Prior Experience	Resume, presentation, onsite behavioral interview
Product Skills	Take-home assignment, phone interview, onsite PM interview (includes strategy), onsite design interview (includes wireframes and usability)
Analytical Skills	Phone interview, onsite engineering interview, onsite analytical interview
Communication Skills	All

Resume review and cover letters

For senior roles, this is often a quick scan to see if they actually have the experience you need. For junior roles, however, there's a wealth of information you can evaluate at this stage; communication, leadership, product-like experience. Be very careful about unintentional bias—if you require an ivy-league degree, you'll be skipping over a lot of talented folks.

One way to evaluate resumes is to create a list of "signs of excellence" that you care about and require one or two of them to advance. Some examples include a good GPA, experience as a teaching assistant, experience as a residential advisor, varsity sports, entrepreneurship, student leadership, fellowships, a great cover letter, attending a top school, or experience at a top company.[9]

---

9   Be mindful of unintentional bias here. Students from privileged, educated families have the resources to support top schools and the networks to teach them how to write great cover letters. This is one reason why it's important to keep an open mind about how someone can demonstrate excellence, rather than requiring one specific way.

Take-home assignment

Take-home assignments are controversial. The people in favor of them say that they're more representative of real PM work than a high-pressure interview and that they allow a company to widen the net to consider candidates without elite credentials. The people against them say it's unfair and biased to ask for unbounded amounts of "free work," especially when some candidates might have gotten outside help on the assignment.

If you choose to use a take-home assignment, here are some things to be mindful of:

- Aim for an assignment that can be completed in 30 - 60 minutes (adapting a phone interview question could work). Beta test it to ensure it doesn't actually take hours. Remember that some candidates will put in extra time, but you want an assignment where people can actually pass it in the time allotted (and where spending extra time doesn't effectively result in bonus points). Be explicit about your time expectations.

- Don't make the assignment directly related to your product. When you do this, it feels like you're trying to get "free work" from them. Even if you aren't, perception matters!

- Consider allowing candidates to combine the assignment with a phone interview. They can see the assignment but not have to prepare anything in advance.

- Make sure candidates are very clear on what you'll be assessing, and not. For example, should they spend more time on research, idea generation, or clear communication? State up front whether they can ask friends for ideas or if they should complete it solo.[10]

- Consider providing materials that will help candidates complete the assignment quicker and more consistently—a template for the answer, research materials, screenshots, sample answers, etc. If your assignment is just testing "can they look up a good template online", it's not a great assignment.

- Consider skipping the assignment for candidates where you already have enough signal on their skills or where you don't want to take the risk that they drop out of the process.

- Assess whether the assignment is effective. What percent of people pass the assignment? What percent of those go on to pass the next interview? Are graders giving consistent scores? Is the benefit worth the cost?

Take a look at all the pros and cons and decide if it's worth it to include a take-home assignment in your interview process.

Intro presentation

An intro presentation is a great alternative to having each interview start with "tell me about yourself." It could range from a 15-minute simple intro for APM candidates, to 45 minutes discussing past projects for experienced candidates. You can adjust the prompt to cover any particular area you want to hear about.

The presentation gives the candidate a chance to shine and lets the 1:1 interviewers manage their time better.

Be aware that very junior candidates, in particular, might have weaker public speaking skills due to a lack of experience. If public speaking is important to the role, it's okay for that to be a factor. But also recognize that this is also a skill that a candidate can significantly improve in with practice—particularly with the company's support.

---

10 Beware of accidentally putting some candidates at a disadvantage. Someone with more close friends who are PMs will have an advantage if they're allowed to ask their friends. This might end up favoring younger, male candidates, who are more likely to have tech-focused social circles.

Product design questions

These are questions like "Can you tell me about a product you like?" or "How would you improve Google Maps?" They can be a little scary to ask because the answers can really go in any direction. It can also be difficult to think of follow-up questions on the spot or to know if their idea is actually good or not.

To help with this, plan your prompts and follow-up questions ahead of time. Pay attention to time and make sure to steer the interview to touch on all the important areas you want to cover—for example, getting them to draw on the whiteboard. If you feel you're getting an answer that's too rehearsed, you can ask them to come up with another product or idea.

One skill to test for in these questions is "Can you design for someone who is different than yourself?" To get at that, you can ask the candidate to design a product for a specific group of people, such as an alarm clock for the blind, Uber for kids, Photoshop for the elderly, Spotify for truck drivers, and so on. People familiar with the group will have an advantage that can be misleading, so beta-test your questions to ensure it doesn't require specialized knowledge to answer well.

To test product mindset, you can either prompt the candidate to think about goals (for APMs), or see if they come up with goals unprompted (for senior candidates). If the candidate asks you what the goals are, spin it around on them and ask them what they think the goals should be. If a candidate is resistant to setting their own goals or has a lot of difficulty, that's a sign they don't have a product mindset.

Once the candidate starts coming up with actual solution ideas, you can see if those solutions tie back to the goals. When you ask them to prioritize, do they choose the things that help the most with the goals? If they get drawn to the sparkly idea and can't articulate why it's better than the impactful ones, that's a sign they don't have a product mindset.

Analytical questions

The best questions for assessing analytical problem solving are hypothetical scenarios inspired by real experiences from your company where analytical skill was important.

Here are some examples of real-world experiences that can lead to good questions:

- Analyzing mixed experiment results.

- Debugging a surprising drop in metrics.

- Choosing between two product directions.

- Creating an algorithm.

- Working around a technical constraint.

Make sure to test your new analytical question on PMs you respect to ensure it's not a trick question, and also to start calibrating yourself on different approaches. Sometimes the key insight appears obvious to you in hindsight, but is tough to spot in an interview. Your question should let you evaluate a person's problem solving process, not require an "aha" moment.

Behavioral questions ("Tell me about a time when...")

A tricky thing about product managers is that it can be very hard to separate out their contributions from the rest of their team. They might have gotten lucky and been put on a great team, rather than really driving the success, or vice versa.

With behavioral questions, you can start to really dive in to figure out the scope of their responsibilities and what their unique contributions were. You can talk about alternatives they considered and what kind of resistance they faced to get a fuller picture of the situation.

You can learn about product mindset by asking how a past project got started and why they made various decisions. If they helped shape the goals (not just setting numeric targets or specific measurements, but actually deciding which problems to go after) and made decisions to support those goals, that's a strong sign that they have a good product mindset. If they've only ever picked obvious goals, or if their reasons were "I wanted to try this new technology," they might not have a product mindset.

As you ask these questions, keep *"signal"* top of mind. What are the core attributes you want to measure? Ask a question that helps you evaluate that, and then keep probing deep until you get there.

Testing for soft skills
Soft skills can be evaluated implicitly or explicitly.

- **Explicit evaluation** is via behavioral questions. You might ask for examples of how they handled conflicts, how they influenced a senior manager, or how they aligned stakeholders behind an idea. Usually, after their response, you will follow up to ask more questions about why they took that approach, or whatever else is needed to evaluate this signal.

- **Implicit evaluation** is by just observing their behavior. For example, you might push back on one of their ideas during a design question and see how they handle this. Ask why they wouldn't design it a different way, and see how open they are to your suggestion. Do they get defensive, dismissive, or do they consider it?

Be careful here. It can be helpful to challenge the candidate in some way, but you want to be sure that you stay friendly and supportive as you do this.

Avoiding trick questions
Many PM interview questions can accidentally become trick questions. A candidate thinks you're testing their analytical skill but actually you were looking for customer focus. These trick questions can cause you to falsely assume a candidate doesn't have a skill, just because they interpreted your question incorrectly.

One way to avoid misinterpretations is to tell them up front what you're looking for in the question: "I'm trying to get a sense of how you debug problems." Another way is to carefully frame the type of answer you're looking for: "What questions would you ask to decide what to do?" instead of "What would you do?"

Some interviewers employ a "trick" where they hide key information in framing the question to assess whether the candidates will ask questions before diving into problem solving. This is challenging and can often backfire; people act differently in an interview setting, especially when they are guessing you want them to jump in or if they're afraid to appear rude to the interviewer.

So, how can you find out if the candidate asks questions appropriately? Try framing the question with the role you're playing. Instead of "How would you build <feature request>" say, "Imagine I'm a salesperson and I ask you to build <feature request>" and choose a realistic scenario where it would be important to ask questions first. Another way to learn if they ask questions is with a direct behavioral question, such as, "Have you ever had a time when what people asked for didn't end up being what they wanted? How did you figure it out?"

Write up rubrics for your questions

After you have your list of questions, a great way to ensure fairness is to write up a rubric for grading the answers. This makes it much faster to decide how someone did on the question, and helps calibrate across multiple people asking the same question.

Sample Rubric:

	Good	Bad
Creativity	Comes up with at least three distinctly different ideas.	All ideas are simple variants on the same theme.
Design	Demonstrates the value of the product early on.	Forces the user to fill out too much information before getting into the product.
Collaboration	Is thoughtful about the interviewer's questions and pushback.	Gets defensive when questioned on the design.

Don't let your rubric get in the way of analysis, though. For example, you might like three different ideas, but did you give the candidate the opportunity to do this? Analyze what the candidate did, and why. Perhaps the candidate's ideas were all variants on the same idea *because* of how you led them down a particular path.

KEY TAKEAWAYS

- **Recruiting is a numbers game:** You might need to reach out to more than one hundred people to make a single hire. The places you choose to source or recruit from make a huge difference in your candidate pool and who you ultimately hire; promoting your job and listing to a diverse set of people is a great start to creating a diverse team. Expect to spend a lot of time recruiting and improving recruiting processes.

- **Align on what you're looking for:** PMs can have many different strengths, interests and skill sets. Some skills can be easily taught, while others are a bigger investment. Figure out what type of a PM you need and which skills you want to evaluate.

- **Clarify the signals you're looking for in each part of the interview process:** Each step of the interview process should be intentional and evaluated consistently. Plan ahead so that you get enough signal on everything you want to assess. Beware of trick questions or those that require too much insider knowledge.

- **They need to choose you, too:** Interviewing goes both directions. Picking a job is a weighty and emotional experience. The better you can pitch the role and the more effort you put into closing the candidate, the better the chance they decide to join your team.

CHAPTER 31

ORGANIZATIONAL EXCELLENCE

ONE YEAR, MY manager at Asana came to me with this challenge: "I want you to turn the PM team into a well-oiled machine." Our team had been doing well, but we were a little fly-by-the-seat-of-our-pants.

We only had a handful of PMs on the team, and we'd been letting each person do their job the way they liked. This mostly worked fine, except when two PMs happened to be working on the same part of the product. For example, there was the time when one PM introduced a big new premium feature at the same time as another PM redesigned the UI to remove the entry point to that feature... oops! It was time for me to move beyond thinking of my team as just a collection of people, and to think about it as an organization.

As you move into upper management, you'll gain the responsibility to design the structures and processes to help your organization run smoothly. It turns out that lots of PMs all running as fast as they can in whatever direction they want doesn't actually lead to the highest velocity and best results overall.

RESPONSIBILITIES

BUILD YOUR TEAM CULTURE ⚡

As the leader of a team, you must be intentional about creating the culture you want.

What values and accomplishments will you emphasize? How do you want people to interact? How will you show recognition? What kind of training will you provide? How will you encourage team bonding?

Most companies have some budget set aside for culture-building activities. You might be able to host special training events, take the team to a conference, go out for fun events, or buy gifts for your team.

Leadership training is a great investment for team culture. You get dedicated team bonding time and learn new shared skills. At Asana, every employee went through Conscious Leadership training, and it created a shared language for collaboration.[1] Enneagram workshops (pg 228) are another great way to learn about each other and how to work better together. Ask around to learn which workshops are well respected.

---

1   See more about their courses at https://conscious.is/services/trainings.

Another important part of culture is how you show recognition and appreciate each other. You could create awards that you give out monthly for demonstrating team values, or you could invite PMs who have done exceptionally well to share their stories at a team meeting. Consider a mix of public and private forms of recognition.

GET YOUR TEAM THE RESOURCES AND SUPPORT THEY NEED ⚡

As a manager, one part of helping your team to run smoothly is making sure everyone on your team has what they need. Do they need money for test devices, a dedicated data scientist, or more support from user researchers? Are they distracted by tension with the sales team? Are they getting everything they need from partner teams?

It's up to you to notice opportunities like these. The PMs on your team might assume that things have to stay the way they've always been, but you should take the time to imagine what ideal relationships and resourcing would look like. Don't wait for someone above you to initiate the change; be proactive and use your relationships with other managers to get your teams working better together.

ESTABLISH PRODUCT PROCESSES ⚡⚡

Most teams follow a product life cycle that's roughly similar to Discover, Define, Design, Develop, Deliver, Debrief as described in "The Product Life Cycle" on pg 14. Each of these stages is an opportunity to add training, templates, guidelines, or reviews.

For each process, consider the tradeoffs between product quality, team autonomy, and the velocity of iteration. Heavier processes can improve pre-launch quality to an extent, but they also discourage post-launch iteration and improvement. Small teams who work closely together may only need one or two "required" reviews, while larger teams with more cross-functional work or less experienced PMs may need more.

Here are some processes to consider.

User research debrief

The debrief is not usually a formal review, but it's a great time for product leaders to learn about the problems the team discovered, ask additional questions, and give early feedback on which direction to pursue. This review is a way for the feature team to bring leaders along in the discovery process, so they'll be more likely to support the team's decisions.

- **When:** At the end of the Discovery stage, or after any significant new user research.
- **Who leads:** User researcher.
- **Who participates:** Product leadership (Head of Product, Head of Design, Head of Research, Head of Product Engineering), Feature team.

Spec review

Spec review, or another kind of pre-design review, is a great way to align on the plan while it's still early enough to make changes. At this stage, product leaders get a chance to learn about the discovery work the team has done and what direction they're proposing. Spec review can also be a team activity where PMs review each other's specs and give each other feedback.

Intentionally set expectations for how feedback is given:

- Do you want people to focus on supportive as well as constructive feedback?

- Should they give a lot of feedback or only the feedback that would affect their team?

- Are you looking for feedback on the formatting of the spec, or just the content?

- Do you encourage people to debate their points, or share and let it go?

- Should the feedback be provided as comments on the document, or shared in a meeting?

You'll also want to make it clear when the PM can move forward from spec review. Do they need to get approval, or are they free to choose to move on after they've heard feedback? Does the manager let them know if they need to iterate?

Specs are an excellent place to add templates. You'll want to keep the template short so that people don't get used to ignoring sections, but when used sparingly, the sections can be a great prompt to think about areas that are often overlooked such as internationalization.

- **When:** At the end of the Define stage

- **Who leads:** PM

- **Who participates:** Product leadership (Head of Product, Head of Design, Head of Research, Head of Product Engineering), Feature team, Other PMs

Design review

Design review is a tricky process because in modern software companies, the design is rarely locked down at a clear point in time. You'll need PMs and designers to work closely together to decide what work to show, at what time, and in what fidelity. Often, it makes sense to have a weekly "Design Crit" (Design Critique) where designers show each other their work and give non-binding feedback.

Make sure teams are clear about where in the design process they are and what kind of feedback they want. Early on, they should show conceptual ideas such as flow diagrams or options of a few directions the solution could go. In the middle, they should show low fidelity mockups or wireframes to discuss interaction design. At the end, they should show high fidelity designs with near-final visuals.

- **When:** During the Design stage.

- **Who leads:** Designer

- **Who participates:** Product leadership (Head of Product, Head of Design, Head of Research, Head of Product Engineering), Feature team

Eng design doc review

Engineers usually run this process, but if it doesn't exist, you might want to nudge your engineering counterpart to implement it. This review is the equivalent to a spec review for PMs; the engineers share how they plan to approach the problem from a technical perspective, and other engineers at the company can point out possible alternatives, things to be careful of, or issues they missed.

- **When:** Near the beginning of the Develop stage.

- **Who leads:** Engineers

- **Who participates:** PM, other engineers

Experiment results review

If your team runs A/B tests, you'll want to get together as a group with data scientists and engineers to analyze the results. It often takes a lot of experience before you start noticing patterns in the results, so it helps to have a regular group of people who look at all results.

- **When:** After A/B tests have run long enough to reach statistical significance.
- **Who leads:** Data Scientist, Engineer, or PM
- **Who participates:** Data Scientists, Head of Data Science, PM, other PMs or engineers who work closely with experiments.

Launch review

If you have a team of independent senior PMs, launch review might be the only required review you need. It gives you a chance to ensure quality and catch major problems before they go out.

The more you can document about your launch review, the more PMs will anticipate your responses and catch problems on their own.

Here are some things to consider:

- What should the team prepare for the launch review? Will you try the product out yourself? Should they prepare the first-time state?
- What standard questions will you ask?
- Under what circumstances do you veto a launch? What kind of changes do you request? What imperfections are you willing to overlook?

In an ideal world, launch review can be more than a quality control checkpoint; it can be a coaching experience where teams absorb company values and product philosophies.

- **When:** Near the end of the deliver stage, about a week before launch.
- **Who leads:** PM
- **Who participates:** Product leadership (Head of Product, Head of Design, Head of Research, Head of Product Engineering), Feature team

BUILD OUT A PRODUCT PLANNING PROCESS ⚡⚡

Surrounding the product process for each individual launch is a larger planning process that determines which problems and goals to go after. The planning process guides decisions across multiple teams and projects, including which new teams will be started and what each team's goals will be.

Planning processes are usually run on an annual or quarterly basis. Tying planning to the calendar, rather than a stage in the product life cycle, ensures that you regularly step back and assess whether or not you're on the right path. It's easy to get caught up in the day-to-day work and miss the bigger picture, such as when it's time to switch priorities or pivot.

Planning works best when it combines top-down and bottom-up processes. Individual contributors across the company will have the widest range of creative ideas and are on the front lines of new trends. Company and product leaders have the broadest context, and hopefully, the strongest strategic thinking to synthesize the ideas and tradeoffs.

As important as the bottom-up part of planning is, it usually requires explicit structures in order to be effective. People outside of the leadership team don't automatically know the right time to share ideas, what kind of ideas to share, or how to effectively make a case. They might also have trouble carving out time from their regular responsibilities to do longer-term thinking.

Here are some approaches:

Publish the planning timeline to the whole company

Many people would like to be involved in planning the future of the product, but they just don't know when they should share their ideas.

Try publishing a timeline of when to submit proposals, when discussions happen, and when each stage of approval and communication happens. This gives people a chance to contribute before the decisions are finalized.

Consider the "W framework" for planning

The W framework helps information flow between leaders and teams.[2]

It consists of 4 steps:

1. **Context:** Leadership shares a high-level strategy with teams.

2. **Plans:** Teams respond with proposed plans.

3. **Integration:** Leadership integrates into a single plan, and shares with teams.

4. **Buy-in:** Teams make final tweaks, confirm buy-in, and get rolling.

This back-and-forth ensures that the plan will work for everyone involved.

Make an open call for requests

People across the company might have great ideas and insights based on their unique perspectives. You can share a template or form to ensure people submit their ideas in the most helpful way.

Host strategy days with your team

To allocate time specifically for strategic planning, you can hold an offsite strategic planning event with activities to solicit ideas from everyone on your team.

By including junior team members in the planning process, you generate more ideas and expose people to strategic work that will help them grow.

---

2   Read more about the W framework at https://firstround.com/review/the-secret-to-a-great-planning-process-lessons-from-airbnb-and-eventbrite/.

GROWTH PRACTICES

USE DEADLINES EFFECTIVELY ⚡⚡

Deadlines are controversial. Those in favor of them say they help teams move faster, make necessary trade-offs, and make it possible to coordinate big events. Those who are against them believe that they demotivate people, reduce quality, and cause people to push problems into the future, slowing teams down overall.

It's important to make intentional decisions around deadlines as part of the planning process so you can avoid miscommunication and misalignment. You don't want the sales team believing a date was a firm commitment when the product team thought it was just a rough estimate.

Here are some examples of the range of possible approaches:

- Have a few "set in stone" dates. For example, hosting a big conference each year.

- Let each team set their own dates in concert with leadership, and ensure they're aware that there are consequences if the dates are missed. For example, receiving a poor performance review.

- Let each team set their own dates, and have the teams hold a retrospective if they miss them.

- Don't set any dates. Teams can estimate when things will be done, but those estimates are not considered commitments.

The best approach to use will vary based on the type of work, company needs, and individual people. The more pressure you put on dates, the more unwanted side effects may happen, such as cutting quality to ship on time, adding excessive buffers that results in slower work, or burnout. On the other hand, dates can bring very useful clarity and constraints to prioritization decisions.

Without dates, teams can get distracted by all kinds of other work that comes in. People might work on side projects or unnecessary features, since the trade-off is less visible. When there's a set deadline, they'll need to think twice about taking on extra work that could cause them to miss it. Deadlines make it easier for the PM to say no to extra work since everyone can see that there's a limited amount of work that can fit in.

As a leader, you'll need to pay close attention to your teams and see what approach works best for them.

ALLOCATE PEOPLE EFFICIENTLY ⚡⚡

Allocation is like solving a Rubik's Cube. Each move has an impact on the rest—shift this piece over here, and the others are popped out of place. Instead, you need to look at each move in the context of the broader puzzle.

Likewise, in team allocation, there are tricky tradeoffs and constraints. You need to find the best way to match your PMs to the work and the other teammates, all while balancing across what's best for each team and individual.

You could choose to stack the highest priority work with all of the best people, or you might choose to distribute the talent more evenly. You'll need to assess how much the allocation will stretch each person, and whether there are gaps where you need to add more support. You'll need to think about whether people are accessing opportunities that will keep them engaged and help them grow. On top of all that, you'll want to consider personalities in order to reduce predictable interpersonal conflicts.

When you do allocation, it's worth it to consider all of your people, even if there's a very obvious solution that only moves one person. If you always move the person whose project is just finishing up, you miss the opportunity to make more strategic allocation choices.

Consider these factors when determining who should work on each team or project:

- How much of a stretch will the work be?

- How senior is the rest of the team? Is there someone who can step up as a leader?

- Is the team under-resourced in any area (e.g., design, data science, user research), and how does that match up with the PM's skill set?

- How critical is the work?

- Does the work and team structure support good mentorship?

- How much do they want to be on the team, and have they been getting the projects they want in the past?

- How does this fit into their growth plan?

Allocation is all about tradeoffs—what's best for the business and what's best for individual people's growth? What's best in the short and the long run? What's best for one team versus another?

You might sometimes get lucky and everyone will end up on their first-choice team, but that won't always happen. It will be up to you to explain why you're allocating people the way you are and to get them excited about their team. Connect the work to the skills they'll build and their career goals.

CONCEPTS AND FRAMEWORKS

HORIZONTAL TASKS

An incredibly valuable part of Google's APM program is what they call "horizontal tasks." Executives at the company come up with a list of business questions, projects, and responsibilities. APMs can then volunteer to take on any of those "horizontal tasks." The tasks themselves are often time consuming and tedious, but they come along with exposure to executives, higher level meetings, and strategy that the APM would otherwise not get until they were much more senior.

Here are some examples of good horizontal tasks:

- Taking notes at an executive meeting.

- Doing the administrative work to run an upper-level staff meeting.

- Putting slides together for board meetings.

- Gathering weekly product metrics.

Horizontal tasks can be a great win-win. Executives benefit from the extra assistance, and the PMs benefit from the exposure. Consider adding horizontal tasks at your company!

ORG DESIGN

As your organization grows, you'll need to think about how to split up the work. When the company is small, you might have a scattered set of distinct teams. But as the company grows, you'll likely need a more complex hierarchy, grouping the teams into divisions.

Here are some signs you need to invest in longer-term org design:

- People spend a large percentage of their time ramping up on new areas as they jump from project to project.

- Teams make short-sighted product decisions.

- Teams are reluctant to make long-term investments.

- The team has grown large enough that you need to delegate management.

There are many ways to organize long-running teams. Often, companies will use multiple options at the same time. For example, they might organize by product at a higher level, and then within products by user type. Or, they might organize by objective, but also organize a few teams by the engineering codebase. It's fairly common for companies to reorganize every one to three years.

To help illustrate the options, consider a hypothetical social media company DogTok where dog owners share videos of their dogs. We'll explore what that might look like, and how they might add a new feature, "Bark Translation," that captions the videos with what the dogs are saying.

Here are some common approaches for organizing teams:

By product

- **What it is:** This is when there is a team or organization for each separate product at the company. There may also be a shared services team to own and invest in components that are used by multiple products.

- **Example:** DogTok might decide that Bark Translation deserves to be its own app. They would spin up a new division with its own general manager and teams of people who work on various features of the app.

- **Benefits:** Dividing by products offers clear boundaries, and each product can usually run autonomously.

- **Drawbacks:** It can be hard to drive consistency across products.

- **Who it works for:** Large companies that need multiple levels of organization hierarchy. Independent products that don't require much cross-product collaboration.

- **How to make It work:** Unless the products are very small, you'll usually need to use another organization style within each product.

By short-term project

- **What it is:** In small organizations, you can assign individual short-term projects such as "Twitter importer" or "Calendar view."

- **Example:** If DogTok organizes by short-term project, the leadership team decides what to work on next. They assign each piece of work to a small, temporary team based on availability, interest, and skills. One team builds the onboarding experience in January, and a different set of people run A/B tests on it in August. The leadership team spins up a "Bark Translation" team who builds the entire feature and integrates it into the existing video player. After it ships, they move on to start building another feature.

- **Benefits:** Leadership gets to clearly dictate what gets worked on. At a small, early-stage startup, the founders probably have a clear vision of what they want to build, and it might be unnecessary to delegate those choices.

- **Drawbacks:** The single-project approach can discourage long-term thinking on both the product and engineering side, leading to accumulating engineering debt and a lack of product expertise. It also increases the percentage of time people spend in a lower-productivity "ramping up" state, both in terms of the project itself, as well as learning to work with new teammates.

- **Who it works for:** This places most of the strategic thinking on leadership and is usually more appropriate for teams led by junior PMs.

- **How to make it work:** If you choose to organize teams by project, you should put extra effort into communicating what you expect to the teams. Make sure they understand the strategic reasons the project was chosen, and what you're hoping to get out of it. Be clear about how strictly they should stick to the initial project idea; should they do their own research, can they consider alternate solutions, what kind of early validation do you expect?

By engineering codebase

- **What it is:** Historically, many teams were organized around the engineering codebase. Each team owned a part of the product that corresponded to specific files and folders in the code repository.

- **Example:** If DogTok organizes by engineering codebase, they create a team for each component and piece of infrastructure. Each file in the codebase belongs to one team. They have a team for the ranking algorithm, one for the search box, one for the comment box, and so on. Someone at the company who had the idea for Bark Translation would try to convince the video team to add it to their roadmap.

- **Benefits:** Engineers can build up expertise in their area and you get clear responsibility over bugs, design decisions, code quality, and long-term maintenance of the code base. It avoids two PMs stepping on each other's toes or making conflicting changes, since each component has a clear owner.

- **Drawbacks:** The codebase usually doesn't map to specific customers, use cases, or problems, and so it's hard to launch impactful changes. It can be challenging to find the highest priority work for your team; it's not straightforward to find the most important customer need that can be solved with your part of the codebase. It's possible that the highest priority work on one part of the codebase is quite low priority for the company overall. Even worse, many important customer problems can't be solved in just one part of the codebase, and this organization adds a lot of friction to solving those problems.

- **Who it works for:** When you have parts of the codebase that require deep technical expertise, this might be the best organization for those teams. It makes sense at most companies to have *some* teams that are split by codebase, but to use this option sparingly. If you don't have enough specialized mobile engineers to embed in each team, you can create a centralized mobile team. Infrastructure teams are often organized around the systems they maintain.

- **How to make it work:** This organizational approach requires strategic leadership at a higher level in order to ensure the teams are appropriately staffed to match company priorities and help guide them towards high-impact strategic work.

By user type

- **What it is:** If your product has distinct types of users with different needs, such as administrators and knowledge workers, or drivers and riders, you can create teams that are each responsible for improving the product for their user type.

- **Example:** If DogTok organizes by user type, they create one team for dog owners, one team for viewers, and one for advertisers. The PMs for each of those teams spends a lot of time with their audience, getting to know their needs and how to increase their usage of the product, and then creating a roadmap for the team. The Bark Translation feature arose out of conversations with dog owners, and so they take on the work.

- **Benefits:** When PMs own a specific user type, they can become experts in those users and assess which problems are the highest impact to solve for that user. They can design holistic solutions across multiple parts of the product.

- **Drawbacks:** A downside of organizing by user type is that multiple PMs might have conflicting ideas regarding in which direction to take different parts of the product, for example, what functionality to highlight on the homepage.

- **Who it works for:** This organization works well when you have distinct customer types who need to be served over the long run. Many companies have a product team focused on IT administrators.

- **How to make it work:** You'll need an approach to moderate conflicting ideas, for example, assigning ownership of contentious areas to teams, or carefully reviewing and moderating the proposed changes.

By use case (or problem)

- **What it is:** When a product has multiple prominent use cases, such as creating content and consuming it, you can create teams that are each responsible for improving their use case. Often, each use case is closely tied to a few parts of the product, for example, the team responsible for content discovery probably owns the search UI. Framing the team's charter around the use case instead of the product area encourages the team to look for the best solution wherever in the product it might go. This can lead to better and more impactful solutions.

- **Example:** If DogTok organizes by use case, they create teams for video creation, exploration, onboarding, and monetization. The video creation team noticed that as they add unique video editing capabilities, people upload more videos. This gave rise to the idea of Bark Translation, which they then built.

- **Benefits:** Organizing by use case shares many of the benefits of organizing by user type, while also giving leadership more fine-grained control over what types of problems teams choose to solve. PMs can become experts in their use cases, and are encouraged to find the highest impact problems to solve within their predefined scope.

- **Drawbacks:** Teams organized around specific use cases might need to be spun up or spun down frequently, as company priorities change. For example, after a year of investing in content discovery or exporting data, the company might decide that those use cases are handled well enough and people should be reallocated to more pressing problems. Relatedly, tackling a newly identified problem often involves spinning up a new team, which can be more overhead than you want.

- **Who it works for:** Organizing by use case works well in smaller organizations where leaders creating the teams are deeply knowledgeable about the priorities of individual problems and use cases.

- **How to make it work:** Look for use cases that are MECE (mutually exclusive, collectively exhaustive) to avoid gaps or PMs stepping on each other's toes. You may also want to have a "special ops" team that tackles high priority short-term projects that don't fit into an existing use case.

By objective

- **What it is:** When your organization is going after a few distinct goals and you have senior product leaders, you can organize teams around objectives such as adoption, monetization, or new user growth. In this model, the team owns a key success metric and can consider a very broad range of ideas to move that metric. For example, at Facebook, the growth team tackled international expansion and even bringing internet connectivity to more parts of the world, in addition to more traditional growth projects like revamping the onboarding experience.

- **Example:** If DogTok organizes by objective, they create teams for increasing uploads from existing dog owners, increasing video views, improving adoption of new viewers, and improving monetization. The team responsible for increasing uploads discovers that people like to upload to explore the fun overlays, and decides to build Bark Translation.

- **Benefits:** Teams have a clear mission and are very empowered to solve it in the way they think is best. Leadership is crystal clear about what results they want, while pushing the "how" down to the PMs who are closer to the problems. This model also encourages good strategic practices in the leadership team; they'll need to think about what objectives matter, and their relative priorities.

- **Drawbacks:** This model might falsely empower teams if they're not actually allowed to choose their own approach. Or, it can lead to stress and wasted efforts if the teams aren't strong enough to choose good projects.

- **Who it works for:** This model works best when you have strong senior PMs and high-level objectives of roughly equal priorities. For example, if you have four high-level priorities of equal importance, you can create four teams. However, if one of those priorities is much more important than the others, you might want three teams working on that priority, and you'll need a different way to differentiate what each of those teams work on.

- **How to make it work:** Set clear expectations with PMs around how much autonomy they have and when to bring plans to you for review. They may need extensive coaching on how to set a good roadmap and what types of risks are "good" risks to take.

KEY TAKEAWAYS

- **Structure helps you scale:** When done well, each PM gets the freedom they need to own an important area and move fast towards ambitious goals. They also get the necessary guardrails to keep teams strategically aligned and prevent excessive conflict or wasted work. Beware of team structures that make it hard to ship end-to-end solutions.

- **The organization is your product:** As a product leader, the quality of your organization is your direct deliverable. Invest in your team culture. Develop the people on your team. Look for systemic opportunities to improve how your team creates products.

CAREERS

PART H

CAREERS

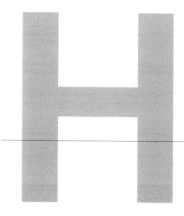

CAREERS

IF YOU'VE JUST landed your first PM job, it might be hard to imagine how your career will progress over the coming decades. Some PMs grow by advancing within a company, while others grow by switching companies, and then there are those who decide to move on to other roles beyond product management.

In this section, we'll learn how to set and achieve our career goals.

- **The Career Ladders** (pg 343) will show us what career progression looks like for product managers. We'll learn about the expectations of each level in the career ladder, and what it will take to advance to the next rung of the ladder.

- **Career Goals** (pg 373) will explain the importance of career goals. We'll learn about the wide variety of potential goals and learn some visualization exercises to help us discover which goals are important to us.

- **Skills for Career Growth** (pg 378) will teach us how to convert our accomplishments into career advancement. We'll learn how to partner with our managers, pick the right company and team, and how to handle bad situations.

- **Extended Learning** (pg 408) will teach us additional ways to develop as a product leader. We'll discuss courses, coaching, and MBA programs.

- **Beyond PM** (pg 410) discusses popular career options outside of product management. We'll learn about roles such as general management, venture capital, and startup founder.

Keep in mind that we're only offering *career* advice; it's completely fine to not follow it. This book is designed to provide you with the tools and education to find and create the career path that suits you best. Ultimately, you should be trying to "optimize" your life. Sometimes that means striving for "bigger and better" jobs. And sometimes, it means that the better job—for you—is the one that offers a better work/life balance, a better location, or something else.

CHAPTER 32

THE CAREER LADDERS

THE FIRST TIME I really thought about my career growth was after a year of working full-time. I was a PM on the Microsoft SharePoint team, and I was asked to write my career goals as part of a self-review. I wondered if it would sound too ambitious to write down "CEO." I looked at the job ladder documentation for a hint, but how could I "set strategy for a product line" when I only owned a few features?

I was eager to grow and learn, but I didn't really understand what it was that I needed to learn. My features were well designed—wasn't that enough? I kept hearing that I would grow through on-the-job experience, but that sounded very vague and unsatisfying. My manager and teammates were constantly sharing useful advice, but I felt like I could grow faster if I just knew which areas to focus on.

Later, at Google, I hit a similar stumbling block. I thought things were going well until I missed out on a promotion. Apparently, the promotion committee expressed concerns that I wasn't strategic enough, and that one of my team's major projects hadn't launched yet. Even though it's obvious to me now, somehow, I hadn't realized those things were so important.

I corrected those things, and it taught me a valuable lesson: think about your career path *early* and know what the next level requires.

This is where the career ladder comes in. It addresses questions such as:

- How does a company decide how much to pay you, and when you get a raise?

- How do they decide who gets new projects and who gets to become a manager?

- What does it mean to be a junior or senior PM at the company?

The details of the career ladder vary across companies, but the underlying concepts are generally the same.

LEVELS AND LADDERS

Similar to how a physical ladder has rungs, a career ladder has levels. You start your career near the bottom of the ladder and get promoted to higher levels as you progress through your career and gain more experience and skills.

Level

Your level is the classification your company assigns you to represent how senior you are and what scope and level of work is expected of you. At some companies, the levels map directly to titles like "Senior" or "Director," but it's also common to have multiple levels within one title. These levels might be semi-secret. For example, at Microsoft as a new college grad PM, you might start off at a level 59. You and your manager know your level, but this isn't displayed publicly to others. You could get promoted to level 60, but your public title may remain the same.

Even if your company doesn't have titles, they still likely have some form of levels behind the scenes. Going up a level is equivalent to getting a promotion, and typically corresponds with a pay raise.

Career ladder

The career ladder is a company's documented path with the skills and competencies expected at each level for a role.

The career ladder is not, however, a complete grading rubric. Your level is determined by the scope and autonomy the company trusts you to handle, and the impact they expect you to deliver. The ladder is just leadership's best attempt at articulating their thought process behind that trust. Many PMs are led astray when they treat the career ladder like a checklist rather than as a guideline.

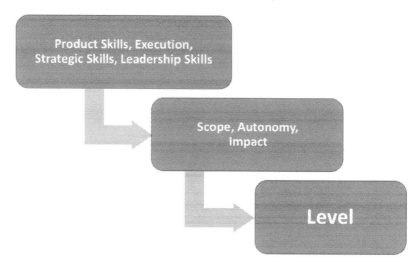

Your skills are a big part of the calculation, but they don't directly determine your level. If you lead a team that requires top-notch execution skills to pull off an important partnership but doesn't have difficult product work, you can get a promotion even if your product skills aren't stellar. If all of your skills are excellent, but your project is canceled by circumstances outside of your control, you probably will not get promoted to the next level.[1]

In this chapter, we'll go into detail about the PM career ladder, and have a look at the core qualities that differentiate each level.

---

1   In practice, there are very few reasons a project would be canceled that are truly outside of a PM's control. When this happens, focus on transitioning quickly and smoothly to the next important area.

A TYPICAL LADDER

The levels tend to vary from one company to another, but most companies have a ladder that generally looks like the chart below. The mappings, number of levels, and years of experience differ by company, but the progression of responsibilities is consistent.[2]

IC Path	Manager Path	Typical Experience	Key Responsibilities
APM		0-4 years of experience.	Learn the basics of PMing. At some companies, this might be a rotational program.
PM 1 & 2[3]		3-8 years of experience.	Ship impactful work.
Senior PM		5+ years of experience.	Set team strategy to prioritize what their team works on.
Principal PM	PM Lead	Industry Expert / Managing 3+ people.	Get a team of PMs to ship excellent work, via strategy and coaching.
	Director	Manager of managers.	Create high-level frameworks and processes to drive strategic and organizational excellence across product teams.
	Head of Product	Executive level.	Drive strategic, managerial, and organizational excellence at a company-wide, cross-functional scope.

The PM role changes significantly as you advance. The early levels focus on launching great products, the middle levels focus on product strategy, and the upper levels focus on organizational excellence.

	Shipping Product	Product Strategy	Organizational Excellence
Learning	APM	PM 1 & 2	PM Lead
Knows How	PM 1 & 2	Sr. PM	Director
Excels	Sr. PM	PM Lead / Principal PM	Head of Product

Because of these shifts, career progression is often more of a zigzag pattern than a single straight line.

---

2   http://levels.fyi has excellent up-to-date comparisons of titles and salaries across companies.

3   The level between APM and Senior PM is often called just "PM," but for clarity we will call it "PM 1 and 2" to distinguish the level from the overall role of Product Manager.

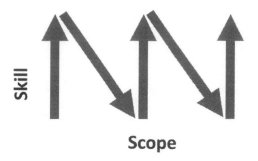

Scope

Inspired by Shreyas Doshi's Scope and Impact Matrix[4]

Each time your scope increases, you go from being the expert to being a novice again. It will take time to learn how to do your new job well. It can be upsetting to feel inadequate at your job after being good at it for so long, but it helps to think of scope increases as a new type of job and to keep a learning mindset.

The zigzag pattern to career progression also explains why, as a new PM, it can be difficult to understand what makes senior people so great. A PM director might not be any better at launching a feature than a PM 2, but they're much better at strategy.

ADVANCEMENT

The rate of advancement is not consistent at each level. At the beginning of your career, you might be promoted every year or two, but as you advance, the promotions tend to space out and become more challenging to achieve.

With enough time, most PMs can and should advance to senior PM. Senior PMs are strong independent contributors. If you stay at the PM 1 level for a long time without growing, your company might decide you require too much oversight. Once you reach senior PM, you don't need to keep advancing if that doesn't align with your career goals. You can have a perfectly healthy and happy career by remaining at the senior PM level.

> People do not get promoted to a level until they have reliably demonstrated the skills for that level. The descriptions for each level are, mostly, the skills you need to demonstrate in order to get to that level, not the skills you need to graduate from it. In many cases, you need to be operating at a higher level for at least six months before you are promoted into it.

Many new PMs get frustrated by this "off by one" aspect of career charts. It makes sense, however, once you understand that PM career progression isn't a linear scale of getting better at PMing. Rather, many of the promotions represent a change in responsibilities. Just like a waiter doesn't get promoted to chef unless they prove they can cook, a PM doesn't get promoted to senior PM unless they demonstrate that they can consistently create product strategies.

---

4   Scope and Impact Matrix: https://twitter.com/shreyas/status/1055718675678814208?s=20

To advance beyond senior PM, you not only need the skills; you also need to match with an appropriate business need. For example, if your company doesn't need a people manager, you won't get promoted to PM lead. If a company doesn't need your specific industry expertise, they won't hire you as a principal PM.

SCOPE, AUTONOMY, AND IMPACT

The hallmarks of PM career progression, both within and across companies, are increasing scope, autonomy, and impact. Together, they represent the value you provide for your company.

Scope, autonomy, and impact have a mutually reinforcing relationship with each other.

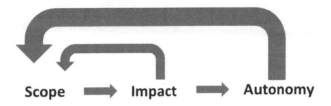

Scope ➡ **Impact** ➡ **Autonomy**

Your scope is a major factor in how much impact you can have. If you're working on a small feature, you might be able to move some local metrics that are important to your team, but it's unlikely you'll move key company metrics no matter how well you PM the feature.

You don't get to choose your scope directly because you're assigned your project or team. To increase your scope, you'll first need to earn trust by showing the appropriate level of autonomy and delivering solid results (making an impact). Then, you'll need to find an available opportunity at a larger scope.

You also don't get full control over your level of autonomy. As a new PM, you might be subject to a lot of oversight, and you'll need to earn the right to act more autonomously through running projects successfully and delivering impact.

> When people advance quickly in their careers, it's often because they take advantage of an opportunity to grow their scope, impact, or autonomy faster than usual.

They might join a fast-growing company, deliver better-than-anticipated results, or show more initiative than expected.

SCOPE

Scope generally refers to the size and complexity of your responsibilities. A big part of advancing in your PM career is being able to handle larger and larger scopes.

There's no foolproof method to determine the scope, but here are a few factors to consider:

- **Amount of product ownership.** Are you responsible for individual features, an area with multiple features and the strategy across them, an entire product, or a suite of products?

- **Team size**. Overseeing more engineers and designers generally corresponds to a bigger responsibility, all else held equal. This isn't always the case, however; some teams are larger just because the work is more eng-heavy.

- **Complexity**. Work will generally have a larger scope when it has more cross-team collaboration, lower tolerance for mistakes, more ambiguous customer needs, and more difficult tradeoffs.

- **Potential impact**. A small feature with a million users could be a larger scope than an entire product that only has a thousand users. Features that have the potential to bring in a lot of revenue might be a larger scope than those that only bring in a little. Building something ambitious and innovative could be a larger scope than merely maintaining a legacy product.

Scope is somewhat subjective. When considering multiple job offers, you'll need to make your own assessment of which scope is larger.

AUTONOMY

Autonomy refers to the independence you're *given*, as well as the independence you *show*. You need to know when and how to seek input.

The amount of autonomy you're given on a project can be a large modifier on its level of difficulty.

A project that usually would be appropriate for a senior PM can be scoped down for an APM by giving them more guidance and less autonomy on it. This could include setting constraints, providing the process and timeline, checking in frequently, giving more feedback, and double-checking decisions.

Likewise, you might be responsible for a scope that usually corresponds to a senior PM, but if you need a lot of help or direction, you won't be performing at the senior PM level. People with impostor syndrome might ask for more help than they truly need, while overconfident people might think they don't need help when their manager thinks they do. It takes self-awareness to know which side of the scale you're on.

See "Make sure your manager knows how your work is going" on pg 383 for a high-autonomy way of sharing your progress and asking for input.

IMPACT

Impact refers to the positive outcomes you deliver.

> As Chaim Gross explained, "Product management is a 'hits' business. You need to have a hit once in a while to be a good product manager." At the end of the day, your reputation as a product manager will be driven primarily by the products you shipped.

An easy way to think about impact is with the formula:

> **How meaningful the improvement is** x **how many people experience the improvement**

Different people care about different types of impact. Some people are more motivated by launching small improvements that affect millions of people, while others seek to make a tangible difference in just a few people's lives. Some people love creating better forms of entertainment, while others prefer to focus on health or education. When people move to another company, they often do so because they believe they can have more impact in the new role.

Within a company, your impact is usually judged by the goals you set and how well you perform to meet and exceed those goals. When you convince leadership that you are able to set and achieve ambitious, strategically-aligned goals, you'll be seen as having a large impact. Without that preemptive calibration, leadership might not appreciate the size of your impact.

PSHE FRAMEWORK

Lane Shackleton wanted to move from sales to PM at YouTube, and the VP of Product, Shishir Mehrotra, offered him a project to prove his skills: skippable ads. This project had been shelved for several years because the sales team hated it.

Mehrotra laid out a playbook. The **problem** was the way they'd tried to put the new ad format into AdWords. The **solution** was to get it into AdWords in a different way. The **how** was setting up meetings with the AdWords team. Mehrotra expected Shackleton to **execute** on that playbook.

Three weeks later, Shackleton had talked to the AdWords team, but came back with a different update. He told Mehrotra, "I decided that our problem is different. I think our problem is the brand." He went on to explain that the framing of "skippable ads" was a value proposition to users, but was a negative value proposition to the real customer—the advertisers who buy the ads. They don't want to think about people skipping their ads.

So, Shackleton decided to switch it around. He ran a naming exercise and came up with the name TrueView. The new name emphasized the advertising value proposition—you only pay for the ad if it's actually watched. The new brand aligned with Google's goal of making better ads. With just this change, the sales team came to love the new ad format and it became their top requested product.

Popularized by Mehrotra, PSHE stands for Problem, Solution, How, and Execution. PSHE represents a way of framing career growth. Junior PMs are handed the problem, solution, and instructions on "how" to execute, and then are expected to execute that playbook well. As they grow they can take a rough solution and figure out the 'how.' Then, they learn how to take a vague problem and come up with a solution. At the most advanced level in their careers, they can take an ambiguous space and determine the problems to go after.

Problem: Given an ambiguous space, they can determine problems to focus on, then develop solutions.

Solution: They can take an ambiguous problem and come up with a solution, then execute on it.

How: Given a problem and rough solution, they can figure out how to execute and get it done.

Execution: They can execute when given problem, solution, and 'how' instructions.

In Shackleton's case, he was originally handed a problem, solution, and 'how' instructions, but he showed his advanced skills by questioning the problem he was handed and finding a better one. This impressed Mehrotra enough that he converted Shackleton over to a PM role, and several years later, recruited him to run product at Coda.

THE LEVELS

Unlike most other leveling guides, we are not going to frame our guide as a rubric that matches skills to each level. If your company provides those, you can look to them for hints of what product leadership values, but they often confuse more than they illuminate. Those rubrics tend to be unhelpfully vague with subjective words or misleadingly specific with bullet points that aren't applied consistently. They might include categories that aren't heavily weighted in actual practice. Often, they just self-referentially describe the scope you've been assigned, such as "sets strategy for a product area."

> The underlying truth is that PM skills don't directly translate into levels.
>
> Instead, your level is determined by your scope, autonomy, and impact. The way to earn a promotion to the next level is by demonstrating autonomy and impact at your current scope and gaining the trust that you can perform at a bigger scope.

In this guide, we'll describe the typical scope, autonomy, and impact expected at each level, and what you can do at your current level to demonstrate that you're ready for the next one.

Note: Titles are not standard across companies. The Group Product Manager (GPM) level, in particular, varies and can be more like "PM lead," or more like "Director." For clarity, we're not using that terminology. Look at levels.fyi to find the mapping for your company.

ASSOCIATE PRODUCT MANAGER (APM)

People at the APM level are learning the ropes of product management.

Some companies have official APM programs that include rotational assignments (switching teams every 6-12 months), official mentorship, training materials, and community building. Other companies may hire new grads directly onto teams without an APM program.

Typical Scope, Autonomy, and Impact

- **Tightly scoped projects:** The problem is well defined and the mentor likely has a good idea of what the solution will look like.

- **Low-risk projects:** If the projects get delayed or fail, it won't hurt the company much.

- **Small set of engineers:** Might only be responsible for a few engineers or part of an engineer's time.

- **Hands-on mentorship:** A mentor provides a playbook and guides the mentee through it. The mentor might tell them what they should be working on and review their work closely.

- **Not given much autonomy:** Anything with the potential for high impact has gatekeeping reviews.

- **Impact on local metrics:** Generally launches are expected to improve feature-level metrics, but not global metrics such as engagement or retention.

To get from APM to PM 1

The promotion from APM to PM 1 is straightforward for PMs who are doing well. It tends to be more closely tied to your time in the role than the details of your performance. Companies with formal APM programs often promote people from APM 1 to APM 2 after the first year, and from APM 2 to PM 1 after the second year, as long as there aren't any performance issues.

At most companies, it's very unlikely for an APM to be promoted to PM 1 ahead of schedule, even if they meet the criteria for PM 1. This is because companies like to keep the class together through completion of the APM program. An early promotion would usually require meeting the criteria for Senior PM—which would be exceptional and highly unusual.

Here are the key elements to focus on for advancing to PM 1.

Learn how to go through the product life cycle independently

APMs are expected to learn the basics of PMing. To get to PM 1, you'll need to demonstrate that you know what to do during the day-to-day job at each stage of the product life cycle without hands-on mentorship.

- When you're dropped onto a team, can you figure out what you're supposed to do, or do you ask your manager?

- Can you kickoff a new project and follow the product team's processes?

- Do you know when to do product discovery and how to get the resources you need?

- Are you able to use spec review and design review effectively?

- Can you pull cross-functional teams together to launch features?

The first time you go through each stage of the product life cycle, you'll have tons of questions and probably need a lot of support. Each subsequent time gets easier. Most people need to go through at least two complete product life cycles before they're ready to be independent PM 1s.

Teams that launch frequently will give you extra practice and extra chances to prove your independence. When you're ready to do this, move away from asking your manager what to do or how to do it; instead, *tell* your manager what you plan to do. It's still great to ask questions and have a learning mindset, but the tone should be more along the lines of "I'd love to hear your perspective," rather than "please tell me what to do; I'm lost!"

If you find yourself on a team with a long product life cycle or don't get a chance to work on all of the stages of the product life cycle, you might need to be more proactive. Ask your manager or their peers if the limited experience will be a problem at promotion time. Look for opportunities to fill in the missing stages, for example, with a side project. You might find that having a small number of launches isn't a problem for internal promotion. Even so, it could make it more difficult to get hired at another company.

Launch features successfully

Here's where all of the product and execution skills come into play.

To get to PM 1, you usually don't need stellar launches, but you do need to design reasonable features and launch them without major issues. In fact, most of the time, the work you're assigned won't have much potential to be stellar.

It's often fine to launch a straightforward feature that people use, even if it doesn't move the metrics significantly. It could be a problem, however, if your feature never launches or if sloppy logistics cause important steps to be missed.

One way success will be measured is whether you're hitting your team's goals and OKRs. This can lead to a point of tension on teams where APMs are responsible for major challenges. Good OKRs usually involve moving the metrics that matter, but sometimes that can't be done with straightforward feature work.

If you're making a risky bet on product work, make sure that you, your manager, and the rest of your team are completely aligned. If your manager believes in the work you're doing, but the experiment is a loss, you'll still be in a good situation. On the other hand, if your experiment is a loss and your manager was never bought in on the idea, it could hold you back. Basically, to get to PM 1, it's more important to show that you can build products that follow someone else's strategy than to design your own strategy.

Be a leader or equal partner on your feature teams

If you've joined a team with strong engineers and designers, you might be tempted to sit back and let them take the lead. PMs in this situation sometimes end up as glorified note-takers who schedule the meetings and then let other people make decisions.

It's not always easy to tell the difference between highly collaborative lead-from-behind PMs and those who neglect their leadership responsibilities. To see where you fall, consider what your teammates would say are your top contributions. If the answers are all administrative, that's a problem. If they're unaware of the ways you're influencing the product and strategy, they won't support your promotion. They might even resent you for not contributing to the team as much as other people do.

> Great lead-from-behind PMs can be humble, but they improve outcomes enough that their teammates notice. If you're going to be quiet, your work needs to speak for itself.

If you are a lead-from-behind PM, make sure your manager understands your contributions. Talk through the challenges your team is facing and how you are addressing them. You might want to invite your manager to some of your meetings to see your subtle style in action.

Get good peer reviews

Peer reviews are incredibly important for PMs because, in a sense, our only purpose is to make our teammates more effective. In that respect, our teammates are the best suited to evaluate our performance.

If your engineers and designers feel the work would have gone just as well without you, something has gone wrong. Peer reviews are the primary way a manager can tell how much credit the PM should get for the team's success. One product area might have a weak PM and strong engineers, while another team has a strong PM and weak engineers. From the outside, it's not always clear who is carrying more than their fair share of the weight, but those differences will come to light in the peer reviews.

Some PMs think, "It's so important to get this launch right that it doesn't matter if I irritate or anger my teammates." Unfortunately, that reasoning falls apart when you realize you'll need to work with those teammates again. It doesn't matter how "right" you were if people refuse to work with you again.

Address any gaps from your performance reviews

A tricky aspect of performance reviews and manager feedback is that it's not always clear which constructive feedback is a gap (a performance issue that will hold you back), and which is just a suggestion on how you could do better. If you're not sure, ask directly:

> Thank you for all this feedback. Can you point out which of these are the top issues I need to address?

Of course, it's worth working on all of the feedback, but the gaps are the highest priority.

PM 1 AND 2

A PM 1 or PM 2 is like a very good APM. They understand the company strategy. They can successfully run a project that is handed to them. If given good context, they'll deliver great results at a feature level. They can make straightforward roadmapping decisions.

At this level, the PM might take on projects that are more complex in terms of execution or collaboration. They may also be able to run multiple projects at once.

People at the PM 1 and 2 levels tend to follow processes and frameworks to the letter. They know how to execute the steps very efficiently, but they don't have a deep understanding as to why each step is there. As a result, they're unable to show good judgment on what to emphasize, when they can skip steps, and when to work outside of the processes.

For example, when people at the PM 1 and 2 levels give presentations, the signal-to-noise ratio is often low because they don't know which details are the most important. As they start to understand the context more, they'll get better at anticipating questions and tailoring their presentations to answer those questions up front.

Typical Scope, Autonomy, and Impact

- **Serves as the PM for a team:** Rather than being assigned individual projects, the PM is responsible for all of the projects on the team. This usually corresponds with owning a part of the product or use case.

- **Sets the roadmap with support:** Partners closely with their manager to choose projects and create a roadmap for the team.

- **Runs a project with limited support:** Knows how to run the team and move things forward throughout the product process.

- **"Go to" person for the team:** People see the PM as the person to answer any questions about the team and its projects. They trust the PM to know the full context and give accurate, useful answers.

- **Aiming for impact on global metrics:** Launches might only move feature metrics, but the goal is to move global metrics.

To get from PM 2 to senior PM

The promotion to senior PM can be challenging. It requires both mastery of the day-to-day product life cycle work *and* new contributions to product strategy.

Execute successful product launches of increasing complexity

While a PM 1 or 2 can do a great job on some types of projects, senior PMs are expected to know how to handle almost any kind of product work and deliver meaningful impact.

More complex projects can include:

- More cross-functional stakeholders
- Larger product changes
- Bigger marketing moments
- Tougher trade-offs

- Less straightforward customer needs
- More ambiguity
- Potential customer backlash
- Longer-term investments

- External partnerships
- Less room for error

- Higher executive scrutiny
- And so on...

At this level, "successful" means not only that you lead the team through launch without issues and hit your goals, but also that the work is strategically important in some way. You'll also be expected to confidently present your work at executive meetings and engage in constructive discussions with company leadership. All of the skills in early chapters come into play here.

This is not to say that it's wrong to build simple solutions to simple problems. A lot of your day-to-day job might involve simple solutions, and it shows good judgment to not over-complicate them. But, you can't demonstrate your seniority if you only take on easy work. You might naturally get assigned to more complex projects as you build your skills, but if not, you'll need to be proactive and look for them.

Make time for strategic work

You don't get to reduce your project workload when you pick up strategic responsibilities. Instead, you *make* the time by learning how to run your projects more efficiently and increasing your capacity.

This might mean that you write specs more quickly, but could also mean that your initial proposals are so good that they don't need much iteration. As you build your intuition, you might save hours of research by going with an educated guess. You'll also save time by giving your teammates clear context so there are fewer misunderstandings to correct. As you gain experience and practice the PM skills, you'll see these efficiency improvements.

> It's important to commit to making time for strategic work. There will always be potential excuses for why you don't have time, but overcoming them is a critical element for becoming a senior PM.

For more advice on time management, see Chapter 13: Get Things Done (pg 149).

Demonstrate nuanced and structured thinking on complex decisions

Junior PMs sometimes jump to solutions without noticing the complexity or tradeoffs of the decision.

They might narrowly focus on their own team's goals and miss the additional valid goals from cross-functional stakeholders. For example, they might launch a feature without realizing that it causes a large increase in the time it takes customer support to answer tickets. When they're told, they might naively disregard the complaint because they haven't considered the customer satisfaction and operating cost repercussions.

The more senior you get, the more you'll be faced with decisions where the right answer is "it depends." You'll need to recognize these decisions and reason through them in a structured way. That doesn't mean you'll take days to make each decision; with practice and increased subject matter expertise, you'll be able to lay out your thought process in minutes.

As you work towards this, you can compensate for some gaps with improved collaboration skills. Instead of noticing the complexity on your own, you might only need to ask stakeholders for their concerns.

Learn your product area and customer needs in more depth than anyone else at the company

When you go to product review, you should be teaching product leadership about your customers. That deep knowledge and your insights are a big part of what makes you a more valuable PM.

> When you're the expert, it shifts the relationship between you and product leadership from student/teacher to peers. It gives you the credibility you need.

Beyond the immediate benefits, learning new insights about your customers positions you to identify new strategic opportunities. A casual statement you hear during a research session might spark a brand new initiative!

Show strategic skills on your own team by crafting excellent goals and prioritizing work strategically

Even when you join a team with a pre-defined strategy, you can still demonstrate strategic skills with the way you write your team's goals and prioritize your team's work.

Make sure that your goals clearly connect to the overall product strategy. Look out for potential conflicts or tradeoffs and resolve them in the goals. Be clear about the mechanism by which you expect your product work to be a win. For example, if you're not sure whether your new feature is primarily meant to win new customers, increase the engagement of existing customers, or make existing customers happier, that's an indication that you haven't thought strategically enough about the work.

Then, make sure the work your team chooses to do matches up with those goals. If your goal is to win new customers, you're hopefully prioritizing acquisition, marketing, and the new user experience. Don't let lower priority work crowd out the most important projects.

Finally, reference those strategic choices when you talk to people about your team's plans. Make sure everyone on the team understands the strategic reasons for your choices. Let product leadership know the tradeoffs you considered. This isn't self-promotional; if others don't know you did the strategic thinking, they'll feel compelled to do their own strategic analysis.

Proactively create and evangelize the long-term strategy within your scope

The best place to start writing strategies is with your own team. Even if your team is working on just one well-defined project, you can start planning ahead to what your team should work on next. Draw up an exciting vision and share it with other people at the company. Teach people on your team, and beyond, why your team's work matters.

When you start on a new team, you might be handed a project to start working on, but you'll soon need to take the driver's seat when it comes to deciding which products to build, which problems to solve, and which goals to pursue.

For more information on creating a strategy, see Part E: Strategic Skills (pg 166).

Contribute to higher-level strategic discussions

To get to senior PM, you'll need to show that you have good judgment on higher-level strategy. This is tricky because you might not be invited to strategic discussions yet. The head of product probably isn't stopping you in the hallway to ask which markets the company should enter next. Instead, you probably receive the strategy after it's finalized.

Here's where you'll need to get creative.

Read and absorb everything you can about the existing strategy. Ask your manager and skip-level managers about the current strategic discussions and open questions.

Look for places where insights you've discovered could be relevant. See if there are any open questions where new research, such as a competitive analysis, could be useful.

Once you have something useful and relevant to contribute, find a way to get it to the right people and make it digestible:

- Discuss it with your manager in a 1:1
- Email people directly
- Attend senior executive's office hours
- Present at hackathons
- Set up meetings
- Approach people in the cafeteria

Learn about the annual planning cadence, and time your contributions for the beginning of the cycle before things are locked down. If your ideas aren't making an impact, talk to your manager to understand why.

> It can take a long time for new ideas to get incorporated into the strategy, especially when you're starting without much credibility. You might need to plant seeds for a while before people come around to the idea. If you're convinced it's important, don't give up.

Analysis—and persistence—will help you get to the next level.

SENIOR PM

Senior PMs are highly competent and strategic. Given an ambiguous problem area, they can rapidly pick out the most important problems to solve and drive the work through to tangible impact. They know when to question the direction they were handed, rather than seeing it as a fixed variable.

Senior PMs take a nuanced and holistic view that acknowledges different points of view and complexities. Instead of believing they have the right answer (and everyone else is stupid), they can get to the heart of the matter and drive alignment even when partners have competing goals and priorities. They quickly hone in on what's most important.

A senior PM drives the strategy and roadmap for their team, making time by gaining efficiency in their tactical work. They create roadmaps that balance multiple goals such as delighting customers, winning market share, and increasing revenue. They evangelize their work to get their team the recognition they deserve. They achieve ambitious goals.

Typical Scope, Autonomy, and Impact

- **Runs one or more teams independently:** Has the efficiency and time management skills to take on more teams with time to spare for strategic work.

- **Solves complex and ambiguous problems with no right answer:** Recognizes difficult tradeoffs and competing priorities, even when they're not obvious. Uses nuanced judgment, structured thinking, and strong collaboration to drive alignment around a decision.

- **Drives end-to-end success of their product:** Takes responsibility for ensuring all functions (including marketing, sales, and customer support) work together to deliver the customer and business results desired.

- **Drives alignment on team strategy and roadmap with limited support:** Creates an ambitious vision based on customer and business insights and determines the path to get there. Thinks through competing priorities and complex tradeoffs to come up with a good strategy. Determines which problems to focus on.

- **Internal expert in their area:** Acts as a partner rather than a student to leaders across the company. Knows their customer and business better than anyone else and develops new insights.

- **Delivers strategically important impact:** Creates results that are important to the company goals and contribute meaningfully to the company's success.

To get from senior PM to PM Lead

A PM Lead is a first-level people manager.

See Chapter 27: Becoming a People Manager (pg 285) for details on how to become a people manager.

To get from senior PM to principal PM

Promotions to principal PM are rare. Becoming a principal PM is not just about doing your job really well, but about being so uniquely excellent at your job that you would be quite difficult to replace. Principal PM is the top of the IC (individual contributor) PM career path, and so reaching that level implies that you are now the top of your game.

Become a recognized industry expert

One of the more objective criteria for principal PMs is that they are recognized as experts in their field. Beyond just being the most knowledgeable person at the company in your area, it also helps to be recognized by people outside of the company as the leading expert in some element of your work.

While there are many ways to raise your external visibility, such as speaking at conferences, becoming an expert is more about the deeper expertise and respect you build up. Industry experts are often people who invented a new approach, serve on standards boards, and mentor people in the community.

Build deep trust with your manager and other company leaders

You'll need the support and advocacy of your manager and company leaders to get the promotion to principal PM.

Much like a manager role, a principal PM title often indicates that you can be trusted with sensitive information and looped into executive-level discussions. Leadership tends to be cautious when inviting new people into that circle of trust.

Contribute and influence at the company level

While principal PMs have their own team, they're also expected to contribute across the company. They often serve as mentors to other PMs. The might guide teams across the company with respect to a large initiative like security or open-source strategy.

Find mission-critical PM roles that require principal level skills

Not every company needs more principal PMs. Senior PMs are already highly competent, so a principal PM wouldn't necessarily do a better job on most projects or teams. In many cases, a company would be overpaying to hire or promote someone to principal PM when a senior PM would do.

To become a principal PM, you need to find an opportunity where your skills are worth the cost. It also needs to be an opportunity where you can be an effective IC PM without direct reports. This generally means it's a small amount of product work that has to be done especially well.

PRINCIPAL PM

Principal PM is the top of the IC PM career path. They take on the work that is especially high stakes: integrating acquired companies, overseeing prominent partnerships, owning decisions that direct large monetary investments, etc. They take on the type of projects that most other PMs wouldn't be trusted to handle.

Typical Scope, Autonomy, and Impact

- **Owns the highest priority, most complex work:** Responsible for critical work with a low margin for error.

- **Creates their own scope:** Identifies a new opportunity, sells a vision to the company, and creates their own team to go after it. Engages cross-functionally to get the resources and partnership they need. Drives from idea to execution.

- **Improves the quality of the PM team:** Serves as a mentor to other PMs. Acts as a role model for company values. Shapes the PM team culture.

- **Highest level of autonomy:** Delivers excellent work without oversight. Creates successful strategies from scratch. Does not rely on their manager to clear barriers, make connections, or drive alignment. Trusted to represent the company in cross-company talks.

- **Industry expert:** Brings unique expertise to the company, usually based on years of experience.

- **Delivers some of the highest impact at the company:** Entrusted to deliver results in the highest impact parts of the company.

PM LEAD

The first level of PM management is sometimes called "PM lead" or "Group Product Manager." PM leads often hold a player-coach role, where they both manage other PMs and are responsible for PMing their own feature team. They usually have limited authority to approve small launches and decisions on their own, but the majority of their work, and their team's work, goes through a higher level product review.

Sometimes, a PM lead manages all the PMs in a product area and owns the unified strategy, but not always. A PM lead might only be responsible for managing and coaching their reports, but not have full accountability over their work.

Typical Scope, Autonomy, and Impact

- **Everything from senior PM:** PM leads not only do everything a senior PM does, but they also do it faster, making time for other responsibilities.

- **Manages 1 to 5 PM direct reports:** Responsible for the management, coaching, and development of a few reports. Usually manages lower level PMs, such as APMs.

- **Sets or influences strategy for reports:** Responsible for ensuring that each team is strategically aligned with higher-level strategies. May or may not create a unified strategy across their PMs.

- **Learning the ropes of people management:** Their manager supports them in people management and is involved in important decisions such as promotions and performance management.

- **Impact through launches and developing people:** In addition to any product launches they own, also delivers impact by developing their direct reports and ensuring they have successful launches.

To get from PM lead to director

The move from PM lead to director is a big leap. Companies may be willing to give someone a chance at the PM lead role when there's a business need for more managers, but they wouldn't promote someone to director unless they were confident that they wanted the person on the product leadership team.

Focus on making the larger organization successful, even when it's worse for your team

At the earlier levels, PMs primarily identify with their teams of engineers and designers. They worry about hitting their launch goals and try to protect their teams from the whims of management.

To get to the director level, you need to shift your mindset. It's no longer acceptable to optimize for your own team without considering the impact it will have on other teams. Instead, you might volunteer engineers from one of your teams to help another team hit an important launch. If that means your team could miss some goals, you must communicate those tradeoffs clearly, but still advocate for what you think is best overall good of the company.

This shift takes confidence and bravery. You need to feel secure in your job and your relationships to take the risk of *not* doing whatever it takes to help your team. You need to be okay with some of your teammates being angry with your choices. It might take some time before you feel comfortable making this shift.

Build trust and deep relationships across the company

When you're promoted to director, the other directors and company leaders become your peer group. You'll work closely with them to set strategy, implement new processes, and resolve issues. The stronger those relationships are, the more you can get done.

The more you build up these relationships in advance, the easier it is to demonstrate that you have the necessary leadership skills. If you are frequently in conflict with someone at the company, that could be a reason to deny you the promotion.

Demonstrate excellent product, business, and strategic judgment

As you advance, you gain more authority as a reviewer. To be entrusted with that authority, you need to show excellent judgment.

You can demonstrate your judgment in many ways:

- Through the decisions you make and how you explain them.

- Through the feedback you give.

- By what you say in meetings.

- By the quality of the work of your direct reports.

You'll want to develop your judgment to the point that your manager would be happy to have you stand in for them at a review meeting.

For building your judgment, see Part C: Product Skills (pg 33) and Part E: Strategic Skills (pg 33).

Build a high-functioning team

You might be surprised that getting your direct reports to love you doesn't have much bearing on the promotion to director. Instead, the most important thing is to build a high performing team. Morale is one component of that, but so is hiring well, coaching and training, and allocating people appropriately.

For more on building a high-functioning team, see Chapter 29: Coaching and Development (pg 302) and Chapter 30: Building a Team (pg 313).

Drive operational excellence

Directors are expected to be competent at operational excellence. Rather than working within the existing systems, you'll need to show that you can improve them, such as adding new processes or training. Many PMs avoid this part of the job, but it becomes a larger part of the role as you advance.

For more, see Chapter 31: Organizational Excellence (pg 328).

Create innovative and impactful multi-team strategies, and see them through to success

For the promotion to director, the track record of success that's most important is your ability to set strategies across teams and see them through to good outcomes.

At the senior PM level, you created strategies for yourself. The strategy was an important planning and communication tool, but at the end of the day, there wasn't much difference between the success of your launches and the success of your strategy. If the strategy wasn't clearly written, you could just remember your own intentions. You weren't using the strategy to expand your influence.

As a director, you are responsible for a strategy that other PMs execute. The stakes are higher, and communication becomes much more important.

PM DIRECTOR

A PM Director is the strategic and operational lead of a product or large product area. Instead of serving as the PM for a team, they create impact by fostering the teams under them to be as successful as possible.

Typical Scope, Autonomy, and Impact

- **Manages several PMs or a few PM Leads:** Responsible for all of the PMs in a given product or product area.

- **Drives an innovative and impactful strategy:** Fully responsible for charting a course that will win the market. Understands the ecosystem and predicts the direction the market will go. Influences higher-level strategies.

- **Builds a high performing team:** Recruits talented people to join their team. Coaches and develops PMs to improve their skills. Intentionally builds a culture where people can thrive and do their best work.

- **Accountable for all of the work in their area:** Reviews product work. Creates product principles. Ensures teams have good goals or OKRs.

- **Achieves operational excellence with support:** Improves processes and removes roadblocks. Partners with their manager and engineer managers to define teams and allocate people. Finds creative ways to use or increase resources to achieve top priorities.

- **Impact through their team:** Responsible for delivering impact that has a strong return on investment relative to the size of their team.

To get to head of product

The path to becoming a head of product tends to be different than earlier promotions. Relationships and reputation are critical. Companies want someone who already knows how to do the job. Instead of promoting internally or posting a job listing, many companies use executive search firms to hire a head of product.

Here are a few paths to head of product, once you've reached PM director:

- Build a relationship of deep trust with the CEO and other executives, and then move into the role when it becomes available. Aim to become a strategic advisor to the CEO or to the current head of product. Demonstrate that you can execute autonomously.

- Move from director at a well-respected company to head of product at a smaller or less prestigious company.

- Develop a strong reputation and work with recruiters from an executive search firm or VC firm.

Companies typically look for the following attributes when hiring a head of product:

- **Experience:** Have you handled a breadth of product, management, strategic and organizational challenges? Have you managed designers and engineers or held a GM role before? Do you have an impressive track record of success? Do you have the specific expertise the company is looking for?

- **Philosophy:** Do you have robust frameworks for how you approach those challenges? Does your philosophy align with the company's values?

- **Autonomy:** Do you run your product organization entirely autonomously? Are you beyond the point of needing coaching on how to manage ICs and managers? Do you proactively create the strategies, processes, and structures that your team needs to deliver?

- **Fit:** Can you collaborate well with the rest of the executive team? Do they trust and respect you? Does your working style mesh well with the CEO? Do you fill an important gap on the executive team?[5]

- **Reputation:** What do past peers, managers, and reports have to say about you? Expect the company to look for back-channel (secret) references from any mutual relationships.

HEAD OF PRODUCT

The head of product role looks very different when you look at it from above or from below.

From the point of view of the CEO and other executives, the head of product is a member of the executive team and an advisor to the CEO. They work cross-functionally with other members of the executive team to drive strategy and operations across the company. They participate as a respected leader all-around, rather than just working on product issues or only representing the product organization.

From the point of view of people who report up into them, the head of product is the top of the product organization. The product organization includes PM, design, user research, and possibly engineering. They

---

5   Assessing for fit is notoriously rife with bias, but it would be disingenuous to pretend it wasn't an important factor in executive recruiting.

drive the overall product vision and strategy. They determine the organizational structure, allocate budget and headcount, and set up processes. They review and approve product work.

Typical scope, autonomy, and impact

- **Drive top-level product strategy:** Sets strategy across all products at the company. Determines the organizational structure to achieve that strategy.

- **Influences company strategy:** Influences company-wide decisions such as setting compensation targets, opening new office locations, acquiring companies, updating the company organizational structure (reorgs), hiring other executives, and setting financial targets. Represents the perspective of the product organization, but also serves as a thought partner to the rest of the executive team.

- **Drive operational excellence across the product organization:** Recruits and trains ICs and managers. Enacts rules and guidelines where necessary. Sets the product culture. Identifies gaps or obstacles that span the product organization and overcomes them. Entirely autonomous. Knows from experience how to handle any situation. Responsible for the product organization budget.

- **Accountable for all product work:** Might review all product work or just the most critical pieces. Ensures quality and consistency across products.

- **Impact at the company level:** Responsible, in collaboration with the rest of the executive team, for the overall success of the company. Responsible for company-level success metrics, including revenue and costs.

LEVELS IN PRACTICE

Let's look at some examples to see how people at various levels might approach problems differently.

Scenario 1: Customers complain about ease of use

Customers frequently write in to customer support to complain that the app is hard to use. These complaints are one of the top three issues that customer support hears about, and sometimes these complaints appear on social media as well.

APM

The APM's manager brings up the problem during a 1:1 and says, "For your next project, I'd like you to own this problem."

The APM replies, "Okay, what should I do?"

The manager then sketches out an outline of the playbook to follow.

> Observe: the PM was told what to do and how to do it.

PM 1 or 2

The PM's manager brings up the problem during a 1:1 and says, "For your next project, I'd like you to own this problem."

The PM replies, "Great! I'll dig into the complaints and find the top usability bugs, and then we'll fix those."

The PM then asks customer support and user research for a breakdown of the top issues, and then reads some of the complaints. They order the list by the number of times each issue was reported and propose that list to their team. The number two item is particularly expensive, so it's removed from the list.

A few months later, the team has addressed four of the top five issues. Customers are happy about the specific improvements, but ease of use is still in the top three list of complaints that customer support hears about. Customers are still complaining on social media. Customer retention has not noticeably improved.

> Observe: the PM figured out their own path, but limited the scope to usability bugs.

Senior PM

The senior PM's manager brings up the problem during a 1:1 and says, "For your next project, I'd like you to own this problem."

The PM replies, "Great! I'll get right on that."

The PM then asks customer support and user research for a breakdown of the top issues and reads many of the complaints. They notice that the top five issues only account for a small fraction of the overall complaints. Many of the complaints are amorphous and are about more than just a particular usability bug. They work with a user researcher to set up several user sessions.

Through talking to customers, the PM realized the ease of use issue seems to be related to a fundamental mismatch between the use cases that the customers have, and what the product was initially designed for. The PM recommends a large redesign, and product leadership agrees.

A year and a half later, the redesign is complete and ease-of-use complaints have dropped to number five on the list of customer support topics. Retention is up 10%.

> Observe: the PM analyzed the data to identify a larger opportunity, leading to a significant improvement.

Principal PM

The principal PM has been investigating potential new markets to enter. One of the most promising directions involves entering a space with several "easy to use" competitors. They know that current customers complain about how hard the app is to use and decide to see what it would take to address the issue.

The principal PM follows the same steps as the senior PM to determine the root issue of the complaints. They consider the option of a large redesign alongside the options of acquiring one of the easy to use competitors or going after a different market altogether. Ultimately, the principal PM recommends a narrower redesign of the app and creating a premium add-on product to capture the value of the new target market.

A year later, the redesign is complete and ease of use complaints have dropped to number five on the list of customer support topics. Acquisition is up 5%, retention is up 5%, and revenue is up 10%.

> Observe: the PM discovered the opportunity and considered an expanded set of options. They connected the usability work to the strategic goal of entering a new market.

PM Lead

The PM lead owns the product initiative of new user adoption and meets regularly with people from sales, customer support, and user research to learn about the biggest blockers and opportunities related to adoption. Ease of use has been a hot topic at those meetings for a few years.

During the annual planning cycle, the PM lead decides to tackle the ease of use problem. They work cross-functionally to create a vision and strategy for making the product easier to use. The strategy balances short-term wins like usability fixes with long-term investments like a redesign.

The PM lead presents the vision and strategy to the executive team and asks for the PM, engineering, and design resources needed to execute on that vision. The executive team agrees and the work is funded for the next year.

The PM lead works with their manager to assign the work to PMs on their team. Throughout the next year, the PM lead supports each PM on their work.

A year later, the redesign, as expected, is still underway. Meanwhile, the team focused on small wins has been able to provide a steady stream of improvements that please customers and satisfy the customer support team.

> Observe: the PM lead identified the opportunity, created a strategic vision, advocated for resources, and created a roadmap that balanced short-term and long-term goals.

Director

A PM who reports to the director comes to a 1:1 and says they'd like to tackle the ease of use problem with a redesign.

The director brings up the company's strategic goals of internationalization and revenue growth and guides the PM to think about the redesign in that context. With that prompting, the PM realizes that the proposed redesign could be adjusted to also make the product easier to internationalize. They also notice that their proposed redesign might decrease the prominence of premium features and come up with a testing plan to ensure that revenue does not drop.

With a 30 minute conversation, the director steered the PM towards a direction that was more valuable for the company, will prevent duplicate work, and will protect against a surprise drop in revenue. This conversation was effective because the director had recruited talented PMs, invested in them, empowered them, and kept them up-to-date on company strategy.

> Observe: the director was able to use a light touch to make a big impact on the product because of their prior investments in building a strong team and setting strategy. This enables them to scale themselves.

Head of Product

The head of product gets off a call with one of the company's biggest customers and reflects on the dozens of topics they discussed. One offhand comment jumped out at the head of product: the customer mentioned how all of their new employees went through a four-hour session to learn how to use the app. The customer was proud of the training they'd built and didn't see it as a problem, but the head of product was shocked.

They knew from past experience how valuable employee onboarding time was and realized if they could cut that time in half, they could use it as a competitive advantage.

At the next 1:1 with the relevant PM director, the head of product brought up the conversation and questioned whether the team should shift gears to tackle this problem sooner. The director agreed.

As the director formed the plans, the head of product realized that the current operational processes would result in a siloed solution. To really improve onboarding time, it would take a cross-functional approach including marketing, customer support, user research, and data science. The head of product worked with the leaders of each of those teams to advocate for a unified approach that would require changing how the teams worked together.

The unified approach worked and the teams were able to deliver an integrated end-to-end solution that resulted in huge improvements across the customer acquisition funnel.

> Observe: the head of product has a "spidey sense" for which feedback is most important and uses organizational solutions to improve product outcomes.

Scenario 2: PMs feel that there's too much "process"

Some of the IC PMs have been complaining that there's too much "process" at the company, and it's slowing down execution.

APM

The APM speaks up at a team meeting and says, "There's too much process and it's slowing us down. Why can't we just skip the reviews and launch 1% experiments like Google does? I just read a blog post that says all specs should be one page or less."

> Observe: the PM surfaces the issue and a proposed solution, but not tactfully. They appeal to authority without demonstrating awareness of context and considering whether the proposed solution would work for their team (e.g., their product probably does not have enough users for a 1% experiment).

PM 1 or 2

The PM brings up the issue during a 1:1 saying, "It takes a lot of time to write these long documents and take our work to three different reviews, even for small projects. Do you think you could change the process? One thing I've heard about is other companies skip the spec review for small projects."

> Observe: the PM surfaces the issue tactfully and suggests a reasonable solution.

Senior PM

The senior PM has taken it upon themself to adjust the process to what they think is appropriate. They've been skipping sections in the spec template, combining reviews, and even launching small changes without any review. They tell their manager about the changes after they ship and assume it's easier to ask for forgiveness than permission. Luckily, their judgment is strong enough that they rarely need to ask for forgiveness.

> Observe: the PM didn't let themselves get blocked or slowed down and showed good judgment on bending the rules.

Principal PM

The principal PM usually works on things that are outside of the standard product processes, so this isn't an issue for them.

PM Lead

When an IC PM complains, the PM lead coaches them on how to use the processes and templates more effectively.

> Observe: the PM lead focuses on guiding people through the system rather than changing the system.

Director

The director checks in with reports quarterly on how they feel about the PM team, and finds out about this issue proactively. Through talking to the team, they understand what parts of the process feel like they're causing the most issues.

The director deeply understands the intention and goals of each part of the process, and so they're able to come up with a few small adjustments that speed up the processes without compromising any of the quality checks. They check with the head of product to make sure the changes are acceptable, then roll out the changes to the entire PM team.

> Observe: the director proactively looked for issues and solved the problem in a systematic way.

Head of Product

The head of product learns about the issue from the yearly engagement survey. They meet with PMs individually to hear people's thoughts and suggestions. Then, they reach out to their network of other heads of product to hear their experience on what they do and what they've found works or doesn't work.

Through that investigation, they find a few infrastructural and organizational changes that would enable a faster and lighter process: making it easier to run small experiments, synchronizing the product and marketing design review schedules, and creating a tool to estimate the number of users impacted by a given change. They work with the cross-functional partners to get broad buy in and excitement about a revised process.

The resulting changes make product launches better for all of the functions.

> Observe: the head of product discovered the root causes and addressed them with organizational changes and investments in infrastructure.

Scenario 3: Annual Planning

It's annual planning time and it's the chance for PMs to influence the future direction of the product.

APM

The APM is assigned a project brief or 1-pager to write on a potential future feature. They write their assigned feature and two additional features they think would be cool.

> Observe: the PM proposes features somewhat capriciously, based on what seems cool or fun.

PM 1 or 2

The PM has a few ideas about what they think the company should work on that they've been thinking of over the past year. They work with their manager to write a compelling brief for each, especially focusing on the most likely areas their own team would tackle.

> Observe: the PM generates relevant proposals for their team.

Senior PM

A month before the planning cycle, the senior PM works with their teammates to create a vision, strategy, and proposed roadmap for the team. The vision outlines an ambitious future that makes a tangible difference in customer's lives and has the potential to make a big impact on company success metrics, such as retention. It's supported by preliminary research and the PM has shared the strategy with senior leadership.

As the annual planning cycle progresses, the PM advocates for their strategy and ensures their ideas stay top-of-mind with leadership. They take care to represent the needs of both their customers and their teammates. As they learn more about the way the company strategy is shaping up, they incorporate key ideas and phrases into their own strategy document.

> Observe: the PM created a product strategy and advocates for it. They approached planning from a higher level than from just a list of features.

Principal PM

The principal PM has been independently researching potential strategic directions throughout the year. After considering multiple options, they believe the most promising direction is to enter into a strategic partnership to enhance distribution. They've created a vision and strategy for this partnership that provides a robust view of what it would take to execute, across not just product, but also legal, finance, sales, partnerships, and marketing.

> Observe: the PM created a comprehensive, cross-functional strategy that goes beyond product work.

THE PM CAREER ► CAREERS

PM Lead

When the head of product asks, the PM lead creates a rough plan for what they think each of the teams that report into them will work on over the next year. They then work with each PM on their team to submit the appropriate documents to the planning process.

> Observe: the PM lead mostly delegates work to the PMs on their team and guides them through the processes.

Director

The director plays an active role in annual planning, working closely with the head of product to create a strategic proposal for the work and resourcing needed for the teams under them. They've read all of the project briefs and strategy documents submitted by PMs and have worked with finance to estimate headcount growth. The portfolio they propose balances investments in key company objectives and has an intentional allocation between low and high risk initiatives. They've worked hand-in-hand with the business teams to ensure the proposed portfolio will satisfy the business needs of teams like sales and marketing.

> Observe: the director takes a holistic view to ensure the annual plans are feasible and strategically aligned.

Head of Product

The head of product works with company leadership to revise the company objectives and resolve any important strategic trade offs. In parallel, they create an inspiring long-term vision that ties all of the proposed work together into a coherent theme.

As the directors share their proposals, the head of product reviews them to ensure the work is ambitious enough and strategically aligned. The head of product is also in constant communication with other executives and aligns with them in advance of the final plans. The head of product reviews the plans within the larger context of important company goals such as fundraising, hitting revenue targets, and demonstrating progress towards the company vision.

> Observe: the head of product sets the company strategy and takes a company-level view of the planning to ensure the company's success.

HOW LEVEL IMPACTS YOUR CAREER

About a year into my first PM role at Microsoft, the company started showing people's levels in the internal directory.

Before that point, my mentors had taught me to count "steps from billg" when I got an email from someone I didn't know. I would open the org chart and see how many managers were between them and Bill Gates, as a way to assess how much credibility they had. If a request or feedback came from someone high up in the org chart, I should take it more seriously than someone lower down.

I took this rough assumption and applied it to my teammates as well. Clearly, the people managers were better role models than the ICs. And for the ICs? I assumed the more years of experience, the better. Subconsciously, I imagined your level at your job was like your grade in school; a few people might be held back or skip a grade, but generally, people advance with the rest of their class.

When the levels came out, I found some big surprises! Some of the ICs were higher levels than some of the managers! And within PMs who had the same years of experience, there were some big differences as well.

For me, at least, this was a big relief; the levels seemed to correspond with my intuition of who the best PMs were. It gave me a lot more confidence to choose which people I wanted to use as my role models.

Levels are more than just a way to earn a fancy title. They affect all parts of your career, from what people expect of you, to which projects you get to work on, to how much money you make.

Here is how your level impacts your career, in the short and long run.

COMPENSATION

Level is the largest factor in compensation. Each level is mapped to a range of compensation (the salary range for the role), and that range is generally only known to managers. The ranges may have some overlap, so someone at a level above you could be earning less than you. These ranges aren't 100% binding, but generally, people will be hired with compensation within range (perhaps excluding signing bonuses) and will receive raises that keep them within range.

If your current compensation is at the lower end of the range, you can earn raises just by keeping up the good work. If your compensation is at the upper end of the range, you might not get a raise even after you've shown consistently strong performance; you'll need to advance to the next level to increase your compensation.

The process for your manager to give you a raise is much easier than the process to get promoted to the next level. If you have the opportunity to negotiate for a higher level, that will set you up for more raises in the future (assuming you can meet expectations at that higher level).

One consequence of this is that if you're negotiating a job offer, you might only be able to secure a small 'bump' in your salary. If you're looking for a more substantial increase, you might need to negotiate a higher level. This is sometimes feasible but may require that you prove you are ready for greater scope, autonomy, and impact. As you'll see in the next section, however, that's not necessarily a good thing.

EXPECTATIONS

Your level guides the expectations your manager has for you. When you get your performance review, your grade will be relative to the expectations for your level. Whether you'll be graded as "exceeds expectations" or, "misses expectations" will depend on where those expectations were set. If you reliably exceed expectations, you can get promoted.

Unfortunately, if you frequently miss expectations, you probably won't get demoted; you'd get fired instead. This is why it's not always good to fight for a higher level. Inappropriate promotions can set you up for failure.

PROJECT ALLOCATION

When hiring and assigning people to projects or teams, managers will have an idea of the level they need for that role. They'll ask questions like, "Could an APM do this role? No, it needs at least a senior PM because of the amount of cross-team collaboration."

At a large company, this happens officially; the recruiters have a level, or minimum level, written down for each role they're filling. At a smaller company, however, this happens unofficially; your boss doesn't think you're ready for the project.

THE PRESSURE TO ADVANCE—AND WHEN IT STOPS

Some companies have an official "up or out" policy: you need to advance to a certain level in a fixed amount of time (e.g., graduate the APM program in two years), or you'll be asked to leave the company. More commonly, there is unofficial pressure to advance. Two years as a PM 1 is probably fine, but if you're not getting a promotion after three years, your manager might prefer to use your headcount on someone who is growing faster.

Luckily, the pressure to advance doesn't last your whole career. Usually, once you reach the senior PM level, you can stay there without risk to your job. As a senior PM, you're a valuable, independent member of the team. Your manager might appreciate having someone on their team who is happy to keep building great products, rather than seeing the IC role as a stepping stone to a larger scope.

Staying at the senior PM level doesn't mean your skills won't be improving. If you choose not to go for future promotions, you'll still improve your craft, get more efficient, and ship better products. At some point, your salary will approach the top of the range, and you'll only get raises as the market rates increase, but you'll likely be making a decent salary by then. You'll have the choice to dedicate your extra time and energy to other interests.

PEOPLE MANAGEMENT

Each company generally has a minimum level for promoting people to manager roles. They need to know that you can do the job well yourself before they start letting you coach other people on it.

It's always good to bring up your career goals with your manager, but you'll look naive or arrogant if you push too much on becoming a people manager before your fundamental skills and impact match the minimum level. Many managers are too polite to directly say, "You're not good enough to be a people manager yet."

See "Partner with your boss on your career goals" on pg 381 for a future-looking way to indicate interest in people management earlier in your career.

LEVELING DURING THE HIRING PROCESS

Your initial level is determined during your interview and hiring process.

The role you interview for may have a set level, or the hiring manager may try to determine your level during the interviews. During the interview, they'll look at your earlier roles, how you approach problems, and how much you proactively take the lead vs. require prompting. The hiring manager and recruiter will also have a general idea about your level based on your prior experience and the compensation range you're looking for.

Here are some of the factors considered:

- **Years as a product manager.** There's no standard way to assess non-PM experience, but product-adjacent work like engineering, design, or product marketing might count as half to full credit. Other work, such as sales or operations, usually doesn't count.

- **Your previous level or title.** Especially if you've worked at a large company, the hiring manager and recruiting team might know how those levels translate. Many large companies have (secret) charts detailing how a title at one company translates to a title at their company.

- **The trajectory of your title increases.** Your title at a lesser-known company won't mean much to the hiring manager, but if you went from APM, to PM, to senior PM, to director at a company, that carries more weight.

- **Your previous scope.** The hiring manager will try to assess how your previous scope translates to the new company. How much strategy were you responsible for, and how much came from other people? How many engineers were on your teams? How many other PMs did you work with?

- **The compensation range you're seeking.**[6] If the hiring manager has a specific level they want to hire for, the recruiter might ask for your desired salary range to determine if your expectations align.

- **The way you approach and answer questions in the interview.** The chart on page 345 shows how the levels vary from "learning," to "knows how," to "can teach" across shipping products, product strategy, and organizational excellence. If you answer questions confidently and correctly, that demonstrates "knows how." If you also share your framework and how you explain the concepts to other PMs, that demonstrates "can teach."

To make sure you're leveled appropriately, aim at a specific level, and frame your experience, salary expectations, and interview performance with the expectations of that specific level. For example, if you're interviewing for a director level, emphasize strategy, cross-team frameworks, and coaching when talking about your past experience. Discuss your leveling expectations with the recruiter to make sure you're interviewing for a role that matches the level you want.

The titles and levels at smaller companies are not standardized, so ask questions and look at carefully to assess the offer. You can look at the reporting hierarchy and equity component to estimate the level. Don't assume that, as the first PM hire at a company, you'll automatically be head of product; ask directly about whether you're a member of the executive team, if you'll be responsible for building out the PM team, and if they might be hiring anyone above you.

---

6   Please note that many states in the US have laws prohibiting employers from asking about a candidate's current salary. They can, however, ask about your desired range.

> You can sometimes negotiate for a higher level after you receive an offer, but do so with caution. If you're working with the people who interviewed you and they see you have a higher level than they recommended, they might be extra critical of your work. It will be harder to make a good first impression.

On the other hand, women and other underrepresented groups are frequently underleveled in the hiring process, and this can result in a much lower lifetime earning potential. It can help to work with a trusted mentor (see "Build genuine relationships with people who can mentor you and might help you" on pg 398), especially one who knows the company or hiring manager.

KEY TAKEAWAYS

- **Your level is what determines your seniority:** Compensation, expectations, project allocations, and whether you're eligible for people management all tie back to your level. Titles map to levels, but the concept of levels exists even when your company doesn't have titles.

- **Doing your job really well isn't always enough to advance:** The middle and upper levels of the PM career ladder are not about doing a better job of running feature teams and shipping products. Instead, the middle levels require shifting focus to product strategy, and the upper levels require shifting focus again to organizational excellence. Each time you shift, you'll feel like a beginner again.

- **Scope, autonomy, and impact define each level:** A guide may describe common actions, capabilities, and skills of a PM at each level, but levels are not directly determined by those things. Checking all the boxes is neither required nor sufficient for promotion. Instead, focus on increasing your scope, autonomy, and impact to advance.

CHAPTER 33

CAREER GOALS

WHEN IT COMES to career advice, remember to be careful. I know this sounds like an odd thing to say in a book about advancing your career. It'd be like a doctor saying, "be careful about medicine!" But in actuality, it's a lot like that because as it turns out, doctors *will* say that quite often—and they're possibly the best people to say so.

You see, I can tell people to move to a tech hub, seek out greater responsibilities, or go to a rapidly growing company—but all of this, while not necessarily incorrect, brushes by bigger questions about your career goals.

What I like to tell people is that I can offer career advice, but I can't offer life advice. Life isn't a video game where you win by reaching the highest level by scoring the most points or making the most money. Life is about being happy, making an impact, and creating good in the world. Or—I don't know. What do *you* think it's about?

FIGURING OUT WHAT MATTERS

By reflecting on your own career goals, you can open up opportunities to move in more rewarding directions. You can make intentional choices about where to spend your time. Which of these seem most important to you?

Money

- Making enough money to be comfortable.

- Making enough money to help others (your family, charity, etc.).

- Making enough money to retire early.

- Making as much money as you possibly can.

Personal connection

- Working on a product or problem that you're passionate about.

- Working on something exciting.

- Innovating and inventing.

- Working on a product your friends and family use.

Learning

- Being part of a well-run team where you can absorb best practices.

- Constantly learning new skills.

- Taking on new challenges and stretching your limits.

Helping the world

- Working on a product that makes a huge impact for the people who use it.

- Working on important issues.

- Making a positive difference in the world through your work.

- Working on a product that millions or billions of people use.

External validation

- Earning a prestigious title.

- Being appreciated for your skills and accomplishments.

- Being recognized as an expert.

- Becoming a well-known public speaker.

- Working at a prestigious company.

Autonomy, scope, and flexibility

- Being in a role with a lot of autonomy.

- Keeping your options open as you grow.

- Starting your own company.

Team

- Being on a team with good hours and a great work/life balance.

- Being part of a really fun and close-knit team.

- Being on a team with smart people.

- Working at a company where you'll make good connections.

Career growth

- Being responsible for increasing scope.

- Climbing the corporate ladder as high as you possibly can.

- Moving into a new role (people manager, venture capital, product coach, board member, general manager, etc.).

- Working at a different kind of company (startup, big company, growth stage, etc.).

Your societal and cultural background might tell you that factors like learning are 'good' and factors like validation are 'bad'. Don't let cultural stereotypes get in the way of understanding yourself!

In truth, at least to some extent, almost everyone wants to make money and have people see them as being important and successful. That is a totally normal drive. So, if those things speak to you, listen. You won't be doing yourself any favors by pretending you're not motivated by something when you are.[1]

VISUALIZATION EXERCISES

Career goals are more like visions than commitments. They don't lock you in, rather, they should motivate decisions about your future. Much like a product vision, career goals should be tested and validated. Sometimes, you set out with one set of goals, but time, experience, and life circumstances shifts these goals. Be open to that change.

---

1   At the same time, it could be good to consider *why* you care about validation. Perhaps, if you relaxed a bit on your need for validation, you could find an even more fulfilling job.

To begin developing goals, or to update them, take some time to think deeply and do some visioning exercises. You'll want at least an hour to start, but you'll probably mull over your ideas for a week or more.

As you do these visioning exercises, remember that it's okay to come up with more than one idea. The goal is to gain some clarity into what appeals to you and what doesn't.

ZONE OF GENIUS

In his book *The Big Leap*, Gay Hendricks introduces the idea of working in your "zone of genius." Many people get stuck spending most of their time in the "zone of excellence" where they are really skilled and valuable, but feel unsatisfied. In contrast, when you work in your "zone of genius," you're excellent *and* it feels great. You get in the flow and lose track of time, and you feel alive and fulfilled. This is the place where you're using your unique talents.

To find your zone of genius, Hendricks presents four questions for you to reflect on:

- What do you love to do most? (You love it so much you can do it for long stretches of time without getting tired or bored.)

- What work do you do that doesn't actually feel like work?

- In your work, what produces the highest ratio of abundance and satisfaction to the amount of time spent?

- What is your unique ability? What unique ability of yours, fully realized and put to work, can provide enormous value to you and/or your company?

Write down ten instances in your life when you felt really fulfilled and proud of what you did. What exactly made each time so special? What aspects were fulfilling? Find a friend or mentor to share with and look for patterns. It's helpful to have an outside perspective since your zone of genius will be so intuitive to you that you might not even notice your unique talents.

IMAGINING YOUR IDEAL JOB

Here are some prompts to help you imagine your ideal job:

- What kind of challenges do you enjoy?

- Which of your strengths do you like to use?

- What are you passionate about?

- What would you do if you had enough money to never have to work again?

- How would you change your current job to make it better?

- What would you want to do if you couldn't work at your current company anymore?

- Who do you admire? Who are your role models? What about them do you want to emulate? What would you like to do differently than them?

- If you imagine three, five, or ten years in the future, what would you love to be doing?

You can also look at Chapter 36: Beyond PM (pg 410) for ideas of roles outside of product management.

PREFERENCES AND TRADEOFFS

Getting into the details, here are some questions to ask yourself. If you're not sure about some of them, you can try talking to people at different companies and in different roles to learn more about them.

WHAT STAGE OF COMPANY DO YOU PREFER?

An early-stage company that hasn't found their product-market fit will feel very different from a growth stage company that's scaling, or an established company.

How much risk can you tolerate? Are you better at finding great ideas, or figuring out the important details? Are you more excited by innovation, or scale? Do you like needing to do a little bit of every job, or would you prefer working around expert marketers, salespeople, and researchers?

ARE YOU DRAWN TO A PARTICULAR TYPE OF PRODUCT, OR DO YOU MOSTLY WANT TO GO WHERE YOU CAN MAKE THE LARGEST IMPACT?

Some PMs have a clear idea of what type of product they'd like to work on. They know that they want to work on a music app, or software that helps healthcare workers, or developer platforms. Others are open to working on any type of product, and find that they are passionate about a wide range of customer problems.

Are you more motivated by impacting a lot of people a tiny bit, or a few people a lot? Do you care more about alleviating pain, or bringing delight? Do you crave cutting edge innovations? Do you prefer the kind of impact that shows up in a user study, or in financial metrics?

WHAT SALARY RANGE WOULD YOU NEED TO FEEL COMFORTABLE?

Large companies tend to pay well. A senior PM with seven years of experience might make as much money as a doctor, but without the medical school debt. If money is a big motivation, you might not need to advance as far as you assume. You can research salary information online to get a better sense of what various levels offer on average.

If you're looking to improve your compensation, the type and size of the company you work for usually matters more than your level. Bigger companies tend to pay more than smaller ones. For-profit companies will typically pay more than non-profits. Modern tech companies often pay more than more traditional companies.

Even among similar companies, compensation philosophies can vary wildly. Some startups put a low cap on salary and compensate mainly in equity, while others don't. Also, pay attention to the cost of living and income tax as those can make a big difference in your take-home (net) pay.

HOW IMPORTANT IS KEEPING YOUR OPTIONS OPEN?

If you choose to gain broad exposure to a diverse set of teams, you'll need to spend more time ramping up and learning. It might take you longer to start delivering a lot of value, but you'll probably find that you can handle a variety of circumstances later on.

"LIVE TO WORK" OR "WORK TO LIVE?"

Do you want your job to be your passion, or do you need time to support your passion outside of work?

Some teams expect you to work long hours and be available on the weekends. On other teams, everyone packs up at the end of the day, and doesn't think about work until the next morning. If there's a mismatch between you and the team culture, you're likely to become frustrated.

It's also worth it to consider what other aspects of team culture are important to you. On some teams, the people become close friends and invite each other over for barbeques on the weekends. Other teams are cordial but keep work and personal life separate. Some teams are chatty during the day, while others keep things strictly professional and stay heads-down working.

WHAT IS YOUR RISK TOLERANCE NOW, AND IN THE FUTURE?

Life events such as taking time off work to travel, starting a family, or supporting a spouse while they go back to school can be an important factor in the level of risk you wish to tolerate.

Take a look at the credentials you've built up, your savings, and your risk tolerance. You might realize that right now is the ideal time for you to take a risk. Or, you might decide to go with something more secure now so you can take risks (or take it easy) in the future.

CREATING A PERSONAL DEVELOPMENT PLAN

It's very easy to let personal development take a back seat when you're busy, and, to a certain extent, it should. The most important aim of your career will usually be shipping successful products, not writing blog posts. That said, you want to make sure you're not so heads-down that you forget to invest in yourself.

Draft a rough outline of some key milestones along your path to achieving your career goals. Then, pick a few milestones for the next 6-12 months and turn them into concrete plans.

What can you do to make progress towards those milestones? Consider action items such as:

- Analyzing a competitor's product and presenting your findings to your team.

- Creating a long-term vision for your product area.

- Reaching out to three people in the industry you're interested in for coffee chats.

- Writing a blog post about how your team runs experiments.

Write your plans down (with dates) and commit to them. Set yourself a reminder to revisit those milestones when the deadlines come.

KEY TAKEAWAYS

- **Take the time to reflect on your career goals:** You don't need to commit to anything, but the world of potential goals might be much broader than you originally imagined. Once you understand your goals, you can make better choices to achieve them.

- **Invest in yourself:** Create a personal development plan and commit to a few milestones. Your action items can be directly related to your current job, or they can be about exploring new paths. Keep in mind, however, that launching successful products is the most important part of a PM career.

CHAPTER 34

SKILLS FOR CAREER GROWTH

ANDREW WAS FRUSTRATED by the feedback from his review. "He needs to invest more in sharing status updates and findings across the company," his manager stated. That kind of self-promotion felt artificial and political. Why should he waste time trying to impress other people? Why didn't his boss appreciate all of his hard work?

I wish I could tell you that he doesn't need to do this—and that all *you* need to do to get promoted is to work hard and ship great products. Listen to your users. Process data. Inspire your developers. Collaborate with marketing and sales. Develop your scope, autonomy, and impact.

No doubt, those are critical pieces—hopefully enough. But, just like how the best candidates don't always get the offer, the best employees aren't always the ones who get promoted. There are false positives and false negatives in both groups.

Andrew's manager had given him good advice. Product managers can only influence as far as their credibility reaches. When it's done with tact, people across the company appreciate any extra signal about which people are good at their jobs. When he started hosting learning lunches and sending his status updates more broadly, he was surprised to see how coworkers started giving him the benefit of the doubt and being more willing to help his team.

WORKING WITH YOUR MANAGER

Your manager has a major influence on your career. It's almost impossible to get a promotion or a raise without having your manager on your side. A good manager can act as your sponsor, finding you stretch opportunities that expand your influence and improve your skills.

MANAGERS ARE ONLY HUMAN

Your manager is a human being, just like you. I know, sometimes they might seem almost god-like, and sometimes, well, the opposite. But they are only human, and it's worth remembering that.

They have the same types of biases, fallacies, emotions, and flaws as everyone else. Just because they have more experience and authority than you doesn't mean they'll always do the right thing. Even the best managers are susceptible.

What could these flaws look like?

- They assume you don't want a challenging new assignment without asking you.

- They don't tell you where you're falling behind because they don't want to have an uncomfortable conversation.

- They don't remember or didn't notice some of your accomplishments.

- They pile undesirable work on the person who doesn't complain about it.

- They resent you for complaining about undesirable work.

- They brush you off when they're stressed.

- They get defensive when you share your ideas for improving their work.

Once you realize that managers are only human, you can find the best ways to partner with them to achieve your career goals. You can "manage up" with the collaboration and customer empathy skills you already have.

> Caveat: While all managers have some problems, you shouldn't stick it out with a terrible manager. See "Bad situations" on pg 399 for more about bad situations.

EMPATHIZE WITH YOUR MANAGER'S MINDSET

If you treat your career like a product, then you can think of your manager as one of your customers. The better you can understand your manager, the easier it will be to form a strong relationship and get the support and sponsorship you want.

If you haven't already, go back and read Part G: People Management Skills (pg 282) to learn what the people management job is like. You'll see some of the challenges that managers face, and you might be surprised by some of the expectations of the role.

You'll also want to learn about your specific manager.

- What are their goals?
- What are their pet peeves?
- What keeps them up at night?
- What is their leadership philosophy?

- What enneagram type are they?
- What's their favorite management book?
- What's their highest priority project?
- What side projects are they passionate about?

You can treat each interaction with them as an opportunity for customer research. Why did they push so hard for that one change? What made them add that new process? What assumptions are behind the strategy they presented? Which PMs do they praise, and for what?

When you really understand and empathize with your manager, your relationship with them will improve. You'll get better at interpreting their questions and suggestions. They'll feel like you understand them. It will be easier to deliver what they consider great work, and all of this will increase the chance that they see you as someone who's exceeding expectations.

A DAY IN THE LIFE OF A PEOPLE MANAGER

A manager's job might be very different from what you imagine. Here's an example of what a typical day might look like:

I start the day with a recruiting meeting. I need to hire three more PMs to support our growing team, but it's been taking a long time to find the right people. We discuss how the pipeline is looking and brainstorm a few avenues for sourcing more candidates; maybe we can host a meetup. I've got three coffee chats scheduled for the week, and we have four candidates coming onsite (I'll interview all of them, along with some other interviews for marketing leads and data science leads). The recruiter points out that one of the PMs has been very slow with her interview feedback, which is causing delays. I'll need to talk to her.

Next, I have a 1:1 with one of my direct reports. He's added a topic about his frustration with his designer, which is lucky because the designer's manager let me know the frustration goes both ways. I want to coach him to improve the collaboration, while also helping him detect and solve problems like this in the future. We talk through a few scenarios and I prompt him to imagine the designer's perspective. He realizes how he contributed to the situation and comes up with some ideas for fixing it. I'll check back with him in a few days to see how it goes.

Our next topic is on the results of his experiment: it went really well and he's planning to roll it out after a few small fixes. He needs my approval before it can launch, and I want to reinforce his good work. I mentally check his plan against the top risks and see that he's appropriately mitigated them. I approve his plan and I point out a few of his earlier choices that helped it be a success.

For our final topic, I bring up a new opportunity for him. We need someone to run a cross-functional process and I think he'd grow a lot from it. I'm a little nervous about bringing it up because I'll have to find someone else if he doesn't want to do it. He accepts, yay!

I run to my manager's team meeting. My manager and all of her direct reports get together every other week. This is when we sync and learn about new strategic initiatives, company risks, or other major topics that will affect the product teams. The managers also help each other out with issues that any of us are having.

One team is at risk of missing an important launch date, and we talk about various strategies to help: moving more people onto the team, helping team members hand off extra responsibilities, or getting more outside mentorship. I suggest that one of my teams might be able to take on some extra work, and make a note to follow up with the PM to see if it's possible. The PM on my team would have to move a deadline to take on the extra work, but it might be worth it in the larger picture.

The next topic is about a new competitor. We discuss the strengths and weaknesses, and whether there's anything we can learn from them or if we should change any plans. We think it would be great to have one of the PMs look into it. After a quick discussion, we decide that a PM on one of the other manager's teams would be a good match because they've needed a chance to demonstrate their strategic skills.

After that meeting, I finally have 30 minutes free! I catch up on my inbox and answer about a dozen quick questions: sharing links to old research, giving quick feedback on some announcement text, reviewing the list of stakeholders for another report, and congratulating a team on the results of their launch. I haven't gotten through all my messages, but I scan the list quickly to make sure I've replied to everyone who would be blocked.

For lunch today, I'm meeting with the product marketing lead. We have a monthly lunch together just to share what's on our mind and keep the relationship strong. She's worried we don't have enough launches planned for September. There are a few teams I know that might be able to launch then, so we talk through the tradeoffs. I'll bring those ideas to the teams later.

After lunch is office hours, where teams will present their work. Two teams are bringing in designs for a design review. I drill into the goals of the project to make sure the team is going after the most impactful problems. As the teams present their prototype, the design manager, eng manager, and I give feedback using the Do, Try, Consider framework.[1] We want to ensure a high product quality without dictating the solution or asking for too much iteration. The first team's work is looking great, and all of our feedback is suggestions for them to "consider." The second team has put a lot of work into their designs, but isn't realistic about how much time users were willing to spend on the flow. We ask them to "try" to validate the length of the flow or come up with something shorter.

My next meeting is the Quarterly Business Review. I'm mostly an observer at this meeting, learning context that will help my teams make better decisions. I learn about how all of our marketing and sales channels are doing, and what the upcoming plans are. We're falling behind in one segment, and that helps me understand some of the questions that salespeople were asking in a stakeholder meeting yesterday. I take notes on the key information to pass along to my team.

Finally, my meetings for the day are finished. I have a few specs to review, and then I'll spend the rest of the time preparing for a vision presentation I'm giving to the business teams next week.

Unfortunately, an hour later, one of my reports surprises me with a big problem. They just found a major bug in the feature that was supposed to launch in two days—it looks like they'll have to move the launch! I'm thankful they brought the issue to me so quickly and calmly. We talk through the options (just moving the launch date, putting a janky workaround in, shortcutting some roll-out processes to get the bug fix out sooner) and figure out a communication plan. I'll start giving other managers a heads-up, and the PM will send out an official message to the stakeholders.

After that, I just have a little time to finish up the vision presentation. Last week, I got approval for increased headcount to support an ambitious roadmap, but most people at the company don't know our new vision yet. This presentation is meant to inspire people across the company and help them see how we'll drive increased revenue and expand our market next year. I've been working on it with my design counterpart, and she's been, thankfully, improving the presentation while I was working on that surprise bug. It looks like we're almost set.

Time to go home!

PARTNER WITH YOUR BOSS ON YOUR CAREER GOALS

Good managers want to support your career ambitions, but you need to be proactive about sharing your goals and looking for your own opportunities. Especially at the more senior levels, you'll need to take the lead on finding possible stretch projects and deciding what to take on. Don't assume that your manager knows your career ambitions or that they will find you the type of assignments you need to keep advancing. Speak up!

---

1   Read more about the Do Try Consider framework on page 299

> ### A PROBLEM WITH MISTAKEN ASSUMPTIONS
>
> One PM noticed he wasn't being invited to give client presentations. His manager had assumed that he wouldn't be interested in giving presentations because of his tics associated with Tourette Syndrome. The PM spoke to his manager and shared his public speaking goals. He explained that the tics subside when he's in "presenter mode," and he really enjoys public speaking. By talking to his manager, he was able to clear up the mistaken assumption and get the growth opportunities he wanted.

Your manager might feel uncomfortable in career conversations, so you don't want to make the conversation combative. If you appear insulting or overly critical of them for not promoting you, they might hold it against you.

To avoid this, frame the conversation as future-looking:

> I'd love to become a director eventually. What areas should I focus on so I'll be ready when the opportunity comes up?

If you're early in your career, you can propose that the two of you brainstorm ways that you can build the skills. If you're more advanced, you'll want to show your seniority by proposing your own suggestions for how you can build and demonstrate the required skills. Treat the conversation as a partnership.

If your manager claims you're missing a skill that you believe you have, don't argue. Instead, discuss how you can demonstrate those skills. Get curious, be coachable, and stay open to feedback.

> Remember: Your manager chooses where to invest their time and energy; if they think you'll listen to them and learn from them, they're more likely to think you're worth the investment.

That's why this approach works well. It takes the pressure off your manager and doesn't force them to commit. At the same time, it makes your intentions clear and demonstrates your willingness to learn. When a great stretch opportunity comes up, they'll know you're interested in it.

SPONSORSHIP

A sponsor is different from a mentor. Mentors help you develop your skills and give you advice, while sponsors advocate for you and help you advance. A sponsor might recommend you for a promotion, hire you into a larger role, or connect you to people in their network. They are people who believe in you and give you the opportunities you need to advance.

The best people to be your sponsor are usually your manager or someone higher in your reporting chain. They're close enough to know your skills, and high enough to have access to opportunities. Not every manager is a great sponsor, however; some don't have the connections, and others don't do a lot of recommending. You'll need to look for a good sponsor, work at building the relationship, and make sure they know what you're looking for.

> ### ASKING FOR WHAT YOU WANT
>
> To get a sponsor, you may have to ask for it directly.

Bangaly Kaba used this approach successfully. When his manager asked him what he cared about in his career as part of a professional development conversation, he answered, "It really matters to me that I'm on a clear path towards this level and this set of scope. I believe that I need sponsorship to get there. I want to know if you're willing to be the sponsor for me or you can help me figure out how I can achieve that."[2]

Being specific about his goals worked.

Much like for mentors, sometimes, the relationship evolves naturally—and other times, it's useful to explicitly ask for this.

BUDDY WITH YOUR BOSS ON THEIR WORK

One of the best ways to learn PM skills is to watch them in action. Strategic skills, in particular, are difficult to learn if you don't have good examples. Luckily, many people enjoy having a work buddy, whether it's having a thought partner to bounce ideas off of or just a scribe to write down notes and put slides together. In either case, you'll get a front-row seat to how it's done.

Talk to your boss about what work they have coming up, and ask if they'd like any help with it. Maybe you can help put together a kickoff presentation or slides for a board meeting. Frame it as help for them, and pay attention to make sure that your "help" isn't creating more work or frustration for them—e.g., dragging them into long arguments that they don't want to have.

To help these opportunities come to you, you can begin paying attention to what your boss is working on and thinking about how you would handle it. You'll get to see how it plays out for them, and if they bring it up, you'll have useful thoughts to share.

MAKE SURE YOUR MANAGER KNOWS HOW YOUR WORK IS GOING

On page 306, we talked about the challenge of managing PMs from the manager's point of view.

If you're not communicating proactively with your manager, you'll end up in one of two bad situations:

1. Your manager starts micromanaging you.

2. Your manager is unaware of what you're doing, and you don't get credit for your good work.

You might be tempted to blame your manager if this happens, but the blame—and the fix—lies with you. You need to realize that your manager is not a mind-reader, and therefore, you must proactively share your work with them. Without this, your manager will either be unable to offer you autonomy or will not be able to fulfill their own responsibility to oversee your work.

Much of a PM's work happens privately or behind the scenes, so the only way your manager will be aware of the challenges you've faced is if you tell them. If you let your manager know about potential problems early, they won't feel the need to hunt for your team's problems themselves. If you keep them up-to-date, they'll represent your work to the rest of the company and share the context your team requires.

When you speak with your manager about your work, keep these three goals in mind:

1. Promote your skills and accomplishments.

2. Equip your manager with the information they need to do their job.

---

2   See the full interview in Chapter 40: Bangaly Kaba (pg 430)

3. Solicit feedback and suggestions to improve your work.

All of these goals apply to every communication, whether the news is good, bad, or neutral. When you combine these goals together, you're able to self-promote without seeming arrogant and rubbing people the wrong way.

An easy approach to combine all three goals is to use this three-part template:

Here's what's happening: <The current challenge>.
This gives them the context they need. You can talk about a designer missing deadlines, a surprising A/B test result, great ideas that were brought up in a brainstorming session, a launch-blocking bug you discovered, a new request from the sales team, or any other interesting pieces of work. Instead of just a basic status report, combine the status with the details of a recent discovery, challenge, or surprise.

Here's how I <handled it/am handling it/am thinking of handling it>.
This promotes your skills and accomplishments. Sometimes, you'll be really proud of the clever way you handled a challenge. Other times, you'll feel lost, but you can take ownership of the problem and share where you're stuck. Sharing your plan lets your manager work with you as a partner and helps them see your skills. Otherwise, they might suggest solutions you've already thought of and get a false impression that you didn't know what to do. If you ask for help without having any plan of your own, you could come across as very junior or low-potential.

Do you have any thoughts?
This invites them to share their suggestions. This invitation softens the self-promotion factor in the second part by putting it in the context of growth and learning. It makes it easy for your manager to give you feedback they might have otherwise held back; if you don't seem open to feedback, they might feel uncomfortable pushing it on you. The phrasing also gives them the option of saying, "That sounds great!"

AMBITION AND SELF-ADVOCACY

Managers can get annoyed when PMs are too focused on their personal ambitions. It can seem like you're trying to succeed at the expense of others, rather than *with* your team. For a high-performing team, individuals need to put the team first. If you're too focused on the next promotion, you might do a bad job on your current work.

This leads you to a catch-22:

- If you ignore your ambition and try to "trust the system," you might miss out on opportunities you need to grow and advance.

- If you push too hard, your manager might see you as entitled, impatient, or self-serving.

This is a little bit of a song and dance. Of course, you care the most about yourself and would leave the job if it wasn't good for you. But, being blatantly obvious about that can be interpreted as a threat and could damage your relationship with your manager, as well as with your team.

The work-around
Whenever possible, try to frame your requests in terms of benefits to your team or company. Ask about ways to improve your skills rather than bringing up promotions. Explain what you could deliver for customers with a bigger team. Offer to lighten your manager's load by taking on some of their reports.

In *Lean In*, Sheryl Sandberg shared how she framed her aggressive salary negotiation as a team benefit: Facebook would benefit from her strong negotiation skills once she was negotiating for them. By discussing what she could do for the company, she was able to negotiate for the salary she wanted without creating any animosity.

The exception

There are exceptions to every rule, however, and it will sometimes make sense to advocate for yourself directly, especially in the context of explicit career conversations.

In those instances, it's helpful to start by getting your manager into the mindset of being on your side and supporting your growth before you make your request. Keep it forward-looking to avoid putting them on the defensive.

Imagine your company is hosting a big conference and you'd like to be on the planning committee. You found out that managers were asked to recommend people on their team, and you weren't recommended.

> **Don't**: "I can't believe you didn't recommend me for the conference planning committee!"
>
> **Do**: "I'd love your advice. Could we have a career growth check-in? Great! I noticed there's a conference planning committee and I think it would be a great growth opportunity for me. Could we have a chat about it and see if you could recommend me for it?"

Use your judgment and pay attention to how your manager reacts. Some managers will require an even subtler approach.

LEARNING FROM FEEDBACK

Feedback is critical for career growth because it's personalized to you and your situation. Every manager, team, and promotion committee puts slightly different weights on what they value, so you'll need feedback to find the perceived gaps.

NOTICE, ASSESS, IMPROVE

Feedback like, "You need to be more decisive," or, "be more customer-focused," can feel really difficult to act on. Breaking it into three steps can make it actionable:

1. **Notice** the relevant opportunities when you should be applying the skill. Gather examples. Ask coworkers to point them out to you. Ask other people how they recognize the moment.

2. **Assess** what went wrong, and why. Was the root cause lack of confidence? Were you prioritizing something else? Is there a pattern?

3. **Improve** on the issue. Come up with a plan to address the root cause.

When you go through these steps, you'll often discover that the real problem is very different from what the initial feedback implied.

SOLICITING FEEDBACK

Getting direct feedback from your peers, manager, and manager's peers is one of the best ways to grow quickly. Unfortunately, many people shy away from giving you the feedback you really need to hear.

To reliably get useful feedback about your work, you need to make it comfortable for people to speak with you honestly. Here are some ways to do that:

- **Proactively ask for feedback**. An anonymous 360° report (including feedback from peers, reports, manager, and cross-functional partners) can be a great way to get a holistic, honest view of how you're doing. You can create one for yourself with a product such as Google Forms.

- **Be transparent about the areas you're working on**. If people know that you're aware you need to work on something, it's easier for them to point it out. For example, "I'm working on clearer communication, so if I say anything that's unclear, can you please let me know so that I can explain it differently?"

- **Frame the request as "What would the next level look like?"** It's common to ask for what you could be doing better and hear, "Nothing, just keep doing what you're doing." When you ask, "If I were one level higher, what would you expect me to do differently?" it can unlock new types of feedback that people might not have thought of.

- **Don't appear to resist the feedback**. Put on a happy (or neutral) face and thank people for the feedback. Be careful your tone doesn't sound like, "Prove it!" if you ask for examples. If your automatic response is to go on the defensive, people will be reluctant to give you feedback in the future and might even assume you don't have a growth mindset. Approach the feedback with as much genuine curiosity as you can.

- **Look for the gem**. Even when you disagree with the feedback, there's often something useful to learn. What do they know or not know that's giving them a different point of view? If their perception was inaccurate, how can you ensure they perceive things accurately in the future so that they'll trust you?

- **Be aware of cultural differences in feedback**. When an American says, "You sometimes talk over people, and you might want to try soliciting opinions more," they often mean, "Stop being such a jerk and listen more!" Americans tend to tone down their negative feedback, but people from other cultures may be more direct. When you work across cultures, take time to learn the other person's feedback style. Remember that harsh feedback might not actually be intended as negative on the part of the speaker, while gentle feedback might be much worse than it seems.

- **Follow up**. If the feedback was actionable, communicate back once you've fixed the problem. This lets the person know you've taken the feedback seriously and addressed the issue so they won't hold on to a negative impression of you.

Remember that feedback can be as uncomfortable to give as it is to receive. Your peers may worry that they've tarnished the relationship by being "mean," especially if they're more junior than you. Show them that you appreciate and value their feedback.

BUILDING RELATIONSHIPS WITH YOUR MANAGER'S PEERS

Don't underestimate the influence your manager's peers can have on your career. They can provide new perspectives on your work, dedicate resources for your initiatives, and support your promotion. These relationships are particularly important during reorganizations or if your manager leaves the company.

So, how can you build these relationships? Aaron Filner, Director of Product Management at Google, shared some advice:

> People sometimes undervalue sending newsletters, status updates, and launch updates far and wide. However, they are read more than people realize. It's important to craft them in a way that people who are far from your project can understand what was done and why it was interesting.
>
> In terms of projects, any time there's interaction or partnership between teams, it's an opportunity to create an impression on that adjacent leader. It gives you an excuse to proactively reach out to them. If you proactively solicit input, people are usually willing to engage.

Once you have established these relationships, you can also ask for advice. People are often happy to give advice, and your manager's peers will be able to give you an outsider's perspective.

CHOOSING THE RIGHT PLACE AT THE RIGHT TIME

If you speak with PMs who have had successful careers, you'll repeatedly hear how much being in the right place at the right time has helped them. While a lot of that comes down to luck, you can be intentional about how you choose your companies and teams.

TOP-REPUTATION COMPANIES

Think about the "cool" tech companies. We're not talking about which ones you think of as having the best technology or culture. We're talking about the *public perception* of which companies are cool, selective, or impressive; the ones that, for example, the top students from the top universities are clamoring to go to.

Spending time at one of the "top reputation" companies can give you a big boost in the long run. Is this superficial, perhaps even unfair? Yes. But nonetheless, collecting such a name on your resume can help you in many ways:

1. **Learning:** You can learn many best practices from an established company. You won't need to reinvent the wheel or possibly pick up bad habits. You can get great mentorship and build a strong network.

2. **Credibility:** That brand name will open doors for you in the future. Once you've worked at a top tech company, you can usually get a phone interview, at least, at many other tech companies. Note that this piece has more to do with *prestige* than *size*. A company can be large but not confer a great deal of prestige. Likewise, small to medium-sized companies can sometimes offer the same credibility that you'd see at one of the "cool" top companies.

3. **Pay:** The big brand-name companies tend to pay better, sometimes even up to double the industry average. This makes a huge difference while you're paying off student loans and can help you build up your savings so you can take greater risks later in your career.

This doesn't mean that you *must* work for a big brand-name company, or that it's always the right decision for your career goals or for your life overall. But we encourage you to consider joining a brand-name company early in your career, even if your long-term goal is more startup-focused.

FAST-GROWING COMPANIES

Fast-growing companies are usually the best places to grow your career.

While it would be amazing to join a small startup right before it takes off, you don't need to be that clair-voyant. Fast-growing companies are, by definition, hiring many people, and so they're easy to spot. You can follow tech news and ask around to learn about the hot companies. If you know recruiters or managers, you can ask which companies they're losing candidates to.

Fast-growing companies are great for your career because as the company grows, your role gets bigger and new opportunities open up. Your knowledge of the product and the trust you've built up will let you take on roles you wouldn't otherwise be qualified for. Things move faster, so the longer you stay, the more new experiences you get, and the more you learn.

However, be aware that these companies will also likely go through growing pains, where their rapid growth causes a certain level of dysfunction. It could also evolve into a company you "don't recognize"—one that's very different from the one you were so excited to join.

STARTUPS

Choosing a startup is much riskier than opting for a large or medium-sized company.

For example, one person joined a hot startup that went bankrupt because it cost more to deliver the service than customers were willing to pay. Another found out his equity was worth $0 after the company was sold for $100M because of liquidation preferences. Another saw her startup dissolve after an ethical scandal.

There's no magic formula for choosing a great startup, but here are some things to consider:

- **The founders:** Have they been successful in the past? Do you trust and respect them? Do you believe they're ethical? Do you think they're smart? Do you believe in them? Do you have any mutual contacts who can tell you more about them and raise any red flags?

- **The team:** How high-quality are the people on the team? Do you believe that these are the people who can win a competitive market? Will you be happy to add these people to your network? Will you enjoy working with them?

- **The mission and product:** Do you believe in the mission? Do you think this product can win in the marketplace? Does the product solve a real problem that a large enough set of people have? Do you want to devote years of your life to becoming an expert in this space? Would the company pivot if the evidence suggests they should?

- **The competition:** Who are the competitors? What makes this company better situated to succeed than the competition? Is the market over-saturated?

- **The business model:** What will it take for the company to become profitable? Can the company acquire customers and provide the service at a cost that customers are willing to pay? Do you believe the business model will work?

- **The investors:** Have reputable investors chosen to invest in the company? Do experts in the space believe in the future of the company?

It can be useful to see a startup much like an investor would. After all, you're investing your time, emotions and career growth in it. If you wouldn't believe in it as an investor, perhaps it's not a good fit as a career either.

First PM at a startup

The first PM or head of product at a startup frequently doesn't work out. Many PMs quit in a huff when they realize the role is nothing like what they had expected. Product-minded founders rarely give up any control to the new PM. Non-product founders rarely accept the cultural changes that are necessary to do product well. If you want things to go well, you need to be realistic about the challenges you'll face and the scope of your autonomy. The role can be immensely rewarding over time, but you don't get to shape everything to your liking on day one.

Gemmy Tsai, head of product at Solv and former head of product at Hired, recommends having an explicit conversation with the startup's founders about what they want in the role and how it might evolve to see if it matches what you're looking for. Then, hold back on the impulse to immediately create a new strategy:

> The best way to build trust is to prove you can execute. It's about building that foundation of trust and then layering on the big strategic stuff because that's always the last thing they want to give up.

In my own experience as the first PM at Asana, I credit my success to the strong working relationship I formed with the product cofounder, Justin Rosenstein. Our strengths and weaknesses complemented each other. Even so, I had some bumpy experiences as I learned not to shut down his ideas and, instead, build on top of them. Unlike at a larger company where I could become the true expert in my area, at Asana, I'd never surpass JR's depth of vision. So, instead of trying to take over the product strategy, I looked for ways to add value to it. That approach helped me build trust and set me up to grow with the company.

CHOOSING THE RIGHT TEAM

Even within a company, the team you're on matters tremendously:

- **Do:** Learn which teams have good managers.

- **Do:** Look for which teams get their PMs promoted quickly.

- **Do:** Work on important company initiatives.

- **Do:** Work on teams with fast cycles early in your career.

- **Do:** Consider teams with measurable results, like growth and monetization.

- **Do:** Take on large enough scoped roles when going for higher-level promotions.

- **Don't:** Join a project that's likely to be canceled.

- **Don't:** Join a team with bad politics.

- **Don't:** Underestimate the potential of internal-facing teams. There's often room to make major improvements with high visibility.

Choosing a team with an appropriate scope is especially important to advance at higher levels. Aarti Bharathan, Senior Director at PayPal, was promoted from GPM to Director after taking on a project that grew to a huge scope:

> My skip-level manager told me he had a problem around what to do with all the marketplaces. I said I'd go figure it out. I started from scratch and ended up creating a whole new product line.

After this, it was obvious to everyone that Bharathan deserved the promotion.

MOVING ON AT THE RIGHT TIME

Career growth within a role tends to follow an S curve. You ramp up, have a period of accelerating growth where you're learning a lot and making a big impact, and eventually hit diminishing returns.

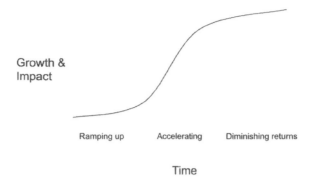

It usually makes sense to stay when you have a great relationship with your manager, you're growing quickly, you're learning a lot, you believe in your product, and your company is doing well. It's especially bad to leave before you ship something meaningful and see the results.

On the other hand, if you've been in the same role for many years, you might be able to grow more quickly and make more money elsewhere. There are a few factors at play:

- The longer you stay at the company, your institutional knowledge grows but the value you bring from outside experiences diminishes.

- In fast-growing companies, your role is probably growing and changing all the time.

- As the company's valuation increases, the value of the equity you vest each month can grow immensely.[3]

- Managers often don't pay close attention to keeping your compensation at market rate.

If you want to learn whether you could be making more money, you can interview at other companies and see if your current company would make a counteroffer. Before you do this, however, assess your company's counter-offering culture. Some companies take an ardent stance *against* counter-offering, figuring that there's no use begging you to stay if you want to leave.

When you switch roles or companies at the point where you hit diminishing returns, you create overlapping S curves and grow much faster.

---

3   While it might make sense emotionally to assume your equity is worth zero at a startup, if you do that while comparing offers, it will never make financial sense to join a startup.

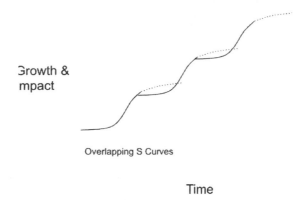

Overlapping S Curves

Time

If you're not sure whether you're hitting diminishing returns, speak with some trusted mentors. Sometimes, the plateau is real, and other times, it represents a valuable "growth edge" where you're on the cusp of major growth.

Whenever you choose to move on, it's important to always leave on a good note. The tech industry is a small world and you may end up working with your former coworkers again at one point; don't burn those bridges.

NEGOTIATION

When you receive an offer, know that it's not set in stone; companies expect you to negotiate. This can be intimidating since the company negotiates offers every day, but you rarely do. Luckily, there are a lot of resources and information available, scripts to follow, and even negotiation specialists you can work with.

It's a good idea to become familiar with these in advance so you'll know how to handle traps like exploding offers. You might also want to check out:

- Candor's comprehensive guide to salary negotiations.[4] Candor is a company that helps with salary negotiations.

- Haseeb Qureshi's *My Ten Rules for Negotiating a Job Offer* (pg 502).

Negotiating is a useful skill to develop, even beyond this specific offer. Here are a few tips to get you started:

- The easiest way to negotiate is to have competing offers. If at all possible, line up your interviews so the offers all arrive around the same time.

- Understand the level you're being offered and research the compensation range for that level. Try to negotiate your level if it is too low, using specific facts from their levelling descriptions.

- Don't accept the offer the moment you receive it; ask for time to make your decision. Time is on your side.

- Stay polite and enthusiastic; "I'd really like to make this work out! I'm sure we can find something that works for both of us." You won't sabotage your offer as long as you stay reasonably nice.

---

4   Review Candor's guide at https://candor.co/guides/salary-negotiation

- Signing bonuses are usually the easiest part of the compensation package to negotiate. As we explained earlier, salary is typically tied in with your level. A significant increase can require going up a level, and you might not be ready for that (or be perceived that way). Signing bonuses, on the other hand, are usually not as strictly tied to your level.

Most of all—just do it. Some people are so hung up on finding the "right" way to negotiate ("Do I use email or the phone?" "Should I act excited about the offer or concerned?" etc.) that they just avoid it entirely. It's much more important that you try to negotiate than that you follow every piece of negotiating advice.

If you're still reluctant to negotiate, think about it this way: A single "uncomfortable" conversation will earn you at least a few hundred, but, often, thousands of dollars. It's a no-brainer.

So, pick up the phone, or write an email, or have someone *else* write an email and you just hit send. But, do it.

NAMING A NUMBER

Pop Quiz: In a negotiation, should you name the first number?

Most people—and conventional wisdom—say no. Let the other person name the first number! You don't want to show your cards too early! See what the other side is thinking!

Some research, however, indicates something different. As Adam Grant, Wharton negotiations professor and author of *Give and Take*, says in his WorkLife podcast:[5]

> First offers serve as anchors. They set the hook for the negotiation, and it's hard to escape the pull. One comprehensive analysis of negotiation experiments showed that every dollar higher in the first offer translates into about 50 cents more in the final agreement.

People often do better in negotiations if they offer the first number. If you're surprised, consider this hypothetical scenario.

> **SO YOU'RE BUYING A USED CAR...**
>
> Imagine you're buying a used car. The seller starts at $20,000, but you were thinking $15,000 to $17,000. What now?
>
> Most likely, you'll say no—and hope that, if you're lucky, you'll be able to pull it down closer to $17,000. What started out as the *high* end of your range is now your optimistic goal. Whoops!
>
> Had you had started with $15,000, they would be working up from *your* number.

But does this apply to *you* negotiating salary? That's where it gets tricky.

Many candidates don't know their own worth. If you name the first number, you *can* anchor the company to a much higher number—or you could low-ball yourself, *or* you could throw out an unrealistic ask.

This is why many people advise to "play it safe" and avoid naming the first number. Then, you just take the company's number and add extra to it.[6]

---

5   Read the full transcript (or listen) at https://www.ted.com/talks/worklife_with_adam_grant_the_science_of_the_deal/transcript

6   Of course, this means that the company has anchored you to a lower number.

There is no clear-cut answer to this dilemma. Your best bet is probably to do enough research that you're well-informed about typical salaries, so you can avoid undershooting. But if you can't do that, then you might wait until the company throws out a number.[7]

Or, there's another option: "The easy solution is to anchor with a range," Adam Grant suggests. A range allows you wiggle room to push for the higher end or move lower if it was an unrealistic ask.

Protecting yourself via research

How do you avoid low-balling yourself or overshooting? Get as much information as you can about what this company (or companies like it) typically pays. Beware of relying too much on websites like Glassdoor for salary information though—it can be a starting point, but their information is often quite inaccurate.

Often, the best way to get this information is to just *ask your friends!* Yes, we know that discussing your salary is a faux pas in many parts of the world, but—in our experience—people are nonetheless okay sharing it. The trick is to acknowledge the awkwardness in the situation, explain what's happening, and ask. Really.

If all of this sounds terribly intimidating, take heart; many tech companies have a range in mind for the level. Even if you offer a number below this range, they'll often bump it up to their range. After all, it's not just about getting you on board, but also about retaining you. Underpaid people tend not to stick around for very long.

OPTIMIZING REVIEW CYCLES

I can always tell when it's perf time for my friends. What is perf time, you might ask? That's when work (and socialization) grinds to a halt for people to do the dreaded *performance reviews*.

They are what's considered a necessary evil. No one really *likes* them, but we know we have to do them. Many tech companies follow the process of "360° peer reviews." This means that people get reviewed not only by their manager but also by their peers. This is actually a good policy because your peers may have insight on your performance that your manager doesn't. However, it also increases the number of reviews by possibly 5x. It also means that not even ICs are free from the burden of writing reviews.

The silver lining with performance reviews is that this is the time when strong performers (that's you, right?) become eligible for raises and promotions.

At most companies, performance reviews are considered quarterly, bi-yearly, or annually as part of an official performance or compensation review. A review cycle might look like this:

1. When review season starts, you write up a self-review and ask peers to write feedback for you.

2. Your manager reads those reviews and writes up a manager evaluation.

3. Depending on the company, either your manager or a committee gives you a performance rating, such as "greatly exceeds expectations," and decides whether to promote you to the next level.

4. If compensation is part of this review, your manager then recommends an increase and submits it upward for approval.

5. You meet with your manager, go over their written evaluation, learn your performance rating, and start working on a personal development plan for next time.

---

7   Note that these will often happen at different times. If you're naming a number, it's usually in the early stages when the company asks what you are expecting to make. If the company is naming a number, it's usually with an offer.

At a small company, the process might be much less structured.

You'll want to hit the sweet spot of optimizing for review cycles. Focusing on them too much will cause you undue stress, annoy your coworkers, and use up energy that would be better utilized to ship better products.

MANAGER DISCRETION VS. BY COMMITTEE

It can make a big difference whether promotions and compensation increases are at the discretion of your manager or decided by a committee.

Manager Discretion

When your manager is the decision-maker, the advice is fairly straightforward.

- Invest heavily in your relationship with your manager.

- Have career discussions with your manager. Learn what they want to see and what exceeding expectations might look like. Share your career goals.

- Make sure your manager knows about the great work you're doing. See pg 383.

- Check in with your manager occasionally to find out whether or not you're on track and focusing on the right things.

- If your manager isn't giving you useful development feedback, you can reach out to your manager's peers for additional mentorship.

- Learn which managers promote people quickly.

Remember that if you have a bad relationship with your manager, it's going to be difficult to get a promotion or raise. It's up to you to repair the relationship, or leave.

By Committee

When promotions and raises are handled by committee (usually higher-level managers and your manager's peers), there's a lot of emphasis on your "packet" of feedback and evaluations. People who might not know you look at the packets of all the PMs of your level and calibrate across them.

Below is some advice you should keep in mind:

- Invest in your relationships with senior teammates; their feedback carries more weight than that of more junior peers.

- Invest in your relationships and reputation with your manager's peers. If they're familiar with your work, they might speak up for you on the committee.

- Talk to a manager who's been at the company for a few years to learn what the committee wants to see in your packet.

- Carefully frame your skills and accomplishments in your self-evaluation so people who don't know you will believe you're performing at the next level.

- When asking for peer feedback, ask them to speak to the skills you need to demonstrate. You can suggest accomplishments or challenges you'd like them to address.

- Enlist your manager to be an ally and help you in your career growth. You may be able to get exceptionally honest feedback by asking, "What might the committee think I'm lacking? How can we help me get that experience?"

A committee adds overhead to the review cycle, but it can make the process less subject to bias and randomness since it's not controlled by only one person.

TIMING

When possible, try to ship your important projects before your review cycle. Even if everything is going well, if you have work that isn't quite ready to be shipped, that's often used as an excuse for the manager or committee to push your promotion or raise to the next cycle.

If you're working on a project that won't ship across multiple review cycles, work closely with your manager to develop intermediate milestones and discuss what "greatly exceeding expectations" would look like at each of them.

GOALS AND OKRS

Goals and OKRs (Objectives and Key Results) are the most objective measurements of your performance, and achieving them can carry a lot of weight on your performance reviews. There's a tricky balance in setting them, however.

When you set your OKRs, make sure your manager is in agreement that they're ambitious enough. You don't want to hit your goals and then have your manager say they were too easy.

Learn about how your manager or the promotion committee feels about hitting and missing OKRs. Some put a lot of importance in hitting them, in which case you want to make sure you don't sign up for too many or make them too difficult to hit. Others pay more attention to context and won't hold it against you if you miss an ambitious OKR, as long as you were doing good work.

SELF-REVIEW

Your manager often uses your self-review as a starting point when writing their manager evaluation. You can use your self-review to remind them of your accomplishments and frame your work in the best possible light. When they're on the border of what score to give you, your self-review can be the tipping point and make it easier for them to give a higher score.

If your company has a job ladder, reference the level you're targeting. You can create headers for each skill and use direct quotes from the job ladder to describe your accomplishments. You can do the same with the growth opportunities from your last manager evaluation. Write down how you addressed and improved each of them.

When you write what you did, explain why it was challenging and important. Talk about the great results you and your team achieved. Repeat lines from your vision or marketing material to explain why it matters.

If you're asked to self-assess, do so proudly, but honestly. Have the self-awareness to know whether you tend to overplay or underplay your accomplishments, and adjust accordingly. However, be careful that you make the correct adjustments, and don't overshoot (underplaying out of fear of overplaying).

PEER FEEDBACK

While peers can offer feedback to help you grow, the performance review probably isn't the best time for this. Seek the critical feedback privately, and let your official peer feedback serve as a glowing report of how much your teammates like working with you, and how much you contributed to the team.

Try the following to get stronger performance reviews from your peers:

- Before the review cycle, ask your peers if there's anything you could be doing to be a better PM for them, and then follow up with them after you address it.

- Throughout the year, let your team know about the work you're doing for them behind the scenes. At standups, you can let the team know when you're working on presentations, customer visits, strategy meetings, cross-team coordination, etc.

- You can let your peer reviewers know what you'd like them to cover, such as, "Could you speak to the work I did analyzing the A/B test?" or, "I'm trying to emphasize my customer insight, so I'd love it if you could share some examples of that." Ask them to speak to specific skills that are mentioned in your company's PM career ladder (pg 343). Peer reviews can be intensive, and many reviewers will actually appreciate this guidance.

- Within reason, choose people you believe will give you good reviews. However, it's important not to skip anyone important, such as your eng lead or design lead.

- After the review cycle, follow up with your peer reviewers again regarding any negative feedback, and how you plan to address it.

This doesn't mean you should expect your peer feedback to be all sunshine and roses. Everyone has some development areas, and you want to pay extra attention to any mentioned in your review.

WRITING PEER FEEDBACK FOR OTHER PEOPLE

Peer feedback is "on the record" documentation. The peer feedback you write will influence whether your teammates get a raise or promotion. Sharing examples of their contributions and what you appreciate about them can help their manager or the promotion committee get a better picture of their capabilities.

That's the straightforward part. The less straightforward aspect is how forthcoming to be about providing "areas of improvement."

Although criticism is essentially explicitly asked for, cultural norms and expectations often suggest a different tactic. Americans, for example, tend to be direct with positive feedback and indirect with negative feedback; that is, Americans tend to "tone down" their negativity—especially with written documentation such as this.

At many companies, peer reviews are often quite positive—more so, even, than the person's performance would dictate. That creates real challenges with how to interpret written feedback. Some managers may read between the lines and interpret any small critical suggestion or even a lack of enthusiasm as harsh feedback. Others read less closely and might miss statements that are intended to convey a severe problem. Most people have a tendency to pay attention to feedback that matches their impression and dismiss feedback that conflicts with it.

Our advice is therefore to "know your audience." Understand your company's culture around feedback and match the tone. This is not dishonest or misleading—quite the opposite. If the manager assumes negative feedback will

---

be toned down, then to convey an accurate impression, you need to do just that. The manager may share your feedback directly with your peer, so write with that in mind.

NETWORKING

Buzz Bruggeman is an incredible networker. Fifteen years ago, Buzz shifted careers and went from being a real-estate lawyer to a tech entrepreneur, moving 2,700 miles to a new city where he knew only six people. Yet now, he boasts an impressive contact list of tech and business leaders. But the thing is, he's not just collecting business cards. He has genuine relationships—friendships—with them.

What's his secret? How has he been able to build such a network? It wasn't through sending hundreds of LinkedIn requests (that won't get you very far), nor was he throwing so much money at startups that people were clamoring to meet him.

His secret is simple. First, he starts by putting in the work. He organizes events, introduces himself to many people, and makes the effort to build relationships.

Next—and this is a big one—he gives so much more than he takes. He wants to be helpful. People like and appreciate him, and they trust that he's kind and honest.

In the real world, relationships matter a lot. Job seekers use their friends, and friends of friends, to discover great roles. Hiring managers use their networks to find great candidates. Everyone can leverage their network to get extra mentorship or get answers to little questions.

Connections in your network generally fall on a spectrum from acquaintances who can help with small requests, to genuine relationships with people who will recommend you for unpublicized opportunities.

A network is like a garden, however. You can't just grow it overnight; every action you take plants a seed (or, sometimes, sprinkles some weed killer), and it requires gentle and consistent tending to grow it.

For more on building an effective network, read *Networking for Introverts*, by Jules Walter (pg 493).

BROADLY REACH OUT WITH SMALL REQUESTS

I get a lot of emails with requests for advice or assistance in some area. Some are from friends, some from acquaintances, and many are from strangers. It's all okay. That's not to say that I respond to every one of them (I wish I could), but I am rarely bothered by them.[8] So ask!

Your chances of getting a response will be higher if you reach out to people you already have some type of connection with. This might be a friend-of-a-friend, a fellow alum from your alma mater, or someone in a shared group. (Strangers are okay, too, but you have a lower chance of receiving a response, particularly if they're a busy person.)

If you're looking for a job, ask them if they'd be up for a quick chat to tell you more about their company. At the end of that chat, you can ask them if they'd be willing to submit your resume. This can help both of you, since they'll usually get a referral bonus if you get hired.

---

8   The rare times when I have been bothered was when someone acts like they are owed a response. For example, one person said, "I'll give you two more chances to respond" (or else what?). Another person—a complete stranger—asked me to provide three times when I'm available to meet, this Monday or Tuesday. I hadn't agreed to meet him at all!

However, be sensitive to different companies and individuals having varying attitudes around "distant" referrals. Some encourage them, figuring that *some* connection is better than none, but others expect referrals to only be from people who can genuinely attest to your skills. Still, it never hurts to ask.

Some schools and organizations also have mailing lists, chat channels, or discussion groups where you can reach out and ask for connections. If you're interested in joining a small startup, you can ask the group if there are any startups you should reach out to. If you've just started an internationalization project, you can ask if anyone has experience in that area.

To make cold outreach more effective, consider the following:

- **Provide the relevant information.** Many people send emails asking if they can ask a question. Just ask! It doesn't help the recipient to have to follow up, asking for more information (or confirming that you can ask the question). It also dramatically reduces the odds of getting useful help; you're counting on the recipient being responsive *twice*, rather than just once.

- **Keep it brief.** Thousand-word emails where the recipient must dig around for the question are time-consuming and typically ignored. The more work you make them do, the less likely they are to punt it to when they have time (which might be never).

- **Be specific and non-googleable.** Asking someone a very broad question like, "How do you launch a product?" isn't a good use of your time, or theirs. There's just *far* too much to say on the topic—particularly to an expert. If you can write a book on the topic, you should probably *look* for a book (or at least a blog post) on it.

- Be polite and appreciative. Be kind, and you often get the same in turn. Show politeness and gratitude, especially if you actually get a response.

All of that being said, it's important to remember that even if you do everything perfectly, many people will still ignore your request. It's okay, and even expected, for most people to say no. You just need one person to say yes!

If you don't have any connections, you can do an online search for "product manager community" or "product manager network." Local product manager groups can also be a good place to start. Some groups are primarily aspiring PMs or filled with self-promotional posts, while others have very helpful mentoring and resource-sharing. Once you've found your first group, you can (discreetly) ask around to find the most helpful groups.

Once you're in these groups, try to be as useful as you can. Be kind and considerate. You'll slowly begin to get recognized—even if only as, "Oh yeah, I recognize that name!"—and your network will start to grow.

BUILD GENUINE RELATIONSHIPS WITH PEOPLE WHO CAN MENTOR YOU AND MIGHT HELP YOU

For a bigger career boost, genuine relationships with people who can vouch for you and who want to help you are incredibly valuable. These can be people who think highly of you because they worked with you in the past or people with whom you've built a relationship over time.

One type of relationship to specifically look for is trusted mentors—people you can turn to when you need honest advice. For example, after getting harsh negative feedback, you might turn to a trusted mentor to double-check if the feedback really is about your skills, or if it's just a sign that the role is a bad match. These trusted mentors are usually people you respect, who are a bit removed from your work, so that you won't worry that they have ulterior motives or that your honesty will work against you. If you can't find the perfect trusted mentor, you can also reach out to your friends for advice.

Once you have built genuine relationships, you'll often find them to be mutually beneficial. You might reach out to them to ask for advice or to see if they are aware of any good job opportunities, and they'll reach out to you when they hear about opportunities, or to ask you to help another person they know.

For a great approach to building these relationships, take a look at Jules Walter's essay, *Networking for Introverts* (pg 493).

WHEN NETWORKING GOES WRONG

Buzz (from 397) is perhaps the best networker I know. The worst? That would be a man we'll just call "Fred." (There's no need to publicly shame anyone.)

Ironically, Fred cares *so much* about networking that he actually became bad at it. He is laser-focused on his career goals and only develops relationships with people when he can see their value-add.

This backfires—big time. First, people see through this insincerity and resent him for it. But second, and more importantly, he can't accurately predict someone's "use." As a tech PM, he might dismiss the doctor he meets, not realizing that this person might have friends whose connections would be useful to him.

> In short, build a diverse network, be kind, and be helpful—to those more experienced than you as well as those less experienced. Be open, and, please, don't see everyone as a stepping stone to something better.

Don't be a Fred.

BAD SITUATIONS

You've made it this far into what's a pretty meaty book (or skipping ahead a bit—hey, we won't tell). We wish we could promise you that, from here on out, everything's on the up and up. You'll get the best jobs, amazing managers, great promotions, and ultimately, the right career growth, whatever that is.

Unfortunately, life doesn't always work that way. You will make mistakes. And as long as you're *trying*, then you're taking risks, and that means putting yourself in the path of potential failure. Not only that, but some things are simply out of your control.

The good news is that you can recover from even the biggest stumbling blocks. People often, in fact, wind up *better off* than they were before, because they've learned and grown—or it ended up being a blessing in disguise, and a good time to start fresh.

RECOVERABLE AND UNRECOVERABLE SITUATIONS

Any bad situation is technically recoverable, but at what cost? If you put yourself through prolonged, chronic stress, you're going to burn out. As product and leadership coach Becca Camp shared, "You'll start to ask yourself if you're cut out for the job, and lose faith in yourself." When you're in the thick of things, it's not always easy to know if it's wiser to stick it out or bail.

A clear indicator you should leave a situation, Camp shared, is if your relationships outside of work are suffering. It's one thing to put up with a tough time at work when you can lean on your friends and family, but it's another when you lose that support. The hardest thing is when you believe you're alone. Find mentors, coaches, and community who can give you advice and provide you with space to vent.

> When you're in a bad situation, be intentional. Either stay on purpose, or leave on purpose. "You don't owe anyone anything, and no one else will rescue you," says Camp.

For example, if you decide to stay with the goal of learning how to ship a product, focus on protecting yourself from stress. You might come to realize that your own baggage is exacerbating the situation, but you have the choice about whether to work on healing those issues in your current role or in a less inflamed environment. The book *Burnout*, by Emily Nagoski, includes more information on "completing the stress cycle," for example by running, seeking safety, or resting.

One pattern Camp noticed is that many bad situations happen because a person is really unhappy with their job. They often unknowingly self-sabotage because the role just isn't a great match. This doesn't mean you need to feel "passionate" about your job, but consider how you want to feel at work. Some people thrive in fast-paced, high-transparency cultures with lots of reviews, while others prefer more space and freedom. Some people can't tolerate managers who are easily distracted, while others won't tolerate managers who turn everything into a debate. Camp says, "You have to sign up for your flavor of dysfunction."

There's no right answer to the question of when you should stay and when you should go. You'll need to be honest with yourself and assess how much effort you're willing to put into repairing the situation.

- How much of a safety net do you have?

- Are you staying out of misguided loyalty or shame?

- What do you hope to get by staying?

- Is this role really a good match for you?

We are all humans who are growing and learning, and it's okay to change your path.

MANAGER PROBLEMS

A good fit with your manager is critical to your career growth. So, if you're having problems with your manager, you'll want to either resolve them quickly or transfer away.

Please note that many problems are repairable, but not all. If you're in an unrepairable situation—regardless of whose fault it is—the best solution is often to just walk away.

Repairable problems

Repairable problems often come from a misunderstanding, oversight, or cultural differences. They can also happen when your manager is still developing their craft. If you fundamentally respect your manager and they feel the same way about you, the problem is probably repairable.

Two of the most common problems are a mismatch in feedback styles, and micromanagement.

Mismatch in feedback styles

Many managers are desensitized to public feedback and debate about work. They're accustomed to saying what they think about product decisions and don't expect PMs to take it personally. Not everybody is comfortable with such openness, however. Some people are horrified the first time their manager disagrees with them or—gasp—playfully teases them in a room full of people.[9]

This is a repairable cultural mismatch and can be addressed from both sides:

1. You can rethink your assumptions that public feedback implies disrespect or disappointment. Often, managers will only debate you in public if they think highly of you; it doesn't occur to them that you might not feel confident in your standing.

2. You can let your manager know how you feel and ask for more private feedback. If you get an apology and a supportive response, there's hope! If they get defensive and the situation escalates, it might be time for you to move on.

It's not necessarily important to assess who's right and who's wrong. What matters most is whether the situation is fixable.

Micromanagement

Managers frequently fall into micromanagement when they haven't yet learned how to get the proactive communication they need. If you're facing this problem, it's better to not directly tell your manager you feel micromanaged. Instead, first consider if you're communicating proactively. Could you let your manager know your plans before they jump in with their own instructions? If that doesn't work, you can talk to them about how you'd like to earn their trust to work more independently, and ask if they have suggestions.

Overall, it's appropriate for your manager to be more hands-on when they haven't seen you successfully handle a type of challenge yet. However, if you feel like your manager is trying to one-up you, or if they aren't able to give you constructive feedback on the skills you'd need to develop to earn their trust, the situation is less promising.

Exclusionary behavior

Some people face the problem that their manager excludes them from important meetings or decisions. Often, this happens when it just hasn't occurred to the manager that it would be valuable to include their report. If your relationship is on steady ground, you can ask if you could be included in the future.

If your manager is concerned by the number of people in the room or doesn't think you're senior enough to attend, you can start by working more closely with them before and after the meeting to make sure they can appropriately represent your team and convey feedback to you. Over time, your manager might decide it's more efficient to invite you to the meeting directly.

Irreparable problems

If your manager doesn't believe in you or doesn't want to invest in you, it will be difficult to repair any problems. Early in your career, it might be easier to recover from a bad first impression. Most managers expect APMs to make mistakes and grow. As you advance, however, it's less likely that they'll change their mind once they've classified you as "low potential." A manager who doesn't believe in you won't recommend you for promotions and might overlook your accomplishments.

---

9   If you're the one "joking around" with others, watch out that you're not crossing the line. Sometimes, people won't admit that they're hurt or embarrassed for fear of looking "weak."

It's important to distinguish between a manager who doesn't believe in you and one who gives you honest, critical feedback. Sometimes, the best manager is the one who is willing to tell you the harsh truth and give you a chance to grow.

- Do you believe your manager is rooting for you?

- Does it feel like they're on your side?

- Do they think it's possible that you can overcome the challenges?

If so, you're in a good situation. But if you think they've given up on you or are merely cataloging your short-comings to justify their evaluation, that problem likely can't be repaired.

Another type of irreparable problem is when your manager mistreats you, belittles you, yells at you, or harasses you. That kind of manager won't change unless they want to, and you deserve better. People who try to stick it out in that kind of a situation often spend years recovering from it. If you stay too long, you might start to believe that's an appropriate way to be treated and lose confidence in your own skills.

Finally, sometimes the problem is just a poor fit between you and your manager. All managers have flaws. Some flaws won't bother you. They might even open up opportunities where you have a chance to shine (for example, when you can step in to help). Other flaws will feel intolerable to you. Not every person is bothered by the same things, so even if someone has a reputation as a great manager, they might not be great for you.

When it's time to move on

Once you've decided the problem isn't repairable, it's time to look at your options.

Internal transfers are a great option because you can ask around to learn which managers are good. Your current manager might be able to block your transfer, so try to placate them and lay low while you're making the move.

Your skip-level manager or other senior people you're close with can be good allies, but don't force them to pick sides. Instead, share the situation with them, placing as little blame as you can, and ask for advice. Some people have had luck telling their HR department the full story, but others have faced retaliation.[10] Be aware of that risk.

If those options don't work, you can always leave the company. It can be helpful to interview for new jobs while you hold your current one. There's a good reason for this: Employers won't expect your current manager to be a reference if you're still working for them.[11] But, if you leave first, you might raise some red flags if you don't provide them as a reference.

Of course, it's not always possible to get a new job before you leave. Just be sure to always speak diplomatically about your old manager; if you complain, they might wonder if you were part of the problem.

---

10 HR is filled with people, and people are mostly good. But if you're asking HR to do something and it increases risk for the company, or the facts are somewhat of a "he said/she said," or it jeopardizes a more senior employee's job, beware. As many would say: HR works for the company, not for you.

11 Note that many large companies in the US have policies prohibiting people from providing references, for current and prior employees. Before you quit your job, you may want to find out your company's policy.

NEGATIVE PERFORMANCE FEEDBACK AND PERFORMANCE IMPROVEMENT PLANS (PIPS)

Review time came around and Carla was shocked to see that she had received "misses expectations." Sure, she'd gotten feedback about a few mistakes, but she never realized it was serious. Could the situation be salvaged?

Sometimes yes, and sometimes no.

Shannon Boon, a product director, says:

> The trick is to know whether the company and manager are trying to help you grow or are trying to push you out. Sometimes, it's the wake-up call you need. If you come at it from a place of curiosity and growth, things can work out. Sometimes, it's a call out that the role or company is not a good fit, and can give you valuable insight into where your talents lie. And sometimes it can be political, and you should just find a better company.

When you're trying to tell the difference, consider these factors:

- Is the PIP specific and actionable?

- Are you getting support and mentorship from your manager, or do they disappear?

- Does the role feel like a good fit for you?

- Do you trust your manager and other leaders at the company?

If the issues in the PIP aren't a surprise to you, be really honest with yourself.[12] Sometimes people say, "No one comes back from a PIP." That is, to be sure, an exaggeration, but it holds some truth, too. PIPs are often for chronic issues—issues that you've known about, have tried to fix, and have failed to do so. Has something *actually* changed now? If not, consider whether you want to wait to get fired or if you'd rather just get out now on your own terms.[13]

This is not intended to discourage you. Rather, this is to encourage you to reflect honestly before proceeding. The safest plan is to start interviewing at other companies, even if you'll also be trying to address the issues and recover. That will give you a backup plan.

Most of the people who go on to recover and succeed in a role after a PIP or negative performance feedback are those who learn something important from the feedback. They felt scared and sad, but they didn't disagree with the feedback.

Consider these scenarios:

---

12 With a good manager, a PIP should generally not be a surprise.

13 Yes, some people genuinely choose this path. They may make a last ditch attempt to fix the issue, but accept that they might be fired. In their minds, being fired is "embarrassing" and burns some bridges, but at least they'll likely collect some severance from it.

> ### FALLING METRICS
>
> One PM had been dutifully reporting on falling metrics, explaining that the data science team didn't know why the metrics were decreasing. In her PIP, she learned that she was responsible for those metrics and was expected to track down the problem, write a clear report, and suggest solutions.
>
> Once she realized what she was responsible for, she was able to demonstrate her strong analytical skills and get things back on track. She went on to expand her scope at the company and take on more challenging projects. The PIP didn't hold her back.

And another one:

> ### JUST A JOKE
>
> Another PM was surprised to hear that his team thought he was a jerk, and his job was now at risk. The PM's manager brought specific examples. The PM was shocked!
>
> Many of the examples were times he'd been joking around with teammates and hadn't realized they'd taken him seriously, but he could now see why those jokes were a bad idea. In another example, he realized he'd put too much pressure on the team to hit a deadline and wanted to do better.
>
> The PM put together a plan for apologizing to the teammates and checking in to make sure the problems didn't reoccur. The first few weeks, his teammates were wary, but by two months later their relationships were stronger than ever.

If you don't agree with the negative feedback, it's unlikely you could address it in a way that would be satisfactory to your manager. If you have other strong connections at the company, you could try to use them to ask for an internal transfer to a team where you'd be a better fit. However, you would need to make a strong case for why your "underperformance" only applied to your current team.

Regardless of how you feel about the feedback, it can be a good signal that can help you in your future job searches. Form your own narrative around what happened and then look for ways to avoid that problem in the future. For example, if you were in over your head, you might want to look for roles at a lower level or with more mentoring. If you couldn't thrive under disorganized leadership, look for a company with strong leadership.

A PIP is not a death sentence for your career. Even if you get fired or leave the company, you can go on to find a role that's a better fit for you where you'll thrive. While they rarely talk about it in public, rest assured that there are PMs, managers, and executives who went on to have successful careers after being put on a PIP.

FAILED PROJECT

Product managers often have a deep emotional investment in their project. When it fails, it hits them personally. It's not just about the missed opportunity for career growth; it's a form of loss, not to mention a bruise to their ego.

Projects can fail for many reasons, both inside and outside of your control. Maybe the executive team canceled your project before it launched. Or, it launched, but customers hated it. Perhaps there were huge data-loss bugs. Or—I don't know—a worldwide pandemic[14] affected your customer base.

---

14   Hello, future readers, from the Gayle and Jackie of November 2020!

A failed project doesn't have to be a disaster. Often, the things you learn from a failure provide the insights for your next success.

The key is to take ownership for the failure and learn from it. The good thing about learning from failure is that you're unlikely to ever forget the lessons.

Ask yourself these questions.

What went wrong?

Whether the problem was your fault or someone else's, try to form an opinion on why the project failed. It might be tempting to forget about the project as quickly as possible and pretend it never happened, but if you don't learn from it, you might repeat the mistake again.

When Arjun Ohri worked as a PM on Microsoft's iPod competitor, Zune, he believed in the product quality and social features. Long before Spotify, Zune offered an unlimited music subscription service with personalized, curated, shareable playlists. When the product failed, he was perplexed. He dedicated himself to understanding what went wrong, and realized that success takes aligning great product, promotion, distribution, and timing. This realization motivated him to get an MBA, and he eventually went on to start his own successful company.

As you explore this question, remember that it's for your own benefit—not to cast blame on your team. Blaming others won't make you look better, but showing a deep understanding of how the organizational context led to the mistakes might.

What could you have done differently?

When the mistakes fall under your responsibility, this is a simple retrospective. Perhaps you'll realize that you could have done more customer research, started with a smaller experiment, or driven more cross-functional alignment. You might learn that you needed to check in with the team more frequently.

When the problems were someone else's fault, the question is still equally important. If you could go back in time, how could you, personally, have avoided this bad outcome? Perhaps the project was doomed from the start and you'll choose to avoid projects that take dependencies on unlaunched infrastructure or on teams where the executives won't talk to each other.

Are there any bright spots that are working well?

The project might be a failure, but sometimes there are parts that are promising. Those can guide your next iteration.

When Burbn, an app for checking into locations, failed to take off, the founder looked into the analytics. Most of the metrics looked disappointing, but there was one bright spot. Users were sharing lots of pictures. He decided to pivot to a photo sharing app. He called it "Instagram."

FAILING COMPANY

There's a lot of talk about taking a seat on a rocketship, but not as much conversation about how to grow at a stagnating or failing company. Sometimes, big opportunities open up as senior people jump ship.

The sweet spot for staying with a company on the decline is when you are early in your career and have a safety net or strong network. You get exposure to senior-level responsibilities and an up-close view of tricky business decisions. These experiences can help you grow faster.

At the more senior levels, it's important to deliver real wins, so it's better not to stay at a company you don't think will succeed. You won't get much credit for launching an amazing product if the company goes out of business and shuts it down a month later.

How can you tell when the company is actually failing, versus when it's just going through a rough patch? Unfortunately, there's no foolproof way to tell. Many startups get to the brink of running out of money and, at the last minute, they either raise another round of funding, get acquired, or go out of business. You'll need to use your business sense and weigh it against your risk tolerance.

If you do decide to leave, remember that you might work with those coworkers again someday. One of the best ways to preserve work relationships is to give the team adequate notice before you leave. Instead of two or three weeks notice, you might stay four weeks to ensure a smooth transition. You can work with your manager to create some talking points that feel honest about why you're leaving, but don't hurt the morale of your teammates.

BURNOUT

Because product managers take on responsibility for the overall success of their product, they are especially susceptible to burnout.

Many PMs try to push through stress or lack of sleep because they don't want to let their team down or let a mistake slip through the cracks. They might feel like scaling back would be admitting failure.

The downsides to pushing through stress usually outweigh the benefits. Teammates notice when you're stressed, and it stresses *them* out. You're also much less effective when you're sleep-deprived.

A few things to consider:

- Start with the basics. Sleep well, eat well, exercise, and take vacations.

- Reduce and remove stressful responsibilities (for example, by letting a difficult report go).

- Add more breaks, walks, and free time to your daily schedule.

- Move to a new team or role where you can start over fresh.

- Work with a coach or therapist.

You deserve to be happy. If you want a long, productive career, you need to set a sustainable pace.

If stress isn't the issue, and it's more that you're demotivated, don't just try to "power through it;" you literally lack the willpower. Rather, take time for some reflection—maybe seek out a career coach who can help guide your analysis. Is it the company? The team? The role? Forcing yourself to fulfill goals simply because you made them years ago is never a good idea.

GENERAL ADVICE FOR SWITCHING COMPANIES

As a PM, you'll be evaluated on your track record of success. Two or three failures over a long career aren't a problem, but two in a row can raise a red flag. As you apply to future jobs, many hiring managers can believe that one bad experience was a fluke, but two in a row will make them suspicious.[15]

---

15 Not all hiring managers take this attitude though. Some hiring managers pride themselves on not holding a career with several short stints against a candidate. They've experienced bad situations for themselves and they'll believe you when you say you had to leave. If you've had to leave several companies quickly, look for a hiring manager like this.

If you're about to leave a job because of a bad situation, consider choosing a lower risk job for your next move. If you have a choice, choose a company that's known for good managers or work with someone you trust. Choose a role that's less of a stretch for you. If you succeed in this next role, your bad situation will quickly fade into memory.

Finally, remember that the tech world is a small place. You might work with old coworkers again. Your new manager might be friends with your old manager. Stay in touch with the coworkers you liked, and never badmouth the ones you didn't.

KEY TAKEAWAYS

- **Your relationships with your manager and their peers are key:** They'll be able to find you great opportunities and advocate for you as you grow. They can share honest feedback on where you need to improve. Try to form strong relationships with them. Enlist them to help you with your career growth. Don't forget they're fallible humans with their own interests and motivations.

- **Choose the right place at the right time:** Early in your career, you'll often benefit from joining a well-established company where you can learn best practices. Then, fast-growing companies often provide the best opportunity for rapid growth. Startups can be great, but they can fail for all kinds of reasons. Pay attention to when your growth hits diminishing returns. When you get a new job offer, negotiate your compensation!

- **Build your network:** A strong network can be helpful at any time, but it's especially important later in your career. People in your network can help you find great job opportunities, sometimes even ones that aren't listed. In addition, as you rise in an organization, you'll have fewer people to learn from inside your company. When that happens, the best source of mentorship and advice might be the network you built.

- **If you're in a bad situation with your boss or company, you can try to fix it, but usually, you should look for a new job:** There's usually an underlying reason why the role isn't a great match for you, so you can take the opportunity to find something better. Many people wish they'd left a bad situation sooner, before they burned out.

CHAPTER 35

EXTENDED LEARNING

THE FIELD OF product management is constantly changing, and there are always new things to learn. Many great PMs share their insights on Twitter, in blog posts, and in email newsletters. There are meetups and product conferences where product leaders share their hard-earned lessons learned. You can join product communities on Facebook and Slack to connect with other PMs.

For an up-to-date list of good resources, visit the resources page of our website: CrackingThePMCareer.com.

Beyond those free resources, here are a few paid ones to consider:

COURSES

Early in your career, or when you start a new specialization, taking a course can help you gain confidence and familiarity with a product toolset. They're especially helpful if you don't have strong product mentors at your company.

Most courses teach materials that you could find online for free, but since the cost of the course should be covered by your company's training budget, they can be a helpful choice for people who learn better in a class setting.

Not all courses are created equal, however. Ask around to learn if people thought the course was a good use of their time and what the most valuable part was.

COACHES

Personalized coaching is especially helpful as you grow into more senior roles and find yourself getting stuck. A coach can provide a new perspective to help you make progress.

One product leader found himself stuck on a team retention problem. He dug in with his coach and they zeroed in on feedback that his reports didn't feel like they could connect with him. They went deeper and found that he shut down during conflicts. Reflecting on this, he realized conflicts stirred up childhood memories. Once he saw that, he was able to reframe how he saw the work conflicts, connect better with his reports, and improve retention on his team.

Becca Camp, a product and leadership coach, says that the most consistent advice she gives is around confidence:

> What gives people confidence is a willingness to experience the full spectrum of human emotion. Confidence is a byproduct of being game to experiment and see the results. Not being afraid to be sad if things don't turn out the way you want. If we can get comfortable with seeing failure as data and stagnation as the actual enemy, a lot of things will be easier.

Finding a good coach is about fit, so take advantage of the free initial calls that many coaches offer to see what your rapport is like.

MBA

Once you've already broken into product management, the top benefit of an MBA is boosting your credentials. Enrolling in a respected MBA program can extend your network and open up better job opportunities, especially if you don't already have a top tier undergraduate school or tech company on your resume.

MBA programs provide a structured environment where you can learn business fundamentals and practice leadership skills. Those skills are helpful, but you not only pay tuition, you also pay the opportunity cost of your salary over two years.

CHAPTER 36

BEYOND PM

WHILE SOME PEOPLE join product management straight out of college and (aim to) stick with it their entire career, for many others, it ends up being a midpoint in their career. Perhaps they joined product management after a few years of working, and then they transition out of it two, five, or twenty years down the road.

Indeed, the wonderful thing about product management is that it combines so many different and transferable skills. This makes the job complex and ambiguous, but it also means that you have so many options for the "next step"—if you choose to do that.

Here are some of the more common options.

GENERAL MANAGER

While people say that a PM is *like* a mini-CEO, a General Manager (GM) is truly a mini-CEO. A GM is responsible not only for product teams, but also for the business teams within their business unit. They're responsible for the full end-to-end success and profitability of their products, including the go-to-market strategy that involves marketing, sales, partnerships, and other teams.

If you're a business-minded PM who loves working across functions to land a product in the market, you might like being a GM. On the other hand, if you get the most energy working on product vision and design and don't enjoy the operational side, it may not be for you.

For more about the PM to GM career path, see the Q&A with April Underwood on page 460.

VENTURE CAPITAL

Venture capital (VC) firms raise money from limited partners (LPs), like pension funds, and then invest it in a portfolio of companies. They make money for the LPs when a portfolio company is acquired or IPOs, hopefully for a significant multiple of the original investment. The VCs often advise the companies in their portfolio, and may be given a seat on the board of directors.

There are many different roles at VC firms:

- **General Partner / Managing Director:** The top deal professionals. They raise money, have the final say on which companies to invest in, and become board members. They typically already have a track record of success as entrepreneurs, executives, or experts in their field.

- **Analysts, Associates, and Principals:** Junior deal professionals who scout companies, exercise due diligence, write memos, and calculate cap tables. They make recommendations, but don't get to make the final decisions. Analysts and associates usually leave the firm to work at a portfolio company after a few years.

- **Operating Partner:** Generally, the operating partners don't decide which companies to invest in. Instead, they support the portfolio companies or the VC firm with their specific expertise.

- **Entrepreneur In Residence (EIR):** A 6-12 month role where you're paid a salary or stipend to explore startup ideas and develop a new venture. The VC firm tries to build strong relationships with the EIR in the hopes of funding the startup.

Hunter Walk, a partner at Homebrew VC and former product lead at YouTube, Google, and Second Life, shared how a PM might know if they'd like being a VC:

> It's a love of seeing the future being built. A love of being in the flow of ideas. A chance to be close to the heat of building.

On the other hand, if you want to stay hands-on building products, you don't enjoy stakeholder management, or you like tight feedback and learning loops, VC might not be for you. In VC, you don't learn which decisions were good or bad until many years later. There are also limited advancement opportunities at VC firms; there are very few partner roles, and they are very challenging to get.

Walk also discusses the importance of taking the time to choose the right firm:

> Some are very collaborative and others are lone wolf. In some, you work closely with each company and others you just write a check. Some firms are trying to rebuild themselves while others are working well. When you're making a 20-year choice, you should wait a while and cultivate relationships to make the right choice, not just look at the roles that are open to you right now.

If you're interested in this space, *Venture Deals* by Brad Feld and Jason A. Mendelson is a great book to check out.

For more on the PM to Venture path, see Q&A with Ken Norton on page 440.

ANGEL INVESTOR

An angel investor invests their own money in very early stage startups. It's only feasible if they have the money to invest and connections to entrepreneurs. If they do have that money, it's a chance to participate in the huge upside of equity, and a chance to support the entrepreneurs they believe in.

People who love hearing very early-stage ideas, and having skin-in-the-game with multiple companies, might like angel investing. If you're not comfortable with the risk, it might not be for you.

For more on the PM to Angel Investing path, see the interviews with April Underwood (page 460) and Oji Udezue (page 456).

FOUNDER/CEO

Founding a company is, perhaps, the most common aspiration for PMs. It's a natural fit, too, because you're already used to leading teams, thinking about users, and building products.

As the founder of a company, you have a lot of flexibility to shape what your role looks like. You might take on the head of product role and leave the operational side to a cofounder. Or, you might own the operational side and deal with finding office space, paying bills, and hiring a sales team.

Most founders describe the role as incredibly stressful, and argue that you should only attempt it if you feel like you're the only person who can successfully solve the important problems you want to tackle. They describe struggling through long periods where no one else believed they would be successful, and they constantly questioned themselves. They talk about the weight of being responsible for other employee's livelihoods and returning investor's money. They recall nightmare board members who were worse than any boss could be. They lament the frustration of handling all the work that no one else wants to do. They point at their new gray hairs.

On the other hand, there are serial entrepreneurs who love the role and constantly yearn to get back to their roots. They've usually paired up with great co-founders who balance their strengths and weaknesses. They don't get demoralized easily. They've learned from their first startups and are eager to apply that learning again.

For more on the PM-to-founder path, see the interviews with Sara Mauskopf (page 436) and Sachin Rekhi (page 447). For more on the PM-to-CEO path, see the interview with Teresa Torres (page 452).

CHIEF OF STAFF

The chief of staff is an executive's "right hand person." They're a close confidant of the executive who helps the executive scale. A chief of staff generally gets involved in many projects on behalf of the executive and takes on a few "special projects" to lead directly.

The role can look very different from company to company and executive to executive. Some of the work may include:

- improving team processes
- driving company processes
- managing investor relations
- researching strategic initiatives
- preparing board slides

- running analyses
- coordinating cross-functional initiatives
- running important meetings
- drafting speeches
- helping the executive prioritize their time

If you're interested in a chief of staff role, it's important to align with the executive on what the role will look like and ensure there's a good fit. Some people have taken the role hoping for broad strategic exposure, and instead find themselves mostly taking care of administrative duties like scheduling meetings and taking notes. Beyond the responsibilities themselves, it's important to work for an executive you respect and with whom you have good rapport.

The chief of staff role can be a great career move for someone who wants a broader view of the business. As a chief of staff you participate in senior meetings across the company and see the bigger picture that surrounds the world of product. It can be a stepping-stone to a general manager role or an accelerant for

PMs who need more strategic exposure. If you love cross-functional coordination and have the people skills and confidence to work with executives, you might love the chief of staff role.

Jennifer Conti-Davies has moved from product management to chief of staff twice in her career and recommends stints as a chief of staff as a way to broaden your skills.

> It was a refreshing change to go from a laser focus on the product to a systems view of the organization. As chief of staff, you get a different strategic vantage point which can ultimately make you a better product manager as well.

If you're too early in your career, chief of staff might not be a great match for you. It takes a lot of competence, confidence, and autonomy to be a great chief of staff. Many early-career people are shy around executives or lack the credibility to have the kind of influence they need. Another sign that you might not like the job is if you really love the ownership and accountability of being a PM. As a chief of staff, you're more often a contributor to work than the owner of it.

PRODUCT COACHING AND CONSULTING

Product coaching and product consulting are paths that capitalize on your PM expertise while gaining independence. Coaches might teach new skills or mentor people through challenges. Consultants step in to fill the PM or product leader role at companies.

If you enjoy variety and are looking for better work-life balance, you might enjoy coaching or consulting. If you really want to stay hands-on and own the results, this might not be for you. Many coaches and consultants are independent and need to handle their own lead generation and business operations, which isn't for everyone.

For more on the PM to coaching path, see the interview with Teresa Torres (page 452).

PRODUCT LEADER Q&A

DYLAN CASEY

BRIAN ELLIS

OSI IMEOKPARIA

BANGALY KABA

SARA MAUSKOPF

KEN NORTON

ANUJ RATHI

SACHIN REKHI

TERESA TORRES

OJI UDEZUE

APRIL UNDERWOOD

PART I

PRODUCT LEADER Q&A

THERE IS NO one path into or out of product management. The needed skills are too diverse for any single undergraduate degree or prior role to fully prepare you. Likewise, the skills you acquire are applicable to so many professions.

In this section, we've selected a handful of exceptional product leaders and charted their winding career paths and words of wisdom. You'll hear from:

We hope that you enjoy their thoughts as much as we do.

416

CHAPTER 37

DYLAN CASEY

DYLAN CASEY is the chief product officer of the Engineering Division at Goldman Sachs. His experience includes leading product management teams at Fair, Yahoo, Path and Google, where he was a founding member of the Google+ team. Also, while at Google, he led Realtime Search and the MyTracks Android app. Dylan is a member of the Product Council at Kleiner Perkins and an advisor to FishBrain and RewardStyle. He's also a co-founder and board member at WEDŪ. Before his career in technology, Dylan was a professional cyclist, competing in the 2000 Olympic Games and winning four national championships.

social: @dylancasey

HOW DID YOU GO FROM CYCLING TO PRODUCT MANAGEMENT?

I was a professional athlete on the US Postal Service team with Lance Armstrong and I became a PM at Google in a non-traditional way. Joining Google was the perfect storm of being in the right place at the right time, and ultimately, paying attention to opportunities around me.

When I walked into my interview at Google in 2003, I told them:

> Look, I have this history of being very successful at accomplishing big things. And I have a methodology for doing that. And I think that same methodology will apply at Google.

I knew, from a very early time, that I got a lot of personal satisfaction out of being methodical about doing things and preparing to deliver on big days or events. This idea that you show up on race day, and you have to perform under pressure—I applied that same methodology when I walked in the door at Google.

WHAT DID YOU DO AT GOOGLE?

Once I was at Google, every request to use Google's products or brand in anything would come to me for approval. As Google grew more popular, this became overwhelming and I realized that it was not a good use of my time. So, I put together a proposal on why we should program-itize the system. I submitted it, and I got approval to do so. All of a sudden, it was like, "Okay, now you have the resources and the opportunity to do this. Go get it done."

One particular request came from the CEO about a partnering opportunity with the movie, *The Da Vinci Code*. Because it was a movie, and Marissa Mayer was known for spearheading movie outings for the company, she was also roped into it. We sat together to figure out what to do and decided to start a team. I sent an email to the internal movies mailing list and invited people to show up at a conference room at 10 AM if they wanted to work with us.

Ultimately, we built a series of puzzles that were contextually relevant to the Da Vinci Code, using things like the Fibonacci sequence. Because iGoogle was a really big, strategic priority for us at the time, we knew that this would be a great place to build it. We launched it and it was wildly successful.

At the time, Google wasn't particularly adept at launching big things on a specific date—things where you flipped the switch and everything had to work. Sony was putting millions of dollars into marketing, so on the day that it launched, it had to work.

Marissa saw that I was good at getting a team of people to work on something very undefined and delivering on a launch date, so she invited me to join her team as a product manager. It was a pivotal moment in my career. I just took the opportunity, volunteered, and convinced a bunch of people to join me on this mission, and it all worked out.

HOW DID YOU MOVE FROM THERE TO PEOPLE MANAGEMENT?

There was a call to employees—if you wanted to build an Android app, the company would provide you the time, resources, and assistance to do that. I signed up and found a couple of engineers that were interested in working on it with me.

We built an app called My Tracks. It used My Maps, Google's custom map creator product, as a backend to track and record where you were going, using your phone. People generally used it for hiking, skiing, and cycling. It became really popular and eventually was folded into the Google Maps team as an official product.

After that, my career started to grow. My role evolved from being an individual contributor to a people manager.

> The most challenging part for me was that, as a product manager, I essentially had all the details and numbers and the roadmap and the vision at my fingertips. But now as a people manager, I didn't know anything. It was a hard transition because I was so comfortable when I had all the details. I had to learn how to rely on others.

WHAT WAS IT LIKE TO BE HEAD OF PRODUCT AT PATH?

While I was at Google, I met Dave Morin who started a company called Path. I had previously worked on real time search, leveraging the Twitter fire hose to build an index that could answer real time queries like "traffic on 101." I grew an affinity for "social" as a signal.

Path was a very intimate social network. Because it was 100% mobile, I had this vision of really increasing the fidelity of the type of relationships that you could have online. There were twenty people when I joined, and I was the first product manager.

I felt like Path was that true, small startup experience where I walked into a whole bunch of chaos. There wasn't a shared language or a shared operating machine in place like we had at Google. I had to build it all from scratch.

> What I learned there is to never say, "this is how we did it at company X." You just have to bite your tongue. It was really about going in and not saying anything for a month. Just quietly observe and really soak everything up that's going on in the organization.

WHERE DID YOU FOCUS YOUR TIME AT PATH?

I knew I was going into an organization where the vision was already set. My job was really to try to bring order to the company.

> As head of product, I learned that it's not so much about owning the product roadmap; it's about owning the problem.

I was so focused on the end result of the journey we were on, that I didn't have the ego or confidence to think, "I'm the product manager; I should be able to make all of these decisions."

I went in and reorganized the way that we worked together. I helped the team create its first set of OKRs, because I needed the OKRs to then go and build the roadmap. I went through the different processes that would then lay the foundation to do the rest of the work. Then I hired a couple of product managers, and later a data science team. We evolved the way that design, product, and engineering all work together.

WHAT WERE THE IMPORTANT THINGS YOU LEARNED FROM THAT EXPERIENCE?

When you start to grow from one team to feature teams, having a shared language and shared rituals is so important. The whole idea behind product reviews or design reviews is to have a regular and predictable venue that people can count on to have a conversation.

Ultimately, we were stuck in a hard place. We had a hypothesis that the smaller and tighter you kept your social network, the better your experience would be—but this ran antithetical to "grow as fast as you can." It was a really hard conflict for us to manage.

It ultimately became clear to me that we weren't going to have the outcome that we wanted and so I started looking around.

WHAT WAS YOUR TIME AT YAHOO AS VP OF PLATFORMS LIKE?

Marissa joined Yahoo as the CEO right around the same time I was looking to leave Path. I wanted to work with her again, so I went to Yahoo. She told me that she knew exactly what team I should work on. I figured coming from Path, it would be the mobile team or some social project. I was really wrong!

She asked me to join the platform organization that runs underneath all of the product verticals. I didn't understand it at all. I'm a mobile, social, consumer-facing, classic product manager. She just shook her head and laughed and said, "No, no you're going to be great at this. This team needs a lot of guidance and direction and leadership, and you'll be great at it."

What I discovered when I walked in was that the team was essentially operating in fire drill mode every day. It was just ad hoc development, ad hoc product planning, and ad hoc road mapping. There were 15 stakeholders saying that they all want a different thing, all on the same day. The end result of that mode is that you have a product that doesn't work very well. You have a team that is really unhappy. And you have a group of stakeholders who are equally unhappy because they think the platform organization is failing.

SO HOW DID YOU BRING ORDER TO THE CHAOS?

It took me about six months to really come up with a clear plan. I really needed that time and perspective to truly understand what to do. In the case of Yahoo, it was that we needed to get very, very clear about why we exist as a team. What's our purpose? What's our mission?

And not only is it important for that to be clear, but it's super important that everybody knows it and understands it. There's a maxim that if you don't say it ten times, it's not true. Say it a hundred times and then say it a hundred times more.

The reality is that while you may have a very clear picture of what the plan and the roadmap is, nobody else does. We would literally write it on the walls and on whiteboards and put it on T-shirts because it just was so critical for that team. We got really, really clear about what our mission was. We got really clear about who we were supporting and serving. In some cases, it was another product. In some cases, it was our own users. We got really clear on how to measure that and know if we're doing a good job. How do we know if all of the work that we did in a quarter actually accomplished what we needed to do for our customers' business or the users?

I'd tell the team that, if they're not working on something that is not directly related to one of these ten priorities on the whiteboard, to stop working on it. It empowered everybody to have a little more control over how they spent their days.

Another big part was communicating to the rest of the organization. As a platform team, I got everybody to take on a developer relations mentality of, "You need to go out into the Yahoo internal ecosystem and evangelize what our platform does and why it's important for the people that are using it." I made a habit on Fridays to do a "walk-around day" where I'd walk around buildings and talk to the people using our product.

HOW DID THE TEAM REACT?

One of the hardest changes for the team was not operating from a center of fear. This was a group of people that had become comfortable with losing. I changed this to say, "No, no, you have to change your mentality to how we are going to win today. Let's take some risks. Let's be bold."

To do that, you get some quick wins. You show progress. Get credibility. There's easy ways to do that. Be very clear about what you're going to do and how you're going to do it. Then remind everybody. And then remind them again.

For example, every Friday, we had a meeting we called "demos and drinks" that served a couple of different purposes. The demos got everybody to start showing what they were working on. That showed progress. It gave people the opportunity to get recognition along the way. It opened up the opportunity for collaboration. It also helped put people's feet to the fire a little bit. I'd say "Hey, I know you're working on something. I want to see it on Friday."

It also gave us the opportunity to remind people, "Remember when we said we were going to do this? Well look, here's an example. We did it." We made a really significant habit out of celebrating all the little wins. As human beings, we have a tendency to not really recognize small accomplishments. Either we're afraid of bragging or we don't think they're big enough. Our team got maniacal about celebrating all those little wins. I think one of the interesting side effects of that kind of ritual is that we built up credibility, especially as a leadership team.

In a lot of ways, it was some of the most personally rewarding work that I've done. We started in such a bad state, and it affected a whole team of people and the work they did every single day. We were able to turn that around.

WHAT HAPPENED AFTER YAHOO?

Over time, it became clear that Wall Street was not going to give Yahoo the time that we wanted to turn the company around. I realized it was a good opportunity for me to move on to the next chapter of my career. I left the company and didn't know where I was going to work next. I took my time to think carefully about it and talked to all of my friends and contacts. I interviewed at a million different companies.

Ultimately, I took a job at a company called Fair as Chief Product Officer. There was total chaos, but also really, really, fast growth and adoption. From a kind of product surface area, it was really interesting to me because it provided an opportunity for massive disruption. This was a company that was trying to disrupt auto sales and auto finance.

HOW DID YOU SPEND YOUR TIME AT FAIR?

I spent a lot of time in the beginning putting things in place, such as a career ladder, a process for performance reviews and promotions, a process for hiring and building teams, and an approach to organizing and managing the teams. I sat down with the executive team to come up with company OKRs, which I then used for my team to build our own OKRs, which then ultimately laid the foundation for performance reviews.

I fundamentally believed that the teams would operate better if all of those things were well defined. If it's not there, they spend their time thinking about, "I want to move forward in my career. How am I going to be rewarded? How is what I'm doing measured?" rather than about how to build great products. The basics really matter.

It was also an opportunity to reinstate some of the lessons of the past which were: be really clear about what we're doing, make sure that we communicate dates, and—if we're going to miss a date—be proactive about communicating that. It was great to see how these practices really helped everybody move forward and evolve.

At the same time, I had a side hustle with my former teammate Lance Armstrong to build a community for endurance athletes who really were energized by the idea that suffering has a purpose. It's a surprising phrase, but typically endurance athletes aspire to it. I worked in my spare time to help him build a company called WEDŪ (we do). It is the answer to "Who wants to go ride 100 miles today?" It just took off and has been really successful.

Most recently, I joined Goldman Sachs as CPO. My engineering counterpart at Yahoo joined as their CTO and I'd wanted to work with him again for a while. A common theme throughout my career and the changes that I've made is that there's always been somebody else I had faith in.

WHAT ADVICE DO YOU HAVE FOR PMS WHO WANT TO SUCCEED IN THEIR CAREERS?

It's common to hear "It's all about the people," but it actually really is.

Since very early in my career, even as an athlete, those relationships mattered. You're so dependent on those relationships, not just to be successful, but also to survive the day. My most inspiring memories and the things that I think about the most in the future are really about "Who am I going to work with?"

I've definitely put a lot of effort into relationships. One example is I'd go to company social events and ask people about what they're working on and the challenges they're facing. You learn so much more doing that than you do just talking about what you're working on, because you already know what you're working on.

CHAPTER 38

BRIAN ELLIS

BRIAN ELLIN is the head of City Products at Ride Report. His previous experience includes product lead at Medium, senior product manager at Twitter, and product manager at Janrain. He's passionate about building platforms that promote creativity and inspire people to learn, collaborate, love life, and do good. He has a strong interest in urban mobility and fighting climate change through systemic decarbonization of our global economy.

twitter: @brianellin

HOW DID YOU GET INTO PRODUCT MANAGEMENT?

I studied computer science and decided to move to Oregon when I graduated in 2002. I connected with an entrepreneur through Craigslist and joined his new company, JanRain, as the second engineer. At the time, I was looking for interesting work and to learn how to build and ship real software that people wanted to use.

I worked at JanRain for eight years experimenting and shipping a lot of different things. Ultimately, the company found some success building a platform product for internet identity and cultivating the OpenID protocol.

During my time at JanRain, I would meet with our partners like Google, Yahoo, and Facebook and learn about their needs and their vision for the future. While I was doing that, I got exposed to the incredible products they were building, which inspired me to make a move into a more consumer-facing product role.

In 2010, I moved to San Francisco and joined Twitter's platform team as a product manager. Our goal was to enable app developers, websites and publishers to do more with less. We built APIs, widgets, and platform products that made it easy to do things like share back into Twitter, follow accounts, and build content around tweets. Our work helped bring the best of Twitter to a wider audience off-network, which was super fun and exciting. Later on, I worked on the home timeline team.

After four years, I was ready to do something different. I'd loved working with Ev Williams at the beginning of my time at Twitter and really liked the mission he had at Medium around elevating good ideas and discourse on the internet. I met the team and they were really thoughtful—they were people I wanted to be around and learn from. I joined Medium as the second PM and got to collaborate across the organization on every part of the platform.

WHAT INSPIRED YOU TO FOCUS ON CLIMATE CHANGE?

At that point, after having two kids, my wife and I decided to move back to Portland, Oregon. I joined a startup as the head of product. One day, I was stuck in traffic, and listening to the audiobook of Whole Earth Discipline, by Steward Brand. There was a section about what would need to happen by 2050 to prevent the worst effects of climate change, and it was absolutely extreme. I sat up and thought, "Why isn't everyone freaking out about this and doing everything within their power to take action? I need to go work on that right now." Something clicked, and I decided I needed to start learning more about it.

I read a lot of books, and one of them was *Drawdown*, by Paul Hawken.

> For someone who is new to thinking about climate change, it quantifies a hundred different solutions based on their impact. It provides a framework for thinking about what problem to go work on. And the impact isn't always obvious.

People tend to think about electric cars, but there are fifteen or twenty things that would have a way larger impact—things like refrigeration technology. And so, I created a giant Airtable spreadsheet of sectors and companies and tried to come up with my own impact score for each company.

As a lifelong bicycle commuter and active transit advocate, the company I chose, Ride Report, ended up being a unique fit because we are building a platform that helps city officials implement sustainable policies for transportation. We currently focus on shared bikes and scooters, and in the future will add in more connected vehicles to cover e-commerce deliveries, ride hailing, and things like that. Cities can try out new policies, like creating a protected bike lane or adding more electric vehicles to the right-of-way and learn what impact that has on congestion, safety, equitable access, and climate pollution.

Our company's mission is to accelerate the transition to a sustainable efficient transportation system, which is really exciting for me because it's directly related to my personal mission to improve climate outcomes for future generations. That connection enables me to work with confidence knowing my energy is being directed towards a problem that I care about and know will have an impact.

WHAT ADVICE WOULD YOU HAVE FOR PMS WHO WANT TO SUCCEED IN THEIR CAREERS?

My top piece of advice is to figure out what your mission is and to find companies that are aligned with that mission.

> If you can find a role with a mission that you deeply believe in, you're going to be so much more satisfied. Your work will be more fun, you'll enjoy it more, and you'll learn a lot more.

I encourage people to spend a lot of time thinking about that and searching for it.

Especially as a senior leader, it's really important to be super mission aligned. It not only energizes your own work, but also the work of everyone around you.

> If you feel strongly about a particular mission or about an outcome that you feel needs to exist, I want to encourage you to chase that down. There are opportunities around almost any outcome that you can think of out there.

I'd always been concerned about the environment and climate, but it hadn't occurred to me that I could take my product skills and apply them to the space. I wish I'd known earlier that I could take my personal passion and explore it as a professional opportunity.

OSI IMEOKPARIA

OSI IMEOKPARIA is a VP at Chan Zuckerberg Initiative (CZI) where she leads the technology teams for the Justice & Opportunity Initiative. Most recently prior to CZI, she was the chief product officer for the Hillary for America presidential campaign. Before working in philanthropy or on political campaigns, she was a product leader at Google working on ad tech platforms like Google AdWords and DoubleClick. She began her career in product at a venture-backed consumer startup before moving on to product roles at eBay.

HOW DID YOU GET INTO PRODUCT MANAGEMENT?

When I was at Stanford, I participated in the Mayfield Fellow Program, which is a twelve month entrepreneurship program done in partnership with VCs. This opened my eyes to product management, and I then joined a startup at graduation.

I learned an incredible amount through reading as well as trial and error, but my coworkers and I were all new to PM. I felt like I didn't really have a solid foundation of skills. So when the company started to go bust, I decided to go to eBay, where I knew there were operationally excellent product managers.

WHAT WAS IT LIKE AT EBAY?

I was surprised to see that I knew more than my impostor syndrome had allowed me to believe. I'd learned a bunch at the startup but hadn't realized it because I didn't get positive reinforcement that told me I was doing it right.

At eBay, I could see the progress I'd made, and I could also learn from my incredible colleagues. The VP of Engineering at that time ran an incredibly tight operational ship where we'd launch in 23 companies and across a dozen languages at a time.

I eventually left because I wanted to go live in New York. I had the good fortune to start working at the Google New York office. My first role was in ad tech and I worked on ad tech for 7 ½ of the almost 10 years I was at Google.

HOW WAS BEING A PM AT EBAY DIFFERENT FROM GOOGLE?

At the time, eBay and Google had very different approaches to products.

With eBay, it was much more of a business-driven product management approach, where you would do things like write the business case and work with your business partners to figure out the actual revenue opportunity.

At Google, our collaboration was much more around finding the interesting tech problems. Technology and engineering were much more the center of how decisions and products were launched at Google.

The other material difference is that eBay was a consumer company and the work I did with the Google ads team, DoubleClick acquisition, and larger agency products were enterprise product management.

TELL ME MORE ABOUT YOUR TIME AT GOOGLE, AND HOW YOU MOVED ON AFTER THAT.

At Google, I ended up finding my role as the fix-it person. I went where I could be the most useful. I paid attention to which products the executives were asking for help on. That's how I ended up on the Double-Click acquisition team, which then led to a big opportunity leading an ad server. A bit of that was also driven by the fact that I was in New York and not in Mountain View. Being in a distributed office, my value-add was filling in where there was a need.

The last product that I worked on at Google was in an autonomous unit called "help out." We were trying to start a new consumer brand within Google. It ultimately failed, but it was an incredible opportunity to not only be the product lead but also the team lead.

Finally, after about a decade at Google, I left to join the Hillary Clinton campaign as Chief Product Officer in 2015.

WHAT DOES PM WORK FOR A POLITICAL CAMPAIGN LOOK LIKE?

It was *nothing* like anything that I've done before, and at the same time it was *everything* like things I'd done before.

One of the things that was most surprising was that a lot of the muscles that you use in commercial product management are the same ones that are necessary to deliver products on a political campaign. You were just doing it under much tighter time constraints with way less control. That was both surprising and relieving.

That experience opened my eyes to the ways in which a lot of skills that we have as product managers are applicable across domains. Particularly for me, what I found most compelling was the question of "How can I use product management skills in a civic tech and social impact space?"

That's what landed me at Chan Zuckerberg Initiative (CZI), which is where I am now.

TELL ME MORE ABOUT YOUR WORK AT CZI.

I currently lead the technology team for our justice and opportunity initiative, which covers three main programmatic areas: criminal justice reform, immigration reform and housing affordability. We partner closely with our programmatic and domain experts to shape and understand the "theory of change" for making an impact in those three spaces.

For example, our theory of change for criminal justice could be that decarceration is an important long-term outcome to have, and the lever that's going to help us get there the fastest is by understanding how prosecutors make decisions in this system and then changing that culture and practice of prosecutorial decision-making. The domain experts figure out the strategy and theory of change. My job as the tech lead is to figure out how tech can help support that theory of change, scale that theory of change, or drive more adoption and understanding and awareness of that theory of change.

HOW IS SOCIAL IMPACT WORK DIFFERENT FROM OTHER PM WORK?

There are several ways that social impact work is different.

The way we envision our role at Chan Zuckerberg, our principles are very invested in system change. When you're thinking about changing the 50 year embedded history of criminal justice behaviors, it's going to have a long arc. The work that you put into the world today might not have an outcome that you can measure for five to ten years. The pace and the feedback loops are very different from commercial product management.

When you're dealing with social impact, you're dealing with vulnerable communities. You're dealing with dynamics of power and inclusion and exclusion. You have to be really thoughtful about how you approach conversations, how you approach partnerships, and how you lift up voices that might not otherwise have a seat at the table. Again, that's a very different set of concerns than you would have as a product manager for the AdWords dashboard.

There are big dimensions of how this work is different from what I did in the past, but just like on the campaign, surprisingly, a lot of the same muscles apply. One of the great things about product management is the skill sets that you learn are so durable, in so many different spaces. It allows you to flex in a way that I find really rewarding. You can show up in a lot of different ways and have an impact.

HOW MIGHT A PM KNOW IF SOCIAL IMPACT WORK IS A GOOD MATCH FOR THEM?

You don't know until you try. Trying could be working with a nonprofit in your spare time. There's no shortage of nonprofits and things they need help with. I see a lot of people finding it hard to imagine where they might be useful, but there is no shortage of need. That's a really interesting market failure that somebody should fix.

There's a ton of need in the nonprofit and social impact space for people with technology skills, and specifically with product management skills. Find an issue that you're interested in and call an organization that works on the issue. 99% of the time, there will be a need for a person with technical skills to fill.

There is benefit and power and necessity in having people flow between the domains of social impact work and the commercial side. The best outcome is to have professionals that move across the two fluidly. They'll get robust and rich professional experience because the problem spaces are very different. The work that we do in social impact would not be possible if not for the contributions of engineers and technologists creating products like Stripe and AWS. There is a symbiosis.

WHAT ADVICE WOULD YOU GIVE TO PMS WHO WANT TO ADVANCE IN THEIR CAREERS?

Never feel like you're too good to do something. No matter how seasoned you are in your career, or how long you've been at a company, you should never feel like it's not your job. When you're in management, if necessary, you should roll up your sleeves and get stuff done. That opens up paths that you might not have been thinking of.

As an example, at Google I helped some leaders with a roadmap process. The work was basically spreadsheet gymnastics and it didn't seem ideal for how far I was into my career. But, I was making myself useful. That got me exposure to start working on larger agency products for AdWords.

CHAPTER 40

BANGALY KABA

BANGALY KABA is an executive in residence at Reforge and a scout investor for Sequoia Capital. His previous experience includes VP of Product at Instacart, head of growth at Instagram, senior product manager at Facebook, and senior manager at DirectTV. He's passionate about business model innovation and growth.

twitter: @iambangaly

HOW DID YOU GET INTO PRODUCT MANAGEMENT?

My start in tech was doing my own startup. It was an opportunity to learn what the ecosystem of technology looks like. I had to teach myself how to code, sell my vision and dream to others, and really forge a path. In the early parts of your career, you have to prove your credibility. The startup opened doors for me because people thought my product was interesting and elegant, but I was never able to find product-market-fit.

After that startup failed, which happens often in Silicon Valley but is rarely talked about, I reached out to my network to find my next job. Since they knew me personally and had context on my startup idea, I wrote and asked for advice on what the next steps were to continue on in tech.

What goes unspoken about a lot of career moves is that you need a safe place to land—a place where you feel like you are going to learn and advance your skills, but also be able to find basic comforts and get a salary. A friend of mine from business school was working in DirectTV's Digital Innovation Lab (DLab) and said I should apply.

I joined DirectTV and helped with new product creation in this 30-person group where we were thinking about the future of media consumption. That lab was the right blend for me: it was like a startup but it also allowed me to codify the things I'd learned in my startup.

> Oftentimes in a startup you are just doing things by the seat of your pants. You don't really think about the process and best practices.

At the DLab, I spent time putting pen to paper around how I wanted to lead a product team, how I wanted to think about data visualization, and what my leadership would look like with intentionality.

> The takeaways for me were around getting good at cross functional communication in a structured environment and figuring out how to be a great partner to data and design. I believe that the superpowers of PMs are being great at data visualization and understanding how to tell the story through data.

HOW DID YOU FIND YOUR NICHE IN GROWTH?

A friend from college submitted my resume to Facebook's internal referral tool, and I was able to get through their very rigorous interview process. I only expected to be there for two years (and then join another startup), but I ultimately stayed for four and a half years. I chose to work on growth because Facebook had built the first consumer product growth team and I knew that it would be the best place to learn a skill that I believed every tech company would eventually need.

> Your career is going to take you to different places, but the best thing you can do is to lean into the strengths of the company you're at. If your company is world class at something, then you should become world class at that thing. You can springboard your career off the back of that competency.

Product management is a very high EQ and high skilled job, but the differentiation in various product management roles is hard to understand. The extent to which you can carve a niche for yourself can make you more hireable and more desirable.

In my case, there's only about two handfuls of PMs who have been in a leadership position for a company that's crossed a billion users. And so, that was my niche.

WHAT LED YOU TO MOVE FROM THE FACEBOOK GROWTH TEAM TO INSTAGRAM?

I worked on the Facebook Growth Team for two years. It was challenging because it was very demanding, and they didn't focus on people development at that time. I didn't feel supported. I felt like I was running 1,000 miles an hour, but not progressing. That was a pretty seminal time in my career because I had to figure out a framework for thinking about if I should leave and why I should leave.

> I had an epiphany one day—my impact at a place was equal to the product of my personal abilities multiplied by the environment.

My personal abilities were the product of my ability to communicate, to execute, to think strategically, to work cross functional teams, and so on. But, the environment was the multiplicative product of things like manager support, resourcing, scope, fairness of evaluation, etc.

If any of the things in the environmental bucket were effectively zero, it didn't matter how much harder I worked on the personal side. The impact would still net out to zero. When I articulated this, I was able to have an honest conversation with myself about the extent to which I believed I could change any of those environmental factors.

I decided to leave the Facebook group and looked at jobs elsewhere. I chose Instagram because it gave me a foundation in terms of being able to stay in the same company with the same infrastructure and communication tools, while pivoting to a new product. I felt like the product was well-loved and ripe for having a breakout, but was also still small and needed the right people.

People internally thought it was a terrible move for me because at the time, Instagram was known for being "design first." The founders had only reluctantly decided to start a growth organization. It turns out it was the perfect lucky opportunity for me.

Because the founders were very design focused and focused on doing the right thing for the customer, it made me a better product manager and product leader. Facebook had a history and reputation of doing whatever it took to grow.

The founders of Instagram were unwilling to compromise the quality of the product for the sake of growth. If we had two options—one with a worse user experience but would increase monthly active users by ten million annually, and another with a far better experience but would only increase by seven million—we would ship the latter. We would leave the three million on the table to offer a better experience.

> I believe over the long term that kind of decision-making—based on product principles and real jobs to be done by users—pays dividends, because the product feels more intentional and less spammy.
>
> Another thing that made this a great outcome was that the team was very small and there was no pressure. It was counterintuitive, but the smaller team effectively allowed us and forced us to focus on what really mattered.

Instead of doing all the things, we could only do a handful of things really, really well. I work in a space where if you don't execute perfectly, nothing works. You have to execute perfectly end to end. I was able to spend time with people and take the time to change the processes and culture without having the founders questioning why we weren't growing fast enough.

WHAT WAS YOUR TIME LEADING GROWTH AT INSTAGRAM LIKE?

Growth is effectively a product group that focuses on what we call the adjacent user.[1] Instead of the power user, it's the person who is struggling to adopt the product. In order to build for them, you need to build products in a way that really solves pain points for people at every step.

When I arrived, the team had just shipped a new registration flow and was planning to move on to the next thing. I convinced them that we needed to change those plans by showing them how there was so much more work to be done. We ended up working on improving registration really intensely for 18 months. I sat down with people and showed them how to think about each step from the lens of the adjacent user.

---

1   Kaba has expanded on this via a guest post on Andrew Chen's blog at https://andrewchen.co/the-adjacent-user-theory/

I explained the importance of implementing logging. We brainstormed around the dropoff on each step. We went over the difference between things that were practical versus beautiful. I helped build reinforcing communication structures so we would learn from whatever we launched.

At the beginning of that time, 65% of people who started registration completed it. We got it up to 95%, which is huge for a registration flow that has 1.5 million people going through it a day. That's orders of magnitude more people who experienced the product for the first time, and it was one of many dramatic improvements we made to our signup, activation, and other core flows for new and resurrected users.

That experience was fantastic. For me, it became a signature win at a known brand because we were able to reach a monumental milestone at a company.

> When I think about career moves, what I recommend to people is to look for the conditions that are right for a signature win. That's more important than optimizing for the title.

After that, the product was doing well and there was a ton of opportunity. I was able to show how we were leaving so much on the table due to lack of resources and lack of people. I made a case that helped us get some of the headcount that we needed. From there, my scope grew naturally and I became a people manager.

I don't want to make it seem like this was all perfectly organic though. I certainly had to self-advocate for things like recognition. What I'd say was important there was having monthly conversations with my manager about professional development and progress towards personal and team goals. I also needed to explicitly call out the constraints under which work got done so that people didn't underestimate the challenge.

For example, my first year at Instagram we grew almost 50%, which was much better than anyone expected. My first-half review reflected that but my second-half review didn't, although we'd done even better during the second half. And, I'd accomplished that while going on parental leave for six weeks and setting up the team so I didn't need a backfill.

> There was a clear gap of awareness of what it took to accomplish those things. Some of that gap was on me and some of that was on the people around me, but it was a good lesson for me about the importance of shared clarity and alignment.

WHAT LED YOU TO MOVE ON FROM INSTAGRAM?

When the founders left Instagram, I needed to decide as a leader if I was willing to make a commitment for the long haul. I felt like if I stayed relatively long at Instagram beyond when the founders left, I owed it to my team to see that through. I had built a great team that could do the work without me, I had a clear successor, and I had a really strong team with really strong processes. I felt like I'd maximized my time at Facebook.

I moved to Instacart as VP of Product because I felt like it was a great opportunity. It appealed to me that they had a huge market and they were the strategic leader. Unfortunately I was very burned out after years of grinding at FB Inc and not taking care of my body. I should have taken time off between roles, and, after a year at Instacart, I decided to take the time to work on my health and spend time with my kids (much more than I ever imagined due to COVID!).

WHAT ADVICE WOULD YOU GIVE TO PMS WHO WANT TO ADVANCE IN THEIR CAREERS?

> Early in your career, you really need to build a lot of muscle around product sense and building things that have clear user value and solve jobs to be done in a simple and impactful way for users.

One way to do that is to be around strong thinkers who can push you to think from first principles by breaking down opportunities to their atomic units, prioritizing and executing effectively, editing down the scope of your product to what really matters, and incorporating a sense of craft and delight. Essentially, you need to be able to take a wide open canvas and figure out how to think about it, identify the right segments, and come up with a solution that's meaningful and differentiated. And you do that again and again with less help over time.

> For mid-career PMs, two things matter: the ability to create and get buy-in around a great strategy and the ability to drive cross functional influence.

Cross-functional influence is really about building relationships and building strong communication channels. There's a lot of overlap with networking for a job search. A lot of things get done behind the scenes in every company. If I'm going to create a new strategy for the growth of Instagram, I'm not going to show up and just deliver this whole thing to the founders and everyone without getting some buy-in or early thinking. You have to understand how to get the right cues so you're not reading the room for the first time during your final presentation.

WHAT HAS HELPED YOU AS A LEADER?

One of the things that was most helpful for me was getting an executive coach.

Finding the right person who fits your communication style and your operating style matters, but they're also valuable because they've seen so much. The challenge is, the more senior you get, the more lumpy the cadence is for seeing certain types of problems. A coach can help you pattern match and work through them.

I've also worked with my coach on professional development the same way I would with a manager, talking about what I want to achieve and breaking down the steps to get there.

> There are challenges, especially in careers like product, where understanding the nuance of certain situations and having shared cultural context is helpful.

I mentor a lot of people of color and women on how to navigate a situation as someone who's not of the majority group in the room. It's helpful to have a coach who's aware of those dynamics and will be honest about it. For example, there are common challenges around how to give feedback and express concerns in a way that you won't be unduly criticized for.

> Another challenge is finding a sponsor. The notion of becoming a sponsor is predicated on pattern matching for people who look like you. What I've learned is that I need to ask for sponsorship.[2]

I've had the sponsorship conversation as part of a professional development question where they ask what I care about in my career. I'd say, "It really matters to me that I'm on a clear path towards this level and this set of scope. I believe that I need sponsorship to get there. I want to know if you're willing to be the sponsor for me or if you can help me figure out how I can achieve that." You have to be explicit about your goals and be your own advocate to break through to the executive levels of an organization.

---

2   Read more about sponsorship in "Sponsorship" on pg 382

CHAPTER 41

SARA MAUSKOPF

SARA MAUSKOPF is the CEO and cofounder of Winnie (winnie.com), a marketplace for daycare and preschool helping millions of parents across the United States. Sara has a background in consumer technology and product management. Prior to founding Winnie, she was the director of product at Postmates, and prior to that held product leadership roles at Twitter, YouTube, and Google. She graduated with a computer science and engineering degree from MIT. She's also a mom of three young children.

twitter: @sm

HOW DID YOU GET INTO PRODUCT MANAGEMENT?

I went to MIT and studied computer science. The cool thing to do at the time when I graduated was to get a job at Google. A lot of people were interviewing for engineering positions, but I hadn't taken very many coding-heavy classes and wasn't sure I could pass the engineering interview. I'd taken a lot of math and theoretical computer science classes. At the time, Google was hiring for a position that was a cross between product management and partnerships. I interviewed for that and got the job. And so, I moved out to California and started working for Google.

I realized that I liked the product management aspects of the job more than the partner management aspects, so I started looking for true product manager positions after three years at Google. I was a big Twitter user at the time and a few of my friends had left Google to go there.

Twitter was hiring for a product manager position on the internal tools team. I thought it would be a great way to get started as a product manager, because the stakes were a little lower. I'd be building tools for the company instead of millions of users. It was a great experience.

> When you join a growing company, there will be more positions that open up and more opportunities.

At one point, the VP of Product had left the company and I looked for a team where I could work on the core product. I found a more experienced PM who took me under his wing and said I could work with his team. When a new product leader came, I was already working on the core product.

> One of the things I learned was that if you can find people and build relationships with them, they will help you. Especially if you're working hard, capable, and smart, they'll give you opportunities to try things out. Take those opportunities to prove yourself.

I ended up spending four years at Twitter as a product manager. I got to grow with the company and manage teams.

WHAT LED YOU TO MOVE ON FROM TWITTER?

I had an amazing career at Twitter. I was rising super fast. Then, I suddenly stopped rising at that rate. I went to an exec and asked what was going on. He said to me, "You're good, but you're not one of those world class guys yet." That phrase hit me and I thought, "Whoa, you only promoted guys to those director positions. There are no women in those roles… because you think that to be world class… you have to be a guy." And so I left.

I joined Postmates as their head of product, reporting to the CEO, and I got to build my product team from scratch. I'd been talking to the CEO for a few months, mostly as a big user of the product. I've always found that when I'm really authentic and I really do like a product or respect a person, they are usually able to give me at least a few minutes if I reach out directly.

I was looking for opportunities where the team was small enough that they would take a chance on me as a product leader, but not so small that the company wouldn't be around in a couple of months. I wanted some job security and some brand reputation associated with the company. I also really wanted to work for a company where I knew the people were very solid.

All of that turned out to be true at Postmates. My current cofounder at Winnie, our head of engineering, and one of our salespeople are all from Postmates. They were really amazing people and I was excited to work with them again.

WHAT INSPIRED YOU TO START YOUR OWN COMPANY?

It was not long into my time at Postmates that I became pregnant and then had my first daughter. I was there about a year when I went out on maternity leave, and I had every intention of my daughter having absolutely no impact on my life or career aspirations.

Of course, like many other parents, I had no idea what I was getting into. My desire to go back to work didn't change, but the problems I cared about solving really did change. The kind of culture and environment I wanted to work at changed. I wanted to go to work, do my best work for the limited hours I was in the office, and then go home and turn off work entirely. Postmates has its busiest hours at night and on the weekends, which was exactly the time I didn't want to be working.

At the same time, I was talking to my coworker, who is now my cofounder at Winnie. We were both bonding over the struggles of working parents and all the things we had to balance. We realized there was an opportunity to actually work on these problems. We decided to quit our jobs and started working on Winnie in January 2016.

> I'd never seen myself as a founder. What motivated me was that there was no company solving this problem.

Parents struggle to find childcare providers (such as daycares and preschools) with capacity and many providers don't even have a web presence. Providers who have excess space struggle to find parents. The opportunity was so big that I just couldn't wrap my head around how I could not do this. It felt like my cofounder and I were uniquely positioned to solve this problem at the intersection of technology and childcare. If we didn't do this, we were passing on a massive opportunity in front of us.

HOW MIGHT A PM KNOW IF BEING A FOUNDER AND CEO WOULD BE A GOOD MATCH FOR THEM?

> Now that I am a CEO, I've learned that it is not even close to being a product manager.

In fact, I don't even work on the product here at Winnie. My cofounder is the chief product officer and I sometimes don't see product improvements until our users see them. Sometimes, my product background even hinders my ability to see solutions that are not about building product but more about building a team.

> The way I think of the CEO role is that you're always working on the next thing for the company and figuring out what should be next.

Right now, I'm spending all my time doing sales, operations and marketing. I'm trying to figure out what teams we put in place to manage those critical but newer functions.

Once I spend long enough doing these jobs, I should either figure out that we need to make an investment here in actual people, or that these are not jobs worth doing. I would say 50% of my time is doing things that I end up deciding are not worth anyone's time. They're the least significant things in the company to do. And the other 50% are realizing that these are actually jobs to be done and they need to be part of someone's role. They need to be hired for or we need to somehow make it so that this work gets done.

My take is that if people actually knew what being a founder was like, fewer people would want to attempt it. It's really, really challenging. But at the end of the day, there's also nothing I'd rather be doing right now with my time. I'm really motivated by the problem I'm solving and the impact I'm having.

WHAT DO YOU THINK MAKES A SUCCESSFUL FOUNDER?

> The key difference between successful founders and unsuccessful founders is often just perseverance.

There's a "trough of despair" that new companies frequently hit where all signs point to the fact that you should quit. You've run out of money. You've run out of employees. Everything is going wrong. You're going to get so many signs that this is no longer something you could possibly feasibly continue working on, and there has to be that speck of motivation that tells you, "Just give it one more try. Keep going for a little longer." That speck is sometimes the difference between success and failure.

There are so many better ways to accomplish fame and fortune than this. So many easier, more foolproof ways.

WHAT ADVICE WOULD YOU GIVE TO A PM WHO WANTS TO ADVANCE IN THEIR CAREER?

One is to get experience outside of your core PM job, because it will make you a better PM. Answer support tickets. Join sales calls. That will expand your brain and make you so much better at what you're trying to do as a product manager and eventually any other job that you want to do.

Understand how the financials of your company work. I spent absolutely no time caring about financials when I was working at these massive companies like Google and Twitter. It turns out, what I spend the majority of my time on as a CEO is just making sure we have enough money in the bank for a long enough time. Having those experiences will help you advance your career and make connections that other people won't see or think of.

Don't be afraid to roll up your sleeves and get your hands dirty. Some of those jobs may feel below you, but they can be great experiences.

Finally, focus on the people more than the results. Focus on how you can help the engineers and designers you're working with every day to be successful. Focus on how you can help the other product managers be successful. It's not just about the success you achieve; it's about how you help other people achieve success.

CHAPTER 42

KEN NORTON

KEN NORTON is director of product at Figma. Before that, he was senior operating partner at GV (originally Google Ventures) where he led investing operations and provided product and engineering support to GV's portfolio companies. His experience includes group product manager at Google, vice president of products at JotSpot, and leading product management at Yahoo. Ken has written extensively about the craft of product management. His classic essay *How To Hire a Product Manager* became the playbook for a generation of product managers.[1]

kennorton.com | twitter: @kennethn

HOW DID YOU GET INTO PRODUCT MANAGEMENT?

I started my career as an engineer and startup founder. I was a member of the Snap founding team. After NBC invested, Snap became NBC Internet and I was promoted to CTO of NBC Internet. While I was there, I built sites like News.com and Download.com. My title was CTO, but that included a lot of work we'd call product management. I was responsible for strategic product planning, corporate technical direction, and management.

From there, I wanted to get back to a startup so I cofounded Grand Central Communications, which was an early cloud integration platform startup. I then went to Inktomi to lead search product strategy. When Yahoo acquired Inktomi, I became senior director of product management for the search products.

After three years, I wanted to go to a small company again and joined Jotspot as VP of product. Jotspot was acquired by Google and our product offering was folded into G Suite as Google Sites and Google Docs.

During my years as a product manager at Google, I was the product lead for Google Mobile Maps, Google Calendar, and Google Docs. I was an early member of the Google Apps team that ultimately became G Suite. It was really rewarding because I helped grow the enterprise business from its early beta state to millions of corporate users.

---

1   Read Ken's essay at https://www.kennorton.com/essays/productmanager.html

WHAT LED YOU TO GOOGLE VENTURES?

I had been at Google for a long time and was wondering if I wanted to get back into the startup world, but I still really loved the culture and people at Google. Moving to Google Ventures (GV) was great because I could move closer to startups and at the same time be a part of the Google platform and take advantage of everything that Google has.

I don't think I would have gone into venture if it hadn't been for GV. The traditional kind of venture capital environment wasn't as appealing to me. It was really just this unique kind of combination of opportunity, luck, and timing.

DO PMS GENERALLY DO WELL IN VC FIRMS?

> Product people make great investors because we naturally have a generalist approach to the world. Investing requires the ability to see something from a lot of different perspectives—being able to know enough about business growth, product market fit, the technology, and the direction the industry is going to go.

Most PMs who make the leap into VC become investors, but there are other interesting roles as well. Some venture firms, including GV, have operating partners that aren't investors who work side-by-side with investors to help the portfolio companies. For earlier stage companies, they might help them find product-market fit. For later stage companies, they might help operationally think about go-to-market, structuring their team, and their processes.

Another role is for people who are thinking about starting a company. You can do the entrepreneur-in-residence route, where you spend time at a venture firm helping them think about the industry, helping them develop a perspective, and helping them with a thesis around a particular opportunity. You use your expertise to help them make investment decisions and then potentially start your own thing.

HOW MIGHT A PM KNOW IF A ROLE AT A VC FIRM MIGHT BE GOOD FOR THEM?

Venture capital isn't right for everyone. It's important to understand the difference between being a hands-on product manager and being in a venture firm.

The first thing is that venture capital is kind of a lonely job. You don't work with a team; you're on your own.

The second thing is that as a PM you get used to being accountable for your product. In venture, you're a step removed from the important decisions, and for good reasons.

> A mistake that former product people make is they try to act like they're still product managers. They'll either try to run the products or do a "swoop and poop," where they go way too deep into product decisions and then disappear to go spend time with other companies. That can really distract and randomize the companies.

As a VC, you are the steward of other people's capital. Your primary job is to make sure that capital makes money. You should be a resource to your companies when they need you. One day, you might help them hire a VP of Sales, the next day, you might connect them to another CEO to unlock a partnership, and the day after that, you help them raise the next round of fundraising. You have to be a Swiss Army knife.

> One area PMs struggle with is the long-term perspective. The exit is what really matters in the long term and it takes five to seven years to know the exit.

Anything that feels measurable in the short term is not the thing that really matters. No one is going to care in ten years if your portfolio had a killer product that was incredible but it failed. What really matters is whether it was a good investment. You are ultimately measured by whether you return money to your LPs.[2]

WHAT ADVICE DO YOU HAVE FOR PMS WHO WANT TO ADVANCE IN THEIR CAREERS?

Luck is a big part of it. People who joined super fast growing companies right before the company exploded saw their careers take off. They were great, but they were also strapped to the side of a rocket ship.

> My advice to earlier stage PMs is to find a strong brand that's growing. It's going to give you lots of opportunity for growth. You're going to get to live and learn so much faster because you're faced with the challenges of scale and growth. Chances are you'll be surrounded by other great people that you can learn from. And, those people will go on to do great things elsewhere. They'll become part of your network later in your career.

Flexibility is also a big part of it. Really good PMs find important things that need to be done and volunteer to lead them. I've seen people say, "Hey, our customer experience is bad. I'm going to raise my hand to go build the customer experience team for the next year, because that's the biggest key to us being successful." You have to be able to contribute in areas that you didn't consider to be part of your job. If you're rigid in your view of what a PM does, you'll miss a lot of the best opportunities in fast growing companies.

As you advance, you have to think about where you're trying to go and whether the moves you're making connect with where you want to be in five years. People sometimes go off the rails a little bit caring about the sexiness of the product or their title. As PMs, we fall in love with the product and tend to be blind to the company's culture, whether a business can be built around that product, and whether there's access to the capital necessary to continue building. And, especially if you're coming from a company like Google or Facebook, you can get a VP title anywhere, but you might have less impact than what you're doing now.

---

2   LPs are limited partners—the people or institutions whose money is being invested

CHAPTER 43

ANUJ RATHI

ANUJ RATHI is VP of product at Swiggy, India's largest food delivery marketplace. At Swiggy, he leads revenue and growth products for consumers and restaurant partners, and new offerings for the company. He's worked with Indian e-commerce companies leading product management for their buyer experience (Flipkart and Snapdeal), and with Walmart.com in California for their multi-channel offerings.

twitter: @anujrathi

HOW DID YOU GET INTO PRODUCT MANAGEMENT?

I was a chemical engineering graduate from IIT Kanpur in 2005 and I always knew that I wanted to build something for consumers on the internet. I started as a front end engineer at a couple of startups and developed a deep empathy for the consumer.

Around that time, Flipkart had started in India, selling books like Amazon. During my interview, the CEO said he thought I'd be great as a product manager. I thought product management would mean I wouldn't be a builder anymore, so I initially resisted—but he insisted. That's how I became a product manager by accident. I've never looked back.

When I joined Flipkart, I saw that nobody had time to look through all the user flows and connect the dots. So, I thought of myself as two things:

- The fluid that connects all of the different areas: business, engineering, leadership, strategy, and so on.
- The subject matter expert on e-commerce.

At the time, India didn't really have product managers, so a few of us decided that we had to set the tone for product management in India. Companies were borrowing concepts from Silicon Valley, but they weren't borrowing the cultural aspects. Founders and CEOs wanted to manage things in a very hands-on way, and they didn't know how to trust a product manager.

> It's still a little tougher to be a product manager in India because you're not only building up your own career, but you also have to develop other people's trust in product management and teach them what to expect from a product manager.

WHAT LED YOU TO WALMART LABS AND SNAPDEAL?

I moved to Walmart Labs because, while Flipkart was doing great, I wanted to see a company at a global scale. I used to lead Store Services, which included anything that started online and ended offline or that started offline and got home-delivered (such as Pharmacy, Photos, or Tires). It was a big charter with big revenue potential. I thought it was great—and it was, if you're only looking for impact. But at the time, it was not great for moving fast. I was still young; I wanted to make a huge impact and didn't want to wait.

I was really getting good at e-commerce, so that's when I joined Snapdeal. It was one of the up-and-coming startups in India. It had the sharpest rise and the largest fall.

I joined as an associate vice president, leading buyers experience. I started with a few PMs reporting to me and grew the team multifold.

When you lead a team of product managers, it's a big responsibility. The decisions you make on strategy need to make sense. You need to think through all of the alternatives and be able to explain why you're deploying capital and manpower in a certain way or why you're prioritizing someone else's project. People need to understand your reasoning and be bought into it so they can explain it to their own teams.

> What success looks like for me is not only building products, but actually developing great product managers. I think the way the Indian startup ecosystem will create great consumer products is if some leaders put in the effort to help build great product managers.

WHAT LED YOU TO SWIGGY?

After Snapdeal, I joined Swiggy, a food delivery app. When I joined, it was very small. I'd been doing e-commerce for a long time and I thought food delivery would be simple compared to what I'd done before.

The complexity with food delivery is that not only do you need to match buyers, sellers, and drivers in real time, but there are also millions of product combinations as well. You have a perishable commodity that is deteriorating with time. You might think you want to eat pizza, but end up buying pasta. The platforms which are most successful are the ones which don't only get you to what you want to buy, but also what the platforms need to sell.

I love this. This problem will keep me interested for the next ten years.

WHAT ARE YOUR THOUGHTS ON PRODUCT MANAGEMENT IN INDIA?

Before 2016, a lot of leaders of product companies came from non-technology companies. They didn't know what product management, or even software development, was, and so PMs would spend a lot of time influencing leadership and convincing them of the value of product management. It was easy for traditional leaders to play to their strength and neglect the technology part. What I've seen is that some PMs got frustrated with that and moved to companies in the US.

But, since around 2016, things have been changing. A lot of good product people have been starting to settle here. The market is huge and the potential is immense. The challenges are complex: there are 25 different languages, a wide variety of age groups, infrastructural challenges, fraud, and so on. As a product person, you have to solve these really challenging problems and it's very exciting, but also a little tough.

> I feel very passionately that if India's startup ecosystem is going to evolve, India's product leaders have to be really, really good. They have to be independent, not just copying another product or taking business requirements.

I want to build an engine of people who can build an engine of people who are all strong, independent product thinkers. When I work with product managers at Swiggy, I'm not training them just for Swiggy; I'm hoping they will help evolve the entire startup ecosystem.

WHAT ADVICE DO YOU HAVE FOR PEOPLE WHO WANT TO ADVANCE IN THEIR CAREER?

If you're an early stage product manager, think about what the next five years will look like for you. Don't think in short-term spurts. If you think about what sector you want to be in, you can plan out the skills you need to develop and which companies or people will help you get there.

Three things are important for product management:

1. To have a lot of grit and passion. With grit comes curiosity and not giving up.

2. Superior written and verbal communication, leading to proper influence. You'll need to represent your product, your company, and your stakeholders with your communication.

3. Problem identification and solving. Product management isn't just about connecting engineers to designers; it's about solving problems.

> At mid-career, you can decide if you want to be a specialist or generalist. If you want to be a generalist, you should make sure you're a generalist who has enough expertise to solve the problems of an entire industry.

For example, with e-commerce, there are seven big areas, including search, reviews, and payments. You can spend six months going deep into each area. Every quarter, when we discuss the review scores of product managers on my team, I'm looking to see them dive deep in a field.

As a PM, you're both very creative and very scientific at the same time.

You break down observations into why and how they happened, which leads to insights. A single insight can lead to multiple hypotheses (how can I use this insight to change behaviour?). A single hypothesis could be (in)validated through different experiments or rollouts. Experiments lead to more observations. It's a loop!

You think about human psychology and habits. Over time, as you follow this process, you start understanding patterns that are specific to your business or industry.

> As a product person, you should be trying to become the best person to understand how the system works and how you can make it work better. Keep evolving your frameworks. Everything else revolves around that.

CHAPTER 44

SACHIN REKHI

SACHIN REKHI is the CEO and founder of Notejoy, a collaborative notes app for you and your team. Prior to Notejoy, Sachin founded Connected (a personal relationship manager) and Anywhere.FM (a web music player later acquired by imeem). He's been an entrepreneur-in-residence at Trinity Ventures and head of Sales Solution Products at LinkedIn. Sachin held marketing, product management, and engineering roles at Microsoft, Paetec Communications, and Goldman Sachs.

SachinRekhi.com

HOW DID YOU GET INTO PRODUCT MANAGEMENT?

I studied computer science at the University of Pennsylvania and got a business degree from Wharton. My initial plan was to spend a few years doing software engineering and then move into the world of entrepreneurship.

Talking to a recruiter at Microsoft was the first time I heard about the product management role. I realized the part I love most about software is building solutions to solve people's real world problems. So, I ended up deciding to do a PM internship at Microsoft and then joined Microsoft full time as a PM.

HOW DID YOU GO FROM MICROSOFT INTO ENTREPRENEURSHIP?

I always saw Microsoft as a place where I'd learn how software was developed in the real world so I'd be better prepared to go start my own company. If you go straight to a career in entrepreneurship, you spin your wheels on what you should do. I saw that at imeem—they didn't have any bug prioritization process and just had an email address to collect bugs. I always advise people who want to be entrepreneurs to spend two years at an established tech company first.

While I was at Microsoft, I used to riff on startup ideas with a group of friends. One of my buddies came to me one day and said we should go start a company. I'd just gotten promoted and didn't want to leave, but he told me he was going to start something with or without me. I knew finding the right cofounders was the most important part of starting a company so I made the hard call and decided to leave Microsoft.

We had no idea what startup we were going to start at the time. Along with a third friend from Amazon, we sat in a room and just started coming up with ideas. We presented our top idea to Paul Graham at Y Combinator. He thought it was a terrible idea but liked us as a team, so he gave us two weeks to come up with a new idea.

At the time—this was in 2006, before Rdio and Spotify—we noticed that when you're in the office and wanted to listen to music, you had two options. One was putting in earphones on an iPod, even though you're sitting in front of this big monitor. Or, you could use a service like Pandora, which wasn't your own music. Our thought was, what if you took your entire music collection from your computer, uploaded it to the web, and then played it through this robust internet web music player. That was the idea behind Anywhere.FM.

We ultimately sold Anywhere.FM to imeem, another music company.

WHAT WAS IT LIKE AT IMEEM?

When I got there, I realized that while they had deals with all four major labels, the biggest challenge was that they were prohibitively expensive. We were losing way more money than we were making. I realized the company was dead unless we figured out monetization. Even though they'd hired us to be feature PMs and UI PMs, I told them I really wanted to solve the monetization problem because otherwise we'd be dead in the water.

What we ended up doing was building a completely new audio ad format. This was before Spotify, when everyone was just doing banner ads. We made an audio ad unit with an eight second audio ad on top of a banner ad. It was a new product innovation. And then we got the complete runaround when we were going to sell it.

We went to all the classic marketing ad agencies, but the digital division told us to talk to the radio division and the radio division told us to talk to the digital division. We didn't know how to sell it. We ultimately figured out we could rebrand it as a rich media banner so we could sell it to the digital division. I eventually built it up to a multi million revenue line. Unfortunately, it was too little on the monetization side too late. Ultimately, imeem did sell to MySpace music, but it wasn't a big exit.

WHAT LED YOU TO TRINITY VENTURES?

I knew I wanted to start another company, but I wanted to be a lot more thoughtful this time around. One of the venture capitalists at Trinity Ventures suggested I join them and think of my startup idea as an entrepreneur in residence.

At Trinity Ventures, I came up with a framework which I describe as the eight hypotheses of product market fit.[1] This was the lens I used to figure out for each idea I came up with whether it was worth pursuing.

1. Who's the target customer you're going after?

2. What is the problem you're solving?

3. What is your core value proposition?

4. What's your strategic differentiation?

---

1   Sachin expands on this at https://www.sachinrekhi.com/a-lean-alternative-to-a-business-plan-documenting-your-product-market-fit-hypotheses

5. Who is your competition?

6. What's your go-to-market strategy of how you're going to attract customers?

7. How are you going to monetize?

8. What are your North Star metrics?

I'd write these up in 1-2 pages for each startup idea.

> That framework was really important and ultimately kept with me, even for building a feature inside a larger company. It helps a PM to be far more strategic upfront.

I went through that process, and then came up with the idea for Connected. The interesting insight from Connected was that it combined my obsession with productivity tools with what I learned from working with salespeople at imeem. I noticed that the salespeople who were closing all our big deals were innately relationship-oriented. When we visited New York, they'd scroll through their iPhone and invite people to catch up and grab a drink. That catch-up would turn into a business meeting and then into a sale.

Our idea was a contact management tool that would not only keep your contacts up-to-date, it would help you build better rapport and maintain those relationships.

HOW DID YOU END UP AT LINKEDIN?

After launching and running Connected for about a year and a half, LinkedIn reached out to us for an acquisition. They told us initially that they'd treat us as a startup and leave us alone, but it turned out that couldn't have been further from the truth. LinkedIn was only 1800 people, but it operated much more like Microsoft than it did a startup.

> My cofounder Ada and I transitioned our style to being much more like Microsoft. Influencing without authority was really important. Executive management was really important. Managing all the stakeholders was super important.

That ultimately made us really successful. LinkedIn then did a series of acquisitions that unfortunately weren't as successful.

WHAT DID YOU LEARN FROM THIS?

> Their biggest learning was that going from a small startup to a large company works only if the founders have worked at a large company before. You really can't maintain, "We will treat you as a startup within the larger company."

I ended up mentoring a bunch of PMs from the other acquisitions on how to be effective at the executive leadership pieces, such as getting resources, cutting through red tape, and how to be compelling with different kinds of people.

While I was there, I kept telling LinkedIn that we should be going after sales professionals directly. I started a small project with a few engineers and got a chance to present it to an executive off-site.

LinkedIn saw our project and said we needed to launch it aggressively. So we ended up launching and grew the team from 8 to 500, including 400 people in direct sales. During my tenure there it grew to about $200 million in revenue. I went from being an IC PM to being GM of a division and managing a public P&L. Every week I met with the CFO, and if our forecast was 10% off from the actual, I got grilled on it.

WHAT INSPIRED YOU TO START NOTEJOY?

I was doing quite well at LinkedIn as the GM of the division, but it wasn't as rewarding to me as being down in the trenches. So, even though I was excelling, I knew I wanted to return to my roots of starting a company.

I started Notejoy with my wife, Ada. We realized the reason we work so well together is because we have complementary skill sets. I lead product, design and engineering. She leads growth, analytics, marketing, legal, finance, accounting, operations, and everything else. That makes a clear separation of roles and responsibilities and works really well.

The insight for Notejoy came from my experience at LinkedIn. We found that 90% of the information people needed to know to do their job well stayed in email, in Slack, or in their heads. So much institutional knowledge was being lost. Our idea was to build a tool that you could use from the beginning of the project that scaled with you to that team collaboration scenario. That thesis has proven out and we now have teams that use us for all sorts of use cases.

It's been super fun to return to my roots in entrepreneurship. What I love about it is that every day my job is different. I'm worrying about monetization versus user acquisition versus core feature development. I talk to my customers every single day. I do a bunch of customer support. I'm absolutely loving it.

HOW WOULD A PM KNOW IF BECOMING A FOUNDER AND CEO MIGHT BE A GOOD PATH FOR THEM?

There are a bunch of dimensions of being a CEO that you don't really experience in a classic product management role. One is P&L responsibility. You have to be very sensitive to costs, such as hiring and server costs. The CEO ultimately owns the budget. Another big difference is that the CEO ends up being the de facto head of sales. Customers want to talk to the CEO.

One of the common things I hear from PMs is that they hate having to spend a lot of time on executive management, influence without authority, and coordination meetings. If that's you, I don't think you'd want to become a CEO because you're still going to have that huge coordination role. There's no getting out of it.

> A big part of enjoying the CEO role is having a deep self awareness of what parts you like and don't like, and what parts you're good and not good at. Initially, you're just going to have to do it all. But you can very quickly get to the point where you realize what your strengths and passions are, and build the right team around you to really solve for it.

Another thing is that too many people conflate starting a company with going down the traditional VC-funded path. Many entrepreneurs assume they have autonomy, but as soon as you take funding and have a board, a board member is worse than any boss that you have ever had.

Notejoy is 100% bootstrapped. We had the opportunity to raise funding, but we chose a bootstrapped process. It changes the very nature of what it means to be an entrepreneur and how you run your company. It enables the company to be much more oriented around our values—for example, not launching until something meets my quality bar, or growing the company at a pace that we think makes sense.

WHAT ADVICE WOULD YOU GIVE TO PMS WHO WANT TO ADVANCE IN THEIR CAREERS?

The first thing is realizing there's so many different kinds of PM roles, and really trying to figure out which one's right for you.

- **A builder** is your classic feature PM, responsible for taking an existing product and coming up with new features to delight the end user. The builder is about talking to and delighting customers. It's really about the customer experience.

- **A tuner PM** is an optimization PM, like a growth or monetization PM. It's much more analytically rigorous and is higher velocity in terms of A/B tests. It's much more about the metrics. If you love being a builder PM, you might not like being a tuner PM.

- **The innovator PM** is about building a brand new product for a new audience. There's a lot of uncertainty in being an innovator. Your project might fail. Maybe the audience was wrong. A lot of people try it and realize they're happier as a builder with more clear wins.

Even if your aspiration is to be an innovator PM, start as a builder PM.

> Early in your career, it's important to get some wins under your belt. I've met PMs that worked at three startups and none of them became household names. Now they're struggling to get that role in a larger company. Innovation roles don't do much to help build your credibility as a successful PM unless they succeed.

Early on in your career, I'd encourage people to try all three roles in a larger company like Facebook, Dropbox, or Airbnb. There are plenty of opportunities to move around every 18 months or so and try something different.

Another dimension is consumer versus B2B. As a consumer PM, you end up in graphs and data. As a B2B PM, you end up talking to a lot of customers and having a relationship with them. I've found B2B to be closer to the idea of delighting customers.

The final dimension is the size of the company. At a small company you do a lot of the pieces yourself. At a large company, you have a UX writer, a UX researcher, a product marketer. You spend a lot more time on coordination.

I think too often people say they want to be a senior PM or a group PM, without really figuring out what they love. They end up in a place where they're senior but not loving their job.

TERESA TORRES

TELL ME ABOUT YOU AND YOUR CAREER PATH.

I work as a product discovery coach. That means I work with teams on making good decisions about what to build, through a focus on continuous discovery with things like interviewing regularly, rapid prototyping, and regularly experimenting.

As an undergraduate, I took design classes at Stanford and was exposed to human computer interaction (HCI). As a 22-year-old, I came into business believing that business was human-centered and that people cared about solving customer problems.

Out of college, I took a role as an interaction designer. My first title, technically, was application software developer, but I was hired because of my HCI background. That was my first introduction to a hybrid role.

The next job I had was a really pivotal point in my career. I was the tenth employee at a really early stage startup, which I discovered through Craigslist.

> I started as a frontend developer and designer and moved to a design and product management role. I came in and said I want to talk to customers and figure out what we should be doing. Our VP of product management was impressed and started bringing me into the executive meetings. I got firsthand exposure to the finances and was involved in M&A conversations.

In my third company, I was hired as a director of UX, but within three weeks of joining the company, I realized they really needed product leadership. So, I became their director of product. I've always blurred the roles between product UX and a bit of engineering.

From there, most of the companies I worked with were early stage startups. I got a pretty good introduction to business and how startups work at a young age. By the time I was 30, I was already a VP of product. By the time I was 32, I was a startup CEO.

HOW DID YOU BECOME CEO?

Being a CEO was pivotal in a way that most people wouldn't think. I'd joined the company as a director, nine months before the VP of product left. He helped me build a relationship with the CEO since I was doing strategic product and positioning work. So, when he left, I became the VP of product.

I joined the executive team and learned that it was really misaligned. Our head of sales wanted to go one way, I wanted to go another way, and our head of engineering wanted to go a third way.

I loved the work that we were doing, but it got to the point where I didn't want to work there anymore. I went to my CEO and I told him I needed to take an extended break. I traveled for six weeks and on my plane flight back, I wrote two or three pages of notes of what I thought had to change for me to want to keep working there. When I got back, I sat down with our CEO and just talked to him about it. He agreed and promoted me to be the VP of operations.

Only six months after that, the economy fell apart in 2008. Our entire business was falling apart, and I intended to tell the CEO that I was going to resign because we couldn't afford to pay both of us. And literally on that day, he pulled me aside and told me he was resigning and that he was going to recommend to the board that I take over.

WHAT WAS IT LIKE TO BE A CEO?

The next two and a half years were easily the hardest years of my life, but also the most rewarding. I mean, I was miserable. It wasn't fun.

People associate so much weight with that title, but I don't think they realize that it comes with a ton of gut-wrenching responsibility. You're responsible for people's paychecks. We were in a situation for six months where I didn't know if we could meet our next payroll.

> Also, some people think that as a CEO, they get to make all the decisions. That's not true. Bringing a team along is really hard. Managing a board is really hard and very political. People think that the boss has no boss. That's not true. The boss has many bosses. The politics involved in venture capital is a nightmare.

But, I also learned more in those two and a half years than any other time period in my career.

At the end of the life of that company, I was really burnt out. I took 14 months off and then started consulting, because I wasn't ready for a job but I needed income.

WHAT INSPIRED YOU TO BECOME A PRODUCT COACH?

After consulting for a while, I took a job as head of product and design at another startup. I was only there for about 13 months when I realized that I couldn't do startups anymore. There was a lot of politics with the CEO and the board, and I saw the worst of the impacts of venture capital. I've seen board members who didn't think about what was best for the company and just thought about what was best for them individually as a shareholder. I saw board members who had fixed opinions and weren't open to strategic discussions.

I took some time to write down all the things I loved and all the things I didn't want. That really helped me see that, even though I love working on products, I didn't want to do the executive team alignment work. I also didn't like doing product work as an outsider because it creates a dependency between you and the company. And, I didn't want to be a crutch, preventing them from being on a path to being successful.

> I realized that I kept seeing the same problem at companies, which was that product teams just don't spend enough time with their customers, and they didn't know how to change. That's when I decided to focus on coaching full time.

I came up with the idea that I wouldn't do the strategic or research work for companies; I would teach them how to do it. Companies were still coming to me and asking me to do research. I took those consulting leads and turned them into hybrid consulting/coaching leads by saying I'd do it if they sent a PM to do it with me and learn how to do it themselves the next time.

Eventually, I started writing very deliberately. I had already been blogging, but I very deliberately changed my writing to appeal to a head of product who knew they needed to develop the team but didn't have time. I started talking about the future of product management and what that future looks like. I wrote about the skills required and what people should be focusing on. That's when my blog shifted to be entirely around discovery and continuous discovery.

When I started writing, I started getting inbound coaching requests. The first email I got was a two sentence email that said "You write about a lot of the things that my team struggles with. Will you coach us?" That was from Hope Gurion, and now she's a big thought leader and consultant in the product space and our businesses have merged together.

HOW WOULD A PM KNOW IF COACHING WOULD BE A GOOD PATH FOR THEM?

> I like to make a distinction between coaching and training. Training has this expert/teacher model of "I'm going to teach you the way to do things," which I don't think works very well with coaching. The coaching model is more "Let's co-create together what's going to work for you." There's a humility to coaching that's very different from teaching.

To know if you'd be good at coaching, it's a little bit of a gut check of how much you can set aside your ego. The term "servant leadership" is becoming trendy, and a bit jargony, but I feel like the concept behind it is really good. If I'm working with a product team, my role as a coach is to serve them in whatever way I can.

That's very different from a traditional training mindset of "I have my method that I'm going to stamp onto you."

With coaching, there are the skills of holding the space, naming things, asking powerful questions, and really helping the team find their way there rather than you leading them there.

Moving away from a product role, I do miss working with engineers. I miss creating something as a team. But, I treat my coaching curriculum like a product and I'm getting to the point where I have collaborators on it.

A nice part of coaching is that you can exclude all of the things you don't like. I don't deal with a board. I don't deal with an executive team. I don't have salespeople. I just have an admin who supports me. My business is really simple, and it supports exactly how I want to work.

WHAT ADVICE WOULD YOU GIVE TO A PM WHO WANTS TO ADVANCE IN THEIR CAREER?

> Take some time to really figure out what you like and don't like. Don't just get stuck climbing the corporate ladder and going after more money and a bigger title.

I know it's easy for me to say because I've been a CEO, but I've had this experience a few times. It's really easy to think that you want something, but then you get that, and you realize it's not at all what you thought it was. Before you waste 20 years going after something you're not sure you want, talk to people in those roles. Try to get a really clear picture of what they look like. For example, I know so many heads of product that miss the product work.

> The other advice is—don't be afraid to create the role you want.

It's easier to do that as a consultant, but you can also do it at an organization. People who take initiative have way more ability to do that than they realize.

CHAPTER 46

OJI UDEZUE

OJI UDEZUE is former VP of Product at Calendly where he led product management, design and content strategy. Prior to Calendly, Oji was the head of product for Atlassian's Communication division where he led product strategy for Hipchat and Stride. He has also held product leadership positions at Spiceworks and at Bridgewater Associates, which he joined after over a decade in product at Microsoft. Oji founded Intermingl, a mobile cloud-based networking app, in 2013. In his free time, he's the managing partner of the Kernel Fund, which invests in startups in Africa, and is a member of the board of directors at Quitch.

ojiudezue.com | twitter: @ojiudezue | medium: @okosisi

HOW DID YOU GET INTO PRODUCT MANAGEMENT?

I was born in Nigeria to middle class parents, but when I was about 15, my dad lost almost all his money. From then on, I resolved to take care of myself. In college, I did a lot of internships and one of them was at a very interesting company. They wanted me to keep writing software for them and paid me what was an extravagant sum for me at the time—enough to pay for me and my brother's school fees and cover rent for an off-campus apartment.

After that, I knew I could do really well monetarily in Nigeria, but I felt I needed to leave so I could make my mark on the world. I worked hard and took the GRE, and I got into a couple of schools. But, after getting those acceptances, the US Embassy said I couldn't go. It nearly broke me.

I decided to try raising money for my first year of school upfront and went to all of my family and family friends with a simple pitch to support my future. I went back to the embassy with the money I'd raised, and someone decided I was okay. I got a student visa, and after my first semester, I got a full-ride scholarship and a masters at USC.

After my masters, I went to work for a startup and then to work for Microsoft. I started at Microsoft doing high-end enterprise support. I enjoyed it, but it wasn't really what I wanted to do.

I knew it would be hard to transition to product management, so I took a product I was working with on the support side. I looked at its weaknesses, coded up a solution, and posted it on the internal tools page of Microsoft. That essentially became my resume, and I became a product manager.

WHAT WAS YOUR TIME AT MICROSOFT LIKE?

As a PM, I joined some of the most complicated projects in Windows and Windows Live. Over my career there, I worked with Office, search, and Microsoft Research, and had twelve patents. At one point, I was so mad that my product wasn't winning the market that I transitioned to marketing to learn how to tell the story of product. I ran a marketing team for two years and got an MBA at Columbia and Berkeley.

My big question at Microsoft was:

> How can I prove to myself that I can solve any technical problem? How do I prove to myself that I can be really original?

This was the reason for the quest for the patents: it was one way I could tally originality. I was looking for a way to say that I could put my stamp on the world, that I could be as innovative as some of the best innovators in the world.

Initially, when I chose my teams, it was all about the problem. The harder the problem, the more original the problem, the more challenge I felt. And the more I thought about it. One time, I came up with a whole new solution to a set of problems while I was in the shower. I evangelized it, and the company ended up spending $20 million to back it.

Eventually, as I matured, it became more about the people. It became about people I trusted, people that I had good working relationships with, people who could advocate for me and my career. I needed advocates because I saw that I had some managers who were good and some who were horrible and really slowed my career down.

As part of my focus on building relationships, I started a community called Africans at Microsoft. I realized that, in addition to the community of Black people at Microsoft, I also needed people around me who understood the African experience. When you come to the United States, you lose your entire network. It's an imperceptible lack that you don't really realize at first.

WHAT INSPIRED YOUR NEXT MOVES?

At the end of my time at Microsoft, I was recruited heavily by a hedge fund, Bridgewater Associates. I'd been at Microsoft for over 10 years. I didn't feel innovative anymore.

After a little over a year at Bridgewater, I decided to found a startup that I had been incubating in my head for some time. I felt I was ready, and I felt it was the right time. I did my startup for two and a half years. It mostly failed—while I could keep plugging away at it, I realized the underlying business model wasn't going to work. I didn't have enough time and money to pivot out of that, so I folded the company.

Around the same time that I started my business, I created a super angel group which we call Kernel Fund. Through Africans at Microsoft, I knew a lot of technologists and I knew there was a core group of people who had been looking for opportunities to invest in Africa. So, I basically cobbled that interest together and laid out the rules for how we would operate in collaboration with a few people. I was doing my startup during the week, but on the weekends I would play VC.

> I like to balance my opportunity costs and to start things that I think I want to do long term before I'm fully ready to commit 100%.

It's worked pretty decently. We have some great investments that are doing really well. We've been lucky.

After my startup folded, I moved to Austin. I joined a smaller company before finding what I thought was my forever company, Atlassian. It just felt much more like home. I was hired to lead the product side of the whole communications division which included HipChat, Stride, and a few other things.

I went into that role because of the people and because it was very connected to some of the things I've had a lot of subject matter expertise in. I've been working on some form of collaboration tools all my career. Three years in, we divested that business to Slack.

I looked around and found in my inbox an opportunity that turned into Calendly. It's a very fast-growing company that was almost entirely bootstrapped and was already profitable. The growth upside and the equity upside for me was interesting. It's a great company and I get to essentially build my dream team.

WHAT ADVICE WOULD YOU GIVE PMS WHO WANT TO ADVANCE IN THEIR CAREER?

> I think the first thing is to understand yourself. It's hard to tell a starting PM to do that because generally when we're super young, we're very optimistic about what we are and what we're good at and what we're bad at. But I'd say over time, try to understand what makes you happy, what you're good at, and what you think you can get better at.

Early on, understand that advancement is governed by the approval of people above you. Understand what they're looking for. Identify it critically. Try to excel at it if it intersects with what you're good at. Remove all objections to your rapid rise.

For example, early on in my career, I wasn't good at writing reports every week. I liked to do the work, but I hated to document it. My manager would say:

> Documenting is the work. Since you don't document it consistently, you can't get promoted. You should work really hard to just document it so that people don't block you.

I think in your middle career you should look to work with or for people who are advocates for you. Advancement is about more than your competence; now it's about people who will push you forward.

Then, later in your career, look for opportunities that will, frankly, make you wealthy. Look for things that will help you escape the need to work, if you can.

I always tell young people there's a trifecta of what should guide your career:

- **The first is brand**. It is governed by the companies you've worked for. In my case, it's ex-Microsoft, ex-Atlassian, ex-Bridgewater. People recognize those names, they have a certain expectation of people who've gone through them. It's very important to align yourself with some of those things. If you're an immigrant, if you're a woman, if you're black, if you're an outsider of the power dynamics, it's even more important.

- **The second is reputation**. That's about you. What have you shipped? What have you built? What are you saying on Twitter? What are you saying on Medium? What are you saying on LinkedIn? What do people know you for? What are they endorsing you for? That is your own thing, and you have to guard it.

- **The third thing is money**.

If you have a perfect triangle of those things, you generally have a good career.

CHAPTER 47

APRIL UNDERWOOD

APRIL UNDERWOOD is the founder and CEO of Local Laboratory and co-founder of #ANGELS. Her earlier experience includes chief product officer at Slack and director of product at Twitter. She serves on the board of directors at Zillow Group.

twitter: @aunder

HOW DID YOU GET INTO PRODUCT MANAGEMENT?

I grew up in Texas, far away from the software development world and Silicon Valley, but I always had an interest in computers. I typed in all the metadata for my baseball card collection so that I knew what baseball cards I had without having to flip through the book.

When I got to college, it never occurred to me to choose computer science, so I fell into programming through my part-time job doing tech support. I taught myself to code so I could make the training modules easier to navigate rather than being on the phone myself.

After college, I started my career as a software engineer at Travelocity, working on partnerships and integrations with sites like Yahoo and AOL. Through that, I got exposure to companies in Silicon Valley and started asking questions about the partnership deals and product choices—the kind of questions that PMs ask.

I wanted to become a PM but was told I needed an MBA, so I applied to business school. After I applied, I got the opportunity to become a PM at Travelocity without said MBA, which I took. When I got my acceptance letter to Haas (Berkeley) a few months later, I decided to go ahead and attend anyway. Then, when I graduated business school and joined Google, the market had changed and I was told I couldn't be a PM because I didn't have a CS degree.

That's an important thing to know:

> This role is always evolving and, particularly early in your career, you can run into a lot of reasons why you can't be a PM. It's about finding the right place where you can have a positive impact and develop your experience to the point where people stop questioning whether or not you're really a PM.

It takes a few practice runs for a lot of people. At some point, you've got to get a break, and then it's much easier to find those opportunities afterwards.

During those years at Google, I advocated for myself trying to make the transition from technology program manager, even moonlighting as a PM on a stealth project. Looking back on it, I was killing myself to try to prove that an exception should be made for me to get back to the role I'd held three years prior before my MBA at Travelocity. Eventually, I left to be a PM at an earlier stage company that was less didactic about the qualifications to be a PM.

A few months later, I got a phone call from a friend at Twitter. I loved the product and couldn't say no. It was the opportunity to work on something at the intersection of a technology shift, which was mobile apps, and a cultural shift around people wanting to express themselves differently online. I joined Twitter as a PM on the tweet button and other platform products.

WHAT WERE SOME KEY DRIVERS OF YOUR CAREER GROWTH?

> In terms of career growth, early in my career, I really had to ask for what I wanted. I asked for more opportunities. I asked to be in the room for certain things. I took on work no one asked me to do, as well. I initiated conversations about promotion opportunities or the next job.

One of those opportunities was at Twitter, when we realized we needed somebody to run part of the newly-forming business development team. We had partnership deals with companies like Google and Microsoft that were really a product exercise. What problems are we trying to solve for our mutual users? How could we do that in a way that served the business goals of each organization?

So, I switched over to do that. Afterwards, I came back to a traditional product management role to build the ads API and then ended up leading a significant portion of both the ads and the data PM teams.

HOW DID YOU GET INTO ANGEL INVESTING?

After I left Twitter, I launched #ANGELS with five of my ex-colleagues, and started angel investing. We saw some of our male peers were getting the opportunity to participate in the upside of interesting companies as angel investors and we thought we could build an umbrella and bring deals to us.

> That was really the point in my career where I started thinking about it as a portfolio rather than "this is my job, and I give my job 200% of myself." I instead started to think about the different pots I want to have a hand in and how to run them simultaneously.

HOW DID YOU JOIN SLACK AND GROW INTO THE CPO ROLE?

I met Stewart Butterfield, the CEO and one of the founders of Slack, while I was angel investing. I ended up joining Slack as the head of platform when it had about 150 employees. This was a GM role and it was a really valuable way for Stewart and I to get to know each other and assess whether or not we could have a working relationship that would be productive.

I built up the platform using all the skills that I'd gained in my previous roles, like engineering and business development. I took what was a great team and an API and really developed a platform strategy around it. Just launching features into the world is never enough for a platform. You need to have a business development team that goes and works with the largest companies to bring them on board. You need a developer relations team that helps bring the broader ecosystem along and helps people understand what's possible with the technology. You need a platform marketing team and somebody that can help translate all of this to your end customers.

We launched the Slack app directory about six months after I joined, and later that week Stewart asked me to be VP of product. In product-founder led companies, the fit between the founder and the first head of product doesn't work a lot of the time. The head of platform role was a great way to see what working together would be like. I ran the product organization over the next three years as VP and then eventually as chief product officer.

HOW MIGHT A PM KNOW IF PRODUCT LEADERSHIP ROLES WOULD BE A GOOD MATCH FOR THEM?

The person that would love the VP of product or CPO role loves the internal communication and leadership aspects of helping the entire company understand what's important and why. They can help people understand the choices that are being made. They can not only communicate a path forward that guides people to make the right decisions at every level in the organization, but can also institute the governance structure that allows for decisions to be made quickly and clearly.

> Ironically, for those senior leadership roles where you're managing a portfolio, you have to step back a little from the skills that got you there, like being incredibly passionate about the problem you're solving and being willing to do whatever it takes to make it successful.

Execs need to maintain some emotional distance from the "what." Instead, they should ensure that people are staying aligned on the "why" and that they understand how to get work done within the organization.

Another difference between somebody that might be a great product manager and a great product leader might be that they are increasingly comfortable working cross functionally and good at reaching across the aisle to the business or the sales counterparts. A product leader needs to be comfortable playing that role—defining go-to-market strategy and even getting up on stage to unveil product launches. You may not use those skills for a long time in an IC PM career, and then all of a sudden, they're absolutely critical. And so that leap can be a little hard and a little rocky at times.

That's the CPO path. Being an executive in general is about clarity of communication, some amount of charismatic leadership skills that make people want to join your organization and want to follow you, and humility to face problems within the organization and tackle them head on.

WHO IS A GOOD FIT FOR ANGEL INVESTING?

You'd enjoy it if you love meeting teams who are working on early ideas—if you are energized by that. I go through periods where I am, and periods where I'm not. A lot of times they are *just* ideas; they're not even products yet. It's very, very different than as a CPO, where you're really in it every single day and the customers and the business and the products are very tactile.

WHO IS A GOOD FIT FOR GM?

The GM role is one of the best jobs out there, in my opinion. It allows you to start having real ownership of connecting the dots between the different functions.

I always say that shipping code to production is not a launch. A launch is when customers actually understand what it is and why they need it. There are lots of different ways to go about that, beyond just marketing.

The GM role is more of the business mold of a product leader than it is the technical- or product -vision piece that sometimes gets glorified. But, the companies that really stand out in terms of their results are the ones that can build a great product, but also are really savvy and work really hard at landing the go-to-market.

WHAT ADVICE WOULD YOU GIVE TO PMS WHO WANT TO ADVANCE IN THEIR CAREERS?

The basics are to take responsibility for building a compelling vision that people want to attach themselves to, for things beyond what you're explicitly asked to do. To me, that's leadership—full stop.

If you only do the things you're asked to do, then you're already in the right place on the org chart.

Companies that are growing fast are the best places to be able to advance in your career because there are new jobs opening up all the time and everybody's job is always getting bigger. There's movement, and where there's movement, there's opportunity.

WHAT DOES GROWTH LOOK LIKE FOR A PM?

There are three axes of growth I think about.

The first is that you **identify adjacencies** to the part of the product you're responsible for. You identify new greenfield opportunities for products that amplify or extend what you're already doing. Over time you're sort of giving yourself a promotion because you're convincing the organization that they should invest in something bigger.

The second, which is more of a GM path, is to identify that there are **other things the organization needs to do, beyond building the product**, that are going to improve the ROI for that investment. I advise people to get good at writing job specs for jobs they'll never take. When you need a marketing partner, write a marketing spec being very clear about what you need. Then use that spec to start a conversation or even start the search yourself with a list of candidates to talk to. Sometimes you'll end up being the person to hire them, and now that's a new experience that you have.

The third is that you can **create connections cross-functionally**. Particularly in an enterprise business, you need to spend time selling customers, closing customers, and dealing with them when they're upset. Almost as important is spending time with the sales team. You need to really have empathy for what it's like for them to go out and sell the product and market it, even when it might have some real gaps.

> The PMs who are willing to face those realities and work with the sales people build trust. Then you can actually be an enabler for the solution rather than a gatekeeper for the engineering resources, which is a trap that can put a PM in a challenging position in their organization.

ADDITIONAL READING

PART J

J ADDITIONAL READING

THERE IS SO much to say about product management. We hope we've included most of the essential information earlier. But depending on your background and your goals, you might find some of the following information handy:

- **Types of PM Roles (pg 469):** This chapter will cover what PMs in different types of industries do, and what sorts of skills you need. We will discuss consumer, B2B, e-commerce, marketplace, gaming, platforms and infrastructure, internal teams, hardware and the internet of things, growth and monetization, machine learning / AI / data, startups, regulated industries, non-tech companies, and government and social impact.

- **Landing a Product Management Role (pg 481):** This chapter will walk through what kinds of experience is useful to land a product management role, and how to do well in the interview.

- **Networking for Introverts (pg 493):** This piece, by Jules Walter, teaches us how introverts—and everyone—can develop authentic relationships.

- **The Paradox of Autonomy and Recognition (pg 496):** In this article, Kate Matsudaira writes about the challenges of measuring contributions when people work autonomously.

- **10 Rules for Negotiating a Job Offer (pg 502):** Haseeb Qureshi explains core principles to negotiate a better job offer.

CHAPTER 48

TYPES OF PM ROLES

ONE OF THE great things about product management is that it's very supportive of generalist PMs. Many product managers switch to a different type of PM role with every new job, from consumer to enterprise, e-commerce to marketplace, growth to machine learning, and big company to startup.

Switching types is welcomed because these PM types share almost all the same skills, and those skills generally drive success more than specialized knowledge. Moreover, switching types can actually be *positive*, as many big contributions come from cross-pollination: applying an idea from one type of team to another.

The main exception to the "generalist" rule is when you have the chance to become a leading expert—one of the people with the most or best experience in that specialty. For example, when the iPhone app store opened in 2008, it brought in a new age of mobile apps. PMs with a few extra years of mobile expertise became highly desirable.

With that in mind, we'll dig into how various PM roles differ, and what skills are especially important for each.

CONSUMER

WHAT IT IS

Consumer PM roles are often the first ones people think of when they think of product management. They work on user-facing features for products that target everyday people, such as Spotify, Instagram, Reddit, YouTube, Google Maps, Yelp, or TikTok. Many PMs choose to work in a consumer role because they love the product.

WHAT YOU DO

Consumer PMs usually focus on success metrics measuring engagement: getting people to use and keep using the product. This might be measured by Daily Active Users (DAUs) or Monthly Active Users (MAUs), or even the ratio of DAU/MAU to track increasing frequency of use in a large and growing user base. Entertainment products often use "time spent" metrics such as minutes listening. PMs might also own usage metrics or transactional metrics for their specific area, such as messages sent or reviews written.

WHAT YOU NEED

Product skills such as customer focus, design, and creativity are especially important for consumer PMs. Consumer-facing products often have heavy competition, and consumers will choose the products where they see compelling value and enjoy the design. Consumer PMs must constantly consider their users, what problems they have, and how to solve those problems in a way that will work for millions of users.

Strong product intuition, customer research, and data analysis skills help you make sure your product works for the "silent majority" and keep you from getting misled by the "vocal minority." For consumer apps, the few users who post on the forums every day and send in feature requests often (the vocal minority) don't have the same needs and use cases as the rest of your users (the silent majority). Often, the loudest users want fancy functionality for their niche use case, while typical users would benefit more from usability improvements and easy-to-use features. Great consumer PMs can look at data to find and advocate for big product opportunities.[1]

When your target users are everyday people, everyone has opinions on what you should do. There is no shortage of ideas, but prioritization and the ability to say no become very important. Engineers and designers often run the show at consumer products, so you'll also need top notch collaboration and leadership skills to have an influence.

B2B

WHAT IT IS

Business-to-business (B2B) products are focused on selling software to businesses, schools, or people at work. This includes products such as Adobe Creative Cloud, Asana, Dropbox, Google AdWords, Gusto, Jira, MailChimp, Microsoft Office, Salesforce, Shopify, Slack, Square, Workday, Zendesk, and Zoom.

WHAT YOU DO

While B2B products often don't have the same name recognition and prestige as consumer products, they're a great place to be a product manager. You build a product or service that people find valuable, and they pay you for it. It's relatively straightforward to learn about what customers want from your product, and to know that you're delivering real value. Unless engineers or designers are the target customer, the team usually relies heavily on the PM to understand customer needs.

B2B product managers often focus on success metrics that measure revenue: getting people to pay and continue to pay. This might be measured by new sales deals your features helped close, annual recurring revenue (ARR), or active premium users, especially with a focus on retention and churn. At a zoomed-in level, PMs often focus on engagement with their features.

---

1   This doesn't mean you should never focus on the needs of small, important groups of users, such as influencers. It means that within a user type, you shouldn't assume that the people who proactively speak up are the same as the people who don't.

WHAT YOU NEED

As a B2B PM, it's critically important to think about multiple users—the people who purchase or administer the software often have different needs than the people who use the software. Great products need to consider all of the users. PMs sometimes focus only on what the purchaser wants and end up building poorly designed software that makes the end users miserable. Don't be that PM!

Strategic skills like market analysis and understanding business models are especially important for B2B product managers. PMs need to figure out what it takes to close deals, beat the competition, expand the market, and balance investments across many competing priorities. Unlike some consumer PMs, B2B PMs don't have the luxury of ignoring monetization.

Mike Ross, Senior Director of Product Management at Skydio, explains:

> My job is twofold. The first part is to ship quickly and get feedback: ship quality products, fast; scope them appropriately; and start the iteration loop. The second part is to influence the pipeline. To push the envelope on who we can sell to. To go build the largest market that I can for our product. That involves talking to folks that are on the edges of our boundaries and understanding where the deltas are, and then going and closing those gaps so that we can continue to grow.

Great B2B PMs spend a lot of time with customers and find the connections between customer needs and business opportunities.

E-COMMERCE

WHAT IT IS

E-commerce companies sell things online (and usually deliver them in the real world). This includes websites such as Amazon, Alibaba, Flipkart, Walmart, and Zappos.

WHAT YOU DO

Unlike many modern tech companies, where everyone is inventing best practices on the fly, e-commerce companies build on the fundamentals of supply chain management.

Rahul Ramkumar, VP of Product Management at Walmart, explained:

> The backbone of e-commerce is the supply chain—you can have a beautiful site, a fantastic experience; you can take the orders. But ultimately, you've got to fulfill those orders and deliver them on time. If you don't do that right, they're not going to come back.

Alongside studying the supply chain, he recommends joining a rotational program where you can spend time managing merchandising, answering support tickets, or joining any other team that touches the customer's order to get the 360-degree view. If that is not an option, he recommends seeking out mentors within the organization.

The main success metric at e-commerce companies is usually successful orders. Leading up to that is the conversion funnel: visiting the site, viewing a product, adding it to the cart, checkout, and, finally, purchasing.

WHAT YOU NEED

The top skills for e-commerce PMs vary by part of the company, but execution skills tend to stand out. E-commerce is a complex system where all the pieces need to work together, and mistakes can have more severe repercussions since you're often dealing with physical goods and financial transactions.

MARKETPLACE

WHAT IT IS

Two-sided marketplace products connect buyers and sellers or service providers. This includes products like Uber, Lyft, DoorDash, Airbnb, Etsy, Ebay, and Alibaba.

WHAT YOU DO

PM roles on the buyer-side of the marketplace are often consumer or e-commerce roles. Roles on the seller-side are often B2B roles. However, great marketplace PMs are always thinking about the interplay between supply and demand. Many new features require work on both the buyer and seller side.

Marketplace PMs look at success metrics that track the overall health of the marketplace: supply, demand, and successful transactions (such as bookings or sales).

WHAT YOU NEED

Strategic skills like business sense and collaboration skills (particularly between different teams) are critical in marketplace products.

GAMING

WHAT IT IS

While desktop and console games didn't historically have product managers, newer online and mobile games, especially free-to-play games, do. This includes games like Farmville, Candy Crush, Pokémon Go, Angry Birds, League of Legends, and Fortnite. Now that most games have an online component, even traditional game studios hire product managers.

WHAT YOU DO

PMs at game companies usually focus on success metrics around the long-term value of players, such as engagement and monetization. It's important to build a game that's appealing enough for people to come back, so metrics like D1 and D7 retention (how many people come back after the first day and first week) matter a lot. Monetization might be measured by average revenue per daily active user (ARPDAU). Mobile games tend to acquire new users primarily through ads, so it's very important to compare the long-term value to the cost per install (CPI).

Successful free-to-play games are built with the business model in mind from the beginning—it's not like consumer apps that can get away with first building a massive user base and then figuring out how to monetize them. The type of gameplay affects what types of monetization strategies will work—for example, paying to skip waiting, paying for cosmetic items, or paying for more powerful characters.

The PM works with the game designer to figure out both the core game and what gaming PMs call "the metagame." The core game is the action of the game, like matching colors in candy crush, while the metagame is all of the surrounding elements, like progression and the game economy.

Games are designed to be live for much longer than they were in initial development, so most gaming PMs don't launch a brand new game. Instead, they're responsible for optimizing and improving a game after it's launched. This is called the live operations, or LiveOps phase. A gaming PM is constantly working on improvements, from adding new content, to building new types of gameplay, to optimizing the first-time experience. PMs spend a lot of time analyzing data on how new features are doing. If you don't already know SQL, you'll be expected to learn it early on.

WHAT YOU NEED

It takes a lot of people working together to create a game: artists, game designers, UI and UX designers, engineers, and so on. Some companies have dedicated project managers, but for those that don't, good project management to keep everyone aligned will be very important.

Beyond strong analytical skills, what does it take to be a great games PM? A lot of experience playing games! As Brian Shih, VP of PM at Pocket Gems, shared:

> If you want to get really good at game design, the first thing I would tell you to do is go play 10,000 hours of video games, go play the top 10 games each for 1,000 hours and really, really understand them. Really feel what it's like to have empathy as a player for all the different systems, and to have references to draw on.

If you love video games, being a gaming PM can be a dream come true.

PLATFORMS AND INFRASTRUCTURE

WHAT IT IS

Platform PMs are responsible for foundational components that other people use to build products, such as APIs, UI widgets, or infrastructure components. Platforms can be internal-facing infrastructure (the customers are product teams at the same company) or external facing (providing functionality for developers at other companies to build on top of).

A key difference between platforms and products is that products solve a known set of use cases directly, while platforms are meant to enable other teams to solve the use cases they choose.

WHAT YOU DO

As a platform PM, you'll need to think about at least two levels of customers: the developers using your platform and the end-users they serve. The level of indirection also adds uncertainty: The product teams might change their goals or have failed to communicate their full context.

Platform PMs generally try to measure platform health, such as the number of successful products using the platform. Ideally, the team can also measure the benefits for the product teams building on the platform, such as a decrease in development time or an increase in their key success metrics. A big part of being a platform or infrastructure PM is helping define the right success metrics for your team.

WHAT YOU NEED

Since your customers are developers, technical skills such as a background in coding can be important. Just like consumer PMs spot usability bugs in a UI, platform PMs can spot usability bugs in an API. Technical skills are also important for imagining what might be possible in a platform, and understanding the opportunities and constraints.

Product skills are important for platform PMs to truly understand the use cases and choose coherent sets of functionality to launch. Without a PM, platform teams tend to launch a grab bag of APIs that mirror the internal code structure and that don't always enable important use cases. For example, a poorly designed API might be missing access to a key object or might require too many round trips to be fast enough for the desired use cases.

A great rule of thumb for platform PMing is to design around three different products you'd like to see built on top of the platform. Choosing at least one ensures the platform will actually be useful, and expanding it to three helps illuminate areas where the platform needs to be flexible.

Strategic skills are also important for platform PMs; you need to be able to set a long-term roadmap based on what the products might need in the future. Unlike most online software, which can be regularly fixed through updates, platform mistakes (particularly externally-facing ones) often can't be easily fixed. If your changes aren't backward compatible, the products built on top of your product will break.

INTERNAL TEAMS

WHAT IT IS

PMs for internal teams build products where the customers are other people at the company. This includes infrastructure teams, as well as teams building tools for salespeople, data scientists, customer support, and marketers at their company. It also includes tools to support the primary function of the company, such as tools for real estate agents at a real estate company, financial advisors at a finance company, healthcare advocates at a healthcare company, or journalists at a news company.

WHAT YOU DO

As an internal team PM, you need to work closely with your customers (other teams), executives, and the rest of the company. Often, there can be tension between the company leaders who spun up the team and the internal customers the team is supposed to help.

For example, there might be a company-wide mandate for product teams to move onto common infrastructure, but each product team sees switching work as a pointless burden. You might be building a tool to assist an operations team in decision-making, but they're worried they won't have a job once your tool is implemented. The automation tool you build might take away all the easy work, leaving the operations team with only the stressful work.

Your job is to understand these conflicts, develop appropriate solutions, address the internal customer's concerns, and roll out solutions.

WHAT YOU NEED

Stakeholder management and relationship-building are critical skills for internal PMs. Great internal PMs tackle tension directly and show strong customer focus for their internal customers, rather than blindly following executive orders. They learn about the needs and fears of internal teams and come up with solutions that address them—even if that includes things that PMs don't typically do, such as suggesting new work an operations team can pursue after their current work is automated. They evangelize their work internally to help teams understand the benefits of switching over.

Strategic skills are also important for internal teams. These teams can often feel like they're at the whim of dozens of stakeholders with frequently changing requirements, and there are constant fires to put out. This makes it hard to launch anything, and hard to tell if your work is actually successful. Creating a clear mission and using it to prioritize the work can help teams get out of firefighting mode.

HARDWARE AND INTERNET OF THINGS

WHAT IT IS

Hardware PMs focus on building and delivering physical products, and the Internet of Things (IoT) refers to products that combine hardware and software. This includes products like the iPhone, Sonos speakers, Nest cameras, and Fitbit trackers.

WHAT YOU DO

Instead of A/B testing, hardware PMs rely a lot more on prototype testing and internal feedback on early prototypes (to avoid leaks). Even though PMs can test several prototypes with customers, it's harder to iterate on the fly. It's important to have strong hypotheses about what might go wrong so you can have the right backup prototype ready.

In terms of execution, hardware follows a fixed product development cycle with phases that go from initial concept to mass production. Hardware PMs need to learn about each phase, how long it lasts, and what kinds of changes are easy or hard to make during this phase. Laide Olambiwonnu, PM Director at Syng (and previously at Ring and Sonos) explains:

> Be really critical about the goals and objectives of each build. This allows you to prioritize efficiently and ensure you get the most out of each build.

There are a lot of aspects of hardware PMing that software PMs never face. Hardware PMs often travel to visit the factories where their products are made or to visit vendors, which can be a pro or a con to the job, depending on how much you enjoy travel. Hardware PMs also are responsible for packaging and will consider things like the unboxing experience and sustainable packaging.

For IoT, Daniel Elizalde writes:

> The Internet of Things will require a new breed of product manager—one who can incorporate the five layers of the IoT technology stack into their product strategy and roadmap.[2]

---

2   Elizalde expands on this at https://danielelizalde.com/iot-primer/.

In his framework, the five layers are device hardware, device software, communication, cloud platform, and cloud applications.

WHAT YOU NEED

Compared to software, hardware takes a lot of time and money to produce. This means that you'll need strategic skills (in predicting which way technology is moving), great product intuition (since you can't do mass A/B testing), and excellent execution (since problems can't be fixed as easily after you launch).

If you're working on a piece of hardware that will launch in three years, you need to be able to make good predictions about the future so that you're not stuck with choices that rapidly make your product obsolete. For example, some hardware products attached to the iPhone via the headphone jack, but when Apple dropped the headphone jack in 2016, the products were left scrambling for alternatives. Whoops!

Olambiwonnu shares how she stays on top of which components to bet on:

> Conferences like CES help a lot, as well as following organizational blogs for the big players, and subscribing to their email list. It's good to be in touch with their upcoming roadmap to make sure you're incorporating the best components that are going to be supported for a very long time by the component makers.

Keeping up-to-date with trends and technologies will help you develop hardware that feels perfectly modern—neither outdated nor ahead of its time.

GROWTH AND MONETIZATION

WHAT IT IS

Growth PM roles exist inside many company types and focus on acquiring or monetizing new users rather than on building new functionality. Growth PMs can work on all parts of the product, but often focus on key flows like signup or purchasing.

WHAT YOU DO

Growth PMs focus on what Bangaly Kaba calls the adjacent user, people who are aware of a product and may have tried using it, but are not able to successfully become an engaged user.[3]

As Kaba writes:

> Our insight was that it is critical for growth teams to be continually defining who the adjacent user is, to understand why they are struggling, to build empathy for the adjacent user, and ultimately to solve their problems.

Growth PMs often directly own success metrics such as revenue or active users, and measure that success via A/B tests.

---

3   For more on the adjacent user, see https://andrewchen.co/the-adjacent-user-theory/ and see page 430 for an interview with Bangaly Kaba.

WHAT YOU NEED

Analytical problem solving, data insight, and execution skills are especially important for growth PMs. Analytical problem solving helps you come up with hypotheses and ask the right questions. Data insight helps you size the opportunities and analyze experiment results. Flawless execution is particularly important when running experiments to test hypotheses, because you don't want to be in a situation where you're not sure if the result was because the hypothesis is wrong or because the execution was bad.

Depending on how established growth and monetization are at your company, you might need to help build the right culture for a growth team. Leadership skills will also be critical, as there are a lot of habits and values that need to be learned.

MACHINE LEARNING, ARTIFICIAL INTELLIGENCE (AI), AND DATA

WHAT IT IS

Machine learning (ML) PM jobs tend to be highly technical roles. The PMs work with ML systems and data scientists to create better product experiences by applying pattern matching across big data sets. Machine learning can be used to improve ads, personalize content, recognize images, suggest products, and much more. While all PM roles have important ethical considerations, as an ML PM, it's especially important to think proactively about potential harms.

WHAT YOU DO

Machine learning PMs find ways to use data to solve customer needs. A PM might identify new use cases or target markets that the company's existing data could solve. They might investigate the output of machine learning algorithms to identify areas for improvement.

Navigating tradeoffs is a large part of the job. There are many types of machine learning models with different pros and cons, and each of them can be tuned in various ways. For example, one could improve recall (how many correct results the algorithm returns) at the expense of precision (how many incorrect results). The PM might be able to identify new features (signals) or sources of training data that improve both. Sometimes the PM recommends looking at *less* data to get faster results when timeliness is important.

WHAT YOU NEED

Machine learning PMs need to understand the technical capabilities and limitations, plus deeply understand the customer or business problem they're trying to solve to help guide the team to the right tradeoffs.

Beyond that, PMs need to be comfortable with data. For example, they may need to open up SQL to see what the raw data looks like, check for any problems, or just browse for potential inspiration.

Luckily, you don't need to go back to school to pick up the technical skills, as long as you have an interest in math and a willingness to learn. There are good online courses and articles about machine learning and data science to ramp up.

Because of the technical nature of the job, strong collaboration with engineers is also important. There are often multiple different technical approaches, each with different tradeoffs around cost and speed, or precision and recall.

Strategic skills can also be important. As Laura Hamilton, VP of Product at Rally Health explained:

> You should have a data strategy and figure out what your moat is.[4] And how can you address it and expand it? If all of the data that you're using for your products is publicly available, it's not a very defensible business.[5]

As the underlying machine learning algorithms become widely available and commoditized, finding good sources of data and identifying good features become more important differentiators.

STARTUPS

WHAT IT IS

At most startups, one of the founders plays the role of the first PM. As the team scales, the startup may choose to bring on new PMs to help remove bottlenecks and free up the founders for more strategic work.

Joining a fast-growing startup can be amazing for your career as new opportunities arise and you're able to grow into roles that are larger than what you could get hired for externally. On the other hand, many startups don't have strong product leaders to learn from. Also, if the startup doesn't take off, it might be harder to find your next job than if you worked at a big name company.

WHAT YOU DO

Product managers at startups need to wear a lot of hats, juggle the extra complexities of working with the founders, and define the role.

The relationship with the product-focused founder is the trickiest and most important relationship for a startup PM. Early PMs sometimes come into a startup with an "I'm the CEO of the product" mindset and can quickly butt heads with the founder who doesn't want to give up control of the product vision, or perhaps even the details of the product. At a startup with a strong product founder, new PMs often need to prove themselves with operational execution and polite advising before they slowly gain strategic responsibility.

It's important to make sure you're very aligned with the founders before you join the company, or you'll find you won't want to stay long. First, you'll want to make sure you're strategically aligned and believe in the product vision. Then, make sure you're aligned with what they want from you as a PM. Some only learn after they join that the founder wanted them focused solely on execution, or that executives will make design-level tweaks to every feature.

A common challenge as an early PM at a startup is helping the rest of the team adapt to having a PM. Engineers or designers might worry that you'll take away their autonomy or add too much process. They might never have worked with a PM before and not know what to expect or when to loop you in. You'll need to show everyone how you can add value and help align expectations.

WHAT YOU NEED

Networking is important for PMs at startups because you often can't rely on people inside your company for advice and mentorship. This especially comes into play when you pick up a task you've never done before, like finding a coworking space, recording tutorial videos, planning a go-to-market campaign, hiring a user

---

4   A moat refers to your sustainable competitive advantage, for example an exclusive partnership.

5   Videos of her talks on ML can be found at https://www.linkedin.com/in/lauradhamilton.

researcher, sending out a monthly newsletter, or running social media accounts. Luckily, people at startups tend to be very open to helping others and sharing what has or hasn't worked for them. When stuck, you can always ask the company's investors and advisors to help make introductions.

Execution skills, especially the ability to create lean MVPs and test hypotheses crisply, are very important for startup PMs. Startups have limited resources; the quicker you can learn, the quicker you can make the right choices to achieve product market fit—hopefully before your startup runs out of money.

REGULATED INDUSTRIES

WHAT IT IS

PM roles in a regulated industry like healthcare, payments, or financial services are very similar to other types of PMing, with a few extra tradeoffs. These industries are subject to government regulations that may add extra requirements to product work.

WHAT YOU DO

The benefit of working in a regulated industry is that you can have a significant impact on a very important part of people's lives. These companies are regulated precisely because of how important they are.

Mariano Capezzani, Group Head of Product at HSBC, explained what he loves about the role:

> We have global reach, and the services and experiences that we build here enrich the lives of millions of people in the many communities that we serve across the world. Working here gives you the ability to meet customers, and meet the people that face these customers, all the way from Vancouver, Mexico, London, Dubai, to Hong Kong, Singapore, and Australia.

If you join an older institution that's new to digital transformation, there's often an untapped wealth of information that can provide huge value and opportunities for innovation.

The tradeoff of working in a regulated industry is that there are more constraints, and things tend to move slower (often because of organizational complexity). You might need to work with your lawyer every day to deeply understand the nuances of regulations, the spirit of the law, and the regulatory environment. There will likely be many stakeholders and multi-step approval processes. You usually aren't able to quickly throw together an A/B test.

WHAT YOU NEED

Great PMs in regulated industries don't treat regulations like black and white checkboxes that they hand over to engineers. Instead, they get creative about how to meet customer needs and regulations at the same time. They understand the environment deeply so they can show good judgment on when to push the boundaries—for example, using e-signatures instead of handwritten ones.

Leadership skills are especially important in regulated industries, particularly in more mature, non-tech companies. PMs often need to convince multiple stakeholders to take a risk or change a process. There are multiple teams to align and drive meaningful conversations.

NON-TECH COMPANIES

If you work at a software or technology company, you're usually working in an environment where everyone already believes in the value of product management and customer-focused approaches. When you leave the tech world, there's an opportunity to bring best practices to other organizations, but it does entail extra work.

Alicia Dixon, who's worked as a senior product manager at hotel chains, shared:

> I moved from software companies to companies where the tech is sold to compliment the core product. The key lesson I learned is that to be good at PM in those situations you have to excel at teaching others what you are doing and why you are doing it. Over communication is key.

A huge benefit of working at non-tech companies is flexibility of location. The top tech companies are mostly clustered in a few cities, but non-tech companies are everywhere. You also gain flexibility of product—there are many more businesses that don't center around software than those that do.

GOVERNMENT AND SOCIAL IMPACT ORGANIZATIONS

PMs sometimes overlook government, nonprofits, and social impact organizations, but they can be a great place to work and make a difference in your community.

Michelle Thong, who led digital services for the city of San Jose, recommends taking a "tour of duty" in these areas:

> If you're burnt out working in the tech industry and are looking for more mission driven work, a tour of duty in government could be really fulfilling. Your potential for impact is huge because you're taking a whole organization that is making a valuable contribution to society and helping them achieve better outcomes through product thinking. You may even end up choosing to stay in the public or non-profit sector as a long term career path, which will give you even more ability to enact positive change over time.

The tradeoff is that you need to put up with a lot of bureaucracy and scrutiny. You'll often be swimming against the tide as you try to transform an organization to be more customer centered.

For more on government and social impact work, *A Civic Technologist's Practice Guide* by Cyd Harrell is highly recommended.

CHAPTER 49

LANDING A PRODUCT MANAGER JOB

IF YOU'RE LOOKING to land a new job, this book can help you deeply understand the PM role and emphasizes the right skills and experiences to get you leveled correctly. That being said, you'll probably want to pair this book with one focused on interview preparation.

Our first co-authored book, *Cracking the PM Interview*, is a comprehensive book covering interview preparation. It gives detailed answers to questions like: What experience should you have? How do you make your existing experience translate? What should a great PM resume and cover letter look like? How do you master the interview—estimation, behavioral, case, product and technical questions, as well as the all-important pitch?

We can't possibly do justice to those topics in this book. For readers who are looking for help landing a job, however, we wanted to offer some basic advice on how to get started.

WHO WANTS TO BE A PRODUCT MANAGER, ANYWAY?

Product management is an incredible role. It's creative, influential, well-paying, and usually has a reasonable work-life balance. You get to work with cutting-edge technology, build things that make people happy, and see the impact of your work. You're seen as a leader, and you develop skills that are useful in any leadership role.

But, being a PM is not for everyone. Many people transfer into product management with dreams of being in charge, but they transfer out once they see the reality of the job.

Product managers have influence, but necessarily power. So, how do you know if product management is right for you?

> Overall, people who are happy and successful as PMs usually care a lot about making a big impact, which balances out the downsides. It's the end results that they really care about.

Reflect honestly on the following questions to see if you'd be a successful product manager, and, most importantly if you would enjoy it.

HOW DO YOU FEEL ABOUT NOT BUILDING THINGS WITH YOUR OWN HANDS?

How much satisfaction do you get from creating things yourself? Are you willing to give that up in order to have an impact by influencing others?

As a PM, you don't write the code yourself, and you may not do the designs, or even come up with the ideas yourself. If things are running behind schedule, or aren't as polished as you'd like, you can't just work extra hours to fix it. You'll have to learn to feel proud of the way you have influenced your team, and of the team's results.

Additionally, when you directly create things, there is a lot of praise, acknowledgment, and small victories. People praise the designer for a beautiful product, they praise the engineers for the functionality, but the contributions of the product manager are often overlooked.

As a PM, your impact is often invisible to others, so you may get less appreciation or recognition than others on the team. It's not always easy to tell when you made the right decision, so you'll need to be able to push forward even when the correct path is unclear.

DO YOU ENJOY THE WORK OF CONVINCING PEOPLE?

Do you envision yourself making decisions, and having people just do what you tell them to do? Fortunately, or unfortunately, being a PM is nothing like that.

As a product manager, you are constantly questioned and need to explain your reasoning and prove yourself. You need to convince your immediate team since they won't blindly go along with your plans if they don't agree with them. You need to convince executives and stakeholders, as they won't allocate people to your team or approve your roadmap if they don't agree with your choices. Across the company, people will tell you what *they* think you ought to be doing, and complain that you're not building their "pet" features.

The more seniority you gain, the more controversial the decision-making process becomes. All the easy problems will already be solved by the time things escalate to you.

CAN YOU BE HAPPY PRIORITIZING INSTEAD OF GETTING EVERYTHING PERFECT?

How important is "perfect" to you? How do you feel when you need to share work that is only 80% good?

As a product manager, there's always more work than can possibly be done. What little time you do have is fragmented and filled with context switching. You'll have frequent meetings and other urgent interruptions that make it hard to focus on complex work. You'll need to get used to sharing unfinished drafts, giving presentations that aren't fully polished, and making calls with incomplete data. You'll need to find joy in prioritizing well.

This goes for your product as well. Every additional month you spend adding features or polishing, is a month that users and the business can't benefit from your product. It takes a lot of prioritization and willingness to say "no" to get by as a PM.

LANDING YOUR FIRST PRODUCT MANAGER JOB

Product management can certainly be a competitive field to break into because there are relatively few jobs compared to the interest. However, because it's such a cross-functional role that requires a broad range of skills, there is really no single career path into it. You have many options for entering.

NEW GRAD → ASSOCIATE PRODUCT MANAGER

The textbook way to become a product manager is to major in computer science (and maybe minor in business or economics), get a summer internship, and then move into a full-time role as an associate product manager (APM). APM roles are competitive, so you'll need multiple signs of excellence to stand out: a high GPA, leadership experience, varsity sports, impressive achievements, student entrepreneurship, or a referral from someone within the company.

TAKING ON PM-LIKE TASKS AT WORK → INTERNAL TRANSFER

For those with more career experience, this is the most common approach. You can lean on your existing credibility to find opportunities to demonstrate your product skills. You could pitch a new feature, help your team with prioritization, or even ask a PM to take on a little of their work. Just be warned, this will probably be done in addition to your current work, not instead of it.

WELL-KNOWN TECH COMPANY → PM AT A SMALLER COMPANY

If you currently have a non-PM job at a top tech company and can't get an internal transfer, you might be able to get hired as a PM at a smaller company who really values your big-company experience. Try to learn as much as you can about how the product teams work at your current company and absorb best practices.

MBA → PRODUCT MANAGER

If you're having trouble transferring internally, or if you're getting PM jobs but they're not at the caliber you're aiming for, an MBA might open doors for you. Many companies recruit directly from business schools. Additionally, alumni networks often help graduates discover job opportunities at any stage of their career. Of course, pursuing further education can be expensive and presents a significant time commitment.

SPECIALIZED EXPERTISE → PM IN THAT FIELD

It's tough to get hired as a PM without any PM experience, but if you have important industry expertise, a company (especially a startup) might be willing to take a chance on you. People have made the leap from doctor to health startup PM, lawyer to legal software PM, or teacher to educational technology PM. Some even land their first PM job by being the app's biggest power user.

NETWORKING → WORKING AT A FRIEND'S COMPANY

A less common path is getting hired directly as a PM through your network. In some ways, this is similar to the internal transfer path; your past reputation and relationships give you the credibility to get a chance at the role. Sometimes, this lands you at a startup where you're the only PM. So, it's important to network with PMs outside the company to get the PM-specific support you need.

COLD OUTREACH TO A SMALL COMPANY → PM AT THE COMPANY

Getting your first PM job by reaching out directly to a hiring manager is a very tricky path, but many PMs credit their careers to this approach, especially when they were already a power user of the product. This requires finding the manager, figuring out the best way to contact them, and having a compelling enough message that they'll take the time to meet with you. Asking for a coffee chat instead of an interview lowers the stakes and increases the chance that the hiring manager will say yes.

For the best chances of success, make sure to bring your ideas and analysis about the app. This demonstrates your ability to think about product in general, and the benefit you could bring to the company in particular.

FOUNDER OF ACQUIRED STARTUP → PM AT THE PARENT COMPANY

If there's one thing that's harder than breaking into product management, it's starting a company and leading it through acquisition. This certainly isn't the easy route, but nevertheless, many great PMs started this way. If you're currently running a startup and want to transition into product management, this is a path worth considering. In fact, even a failed startup can still open doors to a product management job. After all, startup founders and PMs share many of the same responsibilities.

COFFEE CHATS

Coffee chats, also known as "informal chats," "informational interviews," or, "I'd love to learn more about the company," are the secret weapons in your quest for a new job. Even if you've researched everything about the company and you're sure you'd like to work there, it's always a good idea to ask if you can have a coffee chat with a PM at the company before you apply.

Coffee chats are valuable because people tend to switch between "pitch mode" and "interview mode," and it's hard to blend them.[1] During a coffee chat, they're trying to pitch you on the company and convince you to interview with them. They're on your side and feel invested in your success. While they also might be hoping to evaluate whether you're a match, that's usually secondary to getting you to apply.

When someone is in pitch mode, they'll share all kinds of useful information that can help your chances of passing the interview. You can ask them about the product strategy, the challenges they're facing, and what they've learned from their customers. You can ask what they look for in PMs, or even directly ask them for interview tips. At the end of the meeting, you can let them know you're interested in interviewing, and ask what the next steps are.

If you're already talking to a recruiter, they can sometimes help you set up a coffee chat. You can also reach out to PMs at the company directly through social media (such as LinkedIn, Twitter, or sometimes relevant Facebook groups), at a meetup, or even by guessing their email address.[2] Not everyone will say yes to a random coffee chat, but some people will, especially if you're polite and have caught their interest. Use good judgment when reaching out—if you annoy someone at the company, it could hurt your chances later on.

To prepare for the coffee chat, make sure you have your pitch ready. This will be your response to the "Tell me about yourself" question. Keep your answer short and be sure to highlight a few relevant talking points

---

1. Sometimes these informational chats can turn into screening interviews, especially if it is with someone senior. Consider being prepped almost like you would for an interview.

2. Many companies use standardized formats for their email addresses, like firstname.lastname@company.com.

(see "Behavioral questions" on pg 485). Beyond that, just be friendly and curious. Don't try to ask questions to show off, point out flaws in their product, or challenge them on their choices.

INTERVIEW QUESTIONS

There are six core types of interview questions, each requiring a different approach:[3]

1. Define yourself

2. Behavioral questions

3. Estimation questions

4. Product questions

5. Case questions

6. Technical questions

For all of these questions, the key to success is practice, practice, and more practice. Ideally, you'll find a partner to have mock interviews with who will give you honest feedback. Remember that you'll probably be nervous on the day of the interview, so you need your training to be strong.

When you're using a framework or step-by-step approach, make sure to use your judgment and adjust your answers for the specific question. Interviewers often want to ensure that you're not blindly following a framework, and are able to adapt to the kinds of twists and turns that happen in real life. One way this could show up is as a question that seamlessly shifts from one type to another, or questions involving details that invalidate part of a well-known framework.

For the interviewer's perspective on these questions, take a look at page 323.

DEFINE YOURSELF ("THE PITCH")

These are open-ended questions like, "Tell me about yourself." or, "Why do you want to work here?" that give you a chance to shine—or, if you're unprepared, to flop.

Prepare honest answers that show you're a strong match for the role. Rehearse your answers until you don't ramble under pressure.

Great pitches don't just explain how you got from point A to point B, but rather, they explain *why* you did. They add color to your background. For example, one might say, "In customer support, I learned how much I enjoy connecting with customers, and it inspired me to look at product jobs."

Be mindful of the length, however. Typically, you should be aiming for a pitch that is about two minutes. Time yourself as you practice; many candidates have no idea that they're actually speaking for five minutes or longer. Remember, you don't have to explain every detail of your experience. This isn't your autobiography. Give only the information that helps to set context and to boost your candidacy.

BEHAVIORAL QUESTIONS

Behavioral questions come in many forms. The interviewer could ask how you would respond to a hypothetical situation, or ask for specific details about how you handled a particular type of situation. They may

---

3   Each of these question types is covered in-depth with examples and walkthroughs in *Cracking the PM Interview*

also ask you to elaborate on a particular section of your resume. Ultimately, they're looking at the same two factors: your content and your communication. Make sure to nail both.

To prepare, master five key stories that best represent why you're a great PM candidate. These are the stories that you'll try to fit in whenever you have a chance. This is where you get to demonstrate your "wow factor."

It's a good idea to ensure your stories offer coverage for each of the five main topics below. Make sure your key stories represent the scope and complexity that match the level at which you're trying to get hired. Choose recent stories that demonstrate the depth of your skills. Note that many stories might fall into two or more buckets, and that's fine. These five main topics are:

- Leadership/Influence

- Teamwork

- Successes

- Challenges/Conflict

- Mistakes/Failures

Good responses are well-structured, and there are frameworks to help you do this. Many candidates go with the STAR (Situation/Task/Action/Result) or SAR (Situation/Action/Result) framework, but we've found this isn't ideal for many PM questions. It leaves the candidate telling facts about what happened, but leaving out so much of the good stuff.

The best answers focus on a problem they solved and the insights they discovered. And hence the PEARL framework was born.[4]

Problem

Start with the setup of the business or customer problem you faced. Give enough background so the interviewer can see that your boss didn't hand you a fully formed project. You want to highlight the distance between the ambiguous problem you started with and the refined problem you decided to address.

By framing the story as a problem, you're drawing the interviewer in and helping them understand why it's important. You can start with the larger problem that your overall product is solving, and then get into the specific problem that you want to tell a story about. If this is a story about an interpersonal conflict, start with the business problem or goals to set the context, and then describe the interpersonal problem.

Epiphany

Next, share your epiphany or insight. What did you learn or realize that kicked off your action? What did you see that other people were missing? How does that contrast with the "obvious" path? How did you learn this? Did it come from customer research, data analysis, or somewhere else?

This might sound like "Everyone thought we should do X, but based on Y, I realized we should actually do Z."

If there's no epiphany, this probably isn't the best story to demonstrate your skills. If you just did the obvious thing, anyone could have done it.

---

4   I first published this on my blog at https://medium.com/@jackiebo/interview-tips-for-senior-pms-2424f7b7c967, where I also have an example of using this framework to answer a question.

Action

The action is the work you did to make it happen. Keep it short and focus on the things that you did that another PM might not have done as well. You don't need to list out every step of the process—just the difficult or clever parts.

Give your interviewer enough context to understand how challenging your role was. That said, be diplomatic when the challenge was dealing with other people. You don't want to sound too negative or give the impression that you don't work well with others. If the other person was challenging in some way, it might be helpful to show empathy and understanding about why—not only will this demonstrate your empathy, but it also comes off less accusatory.

Result

The result is a happy ending. It's okay to have setbacks and failures in the story, but you should treat those as the middle of the story.

For example, if you're talking about a failed experiment, end with how you iterated and had a successful launch later, or how you used what you learned to avoid a similar problem at your next company. When you have good results, connect them to the larger goals, strategy, and mission. For example, instead of just talking about how people loved your feature, talk about how it improved retention.

Learning

Finally, talk about what you learned. What do you wish you knew earlier? What would you do differently next time? Did you get a chance to use what you learned in a later project?

This is especially important for questions about negative events, like mistakes or failures. How did you learn from that and use this learning to make things better? Whenever you're asked about a negative experience, silently add that part to the question—and to your response.

A great response will deliver a *message* to your interviewer about what type of person you are. Are you *relentless* in pushing through challenges? Are you deeply *analytical* with data? Are you *empathetic*—good at knowing what makes your coworkers "tick"? Are you creative and able to find unusual solutions to problems? Think *adjectives*—the sorts of things you'd find on a list of "strengths and weaknesses."

Your interviewer is trying to extract a signal (pg 323) from you. Make it easy for them to find it.

ESTIMATION QUESTIONS

Estimation questions such as, "How many pizzas are sold in the US each year?" are entirely about the process you take to solve them. Typically, the interviewer doesn't know the actual answer and wouldn't care whether you did either. It's the journey, not the destination.[5]

Interviewers use these questions to evaluate both your problem-solving skills and quantitative skills. These questions can be tackled with an eight-step approach:

- **Step 1:** Clarify the question

- **Step 2:** Catalog what you know (or wish you knew)

---

5   Rumors have swirled over the years that "brain teasers" like these have been banned at certain companies like Google. This is not true. While brain teasers are often banned, these questions are not considered brain teasers.

- **Step 3:** Make an equation

- **Step 4:** Think about edge cases and alternate sources

- **Step 5:** Break it down

- **Step 6:** Review and state your assumptions

- **Step 7:** Do the math

- **Step 8:** Check the answer to see if it's reasonable

Depending on your background and the role, these questions can feel technical ("How many servers does this product need?"), business-like ("How much money does this product make?"), or simply weird ("How many golf balls can fit in a school bus?"). The approach is generally the same, regardless of the topic.

PRODUCT QUESTIONS

The product question is the heart and soul of the PM interview. It gets directly at the core of what a PM does: design, build, and improve products. While the question may come in various formats, there is one key component you need to understand and focus on: the goal.

Product questions come in three basic formats:

- "What is your favorite product, and why?"

- Design a <product> for <a group>. For example, "Design a chair for the elderly" or, "Design a math app for children."

- Improve <an existing product>. For example, "How would you improve our company's sign-in flow?" or "How would you get more people to use Google Maps?"

These three types of questions have a lot in common, but they each require a different focus and approach.

Favorite Products

It's common for interviewers to ask you to discuss some of your favorite products—so much so, that it would be a huge mistake to enter an interview without some idea of what you'll discuss. Going into an interview without preparing for this question could make the difference between getting hired and getting a "thanks, but no thanks" email.

Prepare at least five different products in advance so you don't freeze, or have to start from scratch when they ask you to choose a product. But, be careful not to appear as though you're reciting a prepared answer, or the interviewer might make you switch to a different product—interviewers want to see how you think on your feet.

As you prepare, look for a diverse range of products—websites, mobile applications, and physical products. You wouldn't want to only prepare mobile apps, and then get stuck on a question like, "What's your favorite website?"

Start by discussing why you love it, and look to show product insight. At a minimum, you should discuss the use cases (tip: that's good "PM" language to use), and how the product solves those problems. You should be able to discuss how the product is better than the alternative options. Make sure that you also have ideas for how you would improve the product.

Truly impressive answers go a level deeper. They demonstrate true product insight at a level that non-PMs might struggle to explain. For example, a PM could discuss some unexpected things that Airbnb does to build a sense of community, and how this is integral to the trust required in sharing spaces with strangers. As a rule of thumb, if you can imagine your non-technical and non-PM friends and family outlining the same explanation, you probably haven't gone deep enough.

Designing a new product

Designing a new product requires a holistic view of all the elements that contribute to a successful product launch. You'll usually want to focus on a target audience that your product could actually win, while not narrowing the audience so much that they are no longer big enough to be worth going after.

There is a lot to cover, so make sure to use the whiteboard (or paper, if the interview room doesn't have a whiteboard). It can help keep you organized and communicate a structured process to your interviewer.

Step 1: Ask questions
Ask questions to define exactly what a product, or part of a product, is and who the user is.[6] Think carefully about the user. For example, the term "children" is quite broad, since a small child's needs are quite different from a teenager's. Or, you could be asked to design a remote for blind people—but what kind of remote?

Some of the best candidates also discuss priorities. Are we optimizing for customer experience? Making money? Improving operational efficiency?

Step 2: Provide a structure
It's a great idea to provide a structure for the problem, ideally on the whiteboard. One of your goals is to demonstrate good communication skills, so outlining what you're going to do in the next few steps is handy. Additionally, it can help keep you on track.

Step 3: Discuss users and user segmentation
We've already touched on the users in Step 1, but it can be useful to go a step further and segment our users. For example, you could segment amusement park guests into season pass holders, repeated guests, and first-time guests.

Some products have "hidden" users, so it can be useful to discuss that here. For example, products designed for children might also be used by their parents, teachers, and caregivers.

Once you've done this, you might ask the interviewer if they have a particular segment they'd like you to design for. If they let you choose, look for one which has the biggest pain points (problems with the current system).

Step 4: Discuss use cases and goals
Now, we want to discuss what our users are doing. What are their goals? Why are they using this product? What are their core use cases? Are there any "unexpected" uses we should prepare for, like a young child putting the toy in their mouth?

---

6   Some interviewers will intentionally hold back an important part of the question to test whether you ask questions before jumping in. Don't get caught in the trap!

Excellent answers often go deeper and discuss underlying motivations or values. Small children, for example, often want to feel big and important, while teens may value independence.[7]

Step 5: Current pain points

Of these use cases, what isn't going so well? What are the weak spots or pain points? What are they using right now?

Some use cases might be addressed quite well with current options, but others have major pain points.

Step 6: Solve the problem(s)

Now that you understand who the user is, what their use cases are, and what's bothering them, you can attempt to address their needs.

Be careful not to prematurely dismiss a pain point as unsolvable. For example, if bad weather conditions are a pain point, an app *can* address it. It can't control the weather, but it can provide information about weather conditions.

Step 7: Wrap things up

We can now close with a summary of our app and its core features. At this point, if not earlier, your interviewer will likely ask you some follow-up questions. These questions are often about implementation, priorities, or extensions.

If your interviewer disagrees with you, don't worry, it's normal. They might genuinely disagree, or they might want to see how you react to disagreement. In either case, you should consider their perspective, think, then do whatever is best given the users and our priorities.

Improving a product

Improving a product is closely related to designing a new product, but the focus can be quite different. Make sure you clarify—or decide—what "improve" actually means. For example, it could mean user growth, revenue growth, delight, or enabling a new use case. With this in mind, adapt your process to tackle that specific type of improvement. As you're tackling the problem, remember that you're supposed to come up with the best possible improvement, not just *any* improvement or a scattered set of minor improvements.

In practice, this means you'll want to evaluate each idea against the goal and quickly discard any paths that aren't promising. You'll also want to show the interviewer that you've comprehensively considered every good approach, so they'll be convinced your idea is one of the best, not just the first idea you thought of. As you slice up your user base or problem space, double check the slices you're *not* including to see if they might hold the larger opportunity.

CASE QUESTIONS

Case questions are hypothetical situations that usually revolve around delivering the best product to customers. Interviewers are looking for candidates who will structure the problem, ask appropriate questions, show strong instincts and initiative, and drive (not ride) the conversation.

---

7   There is a delicate balance between generalizations and stereotyping. In practice, your interviewer probably won't be offended if you generalize about what teens value. But if you do the same thing based on gender or race, you might find yourself in riskier territory. This is also quite dependent on the culture. The US, for example, tends to be more sensitive to these topics.

Practice is certainly helpful for these questions. It can also help to stay on top of business and technology news, especially around controversial topics. Follow along with what people say the companies did well or poorly, and what they think should be changed.

You can also study common frameworks such as:

- Customer Purchase Decision-Making Process (pg 187)

- Marketing Mix (4 Ps) (pg 188)

- SWOT Analysis (pg 188)

- The Five Cs (Situational Analysis) (pg 189)

- Porter's Five Forces (pg 190)

Please note that while these frameworks offer useful concepts, interviewers generally aren't testing your knowledge of these frameworks; they may not even be aware of them. Don't try to force a framework where it doesn't belong. Sometimes, you might use these concepts as inspiration for tackling a topic rather than using them directly.

TECHNICAL QUESTIONS

Many companies, including Google, Amazon, and Microsoft, sometimes ask PM candidates coding and algorithm questions—particularly with more junior PM candidates. These questions can range from straightforward coding to more complex algorithms, which may or may not be followed by a request to code.

With that said, the expectations, particularly around syntax, are generally lower than they would be for a developer. Many interviewers will even be satisfied with code-like pseudocode.

To prepare, you should brush up on these:

- Data structures (arrays, hash tables, trees, linked lists, stacks, queues) (pg 99)

- Algorithms (sorting, binary search, graph search)

- Concepts (big O notation, recursion) (pg 99)

You can ask the company if you'll have a technical interview, and if so, of what type (coding, system design, etc.). Don't stress until you need to! Many PMs never see interviews of this sort. And those who get them do often perform much better than they expect.[8] These interviews are primarily about problem-solving and showing a basic technical familiarity. Even if your coding skills are rusty, the skills *actually* being tested in these interviews are likely still strong.

If you have no coding experience, there's little sense worrying about this. A company is unlikely to ask a non-coder to code.[9]

---

8   As an anecdote (or is this data?): I (Gayle) often am brought in as a consultant to prep startups for acquisition interviews. (When a big tech company is considering acquiring a startup, they often assess the team's skills via interviews—coding interviews for the devs, and PM interviews for the CEO.) The startup CEO, if they have some coding background, usually *outperforms* the average dev on their team, on the coding interviews! The CEO's syntax might be weak, but their problem-solving skills are sharp.

9   Also, in the unlikely chance that a non-coding PM got asked to code, they'd have little chance to do well anyway. There's no sense stressing about an improbable event that's out of your control anyway.

You could also be asked questions that are technical, but non-coding. These could be questions about designing system architecture, explaining a technical concept, diagnosing a bug or performance problem, or performing a technical task that relates to their product. These sorts of questions are more common for companies or roles that are very technical. The company wants to validate that you have the right experience.

If you find yourself lost, attempting to solve the problem is always better than giving up.

MISCELLANEOUS QUESTIONS

The earlier categories of questions should mostly cover you, but there are other questions that could fall outside of this—or at least appear to. Mohit, a PM candidate, was asked, "How would you evacuate San Francisco?" How would you classify this sort of question?

When in doubt, try to quickly assess what you *think* the interviewer is trying to assess. Is it user empathy, structured problem solving, creativity, etc? That can often give you a good clue about how to tackle the problem.

After that, try approaching roughly like this:

1. **Ask questions.** Think about the who / what / how / why sorts of questions. You need to understand the constraints of the problem. For example, if you're evacuating San Francisco, you'll want to understand why you're evacuating, how long you have, and who.

2. **Structure the problem solving.** Structuring the problem not only helps you develop a more comprehensive solution, but it also demonstrates that you're a structured sort of person. Interviewers like that!

3. **Solve.** Listen to the interviewer and ask questions as needed, but assume you should be in the driver's seat. Leverage the structure you came up with and solve the problem. If you have a whiteboard or shared text editor, this can be useful to share your thoughts with your interviewer.

Consider a very odd question like, "Find all the uses that you can for a paperclip." Force yourself to ask questions (Uses for me or for anyone? Do I have one paperclip or several—or even millions? Can I modify the paperclip—bend it, melt it, etc?). Then find a structure ("Let me break this down by solutions for one paperclip vs. solutions for a dozen vs. solutions for thousands.") Now, solve for each of these pieces. What are the things you might use a single paperclip for? You can even break that down further.

There are no guarantees—after all, we're talking about questions that *don't* seem to fit a pattern—but asking questions and applying a structure is nearly always a good thing.

CHAPTER 50

NETWORKING FOR INTROVERTS

BY JULES WALTER

JULES WALTER is a product leader at YouTube. Previously, he led monetization at Slack and was a key contributor to Slack's 10X growth in his four years there. He serves on the boards of BlackProductManagers.com and CodePath.org, two organizations he co-founded to support underrepresented people in tech. Jules holds a computer science degree from MIT and an MBA from Harvard Business School.

twitter: @julesdwalt

HOW ANYONE CAN BUILD AUTHENTIC PROFESSIONAL RELATIONSHIPS

Building a network is a common recommendation for career development. A strong network can help you access unique opportunities, and offer advice to help you grow and handle challenging situations. Yet, many people—especially introverts—struggle with networking because they feel they lack the mental energy, time, or know-how.

> They sometimes have the perception that networking requires meeting more people than they can handle, or that the people they want to connect with are inaccessible.

Over time, I've learned to overcome those challenges and grow my own network in a way that is effective and feels authentic to me. Many friends and coworkers have asked me to share my approach, which relies on the principles below. These four principles will increase the likelihood that you create fruitful, long-term relationships with new people, and require a relatively low amount of effort.

1. START WITH LOW-COMMITMENT INTERACTIONS

Let's assume you've identified a potential mentor. For example, you meet a speaker at a conference. You believe you can learn from them and would like to stay in touch.

In new relationships, don't ask for too much too soon; this is a common mistake. Don't ask new contacts for coffee in your first interaction and never explicitly ask them to become your mentor. Instead, ask for their email and reach out within a day or so with a quick question they can answer via email, such as:

> Hi Adam,
>
> I loved the point you made yesterday about finding the heat for products. Do you have an example of a feature that wouldn't have existed without this approach?
>
> Thanks,
>
> Jules

With a quick question, they are less likely to ignore you. Once a new contact interacts with you, even with a short email, you have a foot in the door and can build a relationship from there.

2. BE CONSISTENT AND GRADUAL

Pick a cadence to regularly reach out to a new contact based on the person's availability—e.g., monthly or quarterly. After two or three interactions, new contacts will expect you to continue reaching out and will start seeing the interactions as the start of a relationship. It's human nature to invest in a relationship once you expect to consistently interact with a person in the future.

As you build trust and demonstrate that you're not wasting the person's time—through quick and thoughtful exchanges—then you can start asking for more time (e.g., coffee) or connect in more personal ways (e.g., Instagram).

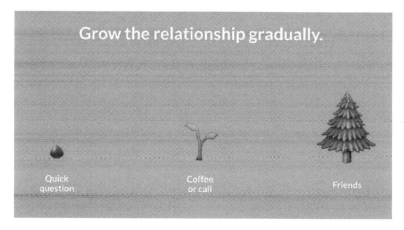

Grow the relationship gradually.

Quick question • Coffee or call • Friends

3. KEEP CONVERSATIONS SPECIFIC AND CONCRETE

Don't ask busy people to "catch up." Be specific in your ask and provide a concrete topic or decision for them to offer input. For example:

> Hi Lawrence,
>
> I'm continuing to think of ways to be a great manager and would love your advice—e.g., how to coach, delegate effectively, manage my schedule and energy.
>
> When's a good time to hop on a call?
>
> Many thanks,
>
> Jules

People often want to help, but have competing demands for their time. The more specific and concise your request, the more confidence they'll have that speaking with you is a good use of time.

4. MAKE THE RELATIONSHIP MUTUALLY BENEFICIAL

For a relationship to last, you need to provide value to the other person, often in intangible ways. For example, let a mentor know how their previous advice helped you, which shows that time spent with you is impactful. It's only when I started mentoring others that I realized how much value I got out of just knowing how they used my advice.

> Get to know a mentor's world and seek ways to help. I often leave a few minutes at the end of a conversation with a mentor to ask them what's on their mind and how I can help. These open-ended questions show genuine care and create unexpected opportunities to provide value.

With these four principles, I've been able to develop a great network that includes mentors and friends like Lawrence Ripsher, who encouraged me to write this post—we met a few years ago at an event. Let me know how this approach plays out for you. I hope it's as helpful to you as it has been to me.

This article was written by Jules Walter and reprinted with permission.[1]

---

1   Reprinted with permission from https://medium.com/@julesdwalt/networking-for-introverts-3544f4287fc1

CHAPTER 51

THE PARADOX OF AUTONOMY AND RECOGNITION
THOUGHTS ON TRUST AND MERIT IN SOFTWARE TEAM CULTURE

BY KATE MATSUDAIRA

KATE MATSUDAIRA works at Google as a director in Core Systems. Her teams help build the infrastructure that powers Google.

Prior to coming to Google, Kate helped build several successful startups that have gone on to get acquired by companies like eBay, O'Reilly Media, and Limelight. Kate started her career as a software engineer and lead at Microsoft and Amazon. She is a keynote speaker, published author, and has been honored with recognition like NCWIT Symons Innovator Award and Seattle's Top 40 under 40.

Find Kate online at katemats.com.

WHO DOESN'T WANT RECOGNITION FOR THEIR HARD WORK AND CONTRIBUTIONS?

Early in my career, I wanted to believe that if you worked hard and added value that you would be rewarded. I wanted to believe in the utopian ideal that hard work, discipline, and contributions were the fuel that propelled you up the corporate ladder. And, boy, was I wrong.

You see, I started my career as a shy, insecure, but smart, programmer. I worked hard (almost every weekend), I wrote code for fun when I wasn't working on my work projects (still do, actually), and I was loyal and dedicated to my company.

MY PROJECT SHOULD HAVE BEEN JUDGED ON MERIT.

Once, for six months, I worked on a project with four other people—and I felt like my contributions in terms of functionality and hours contributed were at the top of the group. So, you can imagine my surprise when at our launch party, the GM of the group stood up and recognized "Josh, and the other team members for their hard work."

I stood there stunned, thinking, WTF?! How was it that the GM was so out of touch with the team? Didn't our manager look at the check-ins and the being resolved? How did Josh, who had probably contributed the second least amount to the project, end up being the only person singled out from the group? Not me, not the most senior person on the project, but the guy who seemed to spend a lot of time talking to my boss and the other people on the project.

So many of us have been there though. We work tirelessly, doing our very best to get things done on time, but somehow we get passed over—in favor of someone else whom you honestly believe didn't contribute nearly as much as you had. What happened to meritocracy and being recognized for your work?

AUTONOMY MAKES MERITOCRACY IMPOSSIBLE

Fast forward to now in the present day. I work with a team of 18 amazing technologists and it is my job to judge their performance. And only recently have I realized that, in many ways, it is near impossible to do so.

> There is no objective, quantifiable way that exists for me to be able to do this at scale without resorting to micromanagement—which is not something you even want to contemplate with a talented team.

If this doesn't make sense to you, let me explain (note that some of these are measurable, but others are more subjective—but all are various ways people have suggested as metrics to judge performance):

- **Hours**. Ugh. I hate hour watchers. Writing code, at least for me, is like art, and when I am just not in the mood, I can't force myself to get things done. To use the measure of time as a productivity measure doesn't fairly represent the creativity and mentation required of a developer. Beyond that, it's not really all that feasible to track hours in a highly virtual environment. I love that people on my team can work from home—or whatever environment where they do their best work (it is the reason we have "no meeting" days)—but how could I possibly track someone's hours if they aren't in the office? Just like counting beans, counting hours sucks. Don't do it.

- **Lines of code**. This measure is flawed for many reasons—from the mantra that "the best code is the lines you don't write" to the simple anecdotal fact it once took me three days to write a single line of code, while another day I wrote over 10,000 lines of code (although admittedly part of that count included some substantial cut and paste). And of course, deleting code can be very productive too.

- **Bug counts**. Of course quality is important, but finding bugs in production belonging to developers that otherwise write great code is not rare. This metric is seriously flawed in a profound way—it does not account for the fact that your best developers often produce a moderate amount of serious bugs because they have been entrusted to design and implement the most complicated and critical pieces of an application/system. Penalizing your best players for having highly impacting bugs is tantamount to rewarding mediocrity.

- **Features**. Functionality is key of course, since when it comes to contributions, the features that are built or added to the product should be directly tied to customer value. Of course, judging on features can get complicated when multiple people contribute to one feature. And of course, the details of the implementation can dramatically impact the efforts and hours involved. For example, recently there was a project to add login to an existing site. Implementing the feature using interstitial pages would have taken a few hours, however the design involved using lightboxes, which added some complexity around security that added days to the project to accommodate. It can be misleading even looking at functionality and features if you don't dive into the technical details of the implementation and trade-offs.

- **Maintainability**. It is hard to measure and track something as subjective as writing solid, maintainable code—but anyone who has had to struggle with legacy spaghetti code will tell you that maintainability is worth the extra time it takes if it's something requiring long-term usage in production. Coders who spend the extra time to write highly-robust, maintainable code are often penalized for it, simply because their true contributions will not be realized until years later.

- **Building skills and knowledge**. And how do you measure the benefit of the time invested learning a new technology enough to be highly effective in its use? Researching and choosing the proper tools that optimize your productivity? And the time spent making careful and deliberate strategic choices that ultimately make a project feasible and successful? Obviously these are critically important, but an outside perspective would note that it seems a lot more work could've been done in the same amount of time.

- **Helping others**. There are many programmers who are great but not for the work they do. Rather, they are great for the way they enable others to be great. Just having these people on the team makes everyone else better. Mentoring and selfless assistance to others is critical to building and preserving a highly-productive and cohesive team, but it can be incredibly difficult to quantify an individual's role in this despite the reality of the contribution.

And of course there are probably another 101 things you could look at to judge someone's achievements—including the way they present themselves (having a good attitude, for example), being very dependable, or a prime contributor of innovative ideas and solutions. However, very few of these are objective, concrete things you can total up and give a grade to—and it is incredibly difficult to do without diving into the minute details or micromanaging the project.

SO IF THERE'S NO RELIABLE MANAGERIAL MEASURE OF YOUR CONTRIBUTIONS HOW DO YOU GET NOTICED?

Really it all comes down to one thing: **Trust**.

> Trust is like a currency; when a manager gives their reports autonomy and independence, they are trusting them to complete the assigned task—making wise and strategic decisions along the way—and proactively communicate problems long before they become a problem.

They are in fact investing their money in you, and when they see the returns on that investment, they, just like any lucky investor, are quite pleased. Trust, though, takes time, patience, and consistency—but if you can't build a relationship with your manager all that means nothing. For someone to invest in you, you have to show you are in fact an investment.

- Does your boss trust you?

- Do your team and your peers trust you?

- Have you done a good job to earn their trust?

- How would your peers describe you to someone else?

- How influential are you within your organization?

As a manager, there have been times when I have been very fond of an employee, but then noticed that their peers didn't care for them or held negative impressions of their performance. In these cases, given the trust level I have with my entire team, the opinions of the collective can easily outweigh my personal preferences. Think of trust like a graph and each arc between the people you interact with as a weight—so when it comes to performance, those weights really matter.

> Projects, products, performance, and companies aren't just judged on the output, but how they produce the output.

In my project, the one thing Josh did differently was he didn't just do the work, but he made sure that the management—my boss and the GM—knew what our team was doing. In retrospect, he was the reason our project was recognized in an organization with so many people. At the time I resented Josh; now, many years later, I realize that his contributions to our team wasn't just his code, but his communication and **the way he did his job**.

As an aside though, I think that certain company cultures may reward this more than others. The problem with some people like Josh is that over time they can optimize on "trust" and create a distorted view of their contributions—and this is what I mean when I say "office politics"—and this isn't good either.

One of my very smart friends told me a story about joining one big company and meeting tons of super-smart, highly functional, and productive people who were all about creating trust with their superiors by being hyper-visible.

> They talked the most at meetings, they interrupted people, they sent extremely verbose emails at 3 am detailing the minutiae of a meeting that took place the previous day, they cc'd long lists of seemingly irrelevant but high-ranking people on their emails, etc. And their bosses loved them and they got the best reviews. After meeting these individuals and being both amazed and disgusted by their shtick, it started to become clear to us that the whole culture self-selects to this type of person. It didn't take us long to understand why so much "work" happens, but so little gets done.

SO WHAT CAN YOU DO IF YOU ARE A MANAGER?

As an employee, I want to be judged by my contributions, and have a team that is a meritocracy. I also want autonomy and the ability to own substantial things and not have someone looking over my shoulder.

As a manager, I want to give recognition and praise to the people who deserve it, and I don't want to micro-manage and spend my days being "big brother."

This implies an implicit contract:

> I will give you autonomy and independence, but it is your responsibility to share status and information with me.

For example, once a team member told me he had worked so hard and really gave it his best, however, from my viewpoint his progress wasn't up to the same level of his teammates. When he was leaving the company he told me all these things he had done—and I asked him "Why didn't you share this with me before?" You see, I would have advised him to spend his time elsewhere on priorities that were more important to the business. He responded with "I thought you would know." Don't make that same mistake.

It is also important that as a manager you recognize improvement. This means understanding a person's strengths and weaknesses. If you observe someone's performance and you see they make substantial improvements in one of their development areas then that is definitely worth recognizing. For example if you have an amazing engineer who is typically a poor communicator, but they step up and not just contribute their great coding prowess to a project but also keep other team members abreast of evolving risk factors— then those sorts of achievements are worth praise.

Just make sure you take in all the factors of a person's involvement in the organization. Take steps to ask good questions and solicit feedback from other members of the organization. And let each person know your expectations around communication and progress.

AND WHAT CAN YOU DO NOW?

And so my end conclusion in all of this is: if you want autonomy, and the ability to own and control your own domain and projects—it is your job to push information and build trust with your team members.

In other words, you need to learn and do the following:

- **Follow through**. Do what you say and consistently deliver on your commitments.

- **Proactively communicate** when a task takes you longer than you thought, and why.

- **Improve your communication skills**. In order for others to hear you, sometimes you have to hone the way you deliver your message.

- **Volunteer information** and make an effort to explain vague or hard to understand ideas and concepts. Make an effort to share the details of your decisions and diversions. This is also important when you make mistakes—letting others know before they figure out on their own will show ownership of the situation and can prevent misunderstandings later.

- **Be forthright and authentic** with your feelings. Even when you may hold a contrary opinion, communicate your thoughts (respectfully and with tact).

- **Don't talk behind the backs of others**. It is very difficult to build trust if someone knows that you will say something negative about your boss, the company leadership, or another coworker.

- **Be objective and neutral** in difficult situations. Learn how to be calm under pressure and act as a diplomat resolving conflicts instead of causing them.

- **Show consistency in your behavior**. Not just in follow-through but by eliminating any double standards that may exist.

- **Learn to trust them**. This is one of the hardest ones, but trust is a two-way street. Giving others the benefit of the doubt and learning how to work with them is essential to a strong mutual working relationship.

In turn, hopefully, you have a good manager that will be able to ask you good questions and take the time to understand your contributions. And if that is not your situation, then make sure you are sharing information with those around you such as your peers, your boss, and other stakeholders.

Good leadership is keeping everyone on the same page; if you want independence, it is on you to make sure people know what you are contributing.

This article was written by Kate Matsudaira and reprinted with permission.[1]

---

1   Reprinted with permission from https://katemats.com/blog/paradox-autonomy-recognition

CHAPTER 52

10 RULES FOR NEGOTIATING JOB OFFERS

BY HASEEB QURESHI

> **HASEEB QURESHI** is a managing partner at Dragonfly Capital, a leading crypto-focused VC. Haseeb's previous experience includes being a general partner at Metastable Capital, and was a software engineer at Earn.com (acquired by Coinbase) and Airbnb. He is an effective altruist and in a previous life was a professional poker player.
>
> Twitter: @hosseeb

10 RULES FOR NEGOTIATING A JOB OFFER

When the story of how I landed a job at Airbnb went viral, I was surprised at how infatuated people were with my negotiations.[1] Media stories portrayed me as some kind of master negotiator—a wily ex-poker-player who was able to con the tech giants into a lucrative job offer.

This is silly. It's silly for a lot of reasons, but one of the main ones is that in reality, my negotiation skills are nothing special. There are lots of job candidates who are better negotiators than I, to speak nothing of recruiters and other professional negotiators.

It just so happens that most people don't negotiate at all, or if they do, they negotiate just enough to satisfy themselves that they did.

Worse yet, most of the advice out there on negotiation is borderline useless. Almost anything you read on the subject will be a vague and long-winded exhortation to "make sure you negotiate" and "never say the first number." Beyond those two morsels of advice, you're pretty much on your own.

---

1   https://haseebq.com/farewell-app-academy-hello-airbnb-part-i/

I thought to myself: why is there so little actionable advice out there about negotiation? I suspect it's because deep down, many people believe that negotiation is inexplicable, that it's something some people can do and others can't, and that there's no real way to break it down so anyone can learn it.

I say that's bullshit. Negotiation is a skill that can be learned just like any other, and I don't believe it's particularly elusive or hard to understand. So I'm going to try to explain how anyone can do it.

Three caveats.

First: I'm not an expert. There are people who really are experts at this, and when my advice contradicts theirs, you should assume I'm wrong.

Second: negotiation is tricky to generalize about because it's deeply intertwined with social dynamics and power. The appropriate advice for an Asian male in Silicon Valley may not be appropriate for a Black woman in Birmingham, Alabama. Racial, sexual, and political dynamics accompany you to the negotiating table.

At the same time, I want to caution against overemphasizing these factors. Being afraid to negotiate out of fear of discrimination can often be just as deleterious as discrimination itself.

Ceteris paribus, negotiate aggressively.[2]

Third: I'm the first to admit that negotiation is stupid. It's a practice that inherently benefits those who are good at it, and is an absurd axis on which to reward people. But it's a reality of our economic system. And like most collective action problems, we're probably not going to be able to abolish it any time soon. In which case, you might as well improve at it.

So here's my guide to negotiation. It's going to be split into two parts: this first part will be about conceptualizing the negotiating process, how to begin the process, and how to set yourself up for maximal success. The second part will be advice on the actual back-and-forth portion of negotiating and how to ask for what you want.

Let's take it from the top.

WHAT IT MEANS TO "GET A JOB"

In our culture we call entering the employment market "trying to get a job." This is an unfortunate turn of phrase. "Getting a job" implies that jobs are a resource out in the world, and you're attempting to secure one of these resources. But that's completely backwards. What you are actually doing is selling your labor, and a company is bidding for it.

> Employment is just striking a mutual deal in the labor market.

Like any market, the labor market only functions well if it's competitive. This is the only way to ensure fair and equitable pricing. Imagine you were a farmer selling watermelons. Would you just sell your watermelons to the first buyer who agreed to purchase them? Or would you survey the marketplace of buyers, see the best price (and business partner) you could get, and then make an informed decision on which buyer to sell to?

And yet, when people talk about the labor market, they think "oh, a company wants to give me a job! What a relief!" As though having a job were in itself some special privilege for which a company is the gatekeeper.

Dispel yourself of this mindset.

---

2   Ceteris paribus is Latin for "all else being equal."

> A job is just a deal. It is a deal between you and a company to exchange labor for money (and other things you value).

This might sound like an abstract point, but you should absolutely approach negotiation from this perspective.

THE ROLE OF NEGOTIATION

Negotiating is a natural and expected part of the process of trying to make a deal. It's also a signal of competence and seriousness. Companies generally respect candidates who negotiate, and most highly attractive candidates negotiate (if for no other reason, because they often have too many options to choose from).

At the risk of spouting truisms: always, always negotiate. Doesn't matter how good or bad you think you are. You never damage a relationship by negotiating.

In all my time as an instructor at App Academy, out of hundreds of offers negotiated, only once or twice were offers ever rescinded in negotiations. It basically never happens. And when it does, usually the candidate was being an unconscionable asshole, or the company was imploding and needed an excuse to rescind the offer.

You might think to yourself: "well, I don't want to set high expectations, and the offer is already generous, so I ought to just take it."

No. Negotiate.

Or maybe: "I don't want to start off on the wrong foot and look greedy with my future employer."

No. Negotiate.

"But this company is small and—"

No. Shut up. Negotiate.

We'll talk more in the next section about why a lot of these objections are bullshit, and fundamentally misapprehend the dynamics of hiring. But for now, just trust me that you should always negotiate.

THE TEN RULES OF NEGOTIATING

I've tried to boil down negotiation to ten rules. The rules, in order of appearance, are:

1. Get everything in writing
2. Always keep the door open
3. Information is power
4. Always be positive
5. Don't be the decision maker
6. Have alternatives
7. Proclaim reasons for everything
8. Be motivated by more than just money
9. Understand what they value

10. Be winnable

We'll only get through some of these in this blog post, and the rest will appear in the second part. But I'll explain each rule as we get to it.

So let's start from the top and try to walk through a negotiation process from the very beginning. For most, that starts when you receive an offer.

THE OFFER CONVERSATION

You've just received the phone call: your interview went well, and after much deliberation they decided they like you. They want to make you an offer. Congratulations!

Don't get too excited though. The fun is just getting started.

Thank your recruiter. Sound excited—hopefully this won't be hard. Before jumping into details, try to ask for specific feedback on your interview performance. If they give it to you, this will help you gauge how much they want you, as well as tell you things you can improve on in your next interview(s).

Now time to explore the offer.

Rule #1 of negotiating: have everything in writing.

Eventually, they'll give you information about the offer. Write it all down. Doesn't matter if they're going to send you a written version later, write everything down. Even if there are things that are not directly monetary, if they relate to the job, write them down. If they tell you "we're working on porting the front end to Angular," write that down. If they say they have 20 employees, write that down. You want as much information as you can. You'll forget a lot of this stuff, and it's going to be important in informing your final decision.

Depending on the company, they'll also tell you about the equity package. We'll look more specifically at equity in part II, but be sure to write everything down.

The rule from here on out is that everything significant you discuss will have some kind of a paper trail. Often, the company won't even send you an official offer letter until a deal is finalized. So it falls to you to confirm all of the important details in subsequent emails.

So yadda yadda, lots of details, writing stuff down, oh there's a joke, time to laugh. Now the recruiter is done talking and you're done asking all of your questions.

Your recruiter will now say something along the lines of "so what do you think?"

This seems innocuous, but your reply here is critical, because there's a lot you can say to weaken your position. This is your first decision point.

A decision point is a moment in the negotiation where your interlocutor wants to compel you to make a decision. If they succeed in tying you to a position, they will close the door on further negotiating. Of course "what do you think?" is a subtle prod. But it is the beginning of many attempts to get you to make a premature commitment.

This leads to rule #2 of negotiating: always keep the door open.

Never give up your negotiating power until you're absolutely ready to make an informed, deliberate final decision.

This means your job is to traverse as many of these decision points as possible without giving up the power to continue negotiating. Very frequently, your interlocutor will try to trick you into making a decision, or tie you to a decision you didn't commit to. You must keep verbally jiu-jitsu-ing out of these antics until you're actually ready to make your final decision.

PROTECTING INFORMATION

There's an uncomfortable silence by now, and their "what do you think?" is hanging in the air.

If you say "yes, that sounds amazing, when do I start?" you implicitly accept the offer and completely close the door on the negotiation. This is your recruiter's number one favorite thing to hear. It stands to reason that you probably shouldn't do this.

But their second favorite thing to hear you say is "can you do 90K instead of 85K?" This also closes the door, but for a different and more subtle reason. And it's the number one reason why most people suck at negotiation.

Rule #3 of negotiating: information is power.

To protect your power in the negotiation, you must protect information as much as possible.

A company doesn't give you insight into what it's thinking. It doesn't tell you its price range, how much it paid the previous candidate with your experience, or anything like that. It intentionally obfuscates those things. But it wants you not to do the same.

A company wants to be like a bidder in a secret auction. But unlike the other bidders, it wants to know exactly how high all of the other bids are. It then openly intends to exploit that knowledge, often by bidding one cent more than the second highest bid.

Yeah, no. Screw that. It's a silent auction, and to keep it that way, you must protect information.

In many situations, the only reason why you have any negotiating power at all is because the employer doesn't actually know what you're thinking. They might not know how good your other offers are, or how much you were making in your last job, or how you weigh salary vs equity, or even how rational you are as a decision-maker. Bottom line, you want them to be uncertain on exactly what it would take to sign you.

When you say, "*can you do 90K instead of 85K*," you've told them exactly what it will take to make you sign. The sheet's pulled back, the secret auction is up, and they're going to bid 90K (or more likely, 87K). And they know there's almost no risk in doing so, because you'll probably accept.

What if you were the kind of person who wouldn't even consider an offer below 110K? Or the kind of person who wouldn't consider an offer below 120K? If you were, you wouldn't ask for 90K, and if they offered it as conciliation, you'd tell them to stop wasting your time.

By staying silent, *they don't actually know which of those kinds of people you are*. In their mind, you could be any of the three.

A corollary of this rule is that you should not reveal to companies what you're currently making. There are some exceptions, but as a rule you should assume this. If you must divulge what you're making, you should be liberal in noting the total value of your package (incorporate bonuses, unvested stock, nearness to promotion etc.), and always mention it in a context like "*[XYZ] is what I'm currently making, and I'm definitely looking for a step up in my career for my next role.*"

Companies will ask about your current compensation at different stages in the process—some before they ever interview you, some after they decide to make you an offer. But be mindful of this and protect information.

So given this offer, don't ask for more money or equity or anything of the sort. Don't comment on any specific details of the offer except to clarify them.

Give away nothing. Retain your power.

Say instead:

> Yeah, [COMPANY_NAME] sounds great! I really thought this was a good fit, and I'm glad that you guys agree. Right now I'm talking with a few other companies so I can't speak to the specific details of the offer until I'm done with the process and get closer to making a decision. But I'm sure we'll be able to find a package that we're both happy with, because I really would love to be a part of the team.

Think like the watermelon farmer. This offer is just the first businessman who's stopped by your watermelon patch, glanced over your crops, and announced "I'll take all of these right now for $2 a melon."

Cool. It's a big market, and you're patient—you're a farmer after all. Just smile and tell them you'll keep their offer in mind.

And this is super important: always be unequivocally positive.

THE IMPORTANCE OF POSITIVITY

Staying positive is rule #4 of negotiation.

Even if the offer is shit, it's extremely important to remain positive and excited about the company. This is because your excitement is one of your most valuable assets in a negotiation.

A company is making you an offer because they think you'll do hard work for them if they pay you. If you lose your excitement for the company during the interview process, then they'll lose confidence that you'll actually want to work hard or stay there for a long time. Each of those makes you less attractive as an investment. Remember, you are the product! If you become less excited, then the product you're selling actually loses value.

Imagine you were negotiating with someone over buying your watermelons, but the negotiation took so long that by the time you'd reached an agreement, your watermelons had gone bad.

Companies are terrified of that. They don't want their candidates to go bad during a negotiation. Hence why they hire professional recruiters to manage the process and make sure they remain amicable. You and the recruiter share the same interest in that regard. If a company feels like you've gone bad, suddenly they're a lot less willing to pay for you.

So despite whatever is happening in the negotiation, give the company the impression that 1) you still like the company, and that 2) you're still excited to work there, even if the numbers or the money or the timing is not working out. Generally, the most convincing way to signal this is to reiterate you love the mission, the team, or the problem they're working on, and really want to see things work out.

DON'T BE THE DECISION-MAKER

You can wrap up the conversation now by saying:

> I'll look over some of these details and discuss it with my [FAMILY/CLOSE_FRIENDS/SIGNIFICANT_OTHER].
> I'll reach out to you if I have any questions. Thanks so much for sharing the good news with me, and I'll
> be in touch!

So not only are you ending the conversation with the power all in your hands, but note there's another important move here: you're roping in other decision-makers.

Rule #5 of negotiation: don't be the decision-maker.

Even if you don't particularly care what your friends/family/husband/mother thinks, by mentioning them, you're no longer the only person the recruiter needs to win over. There's no point in them trying to bully and intimidate you; the "true decision-maker" is beyond their reach.

This is a classic technique in customer support and remediation. It's never the person on the phone's fault, they're just some poor schmuck doing their job. It's not their decision to make. This helps to defuse tension and give them more control of the situation.

It's much harder to pressure someone if they're not the final decision-maker. So take advantage of that.

Okay!

We have our first offer. Send a follow-up email confirming all of the details you discussed with your recruiter so you have a paper trail. Just say "just wanted to confirm I had all the details right."

Groovy. Next step is to leverage this to land other offers and find the best deal we can find in the job market.

GETTING OTHER OFFERS

Turns out, it doesn't matter that much where your first offer is from, or even how much they're offering you. Just having an offer in hand will get the engine running.

If you're already in the pipeline with other companies (which you should be if you're doing it right), you should proactively reach out and let them know that you've just received an offer. Try to build a sense of urgency. Regardless of whether you know the expiration date, all offers expire at some point, so take advantage of that.

> Hello [PERSON],
>
> I just wanted to update you on my own process. I've just received an offer from [COMPANY] which is
> quite strong. That said, I'm really excited about [YOUR AMAZING COMPANY] and really want to see if
> we can make it work. Since my timeline is now compressed, is there anything you can do to expedite
> the process?

Should you specifically mention the company that gave you an offer? Depends. If it's a well-known company or a competitor, then definitely mention it. If it's a no-name or unsexy company, you should just say you received an offer. If it's expiring soon, you should mention that as well.

Either way, send out a letter like this to every single company you're talking to. No matter how hopeless or pointless you think your application is, you want to send this signal to everyone who is considering you in the market.

Second, if there are any other companies you are looking to apply to (whether through referral or cold application), or even companies at which you've already applied but haven't heard back, I would also follow up with a similar email.

So why do this? Isn't this tacky, annoying, or even desperate?

None of the above. It is the oldest method in history to galvanize a marketplace—show that supplies are limited and build urgency. Demand breeds demand. Not every company will respond to this, but many will.

Isn't it stupid that companies respond to this though?

WHY COMPANIES CARE ABOUT OTHER OFFERS

When I wrote about the story of my own job search,[3] I mentioned how having an offer from Google made companies turn around and expedite me through their funnels. Many commentators lamented at the capriciousness of these companies. If Uber or Twitch only talked to me because of Google and until then weren't willing to look at me, what did that say about their hiring processes? What legitimately are they evaluating, if anything at all?

I think this response is totally backwards. The behavior of tech companies here is actually very rational, and you would do well to understand it.

First, you must realize what a company's goal is. A company's goal is to hire someone who will become an effective employee and produce more value than their cost. How do you figure out who will do that? Well, you can't know for certain without actually hiring them, but there are a few proxies. Pedigree is the strongest signal; if they did it at other companies, they can probably do it at yours. And if someone trusted within the organization can vouch for them, that's often a strong signal as well.

But it turns out, almost everything else is a weak signal. Weak in the sense that it's just not very reliable. Interviews, if you think about it, are long, sweaty, uncomfortable affairs that only glancingly resemble actual employment. They're weird and can't tell you that much about whether an individual will be good at their job. There's no way around this. There are a few stronger signals, like bringing someone in for a week or two on a contract-to-hire position, but strong candidates won't consider this. So candidates as a whole have effectively forced companies to assume almost all of the risk in hiring.

The truth is, knowing that someone has passed your interview just doesn't say that much about whether they'll be a good employee. It's as though you knew nothing about a student other than their SAT score. It's just not a lot of data to go off.

Nobody has solved this problem. Not Google nor anyone else.

And this is precisely why it's rational for companies to care that you've received other offers. They care because each company knows that their own process is noisy, and the processes of most other companies are also noisy. But a candidate having multiple offers means that they have multiple weak signals in their favor. Combined, these converge into a much stronger signal than any single interview. It's like knowing that a student has a strong SAT score, and GPA, and won various scholarships. Sure, it's still possible that they're a dunce, but it's much harder for that to be true.

This is not to say that companies respond proportionally to these signals, or that they don't overvalue credentials and brands. They do. But caring about whether you have other offers and valuing you accordingly is completely rational.

---

3   https://haseebq.com/farewell-app-academy-hello-airbnb-part-i/

So this is all to say—tell other companies that you've received offers. Give them more signal so that they know you're a valued and compelling candidate. And understand why this changes their mind about whether to interview you.

As you continue interviewing, remember to keep practicing your interview skills. The single strongest determinant of your final offer will be the number and strength of offers that you receive.

SOME ADVICE ON TIMING

You want to be strategic about the timing of your offers. Generally, you should try to start interviewing at larger companies earlier. Their processes are slower and their offer windows are wider (meaning they allow you more time to decide). Startups are the other way around.

Your goal should be to have as many offers overlapping at the same time as possible. This will maximize your window for negotiating.

When you receive an offer, often the first thing you should ask for is more time to make your decision. Especially in your first offer, more time is by far the most valuable thing you can ask for. It's time that enables you to activate other companies and end up with the strongest possible offer. So be prepared to fight for time.

HOW TO APPROACH EXPLODING OFFERS

Hoo boy.

Exploding offers are offers that expire within 24-72 hours. You won't see this much at big companies, but they're becoming increasingly common among startups and mid-sized companies.

Exploding offers suck, and I share most people's disdain for this practice. But I do understand it. Exploding offers are a natural weapon for employers to combat a strong hiring market for tech workers. Companies know exactly what they're doing with exploding offers—they play on fear and limit your ability to seek out counteroffers.

In a sense, it's unsurprising that if startups have more difficulty attracting and securing talent, they'd resort to this practice. What I don't like is the dishonesty about it. Employers often justify this by saying "If you need more time than this, then that's a sign you're not the kind of person we're looking for."

Please don't buy this crap or feel guilty over it. They're simply doing this to improve their chance of closing candidates. Needing more than three days to make a life decision isn't a sign of anything other than thoughtfulness.

So what should you do if you receive an exploding offer?

Exploding offers are anathema to your ability to effectively navigate the labor market. Thus, there is only one thing to do. Treat the offer as a non-offer unless the expiration window is widened.

In no uncertain terms, convey that if the offer is exploding, it's useless to you.

Example conversation:

> I have one big concern. You mentioned that this offer explodes in 48 hours. I'm afraid this doesn't work at all for me. There's no way that I can make a decision on this offer within a 48-hour window. I'm currently wrapping up my interview process at a few other companies, which is likely to take me another week or so. So I'm going to need more time to make an informed decision.

If they push back and say this is the best they can do, then politely reply:

> That's really unfortunate. I like [YOUR COMPANY] and was really excited about the team, but like I said, there's no way I can consider this offer. 48 hours is just too unreasonable of a window. The next company I join will be a big life decision for me, and I take my commitments very seriously. I also need to consult with my [EXTERNAL_DECISION_MAKER]. There's no way that I can make a decision I'm comfortable with in this short of an amount of time.

Pretty much any company will relent at this point. If they persist, don't be afraid to walk away over it. (They probably won't let that happen, and will come grab you as you're walking out the door. But if they don't, then honestly, screw 'em.)

I was given several exploding offers during my job search. And every time, I did essentially this. Every single offer immediately widened to become more reasonable, sometimes by several weeks.

I want to emphasize, lest I be misunderstood here—what I'm saying is not to just silently let an exploding offer expire, and assume that everything will be fine and they'll still hire you. They won't. For exploding offers to be a credible weapon, a company has to have a reputation of enforcing them. I'm saying explicitly call this out as an issue when they make the offer.

Don't let a company bully you into giving away your negotiating power.

THE NEGOTIATING MINDSET

Before we enter into the actual back-and-forth, I want to examine the mindset you should have as a negotiator. This applies not just to how you approach the conversation, but also to how you think about the company.

Do not fall into the trap of valuing companies solely along one dimension. That means don't just value companies based on salary, equity, or even on prestige. Those are all important dimensions, but so are cultural fit, the challenge of the work, learning potential, later career options, quality of life, growth potential, and just overall happiness. None of these inherently trump any of the others. Anyone who tells you "just choose wherever you think you'll be happiest" is being just as simplistic as someone who says "just choose the one that offers the most money." All of these things matter, and your decision should be genuinely multi-dimensional.

Be open to being surprised as you explore different companies.

It's also important to understand that companies don't all value you along the same dimension either. That is, different companies are genuinely looking for different skills, and there are some companies at which you will be more and less valuable. Even at peer companies, this is true, especially so if you have a specialized skill set.

The more companies you talk to, the more likely you are to find a company to which you are significantly more valuable than the rest. Chances are this is where you'll be able to negotiate your strongest offer. It might surprise you which company this turns out to be; keep an open mind, and remember that a job search is a two-sided process.

One of the most valuable things you can do for yourself in this process is to really try to understand how employers think and what motivates them. Understanding your interlocutor is extremely important in negotiation, and we'll be exploring that a lot in the next blog post.

But most of all, I want to emphasize: be curious about the other side. Try to understand why employers think the way they do. Be sympathetic toward them. Care about what they want and help them try to get it.

Adopting this mindset will make you a much stronger negotiator, and accordingly, a much better employee and team member.

In the next section, I'm going to cover the last four rules of negotiation. I'll also go over the actual back-and-forth process—how to ask for what you want, how to strengthen offers, and how to dismantle the tricks that companies will try to pull on you. Also a lot more on the theory of negotiation, which I really dig.

HOW NOT TO BOMB YOUR OFFER NEGOTIATION

So you know the first 6 rules. You've maneuvered through the initial offer conversation, you've lined up counter offers from other companies, and now it's time to move into the actual negotiating.

Naturally, this is the part where everything goes horribly wrong.

But worry not. Stick with me, and I'm going to make you into a superhuman negotiator. (Or at least an eccentric billionaire negotiator, which is sometimes better?)

Seriously though. In this article I'm going to deep dive on the whole negotiating process, and discuss the final four rules on how to negotiate a job offer.

Right. Let's start from the top.

What does it take to be a good negotiator?

Most people think negotiating well is just looking the other person in the eye, appearing confident, and asking for tons of money. But being a good negotiator is a lot more subtle than that.

WHAT GOOD NEGOTIATORS SOUND LIKE

You probably have a friend or family member who's infamous for refusing to take no for an answer. The kind of person who will march into a department store and bullheadedly argue with the management until they get a purchase refunded.

This person seems like they often get what they want. They make you cringe, but perhaps you should try to be more like them.

Rest assured, this person is actually a terrible negotiator. They're good at being difficult and causing a scene, which can sometimes convince a waitress or shift manager to appease them. But this style of negotiating will get you nowhere when negotiating with a business partner (that is, an employer).

A good negotiator is empathetic and collaborative. They don't try to control you or issue ultimatums. Rather, they try to think creatively about how to fulfill both your and their needs.

So when you think of negotiating a job offer, don't imagine haggling over a used car. Think more like negotiating dinner plans with a group of friends, and you'll fare much better.

SLICING UP THE CAKE

Another important difference between good and bad negotiators is that bad negotiators tend to think of a negotiation as a zero-sum game.

Imagine we're negotiating over a cake. In a zero-sum negotiation, if I get one more slice, you get one less. Any gain I make comes at your expense.

This seems obviously true with cake, right? So what makes a job negotiation any different?

Ah, but it's not actually true for cake. What if I hate corner pieces and you love them? What if I really like the cherries? What if I prefer to scrape off some of the frosting, but you love extra frosting? What if I'm full and you're starving, but you'll agree to treat me to my favorite cake next time?

Of course, when I posed the question, I didn't mention anything about cherries or my feelings on corner pieces. It might seem like I just made shit up.

But this is exactly what good negotiators do. They bend the rules. They question assumptions and ask unexpected questions. They dig to find the core that everyone values and look for creative ways to widen the terrain of negotiation.

While you were thinking about how to haggle over slices, I'm thinking about how to give both of us more than just half of a cake.

Different parties in a negotiation almost always have different value functions. We may value the same things—we both care about cake, after all. But we don't value them in exactly the same way, so there's probably a way to give each of us more of what we want.

Most people go into a job negotiation thinking they need to stubbornly haggle over salary like slices of cake. They don't ever stop to ask—hey, what do I actually value? Why do I value it? What does the company value? Why do they value that?

There are many dimensions in a job negotiation: salary, signing bonus, stock, a year-end or performance bonus, commuter benefits, relocation expenses, equipment, an educational stipend, a childcare stipend, extra vacation time, a later start date, getting a dedicated hour a day to work out or study or meditate or play solitaire. You could choose which team you're assigned to, what your first project will be, what technologies you'll be working with, and sometimes even choose your title.

Maybe you're a frosting person, and the company is more into cherries. You never know if you don't ask.

Hold onto this mindset.

Okay.

Let's pick up the negotiation where we left off. All the offers are in, and recruiters are eagerly awaiting for you to get the ball rolling.

Let's start negotiating.

PHONE VS EMAIL

Your first decision is whether you're going to negotiate over the phone or keep it over email.

Talking on the phone not only signals confidence, but more importantly, it allows you to build a strong relationship with your recruiter.

Talking on the phone enables bantering, telling jokes, and building connection. You want your recruiter to like you, understand you, empathize with you, and want you to succeed. Likewise, you want to care about your recruiter and understand what's motivating them.

The best deals get made between friends. It's hard to make friends over email.

However, if you don't have confidence in your negotiation skills, you should try to push the negotiation to email. Written, asynchronous communication will give you more time to strategize and make it easier to say uncomfortable things without being pressured by a recruiter.

That said, recruiters will always prefer to get you on the phone. It's essentially their home turf. They're also well aware that negotiating is easier over email, and they have little interest in making it easier on you. They'll often be vague about the offer over email and only offer to discuss specific details on the phone.

If you want to stick to email, you have to push back against this. There's no secret to it: just be honest and ask for what you want.

Tell them:

> Hi recruiter, I hope your day is treating you well!
>
> Re: your previous email, I'd prefer to discuss the details of the offer over email. I sometimes get nervous during important phone calls, so discussing the offer over email helps me to keep a clear head and communicate more clearly. I hope this is okay with you. :)

No bullshit, no huff-puffery. Just telling the truth and asking for what you want.

There's tremendous power in honesty and directness. Take advantage of it.

(Also, note how I wrote "discuss the details of the offer" rather than "negotiate." Never describe what you're doing as negotiating—that sounds immediately adversarial and haggley. Describe it instead as a discussion, and they're less likely to recoil.)

HAVING ALTERNATIVES

I mentioned before how essential it is to have multiple offers. I'll reiterate again—it's very, very valuable to have multiple offers.

With other offers on the table, if your negotiation doesn't work out, they know you'll just accept another offer. Your negotiating position suddenly becomes a lot more credible because they know you're willing to walk away.

This effect is strengthened if you get an offer from a prestigious company. And the effect goes through the roof if you have an offer from a company's primary competitor (now they'll really want to poach you from the big bad competitor-corp).

Some of this behavior is stupid tribalism. And some part of it is rational in trying to deprive competitors of talent. Either way, take advantage of it, and be tactical in which companies you aim for.

But what if you don't manage to get any other offers? Does all the negotiating just go out the window?

Not at all. What's important here is not actually having other offers. More specifically, it's in having strong alternatives.

WHICH IS WHY RULE #6 OF NEGOTIATING IS: HAVE ALTERNATIVES.

A negotiation needs stakes. If there were no risk and you knew for sure the other side would sign a contract, what incentive would you have to offer them anything more?

Your alternatives are what give a negotiation its stakes. By signaling your alternatives, you allow your interlocutor to develop a mental model of when and why you'll walk away from the negotiation. Your alternatives also have an anchoring effect on how much the other side thinks you're objectively worth.

In negotiation literature, your best alternative is often referred to as your BATNA (Best Alternative To a Negotiated Agreement). Basically, it's what you'd do if you walked away.

I like the term BATNA a lot, mostly because it sounds like a gadget Batman would lob at bad guys.

So what's your BATNA if you don't have other offers? Do you even have one?

Of course you do. Your best alternative might be "interview at more companies" or "go to grad school" or "stay at your current job" or "go on sabbatical in Morocco for a few months" (as it was for a friend of mine who was deliberating between joining a startup and gallivanting through North Africa).

The point is, you don't need to have another offer to have a strong BATNA.

> Your BATNA's strength comes from 1) how strong the other side perceives it to be, and 2) how strong you perceive it to be.

If your recruiter thinks that going to grad school is an awesome thing to do, then they'll see you as having a very strong alternative, and the stakes of the negotiation will be raised.

But even if they think grad school is ridiculous, if you convince them that you'd be totally happy to go to grad school, then the burden is on them to make this deal more attractive to you than going to grad school.

Thus, you need to communicate your BATNA. This doesn't need to be ham-fisted, but you need to make it a background to the negotiation. (Note: usually whenever you signal your BATNA, you should also re-emphasize your interest in reaching an agreement).

Examples:

> I've received another offer from [OTHER CORP] that's very compelling on salary, but I really love the mission of [YOUR COMPANY] and think that it would overall be a better fit for me.

> I'm also considering going back to grad school and getting a Master's degree in Postmodern Haberdashery. I'm excited about [YOUR COMPANY] though and would love to join the team, but the package has to make sense if I'm going to forego a life of ironic hatmaking.

Note: one of the biggest mistakes I see here is from people who are currently working. If you already have a job, staying where you are is often your BATNA.

This means if you tell your interlocutor that you hate your job, then they know your BATNA sucks, and have no incentive to negotiate with you (on top of potentially thinking that you're a negative person). Always emphasize the pros of your current company, your seniority, your impact, and whatever else you like about where you currently work.

You should make your decision seem genuinely close for it to be a strong BATNA.

WHAT A JOB NEGOTIATION MEANS TO AN EMPLOYER

I've kept saying that to be an effective negotiator you need to understand the other side. So let's take a look at what it's like to negotiate as an employer. (I'm going to have to use the tech industry in my examples here; the details will differ by industry.)

First, we have to rewind and understand what brought us to this offer in the first place. What kind of resources have they spent so far in trying to fill this position?

- Writing and posting a job description on all appropriate channels ($300)[4]

- Reviewing ~100 or more resumes ($1250)

- About 15% of those resumes need to be phone screened, so roughly 15 phone screens ($2250)

- Around 75% of those initial phone screens warrant a technical screen, so roughly 11 technical screens ($9000)

- About 30% pass through to an on-site, so roughly 3 onsites. These onsites require the coordination of 6-7 employees ($10800)

- Finally, they make one offer. The recruiter (and potentially the executive staff) need to spend time on the phone with the offeree convincing and negotiating ($900)

All-in-all this process took about 45 days from start to finish.

Now say you end up turning down their offer. They've spent over $24,000 just extending this single offer to you (to say nothing of opportunity costs), and now they'll essentially have to start over from scratch.

This is what a company faces if you turn them down.

Realize what a gauntlet they've been through!

Realize how important it is that you're the one!

Out of the droves and droves who've shown up on their doorstep, you're the one they want. They want to usher you into their tribe. They went through so much crap to get you here, and now they've found you.

And you're worried that if you negotiate, they'll take it away?

Further yet, understand that salary is only one part of the cost of employing you. An employer also has to pay for your benefits, your equipment, space, utilities, other random expenses, and employment taxes on top of all of that. All-in, your actual salary often comprises less than 50% of the total cost of employing you.[5]

(Which means they expect that your value to the company, in terms of the revenue you'll generate, to be more than 2x your salary. If they didn't believe that, they wouldn't be hiring you at all.)

So, this is all to say: everything is stacked in your favor. It doesn't feel that way, but it absolutely is.

Realize that when you are agonizing over whether to ask for another few thousand dollars, what they're doing is praying with bated breath that you'll sign the offer.

If you don't sign the offer, they lose. Losing a good candidate sucks. No one wants to believe that their company isn't worth working for.

They want to win. They will pay to win.

And yet, you might worry: "but if I end up negotiating more, won't they have higher expectations? Won't my boss end up hating me for negotiating?"

No, and no.

---

4   Numbers nabbed from https://www.quora.com/What-is-the-average-cost-of-recruiting-an-engineer-in-Silicon-Valley/answer/Rick-Brownlow?srid=tvlO

5   Read "How Much Does An Employee Cost" at http://web.mit.edu/e-club/hadzima/pdf/how-much-does-an-employee-cost.pdf

It's your role that will determine your performance expectations, not how much you negotiated. Making 5k more or less in salary doesn't matter at all. Your manager will literally just not care about this.

Remember how expensive it is to even employ you in the first place! Nobody's going to fire you because you're performing 5K worse than they expected you to; the cost of firing you and hiring someone else is a lot more than 5K to begin with.

And no, your boss won't hate you now. And in fact, at most big companies the person you're negotiating with won't even be your boss. Recruiting and management are totally separate departments, completely abstracted from one another. And even if you're at a startup, trust me that your boss is used to negotiating with candidates and doesn't put nearly as much significance in it as you do.

In short: negotiating is easier and more normal than you think, and companies are completely willing to negotiate with you. If your intuition tells you otherwise, trust that your mental model is wrong.

HOW TO GIVE THE FIRST NUMBER

In the beginning, I mentioned how valuable it is not to have to give the first number. But there are times when you can't avoid it. In that case, there are ways to give the first number without giving the first number.

If a company asks you "what are your salary expectations?" you might say:

> I don't have any particular numbers in mind. I'm more interested in learning whether this will be a good mutual fit. If it is, I'm open to exploring any offer so long as it's competitive.

Sounds good. But they push back,

> I understand that, but we need to have a clear idea of what you think is competitive. I need to know whether it's worth going through the interview process. We're a young startup, so I need to make sure we're on the same page as far as compensation.

That's a strong push. But you can still push back.

> I completely hear you, and I agree it's important that we're on the same page. I really have no particular numbers in my head, it all depends on the fit and the composition of the offer. Once we decide we want to work together, I think that's the best time to figure out a compensation package that makes sense.

Most employers will relent here. But there's a small chance they push further:

> Okay, look, you're being difficult. Let's not waste each other's time. What's an offer that you'd be willing to take?

This is a decision point. They're trying to take away your negotiating power and pin you to a premature decision.

That said, you probably will have to say a number at this point, or risk damaging the trust in this relationship. (They are making a valid point that startups can't offer the same kind of cash as large companies, nor should you expect them to. They might be sensing that you're not aware of this.)

But you can give a number here without actually giving a number.

> Well, okay. I know that the average software engineer in Silicon Valley makes roughly 120K a year salary. So I think that's a good place to start.

Notice what I did here. I didn't actually answer the question "what's an offer you'd be willing to take," I merely anchored the conversation around the fulcrum of "the average software engineer salary."

So if you're forced to give a number, do so by appealing to an objective metric, such as an industry average (or your current salary). And make it clear that you're merely starting the negotiation there, not ending it.

HOW TO ASK FOR MORE

Say an offer is out there, and now you want to improve it. As always, be direct and ask for what you want. Here are generally the steps you should take.

First, reiterate your interest in the company. This is as simple as:

> I'm really excited about the problems you guys are working on at Evil Corp…

Now frame why you're asking for more. There are two choices here: you can say that you're on the fence and that an improvement might convince you, or you can go stronger and say that you're outright dissatisfied with the offer. Which approach you choose depends on how much leverage you have, how weak the offer is relative to your BATNA, and whether you have other offers (the weaker your negotiating position, generally the more tentative you should be).

Either way, be unfailingly polite.

If you're dissatisfied with the offer, you might say something like:

> I appreciate the work you guys put into constructing this offer. But there were a couple things I was unsatisfied with.

If you want to be more reserved, you can say something like:

> The offer you guys extended was strong. Right now my decision is basically between you and [XYZ CORP]. It's a genuinely difficult decision for me, but there are a couple of dimensions where, if this offer improved, it would be much more compelling.

Don't just say something like:

> Thanks for the offer. Here are some ways I think it could improve.

This makes you sound like an ass. Be polite, and if you want to strengthen the offer, tell them clearly how you feel about it. This builds trust and conveys seriousness.

Let's say you want to raise the salary. Now that you have a specific ask, it's time to employ **rule #7: proclaim reasons for everything.**

We all implicitly know the catch-22 of negotiation: if you say you want more salary, you'll sound greedy. And no one likes greedy people, right? So why would they want to give more money to a greedy person?

I suspect this is the primary reason why so many candidates recoil from negotiating. They don't want to *feel* greedy. It goes against all of their social conditioning. And yet, there are some situations in which most people would be totally fine negotiating.

Specifically, when they have to.

If you had to raise your salary or you wouldn't be able to afford rent, or if you had to negotiate health insurance to cover a medical condition, you'd negotiate without a twinge of regret. The difference? That you have a reason for what you're requesting.

It's kind of a brain-hack, both for yourself and for your negotiating partner. Just stating a reason—any reason—makes your request feel human and important. It's not you being greedy, it's you trying to fulfill your goals.

The more unobjectionable and sympathetic your reason, the better. If it's medical expenses, or paying off student loans, or taking care of family, you'll bring tears to their eyes. I told employers that I was earning-to-give, so since I was donating 33% of my income to charity, I had negotiated aggressively to leave myself enough to live off.

But honestly, even if your reason is inane and unimpressive, it will still carry this effect.

Just saying "can you improve the salary?" sounds like you're boringly motivated by money. But if you say "I really want to buy a house within the next year; what can we do to improve the salary?", this suddenly seems a lot more legitimate.

If they turn down your request now, they're implicitly telling you "no Jennifer, you can't buy your house. I guess you don't deserve one." No one wants to do that. They want to be the one who says "Alright Jennifer, I talked with the director and I made it happen. You're getting that new house!"

Of course, it goes without saying that the reason you want money is so that you can spend it on things. What do they think you're going to use it for, toilet paper?

I know. It's stupid. It's really stupid, but it works.

Just go with it, state a reason for everything, and you'll find recruiters more willing to become your advocate.

ASSERT YOUR VALUE

One effective move you can make in a negotiation, especially after an ask, is to emphasize the unique value you'll be bringing to the company. Example:

> Blah blah blah, I want X, Y, and Z.
>
> I know that you guys are looking for someone to build out your Android team. I believe I bring a lot of experience leading a team of Android developers and I'm confident that I'll be able to bring your mobile offerings up to parity with your competitors.
>
> Let me know your thoughts.

Be confident without boasting or trying to hold yourself to specific metrics (unless you're supremely confident). Whatever you assert should be something you've touched on earlier in your discussions, but it's okay to repeat it now as a gentle reminder. It reminds them of the carrot and shows that you're still excited to add value.

This is not appropriate in every negotiation, especially for very junior positions, where it's harder to differentiate yourself. But later in your career (or for more specialized/consulting roles) this can be a really valuable nudge.

WHAT TO ASK FOR

This brings me to **rule #8: be motivated by more than just money**. Note, this is not code for "if you seem like you're motivated by more than just money, you'll get more money."

There is no bigger turn-off to a company than somebody who only cares about money. This is something you're not going to be able to fake.

Actually be motivated by other things. You should be motivated by money too, of course, but it should be one among many dimensions you're optimizing for. How much training you get, what your first project will be, which team you join, or even who your mentor will be—these are all things you can and should negotiate.

Among these factors, salary is perhaps the least important.

What do you really value? Be creative. Don't try to haggle over slices of cake when there's so much more on the table.

Of course, to negotiate well you need to understand the other side's preferences. You want to make the deal better for *both of you*. That's why **rule #9 is: understand what the company values**.

How do you figure this out? Well, there are a few good rules of thumb.

First, salary is almost always the hardest thing to give, for a few reasons.

1. It must be paid year after year, so it becomes part of a company's long-term burn rate.

2. It is almost always the thing that people gossip about, so paying someone significantly more salary can cause unrest.

3. It tends to be the most tightly constrained by pay bands, especially at large companies.

So if you want more financial compensation, you should think about structuring as much of it as possible outside of salary. A signing bonus, for example, is easier to give than salary. A signing bonus has the advantage of only needing to be paid once, it gets the candidate excited about joining (because everyone likes wads of cash), and it's generally not as public.

Remember that you can always get salary raises as you continue to work at the company, but there's only one point at which you can get a signing bonus.

The easiest thing for a company to give though is stock (if the company offers stock). Companies like giving stock because it invests you in the company and aligns interests. It also shifts some of the risk from the company over to you and burns less cash.

If you are genuinely risk-neutral or early in your career, then you should generally try to assume as much stock as possible. If you aggressively trade cash for stock, you can end up with a higher expected value offer (albeit with higher risk).

A BRIEF PRIMER ON EQUITY

You can skip this section if you're already pretty familiar with how equity works. I'm going to speak to the totally uninitiated here, because too many people get swindled when it comes to valuing stock.

First, understand there are two completely different classes of companies: public companies and private companies. If the company is public (i.e., it has IPOed and is listed on the stock market), then its stock is as good as cash. You will usually be granted RSUs (Restricted Stock Units), which are just shares like you can purchase on the stock market. Once these shares vest (that is, are released to you), you can turn around and sell them on the stock market. This is how they turn into money.

If the company is private, then things get a lot more complicated. For private companies, most of the time they will not actually issue you stock grants. Usually, they will issue you stock options. An option is a pre-agreed right to purchase shares of stock at a frozen price.

It's important to note that when you want to leave a company, if you have options, your life becomes really complicated. You may have to pay a bunch of money to actually exercise your option (that is, buy your pre-agreed upon stock at the previous frozen price, or risk losing it), with no way to actually sell it yet. The only way to truly liquidate your options is when the company IPOs or is acquired. And many companies don't ever do either.

Thus, options are very risky. It's easier to get screwed by options, especially on tax implications.[6]

EQUITY SHENANIGANS

Many companies will try to play mind games with you when it comes to equity. Several companies pulled these on me.

A common one is presenting the total value of the stock grant rather than the annualized value, despite the stock not vesting evenly, or vesting over 5 years instead of the standard 4.

But the most egregious thing that companies will do is tell you absurd stories about the value of their stock. They'll say: "okay, we're worth this much now, but at the rate we're growing we're going to be worth 10X that in a year. So really, the value of your options is many millions of dollars!"

To not mince words: this is cynically dishonest bullshit. Don't buy it even for a second. I got this a few times, and the only reason I didn't walk away from the offer immediately was because it was always a recruiter pulling this crap. If it was a manager I would've turned down the offer outright.

Here's why this is infuriatingly stupid: a company's valuation is determined by investors. These investors see the financials and the growth rate of the company, and invest at a price that **reflects the current growth rate of the company**. In other words, they invested at a valuation that already took their 10x growth rate into account. Investors are not idiots. And unless you (or your recruiter) think you have privileged information or insight that the company's investors don't, you should probably take the investors' word for it.

(Not to mention a company's nominal valuation is almost always inflated due to preferred shares, debt, and survivorship bias, but let's ignore that for now.)

So if a company gives you this hock of crap, fire back and tell them thank you, but you'll be considering the stock at the same valuation their investors valued it at.

I mean, be nice. But don't let them try to strong-arm you into accepting this garbage.

A job is not a suicide pact. Choose a company that is judicious and transparent, and you'll be much more likely to find yourself respected and taken care of.

---

6   For a lot more information, see Scott Kupor of a16z's post here: https://a16z.com/2016/08/24/options-ownership/

OTHER THINGS YOU CAN ASK FOR

Because I'd be remiss if I didn't point out a few other things.

Relocation expenses often come out of separate budgets at big companies, so this is generally very easy to get.

Look for creative benefits that would be particularly valuable to you. Maybe it's covering your commuter expenses, asking for dedicated volunteer or learning time, getting sponsored for conferences, or even charity donation matching.

Don't assume anything's off the table until you've tried bringing it up.

That said, don't throw the entire kitchen sink at them. A negotiation can quickly become cumbersome for an employer if you bring up a litany of changes. Keep the changeset as pithy as you can.

NEGOTIATING JIU JITSU

Recruiters love trying to trick you into ending the negotiation early. They're going to do this relentlessly. Don't fault them for it—I suspect they can't help themselves.

Just keep breaking out of their shenanigans, and don't let yourself be pressured into ending a negotiation until you're actually ready to make a final decision. This is especially grave if you have multiple offers, and you let one company pressure you into canceling the others. Companies succeed in doing this all the time, so I want to equip you with the skills to jiu jitsu out of these techniques.

Here are two situations you can break out of. (These are both real situations that happened to me during my negotiations, though the numbers and details are invented.)

Situation 1:

I ask for a 10K increase in signing bonus. The company gets back to me and says,

> That's really tough for us to do. I'm going to try, I think you're worth it, but I can't really go to my boss and fight for you unless she knows you're going to sign. Are you going to sign if I get you that 10K?

You should be thinking: ah, this person is trying to force me to a decision point and take away my negotiating power.

I respond:

> Okay, so what I'm hearing is that you'll have to expend some personal reputation to get me a 10K bonus. If you end up going to bat for me, are you confident you'll be able to get that 10K?

They respond:

> I think I can, it just comes down to you Haseeb. If you're serious about joining us, then I'll go fight for you. But I need to know for sure you'll sign.

Great. Time to Jiu Jitsu.

That makes sense. Unfortunately I can't commit to signing yet; I'm not yet at the stage where I can make a final decision. Like I told you before, this weekend I'm going to sit down with my family and talk things over with them. Choosing the company I'm going to spend the next few years at is a commitment I take really seriously, and so I want to be sure I'm making a well-considered decision.

But since you're confident that you can get an extra 10K, let's do this instead: in my mind, I'll pretend this offer is [X + 10K] and as I'm considering my final decision, that's where I'll value it. I know it's tough for you to go and get that from your boss, so I don't want you to do that until I'm certain I'm going to sign.

They then vaguely recant and promptly get approval for the 10K bonus.

Situation 2:

I ask for a 20% increase in stock package. The hiring manager, knowing that I'm negotiating with other companies, then fires back:

I want to get this stock package for you. And I know I can, we've got the budget. But before I do that, I need your word on something.

What's that?

I need you to give me your word that if I improve your offer, you're not going to just turn around and take our counteroffer to [COMPETITOR_COMPANY] to improve your offer with them.

You should be thinking: so basically they're asking me not to negotiate. Cute.

Let me see if I understand what you're saying. You are willing to improve my offer, but only if I agree that I won't tell [COMPETITOR] what you're offering me. Is that correct?

Well no, I can't legally do that. What I mean is…what I mean is, look. I like you. But if I improve your offer and you just take our offer to [COMPETITOR], you'll be violating my trust.

Okay, let me be sure I understand you here. If you give me this offer and I tell [COMPETITOR], I will be violating the trust under which you're granting me this improved offer. Is that correct?

Uhh…Look. How about this. In my mind, I'm going to go get you this stock package okay? And in my head, I'm going to do it with the assumption that you're the kind of person I think you are, and you're going to consider our offer in its own right and not just shop it around. Fair enough?

I nod. He gets the improved offer. I continue to negotiate. Antics averted.

(In case you're wondering, if he had said "yes," I would have turned down the proposal.)

THE PATH TO SIGNING

It's not enough to just continually ask for stuff. Companies need to sense that you're actually moving toward a final decision, and not just playing games with them.

Your goal in a negotiation is not to be difficult or elusive. True, you should assert your value and carefully consider your options, but you can do so in a way that's respectful and considerate toward the companies you're talking to.

Don't go dark on people. Be open and communicative. I keep saying be honest and I mean it—be honest.

Aside: I keep talking about honesty, and you might protest that this is antithetical to my earlier rule of "protect information." It's not. True, you should protect information that might weaken your negotiating position, but you should be as communicative as possible about everything else (which is most things).

Negotiating is all about relationships, and communication is the bedrock of any relationship.

This brings me to **the final rule: be winnable**. This is more than just giving the company the impression that you like them (which you continually should). But more so that you must give any company you're talking to a clear path on how to win you. Don't bullshit them or play stupid games. Be clear and unequivocal with your preferences and timeline.

If there is nothing that a company could do to sign you, or you don't actually want to work for them, then don't negotiate with them. Period.

Don't waste their time or play games for your own purposes. Even if the company isn't your dream company, you must be able to imagine at least some package they could offer you that would make you sign. If not, politely turn them down.

It costs each company money to interview you and to negotiate with you. I didn't negotiate with every company I received an offer from, but if there was one key mistake I made in my job search, it was that I still negotiated with too many (in large part because I didn't think my job search would be successful).

MAKING THE FINAL DECISION

Okay, it's decision time.

(Yes, you do have to make one.)

Three things to keep in mind here:

1. Be clear about your deadline.

2. Assert your deadline continually.

3. Use your final decision as your trump card.

When you start negotiating you don't have to be clear about your timeline because you probably don't have one yet. But once you get into intermediary stages, you should set for yourself a deadline on which you'll sign. It can be for an arbitrary reason (or no reason at all), but just pre-committing to a deadline will allow you to negotiate more clearly and powerfully.

"A weekend with the family." I found works nicely, as it has the added benefit of roping other decision makers in. Then, when companies push you to end negotiations early, you can re-assert this deadline.

Companies should all be totally aware of when you're going to make your decision. This will raise the stakes and galvanize negotiations as the deadline approaches.

This deadline also lets you defer your decision while still improving offers. Your narrative should basically be "I want to see the strongest offer your company can muster. Then I will go into my cave, meditate for 10 days, and when I emerge I will have decided in my heart which company to join." This gives you enormous power to avoid any on-the-spot decision points or premature promises.

Eventually, deadline day will come. Try to make this a business day (say, a Friday or a Monday) so that you can communicate with recruiters during this day. If a hail mary is going to happen, it'll happen here.

Even if there's only one company in the running, you should always *always* wait until the last day to sign your offer. Yes, even if you're certain you're going to sign and even if it's your dream job. I've seen many scenarios in which offers spontaneously improved as deadlines approached, or a fallen player gets up and presents you the holy grail in the 11th hour. Either way, there's no harm.

Finally, your trump card. Save this for the very end. Your trump card is these words: "If you can do X, I will sign." Note, this is NOT "If you give me X, the offer will be more compelling blah blah blah." Fuck that. It's time to make a promise.

Every company that's still on the table, let them know what it would take to sign you (unless there's nothing they could do). And when you make the final ask, don't forget reason-giving, even if it's the same reason as before!

> Hi Joel, I've been thinking it over and it's genuinely a really tough decision for me. I loved everyone at [COMPANY] but the one thing that makes it hard for me is the salary. As you know I'm trying to pay off my student loans so salary is really important to me right now. If you can improve the salary by 10K a year, then I'll be totally ready to sign.

With luck, they meet you half-way. Or, with a little more luck, they'll meet you all the way.

And just because I know someone will ask—yes, once you say you're going to sign, you should always sign. Never go back on your word. It's a small world, people talk, and these kinds of things will come back to haunt you. (More importantly, never go back on your word because you're the kind of person who never goes back on their word.)

Tell all of the other parties that you've made your final decision. Thank them for the negotiation. If you did it well, they'll usually thank you back, tell you to keep in touch, and to reach out again in a couple years next time you're on the market.

And that's it. You did it! Congratulations! You're still alive, right?

…You're not moving.

Well, that's fine. It's time to celebrate your new job, you beautiful fool! (Drinks are on you.)

This article was written by Haseeb Qureshi and reprinted with permission.[7]

---

7   Reprinted with permission from https://haseebq.com/my-ten-rules-for-negotiating-a-job-offer/

APPENDIX

PART K

APPENDIX

CHAPTER 53

KEY PHRASES TO LEARN

PRODUCT MANAGERS ARE expected to think on their toes and often end up being put on the spot. Here are some key phrases that can help you buy time, understand context, and frame your responses. Feel free to adapt them to your own style!

PHRASES FOR PMS OF ALL LEVELS

Phrase	Use it when..
Can you tell me more about that?	Any time you're not sure how to respond or didn't understand someone.
Let me think about that and get back to you.	Any time you're put on the spot and are not sure how to respond. You can then go ask a mentor for help if you need to. Remember to always proactively loop back with them.
Why do you ask? / Are you asking because you're worried about …?	You get a question you weren't expecting.
Ahh, is the problem you're thinking about …?	People bring random feature requests to you and you want to redirect them to the problem, not the solution.
Our top priority right now is…. Can we come back to this idea at the next planning cycle?	You want to say "no" to new work for the team.

I'm focusing on *<top priority>* right now. Maybe *<other person>* would be interested?	You want to say "no" to new work for you.
Let's go back to our goals.	Any time a conversation gets heated
Let's draw out our options.	When a conversation starts to go in circles
Here's how I'm thinking about the pros and cons.	You're put on the spot to make a decision
How can we validate this hypothesis? / Is there an inexpensive way we could learn?	People are stuck in a disagreement because they are making different assumptions.
Here's my plan. Shout if there are any objections.	You need to loop stakeholders in, but you don't want to slow things down by waiting for their approval.
Since we want to move quickly, I propose we go with this decision. Does that sound good enough or would anyone like to escalate?	When people disagree on a decision you're responsible for, this gives you a way to push forward without waiting for consensus. Using the word "escalate" reinforces that they usually should defer to you while giving them a non-combative way to push back if they feel strongly enough.
Here's the problem I'm facing and here's my plan, how does that sound?	Both when you do need help from your manager and when you don't. It shows autonomy and makes room for feedback.
Does this seem like it's on the right track?	You're asking for feedback on your work. It ensures people don't focus only on small changes and avoid telling you directly if you're going in the wrong direction.
Here's an early strawman draft I just threw together quickly. All feedback is welcome!	You feel nervous about sharing work that isn't totally polished.
I wonder … *Eg. "I wonder if this design will work once there's a lot of content"*	You're about to tell someone you think they're wrong or they made a mistake. This phrasing focuses you on positive, constructive feedback.
Thank you for the feedback, I appreciate you sharing it.	You got feedback or a complaint and you need time to process it. Try to say this genuinely, not sarcastically.

PHRASES FOR PM MANAGERS

Manager Phrases	Use it when..
What's your plan? / So what are you thinking?	They've brought a problem to you and are looking expectantly at you to solve it for them. Even if you will eventually help them, this reinforces the expectation that they should be bringing you solutions, not just problems.
Can you walk me through how you got to that decision?	It seems like they've made a bad or surprising decision.
This might already be on your radar... / You might already have thought of this ...	You want to share suggestions without making them feel micro-managed.
I noticed .... What's up with that? *Eg. I noticed the launch date slipped. What's up with that?*	You're bringing up a performance issue for the first time. This phrasing gives them the benefit of the doubt and sets you up to be on their side.

CHAPTER 54

TLAS AND OTHER ACRONYMS

ACRONYM	TERM
AI	Artificial Intelligence
API	Application Programming Interface
APM	Associate Product Manager
ARPDAU	Average Revenue Per Daily Active User
ARPU	Average Revenue Per User
ARR	Annual Recurring Revenue
ASP	Average Selling Price
AWS	Amazon Web Services
B2B	Business-To-Business
B2C	Business-To-Consumer
CAC	Customer Acquisition Cost
CL	Change List
CLI	Command Line Interface
CMS	Content Management System
CPC	Cost Per Click
CPI	Cost Per Install
CPM	Cost Per Thousand Impressions

CSS	Cascading Style Sheet
CTA	Call To Action
CTR	Click Through Rate
DAU	Daily Active Users
DDOS	Distributed Denial of Service
DM	Direct Message
DNS	Domain Name System
EOD	End of Day
EOW	End of Week
ETL	Extract, Transform, Load
FIFO	First In, First Out
GM	General Manager
GMT	Greenwich Mean Time
GPM	Group Product Manager
GTD	Getting Things Done
GUI	Graphical User Interface
GUID	Globally Unique Identifier
HiPPO	Highest Paid Person's Opinion
HR	Human Resources
i18n	Internationalization
IC	Individual Contributor
IDE	Integrated Development Environment
IoT	Internet of Things
IT	Information Technology
JSON	JavaScript Object Notation
KPI	Key Performance Indicator
l10n	Localization
LTV	Long-Term Value
MAU	Monthly Active Users

ML	Machine Learning
MoM	Month over Month
MRR	Monthly Recurring Revenue
MVP	Minimum Viable Product
NPS	Net Reporter Score
OKR	Objectives & Key Results
OOO	Out of Office
perf	Application Performance or Performance Review
PIP	Performance Improvement Plan
PM	Product Manager
PMM	Product Marketing Manager
PPC	Pay Per Click
PR	Pull Request
PRD	Product Requirements Doc
prod	Production (or Production Server)
PTO	Paid Time Off
QA	Quality Assurance
R&D	Research And Development
ROI	Return On Investment
SaaS	Software as a Service
SDK	Software Development Kit
SEM	Search Engine Marketing
SEO	Search Engine Optimization
SERP	Search Enginge Results Page
SLA	Service Level Agreement
spec	Product Specification
SQL	Structured Query Language
SSO	Single Sign On
swag	Scientific Wild-Ass Guess

TDD	Test Driven Development
TLA	Three Letter Acronyms
ToS	Terms of Service
UGC	User Generated Content
UI	User Interface
UTC	Coordinated Universal Time
UUID	Universally Unique Identifier
UX	User Experience
VM	Virtual Machine
VP	Vice President
VPN	Virtual Private Network
WOM	Word Of Mouth
WoW	Week over Week
WYSIWYG	What You See Is What You Get
XSS	Cross Site Scripting
YoY	Year over Year
YTD	Year To Date

CHAPTER 55

ACKNOWLEDGEMENTS

AS PRODUCT MANAGERS, we rely on our teams, and this book is no exception. But while words are sufficient to produce a book, words aren't enough to express our gratitude to everyone who has helped us along the way.

Nonetheless, we'd like to express our deepest thanks to our extended team and stakeholders.

- To Dylan Casey, Brian Ellin, Osi Imeokparia, Bangaly Kaba, Sara Mauskopf, Ken Norton, Anuj Rathi, Sachin Rekhi, Teresa Torres, Oji Udezue, and April Underwood: Thank you for sharing your thoughts on your career path and on excellence as a product manager. We have no doubt that our readers will be inspired by them.

- To Jules Walter, Kate Matsudaira, and Haseeb Qureshi: Thank you for allowing us to share your excellent essays. We've recommended these essays again and again, and we're thrilled to include them.

- To Bryan Jowers, Christina Green, Drew Dillon, Gemmy Tsai, Gibson Biddle, Kasey Alderete, Katie Holden, Krishnan Gupta, Laura Oppenheimer, Marissa Mayer, Olumide Longe, Steven Sinofsky, and Yardley Ip: Thank you for offering your thoughts and opinions on the beta versions of our book. Your contributions have shaped this book for the better.

- To Aaron Filner, Aarti Bharathan, Adam Grant, Adam Thomas, Adrienne Peterson, Alaina Brown, Alicia Dixon, Anna Marie Clifton, Apurva Garware, Ari Janovar, Arjun Ohri, Ashley Fidler, Becca Camp, Ben Gaines, Beth Grant, Brian Shih, Buzz Bruggeman, Carlos González de Villaumbrosia, Chaim Gross, Dare Obasanjo, Dave Hunkins, Demian Borba, Dian Rosanti, Diwakar Kaushik, Ely Lerner, Freia Lobo, Hunter Walk, Jennifer Conti-Davies, Jennifer Nan, Jerry Sparks, Josh Kaplan, Julia Rhodes, Kamal Manchanda, Kate Bennet, Kathy Crothall, Katie Guzman, Kunwardeep Singh, Laide Olambiwonnu, Laika Kayani, Laura Hamilton, Lenny Rachitsky, Lesley Kim Grossblatt, Lili Rachowin, Louis Lecat, Mariano Capezzani, Mckenzie Lock, Michelle Thong, Mikal Lewis, Mike Ross, Molli Simpson, Natalia Baryshnikova, Nate Abbott, Neeraj Mathur, Noa Ganot, Noah Weiss, Nundu Janakiram, Rahul Ramkumar, Sage Kitamorn, Sair Buckle, Salahuddin Choudhary, Sam Goertler, Shannon Boon, Sharon Lo, Shirin Oskooi, Shishir Mehrotra, Shreyas Doshi, Shuo Song, and Tracy Mehoke: Thank you for contributing your time and thoughts in interviews and advice. Your stories bring the book to life.

- To Shana Segal, Bethany Powell James, Jay Slaney, Danielle Macuil, Sophia Dalby, Ian McGuire, Anukha Vusirikala, and Affinity Writing and Editing: Thank you for your feedback and suggestions. You helped polish the book for the better.

- To Alex Hood, Annelène Decaux, Diana Chapman, Dustin Moskovitz, Jack Menzel, Johanna Wright, Justin Rosenstein, Mike Morton, PJ Hough, Tom Stocky, and Yvonne Lopez: Your mentorship and support over the years has been invaluable.

And finally, thank you to our loving families. Your belief in us kept us going.

CHAPTER 56

INDEX

N

O

P

Made in the USA
Monee, IL
17 February 2023

28086841R00302